Biblical Hebrew
and
Discourse Linguistics

edited by
Robert D. Bergen

Summer Institute of Linguistics

© Copyright 1994 Summer Institute of Linguistics, Inc.

ISBN: 1-55671-007-0
Library of Congress Catalog Card Number: 94-68219
Printed in the United States of America

This volume is distributed by Eisenbrauns, Inc., in conjunction with the Summer Institute of Linguistics. Copies may be purchased from

Eisenbrauns, Inc.
P. O. Box 275
Winona Lake, IN 46590-0275
USA

or

International Academic Bookstore
Summer Institute of Linguistics
7500 West Camp Wisdom Road
Dallas, TX 75236
USA

Biblical Hebrew
and
Discourse Linguistics

CONTRIBUTORS

Francis I. Andersen is the David Allan Hubbard Professor of Old Testament at Fuller Theological Seminary. He is also an Academic Associate of the University of Melbourne, Victoria, Department of Classics and Archaeology, and Professor at Large of New College for Advanced Christian Studies, Berkeley. He has served on the Board of Wycliffe Bible Translators in Australia for many years.

T. David Andersen is serving with the Summer Institute of Linguistics (SIL)[1] in a Bible translation project in Indonesia.

Nicholas Andrew Bailey is involved in training and consulting in Bible translation projects in Europe. He has been a member of SIL since 1984.

Robert D. Bergen is Associate Professor of Old Testament and Biblical Languages at Hannibal-LaGrange College. He has also taught intensive introductory courses in Hebrew at the Summer Institute of Linguistics in Dallas, Texas.

Randall Buth is currently serving with the United Bible Societies as a translation consultant in Africa. He has worked in the Luo translation project in Sudan with SIL.

John Callow is a translation consultant with SIL, assisting projects in Europe and Middle Eastern countries.

David J. Clark is a translation consultant with the United Bible Societies, having recently transferred from Thailand to the Europe area.

Lénart J. de Regt teaches in the Bible translation program in the Department of Linguistics, Free University of Amsterdam.

Shin Ja J. Hwang teaches textlinguistics at the University of Texas at Arlington and is a member of SIL.

Hanni Kuhn is a translation consultant with SIL in West Africa, specializing in Old Testament translation.

Bo-Krister Ljungberg is completing doctoral studies in Old Testament exegesis at the University of Lund, Sweden. He and his wife are currently preparing to work with Wycliffe Bible Translators.

Lars Lode has worked as a member of the Lutheran Mission in a Bible translation project in Cameroon.

Robert E. Longacre retired in 1992 from the chair of Linguistics at the University of Texas at Arlington, and has traveled widely as a linguistics consultant with SIL.

Cynthia L. Miller is an Assistant Professor in Old Testament and Hebrew Linguistics in the Department of Philosophy and Religion at North Carolina State University.

Alviero Niccacci is Director of the Studium Biblicum Franciscanum in Jerusalem and has published extensively on the text structure of Biblical Hebrew.

H. Van Dyke Parunak is a scientific fellow at the Industrial Technology Institute in Ann Arbor, Michigan.

Murray Salisbury is a member of SIL, currently completing doctoral studies at the Hebrew University, Jerusalem, and teaching at the Institute of Holy Land Studies, Jerusalem.

Christo H. J. van der Merwe holds the Eric Samson Chair for Biblical Hebrew at the University of Stellenbosch, South Africa.

Ernst R. Wendland is an instructor at the Evangelical Lutheran Seminary in Lusaka, Zambia. He also serves as a translation consultant for the United Bible Societies, supervising projects in seven Bantu languages of East-Central Africa.

Nicolai Winther-Nielsen is working on research into discourse features of Biblical Hebrew at the Free University of Amsterdam. He also serves as the chairman of Wycliffe Bible Translators in Denmark.

---

[1] Members of Wycliffe Bible Translators serve in various parts of the world under the auspices of the Summer Institute of Linguistics.

CONTENTS

Foreword 7
    Francis I. Anderson

Preface 9
    Robert D. Bergen

Part I Grammatical, Syntactical, and Accent Studies

1. Discourse Linguistics and Biblical Hebrew Grammar 13
    Christo H. J. van der Merwe

2. *Weqatal* Forms in Biblical Hebrew Prose 50
    Robert E. Longacre

3. Salience, Implicature, Ambiguity, and Redundancy in Clause–Clause Relationships in Biblical Hebrew 99
    Francis I. Andersen

4. On the Hebrew Verbal System 117
    Alviero Niccacci

5. Methodological Collision between Source Criticism and Discourse Analysis 138
    Randall Buth

6. A Discourse Perspective on the Significance of the Masoretic Accents 155
    Lars Lode

Part II Narrative Genre

7. Analysis of Biblical Narrative 175
    Alviero Niccacci

8. Introducing Direct Discourse in Biblical Hebrew Narrative 199
    Cynthia L. Miller

9. Genealogical Prominence and the Structure of Genesis 242
    T. David Andersen

10. Some Literary and Grammatical Aspects of Genealogies in Genesis 267
    Nicholas Andrew Bailey

11. Is Genesis 27:46 P or J? And How the Answer Affects Translation 283
    Hanni Kuhn

12	The Miraculous Grammar of Joshua 3–4 *Nicolai Winther-Nielsen*	300
13	Evil Spirits and Eccentric Grammar *Robert D. Bergen*	320
14	A Textlinguistic Approach to the Biblical Hebrew Narrative of Jonah *Robert E. Longacre and Shin Ja J. Hwang*	336

Part III Topics Relating to Nonnarrative Genres

15	Functions and Implications of Rhetorical Questions in the Book of Job *Lénart J. de Regt*	361
16	Genre Criticism and the Psalms *Ernst R. Wendland*	374
17	Genre and Form Criticism in Old Testament Exegesis *Bo-Krister Ljungberg*	415
18	Hebrew Proverbs and How to Translate Them *Murray Salisbury*	434
19	Units and Flow in the Song of Songs 1:1–2:6 *John Callow*	462
20	Some Discourse Functions of Prophetic Quotation Formulas in Jeremiah *H. Van Dyke Parunak*	489
21	The Poetic Properties of Prophetic Discourse in the Book of Micah *Francis I. Andersen*	520
22	Vision and Oracle in Zechariah 1–6 *David J. Clark*	529

FOREWORD

The Seminar on Discourse Linguistics and Biblical Hebrew held in Dallas, Texas, in June, 1993, was a remarkable happening. It was encouraging for all present to discover how many people are now doing quality work on discourse grammar as it affects the translation and interpretation of the Hebrew text of the Old Testament.

For two weeks, day after day, paper after paper, a range of topics was explored. Theoretical and practical matters were continually brought into mutual interplay. Of the ninety or so persons present, about sixty were working translators, members of Wycliffe Bible Translators and other societies, whose main vocation is translating the Bible into languages (often of peoples not yet literate) in various parts of the world. This cross-cultural background greatly enhanced the sensitivity to issues of comparative and contrastive linguistics, especially as such studies are applied to translation policies and practices. The other thirty participants were linguists and biblical scholars from all over the world. There was no disagreement about their common interest in fostering the linguistic disciplines of discourse grammar.

What is emerging is a whole new generation of Bible translators who are becoming competent, not only in linguistics, but also in Hebrew language studies. There was a time in the enterprise of Bible translation when the linguistic side was cultivated scientifically, but the biblical end was driven by piety. Prayer is always needed—for everything! But the imbalance between a naive approach to biblical understanding and a sophisticated mastery of modern linguistics, in the minds of these scholar-translators, has given way to a maturity that now promises—and this is particularly exciting—to enrich biblical studies with the contributions that linguistics, especially textlinguistics, can make. It is to be hoped that the present volume will make this vision more widely available.

It is surely needed. Of the thousands of publications that are listed each year in *Old Testament Abstracts* and similar publications, only a handful show any awareness on the part of Old Testament scholars of the enormous benefits to be gained from this kind of cooperation. Sadly, all too many of these publications are invalidated by the limited acquaintance of their authors with the helps coming from contemporary advances in textlinguistics. To mention just two areas of lively debate: textlinguistics interfaces solidly with many issues in current literary approaches to the study of the Bible; and even more, biblical poetics has hardly begun to take advantage of the insights of discourse grammar when addressing questions of prosody and rhetoric.

The research presented to the seminar was driven by a high belief in the unique importance of the Bible as the inspired and trustworthy Word of God. When there is so much unseemly wrangling over this question, it should be said that theology, too, has much to learn from linguistics. But much hard work remains to be done on methodology before we can tread on firm ground from the descriptive analysis of biblical texts to exegesis-interpretation and so to responsible use of the truth revealed by God for evangelism, pastoral care, and the scholarly construction of theological systems.

Against the background of current debate, sometimes acrimonious, it was wonderful at Dallas that persons from a wide range of theological backgrounds and church commitments could work together so courteously and constructively. In more than forty years of participation in assemblies of scholars and learned societies, I have never experienced such respect and fairness in expressing disagreements and such a spirit of eagerness to learn from others.

Francis I. Andersen

PREFACE

The present volume is a repository of twenty-two edited articles that approach Biblical Hebrew topics and texts from a perspective informed by discourse linguistics. Twenty of these studies were originally presented as part of the Seminar on Discourse Linguistics and Biblical Hebrew held in Dallas, Texas, May 31–June 11, 1993. Sponsored by the Summer Institute of Linguistics, the conference was held to assess the present state of knowledge in the interdisciplinary field of Biblical Hebrew discourse analysis and provide a forum in which Hebrew scholars, discourse linguists, and Bible translators might have in-depth interaction with one another. The two-week event included some ninety participants and featured more than seventy papers and presentations. The size and breadth of the conference suggest the degree of interest biblical scholars, linguists, and translators have in examining Biblical Hebrew in the light of textlinguistic presuppositions.

Articles selected for inclusion in the present volume are in three different categories: (1) those dealing with general issues of grammar, syntax, and the Masoretic accent system; (2) those treating narrative texts and issues; and (3) those treating nonnarrative texts and issues. All share an awareness of the field of discourse linguistics and address issues germane to Biblical Hebrew from a discourse-sensitive perspective.

Preparation of this book was a complex task involving many persons. I am especially grateful to Dick and Faith Blight for their tireless efforts to produce error-free, well-formatted electronic copy. The work of David Henne in inserting Hebrew script into the texts was also extremely helpful. Betty Eastman's contributions to the task of copyediting were most appreciated. Finally, I wish to express my thanks to Katy Barnwell, the International Translation Coordinator of the Summer Institute of Linguistics. Her skillful efforts made both the 1993 conference and this book possible.

As a service to persons wishing to have a deeper understanding of Biblical Hebrew and the message of the Hebrew Bible, the following collection of articles is now presented. *Soli deo gloria.*

PART I

GRAMMATICAL, SYNTACTICAL, AND ACCENT STUDIES

1

DISCOURSE LINGUISTICS AND BIBLICAL HEBREW GRAMMAR

Christo H. J. van der Merwe

The aim of this article is to contribute towards a concerted study of Biblical Hebrew grammar from a discourse perspective by identifying some of the most productive avenues for future research in this field. For this purpose, I will first illustrate briefly that the roots of our problem, that is, attempting to describe Biblical Hebrew exclusively in terms of studies of its words and sentences, can be attributed to particular trends in the study of Biblical Hebrew. However, studying Biblical Hebrew from a discourse perspective is also part of a larger development in the study of the language; and in order to identify productive avenues for future studies of Biblical Hebrew from a discourse perspective, it is important to understand where discourse studies fit into this process. The second section presents an overview of the main lines of thought in the new era of the linguistic description of Biblical Hebrew. The third section discusses some of the problematic aspects of the Biblical Hebrew verbal system, word order, participant reference, and the Biblical Hebrew particles. The concluding section summarizes the present state of affairs in studying Biblical Hebrew from a discourse perspective as reflected in this article and some others in this volume. Suggestions are also made concerning how and in what areas future research in Biblical Hebrew grammar may benefit from discourse linguistics.

During the first two weeks of June 1993, about sixty translators and thirty Biblical Hebrew scholars read fifty-three papers at a seminar at the Summer Institute of Linguistics in Dallas on the theme "Discourse Linguistics and Biblical Hebrew." The aim of this DLBH seminar was to bring together those who are seriously interested in the description of Biblical Hebrew from a discourse perspective, both as users and as researchers.

Discourse linguistics may be said to be still in its infancy in that scholars do not agree at all on how texts should be described from a discourse perspective, or even on what a discourse is.[1] However, it cannot be denied that discourse linguistics may open new perspectives on unsolved problems as far as Biblical Hebrew grammatical constructions are concerned.

At the seminar some of these perspectives were presented. Some papers indeed suggested exciting solutions to old problems, some gave rise to new questions, and some provided a foundation for future research.

Others proved to be unproductive dead ends or revealed the provisional status of some of the current discourse linguistic theories and the dangers of uncritical top-down application of these theories.

The aim of this article is to contribute towards a concerted study of Biblical Hebrew grammar[2] from a discourse perspective by identifying some of the most productive avenues for future research in this field. For this purpose I commence by illustrating briefly that the roots of our problem, namely attempting to describe Biblical Hebrew exclusively in terms of studies of its words and sentences, can be attributed to particular trends in the study of Biblical Hebrew. However, studying Biblical Hebrew from a discourse perspective is also part of a larger development in the study of the language. If one would like to identify productive avenues for future studies of Biblical Hebrew from a discourse perspective, it is important to understand where discourse studies fit into this process. In the second section, I therefore give a bird's-eye view of the main lines of thought in a new era in the linguistic description of Biblical Hebrew. Against this background I then discuss, in the third section, some of the perspectives that were provided at the seminar on problematic aspects of the Biblical Hebrew verbal system, word order, participant reference, and the Biblical Hebrew particles. In the conclusion the present state of affairs in studying Biblical Hebrew from the discourse perspective is summarized. A few suggestions are also made as to how future research in Biblical Hebrew grammar may benefit from discourse linguistics.

1. The problem of studying Biblical Hebrew in terms of words and sentences

In the late Middle ages when "the intellectual and demographic center of Jewry" shifted from the Near East to Europe, the study of Biblical Hebrew grammar exchanged its Arabic mold for a Latin one. One of the results of this was that Biblical Hebrew grammar no longer included rhetoric and poetics, but grammar was rather considered to be one of three "co-equal" language sciences (Waltke and O'Connor 1990:37). Unfortunately, Jewish scholars lost interest in Biblical Hebrew grammar when Christian scholars of the Reformation began to study the language with vigor. In the process, Biblical Hebrew grammar was cut off from its only "living" tradition, namely that tradition which survived in the Rabbinic circles. This isolation of the study of Biblical Hebrew grammar from its use was further entrenched by the comparative and historical-comparative studies of Biblical Hebrew that reigned supreme from the late eighteenth century till the sixties of this century.[3] In this entire development the study of Biblical Hebrew was not out of pace with major developments in the European approach to grammatical study of language.[4] The problem was that most of the other languages were living languages. Biblical Hebrew, however, was not being used as a spoken language nor was it backed by a tradition concerning its textgrammatical, speech-act, or sociolinguistic conventions.[5]

2. A new era in the study of Biblical Hebrew

Since the 1970s, many Biblical Hebrew grammarians have no longer been content with the traditional sentence-based approach to grammar. This was due to: (1) the influence of modern linguistics with its insistence that linguistic categories and levels of description be well defined in terms of explicitly stated criteria;[6] (2) discontent with the historical-critical exegetical methods, which led to more text-immanent approaches that again revealed the inadequacies of traditionally oriented Biblical Hebrew word- and sentence-based grammars; and (3) the movement in Bible translation to translate the sense rather than the words of an utterance. This latter phenomenon in the history of Bible translation, according to Orlinsky and Bratcher (1991:155-77), was inaugurated by the RSV in 1952, confronting translators with the shortcomings of the traditional Biblical Hebrew grammars and lexica. The need for tools to understand the use of Biblical Hebrew exposed the too-narrow base (i.e., the sentence) of the traditional grammar. Too many constructions (e.g., the verbal system and word order) were only partly explained or described by means of vague terms (e.g., "emphasis") or not explained at all (e.g., split constituents, differences in participant references, to mention only a few examples).

But since the seventies, research in Biblical Hebrew grammar and lexicography has flourished.[7] Although it is often difficult to distinguish one clearly from another, I identify three main lines of thought among the constant stream of publications since the pioneering works of the early seventies: (1) those that favor an entire reevaluation of existing grammatical knowledge in terms of a new look at all the Biblical Hebrew data—the form-to-function approaches; (2) those that treat specific problem areas in the description of Biblical Hebrew in terms of one particular modern linguistic or discourse theory—the functional approaches; and (3) those that may be regarded as revisions of traditional descriptions of Biblical Hebrew grammar.

2.1 The form-to-function approaches

The form-to-function approaches build classes mainly in terms of formal distributional criteria and demand long and tedious studies that often yield relatively few results.[8] It is assumed that it is necessary to treat the formal data at the lower levels exhaustively before any phenomenon is treated on a higher level, such as semantics or pragmatics, simply because there are no Biblical Hebrew speakers to consult. A significant feature of these approaches is that an interactively created computerized linguistic database is normally an integral part of the research process. Major exponents of this distributional approach are Hoftijzer, Richter, and Talstra. I will discuss only the latter two here.

Wolfgang Richter commenced with an attempt to provide a testable frame of reference for the description of Biblical Hebrew on the level of morphology, morphosyntax, and sentence syntax (1978, 1979, and 1980). A key feature of this frame of reference, in particular the sentence syntax, is the concept of valency, which is useful for the lexical description of verbs.[9] Richter's first contribution to the semantics of Biblical Hebrew was a pair of lexical studies in which the importance of syntax for the proper understanding of verbal lexemes was demonstrated (1985, 1986). Since 1986 Richter has been working on a major Biblical Hebrew linguistic database. In this database the entire Hebrew Bible is divided into sentences and presented in its Massoretic form as well as a transcribed form.[10] At this stage a morphological and morphosyntactic parser has been developed for the database.[11] The first edition of Richter's *Biblia Hebraica Transkripta* also appeared recently. Richter certainly also accepts that levels of descriptions higher than the sentence are important for the understanding of Biblical Hebrew (1985:4).[12] However, he prefers first to make full use of the linguistic data that can be described within the safe boundaries of the sentence before "moving up."[13] Walter Gross, in a certain sense, follows the same road in his major study of the sentence in Biblical Hebrew.[14]

Talstra, unlike Richter, did not start his Biblical Hebrew linguistic database with an explicitly defined grammatical theory.[15] While the point of departure of Richter's database is the sentences as they are identified by Richter in terms of his syntactic theory, Talstra prefers a series of computer programs to analyze the grammatical information of his Biblical Hebrew data successively upwards in the grammatical hierarchy on the basis of mainly surface-level criteria from the morpheme to the text. Talstra's sentences are therefore determined mainly by distributional criteria.[16] Talstra has not yet written a Biblical Hebrew grammar; in fact, his database is not completed for the entire Bible up to the level of syntax. However, his recently launched morphological parser, Quest, represents the first computerized tool available on PC for more complicated searches on the level of Biblical Hebrew morphology and morphosyntax. Furthermore, the linguistic tools that he is developing depart from surface-level phenomena and are hierarchically structured. They therefore allow the encoding of data at the higher levels of description according to different theories while maintaining all the lower levels of mainly surface-level information. This means that if Biblical Hebrew data are encoded in terms of one or another type of discourse linguistic categories, the syntactic features of these categories can easily be retrieved.

At this stage, then, Talstra and Richter provide researchers with basic tools that could be used in the reevaluation of traditional grammars and lexica at all levels of the linguistic description of Biblical Hebrew. Neither is complete as far as the higher levels are concerned, but both are suitable for the experimental encoding of categories at the higher levels. Richter's database could at this stage be regarded as being geared more towards studies in terms of Richter's own grammatical framework, and in particular morphological and lexicographical research, while Talstra's striving towards a surface-level syntax provides researchers with a wealth of syntactic information that may prove invaluable in discourse-related types of research.

2.2 The functional approaches

The functional approaches to Biblical Hebrew normally commence with a hypothesis or theoretical frame of reference on specific linguistic notions and try to explain hitherto problematic Biblical Hebrew phenomena in terms of this hypothesis. The data that are treated are normally determined by the hypothesis. If the data are recorded in terms of a database, they are therefore selective. In contrast, the form-to-function approaches assume that Biblical Hebrew linguistics would be best served if hypotheses could be tested from all the various formal angles that the data we have at our disposal could provide. Their databases try to provide us with as exhaustive as possible a means in this regard. The form-to-functional approaches certainly do not necessarily represent a linguistic theory of language that contradicts that of the functional approaches; they should rather be regarded as complementary to these approaches. They are attempts to provide Biblical Hebrew grammarians with the type of heuristic tools that take the absence of living speakers of Biblical Hebrew fully into account.

As I said before, functional grammars normally commence with a hypothesis on a specific linguistic phenomenon within an explicitly formulated broader frame of reference. In this regard they are in no way unique. However, it is the grounds and the aims of their broader linguistic theory that distinguish them from generative linguistics, the other mainstream in general linguistics.

Since the early Alexandrians, grammarians have been divided on the question as to whether language is a special innate ability or whether it is a set of social conventions that humans cognitively learn. Today the same kinds of opposing views are still current. Most generative approaches, which may be regarded as the mainstream in the general linguistics of the second half of this century, try to explain linguistic phenomena in terms of hypotheses concerning mankind's inherent "language machine." By contrast, the so-called functional approaches try to explain linguistic phenomena in terms of their use in human communication (Berns 1990:1–27). Unlike the generative approaches (most of them, at least), they do not consider only the surface-level features of the sentence to be part of syntax, but also allow elements of meaning and pragmatic use to be treated on the level of the syntax. Moreover, the sentence is for them not the outer boundary of grammatical description. However, leaving these safe boundaries of intrasentence relationships, these linguists were confronted with the problem of their new outer boundary: the text or discourse. A whole array of questions arose. What is a text? What levels exist between the text and the sentence? How does one treat the influence of the text on intrasentence relationships? And there are more such questions.

There is a large variety of approaches to the study of the use of language. For the purpose of this paper I will consider mainly those that study the grammar[17] of the complex linguistic world beyond the sentence and the perspectives it may yield for some problematic intrasentence phenomena, such as word order, verbal aspect and tenses, and participant reference.

Among these studies two types of approaches can be identified. On the one hand, there are those that prefer a bottom-up approach and stay close to the sentence. Dik, for example, in his *Functional Grammar* (1978) supplements the syntactic and semantic level of intrasentence relationships with a pragmatic level: In *The boy is hurt by his brother*, *boy* is syntactically the subject, semantically the patient, and pragmatically the topic of the sentence.[18] (This last could be determined only in the context of the sentence.) Other analysts who use a bottom-up approach go a step further than Dik and concentrate on the centrality of semantic or discourse-functional relations among the parts of a text, in particular between clauselike units. Mann and Thompson (1988:243–81), for example, distinguish twenty-three types of relationships for English.[19]

On the other hand, there are those who prefer a top-down approach. According to this approach the discourse type to which a text belongs could be a useful point of departure in the study of a problematic grammatical construction. Longacre (1983), a pioneer in this field, distinguishes four discourse genres defined in *grammatical* terms: narrative (+ agent, + temporal succession),[20] procedural (− agent, + temporal succession), hortatory or behavioral (+ agent, − temporal succession), and expository (− agent, − temporal succession).

This brings me to the functional line of thought in Biblical Hebrew grammatical studies. The pioneer in this field is without doubt Francis Andersen. Andersen has explored the perspectives that Pike's tagmemic theory provide towards a better understanding of the Biblical Hebrew verbless clause (Andersen 1970) and the Biblical Hebrew sentence (1974). But Andersen, who has sometimes been unfairly criticized,[21] by no means claimed to solve the problems of the sentence in Biblical Hebrew. While giving meticulous attention to a selection of Biblical Hebrew data, Andersen in his 1974 "pilot study" investigated hypotheses concerning a number of deep-structure interclausal relationships in order to determine how they are realized in Biblical Hebrew surface-level constructions. In the process he dealt with a hierarchy of discourse levels (e.g., the phrase, the sentence, the paragraph, and the episode level). Andersen was fully aware that more research should be conducted on three fronts if one wishes to better understand the Biblical Hebrew sentence, Biblical Hebrew discourse, and ultimately the function of Biblical Hebrew conjunctions. First, the theoretical basis of interclause relationships (i.e., the deep grammar) should be strengthened; second, these theories should be tested empirically in the light of all Biblical Hebrew data available; and, third, when the evidence is organized, "the dynamics of structural change in the sentence repertoire, and higher up the hierarchy" (1974:19) could be investigated. Since then, Andersen has been advancing on all three fronts towards a better understanding of Biblical Hebrew conjunctions. A significant feature of his work is his respect for the Biblical Hebrew data. The tools that he has developed in order to account for the data and his studies of the lower levels of description, such as spelling and textual criticism, are witnesses to his achievement in this regard (Andersen 1985, Andersen and Forbes 1986, 1992). Furthermore, in his treatment of higher levels of description, the data are always, where possible, presented in such a way that they could be tested; this was done, for example, in his treatment of the structure of prophetic discourse in Hosea and Amos (Andersen and Freedman 1980, 1989). In sum, Andersen may be regarded as a bottom-up functional grammarian who operates with a number of basic functional assumptions and categories. However, Andersen also scrutinizes the discourse theories he is working with, in particular those at the higher levels, in the light of the evidence provided by the text of the OT.

My earlier reference to Longacre as an exponent of the top-down approach may create a false impression about Longacre. Most of his theories emerged from Pike's tagmemic school of thought (Longacre 1976*b*) and extensive studies in Asian and Pacific languages. These were often necessitated by the shortcomings of the traditional European approach in accounting for a range of phenomena in those languages (Lowery forthcoming). Longacre's views on discourse genres are therefore not always mere theoretical constructions, but are based on his observations in a range of non-European languages. In his 1989 work, Longacre applies a range of his theories to a Biblical Hebrew narrative text, putting forward hypotheses of how episodes and climaxes are linguistically marked in Biblical Hebrew, how the storyline is advanced, how participants are traced, how direct discourse moves a story forward, etc. He also purports to illustrate how the Hebrew verbal system could be better understood in the light of his discourse genres, for example, that the mainline of a narrative text is advanced by *wayyiqtol* forms and that of hortatory texts by *weqatal* forms. However, an important feature of this functional approach is that Longacre puts forward his views, as far as Biblical Hebrew is concerned, as hypotheses, based on particular Biblical Hebrew texts. According to him his views should still be scrutinized in the light of more Biblical Hebrew data. This is exactly what he has been doing since 1989 (personal communication).

Another functional line of thought is that of scholars who treat Biblical Hebrew particles and word order from a functional and discourse perspective. In most grammars both phenomena were traditionally either ignored or described by the vague term "emphasis." The fact that particles may be regarded as lexical items to be treated in a lexicon, and that word order may be regarded as a purely syntactic phenomenon, certainly contributed to this state of affairs. Thus the description of both particles and word order, which can often be properly described only from a discourse perspective, was restricted by the level of description to which it was confined. Muraoka was the pioneer in this regard. In his 1985 work, *Emphatic Words and Structures in Biblical Hebrew,* he deals critically with the trend in traditional works to assign "emphasis" to a number of particles and constructions, such as word order. Bandstra in his 1982 investigation of the particle כִּי, using a tagmemic frame of reference, similarly challenges the so-called "asservative" and "emphatic" meanings so often attached to it. Van der Merwe (1993b) has built on these insights, and also those of Aejmelaus (1986:193–209), utilizing some of the insights of recent German particle lexicography for a better understanding of the different types of causal relationship that may be expressed by כִּי. In his 1990, 1991b work, he explored the role that a bottom-up approach, like that of Richter (1978–80, 1985, 1986), may play in the better understanding of such particles as גַּם, רַק and אַךְ. More recently, van der Merwe (forthcoming a) also demonstrated some of the insights that can be obtained if a bottom-up only approach to the description of these particles is supplemented by a pragmatic approach such as Relevance Theory. As far as word order is concerned, Bandstra (1982, 1992), Buth (forthcoming b), and van der Merwe (1990 and 1991b) use the pragmatic notions *topic* and *focus* for the description of the function of marked word order in Biblical Hebrew. These notions, nowadays generally used by grammarians and linguists, provide Biblical Hebrew scholars with a much more nuanced view of Biblical Hebrew word order than the vague term *emphasis*.

2.3 The traditional approaches revised

Two works that need to be mentioned here are Waltke and O'Connor's (1990) and Joüon and Muraoka's (1991). According to Waltke and O'Connor (p. x), "The great native-speaker tradition of Hebrew grammar associated with medieval Jewry is the first basis" of their study. "The second basis is modern linguistic study, its roots contemporary with Gesenius and its first flowers contemporary with the edition of Gesenius's grammar currently in print in English (1910)." They "resist the strong claims of discourse grammarians" (p. 55) for both theoretical and practical reasons and prefer to gather the great wealth of individual studies carried out in terms of the traditional approach. In this regard, they are indeed a useful up-to-date source of information on Biblical Hebrew syntactic studies since the beginning of this century.

Joüon and Muraoka's 1991 work is not a mere translation of the highly esteemed French traditional Biblical Hebrew grammar by Joüon (published in 1927), but much more than that: "hardly a paragraph...has been left unrevised" (1991:xiii). This revision implies an update in the light of Biblical Hebrew publications since 1920, including those written in Modern Hebrew that are totally absent from Waltke and O'Connor.

2.4 Conclusions

As we have seen, studying Biblical Hebrew from a discourse perspective is part of a greater movement in the study of Biblical Hebrew. Most scholars now would concede that Biblical Hebrew needs to be studied beyond the level of the sentence. But they differ as to the appropriate stage in research for beginning these studies. Some prefer to concentrate first of all on problems within the safe boundaries of the sentence. Others insist that if a higher level of description is investigated, it must always be determined as far as humanly possible whether, and to what extent, the hierarchically structured lower levels can serve as a foundation for that higher level. Others are more adventurous and are prepared to apply theories based on data in other languages to Biblical Hebrew constructions beyond the sentence. However, a feature of even these more adventurous approaches is the prominent role that the Biblical Hebrew data play in the scrutiny of the hypotheses postulated.

A second feature that most of the Biblical Hebrew studies of this greater movement share is that they are problem-oriented. Just as sentence grammarians, who would ultimately want to know what well-formed sentences in Biblical Hebrew look like but who do not yet agree upon the definition of a sentence, discourse linguists ultimately want to know what well-formed Biblical Hebrew texts look like but they also do not yet agree on what constitutes a text or discourse. At the DLBH seminar in Dallas the definition of a text was not discussed, nor were the different discourse theories. This is understandable in view of the fact that most Biblical Hebrew linguists do not strive towards contributing to a specific theory of discourse, but rather want to explore the possibilities of a particular discourse approach for the solution of specific problematic Biblical Hebrew phenomena. In other words, it is assumed that the discourse theories used are nothing but heuristic.

3. The present relationship between Biblical Hebrew studies and discourse linguistics

The DLBH seminar in Dallas should be understood in the light of the state of affairs described in section 2.4. The papers that were read there can be divided into three groups: those that investigated specific Biblical Hebrew constructions from a discourse perspective; those aimed at identifying the features of discourse genres (mostly genres other than narrative); and those that applied existing insights from a discourse perspective to the interpretation of a Biblical Hebrew text. I will not try to summarize them but will rather concentrate on those that in my opinion reflect and/or

Discourse Linguistics and Biblical Hebrew Grammar

advance the current state in the description of Biblical Hebrew grammar from a discourse perspective. For this purpose I will, here in section 3, use as my point of departure the linguistic phenomena that are involved, and not the views of individual scholars.

3.1 The Biblical Hebrew verbal system

As functional approaches, most of the discourse studies of Biblical Hebrew assume that Biblical Hebrew has different registers, or genres, for different communicative functions. Grammatical constructions of a register may therefore be typical of that particular register. The first basic distinction that is maintained is that between prose and poetry.

In prose a number of discourse types are distinguished, such as narrative, instructive, procedural, predictive, descriptive, and expository. In narrative material, a further distinction is made between *narrative* and *dialogue*.[22] A feature of dialogue is that the content of a quotation may belong to any of the discourse types. In all the discourse types, a distinction is also made between the *mainline* and the *subsidiary line* of communication. All the above-mentioned distinctions are made not only on the basis of differences in semantic content, but also on the basis of differences in the verbal forms that occur in each of them. The two constructions that are usually associated with the mainline of communication or primary storyline are *wayyiqtol* and *weqatal*.

3.1.1 *Wayyiqtol*

According to Niccacci (1994b), the mainline of communication in narration is constituted by a chain of *wayyiqtol* forms, as in Jer. 28:10–11:

10 וַיִּקַּח חֲנַנְיָה הַנָּבִיא אֶת־הַמּוֹטָה ... וַיִּשְׁבְּרֵהוּ: 11 וַיֹּאמֶר חֲנַנְיָה
... וַיֵּלֶךְ יִרְמְיָה הַנָּבִיא לְדַרְכּוֹ:

Hananiah, the prophet *then took* the yoke ... *and broke* it. *And* Hananiah said ... *and* Jeremiah the prophet *went* his way.

A *wayyiqtol* form may also start an independent textual unit. It then has a tense value of its own corresponding to the narrative tense of modern languages, as in Lev. 1:1a:

וַיִּקְרָא אֶל־מֹשֶׁה וַיְדַבֵּר יְהוָה אֵלָיו ...

He (Yahweh) called Moses and Yahweh (he) spoke to him ...

This type of *wayyiqtol* form may also introduce a mainline of communication following a secondary line of subsidiary information that introduces a new paragraph, as in Gen. 2:5–7:[23]

5 וְכֹל ׀ שִׂיחַ הַשָּׂדֶה טֶרֶם יִהְיֶה בָאָרֶץ וְכָל־עֵשֶׂב הַשָּׂדֶה טֶרֶם יִצְמָח
כִּי לֹא הִמְטִיר יְהוָה אֱלֹהִים עַל־הָאָרֶץ וְאָדָם אַיִן לַעֲבֹד אֶת־הָאֲדָמָה׃
6 וְאֵד יַעֲלֶה מִן־הָאָרֶץ וְהִשְׁקָה אֶת־כָּל־פְּנֵי־הָאֲדָמָה׃
7 וַיִּיצֶר יְהוָה אֱלֹהִים אֶת־הָאָדָם עָפָר מִן־הָאֲדָמָה וַ . . .

All the wild bush was not yet on the earth nor had any wild plant yet sprung up, for Yahweh God had not sent rain on the earth, nor was there any man to till the soil. 6. However, a flood was rising from the earth and was watering all the surface of the soil. 7. *Then* Yahweh God *fashioned* man of dust from the soil and . . .

More significant, however, is Niccacci's claim that a distinction should be made between the above-mentioned *wayyiqtol* form and those that he regards as the continuative *wayyiqtol* forms. In contrast to the *initial* forms, the *continuative* forms have no tense value of their own.[24]

The major difference between the continuative *wayyiqtol* and initiating *wayyiqtol* is the fact that *only* the continuative forms can occur in dialogue. In other words, a dialogue can never be initiated by a *wayyiqtol* form. A continuative *wayyiqtol*, due to its not having its own tense, can in both narration and dialogue carry on the tense (or aspect) of the form it continues, as in Josh. 24:17:

כִּי יְהוָה אֱלֹהֵינוּ הוּא הַמַּעֲלֶה אֹתָנוּ וְאֶת־אֲבוֹתֵינוּ מֵאֶרֶץ מִצְרַיִם
מִבֵּית עֲבָדִים וַאֲשֶׁר עָשָׂה לְעֵינֵינוּ אֶת־הָאֹתוֹת הַגְּדֹלוֹת הָאֵלֶּה
וַיִּשְׁמְרֵנוּ בְּכָל־הַדֶּרֶךְ אֲשֶׁר הָלַכְנוּ בָהּ . . .

For Yahweh our God brought us and our ancestors out of the land of Egypt, the house of slavery, (it is he) who worked those great wonders before our eyes *and preserved* us on the way in which we traveled . . .

The continuative *wayyiqtol* may also carry on the "tense" of a "habitual" *yiqtol* form as the mainline of a dialogue, as in 1 Sam. 2:29:

לָמָּה תִבְעֲטוּ בְּזִבְחִי וּבְמִנְחָתִי אֲשֶׁר צִוִּיתִי מָעוֹן וַתְּכַבֵּד
אֶת־בָּנֶיךָ מִמֶּנִּי . . .

Why do you *always look* with envious eyes on the sacrifices and the offering I have ordered, *honoring* your sons more than me . . .

It may even continue the narrative tense of the *initial* forms, as in Lev. 1:1a:

וַיִּקְרָא אֶל־מֹשֶׁה וַיְדַבֵּר יְהוָה אֵלָיו . . .

He (Yahweh) called Moses *and* Yahweh (he) *spoke* to him . . .

However, the cases mentioned so far are by definition possible only in narrative material. The "tense value" that is then continued is that which correlates to the "narrative tense of modern languages." Niccacci does not illustrate clearly what he has in mind with this semantic category. I assume that it is supposed to accommodate cases where the *wayyiqtol* form *introduces the conclusion* of a paragraph, as in Gen. 2:1:

וַיְכֻלּוּ הַשָּׁמַיִם וְהָאָרֶץ וְכָל־צְבָאָם

Thus heaven and earth *were completed* with all their array.

Also cases where the *wayyiqtol* form semantically *specifies* the content of a preceding sentence are apparently included here. Exod. 2:10b is an example:

וַתִּקְרָא שְׁמוֹ מֹשֶׁה וַתֹּאמֶר כִּי מִן־הַמַּיִם מְשִׁיתִהוּ׃

She named him Moses, *saying*, "Because I drew him from the water."

The reason the *wayyiqtol* form is used in the two previous cases would be to indicate that the mainline of information is involved. Buth (1994), although differing radically with Niccacci's view on the continuative *wayyiqtol*, suggests that in cases where nonsequential *wayyiqtol*s are involved, too, "the author is primarily concerned in portraying 'mainline' events with the *wayyiqtol*[25] structure." In terms of this view, the *wayyiqtol* form in Judg. 11:1 that "begins a series of several events that the author introduces as part of the main story even though it is out of sequence with the introductory clauses" in 1aa and 1ab may be explained.

1 וְיִפְתָּח הַגִּלְעָדִי הָיָה גִּבּוֹר חַיִל וְהוּא בֶּן־אִשָּׁה זוֹנָה וַיּוֹלֶד גִּלְעָד אֶת־יִפְתָּח׃
2 וַתֵּלֶד אֵשֶׁת־גִּלְעָד לוֹ בָּנִים וַיִּגְדְּלוּ בְנֵי־הָאִשָּׁה וַיְגָרְשׁוּ אֶת־יִפְתָּח

And Jephthah, the Gileadite, was a valiant warrior and he was the son of a prostitute. *And* Gilead *fathered* Jephthah and the wife of Gilead birthed sons for him and the sons of the wife grew up and the drove Jephthah away.

Although Niccacci claims that his description of *wayyiqtol* can account for its use in most Biblical Hebrew narratives, his notion of "narrative tense of modern languages" still needs to be defined more clearly. Illustrations of how this tense operates in modern languages would also be helpful, in particular in the cases where in Biblical Hebrew *wayyiqtol* forms specify a preceding utterance or summarize the outcome of a preceding paragraph.[26] The question as to why Biblical Hebrew has two distinct semantic functions for a construction that has the same discourse function also remains to be answered. Furthermore, the view that a *wayyiqtol* form can introduce a completely new narrative in the OT is not uncontested.[27]

The exact role of many cases of וַיְהִי 'and it was' also eludes us. Why does וַיְהִי repeatedly sometimes elevate "relevant" background information to mainline information? Gen. 39:2 is an example:

וַיְהִי יְהוָה אֶת־יוֹסֵף וַיְהִי אִישׁ מַצְלִיחַ וַיְהִי
בְּבֵית אֲדֹנָיו הַמִּצְרִי׃

And Yahweh *was* with Joseph, *and* everything went well with him *and* he lodged in the house of his Egyptian master.

In other cases, וַיְהִי does not occur where one expects it to occur. 2 Kings 5:1 is an example:

וְנַעֲמָן שַׂר־צְבָא מֶלֶךְ־אֲרָם הָיָה אִישׁ גָּדוֹל לִפְנֵי אֲדֹנָיו וּנְשֻׂא
פָנִים כִּי־בוֹ נָתַן־יְהוָה תְּשׁוּעָה לַאֲרָם
וְהָאִישׁ הָיָה גִּבּוֹר חַיִל מְצֹרָע׃

Naaman, army commander to the king of Aram, was a man who enjoyed his master's respect and favor, since through him Yahweh granted victory to the Aramaens. *But the man was a leper.*

Sometimes it elevates only a part of it, as in 1 Sam. 25:2–3:

2 וְאִישׁ בְּמָעוֹן וּמַעֲשֵׂהוּ בַכַּרְמֶל וְהָאִישׁ גָּדוֹל מְאֹד וְלוֹ צֹאן
שְׁלֹשֶׁת־אֲלָפִים וְאֶלֶף עִזִּים וַיְהִי בִּגְזֹז אֶת־צֹאנוֹ בַּכַּרְמֶל׃
3 וְשֵׁם הָאִישׁ נָבָל וְשֵׁם אִשְׁתּוֹ אֲבִיגָיִל וְהָאִשָּׁה טוֹבַת־שֶׂכֶל וִיפַת
תֹּאַר . . .

There was a man in Maon whose business was in Carmel, a man of means who owned three thousand sheep and a thousand goats. *He was engaged in shearing his sheep in Carmel.* The man's name was Nabal and his wife's name was Abigail. She was a woman of intelligence and beauty . . .

Even more elusive are the reasons why Biblical Hebrew temporal subordinate clauses (as well as some other types of clauses) are sometimes expressed by *wayyiqtol* plus *wayyiqtol* and sometimes by means of וַיְהִי-plus-preposition-בְּ or כְּ plus-infinitive construct. Wheatley-Irving (1994) investigated 1 Samuel and 1 Kings in this regard, but could not identify any differences between the discourse functions of these two constructions.

3.1.2 *Weqatal*

Weqatal is considered to be the counterpart[28] of *wayyiqtol* in predictive, procedural, and instructional[29] discourse. It occurs in 1 Sam. 10:2–3 (predictive discourse):

2 בְּלֶכְתְּךָ הַיּוֹם מֵעִמָּדִי וּמָצָאתָ . . . וְאָמְרוּ אֵלֶיךָ . . . 3 וְחָלַפְתָּ
מִשָּׁם . . . וּבָאתָ עַד־אֵלוֹן תָּבוֹר וּמְצָאוּךָ . . .

Discourse Linguistics and Biblical Hebrew Grammar

When you leave me now, you *will meet* . . . *and* they *will say* to you. . . . *And* you *will go* from there . . . *and* you *will come* to the Oak of Tabor *and* they *will meet* you . . .

It also occurs in Lev. 4:4–6a (procedural discourse):

4 וְהֵבִיא אֶת־הַפָּר . . . וְסָמַךְ אֶת־יָדוֹ . . . וְשָׁחַט . . . 5 וְלָקַח הַכֹּהֵן הַמָּשִׁיחַ . . . וְהֵבִיא . . . 6 וְטָבַל הַכֹּהֵן . . .

4. He *must bring* the bull . . . *and* he *must lay* his hand . . . *and immolate* . . . 5. Then the anointed priest *must take* . . . *and bring* it . . . 6. Then the priest *must dip* . . .

Another example is in Gen. 40:14 (instruction):[30]

כִּי אִם־זְכַרְתַּנִי אִתְּךָ כַּאֲשֶׁר יִיטַב לָךְ וְעָשִׂיתָ־נָּא עִמָּדִי חָסֶד וְהִזְכַּרְתַּנִי אֶל־פַּרְעֹה וְהוֹצֵאתַנִי מִן־הַבַּיִת הַזֶּה:

But remember me when things go well with you *and do* me the kindness *and remind* Pharaoh about *and get* me so out of this place.

When a *weqatal* string occurs in a narrative (not dialogue) section, this is, according to Longacre (1994), a case of procedural discourse that is embedded in the narrative. It represents a tertiary storyline, as in Gen. 29:2–3:

2 וַיַּרְא וְהִנֵּה בְאֵר בַּשָּׂדֶה וְהִנֵּה־שָׁם שְׁלֹשָׁה עֶדְרֵי־צֹאן רֹבְצִים עָלֶיהָ כִּי מִן־הַבְּאֵר הַהִוא יַשְׁקוּ הָעֲדָרִים וְהָאֶבֶן גְּדֹלָה עַל־פִּי הַבְּאֵר: 3 וְנֶאֶסְפוּ־שָׁמָּה כָל־הָעֲדָרִים וְגָלֲלוּ אֶת־הָאֶבֶן מֵעַל פִּי הַבְּאֵר וְהִשְׁקוּ אֶת־הַצֹּאן

He looked and there in the fields was a well with three flocks of sheep lying beside it, for this well was used for watering the flocks. Now the stone on the mouth of the well was a large one; so they *used to gather* all the flocks there, *and then roll* the stone off the mouth of the well *and water* the sheep.

Having put the insights of traditional grammars into his own discourse frame of reference, Longacre proceeds to deal with the residue of cases of *weqatal* that cannot be explained by the traditional grammars. An example is in Judg. 3:20–23:

20 וְאֵהוּד בָּא אֵלָיו . . . וַיֹּאמֶר אֵהוּד . . . 21 וַיִּשְׁלַח אֵהוּד אֶת־יַד שְׂמֹאלוֹ וַיִּקַּח אֶת־הַחֶרֶב . . . וַיִּתְקָעֶהָ בְּבִטְנוֹ: 23 וַיֵּצֵא אֵהוּד הַמִּסְדְּרוֹנָה וַיִּסְגֹּר דַּלְתוֹת הָעֲלִיָּה בַּעֲדוֹ וְנָעָל:

20. Then Ehud went in to him . . . and Ehud said . . . 21. Then Ehud sent out his left hand and drew his sword . . . and thrust it into his (the king's) belly . . . 23. Ehud went out by the porch; he had shut the doors behind him *and locked* (them).

Longacre discusses a substantial number of such cases and concludes that "isolated instances of *weqatal* forms in a narrative framework mark *pivotal/climactic/finalizing events*." Longacre's suggestion as to the function of these types of *weqatal* constructions makes good sense in a number of cases (e.g., 2 Sam. 13:18; 1 Kings 20:21; and 2 Kings 14:14). It may even provide an explanation for Gen. 15:6:

5...הַבֶּט־נָא הַשָּׁמַיְמָה וּסְפֹר הַכּוֹכָבִים אִם־תּוּכַל לִסְפֹּר אֹתָם וַיֹּאמֶר לוֹ כֹּה יִהְיֶה זַרְעֶךָ: 6 וְהֶאֱמִן בַּיהוָה וַיַּחְשְׁבֶהָ לּוֹ צְדָקָה:

"Look up to heaven and count the stars if you can. Such will be your descendants," he told him. *And* Abram *put* his *faith* in Yahweh and he counted this as making him justified.

However, in an equal number of cases, Longacre's explanation of unusual *weqatal* constructions makes less sense, as in 1 Sam. 1:12; 10:9; and 17:37–38 displayed here:

37 ... וַיֹּאמֶר שָׁאוּל אֶל־דָּוִד לֵךְ וַיהוָה יִהְיֶה עִמָּךְ: 38 וַיַּלְבֵּשׁ שָׁאוּל אֶת־דָּוִד מַדָּיו וְנָתַן קוֹבַע נְחֹשֶׁת עַל־רֹאשׁוֹ וַיַּלְבֵּשׁ אֹתוֹ שִׁרְיוֹן:

And Saul said to David, "Go and may God be with you!" Then Saul made David put on his own armor *and put* a bronze helmet on his head and gave him a breastplate to wear.

Particularly unconvincing are Longacre's suggestions that the above-mentioned function is also expressed by וְהָיָה in 1 Sam. 17:47–48:

47 וְיֵדְעוּ כָּל־הַקָּהָל הַזֶּה כִּי־לֹא בְּחֶרֶב וּבַחֲנִית יְהוֹשִׁיעַ יְהוָה... 48 וְהָיָה כִּי־קָם הַפְּלִשְׁתִּי וַיֵּלֶךְ וַיִּקְרַב לִקְרַאת דָּוִד ...

" . . . and that all this assembly may know that it is not by sword or by spear that Yahweh gives the victory." . . . *As* the Philistine had started forward to confront David . . .

Longacre claims that וְהָיָה 'and it is' functions here like the narrative counterpart of וְעַתָּה 'and now' in hortatory discourse: "In both cases we are saying that the preliminaries are over and the substantive saying or action will follow." This is not the function of וְעַתָּה in cases where an imperative follows it. In such cases, וְעַתָּה nearly always introduces a directive that is regarded as a logical consequence of the foregoing state of affairs (*in the light of* x, do y).[31] Longacre's examples of וְהָיָה in Jeremiah need some imaginative reasoning to fit into the above-mentioned mold of introducing pivotal/climactic events. For example, in Jer. 38:28b he assigns to וְהָיָה a cataphoric function that is exactly the opposite of the anaphoric functions elsewhere (see Jer. 3:9; 37:11; and 40:3).³²

38:28 ... וְהָיָה כַּאֲשֶׁר נִלְכְּדָה יְרוּשָׁלָ͏ִם:
39.1 בַּשָּׁנָה הַתְּשִׁעִית לְצִדְקִיָּהוּ מֶלֶךְ־יְהוּדָה ...
בָּא נְבוּכַדְרֶאצַּר ... אֶל־יְרוּשָׁלַ͏ִם וַיָּצֻרוּ עָלֶיהָ:

Now when Jerusalem was captured ... In the ninth year of Zedekiah king of Judah ... Nebuchadnezzar came ... to Jerusalem and besieged it.

Longacre's latest hypothesis of the discourse function of problematic *weqatal* forms provides a possible explanation for some of these constructions, but also raises a number of questions: What exactly is meant by *climactic, pivotal,* and *finalizing*? Are there any differences among them? Are there expressions in other languages that also mark this phenomenon?³³ How are they translated in the various versions?

3.2 The function of marked word order³⁴

Marked word order (i.e., X-V order) in Biblical Hebrew is a construction often associated with the binary opposition foreground versus background in descriptions of the Biblical Hebrew verbal system from a discourse perspective. For example, *(we-)* X *qatal* and *(we-)* X *yiqtol* are considered to be marking subsidiary or background information in Biblical Hebrew narratives, while X *qatal* is regarded as initiating foreground or mainline information, but only in dialogue (Niccacci 1994*a*).

It has been mentioned that most Biblical Hebrew grammarians nowadays agree that the category of "emphasis" is too vague to account for all the finer nuances that may be expressed by means of X-V order in Biblical Hebrew. Bandstra³⁵ and van der Merwe³⁶ attempt to define this concept semantically. However, knowing the semantic meaning of a construction is only a point of departure for understanding its use, and it is Buth (forthcoming *a*) who has contributed much towards a better understanding of the pragmatic functions of marked word order in Biblical Hebrew.

Buth (forthcoming *a* and *b*) is convinced that, from a pragmatic point of view, a clear distinction has to be made between the topic and focus of an utterance. For him focus is "a way of specially marking the salient, important information of a sentence." An example is in Judg. 1:1:

מִי יַעֲלֶה־לָּנוּ אֶל־הַכְּנַעֲנִי בַּתְּחִלָּה לְהִלָּחֶם בּוֹ
וַיֹּאמֶר יְהוָה יְהוּדָה יַעֲלֶה

"Which of us shall march up first against the Canaanites to attack them?" And Yahweh answered, "*Judah* is to attack first."

Another example is in Jer. 1:11:

וַיְהִי דְבַר־יְהוָה אֵלַי לֵאמֹר מָה־אַתָּה רֹאֶה יִרְמְיָהוּ
וָאֹמַר מַקֵּל שָׁקֵד אֲנִי רֹאֶה׃

The Word of Yahweh was addressed to me asking, "Jeremiah, what do you see?" I answered, "*An almond branch* I see."[37]

Topic can be defined as "a constituent that is marked in order to serve as a frame of reference for relating a clause to its context," as in Josh. 2:2:

הִנֵּה אֲנָשִׁים בָּאוּ הֵנָּה הַלַּיְלָה

"Look, *men* are coming here tonight."

However, Buth is aware that the notion of topic has recently been expanded (Dik 1989) to include concepts like discourse topic, new topic, given topic, resumed topic, subtopic, and subject.[38] Buth therefore attempts to demarcate clearly the frame of reference against which his treatment of Biblical Hebrew X-V order must be understood. He commences with the basic distinction of *foreground* versus *background*. For him foreground is a pragmatic concept that is better served by the terms *mainline event* or *thematic continuity*. A mainline event does not communicate referential meaning (e.g., a sequential chain of completed events), but it represents a Biblical Hebrew storyteller's way of advancing his story, as in Jon. 1:16–2:1a:

1:16 וַיִּירְאוּ הָאֲנָשִׁים יִרְאָה גְדוֹלָה אֶת־יְהוָה וַיִּזְבְּחוּ־זֶבַח
לַיהוָה וַיִּדְּרוּ נְדָרִים׃ 2:1 וַיְמַן יְהוָה דָּג גָּדוֹל לִבְלֹעַ אֶת־יוֹנָה . . .

At this the men were seized with dread of Yahweh; they offered a sacrifice to Yahweh and made vows. *And* Yahweh had *arranged* that a great fish should be there to swallow Jonah . . .

Buth agrees with Longacre and Niccacci that Biblical Hebrew has mainly two grammatical devices that speakers may use to advance a story, the *wayyiqtol* and *weqatal* forms, and two that mark background information, *we-X-qatal* and *we-X-yiqtol*. However, he prefers to refer to these two pairs as markers of thematic continuity and discontinuity, respectively.

The functions of X-V order are, on the one hand, to mark focus and, on the other hand, to mark discontinuity. This discontinuity may be a discontinuity either as far as a topic is concerned or a series of events. In Gen. 20:15–16 there is an example of a *we-X-qatal* construction that indicates change of topic:

15 וַיֹּאמֶר אֲבִימֶלֶךְ הִנֵּה אַרְצִי לְפָנֶיךָ בַּטּוֹב בְּעֵינֶיךָ שֵׁב׃

16 וּלְשָׂרָה אָמַר . . .

And Abimelech said (to Abram), "See, my land lies before you. Settle where you please." *To Sarah* he said, . . .

In Gen. 20:4 God is already addressing Abimelech and the X-V order cannot be to mark primarily a changed topic; it is rather to discontinue the series of events in order to provide some background information:

3 וַיָּבֹא אֱלֹהִים אֶל־אֲבִימֶלֶךְ בַּחֲלוֹם הַלָּיְלָה
וַיֹּאמֶר לוֹ הִנְּךָ מֵת . . .
4 וַאֲבִימֶלֶךְ לֹא קָרַב אֵלֶיהָ וַיֹּאמַר . . .

Yahweh visited Abimelech in a dream at night and said to him: "Listen, you are about to die . . ." *Abimelech*, however, did not go near her, and said . . .

In comparing the two preceding examples, it should be noted that in Biblical Hebrew there is a secondary result of introducing such a type of new topic (or contextualizing constituent), namely that the continuity of events is broken, which is the case in Gen. 20:16. A *wayyiqtol* form has been displaced. One may therefore expect to find a newly introduced topic at the head of a paragraph too, as in Gen. 3:1:

וְהַנָּחָשׁ הָיָה עָרוּם מִכֹּל חַיַּת הַשָּׂדֶה אֲשֶׁר עָשָׂה יְהוָה אֱלֹהִים
וַיֹּאמֶר אֶל־הָאִשָּׁה . . .

The serpent was the most subtle of all the wild beasts that Yahweh God had made. It asked the woman . . .

This phenomenon may be explained as follows (Buth forthcoming *b*): A text presupposes one or other type of thematic continuity. This theme or discourse topic is a highly abstract notion that cannot be relegated to a simple function of the grammar. Apart from the overarching thematic continuity there are also smaller continuities in a text, namely, a piece of text/discourse that continues the same situation, the same series of events, or the same topic/character. These continuities resist being broken down in the order that they were mentioned here. In other words, if the topic of a text is changed, there may still be a continuity due to an overarching action that continues. If a series of actions is broken down, there may still be a continuity as far as a larger situation is concerned. In Gen. 20:16 the same type of action—talking—is performed by Abimelech, first to Abram and then to Sarah. In Gen. 20:4 one may say that the situation that is involved is the dialogue between Abimelech and Yahweh. This dialogue is broken up by a "pseudotopic" in order to mark a discontinuity, not of nominal topics, but of the flow of the events that are involved in the dialogue. This role of marked word order to indicate pluperfect reference has been noted by traditional grammarians. Buth goes one step further and argues that this type of discontinuity, where the flow of events is interrupted, may also be used to introduce a new paragraph and episode. Genesis 4:1–2 is a good example of this:

1 וְהָאָדָם יָדַע אֶת־חַוָּה אִשְׁתּוֹ וַתַּהַר וַתֵּלֶד אֶת־קַיִן וַתֹּאמֶר קָנִיתִי אִישׁ אֶת־יְהוָה: 2 וַתֹּסֶף לָלֶדֶת . . .

The man had intercourse with his wife Eve, and she conceived and gave birth to Cain. And she said, "I have acquired a man with the help of Yahweh." 2. She gave again birth . . .

"Adam," the marked nominal item, is not the topic of the sentences following Gen. 4:1a, but rather precedes the verb in order to mark a discontinuity from the events in Genesis 3. A new episode is thus introduced. However, it may happen that the "pseudotopic" is also the topic of the new paragraph or subparagraph, as it is in Gen. 13:14; 18:17; 19:24; 26:26; and 27:6.

In Biblical Hebrew, X-V constructions often break up a sequence of verbs in order to compare two or more topics with one another, as in Gen. 4:4–5:[39]

4 . . . וַיִּשַׁע יְהוָה אֶל־הֶבֶל וְאֶל־מִנְחָתוֹ: 5 וְאֶל־קַיִן וְאֶל־מִנְחָתוֹ לֹא שָׁעָה . . .

Yahweh looked with favor on Abel and his offering. *But on Cain and his offering* he did not look with favor . . .

Buth suggests that because some kind of contrast is usually involved "there is usually a portmanteau with Focus function" (forthcoming *a*). This overlay of the topic and focus function could have been signaled by intonation.[40]

There are also a number of cases where X-V constructions are used in a context where discontinuity is not involved. Genesis 44:3 is an example:[41]

3 הַבֹּקֶר אוֹר וְהָאֲנָשִׁים שֻׁלְּחוּ הֵמָּה וַחֲמֹרֵיהֶם: 4 הֵם יָצְאוּ אֶת־הָעִיר . . . וְיוֹסֵף אָמַר . . .

When morning came and it was light, *the men* were sent off with their donkeys. *They* had scarcely left the city . . . *Joseph* said . . .

Buth (forthcoming *b*) states in this regard:

> The most credible explanation of this is that the author has pragmatically suspended the marking of Foregrounding-Continuity in the story in order to hold the audience's attention at a dramatic Peak . . . It is

the grammatical equivalence of a slow motion technique or of a freezing of a frame at an emotional point of a motion picture film. The X-V structure can be distinguished from a simple Contextualizing Constituent by being used with a sequential event and it can be differentiated from unit-boundary Settings by its logical connections to the surrounding context as non-initial.[42]

We may now summarize the uses of X-V word order as a general marker of discontinuity as follows:

1. Focus marking
2. Contextualizing constituent (topic)
   a. New topic
   b. Comparative topic
   c. Action discontinuity (simultaneous or previous action)
      i. background information
      ii. unit boundaries, both initial and final
3. Dramatic pause

Andersen (forthcoming) investigated the function of fronting in a coordinated clause with a suffixed verb (in Genesis), that is, *we-X-qatal* constructions. He identified six functions that such clauses may have:

1. The true circumstantial clause that reports the events off the mainline.
2. The X element as a negation word.
3. Paragraph-initial clauses that sometimes initiate a new episode.
4. Paragraph-terminal clauses.
5. Paragraph-medial clauses that report the events of the preceding clause.
6. Paragraph-medial clauses that report events that coincide with the event in the preceding clause, a special case being the formation of a chiasmus, in which the two events are presented as two aspects of the same event.

If one compares Buth's catalogue of the pragmatic functions of X-V order in Biblical Hebrew with Andersen's, one immediately realizes that their bases for categorization differ. Andersen asks what the discourse function is of a taxonomy of clauses in Genesis with a *we-X-qatal* form. Buth, on the other hand, uses existing insights from Functional Grammar on the pragmatic function of word order as his point of departure and tries to construct a frame of reference that may account for X-V constructions in Biblical Hebrew. Many of Buth's hypotheses and Andersen's observations complement rather than contradict one another. However, Buth's hypotheses seem to have more explanatory capabilities than those of Andersen. Genesis 31:6 is a case in point:

וְאַתֵּנָה יְדַעְתֶּן כִּי בְּכָל־כֹּחִי עָבַדְתִּי אֶת־אֲבִיכֶן:

You *yourself* know that I have worked for your father with all my strength.

This case does not fit one of Andersen's categories, but in terms of Buth's catalogue the marked subject can be interpreted as the focal constituent (you *yourself*...). Verifying Buth's hypotheses in the light of Andersen's observations would certainly be a worthwhile venture.

3.3 Participant reference

In Biblical Hebrew texts, references to participants sometimes seem overspecified and repeated to us speakers of modern Indo-European languages. Pronominalization occurs at strange places, and different types of split constituents are used relatively often.

De Regt (1991–92), who investigated the way participants are referred to in a corpus of Biblical Hebrew texts, concluded that a number of "normal" Biblical Hebrew conventions may be identified although they differ from European languages. He was able to distinguish between these conventions and marked patterns. Among the normal conventions he noticed two types in particular. The first is that explicit references with a proper name are normally associated with paragraph borders, as in Ruth 1:22 and Gen. 28:10:

וַתָּשָׁב נָעֳמִי וְרוּת הַמּוֹאֲבִיָּה כַלָּתָהּ עִמָּהּ הַשָּׁבָה מִשְּׂדֵי מוֹאָב

This was how *Naomi, she who returned from the country of Moab,* came back with *Ruth the Moabite, her daughter-in-law.*

וַיֵּצֵא יַעֲקֹב מִבְּאֵר שָׁבַע וַיֵּלֶךְ חָרָנָה...

Jacob left for Beersheba and set out for Haran...

The second he saw was that main character participants are referred to differently from others. In his attempt to identify what is normal in Biblical Hebrew, de Regt also found examples that undermine Longacre's (1989) suggestions that there is a difference in the participant reference between lines of direct speech and elsewhere in a discourse. For example, full NP reference (in contrast with pronominal reference) reflects the dominance of the NP referent over the pronominal referent. This may be true in Judg. 6:16:

וַיֹּאמֶר אֵלָיו יְהוָה . . .
And *Yahweh* said to *him*, " . . . "

However, in Judg. 13:13, where Yahweh is of a higher rank than Manoah, the latter is not referred to pronominally.

וַיֹּאמֶר מַלְאַךְ יְהוָה אֶל־מָנוֹחַ . . .
And the *angel of Yahweh* answered *Manoah* . . .

De Regt argues that the use of a pronominal reference in Judg. 6:16 should rather be attributed to the fact that Gideon is "a character in a central role within an already established action sequence" (p. 158).

De Regt could also not detect any difference in meaning between the words וַיֹּאמֶר לוֹ (Gen. 37:13e) and וַיֹּאמֶר (Gen. 22:1), and similar such cases where the addressee is not mentioned pronominally. This is opposed to Longacre's view (1989:169-71, 176-78) that the latter case indicates a stretch of discourse where no tension is present or where something is being glossed over.[43]

Marked ways of referring to participants include the withholding of full reference to a participant (e.g., Gen. 18:1-13, in which the full reference to the Lord as participant appears only in v. 13). De Regt (1992:166) says of the function of this phenomenon that it has a marked stylistic effect in which a persona is developed first and then finally assigned a name. A second marked kind of participant reference is repetition. According to de Regt this repetition may occur for various reasons. For example, it may serve as a climactic point in a text, as in Gen. 37:28:[44]

וַיַּעַבְרוּ אֲנָשִׁים מִדְיָנִים סֹחֲרִים וַיִּמְשְׁכוּ וַיַּעֲלוּ אֶת־יוֹסֵף
מִן־הַבּוֹר וַיִּמְכְּרוּ אֶת־יוֹסֵף לַיִּשְׁמְעֵאלִים בְּעֶשְׂרִים כָּסֶף וַיָּבִיאוּ
אֶת־יוֹסֵף מִצְרָיְמָה׃

Now some Midianite merchants were passing, and they drew *Joseph* up out of the well. They sold *Joseph* to the Ishmaelites for twenty silver pieces, and they took *Joseph* to Egypt.

The repetition of the proper name to refer to a participant may indicate that what he says is important, surprising, or unexpected (e.g., Gen. 18:13; 42:14; 46:30; Judg. 6:13; 8:23). In Ruth 1 and 2 the repetitive reference to "Ruth, the Moabite" serves to remind the reader of Ruth's background. In Jeremiah 28 the repetitive reference to "Jeremiah, the prophet" and "Hananiah the prophet" has a tongue-in-cheek nuance in the quarrel over who is the true prophet.

According to Andersen (forthcoming) the apparently superfluous repetition of "God" in Genesis 1 serves to mark off each of the successive actions that took place as distinct. In Genesis 2, where this subject is not repeated like this, the events are clustered together in units comprising a few sentences.[45] The process is similar when the objects of a number of successive sentences are ellipsed, as in Gen. 3:6.[46]

A third type of marked participant reference is that in which "superfluous" pronouns are used with finite verbal forms that already include the pronominal reference. An example is in Gen. 42:8:

וַיַּכֵּר יוֹסֵף אֶת־אֶחָיו וְהֵם לֹא הִכִּרֻהוּ׃

Joseph recognized his brothers, but *they* did not recognize him.

Other examples are:

וְאַתֵּנָה יְדַעְתֶּן כִּי בְּכָל־כֹּחִי עָבַדְתִּי אֶת־אֲבִיכֶן׃

You *yourself* know that I have worked for your father with all my strength. (Gen. 31:6)

גַּם אָנֹכִי יָדַעְתִּי כִּי בְתָם־לְבָבְךָ עָשִׂיתָ זֹּאת

I too know that you did this with a clear conscience. (Gen. 20:6)

וַתָּקָם הִיא וְכַלֹּתֶיהָ

She stood up, *she* and her daughter-in-law. (Ruth 1:6)

All these cases could be explained in terms of other grammatical constructions. For example, in Gen. 42:8 two topics are compared, in 31:6 a focus constituent is marked, in 20:6 the use of the pronoun is necessitated by the focus particle, and in Ruth 1:6 a so-called split subject is involved. Waltke and O'Connor (1990:294) describe the function of the latter construction as indicating "the chief actor among other actors."

Creason (1993) provides a more nuanced view in this regard. He identifies two main types of split subject: those in which a preposition plus pronominal suffix refers back to the subject (NP1) that is congruent with the verb, and those without this preposition plus suffix.

The following are examples of the first type:

וַתֵּצֵא מִן־הַמָּקוֹם אֲשֶׁר הָיְתָה־שָׁמָּה וּשְׁתֵּי כַלֹּתֶיהָ עִמָּהּ

So *she* and *her two daughters-in-law* **with her** came away from the place where she was. (Ruth 1:7)

וַיִּבְרַח אֲדַד הוּא וַאֲנָשִׁים אֲדֹמִיִּים מֵעַבְדֵי אָבִיו אִתּוֹ לָבוֹא מִצְרָיִם

But *Hadad, he* and *Edomites in his father's service* **with him**, fled to Egypt. (1 Kings 11:17)

Examples of the second type may be seen in Gen. 26:26 and Ruth 1:1:

וַאֲבִימֶלֶךְ הָלַךְ אֵלָיו מִגְּרָר וַאֲחֻזַּת מֵרֵעֵהוּ וּפִיכֹל שַׂר־צְבָאוֹ׃

Abimelech [NP1] came to him from Gerar, with *Ahuzzath, his adviser, and Phicol, the commander of his army* [NP2]. (Gen. 26:26)

וַיֵּלֶךְ אִישׁ מִבֵּית לֶחֶם יְהוּדָה לָגוּר בִּשְׂדֵי מוֹאָב הוּא וְאִשְׁתּוֹ וּשְׁנֵי בָנָיו׃

A man from Bethlehem Judah [NP1] went, *he* [NPron1], *his wife and his two sons* [NP2] to sojourn in the fields of Moab. (Ruth 1:1)

These two main types may be further subdivided—those in which the subject is repeated by means of an independent pronoun and those in which no such repetition is involved. According to Creason (1993), the discourse function of the two main types is basically the same:

> [they are] used to record the activity of two or more participants in a discourse while indicating that they differ with regard to their rank within that discourse. The central participant in the discourse is encoded as NP1 and the participants of lower rank are encoded as NP2.

However, the presence of the preposition in the first type restricts its use in a discourse, because it may be used only if its centrality in a discourse has been established and the NP1 participant will be central in the rest of that episode. When NP1 and NP2 are more or less of equal rank, the optional pronoun (NPron1) is normally used and the NP2 is not defined in terms of the NP1.

3.4 Discourse particles

In the paper that I presented at the DLBH seminar (1993*a*), I proposed a reference grammar for theological students that would include insights from a discourse perspective. Such a grammar would provide, among other things, a particle lexicon dealing (where relevant) with the syntax, semantics, and pragmatics of the Biblical Hebrew particles. As illustrated in that paper, it is important to distinguish between the semantic basis and pragmatic use of the discourse particles. It is particularly important for translators to realize that pragmatic meaning may be lexicalized in one language but not in another one. For example, *even* in English has the same logical basis as *also*. In the case of *even*, the fact that the item to be included or added is an extreme one is encoded in its lexical content. In the Bantu language Xhosa, the notion of *also* is not even lexicalized; rather the equivalent of *and* has to fulfill this role in a particular syntactic position.

Follingstad takes this phenomenon into account in his paper (1993). He uses an in-depth study of הִנֵּה 'behold' by Slager (1989:50–79) as his point of departure and then, with the help of insights provided by Dik's 1978 *Functional Grammar* and Sperber and Wilson's *Relevance* (1986),[47] attempts to put the description of הִנֵּה on a linguistically sound footing. He eventually illustrates how a fronted relative clause, postposed adverbial construction, and focus markers are needed to account for הִנֵּה in the Tyap language.

Traditional grammars and lexica had difficulty in assigning הִנֵּה to a traditional word class. It was often regarded as an interjection. Richter (1978:193) called it a sentence deictic, and Kogut (1986:54) points out that a feature of הִנֵּה is that its presence ensures that some type of sentence will follow. According to Slager (1989:50), הִנֵּה "is used to highlight the noun/proposition that follows it. It raises the relative prominence of the information after it, so that the information has an impact on the reader/listener. Usually, it calls upon the reader to pay attention." Follingstad defines הִנֵּה more narrowly in terms of Dik's notion of focus. For Follingstad, הִנֵּה, as a focus marker, marks a proposition as prominent. It draws attention to what is relatively the most important or salient information in the context, typically because the information is surprising or counter to expectation in some way. He finds support for his view of הִנֵּה in the fact that הִנֵּה has to be translated in Tyap by various focus constructions and a contraexpectation construction. Follingstad's view is an example of the way in which current linguistic theories and descriptions of other languages can help solve problematic constructions in Biblical Hebrew. Similar studies of other particles and conjunctions, such as אָז 'then', לָכֵן[48] 'therefore', and עַל־כֵּן 'therefore', would certainly be worthwhile.

4. Concluding comments

4.1 The most productive way of studying Biblical Hebrew discourse

As part of a larger movement in the study of Biblical Hebrew, the most productive way of studying Biblical Hebrew from a discourse perspective appears to be one that strives to account for all the Biblical Hebrew data at our disposal and building, whenever possible, on the existing insights of the lower levels of linguistic description. We must operate with well-defined categories at all levels of description and attempt to address one clearly defined problem at a time. For these purposes a sophisticated Biblical Hebrew linguistic database is normally required.

To be successful in studying Biblical Hebrew from a discourse perspective, the researcher must also allow imaginative hypotheses to be formulated on the basis of observations of discourse phenomena in other languages. Even if some hypotheses are refuted, our knowledge is furthered by knowing what a construction does *not* mean. It is vital, however, that the hypotheses and categories be defined clearly. No researcher should use categories so vague that they could explain a whole range of strange constructions. (That would put us back at the much-debated "emphasis" category.) Finally, the concepts and categories that are used should be those that can also be understood by fellow scholars in other languages.

4.2 Some insights gained from studying Biblical Hebrew discourse

If the development of Biblical Hebrew discourse linguistics is viewed as I have portrayed it in this article, the reader will now have certain perspectives that will help in a better understanding of Biblical Hebrew: (1) an emerging picture of what a well-formed Biblical Hebrew text may look like,[49] (2) new hypotheses to test, and (3) an awareness of areas that have not yet been investigated at all. To expand on these "perspectives," I will not deal with them separately but will allude to them in the following summaries of some insights for Biblical Hebrew that I gathered from studying discourse:

a. We are fairly certain that the mainline of a narrative is continued by *wayyiqtol* forms, and the mainline of a procedural or predictive discourse by *weqatal* forms. These forms do not necessarily have referential meaning, but are a Biblical Hebrew speaker's presentation of what is continuing his narration. However, as far as instructional discourse is concerned, we are not yet certain what the difference is between a sequence of directive forms and a directive continued by a sequence of *weqatal* forms. The reason why an *infinitivus absolutus* form sometimes initiates such a sequence or is part of such a sequence also still needs to be determined.

b. Discontinuing constructions referring to events that continue a narrative do occur. The function of this marked X-V construction apparently is to create a dramatic pause. On the other hand, background information is sometimes elevated to mainline information by means of a mainline verbal form. Furthermore, *weqatal*, normally not a mainline construction, sometimes occurs in among a series of *wayy-*

iqtol forms. In a number of these cases, but not all, the *weqatal* forms may constitute a tertiary storyline in a narrative referring to events that used to happen. Although some of the residue of this construction may be due to the transmission of the Biblical Hebrew text, others may also be explained as marking climactic/pivotal/ finalizing events. (Of course, the concepts climactic/pivotal/finalizing still need to be more clearly defined, and further research has to be done in this regard.)

c. We know that thematic continuity is a highly abstract notion that should not be equated with a grammatically marked pragmatic notion like topic. X-V constructions are used to (re)introduce a topic or contextualizing constituent, compare two topics, or to mark the break of a series of events to introduce a new paragraph. All these discontinuing constructions may be embedded in a larger unit with the same overarching theme. The function of X-V constructions closing a unit still needs to be investigated.

d. An X-V construction may also mark a focal constituent. If a verbless clause is involved, a predicate-subject order may fulfill the same function. Focal constituents, like new topics, are expected to be more frequent in dialogue and procedural discourse than in narrative discourse.

e. Pilot studies of participant reference indicate that conventions very different from those of European languages may be expected. At this stage a number of hypotheses have been refuted, and only a few patterns have been identified, such as that explicit full NP reference occurs at paragraph borders and that main characters are more pronominalized than subsidiary participants. A few marked ways of participant reference have been identified, such as split subjects, repetitions, and superfluous pronouns. Significant is the way in which explicit NP subject repetition is used to mark events as distinct. We know too that a certain type of split subject construction determines the role of the referents involved in that construction for the rest of the paragraph. However, the function of other split constituents must still be determined. Although the functions of apparently superfluous pronouns that precede a finite verbal form can be fairly well explained, no convincing reason has yet been provided for cases where a pronoun follows a finite verb.

f. We know that discourse particles may reveal crucial information on the relationship between utterances, clusters of utterances, and paragraphs. For the reader they often disambiguate a number of possible relationships between both small and large units of texts. They may also display a speaker's or author's view on the information value of what he is saying (e.g., הִנֵּה). This is an area where more research certainly would improve our understanding of Biblical Hebrew discourse. Questions about the pragmatic function of אַף,⁵⁰ אַךְ, and לָכֵן and the difference between לָכֵן and וְעַתָּה must still be answered.

4.3 Biblical Hebrew studies in relation to discourse genres

As far as discourse genres are concerned, most studies up till now have been done on narrative material. Pioneering efforts have been made by Andersen (Andersen and Freedman 1980, 1989) and Salisbury (1993) on prophetic and poetic literature, but in the words of Longacre, we have only scratched the surface in these areas. The phenomenon of mixed discourse types has also not received much attention.

Notes

1. Lowery (forthcoming) points to the fact that what in the United States is called discourse analysis, is called text linguistics in Europe. (Cf. also Blass 1990:10 in this regard.) Therefore I use the terms *text* and *discourse* as synonyms in this article.

2. I adopt a very wide definition of the grammar of a language. (Cf. also van der Merwe 1991a:167–87.)

3. Cf. van der Merwe 1987:161–90.

4. Cf. Robins 1990.

5. According to Bachmann (1989:87), competence in a language comprises phonological, morphological, syntactic, semantic, textgrammatical, speech-act, and sociolinguistic competence. Knowing a language certainly cannot be equated with knowing its forms.

6. For example, does the term *accusative* refer to a morphological feature of a word, or does it refer to a syntactic function? Does *emphasis* refer to intonational stress, is it a semantic category, or does it refer to an attitude of the speaker towards the content of his utterance? In other words, is it a pragmatic category?

7. Cf. van der Merwe (1987:167–87; 1989:217–41).

8. Cf. Hoftijzer (1981, 1985) and van der Merwe (1990).

9. For a discussion on the roots of so-called valency grammar, as well as its use by mainly German lexicographers, cf. Somers (1987).

10. For the rationale behind his morphological transcription, cf. Richter (1983:3–12).

11. For the most recent progress on Richter's database, consult Rieple (1993:6–28).

12. Schweizer (1981, 1986), a former student of Richter, developed a theoretical framework that includes syntax, semantics, and pragmatics.

13. For the impact of Richter on the study of Biblical Hebrew grammar, cf. Gross, Irsigler, and Seidl (1991).

14. Cf. Gross (1987a, 1987b, 1988, 1991:97–118). The results of a major research project on the Biblical Hebrew sentence by Gross will apparently be published in the near future.

15. For a more detailed description of Talstra's work, cf. Hardmeier and Talstra (1989:408–28), Talstra (1989:9–28; 1991:180–93), and Winther-Nielsen (1994).

16. In this regard Talstra is in line with mainstream general linguistics that restricts syntax to surface-level phenomena and that maintains a strict dichotomy between syntax and semantics. Talstra does not claim that his approach is without any theory. His programs could be described as interactive data-oriented processes and the higher the level of the hierarchy, the more theory-dependent the programs become.

17. Lowery (forthcoming) distinguishes between psychosocial, anthropological (both from a sociological perspective) approaches, and cognitive and grammatical (both from a linguistic perspective) approaches. According to Lowery a basic assumption of the grammatical approach is that speakers "also organize text in some systematic fashion with the *forms* of language."

18. Buth (forthcoming *b*) has a brief introduction to Dik. See also Dik (1978, 1989).

19. See also Mann and Thompson's overview (1992:19–45) of ten different approaches to clauselike structures that appeared since Longacre (1976a). Longacre (1976a:79) distinguished only four basic types of interclause relationships, namely conjoining, alternation, temporal, and implication.

20. Longacre (1983) also defines linguistic criteria that may be used in the analysis of the plot of a narrative.

21. Cf. van der Merwe (1987:71).

22. Also referred to as discursive speech (Niccacci 1994a).

23. Buth (1992:99) cites this text as evidence against the view that a *wayyiqtol* form has no tense or aspect value of its own, because it follows a *weqatal* form that denotes a continuing action, but does not carry it on. However, Niccacci would argue that these forms are not on the same line of communication.

24. This rather traditional view is often represented by theories of a so-called *waw*-consecutive in Biblical Hebrew. Buth (1992:98) categorically refutes this theory.

25. Buth uses a Modern Hebrew pronunciation here.

26. Comparing the results of such an investigation with the semantic values that Buth (1993a) assigns to *wayyiqtol* forms, i.e., definite "past perfective," where continuity/foreground is involved, would be worthwhile. Buth's view certainly includes logical and semantic connections where specification and resultative relationships are involved.

27. Cf. Gross (1981:135, 145).

28. In terms of Niccacci's view (1994*b*) it differs, however, from the *wayyiqtol* form because it cannot start an autonomous textual unit.

29. According to Longacre (1993), instructional discourse differs from predictive and procedural discourse because "it is characterized by sparse use of the imperative, regular *weqatal* backbone, a certain amount of specification data (typically given in nominal, i.e., verbless clauses) second-person orientation, and orientation towards construction and implementation."

30. According to Longacre (1993), a chain of imperatives can be mitigated by using a chain of *weqatal* forms instead. Genesis 40:15 is then an example of this. A study conducted by Randy Garr at UCLA in Santa Barbara (personal conversation) on politeness in the OT may shed more light on these views of Longacre. It may also be asked whether certain lexical constraints are involved in these types of constructions as in Exodus 19:24 (לֵךְ רֵד וְעָלִיתָ אַתָּה וְאַהֲרֹן עִמָּךְ).

31. Cf. van der Merwe (1993*b*).

32. Stipp (1992:544) points to the fact that most of these problematic cases of וְהָיָה occur in the Books of 1 Samuel and Jeremiah. He suggests that these cases of וְהָיָה should rather be attributed to the transmission of the text by people who were acquainted with a version of Hebrew in which וְהָיָה has the same function as that of its *wayyiqtol* counterpart in Biblical Hebrew. He bases his views on the way in which the LXX translated these cases of וְהָיָה in Jeremiah and on a similar tendency of conflating two strands of Hebrew among other Biblical Hebrew constructions in Jeremiah.

33. I regard this as a crucial question because it will enable the grammarian to broaden substantially the corpus on which he bases his definition of this discourse function. Kenneth Pike put a similar question to Bob Bergen as far as his innovative catalogue of peak-producing devices used in Biblical Hebrew narrative is concerned (1993*a*, 1993*b*, 1994). The fact of the matter is, *peak* may also be a vague term if it is not clearly defined. Moreover, if one postulates a catalogue of peak-producing devices in Biblical Hebrew that do not have any counterpart in any other language, this catalogue will barely advance beyond the point of being a heuristic tool for identifying possible peaks in Biblical Hebrew narrative. Nevertheless, the usefulness of Bergen's computer program for this type of study should not be underestimated.

34. Biblical Hebrew is regarded as a VSO or VO language (cf. Bandstra 1992:115 and Buth forthcoming *b*). Marked word order in Biblical Hebrew occurs when the verbal constituent or predicate in Biblical Hebrew is preceded by any other constituent. Only in sentences where the verb is a participle is the unmarked word order subject + verb (participle). (Cf. Buth 1993*b*.)

35. Bandstra states (1992:123): "Emphasis is a function of non-V-(S)-O word order and can better be termed *topicalization*. Topicalization takes what is normally nonsalient information, fronts that constituent, and places it in a position of information prominence."

36. Van der Merwe (1990:39-47) makes use of the concept *focus*. An item is marked for focus when it represents a particular item from at least two or more possible alternatives. In the sentence *John married yesterday*, *John* will be marked for focus in a context in which the speaker and his audience know that *somebody* married yesterday, but with the identity of the person uncertain. In spoken English *John* will then receive intonational stress in order to confirm who it was that was married yesterday. This type of focus where a speaker asserts or confirms the identity of a referent van der Merwe calls the *focus of the illocutionary act*. But when a speaker wants to introduce a new topic, reinstate a referent as the topic of a sentence, or play off topics against one another, he marks an item or items for the *focus of topicalization*. Van der Merwe (1991b) applies this hypothesis to the sentences with X-V order in the book of Joshua. His view that allowing grades of focus may lead to measuring the grade of an item's focus in terms of the amount of intonational stress an item will get in the researcher's mother tongue resulted in a sharply two-dimensional representation of the topics in Joshua, as well as leaving a residue of cases that he could not explain in terms of his hypothesis.

37. Buth (1993b) points out that the unmarked word order in Biblical Hebrew verbless clauses is subject-predicate. In nominal sentences with a participle as predicate the subject will therefore always precede the verb as is the case in Jer. 1:11 when an object is marked as the focus constituent.

38. Buth does not like the term *topic*. He prefers to talk of a "contextualizing constituent." He is of the opinion that the notions of new topic and subtopic are not yet defined clearly enough as part of the grammar. He suggests that the notions of subject and object will cover some of the data.

39. Andersen (unpublished) regards this type of construction as a chiasmus that presents two events as they occur simultaneously and "puts the events on an even footing as far as staging is concerned." They are not like a mainline clause with an off-line circumstantial clause, but both the events that they report are "on-line."

40. This view of Buth has been influenced by Dik (1989:266), who claims that contrastive focus is involved in this type of construction. However, Taglicht (1984:45) points out that "contrastive," if defined as corresponding to marked focus, is really a "pseudo-contextual function." In fact, if one's point of departure is a semantic definition of the concept of focus as described in note 36, focus is by definition contrastive. The apparent additional contrastive focus in the above-mentioned cases can usually be accounted for by the contrastive content of predicates that are compared. Furthermore, Gen. 4:4a is a classic example of how a contrast is played down by a focus particle with the semantic core "addition" (cf. van der Merwe forthcoming *a*).

41. Cf. also Gen. 38:25; Num. 16:3;, 17:13-15; Esther 7:6-10. Buth's explanation may also apply to the X-V order in Gen. 25:34a. According to Andersen (unpublished), "The event reported in v. 34a is not background; it is indeed the climax, since it clinches the deal."

42. Although Buth's category "dramatic peak" is well defined, one may ask here too, as in the case of Longacre's pivotal function of nonsequential *wayyiqtol* forms, whether this pragmatic category is also explicitly marked in other languages.

43. Cf. Gen. 22:12a as a counterexample in this regard.

44. According to Longacre (1989:30, 145), the importance of this event in the life of Joseph's family is marked.

45. So much so that the nonrepetition of the unchanged subject overrides the normal function of the *wayyiqtol* to report events in temporal succession in וַיְבָרֶךְ אֱלֹהִים אֶת־יוֹם . . . וַיְקַדֵּשׁ אֹתוֹ (Gen. 2:3).

46. Irsigler (1984:58-61) uses the notion "Satzbund" to describe the clustering of sentences. Determining all the types of sentence clusters that are possible in Biblical Hebrew and determining whether clustering is influenced by the semantic field of the verbs may yield important insights for both the better understanding of some *wayyiqtol* forms (cf. note 45) and units larger than sentences that could be formed in Biblical Hebrew.

47. As mentioned earlier, van der Merwe (forthcoming *a*) in his description of the particle גַּם also utilizes perspectives from Sperber and Wilson's Relevance Theory as applied by Blakemore (1987) and Blass (1990).

48. The differences between לָכֵן and וְעַתָּה too are not certain.

49. For a synthesis of the state of affairs in 1985, see Lowery (1985). More recently Lowery (forthcoming) has proposed a framework for a Hebrew discourse grammar that shows the broad scope of Biblical Hebrew discourse linguistics.

50. See Mulder 1991:132-42.

References

Aejmelaeus, A. 1986. Function and interpretation of כִּי in Biblical Hebrew. *Journal of Biblical Literature* 105:193-209.

Andersen, F. I. 1970. *The Hebrew verbless clause in the Pentateuch*. JBL Monograph Series XIV. New York: Abingdon.

———. 1974. *The sentence in Biblical Hebrew*. New York: Mouton.

———. 1985. Orthography and text transmission. *Text* 2:25-53.

———. 1994. Salience, implicature, ambiguity and redundancy. (In this volume.)

———. Forthcoming. Discourse features of dialogue in narrative texts, illustrated from Genesis 1-3.

———. Unpublished. Fronting in a coordinated clause with a suffixed verb.

Andersen, F. I., and A. D. Forbes. 1986. *Spelling in the Hebrew Bible: Dahood memorial lecture*. (Biblica et Orientalia 41). Rome: Biblical Institute Press.

———. 1992. *The vocabulary of the Old Testament*. Rome: Pontificio Istituto Biblico.

Andersen, F. I., and D. N. Freedman. 1980. *Hosea: A new translation and Commentary*. Anchor Bible, vol. 24. Garden City, N.Y.: Doubleday.

———. 1989. *Amos: A new translation and commentary*. Anchor Bible, vol. 24. Garden City, N.Y.: Doubleday.

Bachmann, L. F. 1990. *Fundamental considerations in language testing.* Oxford: Oxford University Press.

Bandstra, B. R. 1982. *The syntax of the particle KY in Biblical Hebrew and Ugaritic.* Doctoral thesis, Yale University.

———. 1992. Word order and emphasis in Biblical Hebrew narrative: Syntactic observations on Genesis 22 from a discourse perspective. In Bodine 1992, 109-23.

Bergen, B. 1993*a*. How did Hebrew storytellers produce 'peak'? A catalogue of peak-producing devices used in Biblical Hebrew narrative. (Paper read at DLBH.)

———. 1993*b*. Producing theme by controlling lexical distribution: A lexical distribution analysis of Genesis 1:1-2:3. (Paper read at DLBH.)

———. 1994. Evil spirits and eccentric grammar: A study of the relationship between grammar and meaning in 1 Samuel 16:13-23. (In this volume.)

Berns, M. 1990. *Context of competence: Social and cultural considerations in communicative language teaching.* New York: Plenum Press.

Blakemore, D. 1987. *Semantic constraints on relevance.* Oxford: Basil Blackwell.

Blass, R. 1990. *Relevance relations in discourse: With special reference to Sissala.* Cambridge: Cambridge University Press.

Bodine, W., ed. 1992. *Linguistics and Biblical Hebrew.* Winona Lake: Eisenbrauns.

Brend, R. M., and K. L. Pike, eds. 1976. *Tagmemics.* Vol. 1, *Aspects of the field.* The Hague: Mouton.

Buth, R. 1992. The Hebrew verb in current discussions. *Journal of Translation and Textlinguistics* 5:91-105.

———. 1993*a*. The Hebrew tense-aspect-mood systems. (Paper read at DLBH.)

———. 1993*b*. The Hebrew verbal clause. (Paper read at DLBH.)

———. 1993*c*. Syntax and pragmatics within Hebrew poetry. (Paper read at DLBH.)

———. 1994. Methodological collision between source criticism and discourse: the problem of "unmarked overlay" and the pluperfect *wayyiqtol*. (In this volume.)

———. Forthcoming *a*. Contextualizing constituent as topic, non-sequential background and dramatic pause: Hebrew and Aramaic evidence. In Selected papers from the 4th colloquium on functional grammar, Copenhagen, 1990.

———. Forthcoming *b*. Functional grammar, Hebrew and Aramaic: An integrated, exegetically significant, textlinguistic approach to syntax. *Semeia Studies.*

Creason, S. 1993. Split subjects and participant reference in Hebrew narrative. (Paper read at DLBH.)

de Regt, L. 1991-92. Devices of participant reference in some Biblical Hebrew texts: Their importance in translation. *Jaarbericht "Ex Oriente Lux"* 32:150-71.

Dik, S. C. 1978. *Functional grammar.* London: Academic Press.

———. 1989. *The theory of functional grammar.* Functional Grammar, series 9. Dordrecht, Holland: Foris.

Follingstad, C. M. 1993. *Hinneh* and focus function with application to Tyap. (Paper read at DLBH.)

Gesenius, W., E. Kautzsch, and E. A. Cowley. 1910. *Gesenius' Hebrew grammar.* 2d ed. Oxford: Clarendon.

Gross, W. 1981. Syntaktische Erscheinungen am Anfang althebräischer Erzählungen: Hintergrund und Vordergrund. Congress volume, Vienna 1980, 131-45. VTS 32. Leiden: Brill.

———. 1987a. *Die Pendenskonstruktion im biblischen Hebräisch*. ATS 27. St. Ottilien: EOS Verlag.
———. 1987b. Zur Syntagm-Folge im hebräischen Verbalsatz: Die Stellung des Subjekts in Dtn 1–15. *Biblische Notizen* 40:63–95.
———. 1988. Der Einfluss der Pronominalisierung auf die Syntagmem-Folgen im hebräischen Verbalsatz: untersucht an Dtn 1–25. *Biblische Notizen* 43:49–69.
———. 1991. Satzfolge, Satzteilfolge und Satzart als Kriterien der Subkategorisierung hebräischer Konjunktionalsätze, am Beispiel der כִּי-Sätze untersucht. In Gross, Irsigler, and Seidl. 1991, 97–118.
Gross, W., H. Irsigler, and T. Seidl, eds. 1991. *Text, Methode und Grammatik: Wolfgang Richter zum 65*. St. Ottilien: EOS Verlag.
Hardmeier, C., and E. Talstra. 1989. Sprachgestalt und Sinngehalt: Wege zu neuen Instrumenten der computergestützten Textwahrnehmung. *ZAW* 101:408–28.
Hoftijzer, J. 1981. *A search for method: A study in the syntactical use of the H-locale in classical Hebrew*. Leiden: E. J. Brill.
———. 1985. *The function and use of the imperfect forms with nun-paragogicum in classical Hebrew*. Studia Semitica Neerlandica 21. Assen: Van Gorcum.
Hwang, S. J., and W. R. Merrifield, eds. 1992. *Language in context: Essays for Robert E. Longacre*. Dallas: Summer Institute of Linguistics.
Irsigler, H. 1984. *Psalm 73—Monolog eines Weisen. Text, Programm, Struktur*. ATS 20. St. Ottilien: EOS Verlag.
Japhet, S., ed. 1986. *Studies in Bible*. Jerusalem: Magnes Press.
Jongeling, K., H. L. Murre-Van den Berg, and K. van Rompay, eds. 1991. *Studies in Hebrew and Aramaic syntax: Presented to Professor J. Hoftijzer on the occasion of his sixty-fifth birthday*. Studies in Semitic Languages and Linguistics 17. Leiden: Brill.
Joüon, P., and T. Muraoka. 1991. *A grammar of Biblical Hebrew*. 2 vols. Rome: Pontifical Biblical Institute.
Kogut, S. 1986. On the meaning and syntactic status of הִנֵּה in Biblical Hebrew. In Japhet, pp. 132–54.
Longacre, Robert E. 1976a. *An anatomy of speech notions*. Lisse: Peter de Ridder.
———. 1976b. Discourse. In Brend and Pike, 1–44.
———. 1983. *The grammar of discourse*. Topics in language and linguistics. New York: Plenum.
———. 1989. *Joseph: A story of divine providence: A text theoretical and textlinguistic analysis of Genesis 37 and 39–48*. Winona Lake, Ind.: Eisenbrauns.
———. 1993. WQTL forms in Biblical Hebrew prose: A discourse-modular approach. (Paper read at DLBH.)
Lowery, K. E. 1985. *Toward a discourse grammar of Biblical Hebrew*. Ann Arbor: UMI.
———. Forthcoming. The theoretical foundations of Hebrew discourse grammar. In *Semeia Studies*.
Mann, W. C., and S. A. Thompson. 1988. Rhetorical structure theory: Towards a functional theory of text organization. *Text* 8:243–81.
———. 1992. Relational discourse structure: A comparison of approaches to structuring text by "contrast." In Hwang and Merrifield, p. 35.
Mulder, M. J. 1991. Die Partikel אָז in biblischen Hebräisch. In Jongeling, Murre-Van den Berg, and van Rompay, pp. 132–42.

Muraoka, T. 1985. *Emphatic words and structures in Biblical Hebrew.* Jerusalem: Magnes Press.
Niccacci, A. 1994*a*. Analysis of Biblical narrative. (In this volume.)
———. 1994*b*. The Hebrew verbal system. (In this volume.)
Orlinsky, H. M., and R. G. Bratcher. 1991. *A history of Bible translation and the North American contribution.* Atlanta: Scholar's Press.
Richter, W. 1978. *Grundlagen einer althebräischen Grammatik. A. Grundfragen einer sprachwissenschaftlichen Grammatik. B. Beschreibungsebene: I. Das Wort.* ATS 8. St. Ottilien: EOS Verlag.
———. 1979. *Grundlagen einer althebräischen Grammatik. Bd. II. Die Wortfügung* [Morphosyntax]. ATS 10. St. Ottilien: EOS Verlag.
———. 1980. *Grundlagen einer althebräischen Grammatik. Bd. III. Der Satz.* ATS 13. St. Ottilien: EOS Verlag.
———. 1983. *Transliteration und Transkription. Objekt- und metasprachliche Metazeichensysteme zur Wiedergabe hebräischer Texte.* ATS 19. St. Ottilien: EOS Verlag.
———. 1985. *Untersuchungen zur Valenz althebräischer Verben 1. ʾRK.* ATS 23. St. Ottilien: EOS Verlag.
———. 1986. *Untersuchungen zur Valenz althebräischer Verben 2. GBH, ʿMQ, QSR II.* ATS 25. St. Ottilien: EOS Verlag.
———. 1991. *Biblia Hebraica transcripta.* ATS 33. St. Ottilien: EOS Verlag.
Rieple, C. 1993. *Sind David und Saul berechenbar? Von der sprachlichen Analyse zur literarischen Struktur von 1 Sam 21 und 22.* ATS 39. St. Ottilien: EOS Verlag.
Robins, R. H. 1990. *A short history of linguistics.* London: Longmans.
Salisbury, M. 1994. Hebrew proverbs and how to translate them. (In this volume.)
Schweizer, H. 1981. *Metaphorische Grammatik.* ATS 15. St. Ottilien: EOS Verlag.
———. 1986. *Biblische Texte verstehen.* Stuttgart: Kohlhammer.
Slager, D. 1989. The use of "behold" in the Old Testament. *Occasional Papers in Translation and Textlinguistics* 3:50-79.
Somers, H. L. 1987. *Valency and case in computational linguistics.* Edinburgh: Edinburgh University Press.
Sperber, D., and D. Wilson. 1986. *Relevance: Communication and cognition.* Cambridge, Mass.: Harvard University Press.
Stipp, H. J. 1991. Wəhayā für nichtiterative Vergangenheit? Zu syntaktischen Modernisierungen im masoretischen Jeremiabuch. In Gross, Irsigler, and Seidl, pp. 521-47.
Taglict, J. 1984. *Message and emphasis: On focus and scope in English.* London: Longmans.
Talstra, E. 1989. *Computer assisted analysis of biblical texts.* Amsterdam: Free University Press.
———. 1991. Biblical Hebrew clause types and clause hierarchy. In Jongeling, Murre-van den Berg, and van Rompay, pp. 180-93.
van der Merwe, C. H. J. 1983. Hebrew grammars, exegesis and commentaries. *Journal of Northwest Semitic Languages* 11:143-56.
———. 1987. A short survey of major contributions to the grammatical description of Old Hebrew since 1800 A.D. *Journal of Northwest Semitic Languages* 13:161-90.

———. 1989. Recent trends in the linguistic description of Old Hebrew. *Journal of Northwest Semitic Languages* 15:217-41.
———. 1990. *The Old Hebrew particle gam:. A syntactic-semantic description of gam in Gn-2Kg*. ATS 34. EOS Verlag. St. Ottilien.
———. 1991*a*. Applied linguistics and the teaching of Biblical Hebrew. *Journal of Semitics* 3:167-87.
———. 1991*b*. The function of word order in Old Hebrew—with special reference to cases where a syntagmeme precedes a verb in Joshua. *Journal of Northwest Semitic Languages* 17:129-144.
———. 1991*c*. The Old Hebrew "particles" ʾak and raq (in Genesis to 2 Kings). In Gross, Irsigler, and Seidl, pp. 297-312.
———. 1993*a*. Discourse linguistics and a Biblical Hebrew grammar for theological students. (Paper read at DLBH.)
———. 1993*b*. Particles and the interpretation of Old Testament texts. *Journal for the Study of the Old Testament* 60:27-44.
———. Forthcoming. Pragmatics of the translation value of *gam*. *Journal of Semitics* 4. University of South Africa.
Waltke, B. K., and M. O'Connor. 1990. *An introduction to Biblical Hebrew syntax*. Winona Lake, Indiana: Eisenbrauns.
Wheatley-Irving, L. 1993. Semantics of Biblical Hebrew temporal subordinate clauses in 1 Samuel and 1 Kings: When you say "when"? (Paper read at DLBH.)
Winther-Nielsen, N. 1994. The miraculous grammar of Joshua 3-4: Computer-aided analysis of the rhetorical and syntactic structure. (In this volume.)

2

Weqatal FORMS IN BIBLICAL HEBREW PROSE
A Discourse-modular Approach

Robert E. Longacre

> This article takes issue with the explanations of usages of the *waw* consecutive perfect (*weqatal*) as found in the Gesenius-Kautzsch-Cowley (1910) Hebrew grammar. In attempting to account for various occurrences of this form GKC leave a large number of unexplained residues, even suggesting that in some places the *weqatal* form is simply erroneous. From a discourse-motivated perspective with attention to distinction of text types (genres) and to progress within given texts, I restate what is helpful in GKC and suggest a previously unposited function to explain a sizable proportion of the GKC residues.

Gesenius' Hebrew Grammar (Kautzsch 1910), hereafter GKC, characterizes the perfect with *waw*-consecutive forms (*weqatal*) as primarily consequent on another preceding form (imperfect, imperative, or participle) and as characteristically frequentative in meaning, but "obtaining a kind of independent force—especially for the purpose of announcing future events" in certain passages, and with certain special uses in the apodosis of conditional or quasiconditional forms (330–38). GKC also lists, however, a considerable residue of passages "which cannot be classed with any of these hitherto mentioned" (338–39).

The purpose of this article is to employ a discourse-modular approach in which (1) the consecution of tenses as such is reduced to a place of lesser importance; (2) the role of *weqatal* forms as backbone structures in predictive, procedural, and instructional discourse is recognized as primary; (3) most of GKC's examples of *weqatal* as frequentative in narrative are explained as embedded procedural discourse; and (4) most of GKC's residues in narrative are explained not as consecutive forms but rather as constituting a marker of pivotal/climactic events. I will treat these points in the following order: 2, 3, and 4, and then come back to consider the first towards the end of the article.[1]

Some of these matters I have covered in previous publications, which I will summarize and partly recapitulate here. The data referred to above as 3 are not discussed in any previous publication of mine. The analysis included under 4 involves a suggestion not found in previous literature on Biblical Hebrew grammar.

My analysis will leave some residues. But as far as Biblical Hebrew narrative prose goes, I leave considerably fewer residues than GKC. Furthermore, many of the residues that I do leave are simply ambiguities: forms which can be analyzed as either frequentatives in narrative or as pivotal climactic marking.[2]

1. Predictive, procedural, and instructional discourse

In my approach to Biblical Hebrew prose from a discourse-modular perspective, I consider *weqatal* forms as *backbone structures* in predictive, procedural, and instructional discourses. Here they occur in their own right and not consecutive on other preceding verb forms.

1.1 *Weqatal* in predictive discourse

An example of predictive discourse is from 1 Sam. 10:2-6 (see Longacre 1982), where Samuel predicts what will happen to Saul after Saul departs from him. The passage is introduced with an infinitive construction

בְּלֶכְתְּךָ הַיּוֹם מֵעִמָּדִי
in your leaving my presence today

and proceeds as a string of clauses where *weqatal* clauses dominate:

(1)
 (1) וּמָצָאתָ 'and you will meet' (two men near Rachel's tomb, at Zelzah on the border of Benjamin)
 (2) וְאָמְרוּ 'and they will say' (to you, "The donkeys you set out to look for have been found")
 (3) וְחָלַפְתָּ 'and you will proceed' (from there onward)
 (4) וּבָאתָ 'and you will come' (as far as the great tree of Tabor)
 (5) וּמְצָאוּךָ 'and they will meet you' (there three men going up to God at Bethel)
 (6) וְשָׁאֲלוּ לְךָ לְשָׁלוֹם 'and they will greet you'
 (7) וְנָתְנוּ 'and they will give' (you two loaves of bread)
 (8) וְלָקַחְתָּ 'and you will accept' (from them)
 (9) וּפָגַעְתָּ 'and you will meet' (a procession of prophets coming down from the high place)
 (10) וְצָלְחָה 'and she will come' (upon you the Spirit also)
 (11) וְהִתְנַבִּיתָ 'and you will prophesy' (with them)
 (12) וְנֶהְפַּכְתָּ 'and you will be changed (into a different person)

Other clauses with other verb forms occur, to be sure, along with the backbone forms. Thus in v. 3 (after 5 above), the participle נֹשֵׂא

'carrying' occurs three times in telling us what each of the three men would be carrying. In v. 5 אַחַר כֵּן 'after that' occurs before an imperfect תָּבוֹא 'you will go'—since consecutive forms are clause initial and do not follow particles other than וְ 'and'. A relative nominal clause follows: (you will go to Gibeah of God) "where there (Ø) a Philistine garrison." Verse 5b has an imperfect with a *waw*-conjunctive (rather than the more usual *wayyiqtol*): וִיהִי 'and it will be' (in your entering there, כְּבֹאֲךָ infinitival). In v. 5c a nominal clause depicts the prophets as a musical group: "And before them (Ø) lyre, tambourine, flute, and harp," while later on in v. 5 a participle מִתְנַבְּאִים describes them as "prophesying."

This example illustrates how backbone forms integrate with other elements to give the full text of the discourse. The *weqatal* forms, in exactly parallel fashion to *wayyiqtol* forms in narrative, are *clause initial* and cannot occur after conjunctive or subordinating particles. And whereas *wayyiqtol* forms give way to the perfect in narrative, so *weqatal* forms give way to the imperfect *yiqtol* in prediction—which can be described as a story told in advance of its happening. And like a story, predictive discourse involves particular people in particular places at particular times.

Exodus 6:6-8 is a somewhat different sort of predictive discourse: in a string of eight *weqatal* forms God promises to bring his people out of the yoke of the Egyptians, free them from slavery, redeem them with mighty acts, take them as his people, be their God (and they will know that he is their God), bring them into the promised land, and give it to them as a possession. While there is less storylike movement here, nevertheless there is movement of a sort with some verbs of overlapping semantic content.

1.2 *Weqatal* in procedural discourse

The sacrificial prescriptions of Leviticus are typical of procedural discourse. Such texts are less storylike than predictive texts; they do not predict a given course of action for a given individual at a given time. They do, however, prescribe how a duly qualified individual is to carry out a prescribed cultic routine and the order in which the procedures must be done. They are how-to-do-it texts. Nevertheless, they have essentially the same backbone structure as predictive discourse, that is, a string of *weqatal* forms (see Longacre 1982*a*), where I discuss a procedural discourse, Lev. 4:1-12). The ritual proper for an offering for a sin committed in ignorance as described in Lev. 4:1-12 begins[3] with v. 3b:

וְהִקְרִיב עַל חַטָּאתוֹ אֲשֶׁר חָטָא פַּר
and he shall bring for his sin which he has sinned a bullock

From here on a chain of clauses with *weqatal* forms outlines the major procedures down through the first part of v. 7; I cite these here in English translation with the gloss of the *weqatal* form in italics:

(2)

v. 4 And he shall *bring* the bullock to the door of the tabernacle before Yahweh.
And he shall *lay* his hand on the head of the bullock.
And he shall *kill* the bullock before Yahweh.

v. 5 And he shall *take*, the anointed priest, some of the blood of the bullock.
And he shall *bring* it to the tent of meeting.

v. 6 And he shall *dip*, the priest, his finger in the blood.
And he shall *sprinkle* the blood seven times before Yahweh at the front of the veil of the sanctuary.

v. 7a And he shall *put*, the priest, some of the blood on the horns of the altar of fragrant incense ...

These, it can be argued, are the essential elements of the cultic ritual. Minor (preparatory or resultant) procedures are given in N+*yiqtol* clauses (in this case object-verb with topicalization of the object). Thus, in 7b, such a clause specifies the procedure for disposing of the rest of the blood which was not used in the propitiatory ritual: "And all the blood of the bullock, he shall pour out at the base of the altar of burnt offering." In vv. 8 and 9 instructions are given in considerable detail for the removal of the fat and the kidneys; the clauses here are also N+*yiqtol* clauses. Verse 10 has a כַּאֲשֶׁר clause in which the procedure for the removal of the fat is likened to that used in the fellowship offering of Leviticus 3. This comparison clause has an imperfect, which does not properly encode part of the procedure of the offering but simply compares it to what is (habitually) done in another ritual: "just as the fat is taken from the cow in the peace offering." The offering up of the fat on the altar is, however, a major procedure signaled by the return to the *weqatal* form וְהִקְטִירָם 'and he shall offer them as burnt offering'. Thus the stripping off of the fat is presented as preparatory to offering it.

With v. 11 attention shifts to the disposal of the animal remains which have not figured in the ritual. Verse 11 is a string of accusative phrases (the hide, the flesh, the head, legs, intestines, and dung) for which apparently no main verb is given (the initial *weqatal* of v. 12 cannot be construed with proposed noun phrases). Verse 12 contains two *weqatal* forms ("And he shall carry out and he shall burn") that treat these concluding procedures as part of the main ritual. Notice that this is not a gratuitous assumption to preserve the neatness of the preposed analysis. Rather, the importance of the burning of the carcass is underlined by making 12b a chiastic sentence with "burn" occurring first as a *weqatal* form and lastly as an imperfect (passive).

Thus, major and minor procedures are nicely distinguished in what could be schematized as follows:

Do A
Do B   major procedures
Do C, etc.

As for q, do X
As for r, do Y   minor procedures
As for s, do Z, etc.

It is of interest that topicalization characterizes the minor procedures; the spotlight flickers briefly on each of them before passing on to the next topic. But the topicalization, if we choose to call it that, is not topic-establishing for a section of following discourse.

1.3 *Weqatal* in instructional discourse

Instructional discourse is distinct from predictive and procedural discourse. Logically it should be discussed in connection with hortatory discourse, which is, however, not presented here (see Longacre 1989*a*, chap. 5). Hortatory discourse is essentially a string of command forms (imperative, cohortative, jussive)—not an isolated occurrence of an imperative but a sequence of them. When *weqatal* forms occur in such a string of command forms, they do not simply continue the meaning of the command form but rather express result or outcome. (I will not argue these various claims here; they have been argued in my 1989*a* work. See p. 134 especially.)

Instructional discourse is exemplified in God's instructions to Noah on building the ark (Gen. 6:13–21 and 7:1–4). When I discussed these in 1979, I did not realize that they constituted a special discourse type characterized by sparse use of the imperative, a regular *weqatal* backbone, a certain amount of specification data (typically given in nominal, i.e., verbless clauses), second-person orientation, and orientation towards construction and implementation. Subsequently, Nicolai Winther-Nielsen and I discovered in Exod. 25:1–30:10 a much more extensive example of the same discourse type (Longacre forthcoming *a*). Here the imperative emerges as a topic-establishing introduction to an instructional discourse, whether it be the overall text or some discourse embedded within it. A cleft construction ("and this/these (Ø) what you shall do/make") is likewise initiatory in such texts. But, to repeat, the *weqatal* forms constitute the mainline of development broken by occasional noun-plus-imperfect forms (N+*yiqtol*) which are considered to be secondary. A curious phenomenon, first described by my colleague Winther-Nielsen, is that where a *weqatal* is associated with switch reference (SR), it expresses result (or promise): "Join the curtains together and *it shall be* one tabernacle" (Exod. 26:16) and "You shall sprinkle the blood upon Aaron and his sons and he *will be holy*" (Exod. 29:21). When the SR is from a higher to a lower agent, then promise is expressed: "And they shall make me a sanctuary, and *I will dwell* among them" (Exod. 25:8).

Instructional discourse is an intricate structure involving an occasional imperative, cleft construction, primary backbone *weqatal*, secondary N+*yiqtol*, *weqatal* plus SR, and/or nominal clause, woven together and providing texture. It is distinct from both the predictive and the procedural discourse types.

1.4 *Weqatal* in transformations among discourse types

I interrupt here to point out some relations (one could almost say transformations) among the discourse types. In chapter 5 of my 1989*a* work, I discussed certain relations which hold between hortatory discourse, instructional discourse, and predictive discourse; for example, hortatory discourse with its chain of imperatives can be *mitigated* to instructional discourse. This is seen in Joseph's talking to his brothers before (Gen. 42:18-20) and after (Gen. 45:9-13) his revealing himself to them as their brother (see Longacre 1989*a*:126, 128). But there is still a further possibility: an underlying exhortation can be "toned down" or mitigated even more by reducing it to a predictive discourse. This is, in effect, the nature of Joseph's plea to the cupbearer while Joseph is in prison as the slave and degraded steward of Potiphar's estate. In this passage, Gen. 40:14-15, the only trace of the underlying hortatory intent is the presence of the cohortative particle נָא 'entreaty' on the first of the three *weqatal* forms. The whole passage with its initiatory implication of turning down a reward (כִּי אִם 'rather that . . .') and its appended reason can be freely rendered as follows (Longacre 1989*a*:132):

> No, don't worry about a reward. I'd rather have you keep me in mind when everything turns out good for you. You'll do me a favor, won't you? You'll remember me to Pharaoh. You'll get me out of this prison. For surely I was kidnapped from the land of the Hebrews. And even here I've done nothing to deserve to be put into this hole.

Systematic relations also hold between predictive and narrative, on the one hand, and between instructional and narrative, on the other. Thus, as seen in example 1, Samuel predicts what will happen to Saul in 1 Sam. 10:2–7; and the abbreviated narrative of the fulfillment is in 1 Sam. 10:9–11. Somewhat more strikingly parallel is the instructional discourse in Exodus 25–32 and the narrative of the construction (Exod. 35:4 to the end of the book). In these passages close parallels between instructional *weqatal* sentences and narrative *wayyiqtol* sentences can be found. The moral: discourse types, like grammatical constructions, interrelate in a web of relationships, which may be characterized transformationally if we choose.

2. Narrative frequentatives as embedded procedural discourse

Not only do various discourse types relate to each other quasitransformationally but there is also embedding of one discourse type in the framework of another. This is transparent in the case of reported speech in which the speech content may belong to *any* discourse type in the language. It may be less obvious but nonetheless true that such embedding is frequent in many other kinds of material as well. Thus, for example, description/exposition can characterize setting and background elements in a story, which is a case of expositional discourse being embedded in narrative.

In my 1983 work I suggested that procedural discourse can be plus or minus a parameter that I call projection. Thus, *plus* this parameter, procedural discourse is the "how-to-do-it" procedural discourse as illustrated in example 2. *Minus* this parameter, procedural discourse is "how-it-was-done." Both are "frequentative" in the sense of procedures that can be regularly implemented in the future or that were regularly implemented in the past whenever desired. Thus, we can have procedural discourses of the latter sort concerning house building, burial customs, or making of stone tools (e.g., in the Philippines or Papua New Guinea or parts of Africa before extensive contact with Westerners).

On the other hand, a how-it-was-done procedural discourse can be used to express a customary, script-predictable routine, whether the activity of an individual or within a community, whenever that routine is incorporated into a story. Thus, Howard (1977) posits for Camsa (S. America) a procedural discourse type whose backbone is a nonfinite form. (Why use personal endings on a verb when anyone in any person category can implement the procedures?) But after giving several clear examples of how-to-do-it procedural texts of this sort, Howard mentions another text in which a woman recounts her trip home to her mountain village from

Bogotá, Colombia. In the course of this text she recounts how the bus had to stop in front of a section of highway partially covered by a landslide. At this point the text shifts its form into procedural discourse as it recounts how the people got out, rolled away rocks, shoveled aside earth and gravel, and opened up a roadbed over the face of the avalanche. The shift in discourse type recognizes that such happenings are far from rare and that there is a typical course of activity under such circumstances.

From other parts of the world come other examples of script-predictable routines with a surface form different from the surrounding narrative framework in which they embed. Woods (1980) reports for Halbi (India) a tertiary storyline whose formal marking encodes a stretch of narrative in which, for example, the king is described as sitting in his audience chamber, surrounded by courtiers, hearing petitions, and dispensing justice. Similarly, Leenhouts (1983) reports that in Ténhé (W. Africa) there is a special form for such a routine activity as wifebeating!

The purpose of this excursus into languages of South America, India, and Africa is simply to establish the fact that how-it-was-done procedures, and script-sequenced procedures, when referred to in narrative, can take distinctive surface marking. I suggest, therefore, that whenever in the framework of a Biblical Hebrew narrative a string of *weqatal* forms is found (not in reported speech) we have such a how-it-was-done procedural discourse. Take, for example, Gen. 29:2–3, which gives the routine for watering flocks from a well:

(3)

Setting
   (1) וְהִנֵּה בְאֵר בַּשָּׂדֶה
      And behold (there was) a well in the field.
   (2) וְהִנֵּה־שָׁם שְׁלֹשָׁה עֶדְרֵי־צֹאן רֹבְצִים עָלֶיהָ
      And behold there three flocks of sheep lying near it,
   (3) כִּי מִן־הַבְּאֵר הַהִוא יַשְׁקוּ הָעֲדָרִים
      because from that well they watered the sheep.
   (4) וְהָאֶבֶן גְּדֹלָה עַל־פִּי הַבְּאֵר
      And the great stone (Ø) upon the mouth of the well.

Procedures
   (5) וְנֶאֶסְפוּ־שָׁמָּה כָל־הָעֲדָרִים
      All the flocks would be gathered there.
   (6) וְגָלֲלוּ אֶת־הָאֶבֶן מֵעַל פִּי הַבְּאֵר
      And they would roll the stone from the mouth of the well.
   (7) וְהִשְׁקוּ אֶת־הַצֹּאן
      And they would water the sheep.

(8) וְהֵשִׁיבוּ אֶת־הָאֶבֶן עַל־פִּי הַבְּאֵר
And they would return the stone to the mouth of the well.

Notice in this example that a כִּי clause (in segment 3), with its *yiqtol* verb gives the initial clue that habitual activity is intended: "for they watered the flocks from that well." Four steps, each with its *weqatal* clause, are then described (in segments 5–8), telling "this was how it was done." It needs to be emphasized here that in moving down a narrative discourse some sort of a contextual clue must be given if a shift into a how-it-was-done discourse is intended. This is frequently done with a *yiqtol* form as in example 3. The imperfect (especially N+*yiqtol*) functions as a secondary line in predictive, procedural, and instructional discourse. Its use here serves as an initial clue of a shift from narrative into embedded how-it-was-done procedural discourse.

Example 4, Exod. 34:34–35, is quite similar to the preceding one. It employs a *yiqtol* form as a discourse-switch cue (DSC):

(4)
(1) וּבְבֹא מֹשֶׁה לִפְנֵי יְהוָה לְדַבֵּר אִתּוֹ
And in Moses' going in before Yahweh to speak with him

(2) יָסִיר אֶת־הַמַּסְוֶה עַד־צֵאתוֹ
he removed the veil until his going out.

(3) וְיָצָא
And he went out.

(4) וְדִבֶּר אֶל־בְּנֵי יִשְׂרָאֵל אֵת אֲשֶׁר יְצֻוֶּה
And he spoke to the sons of Israel that which he was commanded.

(5) וְרָאוּ בְנֵי־יִשְׂרָאֵל אֶת־פְּנֵי מֹשֶׁה
And the sons of Israel saw the face of Moses

(6) כִּי קָרַן עוֹר פְּנֵי מֹשֶׁה
that radiated light the face of Moses.

(7) וְהֵשִׁיב מֹשֶׁה אֶת־הַמַּסְוֶה עַל־פָּנָיו עַד־בֹּאוֹ לְדַבֵּר אִתּוֹ
And returned Moses the veil to his face until he went in again to speak with him.

In v. 33 of this narrative framework the veil is introduced in the clause וַיִּתֵּן עַל־פָּנָיו מַסְוֶה 'and put he over his face a veil'—this is the thematic prop of the passage. The infinitive construction וּבְבֹא 'in his going in' and especially the imperfect יָסִיר 'he-removed' give the necessary DSC that the passage is shifting into procedural discourse. Clauses 3–5 and 7 give steps in the procedure, while 6 is an off-the-line כִּי clause.

The Book of 2 Kings ends with a procedural passage, 2 Kings 25:29–30. It states how the captive king Jehoiachin was a pensioner of the king of

Babylon for the last years of his life. Verses 27 and 28, which I do not give here, date the change in Jehoiachin's fortunes relative to his own reign and that of the king of Babylon; explain in a N+*qatal* clause that the king of Babylon "lifted the head of Jehoiachin out of prison"; and then recount in two *wayyiqtol* clauses that he spoke kindly to him and gave him a seat of honor higher than that of the other (presumably captive) kings with him in Babylon. So far the structure is clearly narrative. There follows, however, a shift into procedural discourse, as shown in example 5 (2 Kings 25:29-30):

(5)
(1) וְשִׁנָּא אֵת בִּגְדֵי כִלְאוֹ
And changed he his prison clothes
(2) וְאָכַל לֶחֶם תָּמִיד לְפָנָיו כָּל־יְמֵי חַיָּיו
And ate he bread continually before him all the days of his life
(3) וַאֲרֻחָתוֹ אֲרֻחַת תָּמִיד נִתְּנָה־לּוֹ מֵאֵת הַמֶּלֶךְ דְּבַר־יוֹם בְּיוֹמוֹ כֹּל יְמֵי חַיָּו
And his allowance, a continual allowance, was given to him from the king day by day all the days of his life.

In this passage the clue that the discourse has shifted from narrative to procedural consists in the pervasive references to time duration. Thus, תָּמִיד 'continually' occurs in both v. 29 and v. 30. Likewise, the phrase כֹּל יְמֵי חַיָּו 'all the days of his life' occurs in both these verses, strengthened in v. 30 by the phrase דְּבַר־יוֹם בְּיוֹמוֹ 'each day's concern in its day'. The onset of v. 29 is וְשִׁנָּא אֵת בִּגְדֵי כִלְאוֹ 'and he changed his prison clothes'. Here there is an abrupt change from the *wayyiqtol* forms of the previous narrative (v. 27) to *weqatal*. Why? Presumably, Jehoiachin did not have to change daily from prison clothes to more suitable garments but rather this was an event which could just as well have been signaled by a *wayyiqtol* form. However, once we are freed of the onus of explaining all *weqatal* forms as frequentative, we can simply accept Jehoiachin's changing his clothes as his initial step in his new life as pensioner of the king of Babylon. I, therefore, accept the whole passage (1-3 in example 5) as a how-it-was-done procedural discourse. This passage is not, however, introduced with an initiatory imperfect form (*yiqtol*); rather the DSC consists in scattered but explicit temporal references.

1 Kings 14:26-27 is a similar example:

(6)
(1) וַיִּקַּח אֶת־אֹצְרוֹת בֵּית־יְהוָה וְאֶת־אוֹצְרוֹת בֵּית הַמֶּלֶךְ
And he [Shishak] took the treasures of house of Yahweh and the

treasures of the house of the king.
(2) וְאֶת־הַכֹּל לָקָח
And he took everything.
(3) וַיִּקַּח אֶת־כָּל־מָגִנֵּי הַזָּהָב אֲשֶׁר עָשָׂה שְׁלֹמֹה
And he took all the gold shields which Solomon had made.
(4) וַיַּעַשׂ הַמֶּלֶךְ רְחַבְעָם תַּחְתָּם מָגִנֵּי נְחֹשֶׁת
And King Rehoboam made shields of brass in their place.
(5) וְהִפְקִיד עַל־יַד שָׂרֵי הָרָצִים הַשֹּׁמְרִים פֶּתַח בֵּית הַמֶּלֶךְ
And he delivered (them) to the hand of the commanders of the guard keeping watch at the door of the king's house.
(6) וַיְהִי מִדֵּי־בֹא הַמֶּלֶךְ בֵּית יְהוָה
And so it was that whenever the king went to the house of Yahweh
(7) יִשָּׂאוּם הָרָצִים
the guards bore (the shields)
(8) וֶהֱשִׁיבוּם אֶל־תָּא הָרָצִים
and returned them to the guardhouse.

In this example, 1–4 are regular storyline narrative clauses, and 6–8 are clearly a procedural how-it-was-done discourse. Clues to the latter are found in the phrase מִדֵּי־בֹא הַמֶּלֶךְ 'whenever the king went in' and in the imperfect of 7 followed by the *weqatal* form in 8. But why is 5 also *weqatal*? Here, as in 1 Kings 25:29 (clause 1 of example 5), a nonfrequentative form occurs initially along with the frequentative forms of the following clauses. Again, however, once we recognize 5–8 as an embedded procedural discourse, then 5 takes its form according to the structure of the rest of the passage. We could say that here in 1 Kings 14:27b and also in 2 Kings 25:29a (of example 5) the verb that would otherwise be *wayyiqtol* is "attracted" to the form of the following procedural discourse, but it is simpler to make these problematic forms part and parcel of the procedural discourse that follows.

The lengthy passage, 1 Sam. 2:12–21, contains three how-it-was-done procedural discourses. Verse 12 is introductory to the 12–17 section: "Now the sons of Eli (Ø) sons of Belial [= worthless]; they did not know Yahweh." Its first clause is a nominal (i.e., verbless) clause; the second paraphrases the first and has a negated *qatal* form, לֹא יָדְעוּ אֶת־יְהוָה 'they did not know Yahweh'. Verses 13–14, which go on to outline the usual procedure of the priests in getting their portion of the sacrificial meal, have one dominating *weqatal* form preceded by participial and nominal clauses and followed by imperfects in various constructions, as seen in example 7:

(7)
(1) וּמִשְׁפַּט הַכֹּהֲנִים אֶת־הָעָם
And the custom of the priests with the people:
(2) כָּל־אִישׁ זֹבֵחַ זֶבַח
Every man sacrificing a sacrifice
(3) וּבָא נַעַר הַכֹּהֵן כְּבַשֵּׁל הַבָּשָׂר
and coming up the servant of the priest in the boiling of the meat
(4) וְהַמַּזְלֵג שְׁלֹשׁ־הַשִּׁנַּיִם בְּיָדוֹ
—and the three-toothed fork (∅) in his hand—
(5) וְהִכָּה בַכִּיּוֹר . . .
he would strike it into the caldron . . .
(6) כֹּל אֲשֶׁר יַעֲלֶה הַמַּזְלֵג
Whatever the fork brought up
(7) יִקַּח הַכֹּהֵן בּוֹ
the priest took for himself.
(8) כָּכָה יַעֲשׂוּ לְכָל־יִשְׂרָאֵל הַבָּאִים שָׁם בְּשִׁלֹה
This was what they did to all Israel coming there to Shiloh.

This passage is bracketed with elements that make the theme of the passage explicit: a noun phrase in segment 1 ("the custom/procedure of the priests with the people") and a clause in segment 8 ("thus they did to all Israel coming there to Shiloh"). The noun phrase in segment 2 is perhaps more of a sentence topic (i.e., a *particular* topic): "as for every man sacrificing a sacrifice." Segment 3 is similar to a protasis with a participle: "and coming up the servant of the high priest as the flesh was boiling." Segment 4 is a nominal, almost parenthetical, clause: "And the three-pronged fork (∅) in his hand." Finally the main clause with its *weqatal* form occurs in 5: "And he would strike [with the trident] into the kettle . . ." Segments 6 and 7 together constitute a N+*yiqtol* form such as is common in procedural discourse; 6 itself is a relative clause with an imperfect verb: "whatever the fork brought up." Segment 7 has as its main verb a modal *yiqtol*: "the priest would take for his own." The dominant clause in the passage is rightfully said to be in segment 5: the servant of the priest would plunge the trident into the caldron while the meat was being boiled up. This was precisely the part of the routine that the sons of Eli are described as violating in the next paragraph.

Verses 15-17, the next three verses of 1 Sam. 2:12-21, are displayed in example 8. They depict an opposed scenario—the greedy and peremptory practice of the sons of Eli. The conjunctive complex גַּם בְּטֶרֶם 'even before' certainly is meant here to have adversative form. Verse 16 (i.e., segment 7 in example 8) somewhat surprisingly contains a *wayyiqtol* form. (GKC says it's "perhaps a mere mistake" for וְאָמַר—but such assumptions are often gratuitous.)

(8)
- (1) גַּם בְּטֶרֶם יַקְטִרוּן אֶת־הַחֵלֶב
  But even before they burned the fat
- (2) וּבָא נַעַר הַכֹּהֵן
  and coming up the servant of the priest
- (3) וְאָמַר לָאִישׁ הַזֹּבֵחַ
  then he would say to the man sacrificing,
- (4) תְּנָה בָשָׂר לִצְלוֹת לַכֹּהֵן
  "Give me the flesh for the priest's portion
- (5) וְלֹא־יִקַּח מִמְּךָ בָּשָׂר מְבֻשָּׁל
  (because) he won't take from you boiled meat
- (6) כִּי אִם־חָי
  but rather raw."
- (7) וַיֹּאמֶר אֵלָיו הָאִישׁ
  And then said the man to him,
- (8) קַטֵּר יַקְטִירוּן כַּיּוֹם הַחֵלֶב
  "Surely the fat will be offered first,
- (9) וְקַח־לְךָ כַּאֲשֶׁר תְּאַוֶּה נַפְשֶׁךָ
  then take whatever you want."
- (10) וְאָמַר לוֹ
  And he would say to him,
- (11) כִּי עַתָּה תִתֵּן
  "Give it to me *now*;
- (12) וְאִם־לֹא לָקַחְתִּי בְחָזְקָה
  otherwise, I will take it by force."
- (13) וַתְּהִי חַטַּאת הַנְּעָרִים גְּדוֹלָה מְאֹד אֶת־פְּנֵי יְהוָה
  And the sin of the young men was very great before Yahweh,
- (14) כִּי נִאֲצוּ הָאֲנָשִׁים אֵת מִנְחַת יְהוָה
  for men came to despise the offering of Yahweh.

Essentially, example 8 gives a reported dialogue: what the priest's servant would say to the man sacrificing (4–6), what the man would then say (7–9), and another arrogant threat of the priest's servant (10–12). In 3 and 10 we find the expected *weqatal* forms of אמר 'say'—but in 7 an unexpected *wayyiqtol* narrative form. Aside from GKC's suggestion that this is simply an error, we might settle for saying that the procedure rather incongruously resorts to narrative here in the midst of the procedure. Possibly the narrative form makes more concrete and particular the objection of the sacrificing man. Segments 13 and 14—in v. 17—hark back to v. 12 with which they form a kind of inclusio. Recognizing the narrative thrust of the form וַתְּהִי, we might render it freely: "And thus the sin of the young man came to be great indeed before Yahweh." The second clause of v. 17 (segment 14 in the example) appends the reason, namely "they caused the offering of Yahweh to be held in contempt."

By contrast, after the conflict pictured in the preceding verses, what is depicted in 2:18-21 is almost idyllic: the boy, Samuel, ministering before Yahweh, his mother's tender care for him year by year, and Eli's annual blessing upon her. This stretch, shown as example 9, is also a procedural how-it-was-done discourse.

(9)
(1) וּשְׁמוּאֵל מְשָׁרֵת אֶת־פְּנֵי יְהוָה
And Samuel was ministering before Yahweh,
(2) נַעַר חָגוּר אֵפוֹד בָּד
a boy clad in a linen ephod.
(3) וּמְעִיל קָטֹן תַּעֲשֶׂה־לּוֹ אִמּוֹ
And a little robe his mother would make for him.
(4) וְהַעַלְתָה לוֹ מִיָּמִים יָמִימָה בַּעֲלוֹתָהּ אֶת־אִישָׁהּ לִזְבֹּחַ אֶת־זֶבַח הַיָּמִים
And she would bring it up to him from year to year in her going up with her husband to sacrifice the yearly sacrifice.
(5) וּבֵרַךְ עֵלִי אֶת־אֶלְקָנָה וְאֶת־אִשְׁתּוֹ
And Eli would bless Elkanah and his wife.
(6) וְאָמַר יָשֵׂם יְהוָה לְךָ זֶרַע מִן־הָאִשָּׁה הַזֹּאת תַּחַת הַשְּׁאֵלָה אֲשֶׁר שָׁאַל לַיהוָה
And he would say, "May Yahweh give you children from this woman in place of the one which she asked from/lent to Yahweh."
(7) וְהָלְכוּ לִמְקֹמוֹ
And they would go home.
(8) כִּי־פָקַד יְהוָה אֶת־חַנָּה
And Yahweh visited Hannah.
(9) וַתַּהַר וַתֵּלֶד שְׁלֹשָׁה־בָנִים וּשְׁתֵּי בָנוֹת
And she conceived and bore three sons and two daughters.
(10) וַיִּגְדַּל הַנַּעַר שְׁמוּאֵל עִם־יְהוָה
And the boy Samuel grew up before Yahweh.

Segments 1 and 2 of this passage provide the setting. In 3 the onset of the how-it-was-done procedural discourse is marked by the imperf. תַּעֲשֶׂה 'she would make'. Segment 4 contains the first *weqatal* form, וְהַעַלְתָה 'and she would bring it up', with the repetitive nature of the proceeding doubly indicated in the temporal phrase מִיָּמִים יָמִימָה 'from days to day', but meaning simply 'annually', and in the noun phrase אֶת־זֶבַח הַיָּמִים 'the annual sacrifice'. These elements in 3 and 4 provide the DSC. Together 5 and 6 constitute an extended quotation formula with two *weqatal* forms (speech act verb "bless" plus the generic verb "say"). It identifies Eli as speaker and Elkanah and his wife as addressees. The substance of the blessing is found in 6. In 7 ("And they would return to their place") is another *weqatal* form.

Segments 8-10 (v. 21) are shown, for the sake of completeness, to illustrate how a string of *wayyiqtol* forms signals the shift from the embedded procedural discourse back to the narrative framework. Notice the distinctness with which the embedded discourse stands out from the narrative matrix.

Other examples of how-it-was-done procedure embedded in narrative could of course be cited. Noteworthy here is Exod. 33:7-11, where Moses is described as pitching a "tent of meeting" (אֹהֶל מוֹעֵד) outside the camp and as going in and out of the tent, the people watching, and God's communing with Moses there. An initial *yiqtol* יִקַּח occurs (in "Moses would take a tent ... "), followed by two further *weqatal* forms: "and he would pitch it without the camp, and he would call it the tent of meeting." Three *weqatal* forms of הָיָה occur (medial in v. 7, initial in v. 8 and v. 9): "and it would happen." In a rather intricate tree structure, each כְּ֯ וְ֯ is followed by an imperfect, and in vv. 8 and 9 by *weqatal* forms. This merges into a long string of *weqatal* forms in vv. 10 and 11.

There is another such embedded procedural discourse of the form described here in Judg. 2:18-19. The context in which it is embedded, Judg. 2:10-23, is, however, of a sort not frequently encountered in Hebrew narrative prose: A long string of sixteen *wayyiqtol* forms is used to picture Israel's early apostasy from Yahweh, but the *wayyiqtol* forms are only weakly sequential in that synonyms and even repetitions of the same verb enlarge the series. This departure from the usual narrative norm coincides, however, with the broader function of the passage in marking the whole book's *inciting incident*. An inciting incident resembles narrative peak in its proneness to augment the storyline (Longacre 1990:8-9) even by using synonyms and repetitions as if successive actions were being portrayed. In this respect the Judg. 2:10-23 passage resembles Gen. 7:17-24, the peak of the Flood narrative.

Nevertheless, towards the end of this long passage, the narrative shifts in Judg. 2:18-19 to a procedural discourse. A translation of Judg. 2:18-19 follows (the Hebrew is given for those verbs that are crucial to the structure of the passage):

Weqatal Forms in Biblical Hebrew Prose

And when Yahweh raised up (הֵקִים) judges for them, then Yahweh would be (וְהָיָה) with the judges, and he would deliver them (וְהוֹשִׁיעָם) from the hands of their enemies all the days of the judge. For Yahweh had compassion (יִנָּחֵם) on their groaning before those that oppressed and afflicted them. And it would happen (וְהָיָה) on the death of the judge they would turn back (יָשֻׁבוּ). And they corrupted themselves (וְהִשְׁחִיתוּ) more than their fathers to go after strange gods, to serve them, and to worship them. They did not give up (לֹא הִפִּילוּ) their practices and their stubborn ways.

With the next verse the narrative resumes—although again with a verb which introduces a summary of God's anger over the whole period (cf. the preceding nonconsecutive "consecutive" tenses). The whole passage (vv. 10–23) is in some ways an enlargement of Judg. 2:1–5. Such a paraphrase from a germinal idea to its fuller development befits the structure of an inciting incident.

A procedural discourse embedded in narrative can be minimal in structure. But even the most minimal structure needs to specify the presence of some DSC as to repetitive/durative action plus a *weqatal* form. This is the case in Gen. 2:6, which immediately follows the two negative clauses of v. 5, which reads:

(10)
(1) כִּי לֹא הִמְטִיר יְהוָה אֱלֹהִים עַל־הָאָרֶץ
And Yahweh God had not caused it to rain on the earth
(2) וְאָדָם אַיִן לַעֲבֹד אֶת־הָאֲדָמָה
and there was no man to till the earth.

Next comes the two-sentence procedural discourse of Gen 2:6:

(11)
(1) וְאֵד יַעֲלֶה מִן־הָאָרֶץ
And mist/irrigation waters came up from the earth
(2) וְהִשְׁקָה אֶת־כָּל־פְּנֵי הָאֲדָמָה
and watered all the surface of the earth.

Here the imperfect יַעֲלֶה is the DSC. It marks the shift into the procedural discourse, followed by a *weqatal* verb in the next sentence.

Jeremiah 37:15 presents a problem. I give the passage in full here as example 12:

(12)
(1) וַיִּקְצְפוּ הַשָּׂרִים עַל־יִרְמְיָהוּ
And were-angry the officials with Jeremiah.

(2) וְהִכּוּ אֹתוֹ
And they scourged him.
(3) וְנָתְנוּ אוֹתוֹ בֵּית הָאֵסוּר בֵּית יְהוֹנָתָן הַסֹּפֵר
And they put him in prison in the house of Jonathan the secretary,
(4) כִּי־אֹתוֹ עָשׂוּ לְבֵית הַכֶּלֶא
for they had converted it into a prison.

Here we have two *weqatal* constructions, in 2 and 3, but no overt clue that a repetitive script is involved. Evidently he underwent *one* scourging and was put once (certainly!) into prison. Then why the apparent procedural form? Maybe the scourging can be conceived of as repetitive (they hit him repeatedly) but not the imprisonment as such. Maybe what is pictured is a customary routine of punishment: "they proceeded to give him the customary flogging and imprisonment." If such a routine is pictured, it is not necessary to insist that every verb in it be frequentative in the situation portrayed; clearly 3 is not frequentative here. But possibly the use of the *weqatal* forms is simply to indicate, as we have already suggested, a customary routine. But it remains noteworthy that there is no imperfect verb or adverbial form to mark the transition into a procedural discourse. The possibility remains, therefore, that an analysis such as that proposed in the next section should be invoked.

A question remains. Can one isolated *weqatal* form in the center of a narrative be, in effect, a minimal how-it-was-done procedural discourse? While we cannot rule out such a possibility, an alternative analysis is also possible. This is presented in section 3. (It should be remembered that in a few contexts this analysis may be genuinely ambiguous, as is the construction just discussed.)

3. *Weqatal* forms as marking climactic/pivotal events in narrative

Before I make the main claim embodied in this section, let us consider a few other uses of the sufformative tense. These uses, presented in sections 3.1–3, should not be confused with the use described in section 3.4.

3.1 N+*qatal* as secondary storyline

The idea of a secondary storyline has proven to be a useful concept—especially in the analysis of a number of languages of East Africa (and Halbi of India). The primary storyline in such languages is marked either by the use of a special narrative tense or by the use of a consecutive tense that in narrative is not dependent on the occurrence of some specially marked tense form in front of it (Longacre 1990). Such a primary storyline ideally encodes a series of punctiliar consecutive "happenings": whether actions, motions, cognitive events, contingencies (things that happen to people), or speech acts. In Hebrew the *wayyiqtol* forms perform such a function.

On the other hand, in a given language some events are backgrounded relative to others, especially if such events are more participant oriented than action oriented, if the events portrayed are not strictly sequential, or if some events are regarded either as preparatory to what is reported on the primary storyline or as resultant on such primary events. In these and similar cases a specially marked verb form is employed that can be regarded as constituting a secondary storyline. Characteristically, the secondary tense has a past or perfective meaning, while the meaning of the primary storyline is punctiliar consecutive events in the story world.

Woods's arguments regarding a secondary storyline in Halbi are especially well taken: "While retaining and continuing the temporal sequence of the narrative, secondary events are less prominent than the backbone itself" (1980:123). "Marking an event as less important (through the use of the present incomplete endings) indicates that either the event itself is not the focus or that the participant performing the activity lacks prominence..." (124). She mentions that a secondary storyline can "slow down the reporting of the action and build up suspense" (126), and can "have the effect of further specifying, clarifying, or augmenting the mainline events in the same way" (127). While this description of the functions of the secondary storyline in Halbi may be somewhat generalized to other languages, the secondary storyline in East African languages such as Toposa, Jür-Luwo, Mündü, and Avokaya is characteristically idiosyncratic for each language (Longacre 1990). Furthermore, in most languages a secondary storyline can be promoted to or stand in for the primary storyline in certain contexts.

The perfect tense preceded by a noun phrase (N+*qatal*) functions as a secondary storyline in Biblical Hebrew narrative. I will not here repeat my earlier analyses and arguments but refer the reader to them (see Longacre 1989a:74-83 although I did not term this construction a secondary storyline at the time; 1989b, and 1992a). I summarize by noting that a N+*qatal* clause, like any NV clause in Biblical Hebrew, by its very highlighting of the noun presents an action as a participant-oriented action. The noun is highlighted and the verb is demoted. Nevertheless, in certain contexts—often by default—the secondary storyline can stand in for the primary (see Longacre 1992b).

3.2 *Qatal* forms after particles

Not only must *wayyiqtol* forms be clause initial, they also cannot occur after particles—in which case a *qatal* form must occur. This is observed, for example, where the negative particle לֹא 'not' occurs. I have commonly considered that such a לֹא + *qatal* form is off the storyline by reason of its irrealis status (i.e., it tells what *didn't* happen rather than what happened), following Grimes (1975), who lumped together modal forms of verbs and negative verbs (along with quoted material) as "collateral." But persistent dissatisfaction has been expressed with my work and Grimes's at this point (see Hwang 1992). Certainly in Biblical Hebrew (and possibly in all languages) there are momentous negations which move a story forward. Genesis 8:12 is an example of this: וְלֹא־יָסְפָה שׁוּב־אֵלָיו עוֹד 'and (the dove) did not return to him again'. It could be argued that the failure of the dove to return to Noah is significant in moving the story forward—although even here the positive contingency of the dove returning with the olive leaf in its beak (v. 11) is represented as the crucial event in Noah's coming to realize that the flood waters had abated.

Qatal forms likewise occur after כִּי (causal), כַּאֲשֶׁר (comparative) and אֲשֶׁר (relative marker); here we can generalize to say that *wayyiqtol* narrative forms are limited to positive main clauses and cannot occur in adverbial or relative clauses. In such situations it is not uncommon for the *qatal* forms to have pluperfect meaning, as in Gen. 40:22: כַּאֲשֶׁר פָּתַר לָהֶם יוֹסֵף 'just as Joseph had interpreted to them'. This usage of *qatal* forms after particles is quite distinct; it represents a set of grammatical situations in which storyline forms do not occur. On the other hand, as a sort of grammatically suppressed reporting of an event it is quite distinct from the N+*qatal* forms which function as secondary storyline. I erred in former publications in grouping *qatal* and N+*qatal* forms together as "secondary."

3.3 Evidence for *waw*-conjunctive plus *qatal*

Now we turn to certain uses of *qatal* forms preceded by *waw*-conjunctive that are not the same as the *weqatal* "consecutive" forms that are the subject of this article. The first example (example 13) shows a series of coordinated *qatal* forms after יַעַן אֲשֶׁר 'because'. The next two examples (14 and 15) show a N+*qatal* form coordinated with further *waw*-conjunctive *qatal* forms. The latter could be considered cleft constructions; 'he (was the one who) X'd and Y'd and Z'd.'

Example 13 is 1 Kings 3:11–12:

Weqatal Forms in Biblical Hebrew Prose

(13)
  (1) וַיֹּאמֶר אֱלֹהִים אֵלָיו
     And said God to him,
  (2) יַעַן אֲשֶׁר
     "Because
  (3) שָׁאַלְתָּ אֶת־הַדָּבָר הַזֶּה
     you've asked this thing
  (4) וְלֹא־שָׁאַלְתָּ לְּךָ יָמִים רַבִּים
     and you haven't asked for yourself long life
  (5) וְלֹא־שָׁאַלְתָּ לְּךָ עֹשֶׁר
     and you haven't asked for yourself wealth
  (6) וְלֹא שָׁאַלְתָּ נֶפֶשׁ אֹיְבֶיךָ
     and you haven't asked for the life of your enemies,
  (7) וְשָׁאַלְתָּ לְּךָ הָבִין לִשְׁמֹעַ מִשְׁפָּט
     but you have asked for yourself understanding in administering justice,
  (8) הִנֵּה עָשִׂיתִי כִּדְבָרֶיךָ . . .
     behold I will do according to your words . . ."

It seems plausible that the verbs in 3–7 are all coordinated and dependent on יַעַן אֲשֶׁר 'because'. So not only 3, and not only the negated clauses in 4–6, but also 7 are *qatal* forms, forms that regularly occur in a relative clause. The unusually long coordinated structure after יַעַן אֲשֶׁר can be considered to be an example of a paragraph backlooped into a relative clause (Longacre 1983). Furthermore, the verb in 8 is a predictive verb *qatal* even without being a *weqatal* form. Another such form, הִנֵּה נָתַתִּי 'Behold, I will give' immediately follows. The direct speech here is not narrative discourse; it is more like the cleft constructions described in section 4.

In narrative discourse we find complex constructions such as occur in 2 Kings 14:7, and also in 18:3–4, where an initial הוּא 'he' pronoun is followed by a perfect tense verb and then another one or by a series of coordinated perfects; the latter are not to be considered *waw*-consecutive *qatal* forms but *waw*-conjunctive *qatal* forms. Possibly, as suggested above, a cleft structure is intended. Example 14 is 2 Kings 14:7:

(14)
  (1) הוּא־הִכָּה אֶת־אֱדוֹם בְּגֵיא־הַמֶּלַח עֲשֶׂרֶת אֲלָפִים
     He (was the one who) smote Edom in the Valley of Salt ten thousand men
  (2) וְתָפַשׂ אֶת־הַסֶּלַע בַּמִּלְחָמָה
     (and who) captured Sela in battle

(3) וַיִּקְרָא אֶת־שְׁמָהּ יָקְתְאֵל עַד הַיּוֹם הַזֶּה
And then he called its name, Joktheel, the name it has to this day.

Whether my suggested cleft-structure reading is any more than that proper to any N+*qatal* structure in Biblical Hebrew, the הוּא 'he' of clause 1 can be considered to govern not only the perfect of its own clause (הִכָּה), but the verb in the next clause as well. Again the *waw* of 2 is best considered to be a *waw*-conjunctive.

2 Kings 18:3-4, shown as example 15, is more complex: a string of three *waw*-conjunctive *qatal* forms follows a הוּא *qatal*.

(15)
(1) וַיַּעַשׂ הַיָּשָׁר בְּעֵינֵי יְהוָה כְּכֹל אֲשֶׁר־עָשָׂה דָּוִד אָבִיו
And he did right in the eyes of Yahweh in everything as did David his father.
(2) הוּא הֵסִיר אֶת־הַבָּמוֹת
He (was the one who) removed the high places
(3) וְשִׁבַּר אֶת־הַמַּצֵּבֹת
and broke up the sacred stones
(4) וְכָרַת אֶת־הָאֲשֵׁרָה
and cut down the Asherah
(5) וְכִתַּת נְחַשׁ הַנְּחֹשֶׁת
and broke in pieces the bronze serpent
(6) אֲשֶׁר־עָשָׂה מֹשֶׁה
which Moses had made,
(7) כִּי עַד־הַיָּמִים הָהֵמָּה הָיוּ בְנֵי־יִשְׂרָאֵל מְקַטְּרִים לוֹ
for until those days the Israelites were burning incense to it
(8) וַיִּקְרָא־לוֹ נְחֻשְׁתָּן
and it was called Nehushtan.

In translating 3-5 of this example, I omitted the third-person reference of the Hebrew *qatal* forms in order to bring out the force of the coordination. Again, I believe that the initial *waws* in 3-5 are conjunctive and to be construed with the initial הוּא of clause 2. Notice that we probably have here a *list* of what Hezekiah did, not a set of ordered events. It is interesting that in both examples 14 and 15 the clause that refers to naming is cast into the *wayyiqtol* form.

It is not improbable that *waw*-conjunctive *qatal* forms should occur as well as *waw*-consecutive *qatal* forms (Waltke and O'Connor 1990). Even the *wayyiqtol* form has a parallel *waw*-conjunctive *yiqtol* form; the two forms are formally distinct so there is no problem in recognizing an occasional *waw*-conjunctive *yiqtol* form versus the more frequent *waw*-consecutive form. Such a rare *waw*-conjunctive *yiqtol* form occurs in

1 Sam. 10:5: . . . וִיהִי כְבֹאֲךָ שָׁם הָעִיר 'and it shall be in your approaching the city there . . .' Notice that וַיְהִי would be the *wayyiqtol* form and וְהָיָה the regular *weqatal* consecutive form. What we have in 1 Sam. 10:5 is simply a conjunctive form of *waw* with the third-person imperfect (as in example 1).

3.4 The case for *weqatal* forms as marking climactic/pivotal events

As we saw in previous sections, a sequence of *weqatal* forms in narrative regularly marks the inclusion of a how-it-was-done (or routine sequence) procedural discourse. But even granting N+*qatal* forms as a secondary storyline and some uses of *weqatal* in which the *waw* is conjunctive, we still are left with a stubborn residue of *weqatal* forms in narrative that do not seem to fit any of these functions. My suggestion is this: an isolated *weqatal* in the narrative framework marks a climactic or at least a pivotal event. I will proceed here somewhat inductively through a discussion of a number of examples. Of course, an initial hypothesis might be that if N+*qatal* functions as a secondary storyline, isolated *weqatal* forms could also function this way. This indeed has been my position in previous publications (Longacre 1989a and 1992b). It will, however, become increasingly evident that such a position is untenable.

Example 16 (Judg. 3:20–23) constitutes a rather celebrated case where a *weqatal* form occurs at the end in place of the expected *wayyiqtol* form. The passage is a graphic and detailed description of what is undoubtedly depicted as a high point of the story.

(16)
(1) וְאֵהוּד בָּא אֵלָיו
And Ehud came in to him.
(2) וְהוּא־יֹשֵׁב בַּעֲלִיַּת הַמְּקֵרָה אֲשֶׁר־לוֹ לְבַדּוֹ
And he [Eglon] was sitting alone in the upper room of his summer palace.
(3) וַיֹּאמֶר אֵהוּד
And Ehud said,
(4) דְּבַר־אֱלֹהִים לִי אֵלֶיךָ
"I've a secret message for you."
(5) וַיָּקָם מֵעַל הַכִּסֵּא
And he [Eglon] rose from his seat.
(6) וַיִּשְׁלַח אֵהוּד אֶת־יַד שְׂמֹאלוֹ
And Ehud put out his left hand.
(7) וַיִּקַּח אֶת־הַחֶרֶב מֵעַל יֶרֶךְ יְמִינוֹ
And he took the sword from his right thigh.

(8) וַיִּתְקָעֶהָ בְּבִטְנוֹ
And he stuck it into his belly.
(9) וַיָּבֹא גַם־הַנִּצָּב אַחַר הַלַּהַב
And the haft went in after the blade.
(10) וַיִּסְגֹּר הַחֵלֶב בְּעַד הַלַּהַב
And the fat closed in over the blade
(11) כִּי לֹא שָׁלַף הַחֶרֶב מִבִּטְנוֹ
because he didn't draw out the sword from his stomach.
(12) וַיֵּצֵא הַפַּרְשְׁדֹנָה
And it [the sword] came out his back.
(13) וַיֵּצֵא אֵהוּד הַמִּסְדְּרוֹנָה
And then Ehud went out on the porch.
(14) וַיִּסְגֹּר דַּלְתוֹת הָעֲלִיָּה בַּעֲדוֹ
And he shut the doors of the upper room behind him.
(15) וְנָעָל
And he bolted (them).

The problem here is the occurrence of the *weqatal* form in 15 after the long string of *wayyiqtol* forms. Ingenious attempts have been made to explain it as a frequentative: perhaps there were a series of bolts to draw or bolts on several doors. But if we take this as a special marking, what is the rationale for its use here? Is it climactic or anticlimactic? Is it simply a more specific paraphrase of the verb סגר 'close'? There is a sort of functional inversion here: The use of *weqatal* instead of the expected *wayyiqtol* forms makes what could have been a secondary form (parallel to the regular use of N+*qatal* in this function) in effect a marked form. At any rate, we are at a great moment of a story and we can expect the narrator to indulge in a few tricks.

A parallel example, involving the same verb form נעל 'bolt', occurs at the end of the story of Amnon's rape of Tamar in 2 Sam. 13:18. (The total story occupies 13:1–21.) In v. 18 putting Tamar out and bolting the door after her is presented as the crowning outrage to Tamar, who had said (v. 16), "Sending me away would be a greater wrong than what you have already done to me." Here, as in example 16, the verb 'bolt' is used to mark the climactic event in a scenario of violence.

For example 17 (1 Kings 20:21), not as much preceding context is provided, but it is the denouement of a story that begins in 20:1:

(17)
(1) וַיֵּצֵא מֶלֶךְ יִשְׂרָאֵל
And the king of Israel went forth

Weqatal Forms in Biblical Hebrew Prose

(2) וַיַּךְ אֶת־הַסּוּס וְאֶת־הָרָכֶב
and he struck the horse(s) and chariot(s)

(3) וְהִכָּה בַאֲרָם מַכָּה גְדוֹלָה
And delivered Aram a great blow.

In segment 2 is a *wayyiqtol* form of נכה 'smite/kill', and in 3 a sudden switch to the *weqatal* of the same verb. Again, the effect of the shift may be a way of marking a climax of a story.

In 2 Kings 14:8-14 there is an account of a war between Judah and Israel and the military defeat suffered by Amaziah at the hands of Israel. I give here vv. 12-14 as example 18:

(18)

(1) וַיִּנָּגֶף יְהוּדָה לִפְנֵי יִשְׂרָאֵל
And Judah was routed before Israel.

(2) וַיָּנֻסוּ אִישׁ לְאֹהָלָיו
And every man fled to his tent.

(3) וְאֵת אֲמַצְיָהוּ מֶלֶךְ־יְהוּדָה בֶן־יְהוֹאָשׁ בֶּן־אֲחַזְיָהוּ תָּפַשׂ יְהוֹאָשׁ מֶלֶךְ־יִשְׂרָאֵל בְּבֵית שָׁמֶשׁ
And Jehoash king of Israel captured Amaziah king of Judah, son of Jehoash, son of Ahaziah at Beth-Shemesh.

(4) וַיָּבֹאוּ יְרוּשָׁלַםִ
And he [textual variant: they] went to Jerusalem.

(5) וַיִּפְרֹץ בְּחוֹמַת יְרוּשָׁלַםִ ...
And he broke down the wall of Jerusalem [from point X to point Y distance].

(6) וְלָקַח אֶת־כָּל־הַזָּהָב־וְהַכֶּסֶף וְאֵת כָּל־הַכֵּלִים הַנִּמְצְאִים בֵּית־יְהוָה וּבְאֹצְרוֹת בֵּית הַמֶּלֶךְ וְאֵת בְּנֵי הַתַּעֲרֻבוֹת
And he took all the gold and silver, and all the vessels found in the house of Yahweh, and treasures of the house of the king, and hostages.

(7) וַיָּשָׁב שֹׁמְרוֹנָה
And he returned to Samaria.

In this example, 1, 2, 4, 5, and 7 contain clause-initial *wayyiqtol* narrative forms; 3 contains a N+*qatal* construction in which N represents the preposed object: it was Amaziah the king of Judah, son of Jehoash, son of Amaziah—no less—that the king of Israel took captive. Segment 6 is a *weqatal* clause recounting the spoils to which the king of Israel helped himself, including hostages. While 3 highlights the royal personage who was taken captive, 6 highlights the action of the king of Israel in taking whatever was of value in Jerusalem. This clause is, in effect, final in the series describing the total defeat of Judah. (Segment 7 is simply a motion-verb clause recounting the king of Israel's return to Samaria.) Thus, there is something climactic about segment 6.

Another passage recounting surrender, pillage, and captivity—in this case, Jehoiachin's surrender to Babylon—is 2 Kings 24:10-15. Verse 10 recounts that at that time the officers of Nebuchadnezzar, king of Babylon, went up to Jerusalem and laid siege to it; the construction is N+*qatal* with N representing the phrase "at that time." Verse 11 recounts that Nebuchadnezzar himself came to Jerusalem to join in the siege operations; the clause has an initial narrative *wayyiqtol* form. Verse 12a, which recounts the surrender of the royal family and court, is likewise a narrative *wayyiqtol* clause. Verse 12b, which goes on to recount the king of Babylon's taking Jehoiachin captive in the eighth year of his reign is likewise a *wayyiqtol* clause. Verse 13, with two *wayyiqtol* clauses, recounts the pillaging of the temple and palace and the taking away of gold articles dating from the time of Solomon. Verses 14-16 are displayed here as example 19.

(19)

(1) וְהִגְלָה אֶת־כָּל־יְרוּשָׁלַם וְאֶת־כָּל־הַשָּׂרִים וְאֵת כָּל־גִּבּוֹרֵי הַחַיִל

And he carried into exile all Jerusalem, all the officers, and all the fighting men,

(2) עֲשָׂרָה אֲלָפִים גּוֹלֶה וְכָל־הֶחָרָשׁ וְהַמַּסְגֵּר

ten thousand carrying into exile, and all the artisans and craftsmen.

(3) לֹא נִשְׁאַר זוּלַת דַּלַּת עַם־הָאָרֶץ

He didn't spare except for the poorest of the land.

(4) וַיֶּגֶל אֶת־יְהוֹיָכִין בָּבֶלָה

And he took into exile Jehoiachin to Babylon,

(5) וְאֶת־אֵם הַמֶּלֶךְ וְאֶת־נְשֵׁי הַמֶּלֶךְ וְאֶת־סָרִיסָיו וְאֵת אוּלֵי הָאָרֶץ הוֹלִיךְ גּוֹלָה מִירוּשָׁלַם בָּבֶלָה...

the mother of the king, the wives of the king, his officials and the leading men of the land taking into exile from Jerusalem to Babylon...

(6) וְאֵת כָּל־אַנְשֵׁי הַחַיִל שִׁבְעַת אֲלָפִים וְהֶחָרָשׁ וְהַמַּסְגֵּר אֶלֶף הַכֹּל גִּבּוֹרִים עֹשֵׂי מִלְחָמָה

and all the strong men, seven thousand, and the artisans the craftsmen a thousand, all that were apt for war...

(7) וַיְבִיאֵם מֶלֶךְ־בָּבֶל גּוֹלָה בָּבֶלָה

and took the king of Babylon captive to Babylon.

The syntax of vv. 14-16 is rough and involves an anacoluthon between segment 6 and segment 7. If 6 consists of noun phrases appended

Weqatal Forms in Biblical Hebrew Prose

to those in 5, this is a difficult but possible construction. But 6 cannot be noun phrases preceding the verb of 7, since noun phrases cannot precede a *wayyiqtol*. Perhaps 6 is simply "orphaned" without any explicit governing verb.

Apparently 1, which contains the *weqatal* construction וְהִגְלָה 'and he carried into exile' (the first use of the verb גלה 'carry into exile'), is climactic after the preceding vv. 10–13. Following this, 2 contains a participial phrase involving the same verb, and in 3 a negated perfect, telling who were spared. Segment 4 has a *wayyiqtol* form of גלה 'carry into exile'. Segments 5 and 6 contain various noun phrases of uncertain government as discussed above. The whole passage becomes somewhat repetitious and periphrastic. It is possible, therefore, that the resort to the *weqatal* form in 1 (i.e., v. 14) is indicative of a kind of climax. The difficult and irregular syntax itself may be a kind of peak marker.

The next examples are more problematic, for instance, 1 Sam. 17:38 shown here as example 20:

(20)
(1) וַיַּלְבֵּשׁ שָׁאוּל אֶת־דָּוִד מַדָּיו
And Saul dressed David in his clothing.
(2) וְנָתַן קוֹבַע נְחֹשֶׁת עַל־רֹאשׁוֹ
And he put a helmet of bronze on his head.
(3) וַיַּלְבֵּשׁ אֹתוֹ שִׁרְיוֹן
And he dressed him in a coat of mail.

In this example, while 1 and 3 contain *wayyiqtol* clauses, 2 contains a *weqatal* clause. If I were to doggedly pursue the line of reasoning followed in the analysis of the past examples I would have to say that while 1 and 3 are the expected forms and 2 diverges by the use of *weqatal*, the latter was for some reason marked and singled out. But why? Was there anything of special cultural significance in a warrior's loaning his bronze helmet to someone else? A further possibility is that the passage is chiastic with 2 constituting the key of the chiasm and 1 and 3 the bracketing constructions (they contain the same verb, וַיַּלְבֵּשׁ). If this is a chiastic structure, it gives a certain prominence to 2, which prominence is further reinforced by the *weqatal* in 2.

Another interesting example is 2 Kings 18:36, which follows the long speech of the Assyrian field marshal in 18:19–35:

(21)
(1) וְהֶחֱרִישׁוּ הָעָם
And the people kept silence

(2) וְלֹא־עָנוּ אֹתוֹ דָּבָר
And they didn't answer him a word.

What is interesting here is that, in the parallel account incorporated into chapter 36 of the Book of Isaiah (36:21), the parallel verse has, not a *weqatal* form, but the more expected narrative form: וַיַּחֲרִישׁוּ 'and they kept silent'. While it could, of course, be pleaded that Isa. 36:21 contains the "correct" form and 2 Kings 18:36 an "incorrect" form, a "textual corruption," such ad hoc reasoning is not really necessary. If the *weqatal* can be used as a stylistic marking device (because of its unexpectedness), then all we have to assume is that the narrator/compiler chose to use it in one version of the account while such a choice was not made in the other version of the same event.

The function of the unexpected *weqatal* form in 2 Kings 18:36 is to dramatically mark the end of the scene outside the walls in the hearing of the people. In v. 37 (and what follows in chap. 19) the scene shifts to the royal counsels in the city.

In 1 Kings 13 is the story of the ill-fated prophet who came from Judah and denounced Jeroboam's altar at Bethel. Verse 3 incorporates a brief predictive discourse as a reported speech of Yahweh within the speech of the prophet, and 3a contains a somewhat problematic *weqatal* form. In example 22 (1 Kings 13:1-4) we can see this problem in context:

(22)

(1) וְהִנֵּה אִישׁ אֱלֹהִים בָּא מִיהוּדָה בִּדְבַר יְהוָה אֶל־בֵּית־אֵל
And behold a man of God came from Judah in the word of Yahweh to Bethel.

(2) וְיָרָבְעָם עֹמֵד עַל־הַמִּזְבֵּחַ לְהַקְטִיר
And Jeroboam was standing by the altar to make an offering.

(3) וַיִּקְרָא עַל־הַמִּזְבֵּחַ בִּדְבַר יְהוָה
And he cried out against the altar in the word of Yahweh.

(4) וַיֹּאמֶר
And he said,

(5) מִזְבֵּחַ מִזְבֵּחַ כֹּה אָמַר יְהוָה
"O altar, altar, thus Yahweh has spoken,

(6) הִנֵּה־בֵן נוֹלָד לְבֵית־דָּוִד יֹאשִׁיָּהוּ שְׁמוֹ
'Behold, a son born in the house of David, Josiah by name,

(7) וְזָבַח עָלֶיךָ אֶת־כֹּהֲנֵי הַבָּמוֹת הַמַּקְטִרִים עָלֶיךָ
will sacrifice upon you the priests of the high places, the ones (now) making offerings upon you.

(8) וְעַצְמוֹת אָדָם יִשְׂרְפוּ עָלֶיךָ
And the bones of men he will burn upon you.'"

(9) וְנָתַן בַּיּוֹם הַהוּא מוֹפֵת לֵאמֹר
And he gave a sign that very day, saying,
(10) זֶה הַמּוֹפֵת אֲשֶׁר דִּבֶּר יְהוָה
"This is the sign which Yahweh has spoken:
(11) הִנֵּה הַמִּזְבֵּחַ נִקְרָע
'Behold, the altar shall be split apart
(12) וְנִשְׁפַּךְ הַדֶּשֶׁן אֲשֶׁר־עָלָיו
and the ashes which are on it shall be poured out.'"
(13) וַיְהִי כִשְׁמֹעַ הַמֶּלֶךְ אֶת־דְּבַר אִישׁ־הָאֱלֹהִים אֲשֶׁר קָרָא
עַל־הַמִּזְבֵּחַ בְּבֵית־אֵל
And it happened that when the king heard the word of the man of God
which he cried out against the altar of Bethel,
(14) וַיִּשְׁלַח יָרָבְעָם אֶת־יָדוֹ . . .
Jeroboam put out his hand . . .

Of possible relevance in example 22 is the occurrence in segment 9 of the *weqatal* form, between the preceding 5-8 and the following 10-12, each of which is clearly a predictive discourse. It seems plausible that the וְנָתַן form here is not a use of *weqatal* for special marking in narrative, but belongs rather to the structure of predictive discourse as previously described. On the other hand, the giving of the sign may be climactic in reference to the preceding prophecy and therefore take the special *weqatal* marking.

The next example comes from 2 Sam. 19:11-43 (vv. 12-44 in the Hebrew text), the story of David's return from Transjordan, the gathering of those who came down to the ford to facilitate the royal household's crossing, and David's dealings with Shimei, Mephibosheth, and Barzillai. Verses 11-18a recount the preliminary negotiations and the rallying of certain forces to the ford at the Jordan; vv. 18b-23 recount David's dealing with Shimei, who had cursed him on his flight from Absalom; vv. 24-30 recount his dealings with Mephibosheth; vv. 31-38 recount his dealings with Barzillai the Gileadite; and vv. 39-43 recount the Jordan crossing and the trouble and turbulence that continued over into the following chapter.

The immediate problem here is with two *weqatal* forms found in 18b and 19a of the Hebrew text. Relevant to their occurrence may be the fact that the actual crossing of the king's household is put on hold by the narrator here and does not eventuate until v. 39; the intervening verses recount the dialogue with the three individuals named and matters relevant to those dialogues. Physical trajectory movement (but not storyline movement) ceases during the dialogue portion. Seen in this light, note the following *weqatal* occurrences in 2 Sam. 19:18b-19a:

(23)
(1) וְצָלְחוּ הַיַּרְדֵּן לִפְנֵי הַמֶּלֶךְ
And they [people mentioned in previous context] hastened to the Jordan before the king.
(2) וְעָבְרָה הָעֲבָרָה לַעֲבִיר אֶת־בֵּית הַמֶּלֶךְ וְלַעֲשׂוֹת הַטּוֹב בְּעֵינָו
And they crossed the ford of the Jordan to expedite the crossing of the royal household and to do whatever he desired.

I submit that here, as in other passages, the force of the *weqatal* forms is to mark something climactic in the story: the hurried completion of the plans to bring back the king. The escorting party had to cross the Jordan (west to east) in order to meet the royal household and accompanying forces and to expedite the return crossing (east to west). The two *weqatal* forms—and it is unusual to find two rather then simply one—mark the completion of the preparation; we, the readers and the escorting forces, must wait until the king deals with the three individuals mentioned before the event of the royal crossing takes place.[4]

Looking now at the account of Josiah's reforms in 2 Kings 23:4–30, we see that it has several *weqatal* forms at various points in its narrative framework. Here the *weqatal* as climactic/pivotal marker is used somewhat more freely than in the preceding examples. In vv. 4–7, which can be considered to be a paragraph whose theme is cleansing the temple of idolatrous worship, there is a clear sequence of *wayyiqtol* forms running through vv. 4, 6–7, but at the end of v. 4 and the beginning of v. 5 *weqatal* forms occur. Example 24 is composed of vv. 4–5 (but not 6–7, in which a string of five *wayyiqtol* forms occur).

(24)
(1) וַיְצַו הַמֶּלֶךְ אֶת־חִלְקִיָּהוּ הַכֹּהֵן הַגָּדוֹל וְאֶת־כֹּהֲנֵי הַמִּשְׁנֶה וְאֶת־שֹׁמְרֵי הַסַּף לְהוֹצִיא מֵהֵיכַל יְהוָה אֵת כָּל־הַכֵּלִים הָעֲשׂוּיִם לַבַּעַל ...
And the king ordered Hilkiah the high priest and the priests of the second rank and the doorkeepers to bring out of the temple of Yahweh all the cult objects made for Baal ...
(2) וַיִּשְׂרְפֵם מִחוּץ לִירוּשָׁלַם בְּשַׁדְמוֹת קִדְרוֹן
And he burnt them outside Jerusalem in the fields of Kidron.
(3) וְנָשָׂא אֶת־עֲפָרָם בֵּית־אֵל
And he carried the ashes to Bethel.
(4) וְהִשְׁבִּית אֶת־הַכְּמָרִים
And he did away with the (pagan) priests
(5) אֲשֶׁר נָתְנוּ מַלְכֵי יְהוּדָה
that the kings of Judah had instituted

(6) וַיְקַטֵּר בַּבָּמוֹת בְּעָרֵי יְהוּדָה וּמְסִבֵּי יְרוּשָׁלִָם
And he burnt incense in the high places in the environs of Jerusalem

(7) וְאֶת־הַמְקַטְּרִים לַבַּעַל לַשֶּׁמֶשׁ וְלַיָּרֵחַ וְלַמַּזָּלוֹת וּלְכֹל צְבָא הַשָּׁמָיִם
And those who burnt incense to Baal, to the sun, to the moon, to the constellations, and to the host of heaven.

The theme of the vv. 4-7 paragraph is clearly that of cleansing the temple of idolatry; however, v. 5 (segments 4-7 in the example) does not develop this and therefore could be considered to be parenthetical. But construing the passage this way flies in the face of the highlighting function of *weqatal* in narrative frameworks as seen in previous examples. Certainly segment 3 could be considered to be climactic although Bethel is not mentioned again until v. 15.

There are three points we should mention about the unusual syntax in segments 5 and 6 of example 24: First, the dominating verb is וְהִשְׁבִּית 'and he did away with', a *weqatal* form. Second, the relative clause in 5, which is pluperfect in thrust, seems to govern the *wayyiqtol* form in 6 in spite of the awkwardness of this form's being a singular. Third, the object of "he did away with" resumes in 7. It is evident then, that the verb of 4 governs all that follows, with an intervening relative clause and *wayyiqtol* forms consequent upon the relative clause.

At this point we can turn our analytic liabilities into assets. The great detail and syntactic complexity of segments 4-7 can be considered to mark a high point, a pivotal event of this example.[5] That this is a peak is further established by use of the *weqatal* form in 4 (cf. example 19).

Verses 8-10 later in the same chapter can be considered to be another paragraph. The theme broadens to include bringing in priests from other towns of Judah and giving them a living in Jerusalem—even while abolishing the high places where they had ministered. These verses are displayed as example 25:

(25)

(1) וַיָּבֵא אֶת־הַכֹּהֲנִים מֵעָרֵי יְהוּדָה
And he brought in the priests from the cities of Judah.

(2) וַיְטַמֵּא אֶת־הַבָּמוֹת אֲשֶׁר קִטְּרוּ־שָׁמָּה הַכֹּהֲנִים מִגֶּבַע עַד־בְּאֵר שָׁבַע
And he defiled the high places where the priests had burnt incense from Geba to Beersheba.

(3) וְנָתַץ אֶת־בָּמוֹת הַשְּׁעָרִים אֲשֶׁר־פֶּתַח שַׁעַר יְהוֹשֻׁעַ שַׂר־הָעִיר אֲשֶׁר־עַל־שְׂמֹאול אִישׁ בְּשַׁעַר הָעִיר
And he destroyed the high places of the gates which were at the

entrance of the gate of Joshua, the ruler of the city, to the left of the gate of the city.

(4) אַ֣ךְ לֹ֤א יַעֲלוּ֙ כֹּהֲנֵ֣י הַבָּמ֔וֹת אֶל־מִזְבַּ֥ח יְהוָ֖ה בִּירוּשָׁלָ֑͏ִם
But the priests of the high places were not allowed to minister at the sacrifice of Yahweh in Jerusalem.

(5) כִּ֛י אִם־אָכְל֥וּ מַצּ֖וֹת בְּת֥וֹךְ אֲחֵיהֶֽם
And they ate bread among their brothers.

(6) וְטִמֵּ֣א אֶת־הַתֹּ֔פֶת אֲשֶׁ֖ר בְּגֵ֣י בְנֵֽי־הִנֹּ֑ם
And he defiled Tophet which was in the valley of the sons of Hinnom

(7) לְבִלְתִּ֗י לְהַעֲבִ֨יר אִ֜ישׁ אֶת־בְּנ֧וֹ וְאֶת־בִּתּ֛וֹ בָּאֵ֖שׁ לַמֹּֽלֶךְ
to prevent a man from passing his son or daughter through the fire to Molech.

Again, *weqatal* forms occur at places where we might have expected *wayyiqtol* forms. Segments 1 and 2 have *wayyiqtol* forms, 3 and 6 have *weqatal* forms, 4 and 5 have the *qatal* forms after particles אַךְ, לֹא, and אִם, and 7 mentions the purpose for which Tophet had served. The analytical line we have taken leads us to regard the *weqatal* form in 3 as marking the destruction of the high places as a pivotal/climactic accomplishment, while 4 and 5 constitute accompanying explanation. It is even easier to see that 6, where a *weqatal* form marks the defilement of Tophet (a place of infant sacrifice), indicates a pivotal accomplishment at paragraph's end. In the case of 3 we might wish for more cultural and historic information; possibly the royal suppression of shrines erected by the governor of the city was in itself a significant accomplishment. On the other hand, in view of the prophets' denunciation of infant sacrifice, it is easy to see that the defilement of Tophet was regarded as of special significance.

Verses 11-14 can be considered another paragraph, one that further recounts the destruction of various shrines in and around the temple—especially on the "Hill of Corruption." There is a proliferation of explanatory material in OV (N+*qatal*) clauses with occasional occurrence of *weqatal* forms. Example 26 is 2 Kings 23:11-14 in full:

(26)

(1) וַיַּשְׁבֵּ֣ת אֶת־הַסּוּסִ֗ים אֲשֶׁ֣ר נָתְנוּ֩ מַלְכֵ֨י יְהוּדָ֤ה לַשֶּׁ֙מֶשׁ֙ מִבֹּ֣א בֵית־יְהוָ֔ה אֶל־לִשְׁכַּת֙ נְתַן־מֶ֣לֶךְ הַסָּרִ֔יס אֲשֶׁ֖ר בַּפַּרְוָרִ֑ים
And he removed the horses which the kings of Judah had dedicated to the Sun from the entrance to the house of Yahweh by the chamber of Nathan-Melek, an official in the courtyard.

(2) וְאֶת־מַרְכְּב֥וֹת הַשֶּׁ֖מֶשׁ שָׂרַ֥ף בָּאֵֽשׁ
And the chariots of the Sun he burnt in the fire.

Weqatal Forms in Biblical Hebrew Prose

(3) וְאֶת־הַמִּזְבְּחוֹת אֲשֶׁר עַל־הַגָּג עֲלִיַּת אָחָז אֲשֶׁר־עָשׂוּ מַלְכֵי יְהוּדָה
And the altars which were on the roof of the upper room of Ahaz which the kings of Judah had made

(4) וְאֶת־הַמִּזְבְּחֹת אֲשֶׁר־עָשָׂה מְנַשֶּׁה בִּשְׁתֵּי חַצְרוֹת בֵּית־יְהוָה
and the altars which Manasseh had made in the two courts of the house of Yahweh

(5) נָתַץ הַמֶּלֶךְ
the king destroyed.

(6) וַיָּרָץ מִשָּׁם
And he took them from there.

(7) וְהִשְׁלִיךְ אֶת־עֲפָרָם אֶל־נַחַל קִדְרוֹן
And he took their ashes down to the valley of Kidron.

(8) וְאֶת־הַבָּמוֹת אֲשֶׁר עַל־פְּנֵי יְרוּשָׁלַםִ אֲשֶׁר מִימִין לְהַר־הַמַּשְׁחִית
And the altars which were in front of Jerusalem to the south of The Hill of Corruption,

(9) אֲשֶׁר בָּנָה שְׁלֹמֹה מֶלֶךְ־יִשְׂרָאֵל לְעַשְׁתֹּרֶת שִׁקֻּץ צִידֹנִים וְלִכְמוֹשׁ שִׁקֻּץ מוֹאָב וּלְמִלְכֹּם תּוֹעֲבַת בְּנֵי־עַמּוֹן
which Solomon, king of Israel, had built to Ashtoreth, the abomination of the Sidonians, and to Chemosh, the abomination of Moab, and to Milkom, the abomination of the Ammonites,

(10) טִמֵּא הַמֶּלֶךְ
the king defiled.

(11) וְשִׁבַּר אֶת־הַמַּצֵּבוֹת
And he broke up the sacred stones.

(12) וַיִּכְרֹת אֶת־הָאֲשֵׁרִים
And he cut up the Asherahs.

(13) וַיְמַלֵּא אֶת־מְקוֹמָם עַצְמוֹת אָדָם
And he defiled their places with human bones.

In example 26 *wayyiqtol* forms occur in 1, 6, 12, and 13. Segment 2 is an object *qatal* clause; 3 and 4 are objects preposed to the *qatal* form in 5. Segment 7 involves a *weqatal* form, which may be considered to be climactic in reference to 3–4 (note the reference to disposing of ashes at Bethel in a *weqatal* form in 3 of example 24). Segments 8 and 9 comprise a preposed object with its relative clause for which 10 is the governing *qatal* form. Segment 11 is another *weqatal* form. If this is a marked form—and certainly the incidence of the *weqatal* must be explained—we may well raise the question of the cultural importance attached to the מַצֵּבוֹת 'sacred stones'. The paragraph concludes with two clauses, 12 and 13, that are regular expected *wayyiqtol* forms.

The next example is in 2 Kings 23:15-18, a paragraph that recounts Josiah's carrying his reforms as far as Bethel and desecrating the altar there as prophesied by the nameless prophet of 1 Kings 13. This paragraph alone of the whole 2 Kings 23:4-30 passage has reported dialogue. The paragraph is introduced with the conjunction וְגַם 'and also' and a reference to a change of locale, namely, Bethel. I will not present the total text of vv. 15-18 but only v. 15, since it contains a *weqatal* form whose analysis is germane to this study.

(27)

(1) וְגַם אֶת־הַמִּזְבֵּחַ אֲשֶׁר בְּבֵית־אֵל הַבָּמָה אֲשֶׁר עָשָׂה יָרָבְעָם
בֶּן־נְבָט אֲשֶׁר הֶחֱטִיא אֶת־יִשְׂרָאֵל

And also the altar that was at Bethel, the high place which Jeroboam had made—he who caused Israel to sin—

(2) גַּם אֶת־הַמִּזְבֵּחַ הַהוּא וְאֶת־הַבָּמָה נָתַץ

even that altar and that high place he demolished.

(3) וַיִּשְׂרֹף אֶת־הַבָּמָה

And he burned the high place,

(4) הֵדַק לְעָפָר

ground it to powder,

(5) וְשָׂרַף אֲשֵׁרָה

and burned the Asherah pole.

The verb forms of v. 15 (example 27) are unlike those of 16-18. The latter are *wayyiqtol* forms with reported dialogue (*wayyiqtol* of 'say' in 17-18) in which the men of Bethel speak up and identify a tomb as that of the prophet about whom we read in 1 Kings 13. As to the v. 15 verb forms (in 3-5 of example 27), the first verb is the expected *wayyiqtol* form, the second is a *qatal* (minus *waw*), and the third is a *weqatal* form, is the *weqatal* of the same verb that occurs as *wayyiqtol* in 3.

It may be fruitful, however, to look over the preceding context. Clearly 1, 2, and 3 form one O+*qatal* sentence with the final verb, "demolished." Segments 3 and 4 form one sentence with הַבָּמָה 'the high place' patterning as the common object of the *wayyiqtol* verb of 3 and the *qatal* verb of 4. All of v. 15 appears as background—Josiah in his now familiar role as iconoclast—to the dialogue reported in the following three lines. Possibly, then, the *weqatal* form in 5 is not so much climactic as simply final (i.e., closure of the nondialogue, the weakly narrative setting of a dialogue paragraph).

One paragraph remains of this extended passage: vv. 19-20. (Since it does not contain any *weqatal* forms, I do not present it here.) Verse 19 begins with and shifts the locale to the towns of Samaria; it is a long

O+*qatal*+S construction: וְגַם אֶת־כָּל־XXX הֵסִיר יֹאשִׁיָּהוּ 'And also, all the XXX destroyed Josiah'. After this introductory sentence of the paragraph (cf. v. 15 as introductory in its paragraph), a string of narrative *wayyiqtol* forms sets in.

The reason I have presented this extended passage of 2 Kings 23:4–20 is not so much to support my view that *weqatal* forms in a narrative framework (when not an embedded procedural discourse) mark a climactic/pivotal event as to test it. It is possibly the most difficult passage for anybody's theory of nonfrequentative nonprocedural *weqatal*s in a narrative framework. At first, I was inclined to consider the *weqatal* forms in this passage as parenthetical, a truly "secondary" storyline. But as we have seen, the role of such a secondary storyline is already filled structurally by N+*qatal* forms (of which there are many instances of N as object in this passage). Meanwhile, there are other examples, previously given, which seem to support *weqatal* forms in narrative as marking what in other languages we have called pivotal events, so there seemed no need to jettison that hypothesis here.

The following is a summary of *weqatal* forms in 2 Kings 23:4-20:

Example 24: (3) carrying the ashes of cult objects to Bethel (irregular syntax).
Example 24: (4) doing away with the pagan priesthood instituted by the previous king (irregular syntax).
Example 25: (3) destroyed/defiled high places (where even priests of Yahweh had officiated), culminating with the destruction of the high place at the city gates, by the Gate of Joshua the governor of the city.
Example 25: (6) defiled Tophet—given in detail.
Example 26: (7) threw the rubble into the Kidron Valley.
Example 26: (11) smashed the sacred stones on the Hill of Corruption (but *wayyiqtol* for burning the Asherah and defiling places with human bones).
Example 27: (6) burning the Asherah (grinding to powder *qatal* precedes).

We need to consider one more passage, the final clause of Gen. 37:3, out of respect for those who consider it a *cause celèbre* of a *weqatal* functioning as a frequentative. But I explain it differently:

(28)
(1) וְיִשְׂרָאֵל אָהַב אֶת־יוֹסֵף מִכָּל־בָּנָיו כִּי־בֶן־זְקֻנִים הוּא לוֹ
And Israel loved his son Joseph more than all his other sons, for he was a son of his old age.

(2) וְעָשָׂה לוֹ כְּתֹנֶת פַּסִּים
And he made for him a special cloak.

Possibly Driver was the first to suggest that this *weqatal* form (in 2) is a frequentative. I submit, however, that there is simply no clue here (as in example 9, 1 Sam. 2:18), of a shift to a how-it-was-done embedded procedural discourse (i.e., no DSC). I find it simpler to regard 2 not as saying "he made him a 'cloak' from time to time" but rather marking something climactic and pivotal in the passage. Jacob's favoritism went so far as to lead him to have this special cloak made for Joseph—and therein lay a bitter root of trouble.

3.5 וְהָיָה forms as marking significant background or important events to follow (cataphoric)

The *weqatal* forms of the verb היה are used in a special way, similar to but different from other *weqatal* forms. In narrative, וַיְהִי, the *wayyiqtol* form of היה, occurs plus a temporal element plus material of any status, in other words, primary storyline *wayyiqtol* forms, *qatal* forms, and background material (e.g., participles and nominal clauses) (see Longacre 1989:66–70). Likewise, in predictive and procedural discourse, וְהָיָה regularly fulfills a similar function: וְהָיָה-plus-temporal-plus-main-clause of whatever status. A problem is encountered when וְהָיָה forms occur in a narrative framework where they "shouldn't" occur. In most cases GKC tries to pass such forms off as textual corruptions or just plain "mistakes," peremptorily saying that all such וְהָיָה forms should be read as וַיְהִי (GKC, sec. 112.tt.uu., p. 339). If, however, we can assign a function to the occurrence of וְהָיָה in a narrative framework, such wholesale and unmotivated violence to the text can be avoided.

As an example, consider 2 Kings 3 which recounts the story of a joint expedition of the kings of Israel, Judah, and Edom against Moab. Verse 9 reports that "after a roundabout march of seven days, the army had no water for themselves or for the animals with them." Eventually, at Jehoshaphat's suggestion they call on the prophet Elisha for help. Example 29 presents vv. 14, 15, and 16a:

(29)
(1) וַיֹּאמֶר אֱלִישָׁע חַי־יְהוָה צְבָאוֹת אֲשֶׁר עָמַדְתִּי לְפָנָיו
And Elisha said, "As surely as Yahweh Almighty lives before whom I stand,
(2) כִּי לוּלֵי פְּנֵי יְהוֹשָׁפָט מֶלֶךְ־יְהוּדָה אֲנִי נֹשֵׂא אִם־אַבִּיט אֵלֶיךָ
if it weren't for the presence of Jehoshaphat King of Judah I would not look at you

(3) וְאִם־אֶרְאֶךָּ
or take any notice of you.
(4) וְעַתָּה קְחוּ־לִי מְנַגֵּן
But *now,* bring me a harpist."
(5) וְהָיָה כְּנַגֵּן הַמְנַגֵּן
And it happened that as the harpist was playing
(6) וַתְּהִי עָלָיו יַד־יְהוָה
the hand of Yahweh came upon him
(7) וַיֹּאמֶר כֹּה אָמַר יְהוָה. . .
and he said, "Thus says Yahweh . . ."

What is of interest here is the occurrence of the word וְעַתָּה 'and now', initial in 4, and וְהָיָה, immediately following in 5. The particle complex וְעַתָּה is regularly used to mark the conclusive thrust or appeal of a speech, as in Joseph's speech before Pharaoh (Gen. 41:33) and Judah's speech before Joseph incognito (Gen. 44:33). So Elisha says in 4, "Well, putting aside all the negative considerations which I have mentioned, let's put events into motion by bringing me a harpist; *that* should prove significant." Immediately following this assertion of Elisha's we are told in the narrative framework, in the words of 5 and 6, that something significant happened as the harpist played. Is it not possible to see here a connection between the וְעַתָּה underscoring in Elisha's speech and the וְהָיָה underscoring in the narrative framework? If so, then the וְהָיָה of the narrative is marking a piece of significant background: it was as the harpist played that the hand of Yahweh came upon Elisha and he said, "Thus saith the Lord . . ."

A few examples from the Books of Samuel will now be considered, to test the hypothesis that וְהָיָה is a marker of significant following material (i.e., that it has a cataphoric underlining function). The first is 1 Sam. 1:12-13, which records Eli's first taking notice of Hannah:

(30)
(1) וְהָיָה כִּי הִרְבְּתָה לְהִתְפַּלֵּל לִפְנֵי יְהוָה
And it happened that as she continued to pray before Yahweh
(2) וְעֵלִי שֹׁמֵר אֶת־פִּיהָ
that Eli was watching her mouth.
(3) וְחַנָּה הִיא מְדַבֶּרֶת עַל־לִבָּהּ
Now Hannah was speaking in her heart.
(4) רַק שְׂפָתֶיהָ נָּעוֹת
Only her lips moved.
(5) וְקוֹלָהּ לֹא יִשָּׁמֵעַ
But her voice wasn't heard.

(6) וַיַּחְשְׁבֶהָ עֵלִי לְשִׁכֹּרָה
And Eli considered her to be drunk.
(7) וַיֹּאמֶר אֵלֶיהָ ...
And he said to her, ". . ."

Certainly all that follows in the narrative hinges on Eli's taking notice of Hannah, of her having the opportunity to express her bitterness of heart, and of his pronouncing on her the blessing, "Go in peace and may the God of Israel grant you what you have asked of him" (v. 17)—at which point Hannah believed the prophetic word, went back home, and conceived the child Samuel. Here, then, the unusual presence of וְהָיָה in narrative (it is in segment 1) marks a significant background situation: Eli's taking notice of Hannah at prayer, expressed in participles and *yiqtol* forms.

Another "test case" is 1 Sam. 10:9, a pivot between Samuel's predictive speech in 10:1–8, and its narrative fulfillment in vv. 10–11:

(31)
(1) וְהָיָה כְּהַפְנֹתוֹ שִׁכְמוֹ לָלֶכֶת מֵעִם שְׁמוּאֵל
And it happened that as Saul turned his back to leave Samuel
(2) וַיַּהֲפָךְ־לוֹ אֱלֹהִים לֵב אַחֵר
God gave him another heart.
(3) וַיָּבֹאוּ כָּל־הָאֹתוֹת הָאֵלֶּה בַּיּוֹם הַהוּא
And all these signs were fulfilled that very day.

That this verse as a whole is pivotal between a predictive discourse and its fulfillment seems clear and is possibly sufficient to explain the special tagging with וְהָיָה. Should we say that it was Saul's leaving Samuel that is presented as a backgrounded but triggering event? Or can we simply say that וְהָיָה signals significant events to come?

In 1 Sam. 17:40–51 is a record of David's contest with Goliath. Verses 41–47 record the mutual verbal challenges of the two to each other. Verses 48 and 49, which follow the verbal duel, are shown here as example 32:

(32)
(1) וְהָיָה כִּי־קָם הַפְּלִשְׁתִּי
And it happened that the Philistine arising
(2) וַיֵּלֶךְ
and came
(3) וַיִּקְרַב לִקְרַאת דָּוִד
And came close to meet David.
(4) וַיְמַהֵר דָּוִד
And David hurried

(5) וַיָּרָץ הַמַּעֲרָכָה לִקְרַאת הַפְּלִשְׁתִּי
And ran toward the battle line to meet the Philistine.
(6) וַיִּשְׁלַח אֶת־יָדוֹ אֶל־הַכֶּלִי
And David put his hand into his bag
(7) וַיִּקַּח מִשָּׁם אֶבֶן
And took a stone from there.
(8) וַיְקַלַּע
And he slung (it)
(9) וַיַּךְ אֶת־הַפְּלִשְׁתִּי אֶל־מִצְחוֹ
And he hit the Philistine in the forehead.

This passage (vv. 40–47) along with what precedes (vv. 40–47) has several features that clearly mark it as a great moment of the ongoing story: verbs that carefully detail phases of an action, as in 6–8; nouns for referring to David and the Philistine, thus underscoring the confrontation; and dialogue, holding back the action in the verses that precede vv. 48–49. Another feature that marks this as a "great moment," I should add, is the very use of וְהָיָה in segment 1. The distribution of the latter, at the boundary between the verbal confrontation and the physical action that brings about the Philistine's death, is somewhat striking. It is again as if וְהָיָה were the narrative counterpart of וְעַתָּה 'and now' in hortatory discourse. In both cases the preliminaries are over and the substantive saying or action will follow.

Another example comes from 1 Sam. 25:18–35, the story of Abigail's intervention with David on behalf of her husband, Nabal, and her household. David, whose men had been insulted by Nabal, was on his way to attack Nabal when Abigail and her party met him and his men. It is at this dramatic juncture that וְהָיָה occurs, in 1 Sam. 25:20:

(33)
(1) וְהָיָה הִיא רֹכֶבֶת עַל־הַחֲמוֹר
And it happened that she was riding on her donkey
(2) וְיֹרֶדֶת בְּסֵתֶר הָהָר
and coming down into a ravine of the mountain.
(3) וְהִנֵּה דָוִד וַאֲנָשָׁיו יֹרְדִים לִקְרָאתָהּ
And, behold, David and his men were coming down towards her.
(4) וַתִּפְגֹּשׁ אֹתָם
And she met up with them.

The scene is graphically sketched with participles and הִנֵּה in 3 to focus our attention. A long speech of Abigail follows—and David must have found the encounter a pleasant one, since on Nabal's death he married Abigail (vv. 38–42).

Here again there is a bit of a wordplay between וְעַתָּה in v. 17 and וְהָיָה in v. 20. The former occurs in a speech of one of Nabal's servants to Abigail. He sketches out the situation (vv. 14–16), then in v. 17 advises: וְעַתָּה "think it over and see what you can do." Verse 20 depicts the scene in which Abigail, pursuant to the suggestion, meets up with David—and fittingly labels the scene with וְהָיָה.

In 2 Sam. 6:16 David's first wife, Michal, is watching from a window as the ark of God is brought into the city with David leaping and dancing before the ark:

(34)
(1) וְהָיָה אֲרוֹן יְהוָה בָּא עִיר דָּוִד
And it happened that as the ark of Yahweh came into the City of David
(2) וּמִיכַל בַּת־שָׁאוּל נִשְׁקְפָה בְּעַד הַחַלּוֹן
that Michal, Saul's daughter, watched from a window.
(3) וַתֵּרֶא אֶת־הַמֶּלֶךְ דָּוִד מְפַזֵּז וּמְכַרְכֵּר לִפְנֵי יְהוָה
And she saw King David leaping and dancing before Yahweh.
(4) וַתִּבֶז לוֹ בְּלִבָּהּ
And she despised him in her heart.

In v. 16 וְהָיָה signals a fateful development in the life of Michal, David's first wife, who had been given to another man but had been forcibly retaken by Abner on David's insistence (2 Sam. 3:13–16). Here, in 2 Samuel 16, the unhappy woman watches David's dervishlike worship from a window, thought it conduct unworthy of a king, and told him so later (v. 20). At this point, David resolved to have nothing ever to do with her again. Verse 23 tells us "And Michal, daughter of Saul, had no children until the day of her death." So if Michal is the focus of the story at this point, the וְהָיָה of v. 16 indeed marks the development of an attitude which led to Michal's practical widowhood. As such, the וְהָיָה again marks something more than would be marked by a simple narrative וַיְהִי, had it been used.

Several occurrences of וְהָיָה are found in narrative portions of Jeremiah. Though their function is not so easily determined as those which I have just presented, I believe a case can be made for their being broadly similar, for instance, in Jer. 3:6–10, where there is a first-person narrative in which Yahweh is speaker. Verses 6–8 (NIV) are as follows:

> During the reign of King Josiah, the LORD said to me: "Have you seen what faithless Israel has done? She has gone up on every high hill and under every spreading tree and has committed adultery there. I thought after she had done all this she would return to me, but she

did not, and her unfaithful sister Judah saw it. I gave faithless Israel her certificate of divorce and sent her away because of her iniquities. I saw that her unfaithful sister Judah had no fear; she also went out and committed adultery."

Jer.3:9-10 is shown in example 35:

(35)
(1) וְהָיָה מִקֹּל זְנוּתָהּ
And it happened in the easy acceptance of her adultery
(2) וַתֶּחֱנַף אֶת־הָאָרֶץ
she defiled the land
(3) וַתִּנְאַף אֶת־הָאֶבֶן וְאֶת־הָעֵץ
and committed adultery with stone and wood.
(4) וְגַם־בְּכָל־זֹאת לֹא־שָׁבָה אֵלַי בָּגוֹדָה אֲחוֹתָהּ יְהוּדָה בְּכָל־לִבָּהּ
And yet for all this her treacherous sister Judah did not turn back to me with all her heart
(5) כִּי אִם־בְּשֶׁקֶר
but rather deceitfully,
(6) נְאֻם־יְהוָה
says Yahweh.

Here segment 1 has special marking; perhaps it is a summary (possibly climactic) of what has preceded in vv. 6-8. The lightness of her adultery and the reference to wood and stone in 3 may be indicative of this. Perhaps all of vv. 6-8 is brought to focus in v. 9 (segments 1-3) in order to forcibly underline the denunciation of Judah in v. 10 (i.e., 4-5).

Jeremiah 37:11-13, shown as example 36, records the circumstances of Jeremiah's being put into prison (we are told in 37:4 that he had not previously been imprisoned). In v. 11 וְהָיָה tags the following context as recording the fateful contingency in which the Babylonians lift the siege and Jeremiah sets out from Jerusalem on a personal errand regarding his inheritance back in his hometown.

(36)
(1) וְהָיָה בְּהֵעָלוֹת חֵיל הַכַּשְׂדִּים מֵעַל יְרוּשָׁלִָם מִפְּנֵי חֵיל פַּרְעֹה
And it happened that in the withdrawal of the army of the Chaldeans from Jerusalem before the army of Pharaoh
(2) וַיֵּצֵא יִרְמְיָהוּ מִירוּשָׁלִַם לָלֶכֶת אֶרֶץ בִּנְיָמִן לַחֲלִק מִשָּׁם בְּתוֹךְ הָעָם
Jeremiah started out from Jerusalem to go to the territory of Benjamin to get his share of the property there among his people.

(3) וַיְהִי־הוּא בְּשַׁעַר בִּנְיָמִן
And he was there at the Benjamin Gate.
(4) וְשָׁם בַּעַל פְּקִדֻת
And the captain of the guard was there.
(5) וּשְׁמוֹ יִרְאִיָּיה . . .
And his name was Irijah . . .
(6) וַיִּתְפֹּשׂ אֶת־יִרְמְיָהוּ הַנָּבִיא
And he arrested Jeremiah the prophet,
(7) לֵאמֹר אֶל־הַכַּשְׂדִּים אַתָּה נֹפֵל
saying, "You are defecting to the Chaldeans."

Jeremiah 38:28b is a brief sentence beginning with וְהָיָה. The rest of chapter 39 and all of 40 describe the capture of the city, the fate of king Zedekiah, the carrying of people into exile and how Jeremiah himself fared during the sacking of the city and shortly afterwards. Clearly the thrust of 38:28b is cataphoric:

(37)

וְהָיָה כַּאֲשֶׁר נִלְכְּדָה יְרוּשָׁלָם
and this is how Jerusalem was taken

Certainly, if וְהָיָה is a marker of fateful events to follow, the story of the taking of Jerusalem is such an event, or series of events, as Jer. 40:2–3, part of the context of example 37, shows. These verses record the words of the captain of the guard, Nebuzaradan, to Jeremiah on finding the latter among the captives.

(38)
(1) וַיִּקַּח רַב־טַבָּחִים לְיִרְמְיָהוּ
And the captain of the guard found Jeremiah.
(2) וַיֹּאמֶר אֵלָיו
And he said to him,
(3) יְהוָה אֱלֹהֶיךָ דִּבֶּר אֶת־הָרָעָה הַזֹּאת אֶל־הַמָּקוֹם הַזֶּה
"Yahweh your God decreed this evil against this place.
(4) וַיָּבֵא
And now he has brought (it).
(5) וַיַּעַשׂ יְהוָה כַּאֲשֶׁר דִּבֶּר
And Yahweh has done according to what he said,
(6) כִּי חֲטָאתֶם לַיהוָה
for you have sinned against Yahweh.
(7) וְלֹא־שְׁמַעְתֶּם בְּקוֹלוֹ
And you haven't listened to his voice.
(8) וְהָיָה לָכֶם דָּבָר הַזֶּה
And it has happened to you according to this word."

If וְהָיָה in example 37 is cataphoric, then in example 38 וְהָיָה seems plainly anaphoric, referring back to the immediate words of the captain of the guard in the preceding verse. This is faintly reminiscent of וְהָיָה in example 31 (1 Sam. 10:9), which is pivotal between a prophecy and its fulfillment. At any rate, וְהָיָה in example 38 (also in 37) refers to the taking of Jerusalem, the most fateful event of that day. However, it is a main verb in 38, not a complementizer as in examples 29–37. Consequently, segment 3 in example 38 is best taken as simply a *weqatal* form in climactic/finalizing function.

4. W*eqatal* as an apparently consecutive tense in juridical discourse

The discussion so far has considered discourse types of a thematically connected sort (narrative, predictive, procedural, instructional) . Now we turn our attention to the law codes (e.g., Exodus 21 and 22) where thematic connections are characteristically looser. Although a group of laws on similar subjects is not unusual (e.g., Exod. 21:1-11 on slaves; 21:12-27 on assault and personal injury; 21:28-36 on crimes involving animals), it is not uncommon to have a law constitute its own thematic unity. Instead of any overall tree structure we often find a forest of trees in the same plot. They are essentially sequences of minidiscourses on related subjects.

There is an overall resemblance, however, of such a minidiscourse, or a related set of such minidiscourses, to predictive, procedural (how-to-do-it), and instructional discourses. Like them, the law codes involve a parameter *projection* over against *nonprojection* (i.e., accomplished) in narrative. For this reason we might expect *weqatal* forms to be prominent in juridical discourse. We might also expect an alternation of sorts between *yiqtol* and *weqatal* forms. And this is what we find.

On the other hand, certain features of juridical discourse prohibit the use of *weqatal* forms and make resort to *yiqtol* forms necessary. These features cluster around the fact that conditional sentences are a prominent feature of the law codes.

Let us look at these features in detail: (1) The protasis of such a sentence contains כִּי 'if' at the beginning of a section and אִם 'if' within a section: either particle blocks the use of the *weqatal* form (cf. אֲשֶׁר 'who/which/that'). (2) Some protasis or apodosis verbs are negated with לֹא 'not'; this particle also blocks the use of *weqatal*. (3) A piece of casuistry typically revolves around a hypothetical aggressor or victim; this calls for noun-initial clauses, which again block the occurrence of *weqatal*. (4) Some apodoses (occasionally protases) are strengthened with the use of an infinitive absolute that precedes the finite verb and again blocks the use of a *weqatal* form.

Within this pattern of restrictions *weqatal* forms occur: They occur in non-initial verb clauses within a protasis or an apodosis, and they occur as initial in an apodosis where there is no semantic reason to prepose a noun or to choose an infinitival absolute construction.

This is not to imply that these are the only possible constructions in conditional sentences. We also find an occasional *qatal* or *qatal* conjoined with a conjunctive *weqatal,* all as *pluperfects*. Participles ("the one who..."), and even verbless clauses, are also found.

I do not attempt to identify foregrounded versus backgrounded clauses in these minidiscourses; I do note, however, on the logical ground of truth-tables for the predicate calculus, a certain ascendancy of the constructions in the apodosis. Therefore, in simple laws such as אִם (N) *yiqtol... weqatal*, the latter construction outranks the former. But this reasoning from the ascendancy of the apodosis would also promote N+*yiqtol* to top rank as well as infinitive absolute+*yiqtol* and even an occasional verbless clause. So let it be (at least until further study).

Notice here that I am reversing the line of reasoning hallowed by GKC (1910) and Waltke and O'Connor (1990), who begin by taking sequence of tenses in conditional sentences as basic to the functional understanding of *weqatal* constructions and other more extended uses as special developments. On the contrary, I begin with the latter and regard the distribution of *weqatal* in conditional sentences in the law codes as a special and restricted development. Perhaps GKC and Waltke and O'Connor simply follow early rabbinical tradition reflecting the predilection of the rabbis—who were lawyers—for the law codes![6]

Now for a few rather long statutes where the restricted role of the *weqatal* can be seen in connection with other verb forms. The first example is Exod. 21:5–6:

(39)
  (1) וְאִם־אָמֹר יֹאמַר הָעֶבֶד
      And if truly says the slave,
  (2) אָהַבְתִּי אֶת־אֲדֹנִי אֶת־אִשְׁתִּי וְאֶת־בָּנָי לֹא אֵצֵא חָפְשִׁי
      "I love my master, my wife, and my children; I will not go out free,"
  (3) וְהִגִּישׁוֹ אֲדֹנָיו אֶל־הָאֱלֹהִים
      then his master shall take him before the judges.
  (4) וְהִגִּישׁוֹ אֶל־הַדֶּלֶת אוֹ אֶל־הַמְּזוּזָה
      And he will bring him to the door or to the doorpost
  (5) וְרָצַע אֲדֹנָיו אֶת־אָזְנוֹ בַּמַּרְצֵעַ
      and his master will pierce his ear with an awl

(6) וַעֲבָדוֹ לְעֹלָם
and he will serve him forever.

Example 39 addresses a situation in which a slave declares his love for his master and his own family and declares that he will not go free. So his master brings him before the judges, lines him up against a door or a doorpost, and pierces his ear with an awl. The slave is then a slave for life. A procedure is sketched out to be followed contingent on the slave's declaration. Of some interest here is the occurrence of the infinitive absolute plus *yiqtol* in segment 1 and of a *weqatal*+pronominal-suffix clause in 4. We thus see that an initial *yiqtol* can be strengthened to an infinitive absolute *yiqtol* in the protasis, while a modified *weqatal* clause can express the legal upshot of it all in the apodosis.

A further example is Exod. 21:18-19. Here the complexity is in the protasis instead of in the apodosis and a new topic is implied by an initial כִּי 'if' in v. 18.

(40)
(1) וְכִי־יְרִיבֻן אֲנָשִׁים
And if men are fighting
(2) וְהִכָּה אִישׁ אֶת־רֵעֵהוּ בְּאֶבֶן אוֹ בְאֶגְרֹף
and one man hits the other with a stone or with his fist/tool
(3) וְלֹא יָמוּת
and he doesn't die
(4) וְנָפַל לְמִשְׁכָּב
but takes to his bed,
(5) אִם־יָקוּם
if he gets up
(6) וְהִתְהַלֵּךְ בַּחוּץ עַל־מִשְׁעַנְתּוֹ
and walks around outside on his staff,
(7) וְנִקָּה הַמַּכֶּה
then the smiter will be innocent.
(8) רַק שִׁבְתּוֹ יִתֵּן
Only he will give compensation
(9) וְרַפֹּא יְרַפֵּא
and (the man) must entirely recover.

There are two protases here dependent on the same apodosis. The first (a complex protasis) occurs in segments 1-4, where 1 is necessarily *yiqtol* after כִּי; 2 is *weqatal*; 3 is necessarily *yiqtol* after לֹא; and 4 is, again, *weqatal*. The second protasis occurs in segments 5 and 6, where 5 is necessarily a *yiqtol* form after אִם 'if' and 6 is *weqatal*. In 7 is the apodosis in *weqatal* form: "the smiter will be innocent," while 8 and 9 append two further stipulations after רַק 'only': the (smiter) must provide compensation and the injured man must fully recover. Of some interest here is the customarily implicit way in which participant identification in Biblical Hebrew is handled. In 3, 4, 5, and 6 it is lexically evident that the injured man is the subject of the four clauses. In 7 the subject is the overtly identified "smiter." It remains the subject of 8, but the subject of 9 implicitly reverts to the injured man.

Both of the preceding examples demonstrate the similarity of a lengthier piece of casuistry to a procedural this-is-what-happens discourse. Within either the protasis or apodosis, *weqatal* surfaces wherever it is not blocked by the rules. It is not a matter of mechanical substitution of a *weqatal* for an initial *yiqtol*, for the *weqatal* cannot occur initially in a protasis when an 'if' particle or noun precedes the verb and it is in precisely these situations that the *yiqtol* surfaces. Semantic choice resides, however, in the form of the verb in the apodosis, where *weqatal*, modal *yiqtol*, or infinitive absolute + modal *yiqtol* may occur.

As to the choice of the verb in the apodosis, note that in example 40 the outcome is expressed in 7: the smiter shall be innocent. Further stipulations are expressed, however, in a N+*yiqtol* clause (where *weqatal* cannot occur) and infinitive absolute+*yiqtol*. In example 39 the apodosis is a sequence of *weqatal* forms culminating in a *weqatal*+pronominal suffix clause.

The following examples illustrate the choice of a modal *yiqtol* in the apodosis (example 41, Exod. 21:26) and the choice of an infinitive absolute+modal *yiqtol* in that position (example 42, Exod. 21:12).[7]

(41)
(1) וְכִי־יַכֶּה אִישׁ אֶת־עֵין עַבְדּוֹ
And if he smites a man the eye of his servant
אוֹ־אֶת־עֵין אֲמָתוֹ
or the tooth of his female slave

(2) וְשִׁחֲתָהּ
and he destroys it,

(3) לַחָפְשִׁי יְשַׁלְּחֶנּוּ תַּחַת עֵינוֹ
for freedom he shall release him on account of his eye.

In Exod. 21:26 we see the customary use of *yiqtol* after כִּי 'if/when', a *weqatal* form following in 2, and a noun+modal *yiqtol* in the apodosis in 3. The preposed noun in 3 blocks the occurrence of *weqatal* in that clause.

(42)
(1) מַכֵּה אִישׁ
The smiter of a man

(2) וָמֵת
and he dies
(3) מוֹת יוּמָת
he shall certainly be killed.

Here the *weqatal* in 2 follows a participle in 1; the apodosis in 3 contains an infinitive absolute+*yiqtol* modal form.

5. Conclusion

The *weqatal* form of Biblical Hebrew finds its most characteristic use in the mainline structures of predictive, procedural, and instructional discourse.

Stretches of embedded how-it-was-done procedural discourse occur here and there in narrative. They typically involve a sequence of *weqatal* forms and at least one overt contextual clue that the activity described is durative or repetitive (e.g., a use of the imperfect or a continual/habituative adverb). Isolated instances of *weqatal* forms in a narrative framework mark pivotal/climactic/finalizing events. The *weqatal* forms of הָיָה (the impersonal), aside from their primary use in predictive, procedural, and instructional discourse, occur occasionally in a narrative framework to anticipate cataphorically a pivotal/climactic event in a chain of events further on in the context—often immediately following.

There may be instances where opinions differ as to whether an isolated *weqatal* form in narrative is a minimal one-clause embedded procedural (hence "frequentative") discourse or a pivotal status marker. I regard the former as highly unlikely in such passages as Gen. 37:3 (referred to earlier as example 28).

Juridical discourse (casuistry) resolves into a series of minidiscourses in which *weqatal* forms are presumably basic. But the positing of hypothetical cases via conditional sentences blocks the occurrence of the *weqatal* in many syntactic situations. All of this, it seems to me, points towards a functional explanation of *weqatal* in the law codes that may prove to be preferable to the traditional explanation in terms of consecution of tenses as such.

Notes

1. In that this article is a commentary on and dialogue with GKC's 1910 treatment of the *waw*-consecutive with the perfect, it does not have the breadth of argumentation such as might normally be expected. I note in passing that the GKC approach to the *waw*-consecutive perfect is in essence what we still find today in some Hebrew grammars (e.g., Lambdin 1971 and as recent as Waltke and O'Connor 1990). My approach differs from such previous approaches in that it takes a discourse-pragmatic-typological perspective and exploits insights obtained from the study of a variety of contemporary languages. I do, however, include in the References some previous scholarly work on *weqatal* brought to my attention by Nicolai Winther-Nielsen.

2. Possibly an exhaustive study of accentual features of *weqatal* forms would be relevant to the concerns here, but GKC warns that "the shifting forth of the tone after the *waw*-consecutive of the perfect is, however, not consistently carried out" (1910:135) and says in a footnote on the same page, "The irregularity in the tone of these perfects manifestly results from following conflicting theories, not that of Ben Asher alone."

3. This is actually the apodosis of a conditional sentence. The ritual is embedded in a juridical context (see sec. 4).

4. We cannot, however, discount the possibility that this is an embedded procedural discourse whose verbs have a frequentative meaning: "they were hurrying . . . they were crossing." The fact that two *weqatal* forms occur here rather than only one could reinforce such an alternative analysis. On the other hand, no DSC occurs to mark the transition to a procedural discourse.

5. In Mayan inscriptional material (oral communication of Josseyrand and Hopkins) syntactic irregularity—unusual ordering of main clauses and subordinate clauses—is a rather frequent marker of peak.

6. In considering the consecutive use of *weqatal* in juridical discourse, I also note that a series of injunctions display command forms in simple injunction. These include (a) the imperative (Exod. 20:12, "Honor your father and your mother"); (b) לֹא + *yiqtol* forms as negative commands (Exod. 20:3, 4, 5, 7, 13, 15, 16, i.e., the negative commands of the Decalogue); and (c) the infinitive absolute alone as in Exod. 20:8 ("Remember the Sabbath day").

7. In Exod. 21:33–34 there are three clauses: "he must pay silver," "he must pay the owner," and "the dead animal shall be his." Of these three clauses the first and the third are N+*yiqtol* while the second is simply *yiqtol* (modal).

References

Andrews, Avery. 1985. The major functions of the noun phrase. In *Language typology and syntactic description 1*, ed. T. Shopen, 62–154. Cambridge: University Press.

Bailey, Nicholas A., and Stephen Levinsohn. 1992. The function of preverbal elements in independent clauses in the Hebrew narrative of Genesis. *Journal of Translation and Textlinguistics* 5:179–207.

Bartelmus, Rüdiger. 1985. Ez 37, 1–14, die Verbform w^eqatal und die Anfänge der Auferstehungshoffnung. *Zeitschrift für die Alttestamentliche Wissenschaft* 97:366–89.

Driver, Samuel R. 1892. *A treatise on the use of tenses in Hebrew*. 3d ed. Oxford: Clarendon.

Eskhult, Mats. 1990. Studies in verbal aspect and narrative technique in Biblical Hebrew prose. Acta Universitatis Upsaliensia. *Studia Semitica Upsaliensia*, 12. Uppsala.

Firbas, Jan. 1964. On defining the theme in functional sentence analysis. *Travaux Linguistiques de Prague* 1:267–80.

Grimes, Joseph. 1975. *The thread of discourse*. The Hague: Mouton.

Howard, Linda. 1977. Camsa: Certain features of verb inflection as related to paragraph types. In vol. 2 of *Discourse grammar: Studies in indigenous languages of Colombia, Panama, and Ecuador*, ed. R. E. Longacre and F. Woods. Summer Institute of Linguistics Publications in Linguistics and Related Fields, 52. Arlington, Tex.: Summer Institute of Linguistics.

Hwang, Shin Ja J., 1992. The functions of negation in discourse. In *Language and context: Essays for Robert E. Longacre*, ed. S. J. Hwang and W. R. Merrifield, 321–37. Summer Institute of Linguistics and UTA Publications in Linguistics, 107. Dallas: Summer Institute of Linguistics.

Johnson, Bo. 1979. *Hebräisches Perfekt und Imperfekt mit vorangehenden w^e*. Lund: Gleerup.

Jones, Larry Bert, and Linda K. Jones. 1979. Multiple levels of information in discourse. In *Discourse studies in Mesoamerican languages*, vol. 1, ed. Linda K. Jones, 3–28. SIL Publications in Linguistics, 58. Dallas: Summer Institute of Linguistics and Univ. of Texas at Arlington.

Kautzsch, E., ed. 1910. *Gesenius' Hebrew grammar*, 2d English ed., rev. by A. E. Cowley. Oxford: Clarendon.

Lambdin, Thomas O. 1971. *Introduction to Biblical Hebrew*. New York: Scribner.

Leenhouts, I. 1983. Functions of the verb in Ténhé narrative discourse. Master's thesis, Univ. of Texas at Arlington.

Longacre, Robert E. 1968. *Discourse, paragraph, and sentence structure in selected Philippine languages*. Vol. 2, *Sentence structure*. SIL Publications In Linguistics and Related Fields, 21. Santa Ana, Calif.: Summer Institute of Linguistics.

———. 1972. *Hierarchy and universality of discourse constituents in New Guinea languages*. Vol. 1, *Discussion*. Washington, D.C.: Georgetown Univ. Press.

———. 1976. *An anatomy of speech notions*. Lisse, The Netherlands: Peter de Ridder Press.

———. 1979. The discourse structure of the flood narrative. *Journal of the American Academy of Religion* 47:1, Supplement B (March 1979) 89–133.

———. 1981. A spectrum and profile approach to discourse analysis. *Text* 1:337–59. The Hague: Mouton.
———. 1982*a*. Discourse typology in relation to language typology. In *Text Processing*, ed. Sture Allén, 457–86. Proceedings of the Nobel Symposium 52, Stockholm: Almquist and Wyksell.
———. 1982*b*. Verb ranking and the constituent structure of discourse. *Journal of the Linguistic Association of the Southwest* 5:177–202.
———. 1983. *The grammar of discourse*. Topics in Language and Linguistics, ed. Thomas A. Seboek and Albert Valdman. New York: Plenum.
———. 1985. Discourse peak as zone of turbulence. In *Beyond the sentence: Discourse and sentential form*, ed. J. R. Wirth, 51–98. Ann Arbor: Karoma.
———. 1989*a*. *Joseph: A story of divine providence: A text theoretical and textlinguistic analysis of Genesis 37 and 39–48*. Winona Lake, Ind.: Eisenbrauns.
———. 1989*b*. Two hypotheses regarding text generation and text analysis. *Discourse Processes* 12:413–60.
———. 1990. Storyline concerns and word-order typology in East and West Africa. Studies in African linguistics, supplement 10. Los Angeles: UCLA.
———. 1992*a*. Discourse perspective on the Hebrew verb: Affirmation and restatement. In *Linguistics and Biblical Hebrew*, ed. W. Bodine, 77–189. Winona Lake, Ind.: Eisenbrauns.
———. 1992*b*. The analysis of preverbal nouns in Biblical Hebrew narrative: Some overriding concerns. *Journal of Translation and Textlinguistics* 5:208–24.
———. 1993. Review of *The pragmatics of word order: Typological dimension of verb initial languages*, by Doris Payne. *IJAL* 59:102–8.
———. Forthcoming *a*. Building for the worship of God: Hebrew text of Exodus 25:1–30:10. In press. To appear in a supplement to *Semeia*, ed. Walter Bodine.
———. Forthcoming *b*. Left shifts in strongly VSO languages. To appear in a volume edited by Pamela Downing and growing out of the April 1991 conference on word order and discourse structure at the Univ. of Wisconsin, Milwaukee.
Longacre, Robert E., and Frances Woods. 1976–77. *Discourse grammar: Studies in indigenous languages of Colombia, Panama, and Ecuador*, Parts 1–3. Publications in Linguistics and Related Fields, 52. Dallas, Tex.: Summer Institute of Linguistics and Univ. of Texas at Arlington.
Moran, William L. 1961. The Hebrew language in its Northwest Semitic background. In *The Bible and the ancient Near East: Essays in honor of William Foxwell Albright*, ed. George Ernest Wright, 54–72. Garden City: Doubleday.
Müller, H. P. 1988. Das Bedeutungspotential der Afformativkonjugation. *Zeitschrift für Althebraistik*, vol. 1, pp. 74–98, 159–90.
Payne, Doris. 1990. *The pragmatics of word order: Typological dimensions of verb initial languages*. Empirical Approaches to Languages Typology 7, ed. Georg Bossong and Bernard Comrie. Berlin: Mouton de Gruyter.
Waltke, Bruce, and M. O'Connor. 1990. *An introduction to Biblical Hebrew syntax*. Winona Lake, Ind.: Eisenbrauns.
Woods, Frances. 1980. The interrelationship of cultural information, linguistic structure, and symbolic representations in Halbi myth. Ph.D. diss., Univ. of Texas at Arlington.

3

SALIENCE, IMPLICATURE, AMBIGUITY, AND REDUNDANCY IN CLAUSE–CLAUSE RELATIONSHIPS IN BIBLICAL HEBREW

Francis I. Andersen

Salient readings—those that make the first claim on the listener/reader—are explored for various clause and paragraph structures. Particular emphasis is given to determining strategies employed by classical Hebrew writers to convey the temporal significance of clauses containing *qatal, weqatal, yiqtol,* and *waw + yiqtol* verbs. Biblical Hebrew conventions regarding the establishment of logical, temporal, spatial, and actantial connections between clauses are discussed. Constraints that create obligatorily present elements are also noted. Genesis 3 is then examined to illustrate various aspects of interclausal relationships.

1. Kinds of clause

The repertoire of clause types in Biblical Hebrew can be classified on the basis of several features: first, the verb form used for the main predication (*qatal, yiqtol,* participle, etc.); second, the presence of other clause-level constituents; third, the sequence in which all clause-level constituents occur; fourth, the presence (perhaps absence) of a conjunction or other element (such as anaphora) to signal the connections of a clause with the rest of the discourse. For ease of reference we shall sometimes refer to the suffixed verb form (*qatal*, the so-called perfect(ive)) as VS, to the verb category constituted by the addition of *waw*-consecutive to a "perfect" verb (*weqatal*) as WS, to the prefixed verb form (*yiqtol,* the so-called imperfect(ive)) as VP, and to the *waw*-consecutive (*wayyiqtol*) as WP.

In contrast to the highly constrained and specialized WP and WS verb formations and clause types, VS and VP occur in many different kinds of clauses: independent, coordinated, subordinated, relative. They may occur in any position: clause-initial, clause-medial, clause-terminal. The first and last patterns (i.e., clause-initial and -terminal) coincide when the clause consists of a verb only; the second is possible only when there are three or more words; and we will need to ask, in due course, if there is an important distinction so far as clause-clause relationships are concerned between the clause-initial position and the other sequence patterns in which the signal of the clause-initial position is canceled. Clause-terminal position, as such, might not have any special significance, but even this should not be prejudged. The hasty characterization of Hebrew as a verb-initial language, or even as a VSO language, could degrade the role in the language of other clause types, whose importance is not to be measured simply by their relative frequency.

In the standard Hebrew prose of the classical period, which we take to be the period of the monarchy, the salient mood ("salient" being the reading that makes the first claim on the listener/reader) of VS is indicative, its salient time reference is past, and its implied aspect is perfective. A clause containing VS can be coordinated using ו 'and'. When the verb is clause initial in such a clause, it can happen that the coordinated construction (וְ-VS) and the sequential (WS) are formally identical (homonymous). Thus וְהָיָה might be either 'and it was' or 'and it will be', at least theoretically. For some verbs, however, a minimal contrast is secured by a difference in the stress patterns for וְ-VS and WS (McFall 1982). This kind of distinction is available in the case of only a few positions in the verb paradigms (namely first singular and second masculine singular), and even then it is forfeited when a pronoun suffix object makes only one stress pattern possible. Thus *weqataltihu,* which means either 'and I killed him' or 'and I shall kill him', can be stressed only on the penultimate. This limitation is not only a matter of what is theoretically possible within the phonological constraints of the language, for in the case of *weqatálnu* the theoretically permissible stress on the final syllable is not used; the ambiguous *weqatálnu* serves for both coordinated past (וְ-VS 'and we killed') and sequential future (WS 'and we shall kill'). So most וְ-VS constructions are formally ambiguous, at least so far as the word form in itself is concerned. The most commonly used verb forms are third person, and the contrastive stress patterns for distinguishing וְ-VS and WS are not available.

It is a curiosity of the Biblical Hebrew verbal system that a distinction as important as that between past and future time reference is secured by so very few of the verb forms for which it is pertinent. This feature would not be so much of a puzzle if it should turn out that time (tense) distinctions were not present at all in the Hebrew verb forms during the classical period: if וְהָיָה were not "perfect," but timeless—in keeping with its ancestry as some kind of (con)stative. Yet, given that the differences in stress were important for distinguishing past from future, it is surprising that this distinction did not spread by analogy to other parts of the verb system. We might expect it to have spread to the forms that could have two stress patterns, but in fact it did not. It is likely that this marginal distinction is a late and artificial imposition on Biblical Hebrew as read, but not necessarily a real feature in the pronunciation of the classical

Salience, Implicature, Ambiguity, and Redundancy

language. But it would be going too far to dismiss this detail as no more than a conceit of the medieval scribes.

Even so, the question arises, How much ambiguity of that kind can a language tolerate? Is the homonymity between many pairs of וְ-VS (past) and WS forms (future) resolvable only on the morphological level and then only minimally (through its stress position) and only for those few verb forms which can be stressed either on the last syllable (WS) or on the second last (וְ-VS)? Intuition suggests that a difference as great as that between past and future time would not be left vague in a language that did have a tense system of some kind. If the distinction is not secured (or secured only precariously) on the level of morphology, it should be achieved in another part of the system, namely the syntax. If the two possible meanings of וְהָיָה can be told apart with the aid of differences in their typical syntax, and especially the syntax of clause-clause transitions, then the availability of a stress difference in the case of forms like *weqatalti* is a bonus, not vital for the system.

The methodology of discourse grammar puts this question on an entirely different footing.

A simple way of resolving the formal ambiguity of the clause-initial *weqatal* forms within the confines of the clause itself could be the use of some adverb referring to either future time or past time. When we get down to cases, it will be found that such time adverbs are rarely used. If the use of such adverbs were the main resource, then the time reference of the clause resides in those adverbs, and the verb itself could be quite neutral in the matter of time reference. But the verbs are neutral only in the sense that many of them are formally ambiguous. This is not so in the case of verbs like *weqatalti*, which has a formal contrast. When that kind of verb is used, an adverb of time would simply augment or specify the time reference signaled unequivocally, albeit generally, by the distinctive stress pattern.

One way of mitigating the problems that could arise from using *weqatal* when it might be either וְ-VS (past) or WS (future) would be to use it predominantly or almost exclusively for only one of these two possibilities, with future time as the salient meaning of *weqatal*, so that special markers are needed to override that salient meaning only when *weqatal* is intended to have past time reference. This expectation is borne out by the fact that WS is used far more frequently than וְ-VS, as if the latter was avoided.

Because the *waw*-consecutive in a WS construction serves as an interclause conjunction as well as a morphological marker of the future tense of the suffixed verb to which it is immediately bound, WS (future) is under constraint to be clause initial. (We recognize that this constraint is not absolute—casus pendens can be used—but that depends in part on how *clause* is defined.) VS (past) is under no such constraint. While VS can be used in a coordinated וְ-VS clause, with the danger of being indistinguishable from WS, it can be used without any danger of being misread in medial or final positions in a clause with "and," and in many other kinds of clauses not coordinated, such as relative (subordinated), which are not accessible by WS verbs. A suffixed verb form can thus be future, generally speaking, only when clause-initial (we shall attend to the "exceptions" in due course), that is, in WS. But VS (past) can occur in any clause position. This difference leads us to suspect and to expect that the clause-initial position as such is reserved for WS in order to secure this difference in tense; that the difference in stress will hardly be needed; that the highly specialized and constrained meaning of WS will drive VS (past) away from clause onset, making the latter kind of clause rare. Since "and" is not a part of the verb morphology when VS is past, such a verb can occur, even in a coordinated clause, away from the first position after the conjunction. The comparative rarity of וְ-VS clauses suggests avoidance.

2. Interclause relationships

The ambiguity due to the homonymy of *weqatal* is not eliminated by such a statistical preference. In theory, any *weqatal* form could be either וְ-VS or WS. But a listener's or reader's hesitation could be minimized, if not altogether eliminated, not only by the preferred usage in which most specimens of *weqatal* are sequential future (WS), but even more by structural or cohesive constraints within a piece of discourse in which the future tense of the whole piece (e.g., of a paragraph) is clearly indicated somewhere else and in some other way. WS clauses are used most commonly and characteristically to project, predict, or prescribe a series of actions of states of affairs to be performed or attained in time future from the moment of speaking. That the time reference for the whole paragraph is future is usually indicated by some clear signal at speech onset. The most stereotyped of these onsets is וְהָיָה + a time expression. But וְהָיָה alone can do it, becoming almost lexicalized ("and it will come to pass") as a marker of high-level transition to discourse about future events and states.

Or again such a speech or paragraph can begin with VP or VI (imperative verb). Commencing a speech with an imperative verb makes the whole speech precative, so it would be more accurate to say that a WS clause that follows such an imperative onset is likewise precative.

Pragmatics comes into it too. Pragmatics may be enough to show that the whole discourse is referring to time future, whether in prediction (indicative) or instruction (precative).

So the functions of the several clause types can be set out as follows:

	Past time	Future time / precative
Paragraph onset	VS, וַיְהִי	VP, VI, וְהָיָה
Consequential	WP	WS

Special indicators of the time reference of a whole paragraph might not be needed. In classical Hebrew prose, WP and WS clauses became so specialized and distinctive as to be the sole clause types in an entire paragraph. They were used at paragraph onset to set the time reference of a whole paragraph. An entire paragraph could consist of nothing but a string of WP clauses for past-time narrative or of WS clauses for future projections. WP or WS could mark paragraph onset.

These constraints on the level of paragraph structures are so powerful that they can resolve the ambiguity inherent in certain forms, or even override the salient meaning of some well-defined constructions. Although, as we shall discuss in more detail, both ו-VS and ו-VP clauses were used rather rarely, having conceded the field to WP and WS for past and future respectively, nevertheless a ו-VS clause in a string of WP clauses could be coerced by them into its past-tense option. Similarly a ו-VP clause in a string of WS clauses could be coerced by them into its future-tense option. We are speaking here, needless to say, only of clause-initial VS and VP immediately following "and" that might be mistaken for WS or WP, respectively, especially when reading a consonantal text.

By contrast, ו-...VS and ו-...VP clauses in which something (anything!) comes between the clause-initial conjunction and the verb are unequivocal: ו-...VS clauses are always past tense, and ו-...VP clauses are always future. (The word *always* in this last sentence will doubtless require moderation when we meet various oddities, especially when dealing with archaic grammar in ancient texts.) The first may be embedded within a paragraph whose past time reference is made clear by its onset and/or by the dominating use of WP clauses in its body; and the second (ו-...VP), mutatis mutandis, within a paragraph dominated by WS clauses. The most important thing about such clauses is that the verb (VS or VP) is not clause initial. And, insofar as a ו-...VS (or in future-tense discourse ו-...VP) was chosen rather than WP (or WS), we must ask in each case what difference that choice might have made. For instance, the displacement of the verb from the prominent clause-initial position could be a device for the deliberate announcement of a new topic. (In this case we shall have to ask whether that kind of clause is used to mark the onset of a new paragraph.) Or it could be at least a change of focus when the topic is not entirely new. (See the other articles in this volume that deal with "fronting" from several perspectives.) In any case there is nothing incongruous in using both of the past-tense forms (VS and WP) in the same paragraph; likewise for both of the future-tense forms (VP and WS).

It *would* be incongruous to have a VS clause with VS initial in a paragraph dominated by WS clauses (a VP-initial clause in a paragraph dominated by WP clauses). It seems like a contradiction to speak of a *waw*-consecutive construction that lacks "and," since the conjunction has become an essential part of the verb morphology. But in the extreme case a VS that is the first item in a clause in a string of WS clauses can be coerced into future meaning. Likewise a VP initial in a clause in a string of WP clauses can be coerced into past meaning. When such a VS-initial clause has future time reference through cohesion in a string of WS clauses (or a VP-initial clause has past time reference through cohesion in a string of WP clauses), the irregularity is so blatant that it is no wonder that ancient scribes and modern scholars alike have found the text at fault and supplied the correction by the simple expedient of adding "and." It is always possible, of course, that such a text is flawed, having suffered damage in transmission. But the error is rather unlikely, the "correct" form is so obvious.[1]

It needs to be remembered that the WP construction is itself a fossil syntagma. The retention of archaic ו - is a remarkable token of its antiquity, as is the preterite reference. The tenacity of the ancient vowel of the conjunction has forced doubling of the initial consonant of the verb (or compensatory lengthening before aleph). The use of VP (past) within a context of WP clauses (or anywhere at all, for that matter) is either a pure archaism (in ancestral Hebrew *yiqtol* was preterite) surviving in usage, albeit marginally, or else revitalization of an obsolete usage by analogy. The oddity of such usage inevitably attracts suspicion, but a diachronic approach leaves more room for acceptance of its authenticity.

3. Implication

In the real world, things are happening all the time, and many things happen at the same time. As we tell a story, we can say only one thing at a time. To make the story match the events, we conventionally carry the account along a time line. We choose a few main happenings and report them one after another. The listener/reader expects the narrative to present the events and states of affairs (happenings) in the sequence in which they originally occurred. In this way the story recreates the happenings and the experiences in the imagination of the listener/reader. Even a complex of happenings that occurred simultaneously—coetaneously, contemporaneously, coincidentally, or overlapping—can be reported only one sentence at a time.

It is possible, of course, that a culture might have conventions different from these. Its perceptions and ways of remembering time might be different; for instance, it might be acceptable to unfold a story backwards.[2] Behind our habit of reporting events in temporal sequence lies a perception that effect follows cause, so that causal connections are implied in the sequences as reported, even when causal conjunctions or constructions are not explicitly used. Translators often spell out such implications.

The conventions for storytelling are part of the social equipment of a group; they provide some of the communal bonds that make communication possible. The audience might have to be told when the conventions are not being followed, for instance, when the narrative departs from the time line ("Meanwhile, back at the ranch, ..."). There are conventions for doing that in Biblical Hebrew. At Gen. 39:1 Longacre (1989:224) calls this "re-stage."[3] Eskhult (1990:39) speaks of "a sense of anteriority" in this clause or, more generally, of "narrative resumption" (p. 54). One can backtrack to pick up another thread of narrative at an earlier point. And along the way one can supply background information about previous events as needed rather than supplying such data at the beginning of the story. Even so, an author might decide to disregard, or even flout, such conventions for various reasons—to be deliberately ambiguous, to create an enigma, to set things up so as to lead the audience down the garden path.

4. Conventions of Biblical Hebrew storytelling

Biblical Hebrew text grammar assumes that there is continuity in discourse. If there is any change in the situation—a change in time, location, or identity of any of the participants—this will usually be explicitly indicated by updating the information on any such matter. In the absence of any formal indication of such a change from one clause to the next, the implicit or tacit reading, by default, is that no such change has occurred. Without being specified for each clause, it is inferred (and the author expects the listener to infer) that there has been no change.

For any given clause-level constituent (A)—predicator, complement (referring to actants: subject and objects of various kinds), and adjunct (referring to time, location, and other kinds of "adverbial" modifiers)—that sustains an unchanged contribution to the presentation of the story, movement of the discourse from one clause to the next can involve the following patterns:

	Pattern 1	Pattern 2	Pattern 3
Clause 1	A explicit	A explicit	A undisclosed
Clause 2	A explicit (repeated)	A=Ø (implied)	A explicit

In pattern 1 the movement from clause 1 to clause 2 is unambiguous, but the repetition of the unchanged feature A is uneconomical and might be sensed as bad style. If we locate an event or state of affairs in time by specifying a date in clause 1, we don't have to keep on specifying that date in each new clause. It is assumed that the date remains the same in all succeeding clauses until it is superseded by the supply of a new time reference in a later clause. Pattern 2 is the preferred construction. A continues to operate in clause 2 in the same way it operated in clause 1. A does double duty in both clauses. Because pattern 2 conventionally implies that A is common to both clause 1 and clause 2, the repetition of A in clause 2 would seem to be redundant. It may be doubted, however, if any datum supplied by a text is ever completely redundant. *Everything in a text does something.* The repetition of A in clause 2 is not needed to secure the information that the participation of A has not changed from clause 1; pattern 2 implies that. So the supply of A in clause 2 is available to secure some effect on top of the merely redundant information that A is still the same. This is not a trivial matter. What seems redundant on one level might be doing something extra on another level. It is not enough just to ask what a constituent might be doing in its clause. What seems redundant locally might be securing more long-range cohesive connections. The reiteration of "God" as the subject of clause after clause in chapter one of Genesis, when God is the only actant in the entire story, has been dismissed with disdain as no more than bad style. More patient consideration suggests that this repeated subject does something significant on the higher levels of discourse as viewed by textlinguistics.

We are not impressed by the vacuous explanation, so often found in commentaries, that in such a case A is repeated "for emphasis." Muraoka's monograph (1985) should have disposed of this once and for all. We would still need to ask why the speaker thought such emphasis was needed. But we think it is more important to raise the question of the availability of A in clause 2 to have a formal grammatical function on the level of clause-clause syntax.

My hypothesis is that a seemingly redundant unnecessarily repeated subject noun serves to highlight the distinctiveness of an event, to mark that event as sequential in time more clearly, but not to the extent of giving that event episode status on the main storyline. Hebrew has special high-level transition markers for clustering events into episodes. Fronting a subject is one such device. Sequence patterns add another dimension to the repertoire of clause types.

We are dealing with fine discourse texture here. The clause-clause sequence in which each clause contains the same subject explicitly realized (as in the continual repetition of "God" in the clauses of Genesis 1) works on a level between the sentence and the paragraph. Conversely, a clause that has an unchanged but implicit subject is bound more closely into a cluster with its mate in which their common subject is explicit. After so much repetition of the unchanging subject "God" in Genesis 1, the absence of this word from the second clause in Gen. 2:3 shows that "blessed" and "sanctified" are closely connected.

In the case of the WP clauses that constitute the firm chain of classical Hebrew narrative, the noun subject necessarily follows the predicator, often immediately (the divine name [DN] in 26 out of the 31 cases in Genesis 1). At only one place is the explicit subject "God" needed to indicate a change of subject (v. 12b). Even there, the gender difference in the subjects makes reactivation of the subject "God" unnecessary; by anaphora (quite apart from its formulaic character) one could infer that the subject of "he saw" in v. 12b must be the same as that of the nearest preceding third singular masculine verb. As a matter of fact, v. 12a is the only clause in Genesis 1 in which anyone or anything apart from God does anything at all. It does not seem necessary to keep on repeating "God" just to make that point. The device has a function, not so much in a clause (emphasis) as in clause-clause syntax. Throughout the narrative the seemingly needless repetition of the unchanged subject (always "God") marks off the distinct actions, successive in time. So in Episode 1 (Day 1) there are four distinct acts: "God said ... ; God saw ... ; God divided ... ; God named." Likewise on Day 5: "God said ... ; God created ... ; God saw ... ; God blessed." The thirty-one occurrences of God as the subject of a WP clause mark clearly the thirty-one distinctive events in the creation story.

By contrast, when the subject is not repeated, the events are clustered together. When the second clause does not repeat the subject, the second clause presents another side of the same event. The two clauses thus bound together by specifying the subject only once can even report two simultaneous features of the same event, breaking the chain of temporal succession regularly secured by a string of WP clauses. This is quite clear when the second clause is chiastic, with ו- ... VS (vv. 5, 12a). The effect is the same even when both clauses are WP. Thus the two verbs with only one subject in 2:2—"finished," "rested"—are two sides of the same development. In 2:3 "blessed" and "sanctified" are bound together by the double-duty subject. The nonrepetition of the unchanged subject thus overrides the salient reading of successive WP clauses as reporting events in temporal succession.

The creation story in Genesis 2 (vv. 4b–25) uses this device somewhat differently. It has nothing resembling the highly formal division of Genesis 1 into seven days. The storyline consists of a string of twenty-one WP clauses. Omission of the subject (here "Yahweh God") clusters clauses and so associates certain events as more closely connected than others: event-cluster 1 in v. 7 (three clauses); event-cluster 2 in v. 8 (two clauses); event 3 in vv. 9–14, but only one WP clause; event-cluster 4 in v. 15 (two clauses; a reprise of v. 8); event 5 in vv. 16–17a (one clause); event 6 in v. 18 (one clause); event-cluster 7 in vv. 19–20 (three WP clauses); event-cluster 8 in v. 21 (four clauses);[4] event-cluster 9 in v. 22 (two clauses); event 10 in vv. 23–24 (one clause, new subject indicated); event-cluster 11 in v. 25 (new subject, two clauses).

5. Intraclause sequences and interclause relationships

A full account of each clause in a piece of discourse and of the grammatical relationships between two interconnected clauses has to take into account the use of all the language resources available to the speaker/composer. In particular, it is not just the repetition of an item (A) from clause 1 to clause 2 that could be significant, but also the position of A in each clause. We are interested in the sequence pattern ("line form") of all the constituents in each clause and the corresponding total pattern thus secured in each clause-clause entity.

In the case of pattern 3, clause 1 lacks information about the participant or feature indicated by A. The listener is placed and left in a state of suspense on that point until A comes up in clause 2. Then this information is fed back into clause 1, resolving the suspense; in other words, A in clause 2 does retroactive double duty in clause 1 (see the Appendix).

In every kind of clause-clause construction it is necessary to work out not only what an item such as A is doing in its own clause, but also what it might be doing in a nearby clause in which it is implicit.

6. Obligatoriness

In tracing continuity from clause to clause in a text, distinctions need to be made among the grammatical functions of the various constituents. We distinguish between participants (actants) and background. Constituents that refer to participants (subject and various objects) we call "complements" (of a verbal predicator); constituents that refer to more oblique background matters, such as time and place, we call "adjuncts"

Salience, Implicature, Ambiguity, and Redundancy

("adverbial" modifiers of the predicator). There is a gradient of obligatoriness in the required or optional use of these constituents. Biblical Hebrew narrative is lean, Biblical Hebrew poetry even leaner, often laconic to the point of opaqueness. Many a story is told without saying when or where the action took place. But every finite verb must have a subject, and a transitive verb usually an object. The obligatory subject of every finite verb is minimally indicated by the pronoun affixes of the verb morphology. This means that, strictly speaking, pattern 2 cannot be fully realized when A is the subject in clause 1 and clause 2 has a verb with the same subject. If not as a noun, the subject is unavoidably present in the verb morphology, albeit minimally.

If A is an object in clause 1, that is, if the verb in clause 1 is transitive and the verb in clause 2 is likewise transitive with the same object, can the object be stated only once? In English we can supply an anaphoric pronoun as object in the second clause: John fixed his lunch and ate it. Or we can get around this problem by coordinating the verbs: John fixed and ate his lunch (multidominance) (Ojeda 1987). In Biblical Hebrew it could be enough to state the object once (in clause 1) as in Gen. 3:6 where the object (some of its fruit) continues to operate in clauses 2, 3, and 4:

Clause 1	וַתִּקַּח מִפִּרְיוֹ	and she took some of its fruit
Clause 2	וַתֹּאכַל	and she ate [it]
Clause 3	וַתִּתֵּן גַּם־לְאִישָׁהּ עִמָּהּ	and she gave [it] also to her husband with her
Clause 4	וַיֹּאכַל	and he ate [it]

Compare this with "And Jacob gave Esau bread ... and he ate" (Gen. 25:34). Here it is the pragmatics that tells us that the indirect object of clause 1 is the implied subject of clause 2. The lack of an explicit object in clause 2 (brachylogy) evokes the salient reading that the object has not changed; the inference is drawn that the object in clause 1 does double duty in clause 2 ("Esau ate the bread"). But the pressure to supply clause 2 with an explicit object and not simply to rely on that inference, could be strong. There is grammatical pressure from the transitivity of "ate" to supply an object, and this is readily and sufficiently done by using an anaphoric pronoun ("it") in concord with "fruit" or "bread," whether as a suffixed object or carried by *nota accusativi*. Neither of these devices is used in the previous examples (Gen. 3:6; 25:34). Just as repetition of a (redundant) subject makes successive clauses more distinctive, so ellipsis of an object expected with a transitive verb binds clauses closer together. The term *ellipsis* is not appropriate. There is nothing "missing," so long as we read the two-clause complex as one coherent grammatical entity.

7. Clause-clause relationships in Genesis 3

The narrative line in Genesis 3 is quite simple. Twenty-nine of the clauses are WP. They describe a series of events in temporal succession. The other three are VS clauses (3:1a, 16, 17). The first (3:1a) is an important clause type, וְ- S:N VS. Here it introduces a new character; the snake has not been mentioned before. The preverbal position of the noun subject focuses and topicalizes it. Such a clause initiates a new development in the story. This is a specimen of the well-known clause type called "nominal" by the classical Arabic grammarians.[5] But this term has the disadvantage of including verbless clauses on the grounds that many verbless clauses also begin with וְ- S:N. And it gives too much prominence to a noun (subject) as the fronted element, whereas clauses in which other items such as objects and adverbs are fronted have similar clause-clause functions. The best known and most often mentioned is the "circumstantial" function of adding a reference, usually to a concomitant state of affairs, alongside the main chain of narrated events. Genesis 3:1a is not such a circumstantial clause. Quite the contrary, it brings the snake to the center of the stage.

The outstanding feature of Genesis 3 is the dialogue. There is no dialogue in Genesis 1 and 2. In Genesis 1 only God speaks. In Genesis 2 Yahweh God makes two speeches: the repeated subjects in vv. 16 and 18 show that. Adam makes one speech, but there is no verbal interaction between God and Adam. There are three episodes of verbal interaction in Genesis 3: the snake and the woman (vv. 1–5); Yahweh God and Adam (vv. 9–12); Yahweh God and the woman (v. 13). There are four more speeches made by Yahweh God, but they are not connected with verbal activity of the other protagonists. Verse 22 reports a soliloquy: as in Genesis 1 God talks to himself, using "we." At least no audience is identified.

The verb "said" is used in thirteen clauses. The syntax realizes many of the verb's potentials:

said-he			"Q"	vv. 10, 11
said-he	S:N		"Q"	vv. 12, 13b, 14, 22
said-he		to-him	"Q"	v. 9b
said-he		to-N	"Q"	v. 1b
said-he	S:N	to-N	"Q"	vv. 2, 4, 13a (cf. v. 9a)

In two clauses (vv. 16, 17) the indirect object precedes the verb. The use of the full formula in vv. 2–5 contrasts with the use of the verb alone in vv. 10 and 11. The pragmatics of Question → Answer (1b → 2–3; 9b → 10; 11 → 12; 13a → 13b) is enough to keep track of the speakers without supplying explicit subjects. The contrasting genders of the verbs in vv. 2-5 would have been enough to keep track of the speakers; yet noun subjects are used there. Perhaps this redundancy highlights the fact that the woman is the only actant with whom the snake converses. Oppositely, the identical gender of the verbs in vv. 9b-12 could lead to ambiguity, yet only v. 12 has a noun subject. Here, besides pragmatics, a convention operates that a new "and he said" implies a change of subject, even if the subject is not identified.

The arrangement in vv. 14-17 is particularly interesting. Here the chain of WP clauses is broken. The subject (Yahweh God) does not change and is used only in the first clause (v. 14). The audience is different for each of the three speeches. The addressees are distinguished by the noun indirect objects. The coordination (clause 1, clause 2, *and* clause 3), the chiastic preverbal placement (fronting) of the indirect objects in vv. 16 and 17, along with the use of the divine name as subject only in v. 14, show that these three speeches are closely related and are, in fact, delivered or reported as one "moment" in the drama.

These three speeches to the three culprits are closely interrelated in content as well, and taken together they contribute to the larger rhetorical structure of the chapter. To the snake (vv. 14-15), Yahweh God describes the effects of the incident on the relationship between the snake and the woman. To the woman (v. 16), Yahweh God describes the effects of the incident on the relationship between the woman and the man. To Adam (vv. 17-19), Yahweh God describes the effects of the incident on the relationship between Adam and the earth (not the woman or the snake). This long speech is full of intertextual echoes of chapter 2.

The breaking of the chain of WP clauses by the use of ן-...VS clauses for the speeches to the woman and the man achieves more than one effect. As already mentioned, the dependence of the two ן-...VS clauses on the preceding WP clause (v. 14) makes the three speeches into an integrated set. But the sequence in which the three are addressed achieves an introverted pattern.

    A   Interrogation of Adam (vv. 9b-12)
        B   Interrogation of the woman (v. 13)
            C   Sentence on the snake (vv. 14-15)
        B' Sentence on the woman (v. 16)
    A' Sentence on Adam (vv. 17-19)

8. Changes from clause to clause

There are four possible patterns:

1. Subject does not change and there is no S:N in clause 2 (1b, 6aBa, 6aBb, 6bA, 7aB, 7bA, 7bB, 8a, 8b, 9b, 21b, 24a, 24b).
2. Subject does not change and S:N is repeated in clause 2 (22, 23).
3. Subject changes and there is a new S:N expressed in clause 2 (2, 4, 6aA, 7aA, 9a, 12, 13a, 14, 20, 21a).
4. Subject changes and the new S:N is implied in clause 2 (6bB, 10, 11, 16, 17).

Patterns 1 and 3 are the commonest, as expected. The implication of unindicated subject change (pattern 4) is managed by pragmatics. The two clauses in which the repeated unchanged subject might seem to be redundant (vv. 22, 23) present the closing events of the story (vv. 21–24) as three distinct actions by Yahweh God.

9. Assertion and negation

Most adverbials, once supplied, remain in force from clause to clause until canceled or updated by the provision of a new adverbial such as change of time or place. (There is an exception in 2:2, which repeats the time adverbial.)

One kind of adjunct, however, does not have this power of remaining in force from clause to clause, and that is negation. The salient reading of any clause in Biblical Hebrew is that it is a positive assertion or injunction. It is rare for this positive status of a clause to be enhanced by an assertative adjunct ("surely," "certainly," "indeed"). Such adverbs are available, but their use is frugal. Negation has to be explicit. The salient reading of any clause that does not have a negating particle is as the unmarked positive. In spite of this, however, it is possible for "not" to do double duty, carrying on from one clause to the next.[6] When this occurs, it is probably best to describe the construction as the negation of a whole paragraph consisting of a string of clauses by the one negative particle in the first clause. We have not yet come across a case of retroactive double-duty negation.

Appendix: Double-Duty Retroactive Constituents

When a constituent that is needed grammatically for the completion of well-formedness in a clause is not supplied until the following clause, the first clause would seem to be "ungrammatical." It puts a strain on listener/reader acceptance. Scholars are likely to pronounce a text in which this happens "corrupt." They then take it upon themselves to repair the supposed damage by emendation. Even if they do not venture to rewrite the text, they resort to strained construals in the struggle to interpret the first clause as a stand-alone unit.

This phenomenon occurs in Gen. 25:23, as pointed out to me years ago by David Noel Freedman.

שְׁנֵי גוֹיִים בְּבִטְנֵךְ	Two peoples in your belly
וּשְׁנֵי לְאֻמִּים מִמֵּעַיִךְ יִפָּרֵדוּ	and two nations from your bowels will separate
וּלְאֹם מִלְאֹם יֶאֱמָץ	and people from people will be strong
וְרַב יַעֲבֹד צָעִיר	and great will serve young

This unit is recognized unanimously as a quatrain. It has all the hallmarks of classical Hebrew poetry. The matching word pairs are conventional. The term לְאֹם 'people' is poetic diction, used in the Primary History (Genesis–Kings) only here and in Gen. 27:29. The complete absence of the prose particles leaves many constructions structurally ambiguous. Is the prepositional phrase in the first colon a noun modifier, a predicate, or a verbal adjunct? A congruent and holistic reading of the bicolon requires it to be taken as a verbal adjunct. The verb יִפָּרֵדוּ 'they separate' dominates the whole bicolon and with retroactive double duty; it functions equally in the first and second colons. In other words, the familiar incomplete synonymous parallelism is here inverted. The question even arises whether all the matches force the prepositions into synonymy, with the result that בְּ = 'from'. This insight has not found its way into any translation that we have seen.

We must underscore the importance of accepting the use by Hebrew poets of double-duty items retroactively. O'Connor (1980:123) defines "gapping" as "the removal of the verb of the second clause, provided it is identical to that of the first." Here the verb is "missing" from the first clause, present in the second. Freedman (1985) has pointed out an unimpeachable example in Isa. 1:3, where it is a noun that does retroactive double duty. The recognition of such "backward gapping" has been hampered not only by the expectation that "incomplete parallelism" will occur only in the second colon (which cannot be longer than the first, a dogma widely held by writers on the theory of Hebrew poetry), but also by the theory—almost another dogma—that the Hebrew poetic bicolon consists of "two brief clauses" (Kugel 1981:1).[7]

It is expected that the first colon will be a complete clause. When it is not, instead of recognizing that the missing items are supplied in the second colon, a scholar is likely to take it upon himself or herself to supply something to the apparently incomplete first colon. For example, something seems to be missing from the first colon in Ps. 70:2:

	לְהַצִּילֵנִי	אֱלֹהִים
	to rescue me	God
הוּשָׁה:	לְעֶזְרָתִי	יְהוָה
hasten	to help me	Yahweh

The usual remedy is to import רְצֵה 'be pleased' from Ps. 40:14. BHS proposes further to delete יְהוָה 'Yahweh', presumably to recover Qinah meter, 3:2. Thus both cola are rewritten! It is only when the verb is supplied at the very end of the bicolon that the grammar of the bicolon falls into place. The trope is similar to that in Gen. 25:23. Giving the double-duty verb dominion over the first colon as well as over the second brings everything into line.

We wish to add a methodological observation about Kugel's idea (and others') that the second line of poetry adds something. When it is a more detailed noun phrase and the vital verb is in the first colon, one might, perhaps, accept that analysis. After all, that is the best known and widely used model of "incomplete parallelism with rhythmic compensation (or ballast variant)" that is generally recognized. But it is quite impossible to argue in this way when the "extra" item in the second colon is the vital verb. The verb has to operate retroactively to make sense of the first colon. This is the case with Gen. 25:23, and also with Psalm 70:2.[8]

Notes

1. There are four instances in Exodus where a "consecutive" future construction is found with the conjunction אוֹ 'or': נִשְׁבָּה 'it is taken away' (Exod. 22:9), נִשְׁבַּר 'it is hurt' (Exod. 22:9), מֵת 'it dies' (Exod. 22:13), and מְכָרוֹ 'he sells it' (Exod. 21:37). Other examples are found in Lev. 4:23, 27–28; 5:21–22; Num. 5:14–15 (the VS in v. 14b has the same time reference [or mood] as the WS verbs that surround it); 2 Sam. 17:12 (here the negative particle comes between the *waw* and the [future] VS); 2 Kings. 5:20 (the following verb is standard WS); Isa. 2:11 (VS in a chain of WS clauses); Isa. 8:8 (VS between two WSs—not surprisingly, some MSS have the more "correct" וְשָׁטַף); Isa. 11:8 (VS in chiasmus with WS—both future); Isa. 13:10; 14:24 (VS הָיְתָה is parallel to VP תָקוּם); Isa. 18:5; 19:6 (here the anomaly is the outcome of chiasmus); Isa. 25:8 (a mixture of verb forms, all future in reference); Isa. 30:19–20; 32:14 (the so-called "prophetic" perfect); Isa. 34:5, 14–15, 15 (here is a coherent passage, with nine verbs—WS, VP, VS, WS, VS, WP, WS, WS, VS—all future!); Isa. 47:9; 51:6 (here a future VS is surrounded by "imperfect" verbs); 51:11 (the parallel at Isa. 35:10 has the "correct" WS, and this has crept into some MSS at 51:11); Jer. 6:2–3 (all translations recognize the four verbs in this quatrain as future; the one VP verb overrides the salient past-tense meaning of the three VS verbs); Jer. 31:5 (VP...VS...WS—all future); Jer. 51:38; Ezek. 25:7 (here VS is used in a predictive speech where a participle is more usual); Ezek. 29:5; 39:4 (VP: "...you will fall..."; VS: "...I shall give..."; the use of the same verbs twice attests the acceptability of the usage convincingly).

2. Afanasyeva (1978:19–32) has shown that the time perspective in Mesopotamian art sometimes views events from the present backwards.

3. His characterization of the device of fronting "Joseph" to achieve this effect as casus pendens (p. 26) is not, however, in line with the usual use of that term (see Gross 1987).

4. The new subject ("Adam") of v. 21aB is not indicated; pragmatics makes that unnecessary, overriding the salient reading of an ensuing clause as having the same subject as the preceding one when none is indicated. The subject changes back to "Yahweh God" in v. 21bA, yet the change is not indicated. According to our hypothesis, to have reactivated the subject "Yahweh God" in v. 21bA would have indicated that this clause reports a distinct event. With its omission in the text as it now stands, all four clauses in v. 21 are clustered together as parts of the same development.

5. Eskhult in commenting on the classification of "nominal" and "verbal" clauses says that "formal and functional criteria are consistently mixed up" (1990:41). But his own treatment does not entirely avoid this confusion. While accepting much of the conventional wisdom that regards ו-S:N VS clauses as "circumstantial" (1990:31), he recognizes the cases of which Gen. 3:1 is an excellent example: such clauses, he says, "serve as a device to mark the beginning of a new episode by presenting the prevailing state of affairs, when the new action sets in" (1990:55).

6. One interrogative particle can continue to operate in a string of successive clauses, making them all questions; put differently, the particle dominates a whole paragraph. A full-scale assault is needed on this phenomenon. In the meantime the provisional listing of double-duty items in the Psalter supplied by Dahood and Penar (1970:429-44) is something to go on with.

7. This starting point is a flaw in fundamental theory that invalidates much of what follows in Kugel's book.

8. As other possible examples of a verb in the second colon operating also in the first, Sapan (1987-88) lists Amos 1:3, 6; Zech. 9:17; Ps. 20:8; and Prov. 13:1.

References

Afanasyeva, V. K. 1978. K probleme tolkovaniya shumerskikh rel'yefov. In *Kul'tura Vostoka: Drevnost'i rannee srednevekov'ye*, 19-32. Leningrad: Avrora.

Dahood, Mitchell and Tadeusz Penar. 1970. *Psalms III: 101-150.* The Anchor Bible. Garden City: Doubleday.

Eskhult, Mats. 1990. Studies in verbal aspect and narrative technique in Biblical Hebrew prose. *Acta Universitatis Upsaliensis: Studia Semitica Upsaliensia,* 12. Uppsala: Almqvist and Wiksell.

Freedman, David Noel. 1985. What the ox and the ass know—but the scholars don't. *Bible Review* 1:42-44.

Gross, Walter. 1987. *Die Pendenskonstruktion* in *Biblischen Hebräisch: Studien zum althebräischen Satz* I. St. Ottilien: EOS Verlag.

Kugel, James L. 1981. *The idea of biblical poetry: Parallelism and its history.* New Haven and London: Yale University Press.

Longacre, Robert E. 1989. *Joseph: A story of divine providence: A text theoretical and textlinguistic analysis of Genesis 37 and 39-48.* Winona Lake, Ind.: Eisenbrauns.

McFall, Leslie. 1982. The enigma of the Hebrew verbal system: Solutions from Ewald to the present day. In *Historic texts and interpreters in biblical scholarship,* ed. J. W. Rogerson. Sheffield: Almond Press.

Muraoka, T. 1985. *Emphatic words and structures in Biblical Hebrew.* Jerusalem and Leiden: Magnes Press, The Hebrew University, E. J. Brill.

O'Connor, M. 1980. *Hebrew verse structure.* Winona Lake, Ind.: Eisenbrauns.

Ojeda, A. E. 1987. Discontinuity, multidominance, and unbounded dependency in generalized phrase structure grammar: Some preliminaries. In *Syntax and semantics 20: Discontinuous constituency,* ed. G. J. Huck and A. E. Ojeda 257-82. Orlando: Academic Press.

Sapan, Raphael. 1987-88. Completion from one parallel line to another: Syntactic observations. *Beth Mikra* 33:58-62.

4

ON THE HEBREW VERBAL SYSTEM

Alviero Niccacci

Biblical Hebrew verb forms need to be analyzed in the framework of the text. A basic distinction is necessary between historical narrative and direct speech since Biblical Hebrew, along with other languages, has distinct sets of verb forms for these two genres of the prose. Some verb forms, however, are common to both genres. Two criteria are used in the analysis: position in the sentence (first or second) and level of communication (main or secondary). An attempt is made to show that there is a definite verbal system in Biblical Hebrew. Problems concerning coordination and subordination, as well as tense and aspect, are also discussed in the framework of the system proposed.

Since I wrote "An Outline of the Biblical Hebrew Verbal System in Prose" (1989a),[1] I have met with new challenges and insights as a result of my studies on the syntactical analysis of biblical narrative (1990a), the reviews of colleagues, and a two-week seminar in Dallas on discourse linguistics and Biblical Hebrew. It has become increasingly clear to me that the main problems with the system I am proposing rest on the level of sentence analysis, on the one hand, and on the level of text analysis, or discourse analysis, on the other. I differ with colleagues working on the level of the text on the analysis of the sentence. I differ with traditional grammarians working on the level of the sentence in regard to the value of their kind of analysis.

1. Methodology

When discourse linguists analyze a text, they distinguish between grammar (or syntax), semantics, and pragmatics (Lyons 1977 §4.4). Problems occur when these are confused. For example, scholars give some elements of the sentence a grammatical function, and others a semantic or pragmatic function only. However, in principle, every element of the sentence plays a role on the level of grammar. Only when grammatical analysis shows that a given element has no role in the sentence does one have to look for a semantic or pragmatic role on the higher level, the text level.

Another major problem with discourse linguists lies in the approach they use: the "top-down" methodology. Some (e.g., Longacre 1989:60) begin their analysis by identifying different text types, such as narrative, predictive/ procedural, hortatory, and expository discourse.[2] Then they go on to see which verb forms are characteristic of each type. While this methodology is a considerable improvement upon traditional grammar based on the sentence, it posits too many types of texts, in my opinion. Indeed, an extensive list of text types, important as it is from the point of view of discourse analysis, might blur the understanding of the Hebrew verbal system as a whole, because the same verb forms are used in much the same way in several text types. For instance, many verb forms overlap in predictive/procedural and hortatory discourse, especially *weqatal*. The main disadvantage of this approach is that it becomes difficult to perceive a coherent, overall system of Biblical Hebrew verb forms.

On the other hand, traditional grammarians who work on the level of the sentence are not in a position to solve the main problem of syntax, which is to identify the distinctive function(s) of each verb form in relationship to the others in a coherent overall system. For instance, if one does not take the text level into account, one will not be able to explain why in one case we have a *wayyiqtol* form while in another similar one we have a *waw*-X-*qatal* construction.[3] Consequently, a discourse analysis is a necessary, even indispensable, starting point.

The methodology of my analysis of the Hebrew verbal system is basically a bottom-up (rather than a top-down) approach. Since Biblical Hebrew is a dead language and no competent speaker is available, we learn it from a careful reading of good prose texts, not from our own interpretation, not from ancient or modern translations, and not even from grammars (which are in most cases sentence-based grammars).[4] Through an analysis of prose texts we can hope to establish different sentence types, relationships among sentences, paragraphs, links among paragraphs and sections, and finally text structures. Only a grammar established by means of a careful and flexible textlinguistic research can serve as a firm basis for discourse analysis.

Three different levels of analysis need to be established. Proceeding from the bottom up (from small to broad units), they are: morphological, syntactical, and discourse levels. Morphology is concerned with grammatical analysis of the sentence. Syntax identifies the relationships among sentences and paragraphs in the framework of a text. Discourse analysis brings to the fore macrosyntactic, semantic, and pragmatic devices used by the author to convey his message in a forcible way. I insist that the higher levels be based on the lower ones. Syntax must be based on morphology, and discourse analysis on morphosyntax.

2. Narrative versus direct speech

This bottom-up approach begins, however, with a presupposition of a top-down character. Following Weinrich (1985), I suppose that in Biblical Hebrew, as in other languages, a basic distinction is necessary in order to understand the different verb forms, namely the distinction between historical narrative and direct speech. This distinction is not *a priori*, but rather it is based on the fact that practically every language uses separate sets of verb forms for these two genres. Historical narrative (henceforth simply "narrative") and direct speech are, then, meaningful in reference to the verbal system of various languages.

In previous works I called these two genres "narrative" and "discourse," respectively. Unfortunately, this terminology is confusing when talking of "discourse analysis" instead of textlinguistics. It would involve the use of the word *discourse* in two completely different ways. Therefore I now prefer to call the two genres "narrative" and "direct speech," the latter referring to dialogue, sermon, or prayer. It also indicates indirect speech, as when an author comments in different ways upon the story he is narrating.[5]

This creates an uneasy situation, difficult to clarify: On the one hand, I think discourse linguists posit too many text types; on the other, too few. Predictive/procedural, hortatory, and expository discourses are, from the point of view of the Hebrew verb forms, one and the same genre of "discourse" (in the meaning of direct speech). To this genre also belong the indirect comments an author makes in the course of a narrative (using verb forms of direct speech). On the other hand, discourse linguists do not make the distinction that is really basic from the point of view of the verb forms used, that is, narrative versus direct speech or comment.[6] To distinguish different text types beyond these two is not relevant at this stage because there is not a distinctive set of verb forms; the distinction of narrative and direct speech *is* relevant, however, because the two have a separate set of verb forms in Hebrew (as in many other languages).

The distinction between narrative and direct speech is particularly clear in French, Spanish, Italian and other such languages that possess a rich variety of verb forms. In Table 1 the main verb forms of French, Spanish, and Italian are classified according to the three basic temporal axes.

Table 1. Different sets of verb forms for direct speech and for narrative

Temporal axes	Direct Speech	Narrative
Present	*présent* *presente* *presente*	*imparfait* *imperfecto* *imperfetto*[7]
Past	*passé composé* *pretérito perfecto* *passato prossimo*	*passé simple* *pretérito indefinido* *passato remoto*
Future	*futur* *futuro* *futuro*	*conditionnel* *condicional* *condizionale*[8]

In Hebrew, too, we can posit two different sets of verb forms. This is shown in Table 2.

Table 2. Sets of verb forms for direct speech and narrative in Hebrew

Direct Speech	Narrative
X-*yiqtol* (indicative) *weqatal* volitive forms (cohortative, imperative, and jussive)	*wayyiqtol* *waw*-X-*qatal* —

Biblical Hebrew reveals its limitations in the fact that some verb forms are not distinctive to one or the other of these genres—narrative or direct speech. They function in both, although in a different way, as shown in Table 3 where the different verb forms are distributed along the three temporal axes.

Table 3. Hebrew verb forms according to the three temporal axes

Temporal axes	Comment	Narrative
Present	simple nominal clause volitive forms	simple nominal clause —
Past	*qatal*, or X-*qatal*	*wayyiqtol*
Future	X-*yiqtol* (indicative) *weqatal*	X-*yiqtol* (indicative) *weqatal*

A further distinction is to be made between historical narrative (in German "Erzählung") and oral narrative, or report in the direct speech (in German "Rede," or "Bericht"). These genres are characterized by distinctive verb forms in French, Spanish, and Italian (see the axis "past" in Table 1). Distinctive verb forms are attested in Hebrew, too, insofar as the beginning is concerned. In fact, historical narrative begins with *wayyiqtol* while oral narrative begins with *qatal* or X-*qatal*.[9] This fact needs to be stressed since some discourse linguists posit a "narrative discourse" without caring to distinguish whether it is a historical or an oral narrative. Again, they distinguish too little in this case.[10]

3. The sentence

A sentence that begins with a finite verb form is verbal; any other kind of sentence is nominal. If a sentence contains a finite verb form in the second position, it is a compound nominal clause; if it does not contain any finite verb form, it is a simple nominal clause. The compound nominal clause and the simple nominal clause basically have the same function (see Niccacci 1990c §161ff.).

This analysis of the sentence with a finite verb form in the second position is a cornerstone of the verbal system I am proposing, yet it is a major stumbling block for many contemporary grammarians. I shall try again to show that this definition makes sense in the whole Biblical Hebrew verbal system.

Everybody, I think, would agree that sometimes in Biblical Hebrew a verb form occurs in the second position of the sentence (i.e., X-*qatal*, or X-*yiqtol*) with the purpose of emphasizing the X element promoted to the front. But nobody seems concerned with asking whether or not this brings with it any change in the structure of the sentence.[11] There is, however, enough evidence to show that the sentence with a finite verb in the second position is of a completely different kind from the one with a finite verb in the first position. It does not communicate an event/information as such, as when the finite verb comes first. Rather it states who the subject is, or how, when, where an event/information occurs (depending on the nature of the X element).

The reason is that in Biblical Hebrew the first position in the sentence belongs to the predicate, which is the most prominent component and the element on which the main stress falls. Now the verb belongs to the class traditionally called "universals"; it normally functions as the predicate. The noun belongs to the "particulars" class and normally functions as the subject (Lyons 1977, vol. 2, §12.7, esp. p. 503). When the verb comes in the first position, we have a plain, unmarked sentence precisely because what is normally the predicate comes in the expected place. In this case, normal predicate and first position coincide. When, on the contrary, an element different from the verb comes first, we have a marked sentence, because normal predicate and first position diverge. Because of that, an unmarked sentence informs on the event/information itself, while a marked sentence informs on a detail of it.[12] Another major function of the marked sentence is to signal syntactical subordination.

It is important to understand the designation "nominal sentence." A sentence is nominal not just because it has a noun (normally the subject) in the first place. Actually, it makes no difference at all whether a noun, a pronoun, a prepositional phrase, or an adverb is in the first place. The main point is that it is not the finite verb. Nominal means essentially nonverbal.[13] As noted, a nominal sentence states who the subject or the object is, or how, when, where a given event/information occurs. Still, we have to remember that this is but one function of the nominal sentence (i.e., the function of demoting the verb). Another function of the nominal sentence at the text level is to demote the whole sentence and make it dependent.

Designating a sentence with a finite verb in the second position as compound nominal sentence has the advantage of indicating that its function is equivalent to that of the simple nominal, or verbless clause.[14] Actually both simple and compound play a similar function in narrative, in the sense that they both represent a subsidiary level of the text, the main difference being the temporal reference (past time for the compound nominal sentence, contemporaneity for simple nominal sentence).

In my work on syntax (1990c §6), I illustrated two main syntactic settings capable of substantiating this. They are: independent personal pronoun + finite verb, and interrogative pronoun + finite verb. (Space does not permit me to repeat the evidence here.)

4. Emphasis, topic, focus

Discourse analysis inevitably brings us to such matters as emphasis, topic, and focus. As far as I understand, there are problems here. The first problem is terminology: the same terms are used differently by different authors. The second problem is the relationship between these pragmatic phenomena and the grammatical analysis. While it may be true that emphasis is a much-abused category, called in to easily explain difficulties of Hebrew grammar,[15] nevertheless it is useful in order to clarify the function of certain marked structures that promote a nonverbal element of the sentence to the role of the predicate. For instance, saying that the X element of a X-*qatal* clause is emphasized, or that it is the "focus," means that it is the predicate, or the new information. This seems to me to be an appropriate use of the term *emphasis*.[16]

The main problem, as I see it, is with the grammatical analysis of Biblical Hebrew. As we noted earlier, not every marked structure has the function of putting emphasis on the fronted element and making it the predicate. The compound nominal sentence does have this function on the level of the sentence, but on the broader level of the text, it has the function of making the sentence as a whole dependent on another verb-initial (i.e., verbal) sentence. This is the case, for example, of a *waw-X-qatal* clause conveying background information to a preceding *wayyiqtol*, or antecedent information to a following *wayyiqtol*.[17] Indeed, in this case, there is no question of emphasis; the marked structure is used as a sign of subordination.

The double sentence (protasis–apodosis) is still another structure with a nonverbal element fronted for some reason other than emphasis. This, in modern terminology, is called "topicalization," provided we mean by this a nonemphatic structure with a fronted nonverbal element as the topic of the sentence. Every language has appropriate syntactic structures for this function and we have to be careful not to read the structures of one language into another. In Biblical Hebrew, for instance, grammatical analysis shows that the topic (casus pendens) constitutes a sentence by itself since it is interchangeable with, say, an "if" + finite verb structure (conditional clause), or a "when" + finite verb structure (temporal sentence) (see Niccacci 1990c §119). Vice versa, all the structures capable of filling the first slot of a double sentence are the topic.[18]

A common alternative analysis maintains that the topic (casus pendens) is an extraposed subject, object, or complement, according to its nature and the way it is resumed in the sentence. I do not think this analysis is correct even for English or other European languages.[19] It is certainly not correct for Biblical Hebrew.

5. First-position emphasis

I wish now to prove the assumption that the predicate is the stressed element in the sentence. Let us first study the examples upon which our argument will be based.

(1) Job 32:2-3 וַיִּחַר אַף אֱלִיהוּא בֶן־בַּרַכְאֵל הַבּוּזִי מִמִּשְׁפַּחַת רָם

a | Then the anger of Elihu, son of Berachel the Buzite, of the family of Ram, flared up:

בְּאִיּוֹב חָרָה אַפּוֹ עַל־צַדְּקוֹ נַפְשׁוֹ מֵאֱלֹהִים

b | it is against Job that his anger flared up because he declared himself upright in front of God;

וּבִשְׁלֹשֶׁת רֵעָיו חָרָה אַפּוֹ

c | and it is against his three friends that his anger flared up

עַל אֲשֶׁר לֹא־מָצְאוּ מַעֲנֶה

d | because they had not found any answer

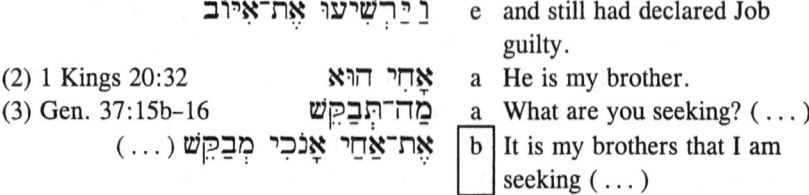

	וַיַּרְשִׁיעוּ אֶת־אִיּוֹב	e and still had declared Job guilty.
(2) 1 Kings 20:32	אָחִי הוּא	a He is my brother.
(3) Gen. 37:15b–16	מַה־תְּבַקֵּשׁ	a What are you seeking? (...)
	אֶת־אַחַי אָנֹכִי מְבַקֵּשׁ (...)	b It is my brothers that I am seeking (...)

Sentence a in example 1 is verbal because the verb comes in the first place. It is a plain, unmarked sentence. On the contrary, sentences b–c are two marked structures, type (waw-)X-qatal, or compound nominal sentences, with the function of stressing the X element. The opposition between wayyiqtol for historical information and X-qatal for comment is here particularly evident. Examples 2 and 3 are simple nominal clauses. The former is a plain, unmarked structure, type predicate–subject, while the latter (sentence b) is a marked structure, also type predicate–subject, stressing the first nominal element that is a "particular term."[20]

Examples 2 and 3 call for a special comment: 1 Kings 20:32 and Gen. 37:16 show an opposition between אָחִי 'my brother' functioning as the predicate in a plain sentence and אַחַי 'my brothers' functioning as the predicate in a marked sentence. In fact, in 1 Kings 20:32 אָחִי is more generic, or "universal," than the personal pronoun הוּא; therefore אָחִי is the expected predicate and the sentence is plain. However, in Gen. 37:16 אֶת־אַחַי is more "particular" than the participial verb form מְבַקֵּשׁ, and therefore it is not the expected predicate and the sentence is marked. The speech situation confirms this analysis. On the one hand, in 1 Kings 20:32 Ahab simply declares something concerning Ben-Hadad (that he is his brother, "my brother" being the predicate, or the new information). On the other hand, the man who meets Joseph in the country sees by himself that he is looking for something, and therefore all he asks for is *what* he is looking for (hence "my brothers" is the predicate, or the new information).

Table 4 shows the structure of the plain unmarked sentence, both verbal and nominal, type predicate–subject.

Table 4. The structure of the plain sentence, verbal and nominal

SUBJECT	PREDICATE	SUBJECT	PREDICATE
אַף אֱלִיהוּ	וַיִּחַר	הוּא	אָחִי
Job 32:2		1 Kings 20:32	

Sentences b–c of example 1 and b of example 3 call for special attention. According to the proposed analysis they are both nominal sentences type predicate–subject. Note, however, that what is called the "subject" consists in both cases of a complete sentence having its own predicate and subject. It is an "embedded clause," and the overall sentence is "superordinate." In Table 5 the subject and predicate of the superordinate sentence are shown in capitals, while those of the embedded sentence are in lowercase letters.

Table 5. The structure of the marked sentence, verbal and nominal

SUBJECT		PREDICATE	SUBJECT		PREDICATE
אֵפוֹ	חָרָה	בְּאִיּוֹב	מְבַקֵּשׁ	אָנֹכִי	אֶת־אַחַי
	Predicate			Subject	
Subject		Job 32:2	Predicate		Gen. 37:16

Now we can show that the predicate is the stressed element in the sentence. We hold that plain and marked sentences, both verbal and nominal (indeed all kinds of sentences), can be viewed as answers to appropriate questions,[21] as, for example, in Job 32:2:

Job 32:2 PREDICATE (first position)   SUBJECT (second position)
Question What   did Elihu's anger do?
Answer   It is | it-flared-up | that | Elihu's anger (did) |

Question Against whom   did Elihu's anger flare up?
Answer   It is | against Job | that | his anger flared up |

An important difference between a plain and a marked sentence is that in the latter, but not the former, the subject of the superordinate sentence is a complete clause (predicate and subject) and the sentence is cleft in two. The same analysis applies to sentences without a finite verb:

1 Kings   PREDICATE (first position)   SUBJECT (second position)
20:22
Question What   is he?
Answer   It is | my brother | that | he (is) |
Gen. 37:16
Question What   are you seeking?
Answer   It is | my brothers | that | I am seeking |

Thus, emphasis is neither an extragrammatical category nor a function of the nonverbal sentence only. Rather, it signals the predicate both in the verbal and in the nominal sentence. Indeed, the first position is the place of the emphasis and of the predicate in Biblical Hebrew.

6. First-position nonemphasis

We now consider the numerous marked sentences that do not signal any emphasis on the initial nonverbal element. I claim that they are dependent sentences. In other words, they do not stand by themselves but rely on a following or preceding verbal sentence. Consider the following examples:

(4) 1 Sam. 19:12	(. . .) וַיִּבְרַח וַיִּמָּלֵט		a	And (David) fled away and escaped (. . .)
1 Sam. 19:18	וְדָוִד בָּרַח	b		Now *(remember that)* David had fled
	וַיִּמָּלֵט	c		and had escaped.
(5) Judg. 8:11	וַיַּךְ אֶת־הַמַּחֲנֶה		a	(Gideon) struck the encampment (of Midian)
	וְהַמַּחֲנֶה הָיָה בֶטַח	b		while the encampment felt secure.

Sentence b of example 4 and b of 5 are of type *waw-X-qatal*: they depend on a verbal sentence with narrative *wayyiqtol*. The former takes up, with a construction of the secondary level, a piece of information communicated earlier, in 4a, with narrative *wayyiqtol*. That piece of information is restated at the beginning of a new episode in the story as "antecedent information." The *waw-X-qatal* construction of 4b relies on the following narrative *wayyiqtol*, וַיָּבֹא 'he went'.[22] But the *waw-X-qatal* in 5b[23] depends on the preceding narrative *wayyiqtol* in 5a as background depends on foreground.

These *waw-X-qatal* constructions do not have any emphatic function at the sentence level but only a subordinating function at the text level. This is the case with most of the examples attested. In some, however, the *waw-X-qatal* form possesses both functions, as in example 1 above where 1b and 1c subordinate to the preceding *wayyiqtol*[24] are also emphatic. That is, they stress the complements "against Job" and "against his three friends." Table 6 shows these two functions of *waw-X-qatal*.

Table 6. The two functions of the *waw-X-qatal* construction

	PREDICATE	SUBJECT (no emphasis)
(4b-c)	בָּרַח וַיִּמָּלֵט	וְדָוִד
(5b)	הָיָה בֶטַח	וְהַמַּחֲנֶה
	SUBJECT	PREDICATE (emphasis)
(1b)	חָרָה אַפּוֹ	בְּאִיּוֹב
(1c)	חָרָה אַפּוֹ	וּבִשְׁלֹשֶׁת רֵעָיו

7. Coordination and subordination

The distinction between a verbal sentence with the finite verb in the first position and a compound nominal sentence with the finite verb in the second position provides us with a criterion for determining if a sentence is main or subordinate. It thus helps us see when we have coordination and subordination. This criterion is valid so far as it is based on the analysis of the Hebrew verbal system and not on the verb forms used in modern translations. (This is obvious, of course; still it is not infrequently disregarded).

At the grammatical level, a sentence is a main sentence when, negatively, it is not governed by a subordinating conjunction like אִם, כִּי, or לְמַעַן, and, positively, the verb is initial. At the textual level, a main sentence is independent when it can stand by itself without relying on another sentence (i.e., when it can start a text unit and marks the main level of communication).

On this basis, let us consider some verb forms. Narrative *wayyiqtol* is a constituent of a main and independent sentence because it occupies the first position in the sentence and starts a text unit. In narrative, a second-position verb form, such as *waw*-X-*qatal* and *waw*-X-*yiqtol*, is a constituent of a main but dependent sentence because syntactically it relies on some first-position verb form and indicates a subsidiary level of communication.

Weqatal is a first-position verb form at the level of the sentence but a second-position verb form at the text level because it is not found at the beginning of an autonomous text unit. In fact, no direct speech is found to begin with *weqatal*.[25] It indicates a grammatically main but syntactically dependent sentence. The same is true of the verb forms used in the apodosis.[26]

Coordination is a sequence of verb forms of the same syntactic status, be they independent or dependent, while subordination is a sequence of verb forms of different syntactic status. For instance, a narrative sequence of the type *waw*-X-*qatal* → *wayyiqtol* or, vice versa, the type *wayyiqtol* → *waw*-X-*qatal*, is not composed of coordinate sentences either syntactically or textlinguistically. At the syntactical level, the first type constitutes a transition from a second-position verb form to a first-position verb form, and vice versa for the second type. At the text level, the first represents a transition from antecedent information to the mainline of narrative, and the second from the mainline of narrative (foreground) to background. For similar reasons, in direct speech (and also in narrative) a sequence of type *weqatal* → *waw*-X-*yiqtol* does not signal coordination but subordination of the second verb form to the first.

In general, then, verbal (unmarked) structures indicate coordination, while nonverbal (marked) structures indicate subordination. A marked structure is subordinate per se, although it is a main clause. Thus, Biblical Hebrew possesses two equally effective ways of producing subordination: one with a subordinating conjunction (grammatical subordination), the other without a subordinating conjunction, by simply putting the finite verb in the second position (syntactical subordination).

Notice that I speak of coordination and subordination without mentioning the conjunction *waw*. I do this because coordination and subordination are not affected by *waw* in any way. In fact, some coordinate verb forms are found not connected by *waw* (e.g., asyndetic imperatives) and, conversely, some subordinate verb forms occur that *are* connected by *waw* (as in the sequence *wayyiqtol* → *waw-X-qatal*). Moreover, we have observed several times that a compound nominal sentence of the X-*qatal* or X-*yiqtol* type plays exactly the same function with or without a preceding *waw*. The reason is, simply, that the function does not depend on the *waw* but on the position of the verb in the sentence.

The *waw* referred to here is the one that connects different verb forms, not the *waw* that constitutes the so-called "inverted" verb forms *wayyiqtol, weqatal,* and *weyiqtol*. Although the diachronic origin of the inverted verb forms may be still obscure, synchronic analysis shows that they are not the result of *waw* + *yiqtol* and *waw* + *qatal* but simply *wayyiqtol, weqatal,* and *weyiqtol*. In other words, they are autonomous verb forms because they possess a distinctive morphology and syntactical function. A simple and yet important consequence of this is that we cannot deduce their function from a supposed virtuality of *waw*.[27]

8. Tense and aspect

From the same basic principles of position in the sentence and level of communication, we can derive criteria to answer a vexing problem of the verbal system. Are there tenses in Biblical Hebrew, or do the verb forms have an aspect value only?[28]

Biblical Hebrew does have tenses. Consider the following examples:

(6) Gen. 42:11 כֻּלָּנוּ a As for all of us,
 בְּנֵי אִישׁ־אֶחָד נָחְנוּ b we are sons of one man.
 כֵּנִים אֲנַחְנוּ c We are honest men.
 לֹא־הָיוּ עֲבָדֶיךָ מְרַגְּלִים d Your servants have never been spying.
(7) Exod. 26:6 וְעָשִׂיתָ חֲמִשִּׁים קַרְסֵי זָהָב a Then you shall make fifty gold clips

וְחִבַּרְתָּ֙ אֶת־הַיְרִיעֹ֤ת אִשָּׁה֙ אֶל־אֲחֹתָ֔הּ בַּקְּרָסִ֑ים	b	and shall join the curtains one to another with the clips.
וְהָיָ֥ה הַמִּשְׁכָּ֖ן אֶחָֽד	c	And so the Tabernacle will be a single unit.
(8) Exod. 36:13 וַיַּ֛עַשׂ חֲמִשִּׁ֥ים קַרְסֵ֖י זָהָ֑ב	a	Then he made fifty gold clips
וַיְחַבֵּ֨ר אֶת־הַיְרִיעֹ֜ת אַחַ֤ת אֶל־אַחַת֙ בַּקְּרָסִ֔ים	b	and joined the curtains one to another with the clips.
וַיְהִ֥י הַמִּשְׁכָּ֖ן אֶחָֽד	c	And so the Tabernacle became a single unit.

There is no justification for denying that the simple nominal clause in 6b–c places the information in the axis of the present (in direct speech), while the (negative) *qatal* in 6d places it in the axis of the past (in direct speech). On the other hand, *weqatal* in 7 places the information in the axis of the future (in direct speech), and *wayyiqtol* in 8 places it in the axis of the past (in narrative).

These are tenses and nothing else. Still, many scholars doubt or do not dare to affirm the existence of tenses in Biblical Hebrew. The reason is, I suppose, that they cannot see any regularity. However, on the basis of our principles (position in the sentence, levels of communication), it is possible to see regularity to a large extent. We can affirm that verb forms have *fixed temporal reference* when they are verbal sentences and/or indicate the mainline of communication both in narrative and in direct speech. On the other hand, they have a *relative temporal reference* when they are nominal clauses and indicate a subsidiary line of communication. In this case, the time reference is not fixed and the tense of translation in modern languages depends on the different functions represented, such as background, retrieved, or prospective information (see Tables 1–3).

Aspect, in the sense of mode of action *(Aktionsart)*, is, then, a legitimate category of the Hebrew verbal system in the subsidiary line of communication. But in the mainline of communication we can readily admit tenses.

In narrative, for instance, *wayyiqtol* is the only verb form for the mainline, but for the subsidiary line we have the simple nominal clause and the compound nominal clause in both its forms, that is, *waw*-X-*qatal* and *waw*-X-*yiqtol*. We have to ask, What is the criterion behind the choice of one on these possibilities? The answer is aspect. In fact, the simple nominal clause is chosen for contemporaneity or for a descriptive function (e.g., Exod. 36:8–13), while *waw*-X-*qatal* indicates a unique event and *waw*-X-*yiqtol* repetition or custom (see Niccacci 1990c §133).

In sum, there is no major overlapping or confusion. Hebrew verb forms and constructions have their own distinctive functions in a well-defined system.

Since my view of tense and aspect is not accepted by a number of my colleagues,[29] some comments are in order here. The two basic criteria for the analysis of the Biblical Hebrew verbal system operate on different levels. The position of the verb operates on the level of the sentence and on the level of the text, while the mainline and subsidiary line of communication operate on the level of the text only.

The situation is complex but neither impossible nor incoherent. Take, for instance, *wayyiqtol*. In narrative it is an initial verb form both at the sentence level and at the text level (in that it can start a historical narrative). In direct speech it is initial at the level of the sentence but not at the level of the text (namely, it is not found at the beginning of a direct speech). The same is true of *weqatal* in direct speech.

A convincing explanation for these facts is, in my opinion, the paucity of verb forms in Biblical Hebrew. The same verb forms are used, although differently, in different genres. They correspond to many different tense forms in European languages (see Tables 1-3). Thus, *wayyiqtol* is used for the past both in narrative and in direct speech, while modern languages have different verb forms for these two genres. Likewise, *weqatal* and *yiqtol* are used both in direct speech and in narrative but correspond to different tense forms in modern languages: future and imperfect, respectively. Finally, the simple nominal clause in Hebrew implies present tense in discourse but contemporaneity in narrative. (This is not simply a theoretical assertion but the result of an extensive reading of texts.)

9. Conclusion

It is possible to see Biblical Hebrew verbs as a system. The system is built from bottom to top upon a coherent binary basis consisting of two types of sentence, one with the verb in the first position, the other with a nonverbal element in the first position. One of the two criteria used to analyze the Hebrew verbal system, then, is *position in the sentence*.

I make a primary distinction between historical narrative and direct speech because a distinctive set of verb forms occurs in each of these two genres. Each of them is characterized by specific verb forms and constructions that indicate the mainline and subsidiary line of communication. This matter of *communication level* is the other of the two criteria used to analyze the Biblical Hebrew verbal system.

The type of sentence that begins with a verb is termed a "verbal sentence." Verbal sentences constitute the mainline both in narrative and direct speech. The type of sentence that begins with a nonverbal element is termed "nominal" and constitutes a subsidiary line of communication.

A narrative text is produced by alternating mainline verb forms (*wayyiqtol*) and secondary-line verb forms (nominal constructions with a finite verb in the second position, or without any finite verb). The first set constitutes a chain of sequential events or pieces of information (foreground). The second set signals a break in the chain for a special purpose, such as to stress a detail of the main information, or to express the writer's comment on his story, or to restage the story and introduce a new character or some other background. Alternation from one set to another provides relief and displays the writer's strategy of communication.

Direct speech is richer than narrative in that it uses more diverse verb forms and constructions. It can freely use the three main temporal axes, while historical narrative is bound to the axis of the past. Given its very nature, direct speech prefers foreground and straight relationship to the addressee. However, especially in large texts, foreground and background are discernible. The mainline in the past axis (oral narrative) begins with *qatal* or X-*qatal*, continues with *wayyiqtol,* and then behaves exactly as historical narrative, with *waw*-X-*qatal* indicating the background. In the present axis, both the mainline and the subsidiary line are represented by simple nominal clauses. In the future axis, the mainline begins with a simple nominal clause (frequently with a participle) or an indicative X-*yiqtol*, and continues with *weqatal,* which constitutes the foreground, while *waw*-X-*yiqtol* indicates the background. Volitive verb forms (cohortative, imperative, and jussive) also play an important role in direct speech. They usually use the mainline, though the secondary line is sometimes indicated by jussive X-*yiqtol*.

Table 7 attempts to show the overall structure of the Hebrew verbal system from the sentence level up to the text level. It is assumed that the two types of sentence (verbal and nominal) are fundamental throughout the processing of a text from small to large units.

Table 7. The overall structure of the Hebrew verbal system

SENTENCE LEVEL	First Position	Second Position
Verbal sentence	Verb	Subject/ Object/ Complement
Compound nominal sentence	Subject/ Object/ Complement	Verb
TEXT LEVEL	*First Position*	*Second Position*
Foreground →	*wayyiqtol* →	
Background (N.a)		*waw*-X-*qatal*
Foreground →	*wayyiqtol* →	
Background (N.b)		*weqatal**
Foreground →	*weqatal* →	
Background (D.c)		*waw*-X-*yiqtol*
Foreground →	(X-)*qatal*** →	
Background (D.d)		*waw*-X-*qatal*
Antecedent Info →	*waw*-X-*qatal*† →	
Storyline (N)***		*wayyiqtol*

D = direct speech. N = narrative.
*Waw-X-*yiqtol* and *waw*-simple nominal clause are also attested.
**After *(X-)qatal* continuative *wayyiqtol* is used for foreground.
***Antecedent information is not attested in D.
†Other nominal clauses are also used.

Notes

1. My previous work (1990c) is a revised translation of the first draft in Italian published by the Franciscan Printing Press in 1986.

2. Longacre puts forward his methodology as a challenge to the traditional way of describing the different uses of Hebrew verb forms found, for instance, in the Gesenius-Kautzsch-Cowley grammar. He writes, "Rather, I posit here that (*a*) every language has a system of discourse types (e.g., narrative, predictive, hortatory, procedural, expository, and others); (*b*) each discourse type has its own characteristic constellation of verb forms that figure in that type; (*c*) the uses of given tense/aspect/mood form are most surely and concretely described in relation to a given discourse type" (1989:59). Longacre's methodology differs from my own in that it posits many text types whereas I posit two.

3. See, e.g., the quotation formulas used in Gen. 3:14, 16, and 17 and my explanation given in "Analysis of Biblical Narrative" in this volume.

4. Such as B. K. Waltke and M. O'Connor's 1990 work. See my review of it (1989*b*).

5. This is a main issue with Weinrich (1985). German possesses a very precise way of expressing this distinction, namely, "Erzählung" (narrative) vs. "Besprechung" (comment). The terms *direct speech* and *indirect speech* as used here have nothing to do with "direct reported speech" (i.e., quotation)

and "indirect reported speech" of the English grammar (see, e.g., R. Huddleston 1984:150-52).

6. For the sake of clarity I shall, from now on, avoid using the term *discourse* to mean direct speech. I shall use *direct speech* or *comment* instead.

7. Imperfect is the "present in the past."

8. Conditional is the "future in the past."

9. See my analysis of "narrative discourse" (1990c §§74-76 and 1989a §4). The fact that no oral narrative (i.e., in the direct speech) begins with *wayyiqtol*, or that *wayyiqtol* is found only as a continuation form, is most noteworthy. See, for instance, Gen. 44:19 and Deut. 1:6; 5:2.

10. A. Verheij (1992) objects, if I understand him correctly, to this distinction of narrative and direct speech stating that it is contrary to Weinrich's method (1985) and is also self-contradicting. However, Weinrich begins his research by classifying the tenses of different modern languages according to their use in narrative and comment *(erzählen, besprechen)*, exactly as I do for Hebrew. As for the definitions, I suppose everybody agrees on what historical narrative and direct speech are. Comment is a "mixed category," an intrusion of direct speech into narrative. When commenting on the event he is narrating, the writer uses the same verb forms as in direct speech, although not all of them nor with the same temporal value. It is as if he were speaking to his reader indirectly. As a way to render this commenting attitude, I used a paraphrase, "Now, the reader should know (or remember) that . . ." (see Niccacci 1990a, e.g., *ad* Josh. 6:1).

11. The position of this grammar changed from the one I am proposing (that was the opinion of the Arab grammarians) to the opinion commonly held by modern grammarians. Please see Gesenius-Kautzsch-Cowley (1910 §142f) for clarification. Nothing new is to be found in the 1991 translation and revision of Joüon (1991:580-3).

12. Compare the "functional sentence perspective" with the "relaxed speech" vs. "excited speech" of V. Malthesius' school (see Garvin 1963:502).

13. See the problem with my position raised by M. Eskhult (1991:96).

14. F. I. Andersen (unpublished) writes: "Among clauses of this type, major attention has been given to those in which the fronted item is a noun, and particularly, if not exclusively, the noun subject. Because this feature has been deemed distinctive, if not definitive, such clauses have been commonly called 'nominal.' This terminology is unfortunate and misleading, for two reasons. First, it inappropriately places such clauses in the same class as verbless clauses in which the noun subject comes first. Secondly, it overlooks or neglects the fact that coordinated verbal clauses in which the noun subject precedes the verb are only a subset of a larger set of clause types that have similar functions on the higher levels of discourse." Andersen lists a series of different functions of the *(waw-)X-qatal* construction, or "*we*-X VS" in his terms, such as "Paragraph-initial: new topic," "Paragraph-initial: known topic," and "Paragraph-medial." These functions, however, are established on the basis of interpretation, not of syntax. In my view, all those functions fall

under two syntactical structures, either (1) *waw*-X-*qatal* → *wayyiqtol*, i.e., a tense transition from antecedent information to mainline of narrative (Niccacci 1990c §§15-19), or (2) *wayyiqtol* → *waw*-X-*qatal*, i.e. a tense transition from main narrative line, or foreground, to background (ibid. §9).

15. Bandstra (1992) would prefer "topicalization" instead of "emphasis." From the examples he gives (pp. 120-22), we see that he brings together under this name constructions that are different from the point of view of grammar: compound nominal sentences and the double sentences (consisting of protasis + apodosis). "Topicalization" is not a designation that can cover both (see Niccacci 1990c §§123-25).

16. I am not speaking of "logical," as distinct from "grammatical," predicate or subject. (For a critique of such a distinction see Jespersen 1924:147ff.) In my opinion, if something is the predicate or the subject, it is such on the level of grammar. Terminological confusion and lack of criteria have led some scholars to the point of avoiding the terms subject and predicate altogether (e.g., Geller 1991, especially footnote 8). But is it possible to analyze a language without asking what the subject is and what the predicate in the sentence?

17. Under these two categories fall the "countless examples" (T. Muraoka 1989) in which an initial nominal element does not bear any emphasis. Despite repeated efforts, I did not succeed in bringing forward my analysis of the nominal sentence at two different levels, that of the sentence and that of the text. See also M. Eskhult (1991:97, esp. footnote 23).

18. I refer here to R. Buth (1992, and forthcoming). In the second of these, Buth, dissatisfied with the term "topic" because of the different meanings it receives, proposes "contextualization," or "contextualizing constituent," instead. He correctly sees that marked sentences in Biblical Hebrew are those with a preposed nonverbal element. He calls this element when it is not emphasized, not salient in the sentence, "topic," or "contextualizing constituent." When it *is* emphasized, or salient, he calls it "focus." Seen in the light of my terminology, focus is the X element of a compound nominal sentence when it bears emphasis. In the case that the X element is not emphasized, however, I would not call it "topic," nor would I call it "contextualizing constituent." In fact, when nonstressed, the X element is simply the subject, or object, or complement, according to its grammatical nature. It is preposed in order to demote the sentence. I would reserve the term *topic* for the casus pendens, the protasis of a double sentence. Possibly Buth proposed the term *contextualizing constituent* under the influence of certain texts that he had studied in which a sentence with a preposed nonverbal element has a contextualizing function (i.e., it gives the stage of a story). This is correct and corresponds to what I call antecedent information. In my opinion, however, the contextualizing function belongs to the sentence as a whole, not to the preposed element only.

19. According to C. Bally (1944 §89), the analysis I am proposing for Biblical Hebrew also applies to French. Bally gives the following example: "*Cet*

élève, je l'aime bien; *cet élève,* je lui ai donné un livre ... = «Pour cet élève, quant à cet élève, puisqu'il est question de ... », etc." (p. 65).

20. In plain, unmarked sentences, the "universals" function as the predicate and the "particulars" as the subject (see Lyons 1968 §8.1.3 and 1977, vol. 2, §12.7, especially p. 503). In marked sentences, however, the reverse occurs. For an application of this principle to Hebrew grammar, see Niccacci (1993). Note that in my example 3 sentence b is an answer to a X-question in 3a, type X-*yiqtol,* namely, a compound nominal clause where the interrogative pronoun is the "predicate," or the new element, and the verb is the "subject," or the given element. The answer follows the same pattern predicate–subject with the only difference that the answer is a nominal sentence without a finite verb. Note, however, that the two kinds of nominal sentence (compound and simple) function exactly the same way. This confirms my definition of the nominal sentence in Biblical Hebrew.

21. The famous passage of G. F. Stout, criticized by Jespersen (1924:146), can be helpful, after all. It says: "All answers to questions are, as such, predicates, and all the predicates may be regarded as answers to possible questions." Lyons (1977, vol. 2, 503) writes: "Every statement that can be made by uttering a simple sentence expresses a proposition, which, if it is informative (...) provides the answer to either an explicit or an implicit question."

22. In 4c the *wayyiqtol* is continuative (not narrative), having the same temporal value of the preceding *waw*-X-*qatal* clause. See Niccacci (1990c §146) for details.

23. I take sentence b in example 5 to be a compound (not simple) nominal clause because in my opinion the verb הָיָה is not a copula but a full verb (see Niccacci 1990*b*).

24. Further examples are found in 2 Kings 18:10; Josh. 4:12-13; and 6:15. See also Niccacci (1990c §48).

25. A summary of *weqatal* is in Niccacci (1990c §156). The וְהָיָה forms found in prophetic literature are not a proof to the contrary since they introduce new sections logically connected to a previous one. Indeed, paying attention to this feature of Hebrew syntax can be fruitful from both a literary and a theological point of view.

26. See my 1987 syntactic discussion of the verb forms of the apodosis (pp. 7-19 and §2). Also see Niccacci (1990c §126).

27. One can even doubt that the *waw* in *wayyiqtol, weqatal,* and *weyiqtol* is the same as the conjunctive *waw*. In any case, I am convinced that *waw,* this unconscious "hero" of Hebrew syntax, simply cannot support all the different functions attributed to it in standard grammars—in the index of Waltke and O'Connor (1990:733) twenty-five entries are listed under the heading "*waw* (conjunction)." From the presence of *waw,* Waltke and O'Connor derive a vague value of consequence and of dependence for *weqatal* and *wayyiqtol*: "Relative *wqtl* [i.e., the conversive or consecutive *qatal*] is subordinate to a primary verb (or equivalent) and in that connection it represents either an

epexegetical situation with imperfective aspect (only in past or present time) or a consequential (logical and/or temporal) situation" (p. 525). Further on they say, "In sum, *wayyqtl* subjectively represents a situation according to the perfective aspect and subordinates it to a preceding statement. Since these two features, subordination and perfective aspect, are distinct and yet always present, we analyze separately the diverse kinds of subordinate connection (33.2) and the diverse functions of the perfective aspect (33.3)" (p. 547). These very equivocal statements are in danger of totally misrepresenting the Biblical Hebrew verbal system (see Niccacci 1989*b*:322-24).

28. Terminology is frequently a problem when one reads modern treatments. I have expressed my reservations on various solutions based on the "aspect" (in Niccacci 1989*b*:314-15 and 1990*a*:36-38). See also Niccacci (1990*c* §133 and 1990*a*:32-33).

29. T. Muraoka (1989:187-93; 1992:190-92), M. Eskhult (1991:95-101), and A. Verheij (1992:214-17) do not believe, after all, in the distinction between the verbal and nonverbal sentence that I propose. The main problem is, of course, to see the coherence of this basic distinction throughout the Biblical Hebrew verbal system. Without that distinction, I think, no real understanding of the Hebrew verbal system is possible.

References

Andersen, F. I. Unpublished. Fronting in a coordinated clause with a suffixed verb.

Bandstra, B. 1992. Word order and emphasis in Biblical Hebrew narrative: Syntactic observations on Genesis 22 from a discourse perspective. In *Linguistics and Biblical Hebrew,* ed. W. R. Bodine, 109-23. Winona Lake, Ind.: Eisenbrauns.

Bally, C. 1944. *Linguistique générale et linguistique française.* 2d ed. Berne: A. Francke.

Buth, R. 1992. Topic and focus in Hebrew poetry—Psalm 51. In *Language in context: Essays for Robert E. Longacre,* ed. S. J. J. Hwang and W. R. Merrifield, 83-96. Dallas: Summer Institute of Linguistics.

———. Forthcoming. Contextualizing constituent as topic, non-sequential background and dramatic pause: Hebrew and Aramaic evidence. In *Selected papers from the 4th Colloquium on Functional Grammar.*

Eshkult, M. 1991. Review of *Lettura sintattica della prosa ebraico-biblica: Principi e applicazioni* by A. Niccacci. *OrSuec* 40:96ff.

Garvin, P. 1963. Czechoslovakia. In *Current trends in linguistics,* vol. 1: *Soviet and East European linguistics,* ed. T. A. Sebeok, 499-502. The Hague: Mouton.

Geller, S. 1991. Cleft sentence with pleonastic pronoun: A syntactic construction of Biblical Hebrew and some of its literary uses. *Journal of the Ancient Near Eastern Society of Columbia University* 20:15-33.

Gesenius, E., E. Kautzsch, and E. Cowley. 1910. *Gesenius' Hebrew grammar.* 2d ed. Oxford: Clarendon.

Huddleston, R. 1984. *Introduction to the grammar of English.* Cambridge: University Press.

Jespersen, O. 1924. *The philosophy of grammar.* London: G. Allen and Unwin.

Joüon, P. 1991. *A grammar of Biblical Hebrew,* vols. 1, 2. Translated and revised by T. Muraoka. Rome: Pontifical Biblical Institute Press.
Longacre, Robert E. 1989. *Joseph: A story of divine providence: A text theoretical and textlinguistic analysis of Genesis 37 and 39-48.* Winona Lake, Ind.: Eisenbrauns.
Lyons, J. 1968. *Introduction to theoretical linguistics.* Cambridge: University Press.
———. 1977. *Semantics,* vols. 1, 2. Cambridge: University Press.
Muraoka, T. 1989. Review of *Sintassi del verbo ebraico nella prosa biblica classica* by A. Niccacci. *AbrNah* 27:188-89.
———. 1992. Review of *Lettura sintattica della prosa ebraico-biblica: Principi e applicazioni* by A. Niccacci. *AbrNah* 30:190-92.
Niccacci, A. 1987. A neglected point of Hebrew syntax: *yiqtol* and position in the sentence. *LA* 39:310-27.
———. 1989*a*. An outline of the Hebrew verbal system in prose. *LA* 39:7-26.
———. 1989*b*. Review of *An introduction to Biblical Hebrew syntax* by B. Waltke and M. O'Connor. *LA* 39:310-27.
———. 1990*a*. *Lettura sintattica della prosa ebraico-biblica: Principi e applicazioni.* SBFAn 31. Jerusalem: Franciscan Printing Press.
———. 1990*b*. Sullo stato sintattico del verbo hāyâ. *LA* 40:9-23.
———. 1990*c*. The syntax of the verb in classical Hebrew prose. *Journal for the Study of the Old Testament.* Supplement 86. (Sheffield: JSOT Press.)
———. 1993. Simple nominal clause (SNC) or verbless clause in Biblical Hebrew prose. *ZAH* 6:216-27.
Verheij, A. 1992. Review of *Syntax of the verb in classical Hebrew prose* by A. Niccacci. *Bibliotheca Orientalis* 49:214-17.
Waltke, B. K., and M. O'Connor. 1990. *An introduction to Biblical Hebrew syntax.* Winona Lake, Ind.: Eisenbrauns.
Weinrich, H. 1985. *Tempus: Besprochene und erzählte Welt.* 4th ed. Stuttgart: Kohlhammer.

5

METHODOLOGICAL COLLISION BETWEEN SOURCE CRITICISM AND DISCOURSE ANALYSIS
The Problem of "Unmarked Temporal Overlay" and the Pluperfect/Nonsequential *wayyiqtol*

Randall Buth

> To one analyst a discontinuity in a text signals a seam between two sources; to another, simply a literary technique. But we will not be able to judge opposing suggestions until we have more precise guidelines about what was proper and possible in biblical storytelling vis-à-vis the signaling (i.e., marking) of discontinuities in time and unit structure.
>
> We also need to take "unmarked overlay" into consideration, since it too is a feature of Hebrew storytelling and nonnarrative as well. "Pluperfect" *wayyiqtol* occurs at junctures of "unmarked overlay" and also as a lower-level literary phenomenon. When is an author "allowed" to go back and overlay or repeat a part of a story? How much lexical marking is necessary? If we can formulate rules about such matters, textlinguistics will be able to contribute to Source Criticism and textual criticism in identifying real problems.
>
> Several texts illustrate proposed parameters. But Judges 14 and Gen. 2:8 and 2:19 are counter-examples; in them the parameters for unmarked overlay are not met and unmarked overlay is not operative. Finally, Numbers 21 and Judges 20 are used to illustrate the contributions of syntax and textlinguistics to exegesis and literary analysis.

A methodological impasse confronts the scholar who would try to explain certain temporal progressions in Hebrew texts. When the natural forward temporal progression is broken, one analyst may suspect that a seam between two sources has been crossed. Another may try to explain the same text by positing either a grammatical or a literary structure in the ancient author's repertoire to fit the incongruity. The question is, Who is right? How do we go about deciding?

The specific problem for this article is the *wayyiqtol* ("*waw-hahippuk*") structure in Hebrew narrative. Everyone recognizes that this *wayyiqtol* verbal structure usually encodes a temporal advancement in a text. That is, when a *wayyiqtol* verb is used, the story usually takes an incremental step forward along a timeline. Of course, various degrees of partial semantic and temporal overlap with a preceding sentence are possible, up to and including a hendiadys like וַיַּעַן וַיֹּאמֶר 'answered and said'. Problems begin to be felt when the *wayyiqtol* form refers to an event (or state) that took place before the previous verb or as a parallel but distinct event.

1. Marked overlay versus unmarked overlay

Hebrew has a structure for marking a break in the temporal succession of a story. Some element is preposed to the verb and a *qatal* verb is used. We can call such a structure a grammatically signaled (i.e., marked) temporal overlay. In other words, the story makes a temporal retreat; it "overlays" a time segment that has already been covered, and the author signals, or "marks,"[1] this overlay with the *waw*-X-*qatal* structure.

Now it is clear that in the Masoretic Hebrew Bible the story will often "retreat" and go back over a temporal segment without using the *waw*-X-*qatal* structure to signal the temporal break. The standard narrative *wayyiqtol* will be used as though the story is marching forward on its timeline but the story actually does an about-face and picks up the time line at an earlier point, one already passed. So the question is posed, Are we looking at a seam caused by an author's use of different sources, perhaps a textual corruption, or are we looking at a literary technique that is not well defined in Hebrew textbooks?

In this article I would like to give a foundation for an answer to this question. I would also like to point the way towards some definitions that can provide guidance in problematic passages. Most of the examples will be taken from Judges, which provides several representative examples and can serve as a starting point for further discussions. Examples of the exegetical value of a fuller understanding of narrative syntax will be given at the end of the article from Genesis 2, Numbers 21, and Judges 20.

2. Examples of marked (grammatically signaled) overlay

Before we directly tackle the problem of "unmarked temporal overlay," it will be good to look at a few "normal" examples of marked overlay (i.e., ones that are grammatically signaled).

(1) Judg. 4:15–17

1a וַיָּהָם יהוה אֶת־סִיסְרָא . . . לְפִי־חֶרֶב לִפְנֵי בָרָק
b וַיֵּרֶד סִיסְרָא מֵעַל הַמֶּרְכָּבָה
c וַיָּנָס בְּרַגְלָיו
d וּבָרָק רָדַף אַחֲרֵי הָרֶכֶב וְאַחֲרֵי הַמַּחֲנֶה עַד חֲרֹשֶׁת הַגּוֹיִם
e וַיִּפֹּל כָּל־מַחֲנֵה סִיסְרָא לְפִי־חֶרֶב
f לֹא נִשְׁאַר עַד־אֶחָד
g וְסִיסְרָא נָס בְּרַגְלָיו אֶל־אֹהֶל יָעֵל אֵשֶׁת חֶבֶר הַקֵּינִי
כִּי שָׁלוֹם בֵּין יָבִין מֶלֶךְ־חָצוֹר וּבֵין בֵּית חֶבֶר הַקֵּינִי

1a 15. And Yhwh routed *(wayyiqtol)* Sisera and all the chariotry and all the camp with the sword before Barak
b and Sisera got down *(wayyiqtol)* from his chariot
c and he fled *(wayyiqtol)* on foot.
d 16. And Barak pursued *(qatal)* the chariotry and the camp all the way to Harosheth-ha-goiim
e and all the camp of Sisera fell *(wayyiqtol)* to the sword,
f not even one remained.
g 17. And Sisera fled *(qatal)* on foot to the tent of Jael, wife of Heber the Kenite, because there was a peace agreement between Jabin, king of Hazor, and the family of Heber the Kenite.

In v. 15, lines a through c, the initial outcome of the battle is recounted in a reasonably natural chronological order. A minor temporal break occurs at v. 16. Although the author has already mentioned that Sisera fled on foot, the storyteller returns to the main battle and picks up the continuing victory and rout of the chariotry. Then at v. 17, line g, the story switches back to the fleeing Sisera. Both of the breaks at 16 (line d) and 17 (line g) are marked by a *qatal* suffix verb with a subject in front of the verb. This is a regular use of the *waw-X-qatal* structure.

(2) Judg. 7:23-24

2a וַיִּצָּעֵק אִישׁ־יִשְׂרָאֵל מִנַּפְתָּלִי וּמִן־כָּל־מְנַשֶּׁה
b וַיִּרְדְּפוּ אַחֲרֵי מִדְיָן
c וּמַלְאָכִים שָׁלַח גִּדְעוֹן בְּכָל־הַר אֶפְרַיִם לֵאמֹר רְדוּ לִקְרַאת מִדְיָן . . .
d וַיִּצָּעֵק כָּל־אִישׁ אֶפְרַיִם
e וַיִּלְכְּדוּ אֶת־הַמַּיִם עַד בֵּית בָּרָה וְאֶת־הַיַּרְדֵּן

2a 23. And the men of Israel were called *(wayyiqtol)*, from Naphtali, Asher and all of Manasseh,
b and they pursued *(wayyiqtol)* Midian.
c 24. And Gideon sent *(qatal)* messengers to the whole hill country of Ephraim, saying,
    "Go down to Midian . . ."
d And all the men of Ephraim were called *(wayyiqtol)*
e and they captured the water-crossing up to Beth-bara and the Jordan.

The calling of the men from Ephraim apparently went on at the same time or slightly before the time that the men of Naphtali, Asher, and Manasseh made pursuit. The reason "messengers" is placed first in the v. 24 clause is not that "messengers" becomes the paragraph-level topic of the following events but that the storyteller wanted to mark the break in temporal succession from the previous verb, "they pursued." Also, the reason "messengers" is chosen over "Gideon" to begin the clause may have to do with the function of "calling" the men of Ephraim, which becomes an issue in 8:1ff.: the messengers carried out that calling.

Judges 19:10b–11a provides an example of a slightly different feature in marking temporal overlay.

(3) Judg. 19:10b–11a

3a	וַיָּקָם וַיֵּלֶךְ וַיָּבֹא עַד־נֹכַח יְבוּס ...
b	וְעִמּוֹ צֶמֶד חֲמוֹרִים חֲבוּשִׁים ...
c	הֵם עִם־יְבוּס
d	וְהַיּוֹם רַד מְאֹד
e	וַיֹּאמֶר הַנַּעַר אֶל־אֲדֹנָיו ...

3a 10b. And he came *(wayyiqtol)* to a point across from Jebus ...
 b and he had with him (no verb) a pair of donkeys ...
 c 11a. They were by Jebus (no verb)
 d and the day was far spent *(qatal,* whether *rad* or *yārad)*
 e And the lad said *(wayyiqtol)*, ...

Verse 11 is a *parenthetical* comment without "and." The *qatal* structure in the second clause of v. 11 (line d) makes it clear that the description of the day covered what *had already taken place* and does not communicate a new, additional temporal development.

In Judg. 6:21 is another twist to the marking of temporal overlay. I label it dramatic pause[2] (see, e.g., Buth 1987:64, 233, 479–80). In this construction *waw-X-qatal* can be used to mark a break in the chronology of the story at points where temporal succession is immediately assumed but the storyteller wants to create an effect of a temporal pause for dramatic effect.

(4) Judg. 6:21

4a	וַיִּשְׁלַח מַלְאַךְ יהוה אֶת־קְצֵה הַמִּשְׁעֶנֶת אֲשֶׁר בְּיָדוֹ
b	וַיִּגַּע בַּבָּשָׂר וּבַמַּצּוֹת
c	וַתַּעַל הָאֵשׁ מִן־הַצּוּר
d	וַתֹּאכַל אֶת־הַבָּשָׂר וְאֶת־הַמַּצּוֹת
e	וּמַלְאַךְ יהוה הָלַךְ מֵעֵינָיו

4a And the angel of Yhwh extended *(wayyiqtol)* the end of the staff in his hand
 b and he touched *(wayyiqtol)* the meat and unleavened bread
 c and fire went up *(wayyiqtol)* from the rock
 d and consumed *(wayyiqtol)* the meat and unleavened bread.

e   And the angel of Yhwh went *(qatal)* from his sight.

This is an instance of a single clause being used (probably) as a dramatic pause. The problem is knowing whether this clause is marked to stop the flow of the story for dramatic effect or marked perhaps as a mini-paragraph unit.[3] Beginnings of paragraphs may also continue the temporal succession of the story while marking discontinuity with the *waw-X-qatal* structure. Here, the potential usefulness of unit-marking seems slight while the surprise of the disappearing angel makes this an appropriate candidate for the dramatic (theoretically "marked") use of the marked (grammatically signaled) nonsequential clause structure.[4]

3. Grammatically unmarked overlay

By definition, when the temporal development of the story pauses and retreats but a *wayyiqtol* structure is used for the verb, then the grammar is not signaling the temporal overlay. As we look at examples of this phenomenon, we will notice two different ways in which the temporal overlay can be signaled outside of the grammar. One method is through lexical reference and/or repetition; the other method is based on culturally natural semantic relationships with the previous sentence. Example 5 comes from a temporally ordered prescription.

(5) Lev. 16:6–11

5a   וְהִקְרִיב אַהֲרֹן אֶת־פַּר הַחַטָּאת אֲשֶׁר־לוֹ
 b   וְכִפֶּר בַּעֲדוֹ וּבְעַד בֵּיתוֹ
 c   וְלָקַח אֶת־שְׁנֵי הַשְּׂעִירִם
 .   ...
 .
 i   וְהִקְרִיב אַהֲרֹן אֶת־פַּר הַחַטָּאת אֲשֶׁר־לוֹ
 j   וְכִפֶּר בַּעֲדוֹ וּבְעַד בֵּיתוֹ
 k   וְשָׁחַט אֶת־פַּר הַחַטָּאת אֲשֶׁר־לוֹ

5a 6. And Aaron will offer his sin-bull
 b and he will make atonement for himself and his house
 c 7. and he will take the two goats ...
 i 11. and Aaron will offer his sin-bull
 j and he will make atonement for himself and his house
 k and he will slaughter his sin-bull

In this outline of duties for the Day of Atonement the author consciously repeats details that have already been mentioned. The *wayyiqtol* system is used throughout for serial actions that are sequential. However, in v. 11 (lines i–j) the description returns to the identical actions of v. 6

(lines a–b). Here, the author not only refers to the same actions, he repeats every word exactly. This can be taken as an extreme case of "overlay."[5]

Not every word need be repeated in order to provide a lexical signal to a grammatically unmarked temporal overlay. The war of Benjamin in Judg. 20:31–47 provides many examples where one or two words suffice to signal to the reader that the author is going over the same material a second time, adding some details. (In order to conserve space only references of unmarked overlay to vv. 31–32 in this complicated battle description are listed here; for further discussion see Revell 1985:417–35.)

(6) Judg. 20:31–47

6a   וַיָּחֵלּוּ לְהַכּוֹת . . . כִּשְׁלֹשִׁים אִישׁ בְּיִשְׂרָאֵל
 b   וַיֹּאמְרוּ בְּנֵי בִנְיָמִן נִגָּפִים הֵם לְפָנֵינוּ . . .
 c   וּבְנֵי יִשְׂרָאֵל אָמְרוּ נָנוּסָה וּנְתַקְנֻהוּ . . .
 d   וְכֹל אִישׁ יִשְׂרָאֵל קָמוּ מִמְּקוֹמוֹ . . .

 e   וַיִּרְאוּ בְּנֵי־בִנְיָמִן כִּי נִגָּפוּ
 f   וַיִּתְּנוּ אִישׁ־יִשְׂרָאֵל מָקוֹם לְבִנְיָמִן . . .

 g   וַיֵּהָפֵךְ אִישׁ־יִשְׂרָאֵל בַּמִּלְחָמָה
 h   וּבִנְיָמִן הֵחֵל לְהַכּוֹת חֲלָלִים בְּאִישׁ־יִשְׂרָאֵל כִּשְׁלֹשִׁים אִישׁ

6a 31b. ... *struck* about *30 dead*
 b 32. and the men of Benjamin said, "They are *beaten* ..."
 c and meanwhile (normally signaled) the men of Israel said, "Let's flee and pull them away ..."
 d 33. and all the men of Israel had (normally signaled) left their *places*

 e 36. and the men of Benjamin saw that they [i.e., Israel, agreeing with Revell] were *beaten*... (referring to (b), v. 32)
 f and the men of Israel gave *place* to Benjamin ...

 g 39. and Israel turned in battle (referring to vv. 32 and 36)
 h and Benjamin began to *strike* about *30 dead* in Israel (marked contextualization as simultaneous to 39a, but the whole is a lexical back-reference to v. 31)

Verse 20:36 (6e) repeats "beaten" as a lexical clause referring to the same event of v. 32 (6b). In 6f, "gave place" reinforces this lexical reference by referring to 6d (v. 33), "had left their places." Even more complicated is v. 39 (6g and 6h): "turned in battle" does not repeat a lexical item but reports the same reversal of vv. 32 and 36. Then 6h reinforces this with the mention of "strike" and "dead" from v. 31 (6a). The back-reference between 6g and 6h is marked with a *waw-X-qatal* and the whole description ties into vv. 31–32 (6a–d) with lexical repetition of 6h.

Another kind of unmarked temporal overlay occurs when one sentence follows another sentence and, from the nature of the events, it is clear that the second sentence describes something that happened before the first sentence:

(7) Judg. 11:1-2

7a	וְיִפְתָּח הַגִּלְעָדִי הָיָה גִּבּוֹר חַיִל
b	וְהוּא בֶּן־אִשָּׁה זוֹנָה
c	וַיּוֹלֶד גִּלְעָד אֶת־יִפְתָּח
d	וַתֵּלֶד אֵשֶׁת־גִּלְעָד לוֹ בָּנִים
e	וַיִּגְדְּלוּ בְנֵי־הָאִשָּׁה
f	וַיְגָרְשׁוּ אֶת־יִפְתָּח

7a And Jephthah the Gileadite was a mighty soldier
 b and he was the son of a prostitute
 c and Gilead (had) fathered Jephthah;
 d and the wife of Gilead birthed sons for him
 e and the sons of the wife grew up
 f and they drove away Jephthah

In 11:1 (7c) Jephthah's father is mentioned; this obviously introduces a prior event. The back-referenced event here is mentioned with a structure that normally relates a "foregrounded" event of a narrative. Knowledge of the real world in v. 1 (7c) prevents any misunderstanding and guarantees that a nonsequential relationship is understood between the sentences a–b and c. This line begins a series of several events that the author introduces as part of the main storyline even though it is out of sequence with the introductory clauses a–b.

3.1 Sources and textual corruption

Not everyone is ready to accept that a function of unmarked temporal overlay existed for *wayyiqtol* in normative Hebrew.[6] Example 8 presents a sequence that resists an explanation from syntax or discourse analysis.

(8) (Judg. 14:14b–17)

8a	... וְלֹא יָכְלוּ לְהַגִּיד הַחִידָה שְׁלֹשֶׁת יָמִים
b	וַיְהִי בַּיּוֹם הַשְּׁבִיעִי וַיֹּאמְרוּ לְאֵשֶׁת־שִׁמְשׁוֹן פַּתִּי אֶת־אִישֵׁךְ
	[according to LXX: ... וַיְהִי בַּיּוֹם הָרְבִיעִי וַיֹּאמְרוּ
c	וַתֵּבְךְּ אֵשֶׁת שִׁמְשׁוֹן עָלָיו וַתֹּאמֶר רַק־שְׂנֵאתַנִי ...
d	וַיֹּאמֶר לָהּ הִנֵּה לְאָבִי וּלְאִמִּי לֹא הִגַּדְתִּי וְלָךְ אַגִּיד

e   וַתֵּבְךְּ עָלָיו שִׁבְעַת הַיָּמִים אֲשֶׁר־הָיָה לָהֶם הַמִּשְׁתֶּה

8a 14c. and they were not able to solve the riddle for three days
 b 15. and on the fourth (LXX, MT: seventh) day they said to Samson's wife, "Deceive your husband . . ."
 c 16. and Samson's wife came *(wayyiqtol)* to him in tears and said, "You hate me . . ."
 d and he said to her, ". . . I haven't even told my parents."
 e 17. And she came to him in tears for the seven days of the feast.

The natural understanding of "she wept"(c) is that she began whining and complaining to Samson after her compatriots requested her aid on the fourth day (or seventh day in MT). Yet the text says that she wept for the whole seven days of the feast (14:17). In order to fit the time together one might interpret this as "she had wept." But this removes any reason for mentioning the third and fourth days in vv. 14–15 (lines a–b). We are left with the conclusion that the text is probably corrupt.[7]

3.2 Hard evidence and other support for unmarked temporal overlay

How do we get evidence for the existence of unmarked temporal overlay as part of the system of the language? Internally, we can examine the attestations in the Hebrew text for consistency, limitation, and motivation of such a structure: *consistency* because that shows that the structure is part of the system of the language; *limitation* because "unmarked temporal overlay" is working against the common structures of the language (without some limitations the whole system would dissolve); *motivation* because Hebrew is a human language and there must be some communicative or psychological purpose for a structure to develop or be accepted beyond mere "static" or "background noise."

Confirmation can be sought in extrabiblical material. We will now look at a good example from the Moabite stone before discussing consistency, limitation, and motivation in the MT.

(9) The Moabite stone

9a   עמרי מלך ישראל
 b   ויענו את מאב ימן רבן
 c   כי יאנף כמש בארצה |
 d   ויחלפה בנה
 e   ויאמר גם הא
 f   אענו את מאב |
 g   בימי אמר כן
 h   וארא בה ובבתה |

i	וישראל אבד אבד עלם
j	וירש עמרי את ארץ מהדבה |
k	וישב בה ימה וחצי ימי בנה ארבען שת
l	וישבה כמש בימי |
m	ואבן את בעלמען
n	ואעש בה האשוח

9a (As for) Omri king of Israel,
 b and he tormented *(wayyiqtol)* Moab many days
 c   for Kemosh was angry with his land.
 d And his son succeeded *(wayyiqtol)* him
 e and he too said *(wayyiqtol)*,
 f   I will torment Moab.
 g It was in my time that he said this.
 h And I got *(wayyiqtol)* the victory over him and his house.
 i and Israel perished (*waw*-X-*qatal*—dramatic pause) forever
 j and Omri conquered *(wayyiqtol!)* the land of Mahdeba
 k and he dwelt *(wayyiqtol)* in it during his days and half of the days of his son, 40 years
 l And Kemosh returned *(wayyiqtol)* it in my days.
 m and I built *(wayyiqtol)* Baal-maon
 n and I made *(wayyiqtol)* the water-works in it . . .

Line j cannot be a suffix verb or an infinitive because there is no motivation for such structures. The verb is not habitual (the normal meaning of *weqatal* in narrative) and it is not continuing a description as normal *qatal* infinitive. Rather than posit in Moabite a unique function, otherwise unattested for *weqatal* in Hebrew, it is certainly better to group this Moabite example with a parallel Hebrew phenomenon, especially since it will be seen that this Moabite example is within the proposed bounds of *wayyiqtol* structures. The mention of Omri in line j returns the narrative to a generation before King Mesha and before the time when Moab subdued Israel. The *wayyiqtol* places the event as part of the mainline of the "narrative" even though this is the second time around.

3.3 Characteristics of unmarked overlay

In view of this outside evidence of the existence of unmarked overlay in the Moabite data, we now try to define the conditions in which it occurs and how to recognize it.

As for the "consistency" requirement (see sec. 3.2, first para.), that cannot be demonstrated in a short article. The grammars give purported examples scattered throughout the Hebrew Bible. Although I have concentrated on Judges, not even all those examples can be discussed.[8]

With "limitation" we are on firmer ground. Two limited environments for unmarked temporal overlay have already been mentioned:

(1) Some lexical redundancy or reference specifically points back to a previous event. The examples from the Moabite Stone, Judg. 20:31-47, and Lev. 16:7-11 fit this environment.

(2) From common cultural experience an event can be interpreted as giving a reason for comment on the immediately preceding events,[9] for example, Judg. 11:1 and Isa. 39:1, the account of the Babylonians' gifts to Hezekiah when they heard *(wayyiqtol)* that he had been sick and subsequently recovered.

(10) Isa. 39:1

a   בָּעֵת הַהִוא שָׁלַח מְרֹדַךְ בַּלְאֲדָן...סְפָרִים וּמִנְחָה אֶל־חִזְקִיָּהוּ
b   וַיִּשְׁמַע כִּי
c   חָלָה וַיֶּחֱזָק

a   At that time Merodach-Baladan ... sent Hezekiah letters and a gift
b   and he (had) heard that
c   he was sick and he recovered

Because we understand sympathy, the most appropriate understanding of the passage is that the news of Hezekiah's sickness and recovery prompted the gifts. Thus, translations regularly use a pluperfect, back-referencing tense and/or a causal connector in this verse.[10]

3.4 Motivation for the existence of unmarked overlay

Finally, we need to posit some motivation for unmarked overlay. Why would the language allow something to exist at cross-purposes with the regular syntax? For the present I can partially answer by observing the communicative effect that this structure might have and by recognizing the symmetry it forms within the narrative system.

With regard to communicative effect, we can say that in back-to-back sentences where the natural relationship of the events provides the proper understanding, the *wayyiqtol* clause is used to report its event as a mainline event. It is not used to mark a semantic relationship (e.g., "reason" or "grounds"). Nor is it used in a construction that breaks up the structure of the narrative with a structurally marked aside or parenthesis.

In cases where lexical reference or repetition signals a back-reference, again we can hypothesize that the author is primarily portraying mainline events with the *wayyiqtol* structure. The constraint of adding details to a passage without also demoting them off the mainline gives rise to this nonsequential use of the *wayyiqtol*. Thus, for both lexically signaled temporal overlay as well as semantically natural temporal overlay the *wayyiqtol* structure lifts a clause to the mainline without making another relationship prominent.

With regard to potential symmetry in the narrative system, a special nonsequential use of *wayyiqtol* presents a pragmatic reversal of normal semantic correlations. There is a similar pragmatic reversal for a sequential use of *waw*-X-*qatal*. *Waw*-X-*qatal* is normally used for marking a break in time or unit structure but extraordinarily it can, for dramatic effect, mark a sequential part of a unit as a "break in expectation" for the audience. This parallels unmarked overlay where a structure is also extraordinarily used. A structure normally marking sequence and connection is used to "normalize" a temporal break. Thus, *wayyiqtol* can be used where *waw*-X-*qatal* would be expected in order to pragmatically make the event a "normal" part of narrative foreground; *waw*-X-*qatal* can be used where *wayyiqtol* would be expected in order to pragmatically make the event a "pause."

So we have extrabiblical attestation, motivation, and a hypothesis about a limiting definition. This gives us something to work with until someone carefully collates all the narratives of the Hebrew Bible for this phenomenon.

3.5 The usefulness of the parameters for exegetical questions

Genesis 2 provides a nice test problem.[11] The differences in order of creation between Genesis 2 and Genesis 1 are well known and do not need elaboration here. The NIV (1978) apparently invoked a pluperfect *wayyiqtol* rule when translating 2:8 and 19, as seen in example 10.

(11) Gen. 2:8, 19

a   וַיִּטַּע יְהוָה אֱלֹהִים גַּן־בְּעֵדֶן מִקֶּדֶם וַיָּשֶׂם שָׁם אֶת־הָאָדָם אֲשֶׁר יָצָר . . .

b   וַיִּצֶר יְהוָה אֱלֹהִים מִן־הָאֲדָמָה כָּל־חַיַּת הַשָּׂדֶה וְאֵת כָּל־עוֹף הַשָּׁמַיִם וַיָּבֵא אֶל־הָאָדָם

a   8. Now the LORD God had [*sic*] planted a garden in the east . . .
b   19. Now the LORD God had [*sic*] formed out of the ground all the beasts of the field and all the birds of the air. He brought them to the man . . .

We must ask, Do these verses meet the criteria for unmarked temporal overlay? The answer, simply, is no. The verbs do not repeat lexical material to refer the reader back to an event that had already been

Methodological Collision between Source Criticism and Discourse Analysis 149

mentioned. There is no earlier נְטִיעָה 'planting' to refer to and there is no previous mention of a garden. Just the opposite is true. The mainline verb "and he formed man" in 2:7 explicitly happens in the midst of a background setting where there was not yet any plant life.

Similarly for v. 19 with יְצִירָה 'form'. This was not mentioned earlier, though one could claim that animals had been mentioned in chapter 1. Even with the animals, however, one does not find a back-reference to which this account in 2:19 can be considered an overlay.[12]

Looking at the question of a natural semantic relationship, we find that neither v. 8 nor v. 19 is readily perceivable as a reason or explanation of the immediately preceding sentences. We must read these verbs as normal sequential *wayyiqtol* verbs. Consequently, the NIV translation of Genesis 2 must be rejected from a discourse syntax perspective as a misuse of a poorly defined older syntax.

What is happening here is that the creation account is purposely told from two different perspectives in chapter 1 and chapter 2. There were certainly different sources but what is important is the final product. Chapter 2 is a kind of macro-overlay but the individual verbs in 2:8 and 2:19 are intended sequentially within that account. That is made clear at the beginning, 2:5-7, where some non-events provide the setting to the first mainline event, the creation of man. More precise grammar allows us to read the passage more accurately. We will avoid a superficial harmonization. On the positive side, we are led to interpreting whole stories as the author/redactor intended.

3.6 Exegetical help from unmarked overlay in Num. 21:25-31

In Numbers 21 the Israelite armies captured Heshbon and the surrounding area from the Amorites (21:24-25). However, in v. 26 the narrator begins to recount that the Amorites had previously taken the land from the Moabites and driven Moab south of the Arnon River. This previous war is explicitly marked with *waw-X-qatal*: וְהוּא נִלְחַם בְּמֶלֶךְ מוֹאָב 'and he (had) fought with the king of Moab'. Verses 27-30 then give a poetic victory quotation introduced with עַל־כֵּן יֹאמְרוּ הַמֹּשְׁלִים 'concerning this the speakers of wisdom used to say'. The question arises, Is this a victory song of the Amorites over Moab or of Israel over the Amorites? Translations and commentators split. The New Jerusalem Bible neatly gives both options in a footnote.[13] *La Bible en Français Courant* explicitly takes the Israelite victory-song interpretation at v. 30: "*Mais nous avons lancé nos flèches sur les Amorites* [But we have shot our arrows at the Amorites]." The Hebrew text, when read as a verb, says only וַנִּירָם 'we have shot *them*'.

Three reasons join together to suggest that the song was intended by the narrator to be seen as an Amorite song. First, the term הַמֹּשְׁלִים 'the speakers of wise-sayings/proverbs' is linked to non-Israelites in the context. Seven times a quotation of the Gentile Balaam is introduced by וַיִּשָּׂא מְשָׁלוֹ 'and he lifted up his wise-saying'. Second, it is difficult to see how an author could expect an audience to switch to an Israelite perspective in v. 30 after mentioning the Amorite victory over Moab in v. 29 without making something explicit. Someone may respond that an abrupt switch is necessary in v. 31 if an Amorite song is assumed. But this brings us to the third reason, namely unmarked overlay, which lends support to the Amorite interpretation. Verse 31 explicitly names Israel as the subject, something that would be expected if a switch from an Amorite perspective to an Israelite perspective takes place. What is more, we have an explicit repetition of vocabulary from 25b.

(12) Num. 21:25b, 31

a   וַיֵּשֶׁב יִשְׂרָאֵל בְּכָל־עָרֵי הָאֱמֹרִי . . .
b   וַיֵּשֶׁב יִשְׂרָאֵל בְּאֶרֶץ הָאֱמֹרִי

a   21:25b And Israel dwelt in all the cities of the Amorite . . .
b   21:31 And Israel dwelt in the land of the Amorite.

An overlay structure is somewhat rare but makes very good sense here. The timeline of the story had broken off at v. 26 where the narrator began to tell about earlier Amorite history. Then, explicitly in v. 31, he signals that he is returning to the time frame of v. 25 by repeating an almost identical statement. It would seem more probable that the author was thinking of the whole section, 21:26–30, as an intrusion and that in good Hebrew storytelling style he has "lexically" marked[14] the end of this with a an overlay. Thus, the whole song is more naturally understood as Amorite.[15]

3.7 Literary use of unmarked overlay in Judges 20

The long and complicated structure of the battle in Judg. 20:31–48 deserves special comment. First of all, it is not reasonable to assume that this is simply the result of a scissors and paste job from sources. The final redactor had to live with the outcome of his work and such a temporal "mess" cannot be satisfactorily explained unless we assume that unmarked overlay was an option within a narrator's repertoire.

If we recognize the option of unmarked overlay, we can proceed to more important questions: Why did the author choose this option so many times in Judges 20? Is there a literary effect that is generated? Is there something more going on than the foregrounding of a few verses or several layers of overlaying?

In the case of the Book of Judges we can explain the exuberance of unmarked overlay in Judg. 20:31-48 as a literary/grammatical imitation of the military and even moral confusion that the author attributed to that episode.[16] The destruction of Benjamin represents the last major piece of evidence against those people who only "did what was right in their own eyes." It was a lawless time and the complications of the unholy, fratricidal battle are highlighted by forcing the audience to untangle the scenes by using the subtle lexical clues of unmarked overlay. This may be included within a relevance theory framework (Sperber and Wilson 1986). The author demands extra grammatical processing energy from the audience for a battle that needs extra moral processing in order to sort out the good from the bad. Thus, there is a reason for the difficult writing. The difficulty of processing the battle description forces the audience to ask what the extra communication intentions are. The author did not want to present easy answers but wanted to force the audience to consider the moral complications. A more precise grammatical description points out a subtle device that contributes to an interpretation of the episode and that must be accounted for. The literary analysis of Judges benefits.

4. Conclusion

As we better understand Hebrew syntax and narrative technique, many passages that we once considered "corrupt" or "unacceptable narrative style" will be exonerated. Some passages, such as Genesis 2 and probably Judges 14, will resist harmonistic exegesis. In those cases the recognition of different sources or corrupted texts will be the more dependable. Exegesis, textual criticism, and larger literary concerns are all helped. Both the "positive" and "negative" results are necessary for better understanding the whole communication.

Notes

1. This is the generic use of the word *mark*. It means "to signal," "to explicitly show," not "special," "nondefault," "less common part of a pair," as in markedness theory. For Hebrew narrative the *wayyiqtol* structure is the "unmarked" structure (i.e., theoretically speaking, the common, default member of a pair) for mainline events, and *waw*-X-*qatal* is the theoretically "marked" structure in the sense of "special" and "nondefault," so the *waw*-X-*qatal* both marks (i.e., signals) the temporal discontinuity and is the (theoretically) marked structure within narrative. In this article "unmarked overlay" means "not grammatically signaled"—it is the generic use of *mark*.

2. I am preparing a separate study of this dramatic function of *waw*-X-*qatal* as seen in the following examples: Esther 7:6-8 (string of 5); Gen. 44:3-4 (string of 4); Gen. 19:23-25 (string of 3); Gen. 38:25 (string of 2 [the participial clause functions equivalently here]); 1 Sam. 4:11 (string of 2 [second clause is not sequential]); Moabite stone, line 7 (a single clause [see example 9i in this article]); Judg. 6:21 (single clause).

3. For example, Judg. 1:9 and 1:16 can be seen as sequential in time but breaking up the unit structure and beginning new units; 3:19 is apparently the same. The *waw*-X-*qatal* structures are used for discontinuities. The discontinuity can be one of temporal sequence or else of structure. A structural discontinuity breaks up the flow of the story and reinforces a unit boundary (beginning or end). See Gen. 37:36, though it also is nonsequential. A new unit can begin with a temporally sequential event. If an X-*qatal* structure is used, it breaks the "packaging" structure rather than the temporal sequence. (See Buth forthcoming *a, b*).

4. There is a pragmatic symmetry here with unmarked overlay (see 3.4).

5. J. Milgrom (1991:1024) calls this "resumptive repetition." See also Talmon (1978:9-26).

6. Waltke and O'Connor (1990:552-53) mention controversy. They allow a pluperfect as an extension of an epexegetical function (e.g., Num. 1:47-49; Exod. 4:11-12, 18 [Samaritan text]-19; 1 Kings 13:12). Driver is often cited against a pluperfect. When pressed, Driver allows *wayyiqtol* "to introduce a statement immediately suggested by a preceding word or phrase, ... or ... in the order in which it naturally presents itself ... or ... amplifying the preceding narrative ... At the beginning of a narrative ... there are ... reasons for presuming that the chronological principle is in abeyance" (1892:82, 89). He denied a "pluperfect": "Some of these apparent instances have arisen, doubtless, from the manner in which the Hebrew historical books are evidently constructed ... that [a circumstantial detail] ... is not equivalent to a true pluperfect is manifest" (88). Actually, Driver felt the need to do what I am here attempting. *Wayyiqtol* cannot be allowed to indiscriminately refer to any tense situation. There were strong restrictions that made the structure quite rare and these must be part of a grammatical description.

7. Alberto Soggin (1981:241) says, "The chronology of the episode is somewhat confused." If we change "the seven days" to שאר הימים or שאר שבעת הימים 'the remainder of the days/week', then we could get some sense out of the passage. The verbs for "weep" seem to have their normal sequential functions in this passage because the natural semantic relationship is one of sequence after the provocation of the men and because the weeping in v. 17 picks up and lexically refers back to the weeping of v. 16. Some doubt remains, though, because the reference to seven days could be said to allow the verb to override the grammar. But it is difficult to find a pragmatically satisfying purpose for the grammatical "unmarking" here. It is not satisfying as an overlay, because it isn't an overlay! Nor is it an upgrading

to foreground. See Y. Kaufman (1978:253-54) for a possible reconstruction and explanation.

8. There are examples of *wayyiqtol* in Judges with temporal irregularities, though they are not necessarily examples of unmarked overlay: Judg. 1:5, 8, 10, 34; 2:1 (mainline event after summary descriptions of chapter 1), 20, 21; 3:4, 7-8 (repeats 2:11-12, contrast 3:12), 10, 16?, (but not 23); 4:5b (habitual?), 21?; 6:2, 4 (habitual?), 5b (habitual?—probably not [see 2:18-21, 3:9]), 24?, 27 (ויעש 2), 35a, b, 40; 7:22, 25; 8:12; 9:56; 11:1; 14:16-17; 17:3, 4, 12; 18:17-18, 20 (cf. 27), 31 (cf. 30); 20:15, (31-47 above), 32, 36 (to 32), (37 is marked), 39 (to 33, 36), (41 is grammatically marked, and not related to ויהפך in 39), 45 (to 42), 46 (to 35), 47 (to 45, 42); 21:23-24. This does not include the *weqatal* problems like 3:23; 7:13; 16:18; or the numerous *waw-X-qatal* examples in various contexts.

9. This is part of what has been called "epexegetical" (cf. Waltke and O'Connor 1990:551-52).

10. Note the parallel in 2 Kings 20:12, כי שמע 'because he (had) heard', rather than a problematic *wayyiqtol*. Driver (1892:83) may have been right in supposing a textual corruption. However, 1QIs^a, from a time when Hebrew was still a living language, agrees with the MT. Together they accept the structure, and our grammatical system would do well to try to incorporate such data.

11. Judges 14:14-17 remains problematic and has been discussed above.

12. Long-range back-references are possible, as in Judg. 3:7: ויעשו בני־ישראל את־הרע בעיני יהוה 'The people of Israel did evil in the eyes of Yahweh'. Judges 3:7 lexically repeats 2:11. It refers to the same specific group of acts and resumes the narrative after a long digression. This is in contrast to Judg. 3:12, where different evil acts are referred to and the line reads, "The people of Israel again [lit.: added to do] did evil in the eyes of Yahweh." Judges 3:7 is a lexically signaled, grammatically unmarked temporal overlay. Such is not the case for Gen. 2:8 and 19.

13. *New Jerusalem Bible* at Num. 21:27 (in a footnote) says, "The poem, of which v. 30 is crucial and also corrupt, can be understood in two ways. 1) It is an Amorite victory-song celebrating Sihon's defeat of Moab, inserted as a commentary on v. 26b; though this requires more radical emendation of v. 30, which would then mean that Heshbon had destroyed Moab. 2) It is an Israelite song, introduced by vv. 25-26, celebrating Israel's victory over Sihon, vv. 27b and 30 (emended), but mentioning Sihon's victory over Moab to enhance the triumph, vv. 28-29: Heshbon devoured the towns of Moab, but we, the Israelites, have destroyed Heshbon. v. 27 would then be an ironic invitation to come and rebuild it."

14. Saʿadia Gaon (882-942 CE) seems to have recognized the recursion. He cryptically commented at 21:31, "וישב — וכאשר ישב 'And he dwelt' means 'and when he dwelt'."

15. The narrator might even have been surprised to know that moderns consider him ambiguous. Translators may be justified in making the partici-

pants clear. The idiom used in v. 27 for "the speakers of wise-sayings" should be used for introducing Balaam's poems and v. 30 can explicitly mention "Moabites" as the referent of "them."

16. This is a case of iconicity where the stylistic choice of grammar reinforces the thing signified.

References

Buth, Randall. 1987. Word order in Aramaic from the perspectives of functional grammar and discourse analysis. Ph.D. diss., UCLA. Ann Arbor, Mich.: University Microfilms.

———. Forthcoming *a*. Contextualizing constituent as topic, non-sequential background, and dramatic pause: Hebrew and Aramaic evidence. In *Selected papers from 4th Colloquium on Functional Grammar, Copenhagen, 1990.*

———. Forthcoming *b*. Functional grammar, Hebrew and Aramaic: An integrated, exegetically significant, textlinguistic approach to syntax. *Semeia Studies.*

Driver, Samuel R. 1892. *A treatise on the use of tenses in Hebrew.* 3d edition. Oxford: Clarendon.

Kaufman, Yehezkel. 1978. ספר שפטים מבואר [Book of Judges, explained]. 5th printing. Jerusalem: Kiryat-Sepher.

Milgrom, Jacob. 1991. *Leviticus 1–16.* Anchor Bible. Garden City: Doubleday.

Revell, E. J. 1985. The battle with Benjamin (Judges 20:29-48) and Hebrew narrative techniques. *Vetus Testamentum* 35:417-35.

Soggin, J. Alberto. 1981. *Judges.* Old Testament Library. Philadelphia: Fortress.

Sperber, Dan, and Deirdre Wilson. 1986. *Relevance: Communication and cognition.* Oxford: Blackwells.

Talmon, Sh. 1978. The presentation of synchroneity and simultaneity in biblical narrative. In *Studies in Hebrew Narrative Art Throughout the Ages*, ed. Joseph Heinemann and Shmuel Werses, pp. 9-26. Scripta Hierosolymitana, 27. Jerusalem: Magnes.

Waltke, Bruce, and Michael O'Connor. 1990. *An introduction to Biblical Hebrew syntax.* Winona Lake, Ind.: Eisenbrauns.

6

A DISCOURSE PERSPECTIVE ON THE SIGNIFICANCE OF THE MASORETIC ACCENTS

Lars Lode

> First the main structures of Biblical Hebrew narrative paragraphs and episodes are briefly presented here, and then the structure and function of the Tiberian accentuation. The end notes present exhaustive data on the distribution in text and the values for each marker in Genesis. The conclusion is that all of the disjunctive accents indicate prominence on the levels of sentence, paragraph, episode, and discourse, except for the most frequent ones, namely Silluq, Atnach, Tifcha, Little Zaqef, and Pashta.

Most Old Testament scholars, both traditional and modern, do not pay much attention to the Masoretic accents. The vast majority of us were taught not to pay any attention to them, or at most we have learned to recognize the middle of a verse by the accent Atnach, the upside-down v-shaped accent which occurs under the last word of the first half of the verse. Some of us have studied the Table of Accents inserted in our Biblia Hebraica, but few of us retain all their names, and rare are those who make constant use of the accents in their study and teaching—except for the rabbis.

The rabbis are right. The Masoretic accents do have meaning. If they are overlooked, we shall miss important parts of the message of the text.

The accents are indicators of the appropriate intonation to be used when reading the sacred texts. This has become stylized in the cantillation of the texts in the synagogue.

But the accents have another function as well. The disjunctive accents are indicators of syntactical breaks within the verse. The generally accepted point of view among Jewish scholars is that of repeated dichotomy. That is, each verse is first divided in two parts by the first cut, usually after Atnach; then each half-verse will be cut in two by the next dichotomy, usually after Little Zaqef; and so on until the entire verse has been sufficiently parsed. The cuts have to be made according to fairly intricate rules, according to which accents occur in the verse.

This point of view has several deficiencies. First, it is rather cumbersome to learn the rules as to where to make the next cut. Second, the cuts do not always correspond to the semantic and syntactic breaks. Third, it takes into consideration only the structure of the verse. For a punctuation system it is rather awkward from a European point of view. And why have as many as eighteen disjunctive markers? After all, English can cope with seven (,;.:!?—), eight if you count parentheses.

In approaching the problem of the Masoretic accents, I have used the same general linguistic method of analysis that has been used by linguists analyzing hundreds of languages all over the world. I myself have used it to analyze the phonologies of several African languages in terms of a hierarchy of several levels, each with a number of different units, and each unit with its particular structural variations and functions. The result of applying it now to Biblical Hebrew is a simple and interesting system.

This is the system presented in this article. It confirms the validity of the traditional main breaks in demonstrating that they are systematic. The essential new element here is the indication that the rarer accents have semantic overtones of focus and emphasis in addition to their traditionally recognized disjunctive value.

In sections 1 and 2 the Hebrew grammatical and phonological structures and the terms I use for them will be presented; and then, in section 3, the structure of the Biblical Hebrew intonational system, represented by the Masoretic accents and, some of its functions. Finally, section 4 treats the functions of the highlighting intonations. (Unless indicated otherwise, the references are from Genesis.)

1. Grammatical terms

Most of the grammatical terms that will be used here are rather traditional: word, phrase, clause, sentence. A phrase is one or more words having a certain function within a clause (e.g., subject phrase, object phrase). A clause is a unit that has one predicate, either verbal or nonverbal. (These terms are not used as in generative grammar or immediate constituents theory.)

The grammatical terms *paragraph* and *episode* need some explanation. A paragraph consists of one or more sentences, an episode of one or more paragraphs. The semantic characteristic of a paragraph is that of interaction, with such relationships as cause-effect, reason-result, etc. A particular type of interaction characterizes *dialogue:* question-answer, proposal-response, and remark-evaluation. These terms have been defined by Longacre (1976, chaps. 3-4) and were first applied to Hebrew by him (1979) and Buth (1977).

Longacre posits five different elements in repartee paragraphs, namely setting, initiating utterances, continuing utterances, resolving utterances, and terminating utterances (1976:165-97). It seems to me that any narrative paragraph may have these five different kinds of constituents, which I prefer to call setting, onset, falling reaction, rising reaction, and conclusion. Onset, reactions, and conclusion constitute deep-level event spans within the paragraph.

An *event span* is a unit characterized by one or more predications attributed to a single referent. Formally, an event span is usually encoded as a sentence.

Setting is background material: temporal relations, circumstances, etc. *Onset* is an animate initiative or an event that triggers reactions.

A *falling reaction* is an event that normally follows an onset; for example, after a host says, "Come in," the visitor enters. It is the expected reaction. This is what Longacre (1976:170) calls a resolving utterance. In this case, though, the resolving "utterance" is nonverbal. Therefore I prefer the more general term *reaction*.

A *rising reaction* is an unexpected or undesired response to an onset. Within a paragraph, it is a complication; for example, a boy says to his friend, "Let's go downtown," and the friend says, "No, I want to stay here."

A *conclusion* closes a paragraph, either by an event indicating the success or frustration of the onset or rising reaction, or by a consecutive event which brings the interchanges to an end. Such a conclusion may often be impressive. For example, a lad crashed his new car (setting). "I'll buy you a new one," his father said (onset). And so he did! (conclusion).

In Biblical Hebrew, onsets and conclusions are usually marked by particular phonological features. Rising reactions have strong markers. Falling reactions are left unmarked. A paragraph-initial setting is often marked phonologically as it introduces a new paragraph. A paragraph-medial setting may be marked if the speaker has particular reasons for doing so.

Paragraphs may be manifested as a sequence of grammatical sentences, one for each event span. Conversely, two or more event spans may be squeezed into one sentence, one event span being marked as focused by being presented in the main clause or clauses, the other event span(s) being marked as less prominent by being presented in subordinate clauses.

A Biblical Hebrew episode in narrative consists of one or more paragraphs. There are different types, the most frequent being the sequential and the thematic. A thematic episode typically has an initial topic sentence or topic paragraph indicating its theme. Then the body develops the theme, and finally there may be a concluding paragraph. A sequential episode is just a string of paragraphs united by a single setting and topic (see Lode forthcoming).

Expository discourse is different structurally in that states are described. Since there are no events in an expository discourse, there will be no interaction of events; therefore such texts may well lack the level of paragraph. Paragraph and episode structures in procedural and hortatory texts in Biblical Hebrew have not been described, so my indications in such contexts should be considered highly tentative.

2. Phonological terms

Each language has its own number of significant levels in the phonology. In most languages there is something like phonological words. They may be marked by word stress as in Biblical Hebrew, or by other features.

Very often one or several words combine into a phonological phrase. In some languages the end is marked by a short pause, in other languages by intonation or some other feature. It is also common to find something like a phonological clause, corresponding more or less to a grammatical clause, a single predication.

Phonological sentences are common. They correspond more or less to grammatical sentences.

Finally, it is fairly common to find a rank above sentence. The phonological paragraph will have its own characteristic features.

In no language that I know of have I ever heard of an absolute correlation between the grammatical and phonological hierarchies. There tends to be only approximate correspondence between the levels in the two hierarchies. It is by using this close correspondence or by "skewing" that each language creates its own dynamics.

All phonological levels may exhibit *contour* and *precontour*. Contour is a turning point usually marked by a musical motif, either rising, falling, sustained, or otherwise discernible. A precontour is the part of the unit that precedes the contour. The precontour, unlike the contour, usually varies little in pitch or stress from syllable to syllable. In a Biblical Hebrew word, the stressed syllable has the contour; in a Biblical Hebrew phrase, the dividing accent marks the contour.

3. The Tiberian Hebrew intonational system

The Tiberian Hebrew intonational system may be described in terms of the following levels: period, sentence, descent, clause, phrase, and word. There is usually a rather loose connection between the grammatical and the phonological hierarchies. For example, Gen. 1:1 contains one simple grammatical sentence. Genesis 1:8 contains two complete sentences. In 1:17-18 the first sentence is distributed over two verses, and 18b contains a complete sentence. Genesis 10:26-29 consists of two sentences, and vv. 27-28 contain only parts of a long object phrase. That is, the skewing between phonology and syntax may be very extensive.

3.1 The phonological word and phrase

The phonological word in Biblical Hebrew consists either of one single grammatical word or of two or more grammatical words joined by Maqqef. The contour is marked by an accent, either conjunctive or disjunctive.

The phonological phrase consists of one or more phonological words. The phrase contour is marked by a disjunctive accent. All immediately preceding conjunctive accents belong to the phrase precontour. This is just another way of describing the distinction between the conjunctive and the disjunctive accents and should need no further comment.

3.2 The phonological period

The largest phonological unit in the Tiberian system seems to be the Masoretic verse. It has been marked phonologically by the final Silluq contour, and graphically by the Silluq accent and the final Soph Pasuq.

3.3 The phonological sentence

There is common consensus that most verses are composed of two main parts: that one ending by Atnach and the final one ending by Silluq. We shall call the two parts the Atnach sentence and the Silluq sentence. These two halves correspond very often to grammatical sentence breaks, but skewing may be considerable, as already mentioned.

Now there are quite a number of verses containing only the "Silluq sentence." They contain the initial or final setting in episodes, details in long lists, or, occasionally, episode-climax paraphrase. An episode-initial case occurs in 2:1: "And was completed the heaven and the earth and all their hosts." An episode conclusion occurs in 1:13: "And became evening and became morning, third day." In 10:16-17 there are new names added to the list of the sons of Canaan. All this is setting and expositional material. In Genesis 1-18 I have noted thirty-eight cases of no Atnach, only two of which occur in a climactic context.[1]

On the other side, the Segolta intonation marks the introduction to a climax, and the text following Segolta contains the climax, as in 3:14:

"And said Yahweh God to the snake, 'Because you did this (Segolta), cursed are you.'" The introductory material may continue until the Atnach contour, as in 3:17, "To the man he said, 'Because you listened to your wife (Segolta) and ate of the tree about which I said, "Do not eat of it" (Atnach), cursed be the land on account of you.'" There is always high tension where Segolta is used. I have noted seventy-six cases of Segolta in Genesis, all of which occur at climaxes or complications in the texts.[2]

Verses with Segolta and those without Atnach occur in complementary contexts; there is, therefore, good reason to say that Segolta marks the end of a phonological sentence, just as Atnach and Silluq do. The presence of only one phonological sentence in the period indicates that it contains background material. The presence of two sentences in the period is neutral. The presence of three sentences indicates a complication or a climax.

3.4 The phonological clause

There is a fair degree of consensus that Zaqef usually is the accent of the strongest disjunctive value in the Silluq and Atnach phonological sentences; and before Zaqef and Segolta, the Revia usually ranks highest. These accents are what I call the markers of "phonological clauses" within the sentences of Silluq, Atnach, and Segolta.

A phonological clause ends with Revia, Zaqef, Segolta, Shalsheleth, Atnach, or Silluq. These accents indicate different clause contours. The clause precontour consists of all preceding phrases back to the previous clause contour. For example, the Little Zaqef may be preceded by one to three phonological phrases marked by Pashta or Yetiv, Revia may be preceded by one or two Legarmeh phrases, Segolta may be preceded by three Zarqa phrases, and Silluq and Atnach may be preceded by a Tifcha phrase and one or two Tevir phrases preceding the Tifcha phrase.

Thus there is a common system: The clause contour phrases may be preceded by two or three precontour phrases, and each clause contour has its characteristic precontour accents. Great Zaqef and Shalsheleth have no precontour phrases.

What then about Pazer, Telisha, and Geresh? They do not belong to any particular phonological clause. They may precede any of the above clauses as "Extra Precontour."

The clauses with their contour and precontour are displayed in the following table. As in Hebrew, the table should be read from right to left.

A Discourse Perspective on the Significance of the Masoretic Accents

Clause contour	Clause precontour		
Revia	Legarmeh	Legarmeh	
Little Zaqef	Pashta (Yetiv)	Pashta (Yetiv)	Pashta
Great Zaqef	none		
Segolta	Zarqa	Zarqa	Zarqa
Shalsheleth	none		
Atnach	Tifcha	Tevir	Tevir
Silluq	Tifcha	Tevir	Tevir
any	Geresh/Garshayim	Telisha	Pazer Pazer

There are some variations. Shalsheleth occurs instead of Segolta under certain phonological circumstances, and the alternation between Pashta and Yetiv is also based on purely phonological grounds. The difference between Little and Great Zaqef is, however, not purely phonological, as even little Zaqef may occur alone in its clause, as in 32:23.

The opinion that Revia might be a transformation of Pashta or vice versa has been completely abandoned. They have different musical motifs and essentially different discourse functions.

3.5 The phonological descent

The aforementioned elements do not occur in random order. Within Silluq and Atnach sentences, the Extra Precontour accents usually precede, followed by Revia clause, Zaqef clause, and finally the Silluq or Atnach clause. This is what I shall call a "complete descent," as the relative pitch level of these clauses seems to be falling towards the end (Yeivin 1980:§195 and Derenbourg 1870:383, 476, 483-89). The Segolta sentences may not have Zaqef clauses. Any deviations from this general pattern will be treated later. This system is presented in the following table:

Silluq sentence may contain	Atnach sentence may contain	Segolta sentence may contain
Extra Precontour	Extra Precontour	Extra Precontour
Revia clause	Revia clause	Revia clause
Zaqef clause	Zaqef clause	Segolta clause
Silluq clause	Atnach clause	

All of these descents may be complete, and any of the elements may be skipped. For example, in a Silluq sentence there may be only the Silluq clause as in 2:1, or only Extra Precontour plus Silluq clause as in 4:3; there may be Revia clause plus Silluq clause as in 2:4, or Zaqef clause + Silluq clause as in 1:2.

Like a phonological descent, which consists of one or more phonological clauses, a sentence also consists of one or more descents. It is especially important to remember that a sentence may have more than one descent where Zaqef clauses occur in sequence.

For example, in the Atnach sentence of 2:19, the first descent consists of one Revia clause and one Little Zaqef clause and the second descent consists of one Zaqef clause and the Atnach clause. It reads: "Yahweh God had shaped from the earth (Revia) every beast of the field and every bird of the air (Zaqef)/ Now he brought them to the man (Zaqef) to see what he would call them (Atnach)." (The break between the descents has been indicated by a slash [/].) The main syntactic break within the phonological sentence is between the descents, at the end of the first Zaqef clause. Thus the first Zaqef will be associated with a stronger disjunction than the second one. (Further details may be found in broader presentations.)

Now the well-informed reader will have a question in mind: What about the cases where the accentuation goes from a lower to a higher pitch level (e.g., from Pashta to Revia)? That is what I call a rising intonation, which we will now consider.

3.6 The rising intonation

A descent may be broken somewhere in the Extra Precontour, in a Revia or in a Zaqef clause. Then the intonation rises to a higher level and redescends from there. In all cases such breaks occur in particular contexts that seem to be calling for attention.

The rising intonation may occur on a prominent circumstance, a prominent event, or a prominent item. Or it may indicate strong emotions. The former is what K. Callow (1974:49-68) calls *focus*; the emotive element she calls *emphasis*. Since theoreticians define these two terms differently, I will stick to her definitions. According to her own use, the emphasis type is essentially a marker of speaker-hearer relationship and indicates emotions such as "I feel strongly about this!" or "You didn't expect this, did you?!" The focus type indicates "This is important!"

In my view, there are four main categories of emphasis, namely insistence, positive and negative emotions, impressive events, and unexpected events. These categories tend to overlap, so my identification of a category is fairly tentative in many cases. However, even a tentative categorization allows us to see more of the tendencies in the data. (All occurrences of emphasis in Genesis are listed in note 3.)

3.6.1 Emphasis showing insistence

Rising intonation is often used at the start of a quotation to indicate insistence, as in 1:9 where the quotation verb has Revia and the following quotation has Extra Precontour, Zaqef, and Atnach clauses: "And God said: (Revia, rising to Geresh) 'Let the waters gather from under the heaven to one place so that the dry land become visible.'" In 1:24 there is a similar example: "And God said: (Revia, rising to Geresh) 'Let the earth bring forth living creatures according to their kind; cattle and creeping creatures and wild game according to their kinds.'" A third example occurs in 1:29.

3.6.2 Emphasis showing emotions, positive and negative

Insistence may be combined with emotions that are kind/happy, or sad/angry, or tense/afraid. In 15:5 the intonation rises from Pashta to Revia. It is combined with a positive attitude. "And he led him out and said/ 'Now look to the sky and count the stars if you can.'"

In 27:37 there are two cases of rising intonation in a sentence that is very emotive. The sad emotions are obvious. "And Isaac spoke to Esau saying/ (Revia to Garshayim) 'Behold, I have made him your lord/ (Pashta to Revia) and all his brothers I have given to him for servants.'" Regardless of which element is predominant (insistence, positive or negative emotions), the element of insistence is almost always present.

3.6.3 Emphasis showing an impressive or unexpected event

Emphasis with rising intonation is far less frequent for the purpose of showing an impressive event or an unexpected event[3] than for showing insistence.

3.6.4 Focus showing relatively more prominence[4]

Rising intonation may be used to mark transition from a setting to the real thing (background to foreground, or setting to onset) as in 25:27. "And the boys grew up, (Zaqef to Revia) and Esau became a hunter, a man of the bush, and Jacob a domestic man." In English we might handle this by making the first clause a subordinate temporal one: "When the boys grew up, Esau became a hunter, whereas Jacob became a domestic man." What English handles by grammar Biblical Hebrew very often handles by phonology.

In 6:9 the transition between the Toledot title and the following text is similarly marked: "This is the book of Noah. (Zaqef to Revia) Noah was a righteous man." In this case both English and Biblical Hebrew mark the transition by phonology. Another example occurs in 26:8.

Rising intonation may also be used to indicate transition to a more prominent clause in the sentence, as in 20:9, where it rises from Revia to Extra=Geresh. "And Abimelech called for Abraham (Revia to Geresh) *and said to him*: 'What have you done to us, and how have I sinned against you, as you have brought over me and over my kingdom a great sin.'" Strong emotions are also involved, but they have been indicated by other means, reversed postverbal word order (Lode 1984 and 1989) and emphatic stress (Lode forthcoming). A similar case is found in 30:32. "Let me pass through your flock today (Revia to Extra) removing from it every speckled and spotted sheep." A corresponding example occurs in 32:23.

Rising intonation may also be used to indicate a climactic event span within a paragraph chain of events as in 18:19. "Because I have revealed myself to him (Revia to Extra) in order that he instruct his sons and his house after him, that they keep the way of Yahweh."

The rising intonation may also be used to introduce a new subject that the speaker thinks is more interesting. Pharaoh does this in 47:6 when the father and brothers of Joseph arrive in Egypt. "Let them stay in Goshen. (Zaqef to Revia) And if you know among them any capable men, you shall put them in charge of my cattle."

All the evidence in Genesis of focus on mainline elements indicated by rising intonation is presented in note 4.

3.6.5 Focus or emphasis on a prominent circumstance[5]

Rising intonation occurs on important circumstances within simple sentences. Genesis 25:20, "And Isaac was 40 years/ (Zaqef to Revia) *when he took Rebecca for wife*," is an example. It is a case of focused circumstance.

A similar example is found in 6:4, rising from Revia to Extra: "The Nefilim were on the earth in those days and even after/ (Rise) when the sons of God came in to the daughters of men, and they bore children to them." (This is probably a case of emphasis, indicating the disapproval of the accentuator.)

In 8:21 there are two examples of rising intonation, the first indicating insistence in the beginning of a quotation, the second one indicating an important circumstance within it. "Yahweh said to himself/ (Revia to Extra) 'Never more will I curse the earth on account of the man/ (Zaqef to Extra) for the thoughts of man are evil from his youth.'" Sad emotions are attached to this circumstance.

3.6.6 Focus on a prominent participant or item[6]

In some cases rising intonation seems to mark an important participant, for example Noah in 5:29. "And he called him Noah, saying: 'This/one (Geresh to Telisha) shall bring us relief.'" In 1:11 "fruit tree" is marked by rising from Revia to Extra; in 1:12 the rising intonation occurs on the main word of an object phrase before a long apposition. Is the rising intonation in 1:11 already alluding to the forbidden fruit of chapters 2–3?

4. The functions of the highlighting intonations

We have seen that rising intonation indicates focus or emphasis. But most of the disjunctive accents do the same even without the rising intonation. The larger context must often be studied to understand the highlighting overtones. The only disjunctives that appear to be neuter are the most frequent ones, namely Silluq, Atnach, Tifcha, Little Zaqef, and Pashta.

That the Segolta sentences always introduce some kind of climax or complication, sometimes in an event span, but more often in a paragraph, an episode, or a discourse has already been mentioned (see note 2). Segolta is a strong focus marker and always has emotional overtones.

Further, Great Zaqef seems to indicate strong emotions. The emotions may be positive or negative, but always strong.[7]

Tevir indicates less prominence, usually with both focus and emphasis value simultaneously. It has a relatively high concentration in contexts that indicate weak emotions, either positive or negative.[8]

The Extra accents (Geresh, Telisha, Pazer) may occur initially in any descent. They indicate a fairly sharp prominence.[9] The more Extra accents, the stronger the prominence. These accents may be used either for focus or emphasis, or both simultaneously.

The Revia is in the middle. It is neither very strong, nor weak, nor sharp. It is used mainly for focusing purposes, indicating the onset of a new, important section of the text, usually more important than the preceding one. It may also focus on participants, and it may be used for focusing on circumstances.[10] The Revia often has emphatic overtones, usually insistent or impressive.

It is interesting to see, in the notes, where these accents do occur. It is even more interesting to see where they never occur. For example, in interaction chains of paragraphs, they may occur on the initial setting, they usually occur on onsets, they often occur on conclusions, they always occur on rising reactions (climaxes), but they never occur on falling reactions. That is, they are obligatorily present for marking the tension of the rising reactions, and they are obligatorily absent on the tensionless falling reactions. This same pattern of presence on high points and absence on low points is fairly clear also on the levels of sentence and episode. Not all the evidence in Genesis is presented in the end notes, but what is not presented shows the same pattern.

As may be seen from the notes, there are no limited contexts where one might expect only a certain highlighting accent and not any of the others. All of them may be used for positive and negative emotions, for focus and for emphasis. It seems that the choice is connected with the intended degree of prominence: weak, sharp, or strong. And as they do co-occur quite frequently, any desired combination may be obtained.

The range of the focus is usually one grammatical sentence, or from the beginning of the focusing intonation to the end of the phonological sentence. Occasionally it may be a single word. Emotional emphasis is rarely longer than a clause. Emotions indicated by Great Zaqef seem to be an exception as the range is usually of focus length (see note 7).

5. Conclusion

The Tiberian accents form an intonational system that is a hierarchy of five levels: the phonological word, marked by any accent; the phonological phrase, marked by disjunctive accents; the clause, marked by Revia, Zaqef, Segolta, Atnach, or Silluq; the descent, marked by descending pitch levels of clauses; the sentence, marked by Segolta, Atnach, or Silluq; and the phonological period, marked by Silluq. The Extra Precontour accents (Pazer, Telisha, and Geresh) may occur initially in any descent.

Only the intonations Silluq, Atnach, Tifcha, Little Zaqef, and Pashta are neutral. They may be used in any type of context. They mark syntactic breaks and indicate progression in the text, but they carry no further overtones. The other disjunctive accents represent intonations that indicate overtones of focus or emphasis in addition to their value as syntactic markers.

Rising intonation within a phonological sentence indicates prominence, with either focus value or emphasis value, or the two combined. There is no evidence of any interrogative intonation such as the rising final intonation in colloquial Jordanian Arabic (e.g., *Hal torid shay?* 'Do you want tea?').

Notes

1. Verses without Atnach in Genesis 1-18 contain episode-initial setting in 2:1; 8:15; 9:8; 13:1; 25:1; episode-final setting in 1:13, 19, 23; 3:21; 6:8; 12:9; 21:34; conclusion in 19:36; paragraph conclusion in 21:24; paragraph-initial setting in 21:9, 28; 22:4; paragraph-reaction setting in 23:5, 7, 12, 14.

Episode-medial details: new expositional paragraph in 10:13, 15; 21:3; 25:5; restriction in 9:4; continuing list of names in 10:14, 16, 17, 27, 28; 15:19, 20, 21; 25:14, 15.

The only climactic context is episode climax paraphrase in 7:22 and 14:11.

2. Segolta or Shalshelet occur immediately before event span climax in 3:3; 24:7, 12; 27:33; 28:16; 29:8; 37:22; 39:8, 9; 42:16, 25; 43:18. In 47:4, the climax occurs after Atnach.

Segolta occur before interaction climax in 3:17; 8:21; 19:16; 26:28; 30:20; 37:10; 47:17; 50:5. The climax is delayed till after Atnach in 3:17 and 24:30.

Segolta occur on episode theme in 43:11; before or introducing episode or discourse complication or climax in 1:7, 28; 2:23; 3:14; 6:4; 14:17; 16:5; 17:20; 19:4; 20:13; 21:17; 22:9; 23:16; 24:15, 47; 27:30; 28:13; 29:33, 34; 30:16, 40, 41; 31:32, 41; 32:10; 34:30; 36:6; 37:25; 38:18; 41:45; 42:21, 34; 43:16, 29, 34; 44:1, 4, 18; 45:9; 46:20; 47:1, 11, 15, 18, 29; 48:13, 16, 20. The climax is delayed till after Atnach in 19:19. Conclusions are in 28:6; 36:39; 39:6.

3. Rising intonation occurs on the unexpected part of the event span in 24:30; 26:8; 32:23; 34:25; and on the event span or longer in 21:22.

An attitude of insistence on a word/phrase is marked by rise after Revia in 6:4; 23:19; 24:7; 35:3; 37:2a; 45:8; rise after Little Zaqef in 1:11; 22:8; 24:27; 25:20; 38:25; after other accents in 1:12; 5:29; 9:12; 17:19; 38:12b.

An attitude of insistence on a clause is marked by rise after Revia in 8:21a; 18:19; 27:37a; 29:2; 30:32; 37:4; 43:23; after Little Zaqef in 6:17; 8:21b; 27:23; 37:2b; 40:16; 43:32; 44:26; 47:9; 50:20; after others in 24:21 and 32:21.

An attitude of insistence on a part of the event span is found in 25:27; 26:7; 27:37b; 31:5; 43:27; on the event span after Revia in 1:24, 29; 15:13; 16:8; 18:6; 19:2; 31:43; 37:14; 46:34; 50:17; after Little Zaqef in 20:11; 22:3; 37:9; after some others in 15:5; insisting on interaction chain in 1:9; 16:2; 20:16; 26:22b; 47:6, 19.

Rising intonation expressing anger/sadness is found in 3:5; 20:9; 35:19; 39:14; 48:7; tension/fear in 26:7; 38:12a; 41:8; 42:28; 43:29; 47:1; kindness/happiness in 7:7; 13:1; 26:22a; 21:14.

4. Rising intonation after Geresh occurs at the start of the list in 13:1 and on the event-span climax in 21:14.

After Revia it occurs on the list climax in 7:7; event-span climax in 20:9; 30:32; 32:23; 42:28; 43:29; interaction onset in 38:12a; 48:7; conclusion in

18:19; higher-level onset in 50:16; theme in 1:9, 24, 29; 8:21; 15:13; 18:6; 19:2; 20:16; 27:37a, b; 31:43; 37:14; 45:8; 46:34; 47:1; climax in 34:25; 43:23. After Pashta it occurs on event-span climax in 27:37b; episode theme in 15:5. After little Zaqef on event-span climax in 22:3; 43:27; 47:9; conclusion in 25:27; 50:20; interaction onset in 26:8; 41:8; climax in 26:22; conclusion in 6:17; 26:7; higher-level theme in 21:22; 27:9; 38:25; 39:14; 40:16; climax in 37:9; 47:6, 19.

Rising intonation after Great Zaqef occurs on event-span climax in 32:21 and conclusion in 24:21.

5. Rising intonation occurs on a prominent circumstance in a clause in 25:20; in event spans in 6:4 and 20:1; in interaction in 27:23 and 43:32; in higher levels in 3:5; 8:21; 9:12; 16:2; 24:7, 27; 26:22; 29:2; 37:2b, 4; 44:26.

6. Rising intonation marks participants which are prominent agents in event spans in 31:52 and 38:12b, and in higher levels in 5:29; 6:9; 17:19; 22:8; 37:2a. It marks theme in a clause in 24:30 and in event spans in 1:12 and 16:8. It marks prop in higher levels in 1:11; 23:19; 35:3, 19.

7. Great Zaqef without Tevir in the descent occurs on unexpected word/phrase in 22:13; part of event span in 5:24; event span in 26:26 and 47:22; impressive word/phrase in 4:22; 13:2; 21:2; 26:18; 33:1; 41:46; 46:5; 47:8; clause in 14:7; 32:30; part of event span in 4:20, 21; event span in 5:6; 7:6; 16:16.

An attitude of insistence is with a word/phrase in 8:3; 9:4, 17; 17:23; 22:17; 23:8, 16; 39:20; 40:3; 41:10, 16; part of event span in 12:7; 22:16, 18; 31:50; 41:27; 44:9, 17; event span or longer in 6:15; 17:11; 20:4; 24:16, 56; 26:5; 37:6; 38:17b; 42:11, 16; 43:4; 44:5, 26; 45:1; 50:4.

An emotion of anger/sadness is with a word/phrase in 2:9; 4:2; 9:18; 50:20; part of event span in 2:20; 3:24; 12:18, 19:9; 30:15; 31:1; 35:22; 37:20b, 35; event span or longer in 3:11; 9:26; 12:14, 19; 27:35; 31:35; 34:31; 37:23; 38:14; 39:10; 42:12, 38; 44:28.

An emotion of tension/fear is with a word/phrase in 20:46; 24:21; 40:9; 41:17; clause in 41:53; part of event span in 24:12; 37:20a; event span or longer in 3:10; 8:6; 12:11; 16:8; 20:4b; 21:30; 24:8, 49; 27:19, 20, 24, 36; 33:5a, 5b, 8b; 37:16, 21; 38:29; 39:18; 41:9; 42:2; 43:14; 44:2, 10, 12, 17; 46:33; 50:16.

An emotion of kindness/happiness is with a word/phrase in 24:24, 60; 33:9; 45:10; clause in 20:4a; part of event span in 8:13; 9:23; 24:31; 26:24; 29:10; 30:7; 45:27; event span or longer in 4:1; 5:32; 6:8; 9:13, 14; 14:16; 17:4a, 4b; 21:6; 24:46; 26:24; 27:2; 30:13, 23; 39:2; 41:1; 43:29; 46:3, 4; 47:30; 48:9.

Great Zaqef with Tevir in the descent occurs on impressive word/phrase in 41:38 and on event span or longer in 5:18 and 27:32. An attitude of insistence is with a word/phrase in 44:16; part of event span in 32:21; event span or

A Discourse Perspective on the Significance of the Masoretic Accents 169

longer in 38:17a; angry/sad event span or longer in 9:24 and 30:3; tense/afraid/ puzzled part of event span in 24:17; event span or longer in 30:25; 32:9; 33:8a; kind/happy word in 50:24; part of event span in 6:18; 8:16; 48:2; event span or longer in 5:28; 9:9; 24:52.

8. Ordinary Tevir with no preceding focus marker occurs on event-span conclusion in 8:9, etc.; chain onset in 1:4, 8, 22; 2:15, 19, 21, 22; 3:6, 9, 13; 5:25, 29; 6:4; 8:3, 10, 20; 9:1, etc.; chain climax in 3:10, 6:12, etc.; conclusion in 6:21, etc.; episode or discourse onset in 2:15; 3:20, etc.; theme in 2:4, etc.; exposition in 9:1 etc.; high-level climax in 1:17, 22; 3:6; 7:18; etc.; conclusion in 2:1; 3:20; 6:14, 16; 7:23; 8:14, etc.

It occurs on background material in chain in 3:20, etc.; in high levels in 2:18; 6:5; 7:16, etc.

Tevir preceded by two or more conjunctive accents but with no other preceding focus marker occurs on event-span climax in 4:4; 7:3; 14:12; 48:11; chain onset in 3:13; 18:15; 45:4, 21; 49:9; climax in 14:15; 27:9; 41:16; conclusion in 16:15; 41:25; paragraph/episode/discourse onset in 2:21; 12:17; 27:7; theme in 2:4; 11:29; 19:32; 24:29, 55; 25:8; 30:41; 31:48; 34:8; 39:4; 46:8; climax in 11:8; 17:16, 19; 21:2; conclusion in 10:32; 33:16; 36:21, 30; 41:49; 48:6.

It occurs on background material in high levels in 41:39 and 47:23; on participants which are prominent as theme in high levels in 23:15; 41:20, 42; 44:9; prop in 3:8.

From the perspective of emphasis Tevir alone occurs on unexpected in 15:12; 17:17; 27:20a, 32a; 30:30a; 43:17; impressive in 5:25; 6:4; 11:23; 18:6, 24a; 21:31b; 23:1; 25:1, 7b, 12a, 19, etc.

An attitude of insistence in 6:14; 17:9, 13b; 18:24b; 19:5; 20:5; 50:19b, etc.; anger/sadness in 3:6; 6:5, 12a; 7:18; 8:9; 11:9; 12:11, 19, 20a; 13:6; 18:20; 24:63; 27:38, 45; 31:14, 15; 35:20a; 37:10; 38:9; 44:4; tension/fear in 3:9, 10; 8:10; 19:20b; 24:23, 43; 27:32; 32:8a, 31; 34:11, 20a; 43:18; kindness/happiness in 1:4, 8, 17, 22; 2:1, 15; 5:29; 6:21; 8:3, 14; 9:1; 10:1; 13:4, 15; 15:14, 15, 16; 16:15a; 17:3, 5a; 22:14, 19; 23:7; 24:61, 67; 29:14; 30:24a; 37:15; 40:7b; 41:51, 52; 42:25; 45:21b, 22, 28; 46:30; 47:3; 48:12; 50:19a, etc.

Residue in 38:13. I ignore how such a fact was usually considered: positively, negatively, or otherwise.

9. Extra Precontour in Zaqef or Atnach phonological clauses occurs after Silluq in Atnach sentences on event climax in 18:5; 24:53; 41:30, 54; 45:23; conclusion in 46:7; chain-initial setting in 14:7 and 24:36; onset in 21:7; 23:13; 25:9a; 27:4; 31:11; 38:21; 40:4, 7; climax in 14:11; 22:2, 12; 34:13; 39:22; 47:20; 48:14; higher-level onset in 2:8, 9; 3:8, 21; 10:13, 19a; 13:1a; 16:7; 18:29, 30, 32; 19:1; 21:3, 9, 14a; 22:11; 24:10; 26:7; 27:15; 34:2; 35:18; 40:5; 46:28; theme in 18:28; 19:15; 22:20; 24:35a; 36:40; 42:30; exposition in 1:12; 19:20a, 35; 23:13; 24:35b; 26:10; 28:11; 37:7; climax in

31:42a and 35:11; conclusion in 5:5; 10:5; 23:20; 24:49; 25:16; 31:53; 39:9; 46:26; 47:26.

Circumstance is prominent in paragraph in 7:9, in higher level in 10:19b and 32:11.

Participant is prominent as agent in higher level in 34:7a; is prominent theme in clause in 6:19 and 7:2; theme in higher level in 41:19; prop in higher level in 34:22 and 49:30.

After Atnach prominence is on start of list in 8:22; event-span climax in 25:6; 28:29; 41:35; 42:35; 47:13, 34; 48:4; 49:28; 50:6.

Prominence is on the chain onset in 4:3; 17:7; 21:19; 27:42; 32:14; 39:1; 41:56; climax in 20:17; 38:9; 47:19; 48:1; conclusion in 4:14; 11:9; 36:7. Prominence is on higher-level theme in 26:11; 27:39; 31:43; 39:17; exposition in 1:28; 21:23; 27:46; conclusion in 18:14; 31:42b; 36:18; 39:5; 44:31; 50:11b.

Circumstances are prominent in event span in 2:5; 6:22; 23:9; 43:32; 47:26; in higher levels in 25:12; 39:11; 43:5; 44:20.

Participant is prominent as agent in higher level in 48:15; theme in sentence in 45:23; in higher levels in 19:8b and 43:12; prop in higher levels in 25:9b and 34:22.

Initially in Segolta sentences prominence is on higher-level onsets in 6:4; 36:6; 44:1a, 4; 34:30; theme in 31:32, 41a; climax in 28:13; 38:9; 42:34; 43:34a; 48:20.

Circumstance is prominent in higher level in 19:19.

After Segolta prominence is on event-span climax in 27:33; higher-level theme in 44:16; exposition in 30:40; 31:41b; 43:11.

Circumstance is prominent in event span in 43:34 and in higher levels in 24:7b and 42:21b.

Participant is prominent as agent in higher level in 19:4.

10. Revia clause without Extra Precontour occurs after Silluq in Atnach sentences on continuing focus on list in 6:20; event-span climaxes in 2:17a; 8:19; 13:11; 19:28a; 20:16; 21:7; 24:18, 20, 27a, 48; 26:8c; 30:38; 31:5, 18; 34:14; 41:21, 43; 46:6; chain-initial setting in 3:16; 6:16; 14:10; 38:7; onsets in 2:21; 9:15; 12:12; 15:13a; 16:8; 19:24; 24:2, 42, 65; 30:36a; 32:30; 37:20; 40:17; 42:13; 43:30; 44:11; 45:13, 27; climax in 4:15; 6:3; 12:4a; 13:10a; 15:2, 9; 17:19; 18:10; 19:9; 23:9; 24:46, 67; 25:2, 33; 27:25; 30:10a, 15a, 18; 31:12, 35; 32:29; 33:10a, 13; 35:4; 37:14; 38:26; 41:35; 42:33; 43:28; 44:16a; 45:10; 46:34a; 47:14, 31; 48:19a; conclusion in 6:7; 15:10; 26:25; 29:19; higher-level onsets in 1:9, 11, 14, 24, 29a; 3:22a; 5:3, 4, 7, 10, 13, 16, 19, 26, 30; 6:21; 7:7; 9:12, 18, 22; 10:15; 11:11, 15, 17, 19, 21, 23, 25; 13:7; 14:1; 15:1a; 18:31; 20:12; 21:28; 22:1, 4, 20; 23:2, 6, 8; 24:22, 54; 25:4, 7, 11, 13, 17; 26:8a, 22a, 32; 28:12; 29:7; 30:1, 8, 12, 37; 31:1, 10; 32:23; 33:5; 34:5; 35:22; 36:12, 14, 17, 18; 37:2, 3, 4; 38:12, 24, 25; 39:7; 40:1; 41:2, 18; 42:35; 43:2; 45:16; 46:10, 12, 17, 21; 48:1, 17a; 49:29;

50:17; themes in 14:2a; 20:7a; 21:23; 22:17; 24:7b; 44:30; 45:5; 47:19; expositions in 7:2, 17; 11:6; 14:24; 24:10; 28:17; 31:8a, 37, 44, 50; 37:9; 44:5, 8a; 48:4; climaxes in 3:15; 6:17; 7:19a; 27:29; 29:3; 32:26; 38:29; 40:13, 19, 20a; 41:4; 44:31; conclusions in 7:16; 13:18; 15:18a; 19:29; 21:31; 23:17; 34:27; 39:23; 43:14; 44:33; 45:8a; 46:15; 49:26.

Circumstance is prominent in event span in 44:8a; in higher levels in 18:19a; 40:14.

Participant is prominent as agent in higher levels in 42:6; 46:4; theme in list in 4:22; event span in 17:14; in chain in 35:12; in higher levels in 1:2; 2:5; 8:5; 24:14, 16; 26:15; 31:16a; 41:26; 48:7; 49:8; prop in event span in 17:12; in higher levels in 27:16; 28:22.

After Atnach it occurs on start of list in 36:2; continuing list in 7:13; 14:2b; clause climax in 13:16; event-span climax in 7:4b; 9:5; 13:12; 17:17; 19:28b; 20:3; 27:31; 30:2; 31:24; 33:7; 35:3; 46:29; 48:19b; 50:23; conclusion in 44:8b; chain onset in 5:2; 9:16; 18:2, 6; 20:2; 21:32; 24:19; 27:19b; 29:10b, 25; 31:8b; 33:1b; 38:28; 40:11; 45:4; 48:17b; 49:1; climax in 12:5b; 22:7; 29:18; 42:28; 45:18; 47:3; conclusion in 7:19b; 18:19b; 27:22; 30:15b; 37:22b; 46:34b; higher-level onsets in 5:1; 18:3; theme in 1:22; 3:22b; 15:1b, 18b; 19:19b; 20:7b; 21:29; 31:51; 37:26, 32; 41:15, 44; 42:14; expositions in 6:15; 24:27b; 27:27; 30:30; 31:52; 36:10; 37:10; 41:22; climax in 31:13; conclusion in 12:4b; 30:36b; 31:16b; 36:43; 50:5c.

Circumstance is prominent in list in 50:8; in event span in 2:17b; 29:32; 31:25; 37:25; 47:9; in higher levels in 2:4; 7:11; 13:10b; 16:13; 22:12b, 16; 26:3; 29:9; 32:11; 35:5, 7.

Participant is prominent as agent in higher levels in 15:7; 40:5; 44:16b; as theme in list in 4:18; in clause in 36:2; in higher levels in 2:11; 3:11; 28:13b; 34:8; 37:19; 41:5; as prop in higher level in 13:3.

In Segolta sentences it occurs chain initially in 3:17; in onset in 30:20; 47:4a; in climax in 26:28a; 43:18; in higher-level onsets in 22:9; 24:15a, 47a; 27:30a; 28:6; 30:41; 43:29a; 47:15; in exposition in 24:30a; in climax in 38:18a; 42:25.

Participant is prominent as agent in higher level in 24:7a.

After Segolta it occurs in a continuing list in 36:6; event-span climax in 19:19a; 26:28b; 27:30b; 29:33, 34; 41:45; 43:18b; 45:9; chain onset in 1:7; 43:29b; 47:2; climax in 42:3; higher-level themes in 2:23; 3:3; 16:5; 17:20; expositions in 37:22a; 47:1; climax in 24:47b; 48:18b.

Circumstance is prominent in event span in 6:4; in chain in 24:30b and 47:4b; in higher levels in 14:17.

Participant is prominent as agent in higher levels in 24:12; 28:13a; as theme in event span in 48:20; in higher levels in 24:15b; as prop in clause in 50:5b.

References

Breuer, Mordechai. 1982. *Biblical accentuation in the 21 books and in the 3 poetical books*. Jerusalem: Hotsa at Mikhlalah.

Buth, Randall. 1977. An introductory study of the paragraph structure of Biblical Hebrew narrative. Thesis, Institute of Holy Land Studies in Jerusalem.

Callow, Kathleen. 1974. *Discourse considerations in translating the Word of God*. Grand Rapids, Mich.: Zondervan.

Derenbourg, J. 1870. Manuel du lecteur. *Journal Asiatique*, 6eme serie, pp. 309–550, tome XVI.

Dotan, A. 1971. Masorah. *Encyclopedia Judaica*, vol. 16, cols 1401–82. Jerusalem.

Lode, Lars. 1984. Postverbal word order in Biblical Hebrew: Structure and function (Part one: Genesis). *Semitics* 9:113–64.

———. 1989. Exodus 1–19, Ezra, Nehemiah, Esther (Part two). *Semitics* 10:24–39.

———. Forthcoming. The narrative discourse structure of Exodus 1:1–15:21. *Semitics*, vol. 11.

Longacre, R. E. 1976. *An anatomy of speech notions*. Lisse, The Netherlands: Peter de Ridder Press.

———. 1979. The discourse structure of the flood narrative. *Journal of the American Academy of Religion* 47:1, Supplement B (March 1979) 89–133.

Wickes, W. 1970 [1887]. *A treatise on the accentuation of the 21 so-called prose books of the Old Testament*. Oxford: Clarendon. Reprint. New York.

Yeivin, I. 1980. *Introduction to the Tiberian Masorah*. Tr. by E. J. Revell. Chico, Calif.: Scholars Press.

PART II

NARRATIVE GENRE

7

ANALYSIS OF BIBLICAL NARRATIVE

Alviero Niccacci

This article illustrates a way of analyzing biblical narrative according to the verb forms used. An effort is made to combine morphology (grammar) with function (syntax), not only on the level of the sentence but also on the level of a text (or discourse), a text being "a logical (i.e., intelligible and consistent) sequence of linguistic signs, placed between two significant breaks in communication" (Weinrich 1985).

A sharp distinction is made between verb forms of connection and verb forms of interruption, that is, between verbal sentences and nominal sentences. Verbal sentences make up the main level of the narrative and nominal sentences a secondary level. By using both verbal and nominal sentences, the writer can indicate progress, pause, and interruption in the communication, allocating all information to either the main or the secondary level (i.e., foreground or background). His choice is indicated by the verb forms used in the narrative. Both a sentence-by-sentence analysis and a global evaluation of a narrative are possible on the basis of the choice of verbs.

1. Verb forms, a vantage point for the analysis of biblical narrative

Although there are many ways of analyzing biblical narrative, it is my conviction that the verb forms in a narrative constitute the main clue to the author's perspective in presenting his information.[1] Therefore my analysis of biblical narrative is on the basis of its verb forms.

One important contribution of H. Weinrich's (1985) textlinguistics is to point out that the author's choice of verb forms reflects his strategy of communication. Verb forms should be seen as linguistic signs at the speaker's or writer's disposal to present his information in a meaningful, forcible way so as to influence and guide the response of the listener or reader.

The starting point of the analysis of narrative should not be the chronology of events *(ordo rerum)* but rather the process of communication. Tenses are not necessarily linked to actual time. Tense and time are distinct. One can narrate the future and predict the past. In addition to being linguistic signs that the author freely uses to express his attitude toward the information he is presenting, tenses are also signs for the reader to understand the author's attitude and conform to it.

To analyze a narrative is to try to detect the author's attitude and strategy. This will, in the end, help determine what the real goal of his communication is.

In the process of communication, two main attitudes are available. The first is narrating the events or information. This, in Weinrich's (1985) terms is *erzählen*. The second is commenting on the events or information, *besprechen*, in Weinrich's (1985) terms. The two literary genres that correspond to these two attitudes are *narrative* and *direct speech* (i.e., comment).

Narrative concerns persons or events that are not present or current in the relationship involving the writer/reader. In narrative the attitude of the writer is one of distance, and therefore the third person is normally used. In direct speech, on the other hand, the speaker/writer addresses the listener/reader directly. Dialogues, sermons, or prayers are forms of direct speech. The attitude is one of involvement and first and second person forms are normally used. Direct speech can also be a comment to the reader; in a narrative, for instance, the writer sometimes holds up the story for a moment to express his own reflections on the events narrated.

2. Verb forms of narrative and verb forms of direct speech

In Hebrew, as in many languages, some verb forms used for narrative are different from those used for direct speech, while other verb forms are commonly used in both. There are two criteria for analyzing the verb forms: first, position in the sentence; second, position in the text. Some verb forms are able to start a text in either narrative or direct speech. As first-position verb forms in the sentence, they are verbal sentences; and as first-position verb forms in the text, they are independent. Verbal and independent sentences constitute the mainline of communication in both narrative and direct speech.

In narrative, only sentences initiatiated by *wayyiqtol* verbs are verbal and independent; they therefore constitute the mainline of communication. *Wayyiqtol* is the only verb form of this kind because it is related to the axis of the past, the only temporal axis viable in narrative. In direct speech, however, all three temporal axes are viable, and therefore a larger variety of verb forms is available: for the past there is *qatal,* for the present the simple nominal clause (SNC), and for the future X-*yiqtol*—not the simple *yiqtol* that has jussive verb function .[2]

Table 1. Mainline of communication

TEMPORAL AXIS	NARRATIVE	DIRECT SPEECH
Past	wayyiqtol*	qatal
Present	—	SNC**
Future	—	weqatal***

   * A chain of wayyiqtol constitutes the mainline of communication in narrative.
  ** Can be preceded by waw although this is optional. The same is true of the compound nominal sentence of the type X-qatal and X-yiqtol.
*** X-yiqtol is the initial verb form. However, a chain of weqatal constitutes the mainline of communication.

Table 2. Subsidiary line of communication

TEMPORAL AXIS	NARRATIVE	DIRECT SPEECH
Past	X-qatal	X-qatal
Present	SNC	SNC
Future	X-yiqtol	X-yiqtol

3. Continuation and interruption in the mainline of communication

According to Weinrich (1985) "a text is a logical (i.e., intelligible and consistent) sequence of linguistic signs, placed between two significant breaks in communication." A biblical text, for the most part, is generated by a chain of the same type of verb forms (the chain of wayyiqtol in narrative and of weqatal in direct speech).

To go a step further, we note that in narrative a verbal sentence is a linguistic sign of *connection,* while a nominal sentence (simple or compound) is a sign of *interruption* in the mainline of communication. The reason for this becomes clear as soon as we remember that wayyiqtol is the only verbal sentence expressing the mainline of communication in narrative.

The chain of wayyiqtol in narrative as well as the chain of weqatal in direct speech goes on without interruption until the author intends to signal a change in his attitude. For instance, he may, for a special purpose, want to communicate a piece of information in a subsidiary line (background) instead of in the mainline (foreground). The verb forms that signal an interruption in narrative are those in the nominal clauses, either simple or compound. They have the same function in direct speech, too. (Note that in direct speech the SNC signals both foreground and background.)

It is of paramount importance for the analyst of biblical narrative to remember that verb forms of interruption are dependent verbs from a syntactic point of view, and from a textlinguistic point of view they express a subsidiary level of communication. As such, they depend on independent verb forms of the mainline of communication. They cannot stand alone in a text.[3]

As a consequence, every time we find a nominal clause in narrative we should look for the *wayyiqtol* form upon which it depends. This *wayyiqtol* can precede or follow. If it precedes, the text shows a tense shift from foreground to background. If it follows, the tense shift is from antecedent information to degree zero, or main level of communication. Table 3 is a list of verb forms that signal an interruption in the mainline of communication. The two possibilities just mentioned are illustrated.

Table 3. Verb forms of interruption (The symbol → means a tense shift)

1. With a preceding independent sentence			
GENRE	VERBAL SENTENCE	→	COMPOUND NOMINAL SENTENCE
Narrative	*wayyiqtol* = foreground	→	X-*qatal** background
Direct speech	*weqatal* = foreground	→ →	X-*yiqtol* background
2. With a following independent sentence			
GENRE	COMPOUND NOMINAL SENTENCE	→	VERBAL SENTENCE
Narrative**	X-*qatal* = antecedent info. ***	→ →	*wayyiqtol* degree zero (main level)

   * Other verb forms attested with the function of background are *weqatal* and simple nominal clause (Niccacci 1990c §§43.46).
  ** Antecedent information is not to be found in direct speech.
 *** Other constructions signaling antecedent information are waw-X-yiqtol, weqatal, and simple nominal clause (Niccacci 1990c §19).

4. How biblical narrative works

Chains of *wayyiqtol* in narrative and of *weqatal* in direct speech enhance the "textuality" of a text; that is, they confer its coherence and consistency. A text with *only* these chains, however, would be too uniform, lacking in information, and foreseeable. Shifts from the main level to subsidiary levels of communication and back again improve a text by arranging the information in a structured whole with foreground and background, beginning and end. They also signal a more-or-less open intervention of the author intended to capture the attention of the reader.

Let me repeat Weinrich's definition of a text: "a logical (i.e., intelligible and consistent) sequence of linguistic signs, placed between two significant breaks in communication." But how do we identify the two significant breaks marking the beginning and the end of a text?

Based on what has been said so far, breaks are indicated by nominal clauses. This statement, however, needs to be elaborated. The tense shift from an independent *wayyiqtol* to a compound nominal sentence, such as *waw*-X-*qatal,* does not actually break the narrative chain because it communicates a piece of information that serves as a background to the preceding information occupying the foreground. In other words, a piece of information is presented not as an independent item but rather in subordination to a preceding one. The two are not successive pieces of information all on the same level as links of the same chain, as they would be if conveyed with *wayyiqtol* verb forms. They are, rather, organized in a close relationship to one another (see Table 3.1, i.e., the upper half of Table 3).

On the contrary, an actual break in the line of communication is represented by the tense shift from antecedent information to degree zero, or beginning of the mainline of narrative. This is a rather common way of starting a narrative or a new episode in narrative in the Bible as in many other forms of literature, including modern (see Table 3.2, i.e., the lower half of Table 3).

Another problem presents itself at this point. We have to establish whether or not the break signaled by the tense shift from antecedent information to degree zero is actually significant. If it is significant, it marks the beginning of a new text. If, on the contrary, it is not significant, it simply marks a new episode of the same text. The solution to this problem cannot be found on purely syntactic or textlinguistic levels. One needs to refer to semantic criteria, such as literary devices, context, change of characters or setting, and meaning. By itself, syntax can only signal a break; it cannot signal the textual significance of that break.

Consequently, a text will extend itself from a significant break in the flow of communication until the next break. In between the two significant breaks, the textuality is enhanced by the chains of *wayyiqtol* clauses in narrative or of *weqatal* clauses in direct speech, as already indicated.

5. Criteria for the analysis of biblical narrative

In order to understand the meaning of a text, we have to understand its structure. For this purpose we begin by dividing the text into complete sentences. Complete sentences from the point of view of grammar consist of what traditionally are called subject and predicate. (In Hebrew we should rather say predicate and subject, because the predicate comes first in the sentence.) Complete sentences can be dependent from the point of view of syntax and/or textlinguistics.

To define the sentence in Biblical Hebrew is not an easy task (see Waltke and O'Connor 1990, sec. 4.8). However, I do not wish to address this issue here (the main criteria I follow are discussed in Niccacci 1990*a* §7.1) except to say that I consider the casus pendens to be a complete sentence by itself. The reason is that it can function as the protasis of a double sentence as do other clauses with אִם 'if' or כַּאֲשֶׁר 'when, like' plus a finite verb form. A prepositional phrase, too, can function as the protasis in a double sentence and as such is a complete sentence by itself. (See the analysis of Gen. 2:17 and 3:3 in sec. 7 and also Niccacci 1990*c* §119.)

In the examples that follow, complete sentences will be arranged in different lines with the purpose of establishing the relationship of one to the other and eventually the structure of the text. In this process difficulties can emerge. For instance, clauses with the relative indicator אֲשֶׁר can be embedded in the main sentence in such a way that it is impossible to arrange them in separate lines (see, e.g., Gen. 2:22 in sec. 7).

6. Three levels of the text

I have established three levels in the Hebrew text: level 1 extends to the right margin, indicating degree zero (the mainline of narrative); level 2 is placed to the left of level 1 and is for antecedent information (the secondary line of narrative); level 3 is to the left of level 2 and is for direct speech.

Nominal clauses connected to a preceding *wayyiqtol* are not assigned to level 2 since they do not signal an interruption of the level 1 mainline, but only a pause. This is the case with a tense shift from *wayyiqtol* to *waw-X-qatal* (see Table 3.1). In fact, the two verb forms together constitute a syntactic unit composed of foreground and background.

I have not assigned a special level to background information in level 3 for various reasons: (1) in order not to make things too complicated; (2) because background information is much more rare in direct speech than it is in narrative; (3) because the tense shifts found in direct speech do not affect the general structure of the narrative if the quotation formulas are in the *wayyiqtol*. In this case, the mainline of communication is carried on by the quotation formulas no matter how long and how complex the direct speech is.

7. Sentence-to-sentence analysis and global evaluation

In order to achieve a global evaluation of a narrative, a sentence-to-sentence analysis of a text should be carried out first, followed by an evaluation of the overall structure. These are the two main steps of my analysis of a biblical narrative. I call the first step "syntactic commentary," the second "macrosyntax," which is narrative syntax (Niccacci 1990*a* §7.3).

By applying the criterion of the verb forms, and diagramming the text according to the three levels just mentioned in section 3, the analyst can detect the extent of a narrative, its different sections, and the relationships of one section to another. As we know already, the extent of a narrative is marked off by two significant breaks in the line of communication.

I hardly need to repeat that background information does not really interrupt the flow of the narrative while antecedent information does. I call antecedent information all the data that an author wishes to communicate to his reader in order to make him understand the following story (see Table 3.2). These data are conveyed in a subsidiary line, or level 2, by means of nominal sentences. Afterwards, the mainline of narrative, or level 1, starts with *wayyiqtol*.

A special case of interruption in the flow of a narrative is the writer's holding up the story in order to recall a piece of information given previously and now necessary to the understanding of the next phase of the narrative. This is a case of "recovered information" in Weinrich's terms.

We are now in a position to appreciate the importance of the verb forms in the processing of a text. They signal connection, background, pause, interruption, and resumption in the flow of the narrative. It is by means of verb forms that an author shapes his information and reveals his strategy of communication.

The choice of verb forms is not subject to any fixed laws but basically depends on the narrator. Some general laws do exist, however. Many times a biblical narrative begins with an introduction providing previous information to the story in a subsidiary line, namely by means of nominal clauses. Sometimes a conclusion of the story is given likewise using a subsidiary line of communication (see, e.g., Gen. 2:25 in sec. 7). The storyline develops by a series of *wayyiqtol* forms. Inside the story the verb forms denoting the background are normally used to convey secondary details, descriptions, or reflections.

In spite of the importance the reader has acquired in recent linguistic literature (see Prince 1982, for example), his task remains subservient to that of the author. He has to try to unravel the writer's strategy of communication and conform himself to it. Since verb forms are the linguistic means at the author's disposal to shape his information and to carry out his strategy, a correct analysis and translation of the verb forms is of paramount importance. Too often it is the case that the translator of a biblical text looks to so-called common sense, or logical development of events, for guidance. Of course, he is just trying to make sense out of an often difficult text. But *which* sense, *which* logic, is he looking for? The answer should not be his *own*, and not even the sense, or logic, of the events themselves. The right answer is, I think, the sense and the logic intended by the author as reflected in the text by means of the verb forms.

The function of a verb form should not be inferred from the tense(s) used in modern translations. Unfortunately, this seems to be a rather common practice. We should not argue, for example, that in such and such a passage a certain verb form can be translated in such and such a way, and therefore, this is the function of that verb form. On the contrary, we should first understand the function of a given verb form in the texts, and then choose the right tense to translate it into modern languages. The criterion should always be the function first, the tense of translation afterwards. In other words, syntactic analysis should always guide the interpretation. Our understanding of syntax should never follow the lead of interpretation and semantics, because it is possible that an author may choose to change the order of events for his own reasons. The interpreter has no right to redress the "real order," giving the verb forms a tense value that he chooses himself. The author is free and sovereign over his information. We interpreters should try to understand and respect the author's choice, whatever the logic and strategy may be.

As an example of how a biblical narrative can be analyzed from the point of view of the verb forms used, I here analyze Genesis 1–3. I first divide the Hebrew text into complete sentences, structuring them according to different levels of communication. Then a syntactic commentary and a macrosyntactic reading follow.

Genesis 1:1–2:4[4]

Level 1 (mainline of narrative)→|
Level 2 (secondary line)→|
Level 3 (direct speech)→|

בְּרֵאשִׁית בָּרָא אֱלֹהִים אֵת הַשָּׁמַיִם וְאֵת הָאָרֶץ	1:1
וְהָאָרֶץ הָיְתָה תֹהוּ וָבֹהוּ	
וְחֹשֶׁךְ עַל־פְּנֵי תְהוֹם	1:2
וְרוּחַ אֱלֹהִים מְרַחֶפֶת עַל־פְּנֵי הַמָּיִם	
וַיֹּאמֶר אֱלֹהִים	1:3

Analysis of Biblical Narrative

	יְהִי אוֹר
	וַיְהִי־אוֹר
1:4	וַיַּרְא אֱלֹהִים אֶת־הָאוֹר
	↑ כִּי־טוֹב
	וַיַּבְדֵּל אֱלֹהִים בֵּין הָאוֹר וּבֵין הַחֹשֶׁךְ
1:5	וַיִּקְרָא אֱלֹהִים לָאוֹר יוֹם
	↑ וְלַחֹשֶׁךְ קָרָא לָיְלָה
	וַיְהִי־עֶרֶב
	וַיְהִי־בֹקֶר יוֹם אֶחָד
1:6	וַיֹּאמֶר אֱלֹהִים
	יְהִי רָקִיעַ בְּתוֹךְ הַמָּיִם
	וִיהִי מַבְדִּיל בֵּין מַיִם לָמָיִם
1:7	וַיַּעַשׂ אֱלֹהִים אֶת־הָרָקִיעַ
	וַיַּבְדֵּל בֵּין הַמַּיִם אֲשֶׁר מִתַּחַת לָרָקִיעַ וּבֵין הַמַּיִם אֲשֶׁר מֵעַל לָרָקִיעַ
	וַיְהִי־כֵן

Genesis 1:1-2 conveys antecedent information before the narrative proper, which begins in v. 3.[5] Then, a chain of *wayyiqtol* goes on without interruption.[6] In 1:5 we find a tense shift from *wayyiqtol* to *waw-X-qatal*. Its effect is to convey the naming of the darkness as background information to the preceding naming of the light. We translate it: "(God) called the light day *while* the darkness *he called* night." The same is true in 1:10: "God called the dry land earth *while* the gathering of the waters *he called* sea." If there had been a *wayyiqtol* instead of *waw-X-qatal*, the various acts of naming would have been on the same level: "God called . . . *and then* he called . . ."

In level 3, the level of direct speech, there are clear examples of the jussive *yiqtol* taking the first position in the sentence, as in 1:3. Its continuation form is *weyiqtol*, also a volitive form (see 1:6).[7]

The text continues without major interruptions until 2:4, where a simple nominal clause breaks the mainline of narrative.

2:4	אֵלֶּה תוֹלְדוֹת הַשָּׁמַיִם וְהָאָרֶץ בְּהִבָּרְאָם בְּיוֹם עֲשׂוֹת
	יְהוָה אֱלֹהִים אֶרֶץ וְשָׁמָיִם

The chiastic arrangement of the text makes it impossible for me to accept the splitting of 2:4 in two halves as literary critics commonly do. The verse is, in fact, one literary unit (see Niccacci 1990c:200, fn. 26).

From the point of view of syntax, it is a nominal clause; as such, it signals a break in the mainline of narrative. The question is whether it should be connected with what precedes or with what follows. Syntax cannot answer this question. In my opinion, semantics and literary analysis suggest that 2:4 is connected with the preceding text. In fact, the key terms of 1:1 are resumed. Actually, the phrases in 2:4 אֶרֶץ וְשָׁמַיִם / הַשָּׁמַיִם וְהָאָרֶץ and עָשׂוֹת / בְּהִבָּרְאָם echo בָּרָא and אֵת הַשָּׁמַיִם וְאֵת הָאָרֶץ of 1:1. Thus the first section of the Bible ends with a nominal clause, that is, with a secondary line of narrative (level 2), as we sometimes find in biblical narrative.[8] Literary analysis shows, however, that 2:4 is background information to the preceding story rather than antecedent information to the following one.

Genesis 2:5-25

וְכֹל שִׂיחַ הַשָּׂדֶה טֶרֶם יִהְיֶה בָאָרֶץ	2:5
וְכָל־עֵשֶׂב הַשָּׂדֶה טֶרֶם יִצְמָח	
↑ כִּי לֹא הִמְטִיר יְהוָה אֱלֹהִים עַל־הָאָרֶץ	
↑ וְאָדָם אַיִן לַעֲבֹד אֶת־הָאֲדָמָה	
וְאֵד יַעֲלֶה מִן־הָאָרֶץ	2:6
וְהִשְׁקָה אֶת־כָּל־פְּנֵי־הָאֲדָמָה	
וַיִּיצֶר יְהוָה אֱלֹהִים אֶת־הָאָדָם עָפָר מִן־הָאֲדָמָה	2:7
וַיִּפַּח בְּאַפָּיו נִשְׁמַת חַיִּים	
וַיְהִי הָאָדָם לְנֶפֶשׁ חַיָּה	
וַיִּטַּע יְהוָה אֱלֹהִים גַּן־בְּעֵדֶן מִקֶּדֶם	2:8
וַיָּשֶׂם שָׁם אֶת־הָאָדָם	
↑ אֲשֶׁר יָצָר	
וַיַּצְמַח יְהוָה אֱלֹהִים מִן־הָאֲדָמָה כָּל־עֵץ נֶחְמָד לְמַרְאֶה	2:9
וְטוֹב לְמַאֲכָל וְעֵץ הַחַיִּים בְּתוֹךְ הַגָּן וְעֵץ הַדַּעַת טוֹב וָרָע	
וְנָהָר יֹצֵא מֵעֵדֶן לְהַשְׁקוֹת אֶת־הַגָּן	2:10
וּמִשָּׁם יִפָּרֵד	
וְהָיָה לְאַרְבָּעָה רָאשִׁים	
שֵׁם הָאֶחָד פִּישׁוֹן	2:11
הוּא הַסֹּבֵב אֵת כָּל־אֶרֶץ הַחֲוִילָה	
אֲשֶׁר־שָׁם הַזָּהָב	
וּזֲהַב הָאָרֶץ הַהִוא טוֹב	2:12
שָׁם הַבְּדֹלַח וְאֶבֶן הַשֹּׁהַם	

| 2:13 | וְשֵׁם־הַנָּהָר הַשֵּׁנִי גִּיחוֹן
הוּא הַסּוֹבֵב אֵת כָּל־אֶרֶץ כּוּשׁ |
| 2:14 | וְשֵׁם הַנָּהָר הַשְּׁלִישִׁי חִדֶּקֶל
הוּא הַהֹלֵךְ קִדְמַת אַשּׁוּר
וְהַנָּהָר הָרְבִיעִי הוּא פְרָת |
| 2:15 | וַיִּקַּח יְהוָה אֱלֹהִים אֶת־הָאָדָם
וַיַּנִּחֵהוּ בְגַן־עֵדֶן לְעָבְדָהּ וּלְשָׁמְרָהּ |
| 2:16 | וַיְצַו יְהוָה אֱלֹהִים עַל־הָאָדָם לֵאמֹר
מִכֹּל עֵץ־הַגָּן אָכֹל תֹּאכֵל |
| 2:17 | וּמֵעֵץ הַדַּעַת טוֹב וָרָע
לֹא תֹאכַל מִמֶּנּוּ
כִּי בְּיוֹם אֲכָלְךָ מִמֶּנּוּ
מוֹת תָּמוּת |
| 2:18 | וַיֹּאמֶר יְהוָה אֱלֹהִים
לֹא־טוֹב הֱיוֹת הָאָדָם לְבַדּוֹ
אֶעֱשֶׂה־לּוֹ עֵזֶר כְּנֶגְדּוֹ |
| 2:19 | וַיִּצֶר יְהוָה אֱלֹהִים מִן־הָאֲדָמָה כָּל־חַיַּת הַשָּׂדֶה וְאֵת כָּל־עוֹף הַשָּׁמַיִם
וַיָּבֵא אֶל־הָאָדָם לִרְאוֹת
↑ מַה־יִּקְרָא־לוֹ
↑ וְכֹל אֲשֶׁר יִקְרָא־לוֹ הָאָדָם נֶפֶשׁ חַיָּה
↑ הוּא שְׁמוֹ |
| 2:20 | וַיִּקְרָא הָאָדָם שֵׁמוֹת לְכָל־הַבְּהֵמָה וּלְעוֹף הַשָּׁמַיִם וּלְכֹל חַיַּת הַשָּׂדֶה
↑ וּלְאָדָם לֹא־מָצָא עֵזֶר כְּנֶגְדּוֹ |
| 2:21 | וַיַּפֵּל יְהוָה אֱלֹהִים תַּרְדֵּמָה עַל־הָאָדָם
וַיִּישָׁן
וַיִּקַּח אַחַת מִצַּלְעֹתָיו
וַיִּסְגֹּר בָּשָׂר תַּחְתֶּנָּה |
| 2:22 | וַיִּבֶן יְהוָה אֱלֹהִים אֶת־הַצֵּלָע אֲשֶׁר־לָקַח מִן־הָאָדָם לְאִשָּׁה
וַיְבִאֶהָ אֶל־הָאָדָם |
| 2:23 | וַיֹּאמֶר הָאָדָם
זֹאת הַפַּעַם עֶצֶם מֵעֲצָמַי |

וּבָשָׂר מִבְּשָׂרִי
לְזֹאת יִקָּרֵא אִשָּׁה
כִּי מֵאִישׁ לֻקֳחָה־זֹּאת
2:24   ↑ עַל־כֵּן יַעֲזָב־אִישׁ אֶת־אָבִיו וְאֶת־אִמּוֹ
↑ וְדָבַק בְּאִשְׁתּוֹ
↑ וְהָיוּ לְבָשָׂר אֶחָד
2:25 וַיִּהְיוּ שְׁנֵיהֶם עֲרוּמִּים הָאָדָם וְאִשְׁתּוֹ
↑ וְלֹא יִתְבֹּשָׁשׁוּ

Syntactic commentary

2:9 A small point of grammar, important for the interpretation of the passage, can be made here. Hebrew grammar does allow both the trees to be found "in the middle of the garden" because this prepositional phrase can modify both the previous and the following nouns.[9]

2:10-14 Different types of nominal clauses are present here. For instance, in 2:10a we find a simple nominal clause (with a participle), and in 2:10b a *waw*-X-*yiqtol*, namely a compound nominal clause, both with the similar function of providing background information.

2:16-17 The divine order in 2:16 is an X-*yiqtol* construction, that is, a sentence in which the X element is a prepositional phrase and the *yiqtol* in the second position is indicative (Niccacci 1987 §§7-19; 1990c §55). Here the indicative *yiqtol* carries a modal value, which I translate "Of every tree of the garden you are allowed to eat freely." In 2:17 the syntax changes. In fact, the presence of the preposition with a resumptive pronoun מִמֶּנּוּ 'from it' shows that the initial prepositional phrase is a *casus pendens*. This phrase functions as the protasis of a double sentence. The apodosis is לֹא תֹאכַל מִמֶּנּוּ. Thus I translate it "But of tree of knowledge of good and evil (protasis), you shall not eat of it (apodosis)."[10] The next sentence has the same structure: "For on the day you shall eat of it (protasis), you shall certainly die (apodosis)."[11]

2:19 There is here a fine example of *yiqtol* in narrative with the function of conveying anticipated information, a pre-vision of the story. Since it expresses future in a past context, it is translated in the conditional mood: God took the animals to the man "to see how *he would name them.*" Literally, it is a singular masculine pronoun: "how he would name *each one of them.*" What follows is a *casus pendens* functioning as the protasis of a double sentence. Taken as a whole, this is a nominal construction governed by a causal conjunction expressing background information to the preceding *wayyiqtol*. We translate it literally, as *"Because, as for* all that the man, who is a living being (see 2:7!), would name them (casus pendens = protasis), this is their name (apodosis) or, less literally, "Because in whatever way the man . . . would name them, etc."[12]

2:20 Despite several problems of interpretation, the syntax of this verse is clear. The second half of 2:20 is a compound nominal clause of the type *waw-X-qatal* expressing background information linked to the previous *wayyiqtol*: "For Adam (*or,* for the man, depending on the vocalization), however, one could not find (*or*, God could not find) a helper fit for him."[13]

2:22 The first sentence contains an אֲשֶׁר 'which, that' clause embedded in such a way that it cannot be separated from the main sentence because, at the end of it, we find the prepositional phrase לְאִשָּׁה 'into a woman' complementing the main verb וַיִּבֶן 'and he made': "Then Yahweh God *built the rib* that he had taken from the man *into a woman.*"

2:23 The direct speech contains two simple nominal clauses that should probably be analyzed as follows: "This one (זֹאת, the subject), at last (an interposed adverbial phrase), is bone of my bones and flesh of my flesh (two predicates)."

Macrosyntax

A new text begins in 2:5-6 with nominal sentences and *weqatal* forms, all of them conveying information antecedent to the story that follows. The main narrative line begins in 2:7 and extends to 2:9. In 2:10-14, again we have a series of nominal verb forms and *weqatal* denoting a secondary line in narrative.

In principle, 2:10-14 can be interpreted as background to the previous *wayyiqtol* forms or as antecedent information to the following *wayyiqtol* forms in 2:15ff. We have to decide the best solution—not an easy task.

According to literary critics, the 2:15 passage shows one of the clearest examples of a doublet marking a different tradition. I do not wish to address this problem here, but I do wish to show how syntax helps interpretation.[14] In fact we have, alternatively, a series of secondary-line verb forms and a series of mainline *wayyiqtol*. The best solution seems to me to be to interpret both series of secondary-line verb forms as antecedent information providing the setting of the following narrative. The first series (2:5-6) provides the setting for the formation of man, the planting of a garden in Eden and the growing in it of all kind of fruit trees, especially the Tree of Life and the Tree of Knowledge. The second series

(2:10-14) provides the setting of another phase of the narrative that takes up again a piece of information already given in 2:7. As we shall propose in the following paragraph, this is a resumption in order to add new information; it is not mere repetition.

Let us look at 2:15 more closely. The first *wayyiqtol* has a resumptive function. That is, it does not add new information but takes up again a bit of information of 2:8b (the man was put in Eden) after the interruption of 2:10-14. We can translate it *"Thus (as already said),* Yahweh God took the man." What follows does, however, contain new information. The main problem is to establish the exact meaning of the following sentence in 2:15b: וַיַּנִּחֵהוּ בְגַן־עֵדֶן לְעָבְדָהּ וּלְשָׁמְרָהּ 'and he put him in the garden of Eden to till it and to keep it'. The verb הִנִּיחַ can simply mean "to put," and thus it would be a semantic variant of the verb שִׂים in 2:8b, as literary critics take for granted. It can, however, have a more precise meaning according to the context. Let us compare 2 Sam. 16:21 (repeated in 20:3) where Ahithophel instructs Absalom with the words: "Go in to your father's concubines, *whom he has left to keep the house* (אֲשֶׁר הִנִּיחַ לִשְׁמוֹר הַבָּיִת)." The similarity of the two sentences is striking. It shows that the exact meaning of Gen. 2:15b is not simply "to put" but "to leave in the same place as before with a special task to carry out" (i.e., to work and keep the place). This interpretation does not agree with the theory of different traditions. Genesis 2:15 is hardly a doublet of 2:8. It is rather a complementing resumption of it. After the background information of 2:10-14, the topic of man in Eden is taken up again and carried on.

A special problem of the passage is the relationship between the secondary-line information of 2:10-14 and the mainline information of 2:15, in other words, between the details concerning the streams of Eden and the primary information regarding the assignment to the man of the task of maintaining the garden.

The rest of Genesis 2 consists of a chain of narrative *wayyiqtol* forms with only direct speech intervening three times. As already noted, direct speech does not actually break the mainline of narrative if the quotation formula is verbal (i.e., in the *wayyiqtol*), keeping the direct speech firmly within the storyline (2:18, 23). Nominal clauses, both simple and compound, and *weqatal* forms are found in 2:19, 20, and 24.[15] However, they do not interrupt the storyline because they are related to the preceding narrative *wayyiqtol* as conveying background information. Verse 2:24 is most likely an explanatory, or etiological, remark of the writer. It can be translated as *"That is why* man shall leave his father and his mother and shall cling to his wife and thus they shall be one flesh."[16]

The narrative chain is not interrupted by the *waw*-negative *yiqtol* construction in 2:25b, either. In fact, this verb form negates a *weqatal*

Analysis of Biblical Narrative

conveying background information related to the preceding *wayyiqtol*. As usual, *weqatal* indicates repetition or habit in narrative (see Niccacci 1990c §156). Since the *wayyiqtol* in 2:25 has a conclusive function, we translate it "*Thus* (i.e., *because they were one flesh*), the two were naked, namely, the man and his wife, *while* (or *although*) they were not feeling shame."

Determining the end of our text depends on the analysis of Gen. 3:1a. This verse is an example of a common difficulty in analyzing a biblical narrative. It contains a *waw*-X-*qatal* form (i.e., a compound nominal clause) and therefore is dependent upon a narrative *wayyiqtol*. The difficulty is to decide whether it should be connected with the preceding or with the following *wayyiqtol*. If with the preceding, 3:1a communicates background information and 2:25-3:1a would be translated as "Thus, the two were naked (עֲרוּמִּים), namely, the man and his wife, while (*or, although*) they were not feeling shame. *The serpent, on his part, was* the most cunning (עָרוּם) among the beasts of the earth."[17] In this case the information concerning the serpent is not given in the mainline of narrative but in a secondary one. Were it given with a *wayyiqtol* form, it would be a further information, successive from the point of view of time: "The two were naked... *And then* the serpent was the most cunning..."

I think, however, that Gen. 3:1a is better understood as connected with the following *wayyiqtol*. The main reason is that a new character is introduced, the serpent, and the serpent is going to be important in the following story. If this understanding is correct, Gen. 3:1a conveys information previous to the main narrative. It is a kind of an indirect appeal of the writer to the reader, as if he were saying that from the outset the reader should know that the serpent was the most cunning beast of the earth. This is "comment" (*besprechen*), not "narrative" (*erzählen*).

If Gen. 3:1a is interpreted as conveying antecedent information to the following story, our text extends from 2:5 down to 2:25. Like Gen. 1:1-2:4, the 2:5-25 text ends with a note of background, although 2:4 is admittedly more independent from the preceding context than 2:25b. This technique of closing in the secondary level of communication leaves the text open to future development.

Genesis 3:1-24

3:1 וְהַנָּחָשׁ הָיָה עָרוּם מִכֹּל חַיַּת הַשָּׂדֶה
↑ אֲשֶׁר עָשָׂה יְהוָה אֱלֹהִים
וַיֹּאמֶר אֶל־הָאִשָּׁה
אַף כִּי־אָמַר אֱלֹהִים
לֹא תֹאכְלוּ מִכֹּל עֵץ הַגָּן

3:2	וַתֹּאמֶר הָאִשָּׁה אֶל־הַנָּחָשׁ
	מִפְּרִי עֵץ־הַגָּן נֹאכֵל
3:3	וּמִפְּרִי הָעֵץ אֲשֶׁר בְּתוֹךְ־הַגָּן
	אָמַר אֱלֹהִים
	לֹא תֹאכְלוּ מִמֶּנּוּ
	וְלֹא תִגְּעוּ בּוֹ
	פֶּן־תְּמֻתוּן
3:4	וַיֹּאמֶר הַנָּחָשׁ אֶל־הָאִשָּׁה
	לֹא־מוֹת תְּמֻתוּן
3:5	כִּי יֹדֵעַ אֱלֹהִים
	כִּי בְּיוֹם אֲכָלְכֶם מִמֶּנּוּ
	וְנִפְקְחוּ עֵינֵיכֶם
	וִהְיִיתֶם כֵּאלֹהִים יֹדְעֵי טוֹב וָרָע
3:6	וַתֵּרֶא הָאִשָּׁה
	↑ כִּי טוֹב הָעֵץ לְמַאֲכָל
	↑ וְכִי תַאֲוָה־הוּא לָעֵינַיִם
	↑ וְנֶחְמָד הָעֵץ לְהַשְׂכִּיל
	וַתִּקַּח מִפִּרְיוֹ
	וַתֹּאכַל
	וַתִּתֵּן גַּם־לְאִישָׁהּ עִמָּהּ
	וַיֹּאכַל
3:7	וַתִּפָּקַחְנָה עֵינֵי שְׁנֵיהֶם
	וַיֵּדְעוּ
	↑ כִּי עֵירֻמִּם הֵם
	וַיִּתְפְּרוּ עֲלֵה תְאֵנָה
	וַיַּעֲשׂוּ לָהֶם חֲגֹרֹת
3:8	וַיִּשְׁמְעוּ אֶת־קוֹל יְהוָה אֱלֹהִים מִתְהַלֵּךְ בַּגָּן לְרוּחַ הַיּוֹם
	וַיִּתְחַבֵּא הָאָדָם וְאִשְׁתּוֹ מִפְּנֵי יְהוָה אֱלֹהִים בְּתוֹךְ עֵץ הַגָּן
3:9	וַיִּקְרָא יְהוָה אֱלֹהִים אֶל־הָאָדָם
	וַיֹּאמֶר לוֹ
	אַיֶּכָּה
3:10	וַיֹּאמֶר
	אֶת־קֹלְךָ שָׁמַעְתִּי בַּגָּן

Analysis of Biblical Narrative

וָאִירָ֔א	
כִּֽי־עֵירֹ֥ם אָנֹ֖כִי	
וָאֵחָבֵֽא	
וַיֹּ֕אמֶר	3:11
מִ֚י הִגִּ֣יד לְךָ֔	
כִּ֥י עֵירֹ֖ם אָ֑תָּה	
הֲמִן־הָעֵ֗ץ אֲשֶׁ֧ר צִוִּיתִ֛יךָ לְבִלְתִּ֥י אֲכָל־מִמֶּ֖נּוּ אָכָֽלְתָּ	
וַיֹּ֖אמֶר הָֽאָדָ֑ם	3:12
הָֽאִשָּׁה֙ אֲשֶׁ֣ר נָתַ֣תָּה עִמָּדִ֔י	
הִ֛וא נָֽתְנָה־לִּ֥י מִן־הָעֵ֖ץ	
וָאֹכֵֽל	
וַיֹּ֨אמֶר יְהוָ֧ה אֱלֹהִ֛ים לָאִשָּׁ֖ה	3:13
מַה־זֹּ֣את עָשִׂ֑ית	
וַתֹּ֙אמֶר֙ הָֽאִשָּׁ֔ה	
הַנָּחָ֥שׁ הִשִּׁיאַ֖נִי	
וָאֹכֵֽל	
וַיֹּאמֶר֩ יְהֹוָ֨ה אֱלֹהִ֥ים ׀ אֶֽל־הַנָּחָשׁ֮	3:14
כִּ֣י עָשִׂ֣יתָ זֹּ֒את	
אָר֤וּר אַתָּה֙ מִכָּל־הַבְּהֵמָ֔ה וּמִכֹּ֖ל חַיַּ֣ת הַשָּׂדֶ֑ה	
עַל־גְּחֹנְךָ֣ תֵלֵ֔ךְ	
וְעָפָ֥ר תֹּאכַ֖ל כָּל־יְמֵ֥י חַיֶּֽיךָ	
וְאֵיבָ֣ה ׀ אָשִׁ֗ית בֵּֽינְךָ֙ וּבֵ֣ין הָֽאִשָּׁ֔ה וּבֵ֥ין זַרְעֲךָ֖ וּבֵ֣ין זַרְעָ֑הּ	3:15
ה֚וּא יְשׁוּפְךָ֣ רֹ֔אשׁ	
וְאַתָּ֖ה תְּשׁוּפֶ֥נּוּ עָקֵֽב	
↑ אֶל־הָאִשָּׁ֣ה אָמַ֗ר	3:16
הַרְבָּ֤ה אַרְבֶּה֙ עִצְּבוֹנֵ֣ךְ וְהֵֽרֹנֵ֔ךְ	
בְּעֶ֖צֶב תֵּֽלְדִ֣י בָנִ֑ים	
וְאֶל־אִישֵׁךְ֙ תְּשׁ֣וּקָתֵ֔ךְ	
וְה֖וּא יִמְשָׁל־בָּֽךְ	
↑ וּלְאָדָ֣ם אָמַ֗ר	3:17
כִּֽי־שָׁמַעְתָּ֮ לְק֣וֹל אִשְׁתֶּךָ֒	
וַתֹּ֙אכַל֙ מִן־הָעֵ֔ץ	
אֲשֶׁ֤ר צִוִּיתִ֙יךָ֙ לֵאמֹ֔ר לֹ֥א תֹאכַ֖ל מִמֶּ֑נּוּ	

	אֲרוּרָה הָאֲדָמָה בַּעֲבוּרֶךָ
	בְּעִצָּבוֹן תֹּאכֲלֶנָּה כֹּל יְמֵי חַיֶּיךָ
3:18	וְקוֹץ וְדַרְדַּר תַּצְמִיחַ לָךְ
	וְאָכַלְתָּ אֶת־עֵשֶׂב הַשָּׂדֶה
3:19	בְּזֵעַת אַפֶּיךָ תֹּאכַל לֶחֶם עַד שׁוּבְךָ אֶל־הָאֲדָמָה
	כִּי מִמֶּנָּה לֻקָּחְתָּ
	כִּי־עָפָר אַתָּה
	וְאֶל־עָפָר תָּשׁוּב
3:20	וַיִּקְרָא הָאָדָם שֵׁם אִשְׁתּוֹ חַוָּה
	↑ כִּי הִוא הָיְתָה אֵם כָּל־חָי
3:21	וַיַּעַשׂ יְהוָה אֱלֹהִים לְאָדָם וּלְאִשְׁתּוֹ כָּתְנוֹת עוֹר
	וַיַּלְבִּשֵׁם
3:22	וַיֹּאמֶר יְהוָה אֱלֹהִים
	הֵן הָאָדָם הָיָה כְּאַחַד מִמֶּנּוּ לָדַעַת טוֹב וָרָע
	וְעַתָּה פֶּן־יִשְׁלַח יָדוֹ
	וְלָקַח גַּם מֵעֵץ הַחַיִּים
	וְאָכַל
	וָחַי לְעֹלָם
3:23	וַיְשַׁלְּחֵהוּ יְהוָה אֱלֹהִים מִגַּן־עֵדֶן לַעֲבֹד אֶת־הָאֲדָמָה
	↑ אֲשֶׁר לֻקַּח מִשָּׁם
3:24	וַיְגָרֶשׁ אֶת־הָאָדָם
	וַיַּשְׁכֵּן מִקֶּדֶם לְגַן־עֵדֶן אֶת־הַכְּרֻבִים וְאֵת לַהַט הַחֶרֶב
	הַמִּתְהַפֶּכֶת לִשְׁמֹר אֶת־דֶּרֶךְ עֵץ הַחַיִּים

Syntactic commentary

3:2-3 The interpretation of אַף כִּי 'also that' is notoriously difficult. In most cases this phrase is found as a second member of a rhetoric remark such as "If it is so with this, how will it be with that!" (Deut. 31:27 and 1 Sam. 14:30, 21:6). Since אַף כִּי is initial here, it could mean "The situation has reached this point" or "God went so far as to say that you should not eat of any of the trees of the garden!" The woman's reply quotes the original divine order in 2:16-17 with only minor additions and changes. (Scholarly opinions differ on this point.) Like 2:16, 3:2b is a X-*yiqtol* construction with an indicative *yiqtol* in the second position carrying a modal value. But compared to 2:17, 3:3 has אָמַר אֱלֹהִים 'God said' added. As in 2:17, the phrase וּמִפְּרִי הָעֵץ אֲשֶׁר בְּתוֹךְ־הַגָּן 'but of the

Analysis of Biblical Narrative

fruit of the tree that is in the middle of the garden' is a *casus pendens* functioning as protasis of a double sentence. The apodosis is the addition introducing God's direct speech: "But of the fruit of the tree that is in the middle of the garden (protasis), God said (apodosis), 'You should not eat of it.'"

3:4–5 The meaning of כִּי 'that' following the negative particle לֹא 'not' is "but" or "on the contrary," not "because." The translation is "You shall not die at all. *On the contrary* God knows ...." A dependent object clause follows, introduced by כִּי. It consists of a double clause as in 2:17. The protasis follows 2:17 closely, while the apodosis has *weqatal* instead of X-*yiqtol* (מוֹת תָּמוּת 'dying you shall die'). This fact shows that in the function of the apodosis X-*yiqtol* and *weqatal* exchange freely, without any difference.[18]

3:10 There is a nice example here of *qatal* used to report orally an event that was related earlier with *wayyiqtol* as historical narrative: "I heard your sound (אֶת־קֹלְךָ שָׁמַעְתִּי, a X-*qatal* construction)," which is for oral narrative. Earlier "they heard (וַיִּשְׁמְעוּ, *wayyiqtol*) the sound of God," for historical narrative, was used (3:8). This fact strongly suggests that *qatal* is at home in direct speech as *wayyiqtol* is at home in narrative. Indeed, it makes a remarkable difference that in oral narrative *wayyiqtol* is not found at the beginning but in the continuation only. On the contrary, in historical narrative *wayyiqtol* is found both at the beginning and in the continuation (see Niccacci 1990c §§22–24). Once the oral narrative has begun with X-*qatal*, it continues with *wayyiqtol* forms: " ... and I was afraid ... and I hid myself."

3:12–13 The answers of the man and the woman are good examples of the compound nominal clause in direct speech. Each one is a sentence with a finite verb form in the second position that functions as subject (the "given element") and a nominal element in the first position that functions as predicate (the "new element"). Let us compare the two sentences:

	Subject	Predicate	Casus pendens
3:12	נָתְנָה־לִּי מִן־הָעֵץ	הִוא	הָאִשָּׁה אֲשֶׁר נָתַתָּה עִמָּדִי
3:13	הִשִּׁיאַנִי	הַנָּחָשׁ	

3:12 The woman that you have put with me, it is she that gave me of the tree ...
3:13 It is the serpent that deceived me.

The reply of the man is clearly a compound nominal clause emphasizing the personal pronoun that becomes the predicate. The woman's reply follows the same pattern. Both the man and the woman try to throw off their own responsibility on to someone else. The context shows, then, that what is commonly the subject becomes the predicate, and vice versa (see Niccacci 1990c).[19]

3:14-17 The quotation formulas of the three divine speeches are worth noting. The first speech involves a *wayyiqtol* form: וַיֹּאמֶר יְהוָה אֱלֹהִים אֶל־הַנָּחָשׁ 'and Yahweh God said to the serpent'. The next two formulas are (*waw-*) X-*qatal*: אֶל־הָאִשָּׁה אָמַר 'to the woman he said' and וּלְאָדָם אָמַר '(and) to the man he said'. This change of verb forms is nicely accounted for in the theory I am proposing. The two X-*qatal* constructions (whether with or without *waw*) are compound nominal clauses signaling a secondary line in narrative. They are not independent but rely upon an independent *wayyiqtol*. Because, in 3:14-17, this *wayyiqtol* precedes, the two X-*qatal* convey background information (see Table 3.1). We can render this as follows: "Then Yahweh God said to the serpent... To the woman, *for her part,* he said... To the man, *for his part,* he said." Thus, the three speeches do not stand on the same level, as the syntax clearly shows, but the second and the third are related to the first. If, on the contrary, they were all expressed with a *wayyiqtol*, they would be successive speeches standing on the same level: "*Then* Yahweh God said to the serpent... *Then* he said to the woman... *Then* he said to the man." (This is the case with the first round of speeches in 3:11, 13, and 14. Note the order in which the three characters are addressed in vv. 11-14: man, woman, and serpent. In 16-17 the order is reversed: following the serpent is woman, then man.)

The beginning of God's words to the serpent, in 3:14, constitutes a double clause with כִּי עָשִׂיתָ זֹּאת 'because you did this' as the protasis, and אָרוּר אַתָּה מִכָּל־הַבְּהֵמָה וּמִכֹּל חַיַּת הַשָּׂדֶה 'you are cursed among all the animals and among all the living things of the earth' as the apodosis. Note that, in the protasis, the verb הָיָה 'be' does not appear. This means that the sentence is an affirmation rather than a command: "*You are* the most cursed among the beasts of the earth."[20] The phrase contrasts, of course, with the affirmation of verse 3:1: "Now, the serpent was the most cunning among the beasts of the earth."

Macrosyntax

The text closes at the end of Genesis 3. This is clear because in 4:1 we find a compound nominal clause that interrupts the mainline of narrative in order to convey antecedent information before the new story on Cain and Abel: "Now *(from the outset the reader should know that)* Adam knew Eve his wife." Between the two significant breaks in the communication (3:1 and 4:1) the text flows without major interruption from beginning to end. Direct speeches are dominant throughout as can easily be seen from the display of the text. Indeed, the speeches are of special importance for the development of the message. In the passages of direct speech, level 1 is normally used in the quotation formulas, and the two cases of (*waw-*)X-*qatal* constructions (3:16, 17) are linked to the preceding *wayyiqtol* (3:14) as background to foreground. Level 2 is never used. The text advances directly and quickly without allowing any pauses and the tension remains high throughout.

Notes

1. See "On the Hebrew Verbal System," my other article in this volume.

2. Examples of indicative X-*yiqtol* are in Gen. 2:16 and 3:3. For jussive *yiqtol*, see my analysis of Gen 1:3, 6, in sec. 7.

3. See my earlier work (1990*b* §135) on the classification of verb forms and grammatical constructions by position in the sentence and linguistic level.

4. An upward arrow ↑ before a sentence means that, although it belongs to a secondary level, it is placed in level 1 because it makes up a syntactical unit with the preceding *wayyiqtol* (see the tense shift *wayyiqtol* → *waw-*X-*qatal* in Table 3.1). Besides *waw-*X-*qatal*, *waw-*X-*yiqtol* (e.g., Gen. 2:19), the simple nominal clause (e.g., 3:6), and *weqatal* (e.g., 2:25, with negative *weqatal*) also play the same function.

5. See Niccacci 1990*c* §18 or 1990*a* §6.1. See also the tense shift X-*qatal* → *wayyiqtol* in Table 3.2. Other constructions functioning as antecedent information are the simple nominal clause (Gen. 1:20) and *waw-*X-*yiqtol* (2:5–6).

6. The first two clauses of 1:4 constitute a syntactical unit consisting of main sentence and object clause, literally "God saw the light, that it is good," an idiomatic construction with verbs of seeing. (This is supported by Joüon 1991 §158d.) In the object clause, the subject is implied.

7. As a volitive verb form *weyiqtol* is distinct from *weqatal*, a nonvolitive verb form (see Niccacci 1990*c* §§61–65).

8. A secondary-level construction (*waw-*X-negative -*qatal*) also comes at the end of 2 Sam. 6:23; the same is true in Judg. 1:36 (*waw-*simple nominal clause) and Ruth 4:18–22 (*waw-*simple nominal clause; *waw-*X-*qatal*). Compare Gen. 2:25 in section 7. Background verb forms also conclude modern stories, as shown by Weinrich (1985). (See Niccacci 1990*a*: 227 and footnote 268.)

9. As is well known, literary critics discover an irreconcilable contradiction between this passage and other mentions of the trees in Gen. 2:17 and 3:3, and posit two distinct stories that have been knit together secondarily. However, the indication "in the middle of the garden" is no argument against the unity of the text. Ancient interpreters did not see this as a problem at all. Ibn Ezra explicitly states that the two trees were in the middle of the garden without seeing any contradiction in it. Ramban (1971:71) elaborates this point as

follows: "we must say, according to the simple meaning of Scripture, that it was a known place in the garden which was 'in the midst' thereof. This is why Onkelos translated: 'in the middle of the garden.' Thus according to Onkelos the tree of life and the tree of knowledge were both in the middle of the garden. And if so, we must say that in the middle of the garden there was the likeness of an enclosed garden-bed made which contained these two trees. The 'middle' means near its middle for with respect to the exact middle they have already said that no one knows the true central point except G-d alone." We can add that the preposition בְּתוֹךְ can mean simply "inside" rather that "in the very middle" if we take into consideration 3:8: "They heard the sound of God walking *in* the garden (בַּגָּן) to the wind of the day and the man and his wife hid themselves from the presence of Yahweh God *in the middle of* the trees of the garden" (בְּתוֹךְ עֵץ הַגָּן). Of course, the clear distinction we read between "the trees *of* the garden" in 3:2, and "the trees that are *in the middle of* the garden" in 3:3 suggests that "the middle" is presented as a special, easily recognizable place, but it cannot be interpreted in a strict mathematical way. Unfortunately, the excesses of literary criticism oblige us to argue on details that would appear obvious to normal readers of the story.

10. Note the difference from the externally similar phrase in 2:16 where the prepositional phrase and the following *yiqtol* make up one single sentence. Niccacci (1990c §§123-25) presents criteria for distinguishing the compound nominal clause (e.g., X-*yiqtol*) from the double clause, or "two-element syntactical construction" (e.g., X = protasis | *yiqtol* = apodosis).

11. A well-known problem is the interpretation of "on the day you shall eat of it you shall certainly die." To override this problem some scholars would attribute to the prepositional phrase בְּיוֹם the meaning "*after* the day." A more recent treatment of this kind is that of S. Kempf (1993:354). This is, however, an unjustified solution in my opinion. The problem is how we should interpret "death" here. Given the wisdom background of the story, "death" can mean more than physical death. The kind of "death" alluded to here did happen in the same day our forefathers sinned. We should not make grammar and plain meaning subservient to subjective interpretation.

12. The word order makes this analysis preferable to the accepted translation: "and whatever the man called every living creature, that was its name" (RSV). Note that the naming is not to be translated as past (as in RSV) but as "future" (i.e., with the conditional in narrative) since it is expressed with a *yiqtol*.

13. Another, perhaps even better, possibility is to take וּלְאָדָם 'and to the man' as casus pendens with the preposition לְ 'to' functioning as the protasis of a double sentence: "But as for Adam, he (= Adam!) did not find a helper fit for himself." In this case, וּלְאָדָם would be a complete clause and have a separate line. An example of לְ introducing a casus pendens is found in Lev. 27:6.

14. Even if it is possible to prove that 2:15 is a doublet with 2:8 and that 2:10-14 is a later addition, we have to presume that the final redactor was a

man capable of writing correct Hebrew syntax. The assumption that difficulties in the syntax signal an intervention of a later glossator is one of the less credible arguments of literary criticism. How much do we know of Hebrew syntax? Who can say that the syntax of a given passage is faulty?

15. The clauses marked with an arrow are to be described as follows: in 2:19, X-*yiqtol*, and casus pendens (= protasis) + simple nominal clause (= apodosis); in 2:20, *waw*-X-negative -*qatal*; in 2:24, X-*yiqtol*, and *weqatal* (twice).

16. Note that *weqatal*, normally translated with the imperfect in modern languages, is translated here with the future, exactly as in direct speech. Indeed, this passage signals an overt intervention in the text on the part of the writer, who wishes to show the permanent effect of the founding encounter of man and woman at the beginning.

17. The connection of 2:25 with 3:1a has been suggested, tentatively, by W. H. Propp (1990 §6). See my review in *LA* 31(1991):554–55.

18. In earlier studies I discussed the special syntactical status of the verb forms found in the apodosis (1990c §126 and 1987 §2). They are all second-position verb forms since the first position in the double sentence is taken by the protasis. As such they are main but dependent sentences since they cannot stand without the protasis. In Biblical Hebrew protasis and apodosis constitute an indivisible syntactical unit.

19. One should reconsider the assumption that the verb is, in traditional terminology, the predicate, while the noun or pronoun is the subject and a prepositional phrase the complement. This is true in plain, nonmarked sentences. In marked sentences, however, where details of an event or information are to be conveyed, every element of the sentence can become the predicate, or the "new element."

20. In an earlier study (1990*b*) I presented a full exposition of the functions of the verb הָיָה 'be'.

References

Joüon, P. 1991. *A grammar of Biblical Hebrew*, vols. 1, 2. Translated and revised by T. Muraoka. Rome: Pontifical Biblical Institute Press.

Kempf, S. 1993. Genesis 3:14-19: Climax of Genesis 2-3? *Journal of Translation and Textlinguistics* 6(4):354-77.

Niccacci, A. 1987. A neglected point of Hebrew syntax: *yiqtol* and position in the sentence. *LA* 37:7-19.

———. 1990a. Lettura sintattica della prosa ebraico-biblica: Principi e applicazioni. SBFAn, 31. Jerusalem: Franciscan Printing Press.

———. 1990b. Sullo stato sintattico del verbo hāyâ. *LA* 40:9-23.

———. 1990c. The syntax of the verb in classical Hebrew prose. Trans. by W. G. E. Watson. *Journal for the Study of the Old Testament*, supplement 86. Sheffield: Sheffield Academic Press.

Prince, G. 1982. *Narratology: The form and functioning of narrative*. Janua Linguarum, Series Maior, 108. Berlin: Mouton.

Propp, W. 1990. Eden sketches. In *The Hebrew Bible and its interpreters*, ed. W. Propp, B. Halpern, and D. Freedman, 189-203. Biblical and Judaic Studies from the University of California, San Diego, 1. Winona Lake: Eisenbrauns.

Ramban [Nachmanides]. 1971. *Commentary on the Torah: Genesis*. Ed. C. Chavel. New York: Shilo Publishing House.

Waltke, B., and M. O'Connor. 1990. *An introduction to Biblical Hebrew syntax*. Winona Lake, Ind.: Eisenbrauns.

Weinrich, H. 1985. *Tempus: Besprochene und erzählte Welt*. 4th ed. Stuttgart: Kohlhammer.

8

INTRODUCING DIRECT DISCOURSE IN BIBLICAL HEBREW NARRATIVE[1]

Cynthia L. Miller

This article examines the syntactic mechanisms for the introduction of direct discourse in Biblical Hebrew and their discourse-pragmatic functions. Three categories of direct discourse are distinguished on the basis of the syntactic form of the quotative frame: (1) single-verb frames with one finite speech verb; (2) multiple-verb frames with two (or more) speech verbs which refer to the same locutionary act; (3) frames with one finite verb and an infinitival form of the verb אמר 'to say' (לֵאמֹר). The last category is particularly noteworthy. Examination of frames with לֵאמֹר shows that when the infinitive is used to introduce reported speech, it is not a gerundive infinitive, but a complementizer. The third category has other interesting syntactic features: it may exhibit unusual patterns of pronominal reference, and it may introduce reported speech in instances where the matrix verb is not a speech verb.

The discourse-pragmatic functions of the various frames depend upon the intersection of a number of syntactic, semantic, and pragmatic features: the semantics of the matrix verb, the distribution of matrix verbs within the three frames, identification of central and marginal configurations, identification of marked and unmarked constructions, and the broader dialogic context.

Reported speech permeates Biblical Hebrew narrative (Alter 1981:65, 70). Almost half of narrative is reported speech,[2] but its importance extends beyond sheer quantity. Reported speech that portrays dialogue often provides the central framework for the plot structure of a story. In addition, reported speech outside of dialogue may be used for various narrative purposes—to introduce characters, to recount their inner thought processes, and to provide background information for the narrative (Bar-Efrat 1989:64–77). Reported speech also finds application in expressing divine action and will as in God's creation of the world (Genesis 1–2), the giving of the law (Exodus 20–24), the establishment of ritual (Leviticus), and instruction concerning building the wilderness sanctuary (Exodus 25–31; 35:1–36:1).[3] An understanding of reported speech is thus critical for understanding biblical narrative.

A token of reported speech is composed of two parts: the *quotation*, which represents the original locution, and the *quotative frame*, the report which introduces the quotation.[4] This article provides a linguistic description of the quotative frames of direct speech in Biblical Hebrew narrative.[5]

First, the salient syntactic features of the various of direct quotative frames are described; then the discourse-pragmatic functions of those forms within narrative are examined. But before discussing these, I review the relevant linguistic features of reported speech in general and direct speech in particular.

1. The linguistic features of reported speech

Reported speech is an interesting linguistic phenomenon in that it is the combination of two distinct discourse events—that in which an utterance was originally expressed and that in which it is cited by another (Sternberg 1982:107). The traditional account of reported speech has described the combination of the two speech events under two broad rubrics—direct speech and indirect speech. By this account, direct speech reports the original locution directly, in the precise wording of the original and with the deictic center of the original (as attested by deictics, exclamatives, vocatives, etc.).[6] Indirect speech, by contrast, reports the original locution indirectly. The reporting speaker takes the original locution and rephrases it to a greater or lesser extent. Minimally, two changes take place. One, the deictic center of the original is changed to reflect that of the reporting speaker. Two, the original locution is syntactically subordinated to the reporting speaker's frame—sentence fragments, exclamatives, and vocatives are excluded. The reporting speaker may, however, reanalyze the original locution to such an extent that the original is entirely irretrievable.[7] The traditional account thus operates in terms of what may be described as two axes: deixis and syntactic subordination. The traditional account is a useful starting point; however, a more insightful description of reported speech can be accomplished by considering the nature of reported speech more closely.

Reported speech is essentially reflexive—it is language describing itself. Language which is used to talk about language is referred to generally as a *metalanguage*.[8] Reported speech, however, may be described more specifically—it is the use of one speech event (the report) to describe another speech event (the original locution). Each of these speech events is pragmatic in two respects (Silverstein 1987:17–38). On the one hand, each is intentional, purposive social behavior and, on the other hand, each bears a relation to its context of use. Because reported speech is the use of one pragmatic event to describe another pragmatic event, we may then refer to reported speech as a specific subcategory of metalanguage, namely, *metapragmatic* (Silverstein 1985:133; 1993:33–58). In the reporting of a speech event, the reporting speaker imposes his or her metapragmatic analysis upon the reported speech event. This analysis of the original locution may be evident in both the quotation and the frame.

The speech verb in the frame is metapragmatic in that it may index the type of speech event and/or its place within the conversation. For example, the verb *ask* indexes the type of speech event being reported (i.e., a question) as in the sentence *John asked Mary, "Are you finished with the shovel?"* The verb *respond* indexes the position of the speech event within the conversation (i.e., in second position after another speech event) as in the sentence *Mary responded, "Not yet."* The frame may index other features of the original locution such as the code or the channel. In the example *Mary asked in Hebrew over the phone, "Mî ʾattâ?"*, the code is Hebrew and the channel is the phone. The frame may also index the speech participants of the original locution such as speaker, addressee, and bystanders. In *Mary said to John in front of the children, "Where have you been?"*, the speaker is Mary, the addressee John, and the bystanders are the children.

The quotation of reported speech may also be metapragmatic to the extent that the reporting speaker provides a metapragmatic analysis of the original speaker's words (Silverstein 1985:135-38). A direct quotation purports to represent the original locution without reanalysis by the reporting speaker. An indirect quotation, however, involves a higher degree of metapragmatic analysis by the reporting speaker. Recognition of reported speech as metapragmatic allows for a more accurate description of reported speech, as well as a means for representing reported speech in scalar terms, rather than bifurcated between the two poles of direct speech and indirect speech.

2. Distinguishing direct speech from indirect speech

Direct speech in Biblical Hebrew is distinguished from indirect speech first and foremost on the basis of deictic indicators, particularly pronominal reference.[9] In indirect speech, pronominal reference is transparent; that is, it is calculated on the basis of the frame.[10] In direct speech, pronominal reference is opaque; that is, it is independent of the frame.[11] Secondarily, direct speech and indirect speech are distinguished on the basis of subordination[12]—the quotation of direct speech is unincorporated into the frame whereas the quotation of indirect speech is incorporated into the frame.[13]

Because direct speech exhibits syntactic independence of the quotation from the frame, direct speech in Hebrew may show four additional permutations which are not found in indirect speech. First, direct speech may be embedded within direct speech for up to three layers of embedding as in example 1.

(1) 2 Kings 1:6

וַיֹּאמְרוּ אֵלָיו
1 אִישׁ עָלָה לִקְרָאתֵנוּ וַיֹּאמֶר אֵלֵינוּ
2 לְכוּ שׁוּבוּ אֶל־הַמֶּלֶךְ אֲשֶׁר־שָׁלַח אֶתְכֶם וְדִבַּרְתֶּם אֵלָיו
3 כֹּה אָמַר יְהוָה
הַמִבְּלִי אֵין־אֱלֹהִים בְּיִשְׂרָאֵל ...

They [the messengers] said to him [the king],
1. "A man came to meet us and he said to us,
2.   'Return to the king who sent you and say to him,
3.   "Thus says Yahweh,
       'Is there no king in Israel? ...'"'"

By contrast, indirect speech may be embedded within direct speech, but not within indirect speech. In example 2, the first embedded quotation (a) is direct; the second embedded quotation (b) is indirect:

(2) 1 Kings 18:9-10

וַיֹּאמֶר מֶה חָטָאתִי כִּי־אַתָּה נֹתֵן אֶת־עַבְדְּךָ בְּיַד־אַחְאָב
לַהֲמִיתֵנִי: חַי יְהוָה אֱלֹהֶיךָ אִם־יֶשׁ־גּוֹי וּמַמְלָכָה אֲשֶׁר
לֹא־שָׁלַח אֲדֹנִי שָׁם לְבַקֶּשְׁךָ
a וְאָמְרוּ אָיִן
b וְהִשְׁבִּיעַ אֶת־הַמַּמְלָכָה וְאֶת־הַגּוֹי כִּי לֹא יִמְצָאֶכָּה:

He [the servant] said, "How have I sinned that you are giving your servant into the hand of Ahab to kill me? As Yahweh your God lives there is no people and no kingdom to whom my lord [Ahab] did not send to seek you,
  a. but they said, 'He is not here.'
  b. So he [Ahab] caused each kingdom and people to swear that they had not found you."

A second feature that distinguishes direct speech is that the frame may appear finally or medially with respect to the quotation. Initial frames are overwhelmingly the most common in prose.[14] Final and medial frames are very rare in prose, but more common in verse.[15] The sole example of a final frame within our corpus is in example 3.

(3) Lev. 13:45

וְהַצָּרוּעַ אֲשֶׁר־בּוֹ הַנֶּגַע בְּגָדָיו יִהְיוּ פְרֻמִים וְרֹאשׁוֹ יִהְיֶה
פָרוּעַ וְעַל־שָׂפָם יַעְטֶה וְטָמֵא טָמֵא יִקְרָא׃

As for the person with the mark of an infectious disease: his clothes must be torn, his hair must be loose, the upper lip he must cover and "Unclean, unclean!" he must cry.

By contrast, the frame of indirect speech necessarily appears only initially since the quotation is syntactically subordinate to the frame.

A third feature that distinguishes direct speech is that the frame of direct speech may be discontinuous with a parenthetical narrative remark interrupting it:[16]

(4) Judg. 20:27-28a

וַיִּשְׁאֲלוּ בְנֵי־יִשְׂרָאֵל בַּיהוָה וְשָׁם אֲרוֹן בְּרִית הָאֱלֹהִים בַּיָּמִים
הָהֵם׃ וּפִינְחָס בֶּן־אֶלְעָזָר בֶּן־אַהֲרֹן עֹמֵד לְפָנָיו בַּיָּמִים הָהֵם
לֵאמֹר הַאוֹסִף עוֹד לָצֵאת לַמִּלְחָמָה עִם־בְּנֵי־בִנְיָמִן אָחִי אִם־אֶחְדָּל

The sons of Israel inquired of Yahweh—now at that place was the ark of the covenant of God in those days, and Phinehas the son of Eleazar the son of Aaron was ministering before it in those days—saying, "Shall we [lit., I] again go out to fight with the Benjaminites, our [lit., my] brother, or shall we [lit., I] cease?"

The parenthetical remark gives information concerning the location of the oracle and the officiating priest.

Finally, direct speech is distinguished in that the frame of direct speech may be entirely absent; that is, the direct quotation is entirely unframed,[17] the only indications of direct speech being the presence of deictics and other elements indicating a switch from the narrative:

(5) 2 Kings 10:15

וַיֵּלֶךְ מִשָּׁם וַיִּמְצָא אֶת־יְהוֹנָדָב בֶּן־רֵכָב לִקְרָאתוֹ
וַיְבָרְכֵהוּ וַיֹּאמֶר אֵלָיו הֲיֵשׁ אֶת־לְבָבְךָ יָשָׁר כַּאֲשֶׁר a
לְבָבִי עִם־לְבָבֶךָ
וַיֹּאמֶר יְהוֹנָדָב יֵשׁ b
וָיֵשׁ תְּנָה אֶת־יָדֶךָ c
וַיִּתֵּן יָדוֹ וַיַּעֲלֵהוּ אֵלָיו אֶל־הַמֶּרְכָּבָה׃ d

After he [Jehu] left there, he came upon Jehonadab son of Recab, who was on his way to meet him.
   a. He [Jehu] greeted him and said, "Are you in accord with me, as I am with you?"

    b. Jehonadab said, "I am."
    c. [Jehu said,] "If so, give (me) your hand."
    d. He [Jehonadab] did, and he [Jehu] helped him [Jehonadab] up into the chariot.

The speech in c is clearly the speech of Jehu, but it is not introduced with a quotative frame.[18]

We have seen that the distinction between direct and indirect speech is clearly maintained in Biblical Hebrew. This discrimination alone, however, is not sufficient to describe adequately the features of reported speech in the Bible. The next section examines the various subcategories of direct speech.

3. The syntactic forms of direct quotative frames

Three syntactic forms of direct speech may be distinguished in Biblical Hebrew based upon the syntactic complexity of the quotative frame.[19] These three categories are summarized in Table 1.

Table 1. Categories of direct speech

Category of Frame	Matrix Verb	Form of אמר 'to say'
Single-verb frame	finite verb	
Multiple-verb frame	finite verb(s)	+ finite form
לֵאמֹר frame	finite verb(s)/ zero verb	+ infinitive construct

In the first category, the quotative frame has one finite speech verb:

(6) 2 Sam. 18:29

וַיֹּאמֶר הַמֶּלֶךְ שָׁלוֹם לַנַּעַר לְאַבְשָׁלוֹם

The king said, "Is the lad Absalom safe?"

Single-verb frames are by far the most common in Biblical Hebrew (over 2,200 tokens), but only when the framing verb is אמר 'to say'.

In the second category, the quotative frame has multiple finite metapragmatic verbs,[20] and each verb refers to the same speech event.[21] Furthermore, the speech participants in each clause are identical and have identical roles in the speech event:

(7) 2 Sam. 18:28a

וַיִּקְרָא אֲחִימַעַץ וַיֹּאמֶר אֶל־הַמֶּלֶךְ שָׁלוֹם

Then Ahimaaz called out to the king [lit., Ahimaaz called and said to the king], "Peace."

Note that in example 7 linguistic expressions referring to the speaker and addressee may be jointly shared. The speaker of the speech event is indexed in the subject of the first clause, the addressee is indexed in a prepositional phrase in the second clause. The fact that the two verbs share arguments is further evidence that they refer to a single speech event.

The metapragmatic verbs in a multiple-verb frame share a number of other features. Each verb is inflected identically with respect to gender and number.[22] In addition, the tense/aspect of each verb is either identical[23] or consecutive.[24]

The arrangement of metapragmatic verbs within the frame is also significant. The final verb conveys the least metapragmatic information. Usually אמר 'to say' occurs in final position;[25] occasionally דבר 'to speak' is found when the preceding verb is ענה 'to answer'.[26] The first verb usually indexes the speaker of the speech event and other metapragmatic features of the speech event.

The third category of direct quotative frame involves quotative frames with one finite speech verb plus לֵאמֹר, the infinitive construct of אמר 'to say' with the preposition ל 'to':

(8) Gen. 41:16

וַיַּעַן יוֹסֵף אֶת־פַּרְעֹה לֵאמֹר בִּלְעָדָי אֱלֹהִים יַעֲנֶה אֶת־שְׁלוֹם פַּרְעֹה׃

Joseph answered Pharaoh לֵאמֹר, "Not I. God will give an answer for the well-being of Pharaoh."

This third category of direct speech is particularly noteworthy. Morphologically, the form is unexpected—לֶאֱמֹר would be the regular form of the infinitive construct. Instead, the form לֵאמֹר exhibits resyllabification in which the sequence /Ceʾĕ/ is simplified to /Ceʾ/. Although resyllabification of this type is attested elsewhere in the language (e.g., *weʾĕlōhîm 'and God' which regularly appears as וֵאלֹהִים),[27] it is not exhibited on any other infinitive construct with an initial aleph (e.g., לֶאֱהֹב 'to love', לֶאֱחֹז 'to grasp', לֶאֱכֹל 'to eat', לֶאֱסֹף 'to add', and לֶאֱסֹר 'to bind').

Frames with לֵאמֹר are also noteworthy in that the syntactic interpretation of this form as an infinitive construct and its significance have been hotly debated (see Miller 1993). The infinitive construct in Hebrew is used in two distinct syntactic constructions and לֵאמֹר appears in each of these. In the first construction, the infinitival phrase is a verbal complement; that is, it is a clause that stands in a grammatical relation (i.e., as subject or object) to the structure in which it is embedded.

(9) 1 Kings 11:40

וַיְבַקֵּשׁ שְׁלֹמֹה לְהָמִית אֶת־יָרָבְעָם

Solomon sought to kill Jeroboam.

There are only two instances of לֵאמֹר used in this way and both occur in early biblical prose. One example appears in 10.

(10) 2 Sam. 2:22

וַיֹּסֶף עוֹד אַבְנֵר לֵאמֹר אֶל־עֲשָׂהאֵל סוּר לְךָ מֵאַחֲרָי . . .

Abner said again [lit., added to say] to Asahel, "Turn aside from following me . . ."

In the second construction, the infinitival clause functions as an embedded clause after a matrix verb to indicate purpose or result as in example 11.

(11) Lev. 14:36

וְאַחַר כֵּן יָבֹא הַכֹּהֵן לִרְאוֹת אֶת־הַבָּיִת

And after that the priest will come to see the house.

All examples of לֵאמֹר in this construction occur in late biblical prose. One example appears in 12.

(12) Esther 6:4

וְהָמָן בָּא לַחֲצַר בֵּית־הַמֶּלֶךְ הַחִיצוֹנָה לֵאמֹר לַמֶּלֶךְ לִתְלוֹת
אֶת־מָרְדֳּכַי עַל־הָעֵץ אֲשֶׁר־הֵכִין לוֹ:

Now Haman had just come into the outer court of the king's palace to say to the king to hang Mordecai upon the gallows which he had erected for him.

There is a third use of the infinitive construct related to the second construction. When the finite verb in connection with the infinitival clause seems to have a meaning other than purpose or result, the infinitive construct is said to "state motives, attendant circumstances, or otherwise define more exactly" (Gesenius and Kautzsch 1910, sec. 114*o*) or to "explain the circumstances or nature of a preceding action" (Waltke and O'Connor 1990, sec. 36.2.3e). It is thus called a "gerundive infinitive," on the basis of its translation into Indo-European languages (especially Latin) by a gerund rather than an infinitive. Examples of the so-called gerundive infinitive are given in 13 and 14.

(13) Gen. 34:7

וּבְנֵי יַעֲקֹב בָּאוּ מִן־הַשָּׂדֶה כְּשָׁמְעָם וַיִּתְעַצְּבוּ הָאֲנָשִׁים וַיִּחַר
לָהֶם מְאֹד כִּי־נְבָלָה עָשָׂה בְיִשְׂרָאֵל לִשְׁכַּב אֶת־בַּת־יַעֲקֹב וְכֵן

לֹא יֵעָשֶׂה:

So the sons of Jacob came in from the field when they heard (it) and they were grieved and very angry because he [Shechem] did a disgraceful thing in Israel by sleeping with Jacob's daughter—a thing which is not done.

(14) Deut. 5:12

שָׁמוֹר אֶת־יוֹם הַשַּׁבָּת לְקַדְּשׁוֹ

Keep the Sabbath day by sanctifying it.

It is this third category into which לֵאמֹר is said to fall.[28]

In evaluating this syntactic analysis of לֵאמֹר as a gerundive infinitive, it is important first to notice that gerundive infinitives in Hebrew share all of the syntactic features of embedded infinitives. They may govern direct and indirect objects, prepositional phrases, and adverbial phrases and may be conjoined with other infinitival phrases. Gerundive infinitives, then, are not a distinct syntactic category of infinitives. Instead, they belong in the category of embedded infinitives, along with infinitives which express purpose or result.

In contrast to gerundive infinitives generally, לֵאמֹר does not share any features of infinitival syntax with embedded infinitives when it introduces direct speech. Three lines of evidence substantiate this claim: (1) לֵאמֹר does not exhibit ordinary features of internal infinitival syntax; (2) the semantics of the matrix verb in the quotative frame may not allow an interpretation in which the infinitive provides "circumstantial information" to the matrix verb in the same way that the so-called gerundive infinitives do; (3) the external syntax of לֵאמֹר shows that it is not a verbal complement.

Let us examine each of these arguments. First, the internal syntax of לֵאמֹר when it introduces a quotation differs significantly from that of true infinitives: לֵאמֹר never governs an object or an adverbial phrase, it does not take pronominal suffixes,[29] and it is never conjoined with another infinitival clause.[30] When the addressees of the speech event are specified by a prepositional phrase, the prepositional phrase precedes לֵאמֹר and is governed by the matrix verb, not the infinitive. That is, we regularly find examples such as וַיְדַבֵּר מֹשֶׁה אֶל־בְּנֵי יִשְׂרָאֵל לֵאמֹר 'Moses spoke to the sons of Israel לֵאמֹר', but not *וַיְדַבֵּר מֹשֶׁה לֵאמֹר אֶל־ בְּנֵי יִשְׂרָאֵל 'Moses spoke לֵאמֹר to the sons of Israel'.[31]

Second, the fact that לֵאמֹר cannot be an embedded or gerundive infinitive is clear from instances in which לֵאמֹר cannot specify the attendant circumstances of the matrix verb.[32] This is particularly the case when the matrix verb is not a speech verb. Consider the following example in which the matrix verb is שׁמע 'to hear' and refers to the reception of information:

(15) 1 Kings 16:16

וַיִּשְׁמַע הָעָם הַחֹנִים לֵאמֹר קָשַׁר זִמְרִי וְגַם הִכָּה אֶת־הַמֶּלֶךְ

The people in the camp heard the following information [lit., heard לֵאמֹר], "Zimri was treacherous and even killed the king."

Note that the infinitive לֵאמֹר cannot be a gerundive infinitive (since one cannot 'hear by saying'), nor can it be an embedded infinitive expressing purpose (since one cannot 'hear in order to say').

In example 16 לֵאמֹר is clearly not an embedded or gerundive infinitive:

(16) Exod. 5:19

וַיִּרְאוּ שֹׁטְרֵי בְנֵי־יִשְׂרָאֵל אֹתָם בְּרָע לֵאמֹר לֹא־תִגְרְעוּ מִלִּבְנֵיכֶם דְּבַר־יוֹם בְּיוֹמוֹ׃

The foremen$_i$ of the sons of Israel saw themselves in trouble with respect to the statement [lit., לֵאמֹר], "You$_i$ will not diminish your daily quantity of bricks."

In this remarkable example, the pronouns in the quotation indicate that the speakers are the Egyptian overseers, not the Israelite foremen, but there is no reference to the Egyptians within the frame.[33] The speakers of the quotation are thus not co-referential with any expressed participant in the frame. If לֵאמֹר were a true infinitive, either the subject or object of the matrix verb would necessarily be the speaker of the quotation.

Third, it is possible for the matrix verb of the quotative frame to have a verbal complement apart from לֵאמֹר. This clearly shows that לֵאמֹר cannot be understood as a verbal complement:

(17) Josh. 18:8

וַיָּקֻמוּ הָאֲנָשִׁים וַיֵּלֵכוּ וַיְצַו יְהוֹשֻׁעַ אֶת־הַהֹלְכִים לִכְתֹּב אֶת־הָאָרֶץ לֵאמֹר לְכוּ וְהִתְהַלְּכוּ בָאָרֶץ וְכִתְבוּ אוֹתָהּ וְשׁוּבוּ אֵלַי

So the men arose and went and Joshua commanded those going to write the land לֵאמֹר, "Go and walk around the land and write it and return to me . . ."

Here the infinitive לִכְתֹּב 'to write' is the complement of the verb צוה 'to command'; לֵאמֹר cannot possibly be understood as a verbal complement.

Thus לֵאמֹר is not a frozen form, since it may appear occasionally as a true infinitive, as in examples 10 and 12. However, when it appears in a quotative frame immediately preceding the quotation (as in 8), it is not a true infinitive. The description of לֵאמֹר as a gerundive infinitive is entirely without syntactic evidence.

A better approach is to see לֵאמֹר as an infinitive that has become grammaticalized as a complementizer introducing the complement of direct speech.[34] This explains two important syntactic features of לֵאמֹר: its appearance always at the end of the quotative frame immediately preceding the quotation and its failure to govern subjects, objects, prepositional phrases, or adverbial phrases.

The quotations introduced by לֵאמֹר frames exhibit interesting features as well. The exclamatives אוֹי 'woe' and חָלִילָה לִי 'far be it from me' do not occur in these quotations, though they do occur in direct speech generally. In addition, the pronouns within the לֵאמֹר quotation may exhibit unusual concordance with the deixis of the frame:

(18) Gen. 50:4–5

a   וַיַּעַבְרוּ יְמֵי בְכִיתוֹ וַיְדַבֵּר יוֹסֵף אֶל־בֵּית פַּרְעֹה לֵאמֹר
b   אִם־נָא מָצָאתִי חֵן בְּעֵינֵיכֶם דַּבְּרוּ־נָא בְּאָזְנֵי פַרְעֹה לֵאמֹר
c   אָבִי הִשְׁבִּיעַנִי לֵאמֹר
d   הִנֵּה אָנֹכִי מֵת בְּקִבְרִי אֲשֶׁר כָּרִיתִי לִי בְּאֶרֶץ כְּנַעַן שָׁמָּה תִּקְבְּרֵנִי

- a. When the days of mourning him [Jacob] were over, Joseph spoke to the house of Pharaoh לֵאמֹר,
- b. "If I have found favor in your eyes, please speak to Pharaoh לֵאמֹר,
- c. 'My father caused me to swear לֵאמֹר,
- d. "Behold I am dying. Bury me in my grave which I dug for myself in the land of Canaan."'"

In b, the embedded quotative frame with לֵאמֹר introduces what Joseph wants Pharaoh's courtiers to say to Pharaoh. However, in the quotation in c, the pronouns ('my', 'me') and the choice of lexical items ('my father' instead of 'Jacob') reflect Joseph's perspective. When the courtiers presented Joseph's message to Pharaoh, they would necessarily say, "Joseph's father (or Jacob) caused him to swear."

In summary, there are various categories of direct speech, distinguishable on the basis of formal, syntactical features of the quotative frame. The function and significance of these categories are examined in the following section.

4. The discourse-pragmatic functions of direct quotative frames

Having examined the syntactic features of the three types of direct quotative frames, we are ready to examine a broader question. What are the discourse-pragmatic functions of the various frames? That is, how does direct speech introduced with one quotative frame (e.g., a multiple-verb frame) differ from direct speech introduced with another quotative frame (e.g., a לֵאמֹר frame)? Are there functional and/or distributional differences between the three types of quotative frames? How does the use of one or another quotative frame contribute to the import of the conversation or narrative within which it appears?[35]

Approaching these questions will involve two levels of analysis. The first level involves the distribution of matrix verbs within the three quotative frames (sec. 4.1). The second level of analysis involves the interaction of three features: the semantics of the matrix verb, the syntax of the quotative frame, and the pragmatics of the speech situation (sec. 4.2).

4.1 Distribution of matrix verbs within quotative frames

Table 2 gives the distribution of matrix metapragmatic verbs and phrasal expressions within the three syntactically distinct types of direct quotative frames.[36] Because the statistics are based upon a corpus of over 4,500 occurrences, the results are reasonably accurate for the more common verbs. However, for verbs that occur only a few times, the conclusions that follow must be considered tentative.

The distributional data are examined from three interrelated perspectives. The first concerns the determination of optional versus obligatory configurations. The second relates to central versus marginal configurations. The third relates to marked versus unmarked constructions.

Table 2. Distribution of metapragmatic verbs in quotative frames

	Single Verb	Multiple Verb	לֵאמֹר
Central Configuration = Single-verb frame			
אמר 'to say'	2172	7	61
מלל 'to say'	1		
ספד 'to mourn'	1		
Central Configuration = Multiple-verb frame			
ענה 'to answer'	5	70	9
קרא 'to call'	9	57	13

	Single Verb	Multiple Verb	לֵאמֹר
בֵּרֵךְ 'to bless'		13	4
נָדַר 'to vow'		3	2
סִפֵּר 'to recount'		4	1
פָּלַל 'to pray'		5	1
הִתֵל 'to mock'		1	
קִלֵּס 'to mock'		1	
מֵאֵן 'to refuse'		4	
נִחַם 'to comfort'		1	
קוֹנֵן 'to lament'		1	
עָתַר 'to pray'		1	
רוֹעַ 'to give a shout'		1	
שִׂים דָּבָר 'to put a word'		2	
הָיָה מָשָׁל 'a proverb was'		1	
נָשָׂא מָשָׁל 'to raise a proverb'		6	
הֵרִים קוֹל 'to cause a shout to rise'		2	
Central Configuration = לֵאמֹר frame			
דִּבֶּר 'to speak'	34	32	175
זָעַק 'to cry out'	1	1	2
נָגַד 'to tell'			
Hophal	4(?)	—	9
Hiphil s.	—	11	11
Hiphil pl.	—	2	16
צִוָּה 'to command'	7	6	56
צָעַק 'to cry out'	1	1	6
שָׁאַל 'to ask/greet'	1	5	12
'to inquire'	2	—	7
שָׁבַע (Niphal) 'to swear'	3	3	16
(Hiphil) 'to cause to swear'	—	1	5
שָׁלַח 'to send [message]'	3	7	42
'to send [messenger]'	1	5	7
בָּכָה 'to weep'		1	3
הֵשִׁיב דָּבָר 'to cause a word to return'		2	4
כָּתַב 'to write'	2		4
שָׁמַע 'to hear'	1		10

	Single Verb	Multiple Verb	לֵאמֹר
אלה (Hiphil) 'to take an oath'			1
באר 'to give news'			1
דין (Niphal) 'to argue with'			1
דרש 'to seek'			2
חנן (Hithpael) 'to implore favor'			2
חרש 'to be silent'			1
כחש 'to lie'			1
נבא (Hithpael) 'to prophesy'			2
סות 'to incite'			4
עוד (Hiphil) 'to testify'			4
פאר (Piel) 'to boast'			1
צחק 'to laugh'			2
רמה 'to deceive'			1
גלה אזן 'to uncover ears'			2
הנה דבר יהוה אל 'behold the word of Yahweh was to'			1
היה דבר יהוה אל 'the word of Yahweh was to'			19
ידע (Hiphil) 'to cause to know'			1
הוציא דבה 'to cause an evil report to go out'			1
מצות 'commandments'			1
ספר 'letter'			1
נתן מופת 'to give a sign'			1
עבר הרנה 'a shout crossed over/through'			1
העביר קול 'to cause the sound to cross over'			1
שים עלילת דברים 'to make baseless charges'			1

Indeterminate Categories

	Single Verb	Multiple Verb	לֵאמֹר
שיר 'to sing'	1	1(?)	1
יעץ (Niphal) 'to take counsel'		1	1
חרף 'to reproach'		1	1
לון 'to grumble'		2	2
ריב 'to strive, contend'		1	1
תקע 'to sound the ram's horn'		1	1

4.1.1 Optional and obligatory configurations

An obligatory configuration[37] is one in which a particular verb invariably occurs in only one syntactic frame. No discourse-pragmatic function may be assigned to the use of that particular syntactic frame when it must obligatorily appear with a particular verb. Optional configurations are in view when a particular verb may appear in two or more syntactic frames. Optional configurations may bear a discourse-pragmatic function. The determination of optional versus obligatory configurations is possible in principle; however, given the nature of our data in this corpus and the impossibility of eliciting new data, it is impossible to determine with certainty.

Based on the data in Table 2, obligatory configurations may be identified as follows. A single-verb frame is obligatory only with the rare verbs מלל 'to say' (a poetic variant for אמר) and ספד 'to mourn'.

Multiple-verb frames are obligatory with eleven verbs or verb phrases; all are uncommon. Seven are metapragmatic verbs—התל 'to mock', קלס 'to mock', מאן 'to refuse', נחם 'to comfort', קנן 'to lament', עתר 'to pray', רוע 'to give a shout'. Four are metapragmatic expressions (phrases referring to communication)—שים דבר 'to put a word' (i.e., to tell someone what to say), היה משל 'a wise saying was' (i.e., to recite a proverb or wise saying), נשא משל 'to raise a wise saying', הרים קול 'to cause a shout to rise' (i.e., to shout).

Frames with לאמר are obligatory with the greatest number of metapragmatic verbs and expressions. The following fourteen verbs occur only with לאמר: אלה (Hiphil) 'to take an oath', באר 'to give news', דין (Niphal) 'to argue with', דרש 'to seek', חנן (Hithpael) 'to implore favor', חרש 'to be silent', ידע (Hiphil) 'to cause to know', כחש 'to lie', נבא (Hithpael) 'to prophesy', סות 'to incite', עוד (Hiphil) 'to testify', פאר (Piel) 'to boast', צחק 'to laugh', רמה 'to deceive'. The following ten expressions occur only with לאמר: גלה אזן 'to uncover ears', הנה היה דבר יהוה אל PN 'behold the word of Yahweh was to PN', היה דבר יהוה אל PN 'the word of Yahweh was to PN', הוציא דבה 'to cause an evil report to go out', מצות 'commandment', ספר 'letter', נתן מופת 'to give a sign', העביר קול 'to cause the sound to cross over/through', עבר רנה 'a shout crossed over/through', שים עלילת דברים 'to put wantonness of words' (i.e., make baseless charges).

These data summarized in Table 2 are significant in two ways, though the caveat concerning the problem of statistical frequency applies here also. First, the data indicate a ranking among the three syntactic frames with respect to obligatory configurations. Single-verb frames are rare in obligatory configurations, לֵאמֹר frames are the most common, and multiple-verb frames are intermediary between them. This may be schematized:

single-verb frames < multiple-verb frames < לֵאמֹר frames.

Second, these data illustrate that communicational expressions (phrases) are most likely to appear (obligatorily) in לֵאמֹר frames.

4.1.2 Central and marginal configurations

The data in Table 2 are arranged in three categories based upon which syntactic construction is the most common, or central, for a given verb.[38] For example, ענה 'to answer' occurs in all three quotative frames, but most commonly in multiple-verb frames. Thus, ענה in a multiple-verb frame is in its central configuration; when ענה occurs in a single-verb frame or a לֵאמֹר frame, it is in a marginal configuration. The verb דבר 'to speak' also occurs in all three frames, but most commonly in לֵאמֹר frames; therefore, לֵאמֹר is the central configuration for דבר. A few verbs occur with equal frequency in more than one syntactic frame; these are listed as indeterminate since it is impossible to specify which configuration is central.

A single-verb frame appears as the central configuration only when the matrix verb is אמר 'to say'. Multiple-verb frames are central configurations with the verbs ענה 'to answer', קרא 'to call', ברך 'to bless', נדר 'to vow', ספר 'to recount', פלל 'to pray'. Frames with לֵאמֹר are central configurations with the verbs דבר 'to speak', זעק and צעק 'to cry out', נגד 'to tell' (both in the Hiphil and Hophal stems), צוה 'to command', שאל 'to ask', שבע 'to swear' (both in the Niphal and the Hiphil), שלח 'to send', בכה 'to weep', כתב 'to write', שמע 'to hear' and with the communication expression השיב דבר 'to cause word to return' (i.e., to send back word).

These data again illustrate that single-verb frames are least likely to be the central configuration in which a matrix verb occurs, whereas לֵאמֹר frames are the most common central configuration. The same ranking occurs as in the earlier schematization:

single-verb frames < multiple-verb frames < לֵאמֹר frames.

The difference, however, between obligatory configurations and central configurations is significant. An obligatory configuration must occur with a particular matrix verb (or verb phrase) and carries *no* discourse-pragmatic function. A central configuration occurs most commonly with a particular matrix verb (or verb phrase) and *does* carry a discourse-pragmatic function.

4.1.3 Marked and unmarked constructions

In general, the notion of markedness refers to the "relationship between the two poles of an opposition" (Batistella 1990:1; see also Comrie 1976:111 and Andrews 1990).[39] For purposes of this analysis, the following features are relevant in determining the classification of the various syntactic constructions as marked or unmarked quotative frames: (1) frequency, (2) complexity, and (3) prototypicality.[40] These features are summarized in Table 3.

Table 3. Marked versus unmarked constructions

	Marked	Unmarked
Frequency	infrequent	frequent
Complexity	lexically complex syntactically complex internal syntax external syntax semantically complex	lexically simplex syntactically simplex internal syntax external syntax semantically simplex
Prototypicality	not prototypical	prototypical

Frequency, which appears first in Table 3, relates to the statistical occurrence of the quotative frames.[41] Complexity of quotative frames, the second feature, may appear as (a) lexical complexity, (b) syntactic complexity, and (c) semantic complexity. Lexical complexity relates to whether the quotative frame has a single verb or a phrasal expression (i.e., a communication expression). Syntactic complexity is of two types. Internal syntactic complexity relates to whether the quotative frame itself has simplex syntax or complex syntax. External syntactic complexity relates to the syntactic contexts within which the quotative frame may appear. Semantic complexity involves the amount of metapragmatic information which is indexed in the matrix verb.

Prototypicality, the third of the features in Table 3, relates to the degree to which a category clearly reflects prototypical or experientially based categories. Prototypicality in reported speech relates to the extent to which the reported speech reflects a prototypical speech event. Any act of verbal communication minimally involves a message transferred between two participants—a speaker (or addresser) and an addressee. The message bears a relation to its referent(s) and is transmitted via a shared code by means of a channel such as speech or writing (Silverstein 1985:135-36; Jakobson 1960:353-54).

A prototypical dialogue involves two participants who alternate speaking and listening in paired turns of talk, or adjacency pairs (Sacks, Schegloff, and Jefferson 1974:696-735). In addition, the dialogue occurs with the two participants speaking face to face and in the same location, not across a distance. The participants in the dialogue speak on their own authority (not as mere animators for others who are the principals of the speech event),[42] and they are presumed to be telling the truth.

Because a reported speech event necessarily analyzes as it reports, reported speech and reported dialogue may radically diverge from a mimetic representation of the supposed original speech situation. Prototypical reported speech and dialogue will, therefore, exhibit the following additional features. The reported speech event is a single event, not iterative (many similar speech events reported as one), nor is the speech retold from a previous conversation. The participants of the speech event are full characters in the narrative, not agents or props; nor are they groups represented as speaking chorally (Silverstein 1985:135-36; Jakobson 1960:353-59, 1980:81-87; Bühler 1934). A prototypical reported dialogue thus purports to mirror, as closely as possible, the supposed original speech situation which is itself prototypically dialogic.

How, then, are the three syntactically distinct categories of direct quotative frames related to one another in terms of markedness? The marked and unmarked oppositions, based on the data presented thus far, may be diagrammed as follows:

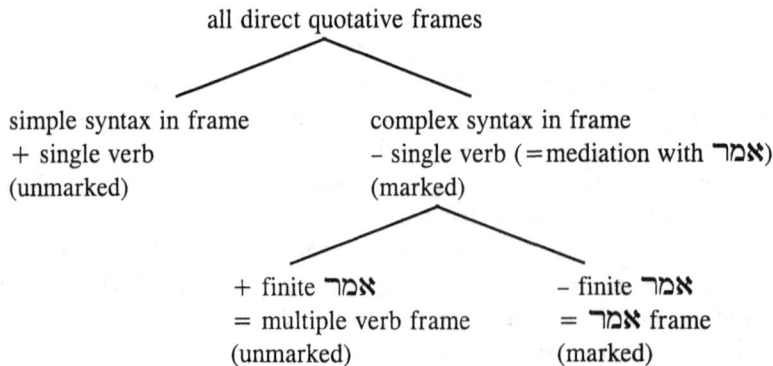

Single-verb frames are unmarked as opposed to frames in which the matrix verb is mediated with a form of אמר by the criterion of complexity. This criterion is significant in two respects. First, single-verb frames are simplex in their internal syntax as opposed to frames mediated with a form of אמר which exhibit internal syntactic complexity. Second, single-verb frames do not have phrasal expressions (lexical complexity) filling the slot of the matrix verb. Single-verb frames (as opposed to mediated frames) convey only the metapragmatic information indexed in the matrix verb; the frame itself does not index additional metapragmatic information.

The choice of verb in a single-verb frame is also significant. We may contrast אמר as the matrix verb with every other verb which may appear in single-verb frames. Single-verb frames with אמר as the matrix verb are the unmarked category by two criteria—frequency and semantic complexity. The verb אמר is the most semantically bare verb with respect to metapragmatic content; only the fact of the speech event is indexed. In contrast, single-verb frames in which the matrix verb is not אמר make up the marked category. Especially noteworthy here is the fact that every other verb (with the exception of the rare verb מלל 'to say') in a single-verb frame indexes an additional feature of the speech event; they are thus semantically more complex in that they convey more metapragmatic information. It is also significant that although אמר does not explicitly index features of the speech event such as 'to answer' or 'to call' or 'to ask', it may be used in contexts where it implicitly has such a meaning.[43] It is thus the more inclusive category, another feature of the unmarked member of an opposition.

The markedness opposition between frames with a finite form of אמר (i.e., multiple-verb frames) and frames with a nonfinite form of אמר (i.e., לֵאמֹר frames) is more difficult to characterize. Both exhibit internal syntactic complexity, so that factor is not decisive. In terms of frequency, we may note that frames with לֵאמֹר occur with a greater number of matrix verbs and communication expressions than do multiple-verb frames, though the actual number of tokens attested for each type is comparable. These, however, are only two features of markedness; the features of external syntactic complexity and prototypicality are also relevant, but require additional explication.

Frames with לֵאמֹר exhibit two features of external syntactic complexity which never occur with multiple-verb frames. First, frames with לֵאמֹר may appear in interrogative constructions:[44]

(19) Josh. 9:22

וַיִּקְרָא לָהֶם יְהוֹשֻׁעַ וַיְדַבֵּר אֲלֵיהֶם לֵאמֹר

לָמָּה רִמִּיתֶם אֹתָנוּ לֵאמֹר
רְחוֹקִים אֲנַחְנוּ מִכֶּם מְאֹד
וְאַתֶּם בְּקִרְבֵּנוּ יֹשְׁבִים:

> Joshua called to them and spoke to them, "Why did you deceive us לֵאמֹר, 'We are from far away from you,' but you live in the midst of us?"

Multiple-verb frames never occur in an interrogative construction.

Second, לֵאמֹר frames may occur within a relative clause in which the head of the relative is co-referential with the quotation:[45]

(20) Gen. 39:19

וַיְהִי כִשְׁמֹעַ אֲדֹנָיו אֶת־דִּבְרֵי אִשְׁתּוֹ אֲשֶׁר דִּבְּרָה אֵלָיו לֵאמֹר
כַּדְּבָרִים הָאֵלֶּה עָשָׂה לִי עַבְדֶּךָ
וַיִּחַר אַפּוֹ:

> When his master heard the words of his wife which she spoke to him, "Your servant behaved like this to me," he got angry.

Multiple-verb frames never occur in such a relative construction. In terms of syntactic complexity, then, לֵאמֹר frames are the marked construction and multiple-verb frames are the unmarked construction.

On the basis of the data presented thus far, it is not yet possible to determine which of the two mediated verb frames represents a more prototypical speech event. In the next section we will consider how to determine prototypicality with respect to quotative frames.

4.2 The intersection of syntax, semantics, pragmatics

Syntax, semantics, and pragmatics are closely interrelated in reported speech. The most salient syntactic facts are those of the quotative frames. The semantic facts under consideration relate to the indexing of metapragmatic features of the speech event in the matrix verb. The syntax and semantics of quotative frames are thus closely connected to the pragmatics of the reported speech event.

The focus of this section is to determine the differences in discourse-pragmatic function between the two types of mediated frames. Single-verb frames will not be considered here, since they are not in opposition to multiple-verb and לֵאמֹר frames in a three-way contrast. (Single-verb frames are used when only the metapragmatic information of the matrix verb is indexed.) It is reasonable, therefore, to consider only the opposition at hand, that between multiple-verb frames and לֵאמֹר frames.

Introducing Direct Discourse in Biblical Hebrew Narrative 219

In order to examine the opposition between the two mediated frames, we shall examine a small section of the verbs that appear most commonly in all three quotative frames. Special attention will be paid to the relationship of the configurations to questions of prototypicality in the reporting of speech events.

4.2.1 Multiple-verb frames as the central configuration: ענה

Of the eleven verbs which appear in all three quotative frames, only two appear with multiple-verb frames as their central configuration, namely, ענה 'to answer' and קרא 'to call'. Both verbs index prototypical features of dialogue: ענה indexes a response to a previous utterance whereas קרא 'to call' indexes the initiation of dialogue or an adjacency pair. This section looks at the use of ענה.[46]

The use of ענה in a multiple-verb frame serves frequently to introduce an appropriate response to a preceding first pair-part such as a question:

(21) 1 Sam. 4:16b–17[47]

וַיֹּאמֶר מֶה־הָיָה הַדָּבָר בְּנִי
וַיַּעַן הַמְבַשֵּׂר וַיֹּאמֶר
נָס יִשְׂרָאֵל לִפְנֵי פְלִשְׁתִּים...

He [Eli] said, "What is the news, my son?"
The one bringing news answered [lit., answered and said], "Israel fled before the Philistines..."

Not surprisingly, ענה may also be used in a multiple-verb frame to introduce the response to a command (Judg. 20:4–7; 1 Sam. 16:18; 2 Sam. 15:21), a protest (Num. 23:12, 26; 1 Sam. 29:9–10), an accusation (1 Sam. 22:14–15; 2 Sam. 20:20–21a), an inquiry directed to Yahweh (1 Sam. 23:14b), or a statement (2 Sam. 4:9–11).

Not all responses, however, are indexed explicitly by ענה. Within a conversation, a multiple-verb frame with ענה is used once or at most twice; other responses in second pair-parts are commonly introduced simply with אמר in a single-verb frame. The use of ענה in a multiple-verb frame thus seems to signal the most salient or important response in the conversation. Example 22 illustrates this. Laban and Bethuel agree to the request by Abraham's servant to take their daughter Rebekah as a wife for Abraham's son. The response culminates a long process in which the servant recounts his travels to their land and his encounter with Rebekah at the well. The pair-part is highly salient:

(22) Gen. 24:50-51

וַיַּעַן לָבָן וּבְתוּאֵל וַיֹּאמְרוּ
מֵיְהוָה יָצָא הַדָּבָר לֹא נוּכַל דַּבֵּר אֵלֶיךָ רַע אוֹ־טוֹב:
הִנֵּה־רִבְקָה לְפָנֶיךָ קַח וָלֵךְ וּתְהִי אִשָּׁה לְבֶן־אֲדֹנֶיךָ כַּאֲשֶׁר דִּבֶּר יְהוָה:

> Laban answered along with Bethuel [lit., answered and said], "The matter was established by Yahweh. We are not able to speak to you either good or evil. Look, Rebekah is before you. Take her and go so that she may become the wife of your master's son, just as Yahweh has spoken."

When two pair-parts introduced with ענה in a multiple-verb frame occur in a single conversation, both are salient.[48]

When there is a mismatch in the adjacency pair, that is, when the designated addressee of the first pair-part is not the speaker of the second pair-part, ענה in a multiple-verb frame may be used. Such a mismatch is particularly common when the second pair-part is spoken by someone who interrupts the conversation to lodge a protest:[49]

(23) Num. 11:27-28

a וַיָּרָץ הַנַּעַר וַיַּגֵּד לְמֹשֶׁה וַיֹּאמַר אֶלְדָּד וּמֵידָד מִתְנַבְּאִים בַּמַּחֲנֶה:
b וַיַּעַן יְהוֹשֻׁעַ בִּן־נוּן מְשָׁרֵת מֹשֶׁה מִבְּחֻרָיו וַיֹּאמַר אֲדֹנִי מֹשֶׁה כְּלָאֵם:

> a. A young man ran and told Moses [lit., told and said], "Eldad and Medad are prophesying in the camp!"
> b. Joshua the son of Nun, the servant of Moses from his youth, answered [lit., answered and said], "My lord, Moses, stop them!"

In this example, a young man runs and tells Moses that Eldad and Medad are prophesying in the camp. Moses, however, does not respond to this information. Instead, Joshua lodges a protest with Moses.[50]

The response of choral participants may be introduced with ענה in a multiple-verb frame in contexts in which the group is presented as an individual participant in the adjacency pair. Often the persons in the group are both known participants in the narrative, and one of them is more prominent than the other.[51] In example 24, Jacob asks his wives, Rachel and Leah, about leaving their father's house. Rachel and Leah respond together, though Rachel as the best-loved wife is prominent; this is indicated by the use of a single verb in the first verb phrase of the quotative frame:

(24) Gen. 31:14

וַתַּעַן רָחֵל וְלֵאָה וַתֹּאמַרְנָה לוֹ הַעוֹד לָנוּ חֵלֶק וְנַחֲלָה בְּבֵית אָבִינוּ:

> Rachel and Leah answered [lit., she answered and they (f.pl.) said to] him, "Is there yet any portion and inheritance in the house of our father?"

Choral participants whose response is introduced with ענה in a multiple-verb frame are never anonymous or unspecified persons, nor is there ever a displacement between principal(s) and animators. Instead, the groups are always specified and identified as, for instance, Balak's princes (Num. 22:18-19), David's servants (1 Sam. 25:10-11), the Gibeonites (Josh. 9:24-25), David's fighting men (1 Sam. 30:22), the women of the town (1 Sam. 9:12-13), the elders of the town (Deut. 21:7-8), the Danites (Judg. 18:14), the Philistines (1 Sam. 14:12a), the Levites (Deut. 27:14-26). Even when the choral speakers are designated simply as 'the people', they are the particular group of Israelites as specified in the narrative.[52] Sometimes the unified nature of their response is further indicated in the quotative frame by phrases such as קוֹל אֶחָד 'with one voice' (Exod. 24:3b) or יַחְדָּו 'together' (Exod. 19:8a).

It is important now to contrast the use of ענה in לֵאמֹר frames with its use in multiple-verb frames.[53] In several instances, a לֵאמֹר frame is obligatorily required syntactically, since the quotative frame is a question (1 Sam. 21:12; 29:5).

The verb ענה may appear in a לֵאמֹר frame in conversation when the pair-part which it introduces is not salient in the conversation. Example 8 illustrates this. Pharaoh tells Joseph that he has had a dream that no one can interpret, but he has heard that Joseph can interpret dreams. Joseph responds that he cannot interpret dreams himself, but God will give him the interpretation. This pair-part is not the most salient in the conversation, since it does not contain the interpretation of the dream. Rather, it is just a polite, negative response to Pharaoh's initial inquiry.

A לֵאמֹר frame may also be used when the adjacency pair within which it appears is an aside (or "side sequence") within a larger conversation. In the larger context of example 25, Jacob's sons speak with their brother Joseph, whom they believe to be the Egyptian ruler. Within that conversation, the sons speak with one another concerning their mistreatment of Joseph:

(25) Gen. 42:21-22

a וַיֹּאמְרוּ אִישׁ אֶל־אָחִיו אֲבָל אֲשֵׁמִים אֲנַחְנוּ עַל־אָחִינוּ אֲשֶׁר

רָאִינוּ צָרַת נַפְשׁוֹ בְּהִתְחַנְנוֹ אֵלֵינוּ וְלֹא שָׁמָעְנוּ עַל־כֵּן
בָּאָה אֵלֵינוּ הַצָּרָה הַזֹּאת:
b וַיַּעַן רְאוּבֵן אֹתָם לֵאמֹר הֲלוֹא אָמַרְתִּי אֲלֵיכֶם לֵאמֹר
אַל־תֶּחֶטְאוּ בַיֶּלֶד וְלֹא שְׁמַעְתֶּם וְגַם־דָּמוֹ הִנֵּה נִדְרָשׁ:

    a. They said to one another, "We certainly sinned against our brother because we saw his distress when he beseeched us and we did not heed him. That is why this distress has come upon us."

    b. Reuben answered them לֵאמֹר "Didn't I say to you, 'Do not harm the boy'? But you did not listen. So, look, we are accountable for his blood."

Reuben's response is marked with לֵאמֹר since it is not the most salient response within the larger conversation.

The verb ענה may appear in a לֵאמֹר frame to indicate a displacement of the principal and animator of the speech event. Example 26, the account of the Amalekite who reported to David that he killed Saul, is instructive. David questions him and then has him executed on the spot. He then stands over the corpse and pronounces a judgment.

(26) 2 Sam. 1:16

וַיֹּאמֶר אֵלָיו דָּוִד דָּמְיךָ עַל־רֹאשֶׁךָ כִּי פִיךָ עָנָה בְךָ לֵאמֹר אָנֹכִי
מֹתַתִּי אֶת־מְשִׁיחַ יְהוָה:

    David said to him, "Your blood be upon your head because your mouth testified against you לֵאמֹר, 'I killed Yahweh's anointed one.'"

It is interesting to note that David attributes to the Amalekite a statement the Amalekite did not utter in the preceding dialogue. David's addition of the charged phrase מְשִׁיחַ יְהוָה 'the anointed of Yahweh', a royal title, to refer to the dead Israelite king, appears to be his own paraphrase of the Amalekite's report, since it is questionable whether an Amalekite would have framed the statement in such terms. As Savran (1988:71–72) suggests, David is probably paraphrasing the quotation for covert purposes—to suppress rumors that he might have been involved in Saul's death. Our analysis of quotative frames with לֵאמֹר permits us to state the nature of the paraphrase more precisely. David has taken the report of the Amalekite (the principal) previously uttered and, as animator, has reworded it for his own ends.

Finally, ענה may introduce choral responses with a לֵאמֹר frame. In some instances the speakers are specified (e.g., the Israelites in Josh.

Introducing Direct Discourse in Biblical Hebrew Narrative

1:16–18; the Gadites and Reubenites in Num. 32:31–32), but it is also possible for the group to be anonymous or unspecified (1 Sam. 29:5).

In summary, the verb ענה appears in multiple-verb frames primarily in instances in which the prototypical dialogic paradigm is met. Choral speakers are identified or specified in the narrative. There is no explicit displacement between principal and animator of the speech event. Within a conversation, the use of a multiple-verb frame with ענה signals the most salient or important response.

The verb ענה appears with far less frequency in לֵאמֹר frames. In a conversation, it introduces a response which is not the most salient within the encompassing conversation and may appear, in fact, within an adjacency pair which is a side sequence. It allows for the displacement of animator and principal and for anonymous, unspecified choral speakers. Thus, ענה לאמר is used in marked instances to indicate a deviation from the prototypical dialogic paradigm.

4.2.2 לֵאמֹר frames as the central configuration

We now turn to the verbs that appear in all three quotative frames, but which have לֵאמֹר frames as their central configuration. The verbs examined in this section are נגד 'to tell' and צוה 'to command'.

4.2.2.1 נגד 'to tell'

The verb נגד 'to tell, relate' appears in two stems, the Hiphil and Hophal; both are used to introduce direct speech.[54] When the Hophal is used, no mention is made of the speaker; instead, the quotation is coreferential with the implied subject of the verb.

(27) Gen. 38:13

וַיֻּגַּד לְתָמָר לֵאמֹר הִנֵּה חָמִיךְ עֹלֶה תִמְנָתָה לָגֹז צֹאנוֹ:

The following was reported to Tamar [lit., it was reported to Tamar לֵאמֹר], "Look, your father-in-law is going up to Timnah to shear his sheep."

Unlike some speech verbs whose position in the adjacency-pair is largely determined by the semantics of the verb, the verb נגד may occur as either the first pair-part or the second pair-part. Although it usually occurs as the first pair-part, its use to introduce the second pair-part is not uncommon, as in example 28.

(28) 1 Sam. 14:43[55]

a   וַיֹּאמֶר שָׁאוּל אֶל־יוֹנָתָן הַגִּידָה לִּי מֶה עָשִׂיתָה

b וַיַּגֶּד־לוֹ יוֹנָתָן וַיֹּאמֶר טָעֹם טָעַמְתִּי בִּקְצֵה הַמַּטֶּה
אֲשֶׁר־בְּיָדִי מְעַט דְּבַשׁ הִנְנִי אָמוּת׃

   a. Then Saul said to Jonathan, "Tell me what you have done."
   b. Jonathan told him [lit., told him and said], "I tasted a little honey with the end of my staff. I am ready to die."

The morphological and syntactic distinctions between the Hiphil and Hophal forms of the verb are also significant to their discourse-pragmatic functions. The Hophal singular is used exclusively when the speaker (or speakers) is anonymous and the principal, or source, of the information is unknown, as in example 27. The Hiphil plural is used similarly, as in example 29. The reported speech serves solely to introduce information into the narrative; ordinarily no response is made to the person who relates the information, though s/he may take action based on the information:[56]

(29) 2 Sam. 11:10

a וַיַּגִּדוּ לְדָוִד לֵאמֹר לֹא־יָרַד אוּרִיָּה אֶל־בֵּיתוֹ
b וַיֹּאמֶר דָּוִד אֶל־אוּרִיָּה הֲלוֹא מִדֶּרֶךְ אַתָּה בָא מַדּוּעַ
לֹא־יָרַדְתָּ אֶל־בֵּיתֶךָ׃

   a. Now they [impersonal plural] reported to David לֵאמֹר, "Uriah did not go to his house."
   b. David said to Uriah, "Haven't you come from a journey? Why didn't you go to your house?"

In this example, David makes no response to the unidentified person (or persons) who relayed the information to him. Instead, he asks Uriah the reason for his behavior.

When the Hiphil singular is used, the speaker is identified in the narrative and is both the animator and the principal of the speech event, regardless of whether the quotation is introduced with a multiple-verb frame, as in example 30, or a לֵאמֹר frame,[57] as in example 31.

(30) 2 Sam. 18:10-11

a וַיַּרְא אִישׁ אֶחָד וַיַּגֵּד לְיוֹאָב וַיֹּאמֶר הִנֵּה רָאִיתִי
אֶת־אַבְשָׁלֹם תָּלוּי בָּאֵלָה׃
b וַיֹּאמֶר יוֹאָב לָאִישׁ הַמַּגִּיד לוֹ וְהִנֵּה רָאִיתָ וּמַדּוּעַ
לֹא־הִכִּיתוֹ שָׁם אָרְצָה ...

   a. Now a certain man saw [it] and he reported to Joab [lit., he reported to Joab and he said], "Hey, I saw Absalom hanging in an oak tree!"

b. And Joab said to the man who reported to him, "What! You saw [him]! Why didn't you strike him down to the ground there . . . ?"

(31) 2 Kings 22:10

וַיַּגֵּד שָׁפָן הַסֹּפֵר לַמֶּלֶךְ לֵאמֹר סֵפֶר נָתַן לִי חִלְקִיָּה הַכֹּהֵן
וַיִּקְרָאֵהוּ שָׁפָן לִפְנֵי הַמֶּלֶךְ:

Shaphan the scribe told the king לֵאמֹר "Hilkiah the priest gave me a book." Then Shaphan read it before the king.

Table 4 summarizes the intersection of two features of direct quotative frames with נגד: (1) the stem of the matrix verb and (2) the syntax of the quotative frame.

Table 4. Distribution of נגד in quotative frames

Type of Frame	Hophal (s.)	Hiphil (s.)	Hiphil (pl.)
Single-verb	unknown speaker	—	—
Multiple-verb	—	known speaker	known speaker
לֵאמֹר	unknown speaker	known speaker	unknown/known speaker

As the table indicates, in multiple-verb frames the speaker is always a known character in the narrative and the principal of the speech event. The matrix verb in multiple-verb frames is always Hiphil (singular or plural). In לֵאמֹר frames, the speaker may be either an unknown person(s) who is not the principal of the speech event or a known person(s) who *is* the principal of the speech event.[58]

This disparity in discourse-pragmatic function between multiple-verb frames and לֵאמֹר frames is understandable in light of the preceding discussion. Multiple-verb frames are more prototypically dialogic, and in a prototypical dialogue the speaker is both identified and the principal of the speech event.[59] In contrast, לֵאמֹר frames allow for features that are not prototypically dialogic. For this reason, the Hophal is found in לֵאמֹר frames, but not in multiple-verb frames. Similarly, the use of the Hiphil plural (the so-called impersonal plural) to represent the speech of unknown, anonymous persons, is attested only in לֵאמֹר frames; the Hiphil plural in multiple-verb frames always has an identifiable speaker who is a principal of the speech event.

How, then, do instances of reported speech with the Hiphil of נגד in multiple-verb frames differ from the same form of the verb in לֵאמֹר frames in cases where they both involve a speaker who is known and the principal? In לֵאמֹר frames, there is often some other feature which is not prototypically dialogic, as the data attest. First, it is more common for no response to be made to the information conveyed in a first pair-part that is introduced by a לֵאמֹר frame. Example 31 ilustrates this.[60] Second, semidirect speech in which the narrator has condensed the "original" quotation is more likely to appear in לֵאמֹר frames than in multiple-verb frames, as in example 32:

(32) 2 Kings 5:4

וַיָּבֹא וַיַּגֵּד לַאדֹנָיו לֵאמֹר כָּזֹאת וְכָזֹאת דִּבְּרָה הַנַּעֲרָה אֲשֶׁר מֵאֶרֶץ יִשְׂרָאֵל׃

He came and he told his master לֵאמֹר, "The maiden who is from the land of Israel told me thus and so."

Third, the reports given by official court personnel who are otherwise merely props in the narrative are often framed with לֵאמֹר (e.g., 2 Kings 9:20 and 10:8a). Fourth, frames with לֵאמֹר often relate hypothetical or future quotations, describing what might be said or ought to be said:[61]

(33) Exod. 13:8

וְהִגַּדְתָּ לְבִנְךָ בַּיּוֹם הַהוּא לֵאמֹר בַּעֲבוּר זֶה עָשָׂה יְהוָה לִי בְּצֵאתִי מִמִּצְרָיִם׃

You must tell your son in that day לֵאמֹר, "On account of this Yahweh did for me when I went out from Egypt."

We have seen, then, that נגד is used in multiple-verb frames in discourse-pragmatic contexts which are prototypically dialogic. The presence of a לֵאמֹר frame signals a less than prototypically dialogic situation.

4.2.2.2 צוה 'to command'

Although the semantics of צוה might suggest that it appears in dialogic contexts with a spoken verbal response to the command, this is almost never the case.[62] Since commands in Biblical Hebrew usually have no verbal response, the difference between multiple-verb frames and frames with לֵאמֹר must relate to other dialogic or nondialogic features of the two types of frames.

Multiple-verb frames with צוה occur in only six examples, none of which exhibit the sorts of nondialogic features found in לֵאמֹר frames. In each instance, the speaker of the utterance is a full character in the narrative (not an agent or prop), an individual (not a group), and both principal and animator of the speech event. The addressee is always specified and identified in the narrative. In addition, in no case is the speech itself iterative, retold, semidirect, hypothetical, or fabricated.

Each of the four examples of multiple-verb frames in narrative seems to introduce an utterance which is highly salient within the conversation.[63] Consider example 34.

(34) Gen. 49:29

וַיְצַו אוֹתָם וַיֹּאמֶר אֲלֵהֶם אֲנִי נֶאֱסָף אֶל־עַמִּי קִבְרוּ אֹתִי
אֶל־אֲבֹתָי אֶל־הַמְּעָרָה אֲשֶׁר בִּשְׂדֵה עֶפְרוֹן הַחִתִּי:

> He [Jacob] commanded them [lit., he commanded them and he said to them], "I will soon be gathered to my people. Bury me with my fathers in the cave which is in the field of Ephron the Hittite . . ."

Here Jacob blesses each of his twelve sons (Gen. 49:1–28) and then gives them the final instructions for his burial back in the land of Canaan (49:29). After these last words, he dies and Joseph mourns for him. Jacob's utterance in 34 is the culmination of his last words to his sons and the climax of the scene.[64]

Instances of צוה in לֵאמֹר frames commonly exhibit nonprototypically dialogic features. With respect to the speech participants, the speaker may be a group (Deut. 27:1–8; Judg. 21:20–22), the addressee may be unspecified and uncertain (2 Kings 17:27), and the roles of principal and animator may be displaced (Gen. 50:16–17; Num. 35:6-9; 36:5-9). With respect to the quotation, a number of nondialogic features are attested. The quotation may be semidirect (Gen. 32:20–21a) or (possibly) fabricated (Gen. 50:16–17). When the speech is iterative, this may be explicitly noted.

(35) Josh. 3:2–3[65]

וַיְהִי מִקְצֵה שְׁלֹשֶׁת יָמִים וַיַּעַבְרוּ הַשֹּׁטְרִים בְּקֶרֶב הַמַּחֲנֶה: וַיְצַוּוּ
אֶת־הָעָם לֵאמֹר כִּרְאוֹתְכֶם אֵת אֲרוֹן בְּרִית־יְהוָה אֱלֹהֵיכֶם וְהַכֹּהֲנִים
הַלְוִיִּם נֹשְׂאִים אֹתוֹ וְאַתֶּם תִּסְעוּ מִמְּקוֹמְכֶם וַהֲלַכְתֶּם אַחֲרָיו:

> At the end of three days, the officers went throughout the camp and they commanded the people לֵאמֹר, "When you see the ark of the covenant of Yahweh your God and the priests and the Levites carrying it, then you will set out from your place and you will go after it."

Sometimes, however, the iterative nature of the speech event introduced with לֵאמֹר is not stated explicitly but may be inferred from the context (e.g., 2 Sam. 18:5).

The quotation may be retold—either as the speech of another character or as a citation,[66] as in example 36.

(36) Gen. 28:6

וַיַּרְא עֵשָׂו כִּי־בֵרַךְ יִצְחָק אֶת־יַעֲקֹב וְשִׁלַּח אֹתוֹ פַּדֶּנָה אֲרָם לָקַחַת־לוֹ מִשָּׁם אִשָּׁה בְּבָרֲכוֹ אֹתוֹ וַיְצַו עָלָיו לֵאמֹר לֹא־תִקַּח אִשָּׁה מִבְּנוֹת כְּנָעַן:

> Esau saw that Isaac had blessed Jacob and had sent him to Paddan Aram to get a wife from there when he blessed him and commanded him לֵאמֹר, "Do not take a wife from the daughters of the Canaanites."

The quotation here is retold from Gen. 28:1, where Isaac gives the command to Jacob using precisely the same wording.

Whereas multiple-verb frames with צוה often give the most salient utterance in the conversation, לֵאמֹר frames with צוה sometimes introduce an utterance that is out of temporal order with respect to the conversation and narrative:

(37) 1 Kings 22:31

וּמֶלֶךְ אֲרָם צִוָּה אֶת־שָׂרֵי הָרֶכֶב אֲשֶׁר־לוֹ שְׁלֹשִׁים וּשְׁנַיִם לֵאמֹר לֹא תִּלָּחֲמוּ אֶת־קָטֹן וְאֶת־גָּדוֹל כִּי אִם־אֶת־מֶלֶךְ יִשְׂרָאֵל לְבַדּוֹ:

> Now the king of Aram had (previously) commanded his thirty-two chariot drivers לֵאמֹר, "Do not engage in battle with anyone, either insignificant or important, except the king of Israel himself."

The preceding context of 1 Kings 22:31 describes the tactics of the Israelites (the king of Israel enters the battle in disguise, the king of Judah wears his royal robes) and then the fact that they go to battle. Thus v. 31 is a flashback to a previous event. It gives the simultaneous command of the king of Aram to his servants as an explanation of the following narrative—why the Arameans thought they had the king of Israel when they saw a man in royal robes. The quotation in v. 31 is out of order in the narrative and describes the earlier command of the king of Aram.[67]

5. Conclusions

We have seen that the intersection of matrix verbs with quotative frames is highly significant. Verbs that appear only in one quotative frame obligatorily appear in that configuration; no discourse-pragmatic function is involved in the use of that construction. Verbs that appear in more than one quotative frame usually appear in one frame more frequently than another; the central configuration of a matrix verb relates to its semantics (in terms of which metapragmatic features it indexes) and/or its pragmatics (in terms of its function in representing the speech event).

Based on the criteria of frequency, complexity, and prototypicality, we argued for the ranking of the three types of quotative frames with respect to markedness. This was demonstrated, not as a three-way opposition, but as hierarchically ordered two-way oppositions.

Single-verb frames are opposed to complex frames in which the matrix verb is mediated by a form of אָמַר, that is, multiple-verb frames and frames with לֵאמֹר. Within single-verb frames, an opposition occurs with respect to the matrix verb: the matrix verb אָמַר is unmarked; all other matrix verbs are marked. The markedness opposition is evidenced by two criteria: semantic complexity (verbs other than אָמַר index more metapragmatic features of the speech event) and frequency (אָמַר is overwhelmingly the most common verb in single-verb frames).

The markedness opposition between the two mediated quotative frames is shown to operate primarily by two criteria: external syntactic complexity and prototypicality. With regard to syntactic complexity, לֵאמֹר frames allow more syntactic complexity, such as relative clauses and questions. In addition, לֵאמֹר frames show more variation in the marking of the addressee(s) of the speech event. With regard to prototypicality, multiple-verb frames more frequently represent a prototypical dialogic situation. In addition, multiple-verb frames often are used to indicate the most salient utterance within a conversation.

By contrast, לֵאמֹר frames allow for the indexing of nondialogic features. These nondialogic features may be found within the frame, the quotation, or the adjacency pair. Within the frame, the speakers may be choral, unidentified, props, or displaced; similarly, the addressees may be unspecified or unidentified. Within the quotation, nondialogic features include quotations that are semidirect, retold, iterative, hypothetical, or fabricated. In addition, the quotation introduced with לֵאמֹר may exhibit pronominal reference indicating that the principal and the animator are distributed between two individuals. With respect to the adjacency pair, two nondialogic features of לֵאמֹר may be mentioned. First, a first pair-part with לֵאמֹר often has no verbal second pair-part. Often a response is not indicated and the narrative switches to a new topic or pericope. When a response is indicated, it may be nonverbal (the addressee performs the specified action) or represented solely by the narrative. Second, when there is a mismatch in the participants of the adjacency pair and the designated addressee of the first pair-part is not the speaker of the second pair-part, the quotation is more likely to be introduced with לֵאמֹר.

The semantics of the verb and the syntax of the frame interact in noteworthy ways, as described in Table 5.

Table 5. Central and marked configurations

Semantics of Verb	Syntax of Frame	
	Multiple-verb frame (unmarked)	לֵאמֹר frame (marked)
Dialogic	ענה 'to answer' קרא 'to call' (central)	צוה 'to command' שאל 'to ask' (central)
Nondialogic	[does not occur]	שלח 'to send' שבע 'to swear' נגד 'to tell' דבר 'to speak' (central)

When the semantics of the verb indexes a dialogic speech situation, the central syntactic configuration may be either a multiple-verb frame or a לֵאמֹר frame. In the former instance, the expected correspondence of frame and verbal semantics is exhibited. In the latter instance, the semantics of the verb indicates a dialogic situation, but the discourse-pragmatic function is nondialogic. The לֵאמֹר frame is used to indicate something unusual with respect to the prototypical dialogic paradigm. When the semantics of the verb is not dialogic, there are no examples of multiple-verb frames as the central configuration; only לֵאמֹר frames are central. This is the expected situation and points as well to the fact that multiple-verb frames find their discourse-pragmatic function in dialogue.

The distinctions among the three quotative frames also elucidate some of the distributional facts of matrix verbs within the frames. No phrasal communicational expressions appear in single-verb frames; rather, a single verb must be in matrix position. This accounts for the distribution of, for example, השיב דבר 'to cause a word to return' (lit., 'to send back word') in multiple-verb frames and לֵאמֹר frames, but not in single-verb frames.[68] This is true even though the expression is roughly synonymous with שלח 'to send', which appears in all three types of frames. By contrast, the verbs כתב 'to write' and שמע 'to hear', which index written communication and the reception of communication respectively, may appear in single-verb frames.

The verb כתב 'to write' indexes written communication which takes place across a distance and in a nonverbal medium. For this reason, it does not appear in a multiple-verb frame, but may appear in a לֵאמֹר frame where the quotation gives the content of the letter. The verb שָׁמַע 'to hear' does not index communication, but rather the reception of communication. Therefore, it does not appear in multiple-verb frames, but it may appear in a לֵאמֹר frame in which the quotation represents the content of the information received. Because these two verbs do not index prototypically dialogic situations, they appear only in לֵאמֹר frames.

In conclusion, the three types of quotative frames which introduce direct speech are relevant to a proper understanding of the conversation and narrative within which they appear. An elucidation of the functions of the quotative frames, however, must be sensitive to the matrix verb that appears in the frame and to the syntax, semantics, and pragmatics thereby entailed.

Notes

1. This article is drawn from my 1992 Ph.D. dissertation at the University of Chicago (Miller 1992). I am grateful to Dennis Pardee, Gene B. Gragg, W. Randall Garr, Amy Dahlstrom, and C. H. J. van der Merwe for their comments and criticisms. The research was completed with the assistance of the National Foundation for Jewish Culture Dissertation Grant (1990-91) and the Memorial Foundation for Jewish Culture Doctoral Scholarship (1990-91).

2. From a random sampling, Rendsburg (1990:160) estimated that 42.5% of narrative is direct quotation. That figure does not take into account indirect speech.

3. For discussion of some of these, see Levenston (1984).

4. Terms for the quotative frame vary: dialogue introducer (Johnstone 1987:34), quotation formula (Silverstein 1985:134), attributive discourse or tagged discourse (Shapiro 1984:71), and transitional formula (Rebera 1981: 129).

5. The discussion is based upon an analysis of all the tokens of reported speech in Genesis through 2 Kings, over 4,500 tokens.

6. As Tannen (1986:311-13) observes, most direct quotation and other forms of reported speech are actually constructed dialogue.

7. This distinction between a direct quotation and an indirect quotation is often described as that between a *de dicto* reading and a *de re* reading. Only direct speech purports to be exclusively a *de dicto* reading of the original locution whereas indirect speech allows for either a *de dicto* or a *de re* reading. The classic example is *Oedipus said that his mother was beautiful.* According to the *de dicto* reading, the original locution would have been something like *My mother is beautiful.* According to the *de re* reading, Oedipus could have made any of several utterances: *Jocasta is beautiful,* or *My wife is beautiful,* etc. If his original utterance were any of the latter sentences, then the

descriptive phrase *his mother* in the indirect report reflects a re-analysis by the reporting speaker (see Coulmas 1986:3-4).

8. The term *metalanguage* was employed by the logician Alfred Tarski to refer to a technical language which describes or characterizes an object language; Jakobson extended the term to include the use of natural language to describe or characterize various aspects of language itself (Jakobson 1980:86). Two common metalinguistic usages of natural language are *definition* (the use of language to refer to the linguistic code) and *reported speech* (the use of language to refer to the linguistic message) (Jakobson 1971:130-33).

9. Goldenberg (1991:85) argues that direct speech and indirect speech are distinguished in Biblical Hebrew on the basis of the *verbum dicendi* in the quotative frame; some verbs (such as אמר) select direct speech, other verbs (such as נגד) indirect speech. While this distinction cannot be maintained, the matrix verb is highly significant, as will be discussed below.

10. See Miller (1992:40-95) for a complete account of indirect speech in Biblical Hebrew narrative.

11. For the phrases "opaque pronominal reference" and "transparent pronominal reference," see Munro (1982:302-3) and Partee (1973:410-18).

12. The syntactic relationship between the quotation and the frame is difficult to characterize. Halliday and Hasan (1976:135) describe the relationship of the reported clause to the matrix clause as hypotactic (i.e., dependent upon another clause), but not embedded (i.e., not structurally integrated as a constituent into the matrix clause). Van Valin (1984:546-47) suggests that direct quotation exemplifies a complement independent of the main clause, yet embedded. In spite of the differences in terminology, both analyses attempt to describe both the connection of the quotation to the frame and the unincorporation of the quotation into the frame.

13. There are three exceptional cases in which no complementizer or other mark of subordination is present in indirect speech: Gen. 12:13, 19; 2 Sam. 21:4. In each case, particular syntactic constraints are present (see Miller 1992:75-77).

14. Rebera (1981) incorrectly states that final frames and unmarked direct speech do not occur in Hebrew narrative.

15. See the discussion and examples in O'Connor (1980:409-14). O'Connor uses "core" to refer to a quotative frame. A "clean core" is a quotative frame which exactly coincides with the poetic line in which it is found. In a "mixed core" the quotative frame occupies only part of the line. An "upfront core" refers to an initial quotative frame, a "postposed core" to a final quotative frame, and an "encased core" to a medial quotative frame.

16. Other examples occur in the quotative frames in Deut. 5:4 and 2 Sam. 7:7.

17. Wright states that when unframed direct speech (in his terminology, "free direct discourse") occurs, "the reader must supply the understanding that

the character is not speaking aloud" (1991:260), but he supplies no convincing evidence for this statement.

18. The versions show a quotative frame, but it is not clear whether the quotative frame has dropped out of the Hebrew or whether the versions have supplied a quotative frame. The LXX supplies a quotative frame: *kai eipen Iou* 'And Jehu said'. The Syriac supplies a quotative frame, but in a different location: *wʾmr ywndb ʾyt wʾyt wʾmr lh hb ʾydk whb ʾydh wʾhʿw lwth lmrkbtʾ* 'Jehonadab said, "It certainly is [lit., it is and it is]." And Jehu said, "Give me your hand." So he gave him his hand and he helped him up into the chariot.' Another example of unmarked direct speech occurs in 2 Sam. 18:22-23. It is similar in that it occurs within a conversation, the quotation is introduced by conjunctive *waw,* and it is textually disputed.

19. These three categories are recognized by Givón (1991:275), though he provides no explanation for their functional distribution.

20. Multiple-verb frames usually contain two speech verbs. Frames with more than two speech verbs are rare, though they do occur. An example is 2 Sam. 11:5: וַתַּהַר הָאִשָּׁה וַתִּשְׁלַח וַתַּגֵּד לְדָוִד וַתֹּאמֶר הָרָה אָנֹכִי 'The woman became pregnant. She sent [a message] and told David and said, "I am pregnant."'

21. Longacre's (1989:160-61) definition of "expanded quotation formulae" (= multiple-verb frames) is too broad. He includes in the frame any clauses preceding the frame which contain either a motion verb (e.g., "they drew near to him and they said") or a psychological verb (e.g., "they feared greatly and they said"). However, by his analysis, it is unclear precisely how much of the preceding narrative should be included. A better option is to recognize only metapragmatic verbs within the quotative frame. This provides a principled means for delimiting the initial boundary of the quotative frame.

22. The person and gender of the metapragmatic verbs are always identical. There are two cases, however, in which the number of the metapragmatic verbs may not be identical. In the first case, the subject is plural and the first metapragmatic verb is singular, agreeing with the more prominent speaker, as for example in Gen. 24:50: וַיַּעַן לָבָן וּבְתוּאֵל וַיֹּאמְרוּ מֵיְהוָה יָצָא הַדָּבָר לֹא נוּכַל דַּבֵּר אֵלֶיךָ רַע אוֹ־טוֹב: 'Laban and Bethuel answered [lit., he answered and they said], "This matter is from Yahweh. We are not able to speak to you bad or good."'

In the second case, a corporate entity is represented as speaking. The metapragmatic verbs in the frame may both be plural (e.g., Exod. 19:8a), or both may be singular (e.g., Exod. 17:3), or the first may be singular and the second plural. An example in which the first verb is singular and the second plural as found in Exod. 24:3b: וַיַּעַן כָּל־הָעָם קוֹל אֶחָד וַיֹּאמְרוּ כָּל־הַדְּבָרִים אֲשֶׁר־דִּבֶּר יהוה נַעֲשֶׂה: 'The people answered (with) one voice [lit., answered (s.) (with) one voice and said (pl.)], "All the words which Yahweh has spoken we will do."'

23. The following patterns of identical metapragmatic verbs are attested: *wayyiqtol* (narrative) (e.g., 1 Kings 20:11), *yiqtol* (e.g., 1 Kings 21:6), cohortative (Gen. 46:31-32).

24. The following consecutive patterns are attested: *qatal* + *wayyiqtol* (e.g., 2 Kings 9:1), participle + *wayyiqtol* (e.g., Judg. 7:13), *yiqtol* + *wayyiqtol* (e.g., Josh. 22:1-5), imperative + perfect consecutive (e.g., Lev. 19:1-2), *yiqtol* + perfect consecutive (e.g., Num. 18:26-29).

25. The only exception in this corpus occurs in Exod. 19:3: כֹּה תֹאמַר לְבֵית יַעֲקֹב וְתַגֵּיד לִבְנֵי יִשְׂרָאֵל 'thus you shall say to the house of Jacob and declare to the sons of Israel'.

26. The four examples of ענה דבר within our corpus are: Josh. 22:21-29; 2 Kings 1:10, 11b, 12.

27. See Malone's (1979:71-79) explanation of the long vowel in the first syllable of וֵאלֹהִים 'and God' as opposed to the short vowel in the first syllable of וַאדֹנָי 'and my lord'.

28. Williams (1976:§195); Waltke and O'Connor (1990:§36.2.3e); Gesenius and Kautzsch (1910:§114o); Joüon (1923:§12o). See also Miller (1970:224); Seow (1987:190).

29. The use of לֵאמֹר should be compared to that of the same infinitive with the prefixed preposition בְּ 'in' which may take pronominal subjective suffixes (e.g., בְּאָמְרִי 'when I said' [lit., in my saying], בְּאָמְרָם 'when they said', and בְּאָמְרְכֶם 'when you [pl.] said').

30. Contrast the use of לֵאמֹר as a true embedded infinitive in 2 Chron. 32:17 where it is conjoined with another infinitive.

31. There are three exceptions to this general rule where a prepositional phrase referring to the addressee of the speech event follows לֵאמֹר. However, each instance is textually problematic and in each the addressee has already been specified within the quotative frame; the prepositional phrase following לֵאמֹר is co-referential with a previous noun phrase referring to the addressee and is entirely redundant. Leviticus 11:1 is an example: וַיְדַבֵּר יְהוָה אֶל־מֹשֶׁה וְאֶל־אַהֲרֹן לֵאמֹר אֲלֵהֶם: 'Yahweh spoke to Moses₍ᵢ₎ and Aaron₍ⱼ₎ saying to them₍ᵢ₊ⱼ₎, "Speak to the Israelites saying, 'These are the creatures which you may eat...'"' The addressees (Moses and Aaron) are specified within the quotative frame; the prepositional phrase ("to them") following לֵאמֹר is co-referential. Thus, this example differs from examples in which לֵאמֹר is a true infinitive governing a following prepositional phrase.

The other two examples in which a prepositional phrase follows לֵאמֹר are Gen. 23:5-6 and 14-15, both of which are textually disputed. In each instance the matrix verb is ענה 'to answer' and the addressees have already been specified within the quotative frame: וַיַּעֲנוּ בְנֵי־חֵת אֶת־אַבְרָהָם לֵאמֹר לוֹ 'the sons of Heth answered Abraham by saying to him' (Gen. 23:5); וַיַּעַן עֶפְרוֹן אֶת־אַבְרָהָם לֵאמֹר לוֹ 'Ephron answered Abraham to say to him' (Gen. 23:14). Instead of לוֹ 'to him', some versions and a few Hebrew manuscripts read לֹא 'not' (cf. verse 11). Sternberg (1991:42-43) suggests that the לֹא/לוֹ

alternation is an intentional ambiguity on the part of the narrator since the sons of Heth were responding negatively to Abraham, but in an oblique fashion.

32. As noted in Meier (1992:97), when the matrix verb is אָמַר, לֵאמֹר cannot add any additional semantic information to the verb.

33. A similar example occurs in 2 Sam. 7:26 (= 1 Chron. 17:24) in which the speakers of the speech event are entirely unspecified: וְיִגְדַּל שִׁמְךָ עַד־ עוֹלָם לֵאמֹר יְהוָה צְבָאוֹת אֱלֹהִים עַל־יִשְׂרָאֵל וּבֵית עַבְדְּךָ דָוִד יִהְיֶה נָכוֹן לְפָנֶיךָ... 'And may your name be great forever (saying), "Yahweh of hosts is God over Israel and may the house of your servant David be established before you..."'

34. For the definition of a complementizer and relevant examples, see Noonan (1985:44–45). The use of a form of the verb 'to say' as a grammaticalized complementizer is widespread cross-linguistically. See the data in Miller (1992:148–52) and the discussion in Heine (1991:158–59).

35. Meier (1992:130–40) argues that frames with לֵאמֹר are used with matrix verbs in the Hiphil and Piel and verbs which indicate the imposition of one's will upon another. This reconstruction is doubtful on two grounds. First, many of the matrix speech verbs used in quotative frames with לֵאמֹר occur only in the Hiphil or Piel, and etymologies that connect them with a causative meaning are highly dubious. More importantly, however, some speech verbs that indicate the imposition of one's will upon another yield a different sense when followed by the complementizer לֵאמֹר as opposed to a true infinitive. Compare the following sentences: "John_i commanded George_j to say, [לֵאמֹר = true infinitive], 'Give me_i asylum'" and "John_i commanded George_j [לֵאמֹר = complementizer], 'Give me_i asylum.'"

In the first example, the subject of the matrix clause (*John*) is not the speaker of the complement clause. In the second example, the subject of the matrix clause is identical to the speaker of the complement clause. If the second sentence were derived from the first, we would expect it to allow the reading that the quotation is spoken by George. But such is never the case with the verb צִוָּה in Biblical Hebrew, nor does לֵאמֹר ever follow צִוָּה as a true infinitive. The use of לֵאמֹר as a complementizer after צִוָּה, however, is widespread.

36. Omitted from consideration here are examples where the matrix verb in a לֵאמֹר frame is not metapragmatic (e.g., וַיָּבֹא לֵאמֹר 'he came לֵאמֹר'). See the discussion in Miller (1992:134–44).

37. For this discussion, a "configuration" is understood to be the combination of a particular matrix verb and a particular syntactic frame.

38. The caveat given above concerning the statistical limitations of the data applies here also.

39. The notion of marked versus unmarked has a long history within linguistics. It was first used by the phonologist Trubetzkoy (1958) to refer to oppositions between phonemes. The use of the term was extended by the Prague School, most notably Jakobson (1971:136).

40. Adapted from Batistella (1990).

41. Determining frequency is problematic in two respects. First, while the data in our corpus are extensive, the corpus is closed. As a result, certain statistical results of the corpus may not be representative of the spoken language. Second, in determining statistical frequency, it is difficult to know how to count. For example, in determining which quotative frame is the most frequent, there are two ways to count. One could count each token of the frame irrespective of the verb(s) appearing in the frame. By that analysis, single-verb frames would be the most frequent, since אָמַר appears most often in single-verb frames.

Another way to count would be to calculate how many different verbs may appear in a frame. By that analysis, לֵאמֹר frames would be the most frequent, though many of the verbs occur only a few times. Because of these difficulties, the criterion of frequency will be used only with respect to the frequency with which a particular verb appears in a particular syntactic frame (i.e., a "configuration"). See also the discussion concerning the problems of determining markedness by statistical frequency in Andrews (1990).

42. Goffman (1981:144) uses the terms "principal," "author," and "animator" to distinguish the various roles of speaker. The principal is the person who is committed to the propositional content of the speech event and stands behind it. The author frames the speech act in language. The animator produces the speech act, whether in writing or orally.

43. For a partial list of these, see Wagner (1979:320).

44. See also Num. 23:26; 1 Sam. 24:10; 29:5; Lachish Letter no. 6, lines 8-10. In late Biblical Hebrew, examples occur in 1 Chron. 17:6 and 2 Chron. 32:11-12.

45. Other examples within our corpus are: Gen. 3:17; 24:7; 39:19; 42:14; Lev. 10:3; Num. 14:17-18; 19:2-22; 36:6-9; Deut. 13:3; 34:4; Josh. 1:13; 1:16; 4:21-24; 14:9; Judg. 8:15; 1 Sam. 20:42; 1 Kings 5:19; 8:15-16; 9:5; 12:10; 12:12; 18:31; 2 Kings 9:36; 15:12. In late Biblical Hebrew, the following examples are attested: Ezra 9:11-12; Neh. 1:8-9; 1 Chron.17:6; 2 Chron. 6:16; 10:9; 10:12.

46. For the uses of קָרָא 'to call', see Miller (1992:271-80).

47. See also 1 Sam. 9:12-13, 19-20; 2 Sam. 14:19b-20.

48. For example, in Gen. 27:33-40, Esau discovers that his brother, Jacob, has deceived their father, Isaac, and acquired his blessing. Esau begs his father to bless him (Gen. 27:36b), but Isaac refuses (Gen. 27:37). The response is highly salient. Esau again begs his father to bless him (Gen. 27:38), and again Isaac refuses (Gen. 27:39-40), this time with finality. Again the response is highly salient.

49. See also 1 Sam. 30:22 and 2 Sam. 19:22.

50. See also the mismatch in 1 Kings 1:28 in which the designated addressee of the first pair-part responds by speaking to someone else.

51. See also the choral responses by Laban and Bethuel (Gen. 24:50-51), in example 22.

52. Exod. 19:8a; 24:36; Deut. 1:14; 1:41; 27:15b; Josh. 24:16-18; 2 Sam. 19:44.

53. The three examples in Genesis 23 and the example in Joshua 1 are not discussed here. Both of these chapters are unusual in that each reported utterance is introduced with a לֵאמֹר frame. I have no explanation for the use of ענה לֵאמֹר in Num. 32:31-32.

54. The addressee of the speech event, if indicated, is always marked with ל 'to'.

55. See also Judg. 16:17.

56. In 1 Kings 1:52 Solomon is informed by Adonijah's actions via a quotation introduced with the Hophal of נגד in a לֵאמֹר frame. Solomon responds not to the person who brought the news, but to Adonijah.

57. The example in 2 Sam. 15:31a has a textual problem: וְדָוִד הִגִּיד לֵאמֹר אֲחִיתֹפֶל בַּקֹּשְׁרִים עִם־אַבְשָׁלוֹם וַיֹּאמֶר דָּוִד סַכֶּל־נָא אֶת־עֲצַת אֲחִיתֹפֶל יְהוָה 'And David reported, "Ahithophel is among the conspirators with Absalom." So David said, "Turn the advice of Ahithophel into foolishness, O Yahweh."' The text probably should read ולדוד הגד 'and to David it was reported', as many of the versions have it.

58. In 2 Sam. 2:4 there is an example of a לֵאמֹר frame introducing a message. It is not clear whether the speakers are the men of Judah (from the first clause of the verse) or anonymous messengers (so NIV, NJPS).

59. Gen. 48:2 is an exception in that the speaker of the speech event is not identified although the quotation is introduced with a multiple-verb frame. The passage, however, is textually disputed. The LXX reading seems to imply that the Vorlage of the LXX had a לֵאמֹר frame rather than a multiple-verb frame.

60. For Hiphil singular in לֵאמֹר frames see, for example, 1 Sam. 19:2-3, 11b; 25:14-17; 2 Kings 4:31; 9:18c; 22:10a. For Hiphil plural in לֵאמֹר frames, see Gen. 42:29-34; 45:26.

61. See also Lev. 14:35.

62. This fact has been noted by Bar-Efrat (1989:73-75). Within our corpus, there is only one instance (2 Kings 17:27) where a quotation with צוה appears as the second pair-part of an adjacency pair. In fact, Num. 32:28-30 is the only example in our corpus of a spoken response to the command and in this case there is a mismatch in the adjacency pair. Moses gives a command concerning the Gadites and Reubenites to Eleazar and Joshua. The Gadites and Reubenites, rather than the designated addressees, verbally agree to the stipulations set down by Moses. Note, however, that a multiple-verb frame introduces the single example of צוה with a spoken response (Num. 32:28-30).

63. See also Num. 32:28-30 (where the utterance by Moses culminates a long discussion with the Gadites and Reubenites concerning their desire to settle in the Transjordan), Deut. 32:32 (where Yahweh and Moses prepare for

Moses' approaching death and Yahweh commands Joshua to be strong and courageous) and 2 Kings 11:15 (where Jehoiada commands the officers to bring Athaliah out of the temple and kill her).

64. The remaining two examples of multiple-verb frames (Num. 28:2; 34:2-12) appear embedded within direct speech and are imperatives: 'command and say'. In each instance, Yahweh tells Moses to issue a command to the Israelites and the succeeding narrative relates that Moses relays the command. Frames with לֵאמֹר appear more frequently in this sort of pragmatic context; there are not enough examples of multiple-verb frames to determine their discourse-pragmatic function in this context.

65. See also Gen. 32:20-21a where the iterative nature of the quotation is explicitly indicated.

66. Gen. 3:17; 50:16-17; Num. 34:13-15; Deut. 1:16-17; 3:18-20, 21-22; 2 Sam. 18:12; 1 Kings 13:9; 2 Kings 14:6.

67. See also Josh. 6:10 (command presumably given before the march around Jericho, but relayed only during the march) and 2 Kings 17:35-39 (the command Yahweh had previously given the Israelites, but which they failed to keep).

68. Other communicational expressions appear only in multiple-verb frames: שִׂים דָּבָר 'to put a word', that is, 'to tell what to say'; הָיָה מָשָׁל 'a wise saying was'; נָשָׂא מָשָׁל 'to raise a wise saying', that is, 'to tell a wise saying'; הָרִים מָשָׁל 'to cause a sound to rise', that is, 'to shout'.

References

Alter, Robert. 1981. *The art of biblical narrative*. New York: Basic Books.
Andrews, Edna. 1990. *Markedness theory: The union of asymmetry and semiosis in language*. Sound and Meaning: The Roman Jakobson Series In Linguistics and Poetics. Durham and London: Duke University Press.
Bar-Efrat, Shimon. 1989. *Narrative art in the Bible*. Translated by Dorothea Shefer-Vanson. Bible and Literature Series, 17. Sheffield: Almond.
Batistella, Edwin L. 1990. *Markedness: The evaluative superstructure of language*. SUNY Series in Linguistics, ed. Mark Aronoff. Albany: State University of New York.
Bühler, Karl. 1934. *Sprachtheorie: Die Darstellungsfunktion der Sprache*. Jena: G. Fischer Verlag.
Comrie, Bernard. 1976. *Aspect: An introduction to the study of verbal aspect and related problems*. Cambridge Textbooks in Linguistics. London: Cambridge University Press.
Coulmas, Florian. 1986. Reported speech: Some general issues. In *Direct and indirect speech,* ed. Florian Coulmas, 1-28. Trends in Linguistics, 31. Berlin: Mouton de Gruyter.
Gesenius, W., and E. Kautzsch, eds. 1910. *Gesenius Hebrew grammar*. 2d ed. rev. from the 28th German ed. and trans. by A. E. Cowley. Oxford and New York: Oxford University Press.

Givón, T. 1991. The evolution of dependent clause morpho-syntax in Biblical Hebrew. In *Focus on types of grammatical markers,* vol. 2 of *Approaches to grammaticalization,* ed. Elizabeth Closs Traugott and Bernd Heine, 259–310. Typological Studies in Language, 19. Amsterdam and Philadelphia: John Benjamins.

Goffman, Erving. 1981. *Forms of talk.* Philadelphia: University of Pennsylvania Press.

Goldenberg, Gideon. 1991. On direct speech and the Hebrew Bible. In *Studies in Hebrew and Aramaic syntax presented to Professor J. Hoftijzer,* ed. by K. Jongeling, H. L. Murre-Van den Berg, and L. van Rompay, 79–96. Leiden: E. J. Brill.

Halliday, M. A. K., and Ruqaiya Hasan. 1976. *Cohesion in English.* English Language Series, 9. London: Longman.

Heine, Bernd, Ulrike Claudi, and Friederike Hünnemeyer. 1991. *Grammaticalization: A conceptual framework.* Chicago: University of Chicago Press.

Jakobson, Roman. 1960. Closing statement: Linguistics and poetics. In *Style in language,* ed. Thomas A. Sebeok, 350–77. Cambridge, Mass.: MIT Press.

———. 1971. Shifters, verbal categories, and the Russian verb. In *Word and Language,* vol. 2 of *Selected Writings*: , 130–47. The Hague: Mouton.

———. 1980. Metalanguage as a linguistic problem. In *The framework of language,* ed. Irwin R. Titunik, 81–92. Michigan Studies in the Humanities, 1. Ann Arbor: University of Michigan.

Johnstone, Barbara. 1987. 'He says . . . so I said': Verb tense alternation and narrative depictions of authority in American English. *Linguistics* 25:33–52.

Joüon, Paul. 1923. *Grammaire de l'hébreu biblique.* Rome: Pontifical Biblical Institute.

Levenston, E. A. 1984. The speech-acts of God. In *Literature and the Arts* 12:129–45. Hebrew University Studies.

Longacre, Robert E. 1989. *Joseph: A story of divine providence: a text theoretical and textlinguistic analysis of Genesis 37 and 39–48.* Winona Lake, Ind.: Eisenbrauns.

Malone, Joseph L. 1979. Textually deviant forms as evidence for phonological analysis: A service of philology to linguistics. *Journal of the Ancient Near East Society* 11:71–79.

Meier, Samuel A. 1992. *Speaking of speaking: Marking direct discourse in the Hebrew Bible.* Supplements to Vetus Testamentum, 46. Leiden: E. J. Brill.

Miller, Charles H. 1970. The infinitive construct in the lawbooks of the Old Testament: A statistical study. *Catholic Biblical Quarterly* 32:222–26.

Miller, Cynthia L. 1992. Reported speech in biblical and epigraphic Hebrew: A linguistic analysis. Ph.D. diss., University of Chicago.

———. 1993. The syntactic status of לאמר in Biblical Hebrew. Paper presented at the American Oriental Society annual meeting.

———. Forthcoming. Discourse functions of quotative frames in Biblical Hebrew narrative. In *Discourse analysis of Biblical Literature: What it is and what it offers,* ed. Walter R. Bodine. Semeia Studies. Atlanta: Scholars Press.

Munro, Pamela. 1982. On the transitivity of 'say' verbs. In *Studies in transitivity,* ed. Paul J. Hopper and Sandra A. Thompson, 301–18. Syntax and Semantics, 15. New York: Academic.

Noonan, Michael. 1985. Complementation. In *Complex constructions*, vol. 2 of *Language typology and syntactic description*, ed. Timothy Shopen, 42–140. Cambridge: Cambridge University Press.

O'Connor, M. 1980. *Hebrew verse structure.* Winona Lake, Ind.: Eisenbrauns.

Partee, Barbara Hall. 1973. The syntax and semantics of quotation. In *A festschrift for Morris Halle*, ed. Paul Kiparsky and S. Anderson, 410–18. New York: Holt, Rinehart and Winston.

Rebera, Basil. 1981. The book of Ruth: Dialogue and narrative, the function and integration of the two modes in an ancient Hebrew story. Ph.D. diss., Macquarie University.

Rendsburg, Gary A. 1990. *Diglossia in ancient Hebrew.* American Oriental Series, 72. New Haven, Conn.: American Oriental Society.

Sacks, Harvey, Emanuel A. Schegloff, and Gail Jefferson. 1974. A simplest systematics for the organization of turn-taking for conversation. *Language* 50:696–735.

Savran, George W. 1988. *Telling and retelling: Quotation in biblical narrative.* Indiana Studies in Biblical Literature. Bloomington: Indiana University Press.

Seow, C. L. 1987. *A grammar for Biblical Hebrew.* Nashville: Abingdon.

Shapiro, Marianne. 1984. How narrators report speech. *Language and Style* 17:67–78.

Silverstein, Michael. 1985. The culture of language in Chinookan narrative texts: Or, on saying that... in Chinook. In *Grammar inside and outside the clause: Some approaches to theory from the field*, ed. Johanna Nichols and Anthony C. Woodbury, 132–71. Cambridge: Cambridge University Press.

———. 1987. The three faces of 'function': Preliminaries to a psychology of language. In *Social and functional approaches to language and thought*, ed. Maya Hickmann, 17–38. New York: Academic.

———. 1993. Metapragmatic discourse and metapragmatic function. In *Reflexive language: Reported speech and metapragmatics*, ed. John A. Lucy, 33–58. Cambridge: Cambridge University Press.

Sternberg, Meir. 1982. Proteus in quotation-land: Mimesis and the forms of reported discourse. *Poetics Today* 3:107–56.

———. 1991. Double cave, double talk: The indirections of biblical dialogue. In *"Not in heaven": Coherence and complexity in biblical narrative*, 28–57. Indiana Studies in Biblical Literature. Bloomington: Indiana University Press.

Tannen, Deborah. 1986. Introducing constructed dialogue in Greek and American conversational and literary narrative. In *Direct and indirect speech*, ed. Florian Coulmas, 311–32. Trends in Linguistics, 31. Berlin: Mouton de Gruyter.

Trubetzkoy, N. 1985. *Grundzüge der Phonologie.* Göttingen: Vandenhoeck and Ruprecht.

Van Valin, Robert D., Jr. 1984. A typology of syntactic relations in clause linkage. In *Proceedings of the tenth annual meeting of the Berkeley Linguistics Society*, ed. Claudia Brugman and Monica Macaulay, 542–58. Berkeley: Berkeley Linguistics Society.

Wagner, Siegfried. 1979. אמר *'āmar.* In *Theological dictionary of the Old Testament*, ed. Johannes G. Botterweck and Helmer Ringgren, trans. John T. Willis, 1:328–45. Grand Rapids: Eerdmans.

Waltke, Bruce K., and M. O'Connor. 1990. *An introduction to Biblical Hebrew syntax.* Winona Lake, Ind.: Eisenbrauns.
Williams, Ronald J. 1976. *Hebrew syntax: An outline.* 2d ed. Toronto: University of Toronto Press.
Wright, Logan Scott. 1991. Reported speech in Hebrew narrative: A typology and analysis of texts in the Book of Genesis. Ph.D. diss., Emory University.

9

GENEALOGICAL PROMINENCE AND THE STRUCTURE OF GENESIS

T. David Andersen

In Genesis, differing degrees of prominence are given to participants by means of a variety of devices, such as the number of episodes a character appears in, type of participant identification, renaming of a character, headings ("these are the generations of"), and information about birth, offspring, and death. Of particular prominence are characters who have a section named after them, and those who have two or more lines of descendants recorded, each line at least two generations. The verb chosen to report the death of a character is another significant device for giving prominence. In this article I will try to calculate the relative prominence of many of the characters in Genesis in the light of these factors.

The way participants are given different degrees of prominence has significant ramifications with regard to the patterned structure of the sections. These sections are classified as genealogical and story sections and also as to whether they represent the chosen family line or the rejected family line. A systematic alternation between the types of section is discerned. Each type of section has a consistent internal structure. The story sections usually contain the following elements in the same order: (1) reintroduction of patriarch, (2) son's birth, (3) choosing/rejection of sons, (4) grandson's birth, (5) choosing/rejection of grandsons, (6) death of daughter-in-law, (7) summary/blessing of descendants, (8) death of patriarch, and (9) death of chosen son. An understanding of the patterns of these discourse macrostructures leads to explanations of various apparent anomalies in the structure of Genesis.

In this article two questions with regard to the Book of Genesis are addressed: the way the author gives differing degrees of prominence to the many characters found in the book, and how the overall structure of the book is organized around some of the more prominent characters. Both of these questions imply an approach which treats the Book of Genesis as a single literary whole. In the past, many scholars have focused on smaller units, such as sources and small literary forms, as well as redactional processes. More recently, however, three factors have laid a firmer basis for investigating Genesis as a unit. These are: (1) appreciation of the literary identity of Genesis as a finished work; (2) appreciation that the composition or compilation of Genesis was motivated by a theological intention later legitimated by its acceptance in the canon; and (3) the application of new approaches in textlinguistics and discourse analysis to biblical books.

1. Four ways of marking a character's prominence in Genesis

One of the concerns of discourse analysis is how different characters in a story are given different degrees of prominence. There are more than three hundred human characters mentioned in Genesis. Which of these many characters has the author made prominent and what techniques does he use to do it?

There are at least four ways relative prominence is indicated in Genesis. The first is the *number of episodes* a character appears in. The more episodes he or she appears in, especially in an active role, the greater the prominence. For example, the following characters play an active role in at least two episodes:[1] Adam, Eve, Cain, Noah, Abraham, Lot, Sarah, Hagar, Ishmael, Abimelech, Isaac, Abraham's servant, Rebekah, Laban, Esau, Jacob, Rachel, Reuben, Judah, Joseph, Tamar, Potiphar, Joseph's Pharaoh, the chief cupbearer, and Joseph's steward.

The second way a character is made prominent is with a *section heading*. Ten characters appear in the formula __ אֵלֶּה תּוֹלְדוֹת 'These are the generations of __': Adam, Noah, Shem, Ham, Japheth, Terah, Ishmael, Isaac, Esau, and Jacob.

The third way relative prominence is shown is in terms of how the different characters are *identified* in the text. (For the theoretical basis of this approach see Grimes 1975 and Fleming 1978.) Longacre (1989:141-57) has analyzed the Joseph story from this point of view. The identification of participants in Biblical Hebrew can be ranked as follows: nouns or proper names plus qualifiers, nouns or proper names without qualifiers, kinship or role nouns, pronouns, object suffixes, subject and possessor affixes, and null references (ellipsis). In general, higher-ranking participants are more likely to be identified by name, and minor participants only by role or kinship nouns. Also, the higher-ranking participants are more likely to be introduced in a distinctive way such as with a descriptive sentence.

A participant is often identified as being locally thematic, or prominent, in a certain episode or paragraph with overt multiple mentions of his or her name or another noun not really needed for unambiguous reference (i.e., even though a pronominal element would be sufficient for clarity). In applying this approach to Genesis, however, the use of proper names to identify major participants may not be of crucial importance since more than 270 characters are identified by name. But *renaming* of characters may be quite significant. There are four characters who are given new names (Abram, Sarai, Jacob, and Joseph), which may be a way of signaling their prominence.[2]

Attention to kinship terms is also a helpful clue to prominence. The locally thematic (higher-ranking) participant can be recognized as dominant in relation to another participant when one is given a kinship role. For example, in the relationship between Abraham and Isaac, if Isaac is referred to as "his son Isaac" (Gen. 22:3), Abraham has the dominant role. If Abraham is referred to as "his father Abraham" (Gen. 22:7), then at that point Isaac has the dominant role and is locally thematic.

In Genesis a fourth way of indicating relative prominence is *information in the genealogies*. The genealogies list three types of information: birth, offspring, and death. But the information varies by kind and amount. Since the presence or absence of particular genealogical information usually has no direct impact on the plot, it is likely that these variations may signal the relative prominence of different characters.

It is this fourth way that is the focus of this article. Sections 2–4 focus on birth, offspring, and death information, the three types of information presented in the genealogies (also at times in the stories). Section 5 focuses on how such information is used to indicate prominence. In section 6, the relationship between participant prominence and the structure of Genesis is treated.

2. Birth

In Genesis information about birth is a frequent means of introducing a participant to the story. Almost 250 characters are introduced this way. Most often it is simply a matter of mentioning a family relationship:

> The sons of Ham: Cush, Mizraim, Put, and Canaan (10:6)
> Tubal-Cain's sister was Naamah (4:22)

In other cases, the verb ילד 'bear' is used:

> וַתֵּלֶד עָדָה אֶת־יָבָל
> Adah gave birth to Jabal (4:20)

> וּמְתוּשָׁאֵל יָלַד אֶת־לָמֶךְ
> and Methushael begat Lamech (4:18)

Information about the age of the father may be given:

> וְשֶׁלַח חַי שְׁלֹשִׁים שָׁנָה וַיּוֹלֶד אֶת־עֵבֶר
> When Shelah had lived 30 years he begat Eber (11:14)

If more information than this is given (e.g., about conception, naming, etc., as in 4:25), it can be regarded as a birth story, not just a genealogical formula.

Based on these features of reporting births, we hypothesize five levels of prominence. From least to greatest they are: no report, relationship only, with verb ילד, verb ילד plus age, and story.

3. Offspring

The number of offspring mentioned varies with different individuals. Of particular interest is the recorded number of generations of descendants. Some individuals have no recorded descendants; they are named as sons or daughters only. This is the case, for example, for Ashkenaz, Riphath, and Togarmah (10:3). Others have one generation of descendants recorded; their genealogical status is that of parents. This is the case for Gomer (10:3), Raamah (10:7), Aram (10:23), Joktan (10:26), Reuben, Simeon, and Levi (46:9-11). For some individuals a group of descendants are mentioned, but without proper names; they are considered forebears, for example:

Reference	Forebear	Descendants
4:21	Jubal	all who play the harp and flute
10:13	Mizraim	the Ludites, Anamites, etc.
19:37	Moab	the Moabites
19:38	Ben-ammi	the Ammonites

Those with at least two generations of named descendants recorded are more prominent. Their genealogical status is that of grandparents. About fifty characters in Genesis have this status. They can be further categorized according to how many separate lines of descendants are recorded. Characters such as Cain and Seth have only one line of descendants recorded. This can be termed a *linear* genealogy. But some characters have two or more lines of descendants, each line at least two generations. This is termed a *segmented* genealogy (see Wilson 1977:9). Table 1 lists all the "double-line grandfathers" found in Genesis.

Joseph does not completely fulfill the criteria for a double-line grandfather since the generation after Ephraim is mentioned but not named. In cases where the names of descendants are scattered and thus not so clear to the reader (e.g., Eber, Terah), the prominence function may not be as clear as in other cases. Other characters with double-line grandparent status in Genesis are wives of those listed in the table, namely Eve, Milcah, Rebekah, Keturah, Rachel, Leah, Zilpah, and Bilhah.

Table 1. Double-line grandfathers

Name	First line	Second line	3rd/4th lines	References
Adam	Cain-Enoch	Seth-Enosh		4:17, 26
Noah	Japheth-Gomer	Ham-Cush	Shem-Elam	10:2, 6, 22
Japheth	Gomer-Ashkenaz	Javan-Elishah		10:2–4
Ham	Cush-Seba	Canaan-Sidon		10:6–7, 15
Shem	Aram-Uz	Arphaxad-Shelah		10:22–24
Eber	Joktan-Almodad	Peleg-Reu		10:26; 11:18
Terah	Haran-Lot	Abram-Ishmael	Nahor-Uz	11:27; 16:15; 22:20
Abraham	Ishmael-Nebaioth	Isaac-Esau	Jokshan-Sheba Midian-Ephah	25:1–4, 13, 25–26
Nahor	Kemuel-Aram	Bethuel-Rebekah		22:20–23
Isaac	Esau-Eliphaz	Jacob-Reuben		35:23; 36:4
Esau	Eliphaz-Teman	Reuel-Nahath		36:10–13
Seir	Lotan-Hori	Shobal-Alvan	Zibeon-Aiah Anah-Dishon (plus 3 more lines)[3]	36:20–28
Jacob	Judah-Er	Joseph-Manasseh	Reuben-Hanoch Simeon-Jemuel (plus 8 more lines)	46:9–24
Joseph	Manasseh-Makir	Ephraim-"Ephraim's children"		50:22–23

A comparison of the list of characters given section headings (Adam, Noah, Shem, Ham, Japheth, Terah, Ishmael, Isaac, Esau, and Jacob) and the list of double-line grandfathers in Table 1 shows how significant the latter category is as a signal of prominence in Genesis. Every single character given a section heading has the status of double-line grandfather except for Ishmael. The correlation is not quite as strong in the other direction: there are four double-line grandfathers (Eber, Abraham, Nahor, and Seir) who are not given section headings.

There are five characters in Table 1 with more than two lines of descendants: Noah, Terah, Abraham, Seir, and Jacob. Is this merely an accident of fecundity, or is it a means of showing them as more prominent than the others? The fact that all of them gain their status as multiple-line grandparents as the result of the addition of a special genealogical section to the text suggests that it is a deliberate device of the author. In Abraham's case, for example, the extra two lines of descendants are mentioned in a short genealogical section inserted just before the account of his death (25:1-4). This contrasts to the genealogies in chapters 5 and 11 which simply use the formula וַיּוֹלֶד בָּנִים וּבָנוֹת 'and he had [other] sons and daughters'. Terah's case is the least clear in that the accounts of his various lines are scattered here and there and not summarized as Jacob's are (35:23-26; 46:8-26). One might argue that the author did not have such information about other characters and that he just included all the information he had. If this were so, it would mean that it was the process of handing down tradition rather than the final author's choice that gave prominence to certain characters. But the end result might be the same.

4. Death

Besides accounts of birth and descendants, accounts of death also contribute to genealogical prominence. Indeed death is more significant than birth. In Genesis some mention of birth is the most common way for a new character to enter the story, but a character's exit is often unmentioned. A death account is given for only about forty characters, whereas almost 250 have some information about birth.

Death accounts are an ideal way to give prominence to certain chosen characters because the presence or absence of a death account usually does not have a crucial effect on the plot. The inclusion of a death account often seems to function only to give prominence to that person.

The use of the verb מֵת 'die' is correlated with this prominence-giving function. For there are some cases where the violent death of a character is part of the plot and does not necessarily mean that that character is being given more prominence than someone who does not die violently. Examples are Abel, Shechem, Hamor, Er, Onan, and Pharaoh's baker. In none of these cases is מֵת used (the later flashback of 46:12 is disregarded). The case of Pharaoh's baker is instructive. Just because he was put to death and the cupbearer spared does not mean the baker is more prominent than the cupbearer. Rather the opposite is the case. So in general we only count a death account as giving special prominence if מֵת is used.

There are some exceptions though. In Shem's section, information about the age of each member of the line is given, but their death is not explicitly mentioned. Genesis 11:11 ("And after he became the father of Arphaxad, Shem lived 500 years and had other sons and daughters") provides an example:

וַיְחִי־שֵׁם אַחֲרֵי הוֹלִידוֹ אֶת־אַרְפַּכְשַׁד
and-lived Shem after his-begetting ACC Arphaxad

חֲמֵשׁ מֵאוֹת שָׁנָה וַיּוֹלֶד בָּנִים וּבָנוֹת
five hundreds year and-he-begot sons and-daughters

Compare this with the formula in 5:4–5 ("After Seth was born Adam lived 800 years and had other sons and daughters. Altogether, Adam lived 930 years, and then he died") in Adam's section:

וַיִּהְיוּ יְמֵי־אָדָם אַחֲרֵי הוֹלִידוֹ אֶת־שֵׁת
and-they-were days-of Adam after his-begetting ACC Seth

שְׁמֹנֶה מֵאֹת שָׁנָה וַיּוֹלֶד בָּנִים וּבָנוֹת
eight hundreds year and-he-begot sons and-daughters

וַיִּהְיוּ כָּל־יְמֵי אָדָם אֲשֶׁר־חַי תְּשַׁע מֵאוֹת
and-they-were all days-of Adam that he-lived nine hundreds

שָׁנָה וּשְׁלֹשִׁים שָׁנָה וַיָּמֹת
year and-thirty year and-he-died.

The presence of this extra clause about total age and death gives more prominence to those in Adam's section compared to those in Shem's section, perhaps because they are the more ancient original forebears.

Another character of whom the verb מֵת is not used is Enoch. Instead וְאֵינֶנּוּ 'and he was not' is used. But we should not interpret this as a lessening of prominence in the case of Enoch.

In the genealogical lists, information about death is generally restricted to the verb מֵת with or without information about age. (Examples without age are found in the kings of Edom list at 36:31–39.) Other commonly added elements are information about burial or formulaic verbs. These extra verbs are seen in the cases of Abraham, Isaac, Ishmael, and Jacob. Ishmael's death in 25:17 ("He breathed his last and died, and he was gathered to his people") is an example:

וַיִּגְוַע וַיָּמָת וַיֵּאָסֶף אֶל־עַמָּיו
and-he-breathed-his-last and-he-died and-he-was-gathered to his-peoples

This obviously does not add anything to the plot but merely gives more prominence. Information about burial also seems important in giving prominence. Other details may be added, including information about place, mourning, deathbed instructions, or a remark about longevity.

The fact that such formulaic verbs give prominence has relevance to the way we translate such verses. The TEV simply omitted the formulaic verbs as redundant and translated Gen. 25:17 "he died." The translators doubtless felt that such repetition was not natural in English. But simple

5. Relative prominence of participants

In Table 2 we see how the various prominence devices combine to determine the relative prominence of different characters. All the major characters and a selection of minor characters are listed with a numerical weighting in terms of the prominence features.

Of course, it is a difficult and doubtful exercise to work out a satisfactory weighting formula. In the scoring that follows Table 2, I have been guided mainly by the number of times a particular feature occurs in Genesis. A feature that occurs with less characters, giving greater relative prominence, is awarded more points. The maximum number of points for any feature is ten, and that is given if it occurs with only a couple of characters. This is gradually scaled down so that, for example, five points are given for a feature that occurs more than thirty times (e.g., מֵת), and one point is given for a feature that occurs more than two hundred times (e.g., mention of birth, named character).[4] In any case, the numerical totals in Table 2 should by no means be considered definitive. (Note that abbreviations in the table are explained in the scoring material.)

The information in Table 2 can be used to investigate how well particular factors or combinations of factors predict overall prominence. At this point, we limit ourselves to two such observations. The best predictor of most central character is a death story that includes the three formulaic verbs plus information about age and burial. There are only three characters who have such a death story and they are the three most prominent characters in Table 2, namely Jacob, Isaac, and Abraham.

The double-grandfather feature is not a completely reliable indicator of greatest prominence, since it also characterizes a relatively less prominent character such as Seir and does not include some major characters such as Ishmael. Similarly the use of the verb מֵת includes some minor characters such as Deborah (who is prominent only because of her death story) and does not include a major character such as Esau. But the *combination* of these two features is a powerful predictor of the major characters. There are seven individuals in Genesis characterized by both of these features, and they are the seven most prominent in Table 2, namely Adam, Noah, Terah, Abraham, Isaac, Jacob, and Joseph. The material in Table 2 gives scope for other observations that could be made on the way the author has carefully treated the large cast found in Genesis.

Table 2. Relative prominence in Genesis

Name	Dom. role[5]	Re-named	Epi-sodes	Sec-tion	Birth	Grand-parent	Death	Total points
Adam	3:8		3	Yes	story	double	MA	33
Eve	3:6		2		story	double		18
Cain	4:8		2		story	single		16
Abel			1		story		(K)	10
Lamech I			1		verb	foreb		8
Seth			1		story	single	MA	19
Enoch			1		age	single	MA	17
Methuselah					age	single	MA	13
Lamech II			1		age	single	MA	17
Noah	9:24		4	Yes	story	triple	MA	36
Shem	10:21		PAS	Yes	age	double	A	25
Ham	9:22		1	shared	age	double		22
Japheth			PAS	shared	age	double		18
Cush					rel.	single		5
Nimrod			1		verb			7
Asshur					rel.			2
Eber					age	double	A	13
Peleg	(10:25)				age	double	A	12
Joktan					verb			3
Terah	11:31		1	Yes	age	triple	MA	32
Abraham	12:5	by God	20		age	mult.	MAFBD	38
Nahor					age	double		9
Haran	11:28		1		age	(sing)	MD	18
Lot	(19:16)		5		verb	(sing)[6]		13
Sarah	16:3	by God	4			single	MABD	25
Milcah						double		6
Bera			1					5
Melchiz-edek			1					5
Hagar	16:4		3			single		12
Ishmael	21:21		2	Yes	story	single	MAF	31
Lot's older daughter	19:33		1			fore-bear		7
Lot's wife			1			(sing)	(K)	6
Abimelech			4					7
Isaac	22:7		9	Yes	story	double	MAFBD	39
Phicol			PAS					3

-continued on next page-

Genealogical Prominence and the Structure of Genesis 251

Name	Dom. role[5]	Re-named	Epi-sodes	Sec-tion	Birth	Grand-parent	Death	Total points
Ephron			1					5
Abraham's servant			2					5
Rebekah	24:55		6			double		15
Laban	29:23		6					10
Deborah							MB	8
Keturah						double		6
Esau	27:32		7	Yes	story	double		29
Jacob	27:30	by God	28	Yes	story	mult.	MAFBD	49
Rachel	30:7		5			double	MBD	23
Leah	30:10		1			mult.	B	18
Zilpah			1			double		10
Bilhah			1			double		10
Reuben	42:37		5		story			15
Simeon			PAS		story			8
Judah	38:20		5		story	single		18
Asher					story	single		9
Issachar					story			6
Dinah	34:11		1		story			12
Joseph	37:10	by man	20		story	(doub)	MABD	32
lead servant								0
Shechem	34:6		1				(K)	7
Hamor	34:20		1				(K)	7
Benjamin	35:18		1		story			12
Seir						mult.		10
Potiphar	(39:19)		3					8
Judah's wife							MD	6
Tamar	38:25		2					8
Perez			1		story			10
warden			1					4
cup-bearer			2					5
baker			1				(K)	4
Pharaoh			6					7
Asenath						(doub)		5
Manasseh			PAS		story			8
Ephraim			PAS		story			8
Joseph's steward			2					5

Scoring

Name	Points
Proper name	1
Noun only	0
Dominant role	
Redundant	2
Not redundant	1
Renamed	
By God	4
By man	2
Episodes	
Shared active or prominent passive (PAS)[7]	2
Active in: 1	4
2	5
3–4	6
5–6	7
7–9	8
20	9
28	10
Section	
Y	8
shared	7

Birth	Points
Relationship only (rel.)	1
With verb	2
With age	3
With story	5
Grandparent	
Forebear	1
Single unnamed (sing)	2
Single	3
Double unnamed (doub)	4
Double	5
Triple	8
Multiple	9
Death	
(K) killed	0
A age only	4
M מֵת (or וַיְרָגְעוּ)	5
MA מֵת + age	6
F formulaic verbs	+1
B burial	+2
D extra details	+1

6. Structure

We have seen how the אֵלֶּה תּוֹלְדֹת section headings give prominence, but this is not their only role. In fact, they constitute one of the most important structural features of Genesis. But there has been disagreement over how these section headings are to be interpreted. The traditional translation, "These are the generations of," and its modern equivalent, "These are the descendants of . . ." (NRSV), lead us to expect an account of the descendants of the "section patriarch" (the term that refers to the character after whom a section is named). Blum (1984:434) argues for this interpretation. But while this fits some sections well enough, in other sections, such as Noah's, most of the material in the section consists of important events in the section patriarch's life. This would justify translating the heading to imply that the section following is a historical account of the section patriarch: "This is the account of . . ." (NIV), or "the life and times of . . ." (Longacre 1989:20).

But many interpreters have been puzzled as to why most sections start after most of the stories about the section patriarch have already been told. This is true of Adam, Japheth, Ham, Shem, Ishmael, Esau, and Jacob.

This caused P. J. Wiseman to suggest that the label was a colophon for the previous section and that it should be translated "These are the historical origins of . . ."[8] Similarly von Rad (1972:63) suggested the translation "story of origin" for the first section heading ("heavens and earth" in 2:4a). In this case he finds the colophon explanation necessary because 2:4 along with the preceding chapter is assigned to the Priestly source, whereas 2:4b signals the start of J. With regard to Jacob's section (popularly known as "the Joseph story"), the Jerusalem Bible tries to solve the apparent problem by changing 37:2 to read, "This is the account of Joseph" (instead of Jacob).

A more fruitful suggestion is that we interpret the section heading to mean, "This is the family (line) of whom _____ is the head." The section patriarch's status is that of current family patriarch.[9] A translation more in accord with this interpretation is the NRSV's (at 37:2): "This is the story of the family of Jacob."

This interpretation helps explain the high correlation between double-line grandfathers and section patriarchs. One reason why double-line grandfathers are prominent is the theme of God's choosing a single family through whom all the families of the earth will be blessed. This theme is worked out generation after generation with one of the two lines being chosen and the other rejected (Kidner 1967:13-14). Having double-line grandfathers as section patriarchs allows for optimum structural development of this thematic pattern. This interpretation also explains why a number of sections end when the current patriarch dies (e.g., Noah, Abraham, Isaac). In these cases the new section marks the accession of his sons to the role of family patriarchs. There is always a pair of sections in these cases, the first a shorter one, dealing with the rejected line, and the second dealing with the chosen line.

We can gain a better understanding of how the sections are used as a structural framework if we classify the sections in various ways. For the purpose of this analysis we take the first section heading in 2:4 as referring to the following section. Chapter 1 is regarded as preliminary to the section structure as such.

A primary division is between genealogical and story sections. Genealogical sections tell about quite a number of generations but have almost no stories. Story sections tell about only one or two generations but they have many stories.

Another way of classifying the sections is based on whether they represent the chosen family line or the rejected family line. For this purpose, the heavens and earth section could perhaps be regarded as a rejected line since it deals with the Fall and with Cain's line.

Table 3. Genealogical depth of sections

Section	Total depth	Until next patriarch
heavens and earth	8	1
Adam	10	9
Noah	2	1
Shem/Ham/Japheth		
Japheth	2	–
Ham	3	–
Shem	5	–
Shem	9	8
Terah	4	2
Ishmael	1	–
Isaac	2	1
Esau	2	–
Jacob	3	–

As exemplified in Table 3, a third way to compare the sections is in terms of "genealogical depth," that is, the number of generations they encompass (for the use of this term see Wilson 1977). There are two ways of counting this. One can count the total number of generations mentioned, or one can count the numbers of generations until the next section patriarch. The latter method does not apply to genealogical rejected-line sections, since no other patriarch emerges from those lines. Neither does it apply to Jacob's section, since it is the last. But in other sections, the two figures tend to differ. For example, the heavens and earth section has a total depth of eight through Cain's line, but there is only one generation to the next section patriarch (if we take heavens and earth as filling the role of patriarch a generation above Adam). The figures for each section are set out in Table 3. Note that the genealogical sections do not necessarily have greater depth than the story sections.

The arrangement of sections can be diagrammed as follows. (Here gen. means "genealogy," the list of those descendants who are either "chosen" or "rejected." The number in parentheses is the number of generations until the next patriarch.)

Genealogical Prominence and the Structure of Genesis 255

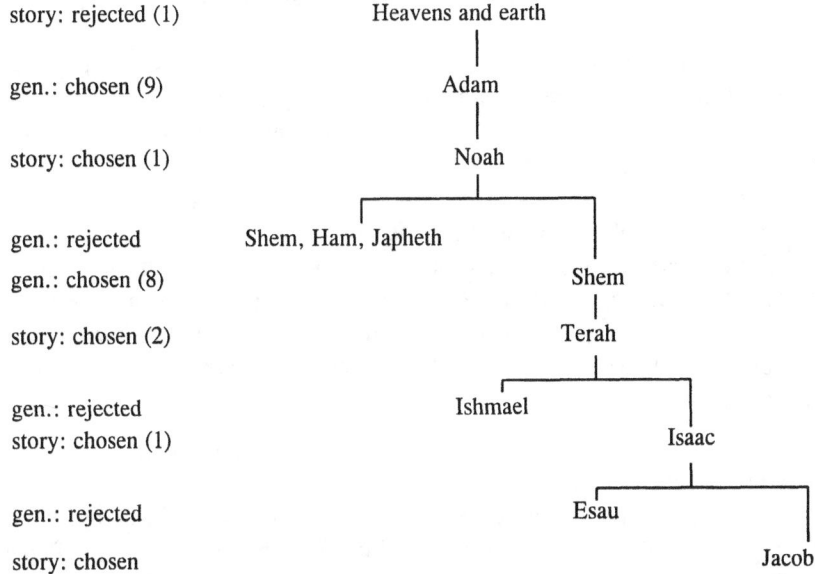

Figure 1. Arrangement of sections

Renaud (1990:8-10) has another way of classifying the תּוֹלְדוֹת sections. He distinguishes between the narrative schema and the enumerative schema. In the former, which is more common, genealogical information is recounted in narrative form with verbs, usually with information about the age of the patriarch as well as his eventual death. In the enumerative schema genealogical information is presented primarily in lists, without verbs. He identifies three תּוֹלְדוֹת sections that follow the enumerative schema: Shem, Ham and Japheth's section; Ishmael's section; and Esau's section. It is significant that these correspond to the rejected sections.

We can see, in the preceding diagram, that there is never a sequence of two identical section types. Generally there is alternation between chosen and rejected and between story and genealogy. There are two places where two chosen-line sections are in sequence (Adam-Noah and Shem-Terah), but in each case the first is genealogical and the second, story. There is one place where two genealogical sections are in sequence (Shem-Ham-Japheth and Shem), in which case the first is rejected and the second is chosen. We never find two rejected-line sections in sequence nor do we find two story sections in sequence. Doubtless this alternation is deliberate in order to maintain a balance between the rejected lines and chosen lines, on the one hand, and the genealogies and stories, on the other.

The other repeated pattern is that every time there is a chosen-line story section it is followed by a pair of sections, the first being the genealogical rejected-line section of the rejected son(s), the second being a chosen-line section (either genealogy or story) of the chosen son. This pattern occurs with Noah, Terah, and Isaac, though not with the chosen-line story section of Jacob since it is the last in the book.

These observations suggest that these sections were arranged using a consistent organizing principle. However, if we hypothesize that the whole book of Genesis is organized according to a consistent pattern, we need to explain apparent irregularities in the hypothesized pattern. Several questions arise:

1. Why is the first section heading labeled "heavens and earth"? Why not a human section patriarch?
2. If a new section begins when the previous patriarch dies, one would expect Noah's section to start immediately after the death of his father, Lamech, in 5:31. But in fact there is an intervening section, 5:32–6:8. Noah's section does not start until 6:9. How can we explain this?
3. Similarly, Adam's section starts unexpectedly late (5:1) after all the stories about him have been told. Since there is no previous patriarch who has to die, how do we explain this?
4. Why don't Cain and Seth follow the normal pattern and have section headings as the heads of the rejected and chosen lines after the patriarch Adam? (The normal pattern is exemplified by Shem versus his brothers, Isaac versus Ishmael, and Jacob versus Esau, all of which have their own section headings.)
5. Why don't all the double-line grandfathers have section headings? Double-line grandfathers Eber, Abraham, Nahor, Seir, and Joseph are not given section headings.
6. Why do Shem (in 10:1 and 11:10) and Esau (in 36:1 and 9) each have two section headings?

In order to answer some of these questions, the elements that recur in the various sections are tabulated in Table 4. The genealogical sections are those of Adam; Shem, Ham and Japheth; Shem; Ishmael; and Esau. If the element is present, this is indicated with Y. Between these elements, stories may be inserted; such insertions are indicated with S. R means that the event was described earlier and that this is a repeated mention. Reintroduction of patriarch may occur either as an introductory description or a repeated mention of birth.

Genealogical Prominence and the Structure of Genesis

Table 4. Recurring elements in genealogical sections

		Adam	Japheth	Ham	Shem 1	Shem 2	Ishmael	Esau 1	Esau 2
1	Reintroduction of patriarch	Y							
2	Son's birth	R	Y	Y	Y	Y	Y	Y S	Y
3	Death of patriarch	Y				Y	Y		
4	Descendants	Y	Y	YSY	Y	Y	Y		Y
4a	Birth of next patriarch	Noah			S	Terah			
4b	Death of next patriarch's father	Lamech							
4c	Birth of next patriarch's sons	Y S				Y			

There are two obligatory elements in the genealogical sections: son's birth and descendants. Genealogical sections have two subtypes depending on whether they trace out a chosen or rejected line. For chosen lines (Adam, Shem 2), a complete list of descendants is given down to the next section patriarch. For rejected lines there is no next section patriarch as descendant. Up to three generations are given in detail, and the rest are often summarized as groups of descendants. The genealogical rejected sections tend to give lists of descendants with less use of verbs.

The story sections are those of heavens and earth, Noah, Terah, Isaac, and Jacob. Among these there are two subtypes: those that tell stories covering one generation (e.g., heavens and earth, Noah, Isaac), and those that cover two generations (e.g., Terah). We classify Jacob's section as being a two-generation section because it parallels the structure of Terah's section. In the case of the section of heavens and earth, we might regard heavens and earth as the patriarch and creation as equivalent to the patriarch's birth. Therefore, in Table 4, Adam is assigned the role of son (cf. Luke 3:38d).

The two obligatory elements in the story sections are the choosing or rejecting of sons and summary or blessing of descendants. Son's birth is almost obligatory, but in Jacob's section while there is reference to some of the sons' births, there is not a repeated report of it as in the other sections. This may be due to a summary of Jacob's sons having just been given at the end of the previous Isaac section (35:22-26), where it functions as the summary of descendants for that section.

Table 5. Recurring elements in story sections

Element		heavens, earth	Noah	Terah	Isaac	Jacob
	Number of generations	1	1	2	1	2
1	Reintroduction of patriarch	2:4	6:9		25:19	
2	Son's birth	R 2:7	R 6:10 S	R 11:27 S	25:21-26	(R 37:3)
(8a)	Early death of patriarch			11:32		
3	Choosing/rejecting of sons	ch. 3	9:20-24	12:1-8 S	25:27-34 S, ch. 27, S	37:3-11 S
4	Grandson's birth	4:1-2		ch. 16S 21:1-7	29:31-32 30:24 S	ch. 38 S 46:8-25 S
5	Choosing/rejecting of grandsons	4:3-16		21:8-21 S		ch. 48
6	Death of daughter-in-law			ch. 23 S	35:16-20	
7	Summary/blessing of descendants	4:17-26	9:25-27	25:1-6	35:22-26	49:1-28
8	Death of patriarch		9:28-29		35:27-29	49:29-50:14
9	Death of chosen son			25:7-11		50:24-26

There are some correspondences between the last three events of the chosen genealogical sections (4a, 4b, 4c in Table 4) and elements of the story sections (Table 5). Birth of next patriarch (4a) is the same as son's birth in a one-generation story section (heavens and earth, Noah, Isaac) or grandson's birth in a two-generation section (Terah). Death of next patriarch's father (4b) is the same as death of patriarch in a one-generation section (Noah, Isaac) or death of chosen son in a two-generation section (Terah). Birth of next patriarch's sons is the same as grandson's birth in a one-generation section (heavens and earth, Isaac).

Though genealogical and story sections have similar elements of birth and death, there are significant differences. The story sections have more narratives, most particularly accounts of choosing and rejecting sons and grandsons. Another repeated type of story is an account of the death of the patriarch's daughter-in-law. In Terah and Isaac's sections this occurs prominently shortly before the final summary of descendants. A death of daughter-in-law is also recounted in Jacob's section, namely that of Judah's wife (38:12), but its sequence is different and it is much less prominent. With regard to sequence, a main difference between story sections and genealogical sections is that in the genealogical sections the patriarch's death comes before the account of descendants, whereas in the story sections the order is reversed. Death of patriarch tends to be at the end of the section. One exception, 8a in Table 4, is Terah's section in which the early death of patriarch[10] corresponds to the genealogical-section pattern. If a story section has one generation (Noah, Isaac), it ends with the patriarch's death. If it has two (Terah, Jacob), it ends with the chosen son's death. In Jacob's section, since the patriarch did not die early as Terah did, the section ends with the death of both patriarch and chosen son. In the heavens and earth section there is no death of chosen son because it is a one-generation section; there is no death of patriarch because the patriarch, heavens and earth, cannot die.

Another area of variation in the five story sections is with regard to stories about grandsons. Three of the sections have stories both about the birth and the choosing/rejecting of grandsons; Isaac's section recounts only the birth; Noah's section has nothing. What explains the differences? The two-generation sections (Terah, Jacob) need to have all the stories of the grandsons. Isaac's section recounts the grandson's birth since it happened while he was still alive, whereas the choosing and rejecting is left for Jacob's section since it presumably happened after his death. In Noah's case there are no stories of choosing/rejecting of grandsons to recount, and no actual birth stories either—the grandsons simply appear in the genealogical lists of the following section.

As for the section of the heavens and earth, the explanation ties in with some of the questions listed earlier. First, why do the heavens and the earth have a section? It is to put the material dealing with the creation and fall of man and woman, as well as the stories of the rejection of Cain, into the same pattern as the other sections. The parallelism is thereby heightened. A patriarch is always introduced in a previous section before his section starts. This is one reason why chapter 1 falls outside the section structure. Once the initial creation story is told, the section of the generations of the heavens and earth can begin. Similarly, Adam's section can begin only after Adam has been introduced in the previous section.

But why couldn't Adam's section begin earlier? The best way to answer this sort of question is to show the pattern incongruity that would arise with any other arrangement. It might be felt that Adam's section could have begun at the beginning of chapter 4, commencing with the story of his sons' births and then their choosing/rejecting (as in Isaac's section, for example). In this case the section would be in the pattern of a story section. But if Adam's section *were* a story section, then a new section would need to be started with the next generation. Otherwise Adam's section would include both Cain's rejected line and Shem's chosen line, a condition which would really be going against the structural pattern.

So this leads to the question of why Cain and Seth do not have sections, parallel to the other pair of rejected and chosen brothers later in the books. If Cain and Seth were to have sections, the sections would have to start after Adam's death in 5:5. The material about Cain's line (4:17-24) would have to be transferred there. The arrangement of sections would then be:

Heavens and earth	Story: rejected	2:4-3:24
Adam	Story: rejected?	4:1-16, 4:25-5:5
Cain	Genealogy: rejected	4:17-24
Seth	Genealogy: chosen	5:5-6:8

Such an arrangement would ruin the pattern of alternations shown in Figure 1. There would be two story sections in a row, which never happens elsewhere. And these two story sections would be quite short, especially Adam's section, whereas the pattern for story sections is to have quite a lot of stories. The status of Adam's section as chosen or rejected would be unclear. The present arrangement has none of these problems. All the stories of rejection (Adam and Eve, Cain) are put in the heavens and earth section to be balanced by the chosen line of Adam through Seth. Incorporating the stories of Cain and Abel and Cain's line into the heavens and earth section makes it congruent with the other story sections, as was shown in Table 5.

The next question to be answered is, Why doesn't Noah's section begin earlier, for instance, at 6:1 after Noah has been introduced? This would be in keeping with Terah's section (11:27). And why isn't the section on the Nephilim and man's wickedness (6:1-8) included in Noah's section? The answer is that a story section always begins with the patriarch's son's birth, whereas most of the events in 6:1-8 happened before Noah's time. The pattern of having a story at the end of a genealogical section (in this case Adam's) is paralleled in the sections of Shem, Ham, and Japheth (the story of Babel) and the first Esau section. The function of such stories may be to pose a problem for which the following chosen line will be the solution. In the case of Noah, the problem is the wickedness of man and the solution is saving Noah's line in the ark. In the case of the story of Babel, the problem is the scattering of the nations, and the solution is the blessing of all the peoples of the earth through Shem's line.

Another question: Why does Shem have two sections? This is connected with the question of why double-line grandfather Eber does not have a section. True, Eber seems much less prominent than other section patriarchs. He does, however, have some characteristics that set him apart from others in his line. He had two sons, Peleg and Joktan, of whom Peleg's line was chosen and Joktan's rejected. A momentous event happened during his time: the earth was divided (10:25). (The name Peleg, if given at birth, was a reflection of the events of his father's time.) And for some reason Eber was the ancestor the Hebrews were named after. He must have done something to leave a lasting impression on his descendants. Perhaps it had to do with his being a migrant. If an ancestor migrates to a new place, his descendants there are likely to think of him as their direct forebear. Biblical examples of such migrants after whom their descendants named themselves are Abraham (who migrated to Canaan) and Israel (who migrated to Egypt). Extrabiblical examples include the Bataks of North Sumatra, all of whom have surnames based on the name of their particular ancestor who was supposed to have migrated to the Batak area hundreds of years ago. In Eber's case, he may have migrated to the vicinity of Ur, where his descendants were found five generations later.[11] His migration may be related to whatever event is meant by the expression "the earth was divided." Despite all these interesting things about Eber, it is not sufficient for the author to give him a section. There is a lack of stories to put in a story section. The theme of choosing and rejecting is very faint in the case of his sons Peleg and Joktan and there would not be any point in splitting Shem's genealogical section in two at 11:17. That would result in two genealogical chosen sections in a row. Instead, what the author has done is give two sections to Shem. The first one focuses on the descendants of Shem who were not part of the chosen line, such as the sons of Aram and the sons of Joktan. The second section recounts the chosen line that goes through Eber and Peleg. This line is given more prominence by giving more details of the birth and the age of each descendant in the line.

The next question is, Why doesn't Abraham have a section? This seems strange, especially since Abraham is such a prominent character. A number of commentators have addressed this question. Weimar (1974: 89ff.) suggests that the תּוֹלְדוֹת formula is associated with the theme of blessing and Abraham is the man of the covenant rather than the man of blessing. Renaud (1990:23) rightly rejects Weimar's weak argument; his explanation (p. 28, n. 44) is that Abraham's genealogy is tightly linked to Terah's in a sort of short series. But this is more a description than an explanation.

It should be realized that if Abraham gets a section, his brothers ought to get one too, according to the normal pattern. Of the three brothers, Abraham would represent the chosen line and Haran and Nahor the rejected lines. However, although Haran's line clearly has the characteristics of a rejected line, the status of Nahor's line is ambiguous. For two generations the wives for the chosen line came from Nahor's descendants. On the other hand, Laban in his confrontation with Jacob displayed characteristics typical of a rejected line. In any case, the ambiguous status of Nahor's line is preserved by not putting it into the parallel structure of rejected and chosen lines such as Ishmael/Isaac and Esau/Jacob.

Another possible reason that Abraham is not given a section is the late birth of his sons. Story sections always begin with mention of the patriarch's sons. If Abraham had a section it ought to start at 12:1 after Terah's death. But his first son is not born until 16:15. However, by letting Terah's section go for two generations, it fits the pattern of the other sections, especially Jacob's section.

Abraham's childlessness is a major source of tension in the narrative. How can he become a great nation without offspring? The lack of Abraham's section increases this tension.[12] If, at the very beginning of the stories about Abraham, the author had said, "These are the descendants of Abraham," the readers would have known for certain at that point that Abraham had offspring. But since this section heading is omitted, the question remains hanging for quite a number of chapters.

The remaining questions of those we listed earlier are: Why do Seir and Joseph not have sections, and why does Esau have two section headings? Seir does not qualify for a section heading since he is not part of the genealogical line traced from Adam. Joseph cannot have a section until Jacob dies, and he dies virtually at the end of the book. Esau's two section headings are difficult to explain in terms of pattern congruity for they seem to break the pattern. We can only note the observation made earlier that the short story about Esau at the end of the first Esau section (36:6–8) is in keeping with the pattern of stories at the end of genealogical sections. Its function may therefore be similar, posing a problem for which the following line of descendants provides a solution. In this case the problem is not enough room for both Jacob and Esau in Canaan. The solution is for Esau to move to Seir and multiply there. This hypothesis is supported by the contrasting locative references in the two genealogical lists. In the first genealogy there are two references to Canaan (36:2, 5). In the second there are repeated references to Seir and the land of Edom (36:9, 16-17, 20, 29). Hence the first short section is oriented towards Esau's sojourn in Canaan, and the second longer section to his longer sojourn in Edom.[13]

7. Conclusions

Francis Andersen (personal communication) has made the following observation with regard to the importance of the genealogies. He suggests that they are what is driving Genesis. In other words, the genealogical framework provides the overall structure of the book. Moreover, Genesis is what drives the whole primary history from Genesis to Kings. The remaining section of the Hebrew Bible, the Writings, is commonly thought to begin with Psalms. However in the Aleppo Codex and the Leningrad Codex, the Writings begin with Chronicles. Chronicles, of course, begins with a long genealogical section. The New Testament also begins with a genealogy. Hence, it may be concluded that genealogies are what gives the initializing, organizing principle for the entire Bible.

Clearly the way participants are given different degrees of prominence has significant ramifications for the overall structure of Genesis. The genealogies and the stories work together in a complementary way to indicate who the most important participants are. This is one indication of the considerable integration between the genealogical portions and the story portions of Genesis. It is not simply a case of two independent sources being cut and pasted together. The genealogical information may well have been originally separate, but it has been intricately fashioned together with the stories as the common elements in Tables 4 and 5 show.

Robinson (1986) suggests that the genealogies convey a message of profound order concerning the elemental rhythm of life as well as the fixity of God's purpose in his promise. As such, they stand in counterpoise and tension with the untidy uncertainty of the narratives.

While this may be true, perhaps the more crucial opposition in Genesis is that between rejection and blessing rather than between genealogy and narrative. For, as we have seen, both genealogical and story sections can expound the rejected line and both can expound the chosen line. Thus while their forms are different, their literary functions overlap.

With regard to the story sections, the parallel structure of many of them seems to be a deliberate device designed to develop, in a systematic way, some of the main themes of the book. Once this pattern is perceived, it enables us to explain many of the structural peculiarities of Genesis.

These structural peculiarities can be seen as motivated and deliberate, in fact, not just an accident of editorial juxtaposition.

The parallelism in the story sections has, in my view, a thematic purpose: it indicates the constancy of the pattern of interrelationship between God and humanity. God's purpose in blessing and choosing is constant and works itself out in similar ways generation after generation. If we want to hear the message of Genesis, we need to understand the structure and let it speak to us, especially if we believe (as the author of Genesis doubtless believed) that the same God relates to our generation now just as he related to the past generations.

Notes

1. "Active role" is defined as being the singular subject of an active verb (not stative). We exclude the formulaic verbs found in the genealogies (ילד 'bear', מֵת 'die'). A new episode is marked by an introductory background clause plus a new location, time, or set of characters.

2. For a discussion of renaming, see T. D. Andersen (1986).

3. The exact number of lines Seir has depends on whether there are one or two people named Anah and Dishon/Dishan.

4. Approximate number of participants who have various features are as follows:

Unnamed sg. human participants	22	Active in 20 episodes	2
Named human participants	270	Active in 28 episodes	1
Dominant role in relationship	31	Birth by relationship only	140
Section patriarchs	10	Birth with verb	49
Active in 1 episode	32	Birth with age of father	22
Active in 2 episodes	7	Birth with story	32
Active in 3 episodes	3	Grandparents— single	28
Active in 4 episodes	3	double	16
Active in 5 episodes	4	triple	2
Active in 6 episodes	3	multiple	4
Active in 7 episodes	1	Death— age only	8
Active in 9 episodes	1	with מֵת	30

5. In most cases when a named participant is identified via a kinship or social relationship, such identification can be seen as redundant since the name itself would be sufficient. For example in 27:1 when Isaac summons "Esau his older son," the additional identification "his older son" is not strictly necessary, and hence Isaac's dominant role (signaled by "his") gives him prominence. But there are two cases where such identification is *not* redundant. The first is where a participant is being introduced for the first time, e.g., "his [Peleg's] brother was named Joktan" (10:25). The other is where a participant is not named and hence is always identified by relationship, e.g., Lot's wife

and daughters. Such cases are in parentheses in Table 2 and are given only one point since the function of giving prominence to the participant with the dominant role is not so certain.

6. The entries "(sing)" or "(doub)" mean that one of the descendants is an unnamed participant.

7. A participant that is the subject of an active verb only when conjoined with another participant (e.g., Shem and Japheth in 9:23) or a participant that has a prominent but passive role in an episode (e.g., Manasseh and Ephraim in Genesis 48).

8. D. J. Wiseman (1936). Cited in Kidner (1967:23).

9. This suggestion is from F. I. Andersen (1984), whose taped talk was the stimulus to the production of this article.

10. Terah's death was early in the sense that it is mentioned early in the section. As to the actual time of his death, a little calculation will show that he died when Isaac was about 35 years old (205 −70 −100 = 35). Since Sarah bore Isaac when she was 91 and died when she was 127 (36 years later), then chronologically Terah's death would have occurred at the end of chapter 22. If it had been reported at that point, it would not fit the pattern of any other section. Moving it forward to chapter 11 makes it congruent with the genealogical sections. The fact that Terah died in Haran out of contact with his descendants may also be a factor.

11. For a discussion of the significance of the names Eber and Peleg and the possible relationship between עֵבֶר and *habiru*, see D. J. Wiseman (1959: 11–12) and J. Bottero (1954).

12. Thanks to Nicholas Bailey for this observation.

13. For more detailed analysis of the possible functions of the different genealogies in chapter 36, see Wilson (1977:175–83).

References

Andersen, Francis I. 1984. Introduction to Old Testament: Genesis. Taped lecture, Kenmore Anglican Church, Brisbane, Australia.
Andersen, T. David. 1986. Renaming and wedding imagery in Isaiah 62. *Biblica* 67(1):75–80.
Blum, E. 1984. *Die Komposition der Vätergeschichte*. Neukirchen-Vluyn.
Bottero, J. 1954. *Le problème des Habiru*. Paris.
Fleming, Ilah. 1978. Participant identification in C. A. Carib discourse. In *Papers of the 1978 Mid-America Linguistics Conference at Oklahoma*, ed. Ralph Cooley, M. R. Barnes, and John Dunn. Norman: University of Oklahoma.
Grimes, Joseph. 1975. *The thread of discourse*. The Hague: Mouton.
Kidner, Derek. 1967. *Genesis: An introduction and commentary*. Leicester: Inter-Varsity Press.

Longacre, Robert E. 1989. *Joseph: A story of divine providence:A text theoretical and textlinguistic analysis of Genesis 37 and 39–48.* Winona Lake, Ind.: Eisenbrauns.

Renaud, B. 1990. Les généalogies et la structure de l'histoire sacerdotale dans le Livre de la Genèse. *Revue Biblique* 97(1):5–30.

Robinson, Robert R. 1986. Literary functions of the genealogies of Genesis. *Catholic Biblical Quarterly* 48:595–608.

von Rad, Gerhard. 1972. *Genesis: A commentary.* Philadelphia: Westminster Press.

Weimar, P. 1974. Die Toledotformel in der priester-schriftlichen Geschichtsdarstellung. *BZ* 18:65–93.

Wilson, Robert R. 1977. *Genealogy and history in the biblical world.* New Haven: Yale University Press.

Wiseman, D. J. 1936. *New Discoveries in Babylonia about Genesis.* London: Marshall, Morgan and Scott.

———. 1959. *The Word of God for Abraham and today.* London: Westminster Chapel Bookroom.

10

SOME LITERARY AND GRAMMATICAL ASPECTS OF GENEALOGIES IN GENESIS

Nicholas Andrew Bailey

While the theological and sociological functions of biblical genealogies have been recognized and studied to some degree, their literary details have been greatly overlooked. This has been especially apparent in how commentators have misunderstood or not even considered how the individual genealogies relate to the greater contexts in which they occur. The present study is devoted to investigating some of the rhetorical aspects of several genealogies in Genesis, including especially how they fit into the greater narratives in which they occur. Certain grammatical aspects of these genealogies are also discussed. It is apparent from this study that the genealogies of Genesis form a crucial part of the backbone of the narrative and its main themes. They also employ many of the same literary devices as do narrative and poetry, including the following devices: inverted parallelism (i.e., chiasm), noninverted parallelism, paronomasia, irony, and especially foreshadowing/highlighting characters and situations currently or soon to be important in the narrative. Finally, it is shown how the grammar can be an important clue to the function of genealogical material.

Most modern Western readers do not count genealogies and name lists among their favorite parts of the Bible. They are too predictable: "Man has son(s); next generation." Not only do genealogies lack the appeal that comes from the drama and plot of a story, but they bear little, if any, relevance to the literary or theological interests of Western Bible readers. At best, they are viewed as a means to identify the relationships between characters in the greater story.

Like readers in general, most scholars have not had great expectations of genealogies. They have not expected to discover any literary gems hidden among them. This neglect of the literary aspects of genealogies has been due, no doubt, to the long-time preoccupation with dissecting the texts into sources[1] rather than looking at how they fit into their larger linguistic contexts. Commentators have often described the genealogies and name lists as being unrelated to and totally isolated from the immediate surrounding narratives.

The little attention that has been concentrated on genealogies in recent years has focused on defining their original theological and sociological meaning. Another goal has been to establish the historical development of the individual genealogies in oral and written forms (Wilson 1977, Johnson 1969).

There continues to be a serious lack in the analysis of genealogies. In view of this, the present study[2] is devoted to investigating some of the literary aspects of several genealogies in Genesis, especially how they fit into the narratives in which they occur (sec. 1 and 2.1-4).[3] Certain grammatical forms used in genealogies will also be discussed (sec. 2.5). A few concluding comments relevant to Bible translation will be made as well (sec. 3).

1. The themes of Genesis and the Pentateuch

There are some fresh insights into the function of genealogies in Genesis that have come from a new quarter of biblical scholarship. Using the tools of literary and rhetorical criticism, Clines (1978), Robinson (1986), and Fokkelman (1987) have shown how, in general terms, the genealogies fit well within the greater themes of Genesis and even of the Pentateuch.

Fokkelman (1987:40-41) writes:

> Genesis is part of a grand design which unites the books of the Torah with Joshua, Judges, Samuel, and Kings in one configuration: from the creation of the world through the choosing of the people of Israel and their settlement in Canaan up to the Babylonian Captivity. Genesis contributes two building blocks to this overarching plot: the primeval history (1-11) and the protohistory of the people of Israel...

For Fokkelman, the word תּוֹלְדֹת (5:1, 10:1, 11:10, 25:12, 36:1; 2:4, 6:9, 11:27, 25:19, 37:2), literally "begettings" is a key structural element for the various sections of Genesis.

Both Robinson (1986:600) and Fokkelman (1987:42) emphasize that the various genealogies are man's execution of God's first command (1:28) to "be fruitful and multiply, and fill the earth" (see also Clines 1978:66). In light of this command, Robinson (1986:600) calls the genealogy in Gen. 4:7-24, which leads from Cain to Lamech, or "from one murderer to another," an "antigenealogy," since it "expresses genealogically the sequelae of human decisions undertaken outside of the order established by God at creation." By means of this ironic use of a genealogy, that is, an "antigenealogy," another theme of Genesis is underlined: "human sin stands in profound contradiction to the created order of God" (Robinson 1986:600). But God's purposes through the created order have the last word, and the narrative continues with Seth's line, which leads to Noah.

In an attempt to discover the main theme of the Pentateuch, Clines (1978:61-79) discusses three thematic patterns in Genesis 1-11:

(1) creation/uncreation/re-creation
(2) spread of sin/spread of grace
(3) sin/speech/mitigation/punishment

(For these three patterns, Clines draws especially on the work of von Rad 1976, Westermann 1964, and Kidner 1967:13). In my own terms, a simplified version of the last pattern would be sin/punishment/grace. The genealogical material of these chapters can be shown to form a crucial element of this pattern. Thus, man disobeys God by eating of the tree; doomed to die, God then casts him out of the garden; but in his mercy God provides clothing and, more importantly, children. The pattern occurs again: Cain murders Seth; Cain is then ostracized; but God graciously provides another son to Adam and Eve. Then again, this time in the face of universal sin and violence, God destroys all mankind except Noah's family, who is a direct descendant of Seth. Then, for a last time in the primeval history, the pattern repeats itself: Through pride, man sins by trying to build a tower, and God punishes him by scattering him. But where is the grace, the last element of the pattern? Having reviewed these patterns and other minor themes, Clines (1978:76-79) actually concludes that the primary theme of Genesis 1-11 and ultimately of the entire Pentateuch is that "no matter how drastic man's sin becomes... God's grace never fails to deliver man from the consequences of his sin... God's commitment to his world stands firm, and sinful man experiences the favour of God as well as his righteous judgement." In light of this, God's reaching out to Abraham and his line through the great promise is the final act of grace, thereby completing the sin/punishment/grace pattern (Clines 1978:78). The patriarchal narratives, beginning with Abraham, are thus related to the primeval history; they constitute the record of God's grace and special blessing through Abraham's line, continuing through the rest of Genesis and the Pentateuch.

Now after the incident at Babel, the blessing and commands of 1:28 take on a new twist. They now apply specifically to Abraham and his line. The rest of Genesis leads us through the ever-narrowing genealogy of the patriarchs, culminating with Israel and his twelve sons (described by T. David Andersen in this volume as God's "choosing or rejecting" certain individuals and their lines). In one sense, the rest of the book is nothing more than a glorified genealogy. But now the genealogy is completely unpredictable (Robinson 1986:598). It has become a full-fledged family drama. The way of the patriarchs is dangerous and threats against their line are ever present: There is barrenness, their wives are absconded, there is deceit, jealousy, hate, and family scandals. In the end, the greatest irony is that, somehow, through the apparently insignificant individual, Abraham, and his peculiar line, this blessing will ultimately be for all mankind (12:3).[4]

2. Examples of the literary structures of the genealogies

Rhetorical devices seen in the genealogies of Genesis include parallelism, inverted parallelism (i.e., chiasm), foreshadowing, irony, and paronomasia, among others.

2.1 Gen. 35:22e–26

Consider Gen. 35:22e–26 (in which all independent clauses except 22e are verbless). This carefully constructed text forms a chiasm:

A 22e   וַיִּהְיוּ בְנֵי־יַעֲקֹב שְׁנֵים עָשָׂר
       and-they-were sons-of Jacob twelve

B 23   בְּנֵי לֵאָה בְּכוֹר יַעֲקֹב רְאוּבֵן וְשִׁמְעוֹן וְלֵוִי וִיהוּדָה וְיִשָּׂשכָר וּזְבוּלֻן
       sons-of Leah firstborn-of Jacob Reuben and-Simeon and-Levi and-Judah and-Issachar and-Zebulun

C 24   בְּנֵי רָחֵל יוֹסֵף וּבִנְיָמִן
       sons-of Rachel Joseph and-Benjamin

C' 25   וּבְנֵי בִלְהָה שִׁפְחַת רָחֵל דָּן וְנַפְתָּלִי
       and-sons-of Bilhah maid-of Rachel Dan and-Naphtali

B' 26a   וּבְנֵי זִלְפָּה שִׁפְחַת לֵאָה גָּד וְאָשֵׁר
       and-sons-of Zilpah maid-of Leah Gad and-Asher

A' 26b   אֵלֶּה בְּנֵי יַעֲקֹב אֲשֶׁר יֻלַּד־לוֹ בְּפַדַּן אֲרָם
       These sons-of Jacob who were-born to-him in-Paddan Aram

Note that in this chiasm the outermost units, A and A', mark the most general category and main topic, Jacob's sons. They function as the title and summary comment, while the next units inward, B and B', present Jacob's first wife's sons, that is, Leah's sons, first by her in B, and then by her maid in B'. Curiously, this situates Rachel and her sons in the center of the chiasm, units C and C', as if the whole family revolved around them.

Jacob (1934:669) is one of the only modern commentators who noted the chiasm, but he did not go on to discuss its significance. Coats, who seems representative of most other moderns, misses the chiasm (1983:243):

This unit is totally isolated in its context. No itinerary formula binds it to its surroundings. No apparent logic calls for a list of the sons of Jacob at just this point, unless it should be to show that Reuben, the subject of vv. 21-22a, is properly ordered as the firstborn in the series.

However, it would seem suspicious if Reuben were highlighted as the firstborn immediately after it is said that he slept with his father's concubine in v. 22. Indeed, that these two comments about Reuben should be contiguous is ironic. Although Reuben is firstborn, he will soon lose his natural prominence in the narrative. In the story about Joseph and his brothers, Reuben is depicted as emotional and incompetent: he fails to rescue his brother Joseph from the other brothers, and is later usurped by Judah (see also Longacre 1989:54-55). In case of any doubt, it is all summarized later in chapter 49 when Jacob blesses his twelve sons and says of Reuben: "You are my firstborn, my might, the first sign of my strength, excelling in honor, excelling in power. Turbulent as the waters, you will no longer excel, for you went up onto your father's bed, onto my couch and defiled it."

Thus, the rhetorical function of this chiasm (which has Rachel and her sons, including those of her handmaids, in central position) is to emphasize—we might say favor—Rachel and her sons over Leah and hers (especially Reuben) and to foreshadow events to come.[5] The greater narrative of Genesis supports this analysis. In the preceding episodes, Jacob has favored Rachel over Leah, and in the following episodes, the drama will revolve around her two sons, Joseph and Benjamin, the favorites of their father, a drama, ironically, initiated by this very favoritism. This short genealogy could, of course, have been presented in many other ways (other lists of the twelve sons are presented differently), but the effect here has been clearly and appropriately to emphasize Rachel and her sons.

2.2 Gen. 46:8-27

The text of Gen. 46:8-27, which comes near the end of the story about Joseph and his brothers, is in like manner carefully constructed. The following diagram summarizes the passage:

X   8   OPENING STATEMENT: and these [are] the names of
          Israel's sons who came to Egypt.

A   9-15 Reuben's sons, Simeon's sons, Levi's sons, Judah's sons,
          Judah's son's (Perez's) sons, Issachar's sons, and Zebulun's
          sons.
          ENDING: These [are] the sons of Leah . . . 33.

B 16–18 Gad's sons, Asher's sons, Asher's son's (Beriah's) sons.
ENDING: These [are] the sons of Zilpah . . . 16.

A'' 19 בְּנֵי רָחֵל אֵשֶׁת יַעֲקֹב יוֹסֵף וּבִנְיָמִן
sons-of Rachel WIFE-OF JACOB Joseph and-Benjamin

A' 20–22 Joseph's sons and Benjamin's sons.
וַיִּוָּלֵד לְיוֹסֵף בְּאֶרֶץ מִצְרַיִם אֲשֶׁר . . .
and-were-born to-Joseph in-land-of Egypt which (. . . Asenath, the daughter of Potiphera, the priest of On bore him, Manasseh and Ephraim.)
ENDING: These [are] the sons Rachel . . . 14.

B' 23–25 Dan's sons and Naphtali's sons.
ENDING: These [are] the sons of Bilhah . . . 7.

X' 26–27 CONCLUDING STATEMENTS:
Total coming to Egypt with Jacob: 66.
Total of Jacob's family who came to Egypt: 70.

The general purpose of this list is, as stated in the first clause, to list "the names of the sons of Israel who came to Egypt." More specifically, however, the list turns out to have a threefold purpose: (1) to list and count the total number of Jacob's descendants who came to Egypt with him (total of 66 is given in v. 26); (2) to count all those who, sooner or later in the story, came to Egypt (total of 70 is given in v. 27); and (3) to list *all* his relevant offspring, including two of Judah's sons who died in Canaan before coming to Egypt. These multiple purposes plus other complications (such as how the totals of 66 and 70 must be arrived at) are considered evidence by Westermann (1986:158–60), for example, that the text has been reworked at various stages of development.

However, the text does hang together in its final form. The counting works out (Kidner 1967:209, Jacob 1934:832–34), and the text displays symmetry and regularity through its structure. Structurally, the text divides into four parallel subsets (units A, B, A', and B'). They list the children and grandchildren in the following groups: first, Leah's sons' sons, unit A; then Zilpah's, unit B; then Rachel's, unit A'; and finally, Bilhah's, unit B'. Each unit uniformly concludes with the statement "These are the sons of mother X . . ." followed by the total number of those sons by that mother. In light of the regularity of the list, what stands out is the special emphasis (once again) on Rachel and her sons, Joseph and Benjamin. In the very center of the text comes the unparalleled statement (A'') "the sons of Rachel, the wife of Jacob, [are] Joseph and Benjamin." None of the other units begin with such a summarizing statement. Nor are any of the

Some Literary and Grammatical Aspects of Genealogies in Genesis 273

other women given the title "the wife of Jacob." Additionally, this clause occurs in apposition, lacking the typical conjunction וְ. The effect of syntactic abruptness here is probably to emphasize the clause rhetorically (see Andersen 1974:39-44).

The syntax of 46:20 also stands out as being irregular. Instead of a verbless clause like "and the sons of Joseph [were] Manasseh and Ephraim," there is a *wayyiqtol* (*waw*-consecutive plus prefixed verb, the "narrative" tense) clause. It reads: "and-were-born (וַיִּוָּלֵד) to Joseph in the Land of Egypt Manasseh and Ephraim which Asenath, the daughter of Potiphera, priest of On bore him." Such details are parenthetical to the *primary purpose* of the list, just as in 46:12b the details about two of Judah's sons who are said to have previously died—also *wayyiqtol* clauses—while in Canaan are also parenthetical (see discussion in sec. 2.5 about the grammar of such parenthetical information in the context of descriptive discourse). However, for the *secondary purpose* of the list, these facts *are* relevant, since they list Jacob's descendants at the time of this move to Egypt. Thus, Joseph and his sons, who are already in Egypt, are not counted among those who traveled to Egypt with Israel in v. 26, but are counted among Israel's descendants in v. 27. The end effect, however, has been to emphasize Joseph and his sons over all the other sons and grandsons of Jacob by means of the relatively numerous parenthetical comments about them.[6]

As to the greater context in which this list of Israel's sons occurs, we see once again the narrator's art of weaving details of the greater story into a list: Jacob's favorite wife, Rachel, is highlighted as she was earlier in the narrative of Genesis; her sons, Joseph and Benjamin, are emphasized over the other brothers just as in the contiguous Joseph story; and Joseph's sons, Manasseh and Ephraim, are mentioned parenthetically in order to foreshadow their importance in the coming narrative, as well as in the greater history of the twelve tribes.

2.3 Foreshadowing

Foreshadowing, as we have seen used in the genealogies of 35:22e-26 and 46:8-27, is a subtle rhetorical device that ties the genealogies into the greater Genesis narrative. Another example of foreshadowing in genealogies is the mention in 10:10 of Nimrod and his kingdom, which included Babel in the land of Shinar. This foreshadows the story of the tower of Babel in the following chapter. The birth notice proclaimed to Abraham in 22:20-24 concerning his brother Nahor's children mentions Bethuel and Bethuel's daughter, Rebekah, preparing readers for the story of the marriage of Rebekah to Isaac in chapter 24. The special emphasis on the birth of Noah in the genealogy of chapter 5, where for him alone a name etymology is given, also serves to underscore his importance in the coming narrative.

2.4 Genesis 10 and 11

Now let us consider briefly the structure of chapters 10 and 11. It involves a network of relationships between three sections: (1) the segmented genealogy[7] of Noah's three sons in 10:1–32; (2) the story of the tower of Babel in 11:1–9; and (3) Shem's line in 11:10–32. Many commentators view these different sections as having contradictory agendas; but, in fact, they have been very cleverly interwoven with each other.

A	10:1	שֵׁם (Shem)	וְאֵלֶּה תּוֹלְדֹת בְּנֵי־נֹחַ
B		חָם (Ham)	and-this account-of sons-of-Noah
C		יֶפֶת (Japheth)	שֵׁם חָם וָיָפֶת
			Shem, Ham, and-Japheth

C'	10:2–5	Japheth's descendants
B'	6–20	Ham's descendants
A'	21–31	שֵׁם's descendants
	32	Summary of 10:1–31

A'' 11:1–9 Babel (with puns on שֵׁם 'name' and שָׁם 'there')

A''' 11:10–32 שֵׁם's line to Abraham (linear genealogy)[8]

Chapter 10, the segmented genealogies of Shem, Ham, and Japheth, is a natural fulfillment of God's command to Noah and his sons (9:1, 7) to be fruitful and fill the earth. But note that the order of the names of Noah's sons in 10:1—Shem, Ham, Japheth—is not according to age but rather according to their relative importance to the nation of Israel (Cassuto 1964:198, 217; Jacob 1934:273).[9] Once the sons are introduced, their segmented genealogies are then dealt with in reverse order, beginning with Japheth, the least important to Israel's history, and concluding with Shem, Israel's ancestor. In this way the order of the three genealogies forms a chiasm to the opening title, but in this case the chiasm should not be viewed as emphasizing Japheth in center position.[10] Rather the chiasm occurs to make Shem, as the most important of the brothers, both first and last topics of discussion.[11]

The discussion of Shem's line, however, does not finish with A' (10:21–31). Following the brief interruption of the story of the tower of Babel comes the most important genealogy of chapters 10 and 11, A''', Shem's linear genealogy in 11:10–32. His linear genealogy provides the next step for the greater narrative of Genesis, recounting his direct line

Some Literary and Grammatical Aspects of Genealogies in Genesis 275

down to Abraham. The segmented genealogies of chapter 10, therefore, are secondary in relation to the greater purposes of Genesis.

Between the two Shem genealogies comes the story of Babel in 11:1–9, which recounts God's response to people's pride and desire to make a name for themselves. Its placement in the general vicinity of chapters 10 and 11 makes sense, because, among other things, it further explains the dispersion of mankind, a theme begun in chapter 10 (Jacob 1934:303).

But there is another reason, quite subtle, that explains the placement of the story of the tower of Babel precisely between the two Shem genealogies. As pointed out by Fokkelman (1975:11–45), there is a complex system of parallelisms between the "two halves" of the Babel story, including both inverted parallelism (that is, chiasm) and non-inverted parallelism, as well as many puns and alliteration. As to the puns and alliteration of the passage, note particularly those that involve the consonants שׁ (shin) and מ (mem). The Babel story is sandwiched between two comments employing the word שָׁם: the last clause of the introduction of the story reads וַיֵּשְׁבוּ שָׁם 'and they dwelt *there*', that is, in the land of Shinar; and the story's closing statement reads מִשָּׁם '*and from there* the Lord scattered them over the face of the all the earth'. A number of other words play with the sounds of שׁ and מ, but the reader should especially not miss the fact that the people wish to make a tower that reaches to the שָׁמַיִם 'heavens' and that they want to make a שֵׁם 'name' for themselves. So with these details in mind, the subtle logic behind the placement of this elegant little text between the two שֵׁם genealogies becomes apparent. Robinson's analysis (1986:603), which is in accord with mine, concludes that "the play on the word שֵׁם reveals profound irony. The whole earth marshals its energy to make a שֵׁם for itself. But . . . God had already provided a Shem through the orderly process of procreation."

2.5 Differing grammatical forms

The different grammatical forms of linear genealogies correspond to different literary and textlinguistic functions. Consider, for example, the following three versions of the linear genealogy of Shem to Abraham:

VERSION 1: The simplest form of the Shem-to-Abraham genealogy occurs in 1 Chron. 1:24–27. It lists the names of the patriarchs in successive order: "Shem, Arphaxad, Shelah, Eber, Peleg, Reu, Serug, Nahor, Terah, Abram (that is, Abraham)."

VERSION 2: We could reconstruct the same list following the pattern of the partial linear list of Gen. 10:24a–b (which is embedded in the greater segmented genealogy of Shem in 10:21–31). It would be composed of verbal clauses, each beginning with a noun followed by a *qatal* verb (suffixed or perfect) as follows:

*	וְשֵׁם יָלַד אֶת־אַרְפַּכְשָׁד	
	and-Shem he-begat DO-Arphaxad	
24a	וְאַרְפַּכְשַׁד יָלַד אֶת־שָׁלַח	
	and-Arphaxad he-begat DO-Shelah	
b	וְשֶׁלַח יָלַד אֶת־עֵבֶר	
	and-Shelah he-begat DO-Eber	
*	וְעֵבֶר יָלַד אֶת־פֶּלֶג	
	and-Eber he-begat DO-Peleg	
*	וּפֶלֶג יָלַד אֶת־רְעוּ	
	and-Peleg he-begat DO-Reu	
*	וּרְעוּ יָלַד אֶת־שְׂרוּג	
	and-Reu he-begat DO-Serug . . . [down through Abraham]	

VERSION 3: A third possibility is the actual list in chapter 11. It is composed of what Longacre (1989:85ff.) would call "narrative paragraphs." "Narrative," or *wayyiqtol,* clauses carry the genealogy forward. (The structure of this list is very similar to that in Genesis 5, the line from Adam to Noah.)

10a	אֵלֶּה תּוֹלְדֹת שֵׁם
	these generations-of Shem [verbless clause]

PARAGRAPH 1

b	שֵׁם בֶּן־מְאַת שָׁנָה
	Shem son-of 100 year (=When Shem [was] a 100 years old)
c	וַיּוֹלֶד אֶת־אַרְפַּכְשָׁד שְׁנָתַיִם אַחַר הַמַּבּוּל
	and-he-begat DO-Arphaxad 2-years after the-flood
11a	וַיְחִי־שֵׁם אַחֲרֵי הוֹלִידוֹ אֶת־אַפְכְשַׁד חֲמֵשׁ מֵאוֹת שָׁנָה
	and-he-lived Shem after his-begetting DO-Arphaxad 500 years
b	וַיּוֹלֶד בָּנִים וּבָנוֹת
	and-he-begat sons and-daughters

PARAGRAPH 2

12a	וְאַרְפַּכְשַׁד חַי חָמֵשׁ וּשְׁלֹשִׁים שָׁנָה
	and-Arphaxad he-lived 35 years

Some Literary and Grammatical Aspects of Genealogies in Genesis

b   וַיּוֹלֶד אֶת־שָׁלַח
        and-he-begat DO-Shelah

13a   וַיְחִי אַרְפַּכְשַׁד אַחֲרֵי הוֹלִידוֹ אֶת־שֶׁלַח שָׁלֹשׁ שָׁנִים
       וְאַרְבַּע מֵאוֹת שָׁנָה
       and-he-lived Arphaxad after his-begetting DO-Shelah 403 years

b   וַיּוֹלֶד בָּנִים וּבָנוֹת
       and-he-begat sons and-daughters

PARAGRAPH 3

14a   וְשֶׁלַח חַי שְׁלֹשִׁים שָׁנָה
       and-Shelah he-lived 30 years

b   וַיּוֹלֶד אֶת־עֵבֶר . . .
       and-he-begat DO-Eber . . . [following the same pattern down to Abraham, with only a few minor differences]

The differences between these three versions correspond to the concerns of the greater narrative, that is, the contexts in which they occur.

VERSION 1: The simple name list in 1 Chronicles is most static and abbreviated, but sufficient for the Chronicler, who does not need to recount this famous list in more detail.

VERSION 2: The syntax of the second version in Gen. 10:24 might strike some as peculiar, composed as it is, of two noun-initial *qatal* verb clauses that relate successive "begettings." Andersen (1974:88), for example, wondered why these "begettings" in 10:24 were not rendered by *wayyiqtol* clauses, since they are clearly sequential. (See the discussion of 4:18–19 on the next page; these verses similarly list successive "begettings" in Cain's line, from Enoch to Lamech.)

At this point it is helpful to contrast descriptive and narrative discourse types. Descriptions are prototypically topic oriented and temporally static, whereas narrative is action oriented and temporally dynamic. In Biblical Hebrew this means that, in descriptive discourse, as elements are frequently topicalized (for various pragmatic purposes), they occur preceding the predicate, whether the clause is verbless or not.[12] Actions reported are generally few and/or peripheral. Such sections are characterized by verbless clauses and clauses with the verb "be" or other stative verbs.[13] In narrative, verb-initial clauses—specifically *wayyiqtol* clauses—predominate. Both temporal sequence and continuity in the story line is the norm. Topicalization, which indicates discontinuity in the story line, occurs relatively infrequently (Bailey and Levinsohn 1992:193–94).

Now the genealogies of Genesis fall on a continuum somewhere between descriptive and narrative discourse. With a couple of very important exceptions (see the discussion of version 3 below), most of the genealogies of Genesis pattern as descriptive discourse; and actions, if mentioned at all, are secondary to the description of topics. This is the actual situation in 10:24. The change or "switch" of topic (Bailey and Levinsohn 1992:179–207) from one ancestor to the next is the pragmatic means by which the clauses are related, rather than by continuity of the storyline (chronological sequence). Although the events reported occur sequentially, this is not the means by which they have been syntactically related.

The details mentioned in 10:24a–b may actually be parenthetical to the main description in which they occur. Arphaxad's begetting of Shelah and Shelah's begetting of Eber appears to be mentioned in anticipation of who was begotten by Eber, Peleg and Joktan, whose lines are described in more detail.[10] Likewise, 4:18–19 (illustrated below) hastily brings us from Enoch down four generations to tell us about the notorious sinner Lamech. The episode in which 4:18 occurs (4:2b–24, which is embedded in 4:1–26) concerns Cain and details of his line, especially the increase of their wickedness, culminating with Lamech, who is not only a murderer like Cain, but also the first person to take two wives and curse another man.

18a	וַיִּוָּלֵד לַחֲנוֹךְ אֶת־עִירָד and-was-born to-Enoch DO-Irad		[*wayyiqtol*]
b	וְעִירָד יָלַד אֶת־מְחוּיָאֵל and-Irad he-begat Mehujael		[noun+*qatal*]
c	וּמְחִיָּיאֵל יָלַד אֶת־מְתוּשָׁאֵל and-Mehujael he-begat Methushael		[noun+*qatal*]
d	וּמְתוּשָׁאֵל יָלַד אֶת־לָמֶךְ and-Methushael he-begat Lamech		[noun+*qatal*]
19a	וַיִּקַּח־לוֹ לֶמֶךְ שְׁתֵּי נָשִׁים and-he-took-himself Lamech two wives		[*wayyiqtol*]

VERSION 3: The third version of the Shem to Abraham genealogy has a conspicuous form. Whereas this line could have been presented in a simpler and more condensed fashion, the individual generations are presented as full-blown sections (Longacre's "narrative" paragraphs, composed mostly of *wayyiqtol* clauses) that give the appearance of little narrative "episodes" of the greater narrative. This is precisely because the genealogy from Shem to Abraham is a crucial episode in Genesis. Even though it lacks any plot structure (according to conventional definitions of

plot), it nonetheless serves the important function of continuing the main narrative from Shem down to Abraham. Since part of the theme of Genesis is to trace the ever-narrowing divine selection from Adam to Israel, it is appropriate that this list not be dispensed with too quickly. Similarly, the line from Adam to Noah in chapter 5, which has the same basic structure as this genealogy, is also part of the main Genesis narrative. To do justice to each of these great ancestors, the crucial events of their lives—begetting the heir, living, and more begetting (and dying)—are formulaically narrated as if it were a solemn ritual.

These two "expanded" linear genealogies of Genesis 5 and 11 also exhibit other literary features, including the significant use of numbers and ages (see Cassuto 1964:175–80, 250–59). For example, as a climax, it is the tenth descendant in both passages who marks a significant change in the development of the narrative (Noah in chapter 5, and Abraham in 11). Enoch (who "walked with God and was not, for God took him") is, incidentally, the seventh in the list from Adam to Noah.

3. Summary and implications for Bible translators

In conclusion, while the theological and sociological functions of biblical genealogies have been recognized and studied to some degree, literary details have been greatly overlooked. This has been especially apparent in how commentators have misunderstood or not even considered the relation of the individual texts to the greater contexts in which they occur. Indeed, the genealogies of Genesis form a crucial part of the backbone of the narrative and its main themes. It is also apparent from this brief study that genealogies employ many of the same literary devices as narrative and poetry: inverted parallelism (i.e., chiasm), non-inverted parallelism, paronomasia, irony, and the highlighting/foreshadowing of characters and situations that are, or soon will be, important in the narrative. Also, the grammar can be an important clue to the function of genealogical material, as pointed out in section 2.5.

Genealogies often appeal more to non-Western audiences than to Western audiences. The translator should be aware that the biblical genealogies may have important implications in the receptor language.

Incorporating the linguistic functions of the various rhetorical devices employed in Biblical Hebrew into a translation of the genealogies is no simple task. The translator must be well acquainted with the arsenal of rhetorical devices and their functions in Hebrew and their equivalents in the receptor language. As de Waard and Nida (1986:119–20) write:

> in treating rhetorical features it is often useless, and generally unwise, to attempt to match form for form. What one must try to do, there-

fore, is to match function for function, in other words, to attempt to discover in the receptor language the closest functional equivalent of the rhetorical structure in the source text. The particular set of forms used for different rhetorical functions is largely language specific, but the functions . . . are universals.

Notes

1. The Genesis genealogical passages are not all attributed to the Priestly tradition. According to Speiser (1964), chapters 5; 10:1-7, 20, 22-23, 31-32; 11:10-27, 31-32; 35:22e-26; and 46:8-27 belong to the Priestly tradition, while the material in chapter 4; 10:8-19, 21; (11:28-30); and 24:30 belong to the Yahwist. The Yahwist material is freer in style and more integrated into the narratives while that of the Priestly tradition is more cryptic, stylized, and stereotyped (Westermann 1984:9). The elegant account of the tower of Babel is, of course, attributed to the Yahwist.

2. An earlier version of this article was read at the Society of Biblical Literature International Meeting, Sheffield, England, 1-3 August, 1988. For the present version, I am especially thankful to my primary proofreader, Denise Louise Bailey.

3. Alter's (1987:16) assessment of the situation is particularly instructive: "the Hebrew Bible quite frequently incorporates as integral elements of its literary structures kinds of writing that, according to most modern preconceptions, have nothing to do with 'literature.' I am thinking in particular of genealogies, etiological tales, laws . . . Those who view the Bible as literature in conventional terms have quietly ignored these materials as unfortunate encumbrances, while most modern historical scholarship has seen in them either an inscrutable ancient impulse to cherish traditions for their own sake or an effort to provide quasi-documentary authentication for political realities of the later biblical period. As a result, the sundry lists have been chiefly analyzed by scholars for whatever hints of long-lost history they might preserve in fossilized form or for whatever oblique reflections they might offer of the situation of the writers and redactors. One need not reject such considerations to note, as several recent literary students of these texts have persuasively argued, that the lists are very effectively employed to amplify the themes and to effect a complementary imaginative realization, in another genre, of the purposes of the narratives in which they are embedded."

4. In Matt. 1:1-2 Matthew's intention is clear in that he traces Jesus' line back only to Abraham. The implications would have been immediately apparent to Jews, who were commonly assumed to be Matthew's intended audience.

5. The function of chiastic patterns such as AB C B'A' or ABC D C'B'A' is commonly assumed to emphasize the center element, since the center element is unique (Parunak 1981:165; Bliese 1990:265). It is less certain whether or not a central pair of elements (such as CC' as in ABC C'B'A') is always emphasized, as we find here in 35:24-25. In this regard Bliese

(1990:266) states that "when the poem has two lines in the center instead of only one, there seems to be reason to identify the first and last lines of the poem as secondary peaks in addition to the main peak in the center."

6. Similarly, one must take note that Judah's grandsons by Perez are mentioned in a *wayyiqtol* clause (12c). Except for the fact that they are *great-grandsons* of Jacob, it would seem counterintuitive to argue that this comment is parenthetical, because they are included in the main census (purpose 1). The end effect, however, may be again to emphasize or bring attention to Judah and his line, including their past negative (chap. 38) and positive (chaps. 43-44) portrayals and to foreshadow their future importance in the nation of Israel (e.g., 49:1, Ruth 4:12-21, Ps. 78:67-70).

7. A "segmented" (horizontal or divergent) genealogy traces multiple lines of descent from a single person.

8. A "linear" genealogy traces a single line down through several generations where only one individual in each generation is mentioned. Linear genealogies are also known as vertical or invergent genealogies.

9. Following Cassuto (1964:164-65, 198, 217), Japheth is the oldest, Shem is the middle son, and Ham is the youngest (cf. Jacob 1934:262-65, 273, 291).

10. Parunak (1981:163) calls this "chiastic summary." It is merely a structuring device and does not serve to rhetorically underline any salient part of the linguistic unit.

11. Earlier, in the discussion of 35:24 and 46:19, I noted the special emphasis given to Rachel as the "wife of Jacob" and to her sons, especially Joseph and Benjamin. Likewise, in this genealogy extra emphasis has been given to Shem and his line in 10:21, which has no parallel in the Japheth and Ham lists (see Cassuto 1964:217).

12. Some might contend that the rules governing word order in verbal clauses differ to some degree for verbless clauses in Biblical Hebrew. These concerns are beyond the scope of this study.

13. See Bailey and Levinsohn (1992:194, 199) and Longacre (1989:111-12) on expository discourse. Longacre (1989:80-82, 106-8, 111-12, 120-23) discusses verb/clause-type ranking schemes for narrative, predictive, hortatory, and expository discourse/text types in the Joseph story. The verb/clause types are ranked from those verb/clause types which encode information most salient to the "main (story/discourse) line" or "foreground information" down to what is "off (the story/discourse) line" or background, circumstantial to varying degrees. Although I do not agree with all of Longacre's conclusions in this regard (see Bailey and Levinsohn 1992), his observations are helpful. For genealogical lists such as the one in 46:8-27, which are clearly descriptive (or expository) discourse, we could posit that the verbless clause ranks highest as presenting information most salient to the discourse. Verbal clauses would naturally fall much lower on the continuum.

14. Even if we cannot prove that these details are parenthetical, the explanation for the grammar remains the same; fronting occurs merely as a topic-changing device.

References

Alter, Robert. 1987. Introduction to the Old Testament. In *The literary guide to the Bible,* ed. Robert Alter and Frank Kermode, 11–35. Cambridge: Harvard University Press.

Andersen, Francis I. 1974. *The sentence in Biblical Hebrew.* Janua Linguarum, Series Practica, 231. The Hague: Mouton.

Bailey, Nicholas A., and Stephen H. Levinsohn. 1992. The function of preverbal elements in independent clauses in the Hebrew narrative of Genesis. *Journal of Translation and Textlinguistics* 5:179–207.

Bliese, Loren F. 1990. Structurally marked peak in Psalms 1–24. *Occasional Papers in Translation and Textlinguistics* 4(4):265–321.

Cassuto, Umberto. 1964. *From Noah to Abraham: A commentary on the book of Genesis.* Vol. 2. Jerusalem: Magnes.

Clines, David J. A. 1978. *The theme of the Pentateuch.* Journal for the Study of the Old Testament, supplement series, 10. Sheffield: JSOT.

Coats, George W. 1983. *Genesis. The Forms of the Old Testament Literature,* vol. 1, eds. Rolf Knierim and Gene M. Tucker. Grand Rapids: Eerdmans.

de Waard, Jan, and Eugene A. Nida. 1986. *From one language to another: Functional equivalence in Bible translating.* Nashville: Thomas Nelson.

Fokkelman, J. P. 1975. *Narrative art in Genesis.* Amsterdam: Van Gorcum.

———. 1987. Genesis. In *The literary guide to the Bible,* eds. Robert Alter and Frank Kermode, 36–55. Cambridge: Harvard University Press.

Jacob, B. 1934. *Genesis.* Berlin: Schocken.

Johnson, Marshall D. 1969. *The purpose of the biblical genealogies: With special reference to the setting of the genealogies of Jesus.* Cambridge: University Press.

Kidner, Derek. 1967. *Genesis.* Tyndale Old Testament Commentaries. Leicester: Inter-Varsity.

Longacre, Robert E. 1989. *Joseph: A story of divine providence:A text theoretical and textlinguistic analysis of Genesis 37 and 39–48.* Winona Lake, Ind.: Eisenbrauns.

Parunak, H. V. D. 1981. Oral typesetting: Some uses of biblical structure. *Biblica* 62(2):153–68.

Robinson, Robert B. 1986. Literary functions of the genealogies of Genesis. *Catholic Biblical Quarterly* 48:595–608.

Speiser, E. A. 1964. Genesis. *The Anchor Bible,* vol. 1 . Garden City: Doubleday.

von Rad, Gerhard. 1976. *Das erste Buch Mose: Genesis.* Goettingen: Vandenhoeck and Ruprecht.

Westermann, Claus. 1964. Arten der Erzählung in der Genesis. *Forschung am Alten Testament,* 9–91. Munich: Kaiser.

———. 1984. *Genesis 1–11.* Tr. John J. Scullion. Minneapolis: Augsburg.

———. 1986. *Genesis 37–50.* Tr. John J. Scullion. Minneapolis: Augsburg.

Wilson, Robert R. 1977. *Genealogy and history in the biblical world.* New Haven: Yale University Press.

11

IS GEN. 27:46 P OR J? AND HOW THE ANSWER AFFECTS TRANSLATION

Hanni Kuhn

The so-called "Jacob cycle" consists of several discourse units. The one of interest here is the one that deals with Jacob getting his blessing by fraud (chap. 27). But where exactly does this unit start and where does it end?

Source-critical analysis, reflected in some modern English translations, assigns 25:34-35 and 27:46-28:9 to P, and the main body of the discourse to J. If this view is accepted, the main story ends in 27:45 with Rebekah's suggestion to Jacob to flee to Haran to save his life. But the reason Rebekah uses to get Isaac to send Jacob to Haran (v. 46), namely the purity of the family line, is said to come from the P-tradition: the redactor added this motif, not to contradict the former, but to supplement it since they both speak to the same context. Another common view is that the redactor penned v. 46 in order to provide the necessary link between 26:34-35 and 28:2-9, sections which would otherwise be too far apart.

My contention, however, is that 27:41-46 forms a unified episode in two acts: We see Rebekah, "the manager," giving consciously and intentionally different reasons to Jacob and to Isaac. It can be shown by looking at features of discourse structure, literary composition, and even vocabulary that 27:46 (and also 26:35) were written by the same hand as the intervening story in 27:1-45.

In translations where section headings are used, my analysis suggests that headings be placed differently from those in GNB, NJB, and NAB. The proposed heading placement permits the reader to perceive Rebekah's clever action more readily.

On what basis do modern translations divide lengthy stretches of narrative into sections? This question I had to ask myself while working on the passage concerning the aftereffects of Jacob's fraudulent acquisition of the blessing (Gen. 27:41ff.). Verse 41 tells of Esau's grudge and his plan to murder Jacob after Isaac's death. Then, in v. 42, Rebekah comes into action, first warning Jacob to flee to Haran to her own family until the storm blows over and next, by way of a suggestive statement, getting Isaac to send Jacob to Haran.

As I was reading the Hebrew text, I was impressed again by Rebekah's skills in managing people; in this case she gets Isaac to do what she wants without his realizing it. Then I looked at some English translations and noticed, to my surprise, that some of them (GNB, NJB, NAB,

Oxford annotated NRSV) divided the narrative with a subtitle in the middle of this most fascinating display of shrewd calculation, namely between v. 45 and v. 46, thereby deflating the tension of the plot.

The reason why these translations segmented the text as they did is brought out in certain commentaries. Speiser (1964:215) succinctly states concerning v. 46 that it "is a direct sequel to 26:34–35"; while Westermann (1981:429) comments on 26:34–35 that "These two verses belong to P and are continued in Gen. 27:46–28:9."

NAB provides the following footnote concerning 27:46–28:9:

> This section, which is from the Priestly source and a direct sequel of 26:34f, presents a different, though not contradictory, reason for Jacob's going to Paddan-aram: namely, to preserve racial purity among the chosen people. The account of Esau's marriages is given for the purpose of explaining the racial mixture of the Edomites, who were descended in part from tribes related to Israel, in part from older peoples in Edom called Hittites, Horites or Hivites, and in part from the Ishmaelite (Arabian) tribes who later invaded the region.

But there are other commentaries and translations which seem to take the text as I did. Sarna (1989:195), for example, writes,

> Rebekah realizes that, for his own safety, Jacob must be sent away at once. But how can this be achieved? She needs her husband's agreement, yet she dare not divulge the true reason—both because she wishes to spare him further anguish and because she fears that her own involvement in the deception might thereby be exposed. She hits upon the pretext of his need to get married.

What we have then are two quite different interpretations of what happened in 27:41–28:5. According to the first, there are two separate incidents, each giving the reason for Jacob's travel to Haran. The two are different (though not contradictory) because they are from different sources: the first from the Yahwist, the second from the Priestly source. The second interpretation takes 27:41–28:5 as one incident only, consisting of two closely linked scenes that show Rebekah talking from the two sides of her mouth, so to speak.

The question we have to ask is: Are there any signs in this narrative sequence to indicate the author's, or redactor's, intention? When the author or redactor compiled the Jacob cycle, did he juxtapose 27:46–28:5 to 27:40–45 simply because these two passages are similar in that they have the same topic (sending Jacob to Haran), or did he understand them as two chronologically sequential episodes in a narrative?

The following steps will help us answer: First, we will establish the extent of the unit to which the two passages belong by determining its boundaries (sec. 1), then investigate the composite nature of the unit (sec. 2), then the thematic structure of the unit (sec. 3), and finally the discourse structure of the unit (sec. 4).

1. The extent of the unit

1.1 The wider context: the Jacob-Esau cycle

What is commonly called "the Jacob story" extends from 25:19 to 35:29. Interestingly, the Jewish lectionary division, which allocates three *parshiyot* to this story, runs from 25:19-36:42; in other words, it includes Esau's genealogy in chapter 36 and thus covers the story of Jacob *and Esau*. Fishbane (1979:40), on the other hand, delimits the Jacob cycle at 25:19 and 35:22; that is, he excludes, in particular, Esau's genealogy. His reason is that he sees the Jacob cycle as a series of episodes in the life of Jacob framed by the genealogical lists of Ishmael and Esau, the two excluded sons. This is indeed a pertinent observation. The only reason I do not follow it is that Esau plays a far more prominent role in the patriarchal narrative than Ishmael. I, therefore, take the wider context as identical with the three *parshiyot* and label this unit, with Westermann, the Jacob-Esau cycle.

1.2 The immediate context

Preceding the events described in 27:41-28:5 is the story of Jacob's obtaining Isaac's blessing by fraud (27:1-40). This is the action that creates the need for sending Jacob to Haran out of harm's way.

This story is preceded by two verses, 26:34-35, that inform us of Esau's age and marriages and their disastrous effect on his parents. Whether there exists any link to the main story is open to question at this point.

Preceding *this* information is a series of episodes in the life of Isaac which must have taken place before the birth of the twins. There is certainly no direct link between the information in 26:1-33 and what is in 26:34-35. Thus we can say at this point that the beginning of the discourse unit to which 27:41-28:5 belongs is either 26:34 or 27:1.

Returning now to the verses which relate Rebekah's suggestion to send Jacob to Haran (27:41-28:5), we find that they are followed by the account of Esau's taking one more wife. The vocabulary in 28:9 makes it clear that Esau's action is intended to be seen as a parallel to, or an imitation of, Jacob's action: Jacob goes off to foreign lands to get a wife from his mother's family, so Esau goes off to get a wife from his father's family. This episode clearly belongs with the preceding verses. At the same time it is the last we hear of Esau before he goes offstage and Jacob takes over. Thus the final boundary of the unit is established.

Two details in 28:6-9 (the account of Esau's taking another wife and the displeasure his first two marriages had caused his father) remind us of 26:34-35. There is a difference, however. In 28:6-9 Esau takes another wife in order to please his father Isaac. This is evident from the words in v. 8, וַיַּרְא עֵשָׂו כִּי רָעוֹת בְּנוֹת כְּנָעַן בְּעֵינֵי יִצְחָק אָבִיו 'And Esau saw that Canaanite women were a displeasure to his father Isaac', and also from v. 9, where he goes off to marry a paternal cousin. This is an "antidote": it acts as a resolution to the problem with which the unit started in 26:34-35.

We can draw now the following conclusions: (1) The initial boundary of the discourse unit is not 27:1, but 26:34. (2) The final boundary is 28:9. (3) Structurally, the two passages, 26:34-35 and 28:6-9, which both have the same topic, form an inclusio to the blessing-by-fraud narrative. This can be diagrammed as follows:

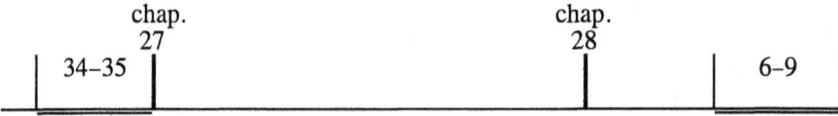

2. The composite nature of the unit

Commentaries that look at the text of Genesis from a source-critical point of view see two sources in the discourse unit under discussion, J and P. They view the central narrative about the blessing by fraudulent means as coming from the pen of the Yahwistic writer, the unsurpassed master storyteller; and they attribute the two parts of the frame or inclusio to P because its features are typical of the Priestly source: interest in genealogical details—here details of age and marital status—plus vocabulary, topic, and style.

The passage at the center of our interest, 27:41-28:5, is also allocated to different sources. J is considered the source of Rebekah's suggestion to Jacob to flee to Haran, and P of Rebekah's suggestion to Isaac that Jacob should not marry outside, plus Isaac's consequent action in sending Jacob off to Haran.

Using the parameters which the source-critical school has set up, we arrive at the following analysis of the composite nature of our discourse unit:

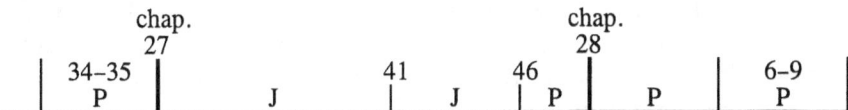

This might seem to be correct, but there is a nagging doubt. Hadn't it been the second performance of Rebekah that had particularly impressed me when I read the text in Hebrew? Before accepting the source-critical analysis out of hand, let us look briefly at some of their arguments for this type of text division.

2.1 Are the source-critical arguments valid for 26:34-35?

Source-critical scholars unanimously ascribe the first two verses of our discourse unit, which form the first half of the frame, to P. But what exactly in these two verses is indicative of P? The first clause gives us Esau's age, while the second informs us of his marriage to two Hittite wives and their names. P at his dry best, it is said, with facts, names, and numbers. But what if J needed a number in order to make a point? Even an author who excels in keeping his readers spellbound may want to pass on some dry facts on occasion, if they serve his purpose. And his purpose in this case, I believe, is to trigger the memory of the readers to see similarities and contrasts.

Now the first clause of v. 34, וַיְהִי עֵשָׂו בֶּן־אַרְבָּעִים שָׁנָה 'and Esau was 40 years old', is the same as the one found in 25:20 concerning Isaac. Reference is here made to age at the time of their respective marriages. The reader is meant to see this similarity between father and son. Then, by mentioning the fact that Esau married two wives (either at the same time or in short succession), the author draws attention to a character trait of Esau's already hinted at in the lentil-soup-and-birthright episode (25:27-34), namely that he was a person of strong physical appetites calling for "instant gratification." The reader is again reminded of Isaac, but this time in a contrastive way, for Isaac waited for and married one wife, who was brought to him from his own clan, whereas Esau married two wives whom he went to find among the people of the land.

The five words of v. 35 form the type of simple statement which could be found in any narrative, but particularly one with a plot structure, for it makes the reader expect a development either for the better or for the worse. Thus it can hardly be said to be typical of P.

Looking at the component parts of v. 35, we find, besides the two names Isaac and Rebekah, the genitive construction מֹרַת רוּחַ 'bitterness of spirit', a unique expression. As for the adjective מַר 'bitter', it occurs in the figurative sense only once in the entire Pentateuch and that is in the very discourse under discussion, in 27:34, a J text, where Esau let out a צְעָקָה גְּדֹלָה וּמָרָה 'a great and bitter cry'. This is a fact not to be taken too lightly, I think.

In summary, then, we can say that the vocabulary of 26:34 serves first to remind the hearers or readers of the similarity between Esau and his father, Isaac (same age when they married), and of the close emotional tie between Isaac and Esau (a fact stated in 25:28a). But v. 34 also serves to allude to the difference that existed between Esau and his father. The description of the difference is more detailed (two wives, foreigners at that), thus more prominent. This change in perspective from similarity to difference serves to prepare the audience for the harsh blow that the following story will deal to their sense of fairness.

The information in v. 35 serves two purposes, one immediate and one more long-term. The immediate one is to add to Esau's negative image (his wives are a source of sorrow to his mother and, more importantly, to his father). The more long-term purpose will only become apparent in the aftermath of the deception story when Rebekah will use it to influence her husband. At present it simply needs to be stored for a purpose the audience does not yet know.

My contention, then, is that these two verses are an integral part of the blessing-by-fraud story. They were written by the same author as the blessing-by-fraud story, and he chose these words carefully and intentionally.

2.2 Are the source-critical arguments valid for 27:46–28:9?

Concerning Gen. 27:46–28:9, Speiser (1964:215) states that it "differs sharply from the preceding narrative in style, phraseology, motivation, and timetable." He considers v. 46 to originate from P because it introduces a different motive for sending Jacob away. Duplications and repetitions are, by definition, suspect to a source critic, so it is not surprising that he would consider the repetition of a similar event as originating from a different source. Furthermore, the topic referred to by Rebekah, namely the unpleasantness of Esau's wives, was recorded for the first time in a text Speiser takes to be a P text (26:35). And finally, the style and vocabulary of 28:1–5 are clearly different from what precedes.

As regards Isaac's motive for sending Jacob away, of course this is a different motive. But since it comes from the lips of Rebekah, whom we have just seen perform a clever act of manipulation and deception, it should not surprise us at all to find her now giving different reasons to different people in order to achieve her aims. If the two motives are left together, we have Rebekah acting in character. If we separate them, the end of the story is something of a letdown: the proper resolution (Jacob's departure) is missing. In addition, as we saw earlier, there is no basis for considering 26:35 (Rebekah's reason) as P material anyway.

Concerning the vocabulary and style of 28:1-5, which are said to be typical of P, three comments are in order:

(1) Isaac is the first man to pronounce what has become known as "the patriarchal blessing." In the case of his father and himself, it was God in person who had bestowed this blessing. Now he, Isaac, has to take on this awesome responsibility. So Isaac can be expected to be more formal on this occasion than he had been previously.

(2) In Genesis a notable difference exists between the features of human speech and divine speech, as shown by the computer-assisted study of Yehuda Radday and Chaim Shore (1985). In this book, Rabin lists features such as long utterances, greater explicitness, and, often, rhythm as characteristics of divine speech. And he states that "even in dialogues the Almighty speaks at greater length, and the phrasing is less dependent on what was said by the human partner" (1985:221). This would support the intuitive conclusion expressed above that Isaac's way of speaking while passing on "divine speech" would differ from his normal speech pattern.

(3) In 28:2-4 six expressions occur which are said to be typical for P: *Paddan-aram*, *El Shaddai*, "fruitful and numerous," "assembly of peoples," "with you" following an enumeration, and "land of your sojourning." Although it is not within the scope of this article to make a detailed analysis and comparison of these terms, the list in the following diagram is instructive:

	Occurrence	Divine speech	Human speech repeat D	Human speech direct	Narrator
Paddan-aram/ Paddan (once)	total 11			2	9
El Shaddai/ Shaddai (once)	Pentateuch 7	3	1	3	0
"fruitful and numerous"	total 12	10	2		2
"assembly of peoples"	Pentateuch and Ezek. 5	3	2		0
'with you/him'	Pentateuch 24	15	3		6
"land of sojourning"	Pentateuch and Ezek. 6	3	1		2

The above terms are said to be typical of P. They occur mostly, and in one case exclusively, in divine speech (D). (*Paddan-aram*, however, occurs exclusively in human speech and in narrator's comments.) Note that these expressions occur in vv. 3-4, Isaac's version of the patriarchal blessing in which he is loosely quoting divine speech. More work is obviously necessary to deal with this question of vocabulary. But, as a preliminary conclusion, I suggest that the vocabulary used in Isaac's rendition of the patriarchal blessing is not necessarily indicative of a specific "source." Rather it is typical of divine speech.

3. The thematic structure of the unit

Fishbane (1979:45) sees struggle and strife as the "recurrent thematic emblem" of the entire Jacob cycle. And indeed there are several simultaneous layers of conflict in this cycle. Moreover, some of the conflicts are interrelated as though interwoven. The Gen. 26:34-28:9 unit provides an example of this. The first part of the frame (26:34-35) presents Conflict 1 (Esau marries two Hittite wives) while the second part of the frame (28:6-9) brings its Resolution, albeit a partial one, as it is aimed only at pleasing Isaac (Esau marries within the family). Then, the first part of the main story (27:1-45) presents Conflict 2 (the blessing obtained by fraud) while the second part (28:1-5) brings its Resolution, again only a partial and momentary one (patriarchal blessing is given willingly; flight to safety). These two layers of conflict are woven together by v. 46 where, following Conflict 2, Conflict 1 is used as argument to suggest and justify the resolution of Conflict 2. It is the interweaving, then, of two variants of the same theme, "conflict and resolution," which provides the entire unit with cohesion. The thematic structure of the Gen. 26:34–28:9 unit may be diagrammed as follows:

chap. 27		chap. 28 v. 46	6–9
Conflict 1	Conflict 2	Partial resolution 2	Partial resolution 1

4. The discourse structure of the unit

The discourse genre of the Jacob-Esau cycle is, on the whole, narrative prose, and this is also true for the frame of the unit under discussion (26:34–35 and 28:6–9). The main body of the story, however, consists almost entirely of speech acts such as monologue, dialogue, and reported speech; so in order to establish the discourse structure of this unit, it is essential to discover who takes the lead in all this speaking and where the speaking is done.

A further characteristic of the main body of the story is that, with one exception only, there are always two participants on the stage. When one leaves another takes over. Often a change of locale goes along with the change of participant. I shall, therefore, take change of participant and change of locale as parameters for delimiting the episodes in the story. Then I shall demonstrate that my divisions are not arbitrary but indeed supported and justified by structural features of the discourse.

4.1 Participants and locales

The 26:34–28:9 unit may be divided into sections based on change of participant and change of locale. The change of participants, which can be observed in the following diagram, is the basis for dividing the text into eleven sections, and the change of locale confirms this division. The reason for making Rebekah's intervention with Jacob into two sections (section 3 and section 4) even though both take place in Rebekah's tent, lies in Jacob's going offstage. Since this involves time, it would call for a curtain if this were a play.

This narrative is clearly a story with a plot; we can, therefore, expect a climax. In the surface structure, the climax appears as the peak. (I will not go into the question of whether the post-peak episodes contain a secondary peak or whether they depict a gradual winding down towards the resolutions of the two conflicts.)

	Sections	Onstage	Offstage	Locale
1	26:34–35	E		land of the Hittitescamp
2	27:1–5	I + E		Isaac's tent
3	27:6–13	R + J		Rebekah's tent
			J to flocks	
4	27:14–17	J + R		Rebekah's tent
5	27:18–29	J + I		Isaac's tent
6	27:30–40	E + I		Isaac's tent
7	27:41	E (+ listener)		camp
8	27:42–45	R + J		Rebekah's tent
9	27:46	R + I		Isaac's tent
10	28:1–5	I + J		Isaac's tent
11	28:6–9	E		campat Ishmael's

Now let us consider the structural features and thematic participants of the eleven sections.

Section 1 (Stage and Inciting Incident of Conflict 1) starts with the paragraph marker וַיְהִי followed by a circumstantial clause about Esau's age. It is clearly the beginning of a new section, as indicated also by the masoretic division marker (sᵊtuma ס). Esau is the thematic participant. He is introduced in detail, and he is the only one who is onstage (i.e., active). His wives and his parents serve as human props.

Section 2 (Stage and Inciting Incident of Conflict 2) starts, like Section 1, with the division marker plus וַיְהִי and two explanatory clauses concerning Isaac's eyes, the second clause being on the storyline. It ends with Esau going offstage. The thematic participant is Isaac. Besides being introduced with some detail, Isaac is also the subject of three *wayyiqtol* verbs. He takes the initiative. Esau, on the other hand, with two storyline verbs, merely responds, both in words and in deed.

Section 1 and Section 2 are tightly linked. They have the same initial structure (וַיְהִי 'and it was' plus background information about the age of thematic participant), and there is also assonance between וַתִּהְיֶיןָ 'and they were' of v. 35 and וַתִּכְהֶיןָ 'and they became dim' of 27:1, and between מֹרַת 'bitterness' of v. 35 and מֵרְאֹת 'from seeing' of 27:1.

Isaac's blindness could have been introduced as background material. However, it occurs on the storyline, and I suggest that this is intentional for two reasons: (1) In the *wayyiqtol* form וַתִּכְהֶיןָ we have assonance with וַתְּהָרֶיךָ, and (2) by being on the storyline, it draws more attention. This is intended in order to put the spotlight on Isaac's blindness: his physical blindness is the condition which makes Jacob's act of deception possible; his perception of reality appears to be clouded (Sarna 1989:190) causing him to overlook the fact that Esau was unsuitable to receive the patriarchal blessing because of his foreign marriages (v. 35).

Section 3 (First Pre-Peak Episode) could begin either in v. 5 or v. 6 since both verses start with a subject-initial clause that interrupts the flow of the *wayyiqtol* verbs of the storyline. But the verb in the first of these two circumstantial clauses is a participle followed on the storyline by further information about Esau, וַיֵּלֶךְ עֵשָׂו הַשָּׂדֶה 'And Esau went off to the bush'; I take it, therefore, as simultaneous with the preceding action on the eventline (i.e., 'Now/As for Rebekah, she was listening to Isaac speaking to his son Esau'). It is background information. It serves to introduce Rebekah and permit her to take the stage. Therefore I consider that Section 3 starts at v. 6 with the second of these break-marking *waw-X-qatal* clauses, whose function, this time, is the introduction of a new participant: וְרִבְקָה אָמְרָה אֶל־יַעֲקֹב בְּנָהּ 'And/Then Rebekah said to her son Jacob'. Rebekah is the thematic participant. This is shown by her explicit introduction as subject. Jacob, in contrast, appears only as addressee in vv. 6–10. Rebekah is the one who lays out the plan and who, upon the protest of her son (vv. 11–12), makes it clear that she is fully in charge here: אַךְ שְׁמַע בְּקֹלִי וְלֵךְ קַח־לִי 'Just listen to my voice, and go, get (it) for me'.

Section 4 (Second Pre-Peak Episode) starts with an execution paragraph. Jacob goes offstage to carry out his mother's orders. In addition, this section is strikingly marked by its complete absence of speech in this otherwise speech-laden story. This is quite the opposite of Section 3 which consists solely of dialogue. (It constitutes a further reason, by the way, for starting Section 3 with v. 6 where the verb is אָמְרָה 'she said'.) The thematic participant is, again, Rebekah. Jacob's action is described in the briefest possible way. The instruction was וְלֵךְ קַח־לִי 'and go, get it for me', and so his action is described as וַיֵּלֶךְ וַיִּקַּח וַיָּבֵא לְאִמּוֹ 'and he went, and he took, and he brought (it) to his mother'. Rebekah's activity, on the other hand, is described with four *wayyiqtol* verbs on the eventline and two *qatal* verbs (הִלְבִּישָׁה 'she clothed' in v. 16 and עָשְׂתָה 'she prepared' in v. 17), which are off the eventline.

Section 5 (Third Pre-Peak Episode) is marked by a change of subject as well as location. Jacob now takes the initiative and Isaac reappears onstage, and the two remain there till v. 29. The entire section consists of one long string of *wayyiqtol* verbs on the storyline with one single interruption only: the comment by the narrator in v. 23, וְלֹא הִכִּירוֹ כִּי־הָיוּ יָדָיו כִּידֵי עֵשָׂו אָחִיו שְׂעִרֹת 'but he did not recognize him because his hands were hairy like the hands of Esau, his brother'. The section is bounded by the pronouncement of the blessing.

When we look for the thematic participant, we find that in vv. 18–23 Jacob is thematic, and in vv. 24–29, Isaac. I see proof for this analysis in the following details:

(1) Jacob is the initiator in this section: he goes to his father and addresses him first.
(2) The name of Jacob occurs first (v. 19), before the name of his father, Isaac (v. 20).
(3) Jacob's claim that יְהוָה אֱלֹהֶיךָ 'Yahweh your God' had helped him puts him into the position of the winner.
(4) The narrator's comment, וְלֹא הִכִּירוֹ כִּי־הָיוּ יָדָיו כִּידֵי עֵשָׂו אָחִיו שְׂעִרֹת 'and he did not recognize him because his hands were like the hands of Esau his brother, hairy', shows that Jacob is successful.
(5) The first occurrence of וַיְבָרְכֵהוּ 'and he blessed him' (v. 23) is not yet the action; it even sounds as though Isaac's decision to bless Jacob was made under duress, so to speak, not out of conviction. In other words, Jacob dominated the blind old man.
(6) In vv. 24–29, Isaac, after having decided that he would bless the son before him, now takes the initiative with his question in v. 24, אַתָּה זֶה בְּנִי עֵשָׂו 'Is it you, my son Esau?'.
(7) Isaac speaks a total of seventeen words in vv. 24–29 against just the single אָנִי 'I' of Jacob in these verses.
(8) In v. 26, Isaac's name is given explicitly, together with the appellation אָבִיו 'his father'.
(9) Isaac gives the blessing, an action marked as the high point by its poetic form; and since it brings the episode to an end, it acts as the final boundary of Section 5.

Section 5, then, is one episode consisting of two structural paragraphs, in the first of which Jacob is the thematic participant and in the second of which Isaac is the thematic participant.

Section 6 (Peak) is clearly set off by an amazing construction consisting of וַיְהִי 'and it was' plus a temporal clause, וַיְהִי, plus a circumstantial clause, and a *waw*-X-*qatal* clause. This construction serves to slow down the pace and, at the same time, heighten the tension. Esau enters as the new participant while Jacob goes offstage.

Like Section 5, Section 6 consists of two structural paragraphs. Esau is the thematic participant in the first (vv. 30–38) and Isaac in the second (vv. 39–40). Section 6 represents the climax of the story; in terms of plot structure, it is the Peak and is marked as such by the following features:

(1) An unusual heaping up of off-the-storyline clauses.
(2) Its length. (This is the longest section in the entire unit—177 words as against 156 in Section 5, the second longest.)
(3) Its emotional content. There are two heart-rending statements, וַיֶּחֱרַד יִצְחָק חֲרָדָה גְּדֹלָה עַד־מְאֹד 'and Isaac trembled a very big trembling' in v. 33 and וַיִּצְעַק צְעָקָה גְּדֹלָה וּמָרָה עַד־מְאֹד 'and (Esau) cried a very big and bitter cry' in v. 34. The plea בָּרֲכֵנִי גַם־אָנִי אָבִי 'bless me too, my father' occurs twice, in v. 34 and v. 38. The final desperation is expressed in v. 38: וַיִּשָּׂא עֵשָׂו קֹלוֹ וַיֵּבְךְּ 'and Esau lifted up his voice and cried'.

That Esau is the thematic participant in vv. 30–38 is indicated by the following structural devices:

(1) He is explicitly introduced in v. 30, and his name occurs twice more, in subject position, at the end of this paragraph.
(2) He takes the initiative in v. 31.
(3) The beginning and the end of the 30–38 paragraph are marked by three *wayyiqtol* verbs each, in v. 31 and v. 38. They are arranged in chiastic order: וַיַּעַשׂ ... וַיָּבֵא ... וַיֹּאמֶר 'and he prepared ... and he brought ... and he said' versus וַיֹּאמֶר ... וַיִּשָּׂא ... וַיֵּבְךְּ ... 'and he said ... and he lifted ... and he cried'.

Isaac is the thematic participant in vv. 39–40, a paragraph that is bounded, as in Section 5, by the blessing, thus bringing this climactic episode to an end.

Section 7 (First Post-Peak Episode) There is nothing in the immediate structure to indicate a new episode, as the storyline continues uninterrupted with two *wayyiqtol* verbs. However, Section 6 was marked by a final boundary, the blessing. Furthermore, there is a change of locale. Esau must have left his father's tent since he is now alone onstage, speaking "in his heart."

Section 8 (Second Post-Peak Episode) starts with the passive וַיֻּגַּד לְרִבְקָה 'and Rebekah was told'. Now it is true that this is a *wayyiqtol* verb, but its function here is off the eventline. Rebekah needs to be informed of Esau's intention. This could be done either by introducing a minor participant on the storyline, thus creating a new episode, or with a *waw*-X-*qatal* clause in which Rebekah could be said to have heard the rumor. In either case the effect would be to prolong the winding down towards the resolution, and this is not desirable. So the author, by means of a passive, provides background information that lets Rebekah know what she needs to know; but he does it on the storyline so as not to disturb the pattern by introducing a new participant or making another break in the storyline, which would prolong the denouement.

Rebekah is thus reintroduced. She takes over by calling for Jacob, and she remains the thematic participant of this episode. Jacob does not utter a single sound.

Section 9 (Third Post-Peak Episode) has two participants: Rebekah and Isaac, Rebekah being thematic. That the locale has changed is evident from the syntax of the clause on the storyline. If Isaac had been present during Rebekah's speech to Jacob, then the clause would have to read וְאֶל־יִצְחָק אָמְרָה (רִבְקָה) 'and/but to Isaac she (= Rebekah) said'. (This is evident from Gen. 3:16–17, אֶל־הָאִשָּׁה אָמַר ... וּלְאָדָם אָמַר 'to the woman he said . . . and to the man he said', and Gen. 20:15–16, וּלְשָׂרָה אָמַר 'and to Sarah he said'.)

Section 10 (Fourth Post-Peak Episode) is an execution paragraph in which Isaac acts, seemingly independently, upon the idea that Rebekah put into his mind by referring to their problems with their foreign daughters-in-law. Isaac calls, gives instructions, blesses, and sends off, while we hear not a syllable from Jacob. For the author, the story has to come to a quick end now. The emotional scenes are over; now it is just business. The final boundary is marked by וַיֵּלֶךְ פַּדֶּנָה אֲרָם 'and he went to Paddan-aram'. That is, Jacob explicitly goes offstage.

Section 11 has a change of participants and locale. This is reason enough to establish a new section. Esau reappears onstage alone. He has learnt something, he acts upon it, and thus he provides the resolution to the initial conflict of Section 1.

4.2 The technique of composition

By lining up the thirteen thematic participants of this unit, we find that there exists a striking pattern, what Fishbane (1979:42) would call a bilateral symmetry.

The thematic participants in the first and last section are identical, and the same is true for the following pairs: 2 and 10; 3 and 9; 4 and 8; and 5b and 6b. The one pair that has different participants, namely 5a and 7, is different only on the surface, for it is in these two sections that the two brothers are shown to act alike, by acting or plotting against each other. Even if Sections 5 and 6 had only one thematic participant, the analysis would still show the same pattern. This pattern can be diagrammed:

Section	Thematic Participant	
1	Esau	
2	Isaac	
3	Rebekah	
4	Rebekah	
5a	Jacob (against E)	
5b	Isaac	
6a	Esau	central character
6b	Isaac	
7	Esau (against J)	
8	Rebekah	
9	Rebekah	
10	Isaac	
11	Esau	

That Esau is indeed the central character in this unit can be seen in the following additional facts:
(1) Mention of him occurs both at the beginning and at the end as well as at the very center of this narrative unit.
(2) He is the only one to have the stage for himself with either only human props (26:34–35 and 28:9) or possibly minor participants (27:41).
(3) He is the only participant whose inner thoughts are reported, and thus we get a more complete picture of him (Berlin 1983:61).

It is notable that the three people who were introduced (explicitly or indirectly) in the frame each appear four times as a thematic participant. Jacob, on the other hand, who is not introduced until Section 3, acts in only one section as thematic participant.

Based on this analysis I conclude that the frame (26:34–35 and 28:6–9) and also 27:46–28:5 are integral parts of this literary masterpiece, even though some others have attributed them to the P source. In coming to this conclusion I consulted twenty-two translations (ten English, six French, six German). Of them all, only two translate in such a way that it is clear that Rebekah's speeches are part of one scheme. Buber and Rosenzweig (1987) and also *Einheitsübersetzung,* translate it: "But to Isaac she (= Rebekah) said." The translators of the *Traduction oecuménique de la Bible* indicate through their use of major and minor titles that they, too, have understood the intention of the redactor. (But in the notes of that translation the idea that the J-story is framed by two elements from P is nevertheless expounded.

5. Summary

The problem that I felt is regard to Gen. 27:46 was a text division that seemed somehow wrong. This caused me to look at the arguments for the composite nature of this text. I then investigated the discourse structure of the 26:34–28:9 passage and concluded that it represents a unified whole with a subtle but nevertheless strikingly clear structure. To divide this text between the two parts of Rebekah's second plot not only makes the story end in an unsatisfactory and unfinished way, but it violates the intention of the author (or redactor if this amazing work is his) as clearly shown by the very balanced structure of this text.

References

Bar-Efrat, S. 1989. *Narrative art in the Bible.* Sheffield: Almond Press.
Berlin, A. 1983. *Poetics and interpretation of biblical narrative.* Sheffield: Almond Press.
Buber, M., and F. Rosenzweig. 1987. *Die fünf Bücher der Weisung.* Darmstadt: Wissenschaftliche Buchgesellschaft.
Die Bibel, Altes und Neues Testament: Einheitsübersetzung. 1980. Freiburg: Herder.
Driver, S. R. 1913. *An introduction to the literature of the Old Testament.* Edinburgh: T. and T. Clark.
Ehrlich, A. B. 1968. *Randglossen zur hebräischen Bibel,* vol. 1. Hildesheim: Georg Olms Verlagsbuchhandlung.
Fishbane, M. 1979. *Text and texture.* New York: Schocken Books.
Fokkelman, J. P. 1975. *Narrative art in Genesis.* Assen/Amsterdam: Van Gorcum.
Longacre, R. E. 1976. *An anatomy of speech notions.* Lisse: Peter de Ridder.
———. 1979. The discourse structure of the flood narrative. *Journal of the American Academy of Religion* 47, Supplement B: 89–133.
———. 1989. *Joseph: A story of divine providence: A text theoretical and textlinguistic analysis of Genesis 37 and 39–48.* Winona Lake, Ind.: Eisenbrauns.
Rabin, Chaim. 1985. Linguistic Aspects. In Radday and Shore, part 6.
Radday, Yehuda Thomas, and Haim Shore, eds. 1985. *Genesis: An authorship study in computer-assisted statistical linguistics.* Series: Analecta Biblica 103. Rome: Biblical Institute Press.

Sarna, N. 1989. *The JPS Torah commentary: Genesis*. Philadelphia: Jewish Publication Society.
Skinner, J. 1930. *A critical and exegetical commentary on Genesis*. 2d ed. International Critical Commentary. Edinburgh: T. and T. Clark.
Speiser, E. A. 1964. *Genesis*. Anchor Bible. Garden City, N.Y.: Doubleday.
Westermann, C. 1981. *Genesis*. Vol. 2, *Genesis 12–36*. Neukirchen-Vluyn: Neukirchner Verlag.

12

THE MIRACULOUS GRAMMAR OF JOSHUA 3-4
Computer-aided Analysis of the Rhetorical
and Syntactic Structure

Nicolai Winther-Nielsen

> The *Werkgroep Informatica* of the Free University in Amsterdam has developed programs for computer-aided analysis of the Hebrew Bible at all levels: word, phrase, clause, and text. A linguist can use them to perform a precise and consistent textual description based on morphological and syntactic criteria. Computer-oriented analysis is consistently sign-oriented, but it can also capture the functions of grammar in text and human communication. The gap between description and interpretation can be bridged by functional grammar and rhetorical analysis of interclausal relations. My analysis of Joshua 3-4 (the crossing of Jordan) illustrates how a computer-aided description and rhetorical interpretation can explain miraculous grammar at climactic peaks, thematicity, and coherence.

Discourse grammar hit the Hebrew Bible like a flood in the late seventies. Longacre's 1979 seminal work on the Flood Story of Genesis 6-9 showed how the grammar and text of a story of universal cataclysm could be explained. He traced the twisting of regular verb functions as the episodes flowed towards a climactic peak of extinction of life in the rising waters.

Since then this analytic current has strengthened. The postflood Hebrew discourse grammarians have exploited new textual data from old exotic languages. Many are heading in the direction of pragmatics: they focus on user-oriented and communicative functions of texts. And some are deeply enmeshed in computational research for fast retrieval of massive pools of Hebrew discourse.

A computer-assisted discourse-pragmatic analysis might well explain a number of grammatical, literary, and thematic problems. For example, could it explain problems such as the boundaries of the story of the crossing of the Jordan in Joshua 3-4? This passage has boundaries of the sort that challenge discourse grammarians, even though it is thoroughly permeated by climactic marking. It also shares with the Genesis Flood Story its intriguing miraculous reporting. The question is to what extent a computer can aid in analyzing a story so heavily permeated by mysterious grammar.

The following overview of the crossing of Jordan will show that computational tools can indeed describe the structural features of the text. The functional and rhetorical aspects of the grammar and the text, however, can better be explained within a broad discourse-pragmatic framework.

1. Computer-aided analysis

The gap between computer programming and all the diverse communicative functions of language in the minds of readers is very wide. However, more restricted and less ambitious goals can be set for the computer, such as letting the computer register and evaluate linguistic features of rhetorical and syntactic structures.

Nobody imagined the full potential of computers twenty-five years ago when the first electronic work on the Bible started. Yet at present biblical studies are increasingly being inundated by computational applications. The outputs increase as the speed of the computers increases.[1] With a personal computer almost anyone can integrate the text of the Hebrew Bible with a translation. Even the average linguist and translator has access to tools for semantic analysis and unique syntactical queries, and complex analyses can be performed with impressive speed.[2]

This wonderful power reaches beyond mere word retrieval and intersentential searching. Today computational research applications can contribute even to the descriptive procedures required for textual analysis.

This potential is found in the computer-assisted research directed by Professor Talstra of the *Werkgroep Informatica* at the Free University in Amsterdam. Over the years he and his team have developed a simple morphologically coded text of the Hebrew Bible that can be used for various linguistic analyses at the word, phrase, clause, and text levels (Talstra and Postma 1989).

The most advanced programs at present are designed for interactive research into interclausal syntactical relations. A linguist can use the programs to perform a precise textual description based on morphological and syntactic information from the lower levels of the language. The textual information is not tagged into the database on the basis of a linguistic theory.[3] Instead, it is produced by using a series of programs that accumulate linguistic information successively upwards in the grammatical hierarchy from morpheme to text. The flow of these programs, named Syn01-05, is as follows:

Name	Function	Output
Syn01	morphological analysis	grammatical functions are listed
Syn02	semantic analysis	lexical part of speech information is added
Syn03	phrase structure analysis	phrases are produced and checked
Syn04	clause division	"clause atoms" are demarcated
Syn05	clause relations	clause relations are set up and coded

The phrase, clause, and clause relations programs work in an interactive data-oriented process (Talstra 1992*b*:135). The idea is that at any stage the computer will propose a construction type based on an earlier registered structural pattern, by recognition matches. The more established patterns there are, the more new data can be treated from previously unanalyzed corpora.

Thus the textual analysis must be performed at several preliminary stages. The most crucial, but also the most problematic, is the demarcation of clause units within larger complex clauses (Andersen and Forbes 1992). The clause–division program, Syn04, delimits these structures into continuous strings of "clause atoms." These clause or clause-fragment units are demarcated according to the following hierarchy of clause-initial elements (Verheij and Talstra 1992:23):

verb > connective + verb > conn. + adverb (+ noun) + verb

The textual description starts with these demarcated clausal units. First, the clause types are determined. For every unit without a verbal predicate the analyst has to decide the actual verbless construction type through the following series of questions:

Is it a verbless *clause*?
- If no, is it an incomplete clause?
    - defective (because of preceding or following embedding)?
    - discourse marker?
    - left-detached position (fronted clause-external)?
    - vocative?
- If no, is it an elliptic clause (a reduced clause with deletion)?

In the next step the program establishes the clause hierarchy. It offers choices of linkage possibilities based on calculation of grammatical similarities, number of similar occurrences in previously analyzed data, and distance to a preceding potential clause link. All three parameters are ranked into a combined score for every connected link (Talstra 1992*b*: 141). The analyst can choose to follow the program's suggestions, but is also free to make his own choice and link as he likes. The program then tabulates these decisions into indentations for parallel or dependent relations between linked clauses.

Other programs can convert these linkage decisions into a syntactic code unique to each clausal unit. The decisions can be monitored in a textual display with groups of phrases demarcated into clausal units; each unit is accompanied by a code for its relational type, line diagrams graphically indicating the linkage. Figure 1 shows this output.

```
   !---------------------- 03,01a [W-]  [JCKM] [JHWC<] [B--BQR]
<203>
   !-----------!-----!---- 03,01b [W-]  [JS<W]  [M-H-CVJM]
<203>        <200> <200>
   !           !     !---- 03,01c [W-]  [JB<W]  [<D H-JRDN]
   !           !                        [HW>  /W-  /KL BNJ JFR>L]
   !           !---------- 03,01d [W-]  [JLNW]  [CM]
   !          <717>
   !           !---------- 03,01e [VRM]  [J<BRW]
```

Figure 1. A syntactic hierarchy of Josh. 3:1 (Syn05 display)

The syntactic code utilized in Syn05 displays can be illustrated by looking at code <717> for 3,01e. The first digit <7..> signals that the clause has the temporal conjunction טֶרֶם 'before'. The second digit <.1.> registers that the clause contains a *yiqtol* form, the Hebrew imperfective. The last digit <..7> specifies that this verb links backwards to a *wayyiqtol* form. Other codes can specify that the relation to the preceding is completely identical, i.e., code <200>.[4]

This kind of syntactic analysis provides the discourse grammarian with full syntactic information on sequences of clauses and predicate types. He can now sort, search, and compare the data with other grammatical information. New grammatical solutions can be experimentally checked, developed, or refuted in an interactive process. Relations can be changed when other solutions to connectivity seem more likely or when some grammatical information needs correction.

With these computational tools it is possible to describe relations in textual structure, and the researcher is still in full command of the tools.

2. A functional and rhetorical perspective on discourse grammar

Nevertheless, the limitations in a formal registration of syntactical relations are obvious. A syntactic relations hierarchy, though crucial, can only be a first step. Any full account of grammar in text and human communication must include such broader aspects as semantic structure, pragmatic purpose, and discourse-holistic structure (Hardmeier 1992).

This is inevitably so, because the language code is multifunctional. Diverse uses of syntax in human communication are marked in the same limited coding material of individual clauses, and text-level functions are not always coded uniformly in the morphosyntax or are only sparingly marked. Linguistic communication is essentially a matter of how to tangle with predicate forms, word forms, word order, connectives, clause reduction, sentence expansion, and other areas of the grammar in order to code the vast cultural, situational, and textual interrelations that go into a text.

Syntactical relation hierarchies are therefore indispensable as a first step, but they must be thoroughly rechecked in relation to pragmatic functions on the discourse level. Talstra has correctly pressed the point that a computer-aided description has to be a consistent sign-oriented exploration of a formalized nature. He has repeatedly pointed to the weakness of any approach that does not start with syntactic marking; only after syntactic marking should the analyst then proceed across the border into textual interpretation (1991:180-81). He has also repeatedly advocated the use of a formalized structural syntax (1992*a*).

However, a new data-oriented concept of linguistic inventories and a more object-oriented approach to programming is currently developing in the *Werkgroep*. The new perspective reduces the reliance on a restricted formalized scope, allowing for a more functionally oriented approach. The work on the "miraculous" grammar of Joshua 3-4 also shows that there is ample room for a functional grammar and a rhetorical interpretation within the computational framework. Both kinds of explanatory and interpretative information can be added to the computational registration of syntactic relations in order to provide a fuller and more adequate understanding of the grammar of a discourse. As a further step I therefore convert the syntactic display into an expanded format that enumerates full clauses in one column and lists grammatical and textual interpretations in a second column as in Figure 2.

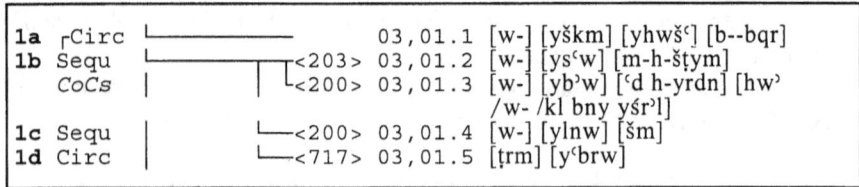

Figure 2. Syntactic and rhetorical relations in Josh. 3:1

The purely syntactic aspects of clause linkages are explained by a functional grammar. A functional theory combines semantics, syntax, and pragmatics at the clause level without transformation from deep structure (Dik 1989:17-20). A particularly powerful discourse syntactic theory is developed in the structuralist-functional grammar known as Role and Reference Grammar, formulated by Foley and Van Valin (1984). In this functional framework for a formal grammar, semantic relations are treated within a layering of predicates, argument roles, and setting adjuncts. More important, its theory of clause-internal layering is extended into clause combining, so that the same grammatical framework operates from morphology to interclausal linkage. Discourse-pragmatic functions are thus closely tied to the syntactic twisting of the semantic content of clauses, sentences, and paragraphs.

The usefulness of a functional explanation can be illustrated by the syntax of Josh 3:1. After the opening of the discourse by וַיַּשְׁכֵּם יְהוֹשֻׁעַ בַּבֹּקֶר 'and-(he)-arose Joshua in-the-morning' (3:1a), another story-initial staging function occurs in the following biclausal sentence, וַיִּסְעוּ מֵהַשִּׁטִּים וַיָּבֹאוּ עַד־הַיַּרְדֵּן (1b). A functional grammar can explain this as a core cosubordination (the CoCs of Fig. 2). Its structure consists of a combination of two predicates with their arguments, which share both source ('from Shittim') and direction ('to Jordan') arguments.[5] The evidence for this explanation is that the compound subject הוּא וְכָל־בְּנֵי יִשְׂרָאֵל 'he and all the Israelites' occurs in a right-detached position of the second core, but is equally closely related to the first core. This functional explanation avoids the necessity of emending the plural verb form in the first core ([03,01.2]). The clause combining is just a discourse-staging statement in the sense of "and they went away from Shittim to get to Jordan, he along with all the Israelites."

Another reason for positing a single extended clause is that this pair of cores does not have any independent rhetorical function in the story, and only in combination mark the movement to a new location. This decision is supported by the Rhetorical Structure Theory formulated by Mann, Matthiessen, and Thompson (1992) to clarify the nature of interclausal and higher-level relations in texts. Their theory continues earlier semantic work on the thread of discourse, but it is formulated as a comprehensive and consistent pragmatic theory on the organization of discourse. It sets out how textual coherence is mostly shaped by relations between heads and modifiers. The latter type of unit, the so-called satellite, supports a nucleus whether preceding or following, and together they may serve as a satellite for a higher-level nucleus. This, in turn, may serve as a satellite for a unit at a still higher level. In this theory only a few relation types are multinuclear or nonsatellitic in nature. About twenty-five different kinds of such textual relations are posited, from the bottom level all the way up through higher levels of textual structure. The discourse topic is then expressed by the highest and most central nuclear element of a given linguistic unit.

Rhetorical Structure Theory has exchanged semantic or logical formalizations for a pragmatic view on clause and text relations. These relations are determined by their intended rhetorical effects on the reader. Because relations need not be marked in the syntax, this pragmatic framework is extremely valuable as an independent account of textual structure. It matches perfectly with a computational registration of hierarchical relations in cross-clausal syntax that describes only morphosyntactic parameters of clause combining.

The theory in its standard form draws relations in diagrams with a graphic representation of how clauses cluster in groups. But they can also be mapped onto a display of syntactic relations as rhetorical satellite nodes. (This is illustrated by the representation of rhetorical and syntactical relations in Fig. 2.) The initial clause, וַיַּשְׁכֵּם יְהוֹשֻׁעַ בַּבֹּקֶר 'Joshua arose in the morning' (3:1a), is a discourse opener after an embedded story in Joshua 2. It resumes events of three days earlier following the end of Josh. 1:18, and specifies the textually accessible implicit subject. Accordingly, a rhetorical reading will classify it as a circumstance, defined as follows:

Relation	Nature of Satellite (S)	Function of S for Nucleus
Circumstance (Circ)	Situation	S as framework for situation

The next two closely combined clauses are sequence relations (Sequ), and so is the final וַיָּלִנוּ שָׁם 'and they spent the night there' (3:1c), which grammatically is a clausal cosubordination with deleted subject. The segment then concludes with a time circumstance, טֶרֶם יַעֲבֹרוּ 'before they crossed', hinting at the theme in the following story. This rhetorical analysis also indicates that the discourse-pragmatic functions of adverbial clauses are always significant, while sometimes extended clauses have less independent functions as core cosubordinations.[6]

Accordingly, both functional grammar and rhetorical reading can be deployed along with computational descriptions of syntactic relations. Both are pragmatically defined, and therefore useful additions to a syntactic registration of relations. Pragmatic and syntactic relations support and complement each other, yet they also retain their individual independence.

This kind of computer-aided analysis of rhetorical and syntactic structure is significant for three different aspects of textual analysis. It plays a role in discourse-pragmatic analysis of textual wholes. It is crucial for analysis of coherence in the storyline and theme. And it may have a bearing on specific problems of interpretation.

We will now consider how this applies to the story of Joshua 3–4.

3. The discourse structure of Joshua 3-4

To begin with, cross-clausal information on both the rhetorical and syntactic relations expounds the overall structure of a discourse. This is apparent in theories of discourse grammar that focus on pragmatic goals and rhetorical strategies (Van Dijk and Kintsch 1983). Such theories explore the nature of constituents, coherence, and content, the three major areas of any textual interpretation (cf. Longacre 1992). These areas can be subsumed under the following definitions:

- superstructure: which constituents build the story and how they are delimited individually according their intentional strategy
- interclausal coherence: how the story unfolds through grammatical means
- macrostructure: how style and dialogue express the story's theme

These three aspects of textual interpretation explain the story in Joshua 3-4. The aspect of the constituents is a major problem. Many scholars agree with Soggin that in Joshua 3-4 "a series of episodes... lack any original internal unity" (1972:50).[7] This seems to be corroborated by a superficial division of the story by content (1972:51):

Unit	Theme
3:1-13	preparations for crossing
3:14-16a	miracle of the waters
3:16b-17; 4:10-11, 14-18	crossing
4:1-9	the twelve stones
4:19-5:1	the arrival at Gilgal

Yet, discourse grammar can establish a more coherent grammatical demarcation of the episode structure. It recognizes that a stage opens the story of the crossing in 3:1 and that several sub-units are marked off by וַיְהִי 'and-it-was' (3:2, 14; 4:1, 11). The two sub-units marked off by 4:1 and 4:11 are similar and strongly marked; they both repeat the fact that the people had crossed and both follow a note on the priests' standing in the middle of the river. A more peculiar type of boundary marker is found in וַיֹּאמֶר יְהוֹשֻׁעַ אֶל־הַכֹּהֲנִים לֵאמֹר 'and-he-said Joshua to-the-priests saying' in 3:6a. It is marked only by the double explicit participant reference and לֵאמֹר, but the context makes clear that an additional day has elapsed. A similar clause structure is present in the beginning of a segment on the return of the waters in 4:15. Unit marking, content, internal composition, and other textual features thus cooperate in demarcating the following discourse profile:

Constituents	Extent	Content	Superstructure
Stage	3:1	March to Jordan	Exposition
Ep1	3:2-5	Preparatory orders for crossing	Inciting incident
Ep2	3:6-13	Orders for crossing	Mounting tension
Ep3 (Peak)	3:14-17	Crossing into water	Climax
Ep4 (Inter-peak)	4:1-10	Orders for stone collection	Interpeak tension
Ep5	4:11-14	Crossing in front of people	Lessening tension
Ep6 (Peak')	4:15-18	Crossing out of water	Resolution
Closure	4:19-24	Arrival at Gilgal	Conclusion
Summary	5:1	Canaanite demoralization	Discourse summary

The aspect of coherence is also problematic because the crossing is believed to disintegrate into two or more sources due to its diachronic evolution (Otto 1973:25-26). The primary evidence in support of this is that a second set of twelve stones suddenly appears in Josh. 4:9. But these stones are just the most visible tokens of other duplications, from the selection and instruction of the twelve men (cf. 3:12, 4:4-5, and 4:1b-3) to the setting up of the stones (cf. 4:9 and 4:20) and their so-called etiological explanation (cf. 4:6-7 and 4:21-24).

The problem of coherence is very important in computer-assisted analysis of rhetorical and syntactic structure as can be illustrated by an analysis of the descent and ascent of the priests as peak constituents in the superstructure. An analysis of relations is also significant for an understanding of the theme, although in the Jordan-crossing story the content is largely uncontested (the crossing theme is difficult to miss in the story).

4. The miraculous syntax of 3:14-17 and 4:18

Rhetorical relations and functional grammar can be deployed to explain a computational description of the syntax at narrative peaks. Thus a new episode opens in 3:14 after extensive dialogue. It reports the miraculous disappearance of the water by a very mysterious grammar.[8] Several temporal descriptive clauses in slow motion describe how the waters suddenly stopped when the feet of the priests were dipped into the water. The rhetorical and syntactic relations are seen in figure 3:[9]

The Miraculous Grammar of Joshua 3-4

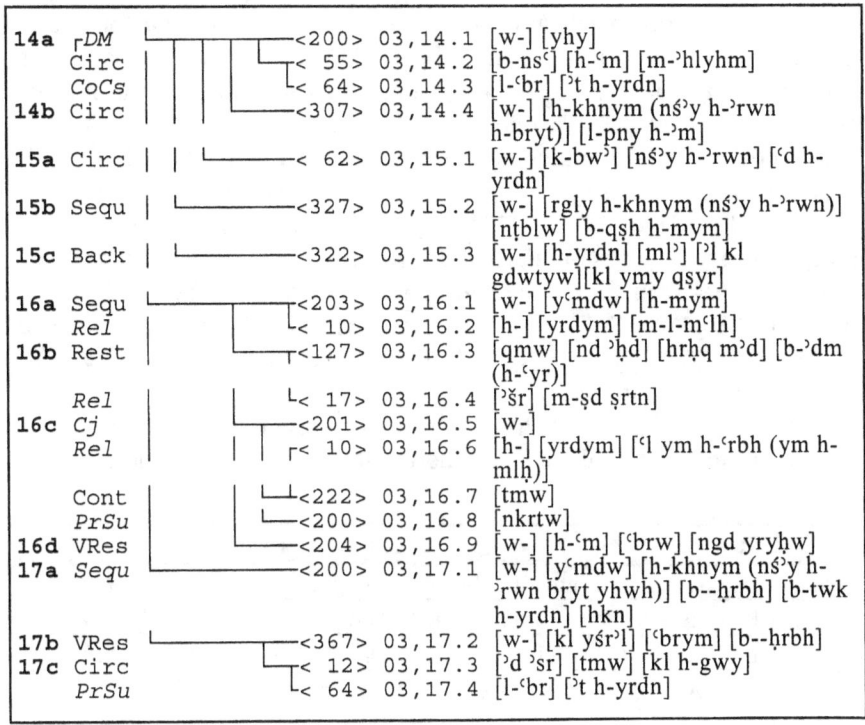

Figure 3. Relations in Josh. 3:14-17

After the initial episode introduction (14a) comes a descriptive clause וְהַכֹּהֲנִים נֹשְׂאֵי הָאָרוֹן הַבְּרִית לִפְנֵי הָעָם (14b [14.4]). This is a verbless clause with *waw* after *wayyiqtol* <307> noting that the priests were in front of the procession as commanded (3:3). The clause functions as a circumstance satellitic to what follows. It is followed by yet another temporal adverbial clause specifying the priests' arrival at the Jordan (15a). Only then does the primary storyline begin, when the feet of the priests touch the water (15b). However, here the storyline is narrated by a passive verb, נִטְבְּלוּ 'were dipped', preceded by וְ and following after *wayyiqtol* ([15.2]: <324>). This *waw*-X-*qatal* construction promotes the object וְרַגְלֵי 'feet' to the pre-core slot for reactivation from 3:13a. It also demotes the agent status of the priests, so that an event rather than an action is described. Another similar *waw*-X-*qatal* construction follows in וְהַיַּרְדֵּן מָלֵא עַל־כָּל־גְּדוֹתָיו 'and the Jordan was flooding all its banks' (15c). This is clearly a parenthetical background satellite. It delays the climax and heightens the miracle by commenting that the Jordan was until now in "brutal" force (Butler 1983:48).

After this prolonged introduction, the expected *wayyiqtol* form is at last used to describe the absolute climax: וַיַּעַמְדוּ הַמַּיִם 'the waters stopped' (16a). But even here the semantic content of the form is still not agentive. The event is barely more dynamic than the *waw-X-qatal* construction used for the dipping of the priest's feet (15b).[10] And after this major event the story stops completely. The *wayyiqtol* form is just restated by the satellite קָמוּ נֵד־אֶחָד הַרְחֵק מְאֹד 'it stood like a wall very far away' (16b) with clause-initial *qatal* ([16.3]: <127>). This restatement sentence (16a–b) in turn is combined with 16c to contrast the upstream waters (הַמַּיִם הַיֹּרְדִים מִלְמַעְלָה [16.2–3]) with the downstream ones (וְהַיֹּרְדִים עַל יָם הָעֲרָבָה יָם־הַמֶּלַח [16.5–6]), which תַּמּוּ נִכְרָתוּ 'completed cutting up' (16c).[11]

A similar grammatical structure is used for the return of the waters in episode 6 in 4:18, although in shortened form. The parallels are as follows:

Joshua 3: descent	Joshua 4: ascent
when people depart, ark in front (14)	[dialogue and execution (4:15–17)]
when ark carriers come to Jordan (15a)	when priests ascend Jordan (18a)
feet were dipped in waters (15b)	foot soles slipped on dry (18b)
Jordan went over banks all summer (15c)	ש Jordan returned (18c)
waters stopped (16a)	ת went over banks (18d)

The interchange of *wayyiqtol* (3:16a) and simultaneous *waw-X-qatal* (3:15b) forms also continues in chapter 3 after the stopping of the waters. In 16d a pre-core slot וְהָעָם is followed by עָבְרוּ. It adds as a background comment to 16b that they crossed in the region of Jericho far away from the damming point. After that a new paragraph opens with a storyline verb, but this time the *wayyiqtol* form narrates that the priests stopped when they got to the middle of the Jordan. This is told by means of a repetition of the וַיַּעַמְדוּ form (17a = 16a). The continuous crossing of the people on the dry ground is then described by a participle, עֹבְרִים (17b), and they continue passing past the ark until all the nation has completed crossing (תַּמּוּ כָּל־הַגּוֹי לַעֲבֹר in 17c).

The "miraculous" syntax of 3:14–17 and 4:18 grammatically twists the action into descriptive events. It lends depictive force to the situation, creating a dramatic pause of the sort that often occurs at peak climaxes and resolutions. All dialogue is faded out, and action is described by turbulent predicate functions. This is quite similar to the Flood Story where the primary and secondary storylines in Gen. 7:18–24 are also restructured (Longacre 1979).

5. The thematic teaching of 4:6-7 and 4:21-24

Computer-aided analysis of rhetorical relations likewise aids in comprehension of content. Here in this narration from Joshua 4 the theme is in two embedded instructions of Joshua's on how the people should explain the events to their children. The first one occurs in an address to the twelve men in the presence of all the people in episode 4 (4:6-7) and the second one at the night camp in the closure (4:21-24). Both expound the meaning of the twelve stones to be carried to Gilgal (4:20) as a sign among them (4:6a). Both are instructional question-and-answer dialogues rather than cathechesis (Boling 1982:174). Their structural similarities are quite clear:

		Speech to twelve (people)	Speech to people
Circ	6b	When your children ask	21b When your children ask their fathers
Q	6c	What are these stones to you	21c What are these stones
Sequ	7a	You shall tell them	22a You shall teach your children
A	7b	The waters were cut	22b You crossed on dry ground

One of the differences between the two instructions is that the question in 4:6c adds לָכֶם 'to you'. This contextualizes the first dialogue more tightly into the actual crossing of the Jordan. It also includes the situationally accessible Israelites in its reference, rather than just the twelve men alone. In contrast the second speech is phrased as a more general rule by opposing 'your sons' and 'their fathers' (= you) in 21b, and the answer to the question in 21c is solemnly introduced by the word וְהוֹדַעְתֶּם 'inform, teach' (22a).

Other differences between the two answers are apparent. The first answer is tied to the crossing situation and focuses on the ark (see Fig. 4).

```
7b  A     |     |   └─<999>  04,07.2  [ʾšr] [nkrtw] [mymy h-yrdn]
                                      [m-pny ʾrwn bryt yhwh]
7c  Circ  |         ┌<142>   04,07.3  [b-ʿbrw] [b--yrdn]
7d  Elab  |         └<204>   04,07.4  [nkrtw] [my h-yrdn]
7e  Purp  |          └─<202> 04,07.5  [w-] [hyw] [h-ʾbnym h-ʾlh]
                                      [l-zkrwn] [l-bny yśrʾl] [ʿd ʿwlm]
```

Figure 4. Relations in the answer of 4:7

It opens with an אֲשֶׁר (7b), which is best interpreted as the complementizer 'that'. It is thus an elliptic clause fragment, '(these stones mean) that . . .', presupposing the question. This is in turn emphatically restated in 7c-d. The final clause (7e) is more difficult to connect וְהָיוּ הָאֲבָנִים הָאֵלֶּה לְזִכָּרוֹן לִבְנֵי יִשְׂרָאֵל עַד־עוֹלָם 'and these stones shall serve as a memory for the Israelites forever'. But because the answer of 7b-d only implicitly refers to the stones ([07.2]), it probably continues the question and answer as a whole. The clause is therefore part of Joshua's further instruction concerning the stones rather than of the Israelites' answer to the sons on the meaning of the stones. The answer proper is therefore very short and only emphasizes that the waters were split when they crossed.

The second answer has a more solemn and formalized structure (see Fig. 5).

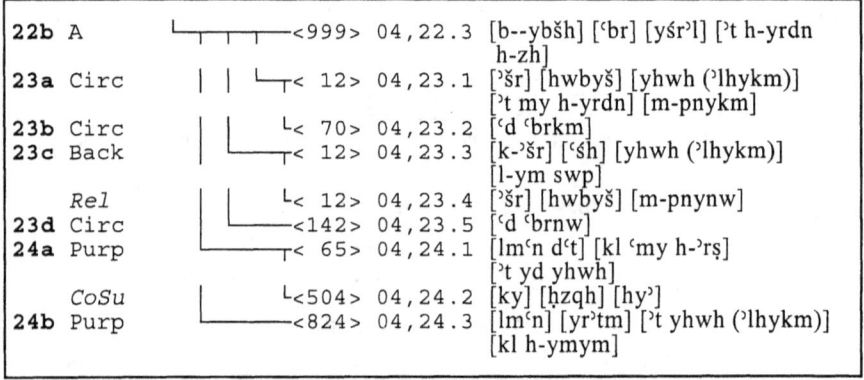

22b	A	<999>	04,22.3	[b--ybšh] ['br] [yśr'l] ['t h-yrdn h-zh]
23a	Circ	< 12>	04,23.1	['šr] [hwbyš] [yhwh ('lhykm)] ['t my h-yrdn] [m-pnykm]
23b	Circ	< 70>	04,23.2	['d 'brkm]
23c	Back	< 12>	04,23.3	[k-'šr] ['śh] [yhwh ('lhykm)] [l-ym swp]
	Rel	< 12>	04,23.4	['šr] [hwbyš] [m-pnynw]
23d	Circ	<142>	04,23.5	['d 'brnw]
24a	Purp	< 65>	04,24.1	[lm'n d't] [kl 'my h-'rṣ] ['t yd yhwh]
	CoSu	<504>	04,24.2	[ky] [ḥzqh] [hy']
24b	Purp	<824>	04,24.3	[lm'n] [yr'tm] ['t yhwh ('lhykm)] [kl h-ymym]

Figure 5. Relations in the second answer of 4:22b-24b

In 4:22b, a locative adjunct, בַּיַּבָּשָׁה 'on-the-dry-ground', is placed in the pre-core slot for focus. A temporal adverbial clause "when Yahweh your God dried out the waters of the Jordan in front of you" (23a) therefore has to follow the main clause. It is introduced with אֲשֶׁר as a temporal subordinator, and in the sequel אֲשֶׁר is also used as a comparative coordinator ([23.3]) and as a relative pronoun ([23.4]).

In this answer Joshua includes the salvation-historical events of Exodus as confessional background in the same way Rahab had done earlier (2:10a). It is therefore thematically important in the Book of Joshua. This is also indicated by two parallel purpose clauses with לְמַעַן 'in order that', which close the answer. The first draws the lesson for the other people that they will now get to know that Yahweh's hand is strong (24a). If כָּל־עַמֵּי הָאָרֶץ is translated 'peoples of the land', it refers directly to the nations mentioned afterwards in 5:1 and also reiterates the final theme of the spy story (2:24b-c). The second purpose clause draws the lesson in terms of their own increased fear or reverence for the Lord (4:24b).

6. The stones picked up in the Jordan in 4:9

A final quite astonishing example shows how a rhetorical reading can guide syntactic description and clarify difficulties posed by individual constructions. In 4:9 we read how an extra set of twelve stones was taken from the middle of the Jordan:

וּשְׁתֵּים עֶשְׂרֵה אֲבָנִים הֵקִים יְהוֹשֻׁעַ בְּתוֹךְ הַיַּרְדֵּן תַּחַת
and-12 (-) stones (he-)rose Joshua in-middle-of the-Jordan beneath
מַצַּב רַגְלֵי הַכֹּהֲנִים נֹשְׂאֵי אֲרוֹן הַבְּרִית (4:9a)
resting-place-of feet-of the-priests carriers-of ark-of the-covenant
וַיִּהְיוּ שָׁם עַד הַיּוֹם הַזֶּה (9b)
and(-they)-were there until the-day (the-)this

This additional set of stones is quite surprising for several reasons. God had not previously ordered Joshua to set them up. They play no role later in the story or in history. Joshua sets them up himself even if he is by now on the western bank with the rest of the people. The place is specified as תַּחַת מַצַּב רַגְלֵי 'under the resting place of the feet', which has earlier been used only in reference to the other set of twelve stones (4:3b). Finally, it is not clear why the narrator insists on their presence there forever, but never says so of the more visual and important set of stones in Gilgal.

So far no convincing explanation for the extra set of stones has been given. They can be removed as an interpolation and the story will run smoothly (Saydon 1950:203), but this solution removes evidence arbitrarily. They can be explained historically as a platform for the priests carrying the ark. Some say this "makes excellent sense as a subject of didactic interest here" (Boling 1982:175). But why set them up only after the priests' arrival, and why insist that they remain there forever if they are only of academic interest? The literary critic Polzin (1980:109) has interpreted them as Joshua's excesses in fulfilling the commands of the Lord, but this is at best only a possible reading and hard to prove as the writer's intention.

On the other hand, it is remarkable that the stones are referred to in the same language as the first set of twelve stones. This might suggest that the second set is identical with the first; however, an identification of the two sets is grammatically difficult. It requires that the וְ-X-הֵקִים construction 'and twelve stones he raised up' has a pre-core slot fronted object, detached from its locative modifier. The extremely long phrase opened by בְּתוֹךְ הַיַּרְדֵּן would then modify the twelve stones, but remain in its postverbal position because of its heavy load. The clause would then be a very unusual discontinuous O_1-V-S-O_2 construction derived from the following:

> and Joshua had erected (the) twelve stones [moved to the pre-core slot] in the middle of the Jordan below the place where the feet of the priests, the carriers of the ark, were standing

The determination of שְׁתֵּים עֶשְׂרֵה אֲבָנִים is also problematic, but can be explained in various ways.[12]

Despite the weak grammatical support, the discourse context seems to favor the identification of these stones with those mentioned in 4:8. The following clause, וַיִּהְיוּ שָׁם עַד הַיּוֹם הַזֶּה 'and they have been there until this day', naturally connects with the *wayyiqtol* clauses of 4:8 and especially the campsite referred to by וַיַּנִּחוּם שָׁם 'and they placed them there' in 8f. This linkage device also received the highest score in the computer-aided syntactic analysis by means of the Syn05 program. An identification is also supported by the language of 4:20a, which again repeats הֵקִים יְהוֹשֻׁעַ 'Joshua set up' now clearly in reference to the twelve Gilgal stones. Finally, it avoids the problem of having just one single reference to a completely new topic, which would be rare in the grammar of Hebrew narrative.[13]

The second set may of course just give an isolated piece of information with no other traces and no further significance. However, the grammatical solution would be further discourse-pragmatic evidence for peak-marking turbulence. In this case 4:9a would not add any new information, but only specify that ultimately Joshua was responsible for erecting the Gilgal stones. Rhetorically it would be a restatement. It would also be on line with 4:10, which continues with further background commentary on how the priests were still standing in the river (participle עֹמְדִים in 10a) where they had stopped (*wayyiqtol* in 3:16a). The words that follow, וַיְמַהֲרוּ הָעָם וַיַּעֲבֹרוּ (4:10c), are *wayyiqtol* continuation forms functioning in an embedded story in the sense of 'and the people had hurriedly crossed', repeating 3:16a and 17b to mark the conclusion of the segment.[14] The segment thus has the rhetorical and syntactic relations shown in Figure 6.

The Miraculous Grammar of Joshua 3-4

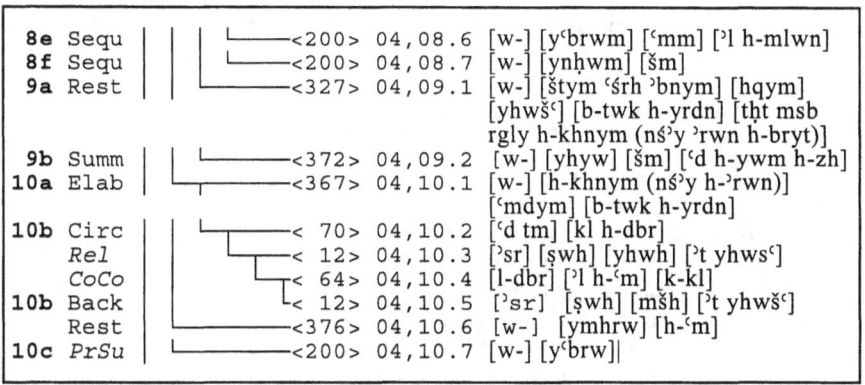

Figure 6. Relations in 4:8e-10d

7. Conclusion

As shown by the examples of miraculous grammar in Joshua 3-4, the most formal of all formal tools, a computer-aided registration of explicit linguistic markings, can assist the discourse grammarian in exploring the rhetorical and syntactic structure of connected Hebrew text. The story of the crossing of Jordan also shows that the gap between computational description and pragmatic interpretation can be bridged by a functional grammar and a theory of rhetorical structure, both of which are user-orientated and can contribute much to an understanding of interclausal connectivity. Both overcome the restrictions of an exclusively formal account of syntactic relations. Yet, the computer helps analysts to clarify the syntactic structure, forcing them to justify whatever function they claim for the grammar or the text in terms of explicit linguistic structures.

The analysis of the story of the crossing of the Jordan has shown the value of computer-aided description for a Hebrew discourse grammar. The computer proved helpful in describing the structural elements of the constituents, coherence, and content. In our example it uncovered the miraculous language at the peaks of the story (3:14-17 and 4:15-18). It clarified the analysis of the thematically central miracle in the dialogues (4:7 and 22-24). It shed some light on a new suggestion for a turbulent peak (4:9).

Thus we have seen the great potential computer-aided analysis has for registration and discovery of syntactic structures. Our illustrative analysis has also shown how necessary it is to tie computer analysis into broader aspects of textual analysis. The computer should be used *in conjunction with* the various grammatical or textual theories, and for *different* analytical tasks. Continued work on the computer will no doubt lead to the discovery of new grammatical features of Hebrew discourse. In the end such new discoveries in the grammar of discourse can be utilized in programming new applications for syntactic and rhetorical analysis.

List of syntactic codes employed

- 10: Attributive clause with hă-relative
- 12: Relative clause (ʾăšer) with qatal verb
- 17: Relative clause (ʾăšer) without verb (verbless clause)
- 55: Infinitive clause with preposition bə 'in'
- 62: Infinitive clause with preposition kə 'like'
- 64: Infinitive clause with preposition lə 'for'
- 65: Infinitive clause with preposition ləmaʿan 'in order to'
- 70: Infinitive clause with preposition ʿad 'until'
- 127: Asyndetic clause with qatal, preceded by wayyiqtol
- 142: Asyndetic clause with infinitive, preceded by qatal
- 200: Identical clauses without any changes in the verb of the second clause
- 201: Identical clauses, but with the verb of the second clause preceded by wə 'and'
- 202: Identical verbs except for shift of person in the second verb
- 203: Identical verbs except for shift of number in the second verb
- 204: Identical verbs, but second clause with explicit subject
- 222: A part of a clause after an embedding, this part containing the verb
- 223: A part of a clause after an embedding, with the verb occurring before the embedding
- 307: Conjunction wə 'and' before verbless clause, preceded by wayyiqtol clause
- 322: Conjunction wə 'and' before qatal verb, preceded by qatal clause
- 327: Conjunction wə 'and' before qatal verb, preceded by wayyiqtol clause
- 367: Conjunction wə 'and' before participle, preceded by qatal clause
- 372: Conjunction wa- 'and' before wayyiqtol, preceded by qatal clause
- 376: Conjunction wa- 'and' before wayyiqtol, preceded by participle clause
- 504: Conjunction kî 'for' before verbless clause, preceded by infinitive clause
- 717: Conjunction ṭerem 'before' before yiqtol, preceded by wayyiqtol clause
- 824: Conjunction ləmaʿan 'in order to' before yiqtol, preceded by wayyiqtol clause
- 999: Start of direct speech

List of abbreviated terms

Rhetorical terms: background (Back), circumstance (Circ), contrast (Cont), elaboration (Elab), purpose (Purp), restatement (Rest), sequence (Sequ), summary (Summ), volitional result (VRes).

Grammatical terms: discourse marker (*DM*), conjunction (*Cj*), core coordination (*CoCo*), core subordination (*CoSu*), core cosubordination (*CoCs*), predicate subordination (*PrSu*), relative clause (*Rel*).

Notes

1. Groves (1989) has tagged the Michigan-Westminster text morphologically, Andersen and Forbes (1983, 1992) have coded particles and clause divisions, Lowery (1985) has analyzed coherence statistically, and Bergen (1984) has developed a program for description of verb structural profiles.

2. Commercial software for lexical retrieval (e.g., Bible Windows) is now being succeeded by syntactic concordance applications in the ECA program (Talstra 1992c).

3. Cf. Talstra's criticism (1991a:181) of merely labeling elements in a data base instead of letting linguistic programs do the analysis.

4. For the full system of codes, see Groves et al.(1992:124-27) and the list of syntactic codes following this article.

5. The grammar thus explicates how Hebrew can have "two or three links [that] form . . . a complex within the whole" (Longacre 1989:70).

6. Note the discussion of hypotaxis in Mann, Matthiessen, and Thompson (1992:66-68).

7. A notable exception is Peckham's (1984) structural exposition.

8. The syntax of vv. 14-18 is overloaded (Butler 1983:39; Soggin 1972:48) by an expansive style (Boling 1982:168). For its grammar, see especially Otto (1973:33).

9. For abbreviations like discourse marker (*DM*), relative clause (*Rel*), conjunction (*Cj*), and predicate subordination (*PrCs*), see the list of grammatical and rhetorical terms at the end of this article.

10. It is thus only partly true that "tradition has tried to locate the miracle exactly in 3:16" (Butler 1983:48), because the feet touching the water is highly foregrounded.

11. The predicate subordination תָּמּוּ נִכְרָתוּ has completive aspect before a semantic verb.

12. Indetermination may be caused by an adaptation to the forms of 4:3b and 8c (Vogt 1965:136, n. 3), or the article left out to avoid cacophony before א (Gesenius and Kautzsch 1909:126z [429]). Otto (1973:38-39, n. 3, and 103) rejects this only because he needs a set for each of his sources.

13. Usually "Biblical Hebrew is extremely circumspect in the identification of new participants (especially minor ones) who are brought into a narrative" (Longacre 1989:31).

14. This is out of chronological order, but it is in a clear logical contrastive relationship to the preceding still-standing priests. Thus it is a parenthetical remark (Saydon 1950:203).

References

Actes du Troisieme Colloque. 1992. *Actes du Troisieme Colloque International Bible et Informatique: Interpretation, hermeneutique, competance informatique.* Paris and Geneve: Champion-Slatkine.

Andersen, Francis I., and Dean A. Forbes. 1983. "Prose particle" counts of the Hebrew Bible. In *The Word of the Lord shall go forth: Essays in honor of David Noel Freedman*, ed. Carol L. Meyers and M. O'Connor, 165-83. Winona Lake: Eisenbrauns.

———. 1992. On marking clause boundaries. In *Actes du Troisiem Colloque*, 181-202.

Bergen, R. 1984. *Discourse analysis software.* Hannibal, Mo.: Center for the Study of Technology in Ministry

Boling, Robert G. 1982. *Joshua: A new translation with notes and commentary.* Anchor Bible. Garden City: Doubleday.

Butler, Trent C. 1983. *Joshua.* Word biblical commentary, vol. 7. Waco: Word.

Dik, Simon. 1989. The structure of the clause. In *The theory of functional grammar.* Dordrecht: Foris.

Foley, William A., and Robert D. Van Valin. 1984. *Functional syntax and universal grammar.* Cambridge Studies in Linguistics, 38. Cambridge University Press.

Gesenius, Wilhelm, and E. Kautzsch. 1909. *Wilhelm Gesenius' Hebräische Grammatik völlig umgearbeitet von E Kautzsch.* 28th ed. Leipzig: Verlag von F. C. Vogel.

Gesenius, W., E. Kautzsch, and E. Cowley. 1910. *Gesenius' Hebrew grammar.* 2d ed. Oxford: Clarendon.

Groves, J. Alan. 1989. On computers and Hebrew morphology. In *Computer assisted analysis of biblical texts: Papers read at the workshop on the occasion of the tenth anniversary of the "Werkgroep Informatica,"* ed. Eep Talstra. Applicatio, vol. 7, pp. 45-86. Amsterdam: VU University Press.

Groves, J. Alan, Hendrik-Jan Bosman, J. Henk Harsen, and Eep Talstra. 1992. *User manual quest: Eelectronic concordance qpplication for the Hebrew Bible.* Haarlem: Nederlands Bijbelgenootschap.

Hardmeier, Christof. 1992. Computer-assisted perception of texts and its hermeneutic relevance. In Actes du Troisieme Colloque 1992, 365-76.

Longacre, Robert E. 1979. The discourse structure of the flood narrative. *Journal of the American Academy of Religion*, Supplement Series 47.1 (March):89-133.

———. 1989. *Joseph: A story of divine providence: a text theoretical and textlinguistic analysis of Genesis 37 and 39-48.* Winona Lake, Ind.: Eisenbrauns.

———. 1992. The discourse strategy of an appeals letter. In *Discourse description: Diverse linguistic analyses of a fund-raising text*, ed. William C. Mann and Sandra A. Thompson, 109-30. Pragmatics and Beyond, New Series, 16. Amsterdam and Philadelphia: John Benjamins.

Lowery, Kirk Edward. 1985. *Toward a discourse grammar of Biblical Hebrew.* Ph.D. diss., Ann Arbor, Mich. (PR:UMI no. 8519127.)

Mann, William C., Christian M. I. M. Matthiessen, and Sandra A. Thompson. 1992. Rhetorical structure theory and text analysis. In *Discourse description: Diverse linguistic analyses of a fund-raising text*, ed. William C. Mann and Sandra A. Thompson. Pragmatics and Beyond, New Series, 16. Amsterdam and Philadelphia: John Benjamins.

Otto, Eckart. 1973. *Das Mazzotfest in Gilgal.* Beiträge zur Wissenschaft vom Alten und Neuen Testaments, 107. Stuttgart: W. Kohlhammer Verlag.

Peckham, Brian. 1984. The composition of Joshua 3-4. *Catholic Biblical Quarterly* 46:413-31.
Polzin, Robert M. 1980. Deuteronomy, Joshua, Judges. In *Moses and the Deuteronomist: A literary study of the deuteronomic history*. New York: Seabury Press.
Saydon, Paul P. 1950. The crossing of the Jordan: Josue 3; 4. *Catholic Biblical Quarterly* 12:194-207.
Soggin, J. Alberto. 1972. *Joshua: A commentary*. Old Testament Library. Philadelphia and London: SCM and Westminster.
Talstra, Eep. 1991. Hebrew syntax: Clause types and clause hierarchy. In *Studies in Hebrew and Aramaic syntax presented to Professor J. Hoftijzer*, ed. K. Jongeling, H. L. Murre-van den Berg, and L. van Rompay, 180-93. Leiden: J. Brill.
———. 1992a. Text grammar and Biblical Hebrew: The viewpoint of Wolfgang Schneider. *Journal of Translation and Textlinguistics* 5:269-97.
———. 1992b. Text grammar and computer: The balance of interpretation and calculation. In Actes du Troisieme Colloque, 135-49.
———. 1992c. Demonstration ECA database and retrieval software. In Actes du Troisieme Colloque, 605-11.
Talstra, Eep, and Ferenc Postma. 1989. On texts and tools: A short history of the Werkgroep Informatica (1977-1987). In *Computer assisted analysis of biblical texts: Papers read at the workshop on the occasion of the tenth anniversary of the "Werkgroep Informatica,"* ed. Eep Talstra. Applicatio, vol. 7, pp. 9-27. Amsterdam: VU University Press.
Van Dijk, Teun, and Walter Kintsch. 1983. *Strategies of discourse comprehension*. New York: Academic Press.
Van Valin, Robert D. 1993. A synopsis of role and reference grammar. In *Advances in Role and Reference Grammar*, ed. R. D. van Valin. *Current Issues in Linguistic Theory*, vol. 82, pp. 1-164. Amsterdam and Philadelphia: John Benjamins.
Verheij, A. J. C., and Eep Talstra. 1992. Crunching participles: An aspect of computer assisted syntactical analysis demonstrated on Isaiah 1-12. In *A prophet on the screen: Computerized description of Isaianic texts,* ed. Eep Talstra and A. L. H. M. Van Wieringen, Applicatio, vol. 9, pp. 21-33. Amsterdam: VU University Press.
Vogt, E. 1965. Die Erzählung vom Jordanübergang, Josue 3-4. *Biblica* 46:125-48.

13

EVIL SPIRITS AND ECCENTRIC GRAMMAR
A Study of the Relationship between Text and Meaning in Hebrew Narrative

Robert D. Bergen

> This textlinguistic study of 1 Sam. 16:13–23 correlates the passage's lexical and grammatical features with its semantic content and demonstrates that a significant relationship exists between the occurrence of statistically rare morphosyntactic structures and significant semantic content. The three most morphosyntactically marked sections are 14a–b, 21c–e, and 22b–23g. These sections also convey the unit's central semantic themes: (1) David's fitness, as God's anointed, to be Israel's king; (2) Saul's unfitness, as God's rejected, to be Israel's king; and (3) the sterling quality of David's actions toward Saul. The conclusion is drawn that adequate textual analysis ought to account for the presence and location of statistically deviant lexical and clause features within a text, since such features serve as clues to the author's semantic intentions for the text.

Within recent years the field of linguistics has produced a series of insights that are fundamentally altering the modern view of language. Led by American discourse linguists such as Robert Longacre and Ilah Fleming, a new foundation of presuppositions about language has been laid that promises to support productive research in language studies. I believe that this foundation will support meaningful research in the world of biblical studies as well. This article is based on axioms associated with the new linguistics.

1. Assumptions and insights from modern linguistics

1.1 Written language is communication

The most basic axiom about language is that it involves communication, the transference of facts, ideas, beliefs, and/or attitudes from one being to another. Written language, too, is a medium for communicating. This axiom serves as the primary assumption upon which all discourse linguistics is based.

1.2 Written language is a shared hierarchical code

In order for written communication to occur, it is necessary for both the writer and reader to share a mutually understood set of symbols which possess agreed-upon meanings. In other words, communication requires a "convention of significance."

This basic truth about language presents something of a problem for those who study the biblical text, for many aspects of the convention of significance for the original languages are either no longer accessible to us or have not yet been identified. Anyone who doubts this need only review scholars' opinions of the Hebrew verbal system (see McFall 1982). To say that we do not yet understand all of the language code of the biblical languages is not to say that we cannot recover any more of the code than we now possess. In fact, modern discourse linguistics suggests that it can be done.

Written language texts can be understood to consist of a highly limited set of repeated physical marks. In the case of Biblical Hebrew, that set originally consisted of twenty-two members (letters); in the case of Greek, twenty-four. These letters are the "atoms" of which all the "molecules," "crystals," and "granites" of the language are composed. Units at one level of language organization serve as the formative basis for the units of successively higher levels of language structure.

These building blocks function as symbols that simultaneously represent two different kinds of metaphysical structures—morphosyntactic and semantic. That is, all structures within text possess (1) grammatical function and (2) meaning. For example, a word may simultaneously be a direct object and possess the meaning "house."

The building blocks are given unique identities by modifying the order, kind, and quantity of materials present in them. Within a given language, a relatively small number of structures are utilized far more frequently than others. Belonging to the "subset of the chosen," they perform specific, common communication tasks. Other less frequently employed structures are reserved for special purposes.

1.3 Some parts of a text are marked as more important than others

Since written language is a medium for the transference of facts, ideas, beliefs, and attitudes, it follows that a writer will drop some hints within a text to assist the reader in the task of figuring out which parts are more important than others. In other words, language texts are both semantically and grammatically contoured. The creator of a text *intends* some of the materials to be interpreted as more important than others.

One means that authors often use to mark semantically noteworthy materials is with statistically rare morphosyntactic features such as rare spellings, odd lexical items, irregular clause structures, and other higher-level deviations from established norms within a given genre. Prominent semantic features may often be identified by locating the unusual morphosyntactic grammatical features. Writers often encode one portion of a text as more important than others through the use of these statistically unusual features, so by identifying them a text analyst may predict with some degree of accuracy those portions of a text that the writer intended to be most important. Portions of a text identifiable by this means are considered to be "grammatically marked."[1]

2. An example from Hebrew narrative: 1 Sam. 16:13-23

The linkage between morphosyntactic *structure* and textual *meaning* can be illustrated with numerous examples in Hebrew narrative. For my purposes here, a pericope of eleven verses from 1 Samuel will be examined to demonstrate how unusual structures at two levels of morphosyntactic textual organization are used to highlight the unusual aspects of the semantics.

2.1 A semantic analysis of 1 Sam. 16:13-23

This passage relates events associated with David's selection as the Lord's מָשִׁיחַ 'anointed one' and his early rise to prominence within Saul's household.[2] In keeping with the Israelite ideal of leadership during the pre-monarchical era, David is portrayed as a man chosen and empowered by Yahweh for the challenging tasks before him.[3] As Yahweh's anointed, he fitly performs a task beyond the capacity of other royal servants, namely the removal of a malicious evil spirit from Israel's first citizen.

The initial two verses of this passage strike a surprising contrast between God's actions toward David and Saul. Even as God's Spirit penetrates the young shepherd, it departs from the venerable king.[4] However, God has not entirely abandoned Saul; a tormenting evil spirit is sent as a sometime substitute for the divine presence.

Verses 15-22 outline the series of events leading to David's position of favor in the household of Saul. Having been informed by his servants that he is afflicted by a God-sent evil spirit,[5] the king is now counseled to secure the services of a musician to foil the effects of the tormentor. A brave, powerful, and handsome harpist is recommended, and then summoned by Saul. Dutifully sent by his generous father, David ben Jesse enters the king's service on a trial basis. The evident skills of young David so impress the king that he is made a member of the royal retinue.

Verse 23 climaxes the narrative unit by depicting David's salvific activities in behalf of the king. His skillful use of the harp brings deliverance and rest for Saul's soul whenever the evil spirit strikes. Like Spirit-anointed judges of previous generations, David effects the needed deliverance from a troublesome oppressor. Unlike the judges, however, David's victory is a cosmic one; it is a triumph over the supernatural demonic world, not merely earthly foes.

From the point of view of its semantics only, the passage may be outlined as follows:
1. David is filled with the Spirit of Yahweh (16:13).
2. King Saul, abandoned by Yahweh's Spirit, is tormented by an evil spirit (16:14).
3. Saul seeks relief from the evil spirit (16:15–22).
4. David provides Saul with relief from the evil spirit (16:23).

2.2 A morphosyntactic analysis of 1 Sam. 16:13–23

In this section the results of three different types of linguistic analysis will be applied to traditionally overlooked dimensions of 1 Sam. 16:13–23.

2.2.1 A clause-level contour analysis

The Center for the Study of Technology in Ministry (hereafter CSTIM) at Hannibal-LaGrange College in Hannibal, Missouri, is using a language-research technique called "clause-level contouring." In narrative texts, clause-level contouring is performed by first of all separating quotational from nonquotational materials. Then the nonquotational materials, which include the narrative genre clauses and occasional embedded nonnarrative materials (e.g., descriptions, evaluative comments) are examined. The morphology of each nonquotational clause is noted, and the structure of each successive clause is indicated on a linear chart.

In order to produce a clause-level grammatical contour of a given text, clause morphologies can be categorized in a general way by identifying the grammatical features within the two primary parts of the overall structure: those of the preverb and verb slots.[6] At the CSTIM a set of abbreviations has been worked out to identify features associated with Hebrew narrative materials. These are used in Table 1.

Table 1. A grammatical contour of 1 Sam. 16:13-23

Location	Pre-Verb Mat.	Verb Mat.	Prominence Value
16:13a	–	WI	1.9
16:13b	–	WI	1.9
16:13c	–	WI	1.9
16:13d	–	WI	1.9
16:13e	–	WI	1.9
16:14a	WS	P	54.1
16:14b	–	WPSf	2840.7
16:15a	–	WI	1.9
16:17a	–	WI	1.9
16:18a	–	WI	1.9
16:18b	–	WI	1.9
16:19a	–	WI	1.9
16:19b	–	WI	1.9
16:20a	–	WI	1.9
16:20b	–	WI	1.9
16:21a	–	WI	1.9
16:21b	–	WI	1.9
16:21c	–	WISf	49.0
16:21d	–	WIx	29.0
16:21e	–	Pt	43.0
16:22a	–	WI	1.9
16:22b	–	PrIf	15.6
16:23a	–	WPx	454.5
16:23b	–	PrIfx	1623.3
16:23c	–	WP	96.3
16:23d	–	WP	96.3
16:23e	–	WP	96.3
16:23f	–	WP	96.3
16:23g	–	WP	96.3

Key:
- – = Empty slot
- I = Imperfect verb
- If = Infinitive
- Ifx = Infinitive of existential verb
- Ix = Imperfect of existential verb
- P = Perfect verb
- Pr = Prepositional prefix
- Pt = Participle
- S = Subject
- Sf = Pronominal suffix
- W = *waw*

The next step is to identify points of grammatical prominence (those that are "marked") among the more common ("unmarked") structures. Within 1 Sam. 16:13-23 are contained 29 different narrative framework clause structures. As might be expected by anyone who has studied Biblical Hebrew, the majority, 55 percent (16), of these clauses begin with a *wayyiqtol* verb. This percentage is in keeping with nonquotational narrative framework materials generally.[7] *Wayyiqtol* clauses are the structures of choice in Biblical Hebrew for presenting chronologically successive events. Because these structures are used so frequently, materials contained in them are structurally unmarked at the clause level.

The plane of *wayyiqtol* verbs in 16:13-23 is interrupted at three points with variant structures. The first of these points of grammatical irregularity is found in 14a-b. The constructions contained in this dyad are: (1) a *waw*-plus-subject-plus-*qatal*-verb clause (hereafter WSP) and (2) a *weqatal*-plus-pronominal suffix clause (hereafter WPSf). WSP constructions occur less than two percent of the time in standard Hebrew narrative, while WPSf clauses occur less than one thirtieth of one percent of the time. These clauses express Yahweh's removal of his Spirit from Saul and the tormenting of the king by an evil spirit.

The second zone of clause-level irregularity is 16:21c-e. In these three clauses Saul's appreciation of David is given grammatical highlighting. Saul "loves" David and takes steps to incorporate him into his permanent staff.

The final and most extensive highlighted portion stretches across eight clauses from 22b-23g. Four different statistically deviant structural types are employed in this region. The predominant type employs a *weqatal* verb in a structural pattern that occurs only about one percent of the time in Biblical Hebrew narrative. Such clauses normally convey intermittently repeated actions without definite reference to time. An examination of the semantic content of 22b-23g suggests that David brought relief to Saul on a number of occasions.[8] David's ongoing and consistent success in combating Saul's ills is thus given prominence through a conglomeration of unusual constructions.

Table 2 identifies the frequency of occurrence of the clause morphologies present in 1 Sam. 16:13-23 in comparison with a body of data collected from all the nonquotational passages of the Pentateuch, the nonquotational passages of 1-2 Samuel, and the nonquotational passages of the Book of Jonah.

On the basis of this table it is clear that the most unusual structure present in the nonquotational features of 16:13-23 is the WPSf structure in

14b. This clause utilizes a morphology found only three times within the entire comparative database. The magnitude of statistical deviation is great enough to suggest that the clause would have caught the attention of a fluent speaker of Biblical Hebrew. Because the grammatical pattern differed so significantly from the established norms, the auditor's brain would have had to perform additional tasks in its efforts to cope with this clause structure. The increased effort expended in the process would have had the practical effect of causing information in that clause to be highlighted. Thus, the information receiving the most clause-level grammatical highlighting in the pericope is the statement that an evil spirit from Yahweh was tormenting Saul.[9]

Table 2. Comparative frequency of clause structures

Construction		Frequency in Database (percentage)	Frequency in 16:13–23 (percentage)
Pre-Verb	Verb		
–	WI	50.70	55.17
–	PrIf	6.39	3.45
–	WIx	3.36	3.4
–	Pt	2.40	3.45
–	WISf	1.89	3.45
WS	P	1.71	3.45
–	WP	1.04	17.24
–	WPx	0.24	3.45
–	PrIfx	0.07	3.45
–	WPSf	0.03	3.45

2.2.2 A verb-prominence contour analysis

Verb-prominence contouring is a form of analysis developed specifically for text-level language research. Its purpose is to identify portions of text that portray actions that are unusual within the society or portray common actions in unusual ways. The underlying assumption is that the employment of odd verbs produces a natural highlighting of the actions denoted by these verbs.

In order to produce a verb-prominence contour, verb-prominence values are assigned to clauses based on the relative rarity of the lexical root of the verb found at the center of each clause. The larger the verb-prominence value, the less frequently the verbal root is found in the database of comparable materials. Table 3 lists the lexical forms and associated prominence values for each of the twenty-nine structures found in the nonquotational sections of 1 Sam. 16:13-23.

Table 3. Verb-prominence contour of 1 Sam. 16:13-23

Location	Prominence Verb	Value	Location	Prominence Verb	Value
16:13a	לקח 'take'	50.9	16:21a	בוא 'come'	24.4
16:13b	משח 'anoint'	811.4	16:21b	עמד 'stand'	180.3
16:13c	צלח 'be strong'	1262.1	16:21c	אהב 'love'	568.0
16:13d	קום 'be high'	104.1	16:21d	היה 'be'	20.4
16:13e	הלך 'go'	43.7	16:21e	נשא 'raise'	105.2
16:14a	סור 'turn aside'	420.7	16:22a	שלח 'send'	76.8
16:14b	בעת 'be terrified'	11359.0	16:22b	אמר 'say'	6.4
16:15a	אמר 'say'	6.4	16:23a	היה 'be'	20.4
16:17a	אמר 'say'	6.4	16:23b	היה 'be'	20.4
16:18a	ענה 'reply'	147.5	16:23c	לקח 'take'	50.9
16:18b	אמר 'say'	6.4	16:23d	נגן 'play an instrument'	3786.3
16:19a	שלח 'send'	76.8	16:23e	רוח 'be relieved'	11359.0
16:19b	אמר 'say'	6.4	16:23f	טוב 'be good'	757.3
16:20a	לקח 'take'	50.9	16:23g	סור 'turn aside'	420.7
16:20b	שלח 'send'	76.8			

The verb prominence chart indicates that a number of events within 16:13-23 stand out as unusual. The most unusual ones seem to have occurred in three primary clusters: 13b-c, 14a-b, and 23d-g.

The first pair of clauses portrays David's anointing with the attendant bestowal of the Spirit of Yahweh on him. The verbs משח 'anoint' and צלח 'be strong' were employed only 14 and 9 times respectively in the 11,359 constructions included in the database. Word-level prominencing, like clause-level prominencing, has the effect of drawing attention to these actions.

The second dyad of prominent verbs is found in 14a–b, a section that informs the reader of Saul's loss of the Spirit of Yahweh and his torment from a divinely sent evil spirit. The lexical roots of the verbs used here are סור 'turn aside' and בעת 'be terrified'. The more common of the two, סור, is found 27 times out of 11,359. Within the context of the database בעת is a hapax legomenon.[10] This fact suggests that 14b, the depiction of the evil spirit's malevolent actions against Saul, is at the top of the verb-prominence table for the pericope.

The final section occurs in the latter portion of v. 23, with the depiction of David playing the harp, Saul's experience of relief, and the evil spirit's departure from the king. The verb roots of this section, along with their frequency of employment, are as follows: נגן 'play an instrument' (3), רוח 'be relieved' (1), טוב 'be good' (15), and סור 'turn aside' (27). It is within this section that the only other unique verb is found (רוח), in 23e, a clause that describes Saul's relief from the evil spirit. Thus it stands as a statistical pinnacle complementing and answering 14b's portrayal of Saul's agony.

2.2.3 A Bergen Value contour analysis

A third means of producing a contour of extended stretches of Hebrew narrative is through the use of a computer program under development at the CSTIM.[11] Among other things, the program analyzes data related to seven different variable factors within Biblical Hebrew clauses and determines on the basis of these features how relatively normal or abnormal a given clause is.

The degree of normalcy is expressed numerically through a statistic known as the Bergen Value. The higher the value, the more unusual the clause profile. The seven factors used in the production of the value are: pre-verb grammatical features, verb-slot grammatical features, verb stem, verb triconsonant frequency, unit length, quote length, and subject type. The Bergen Value thus incorporates the results of the two previous studies, yet goes beyond them to produce a broader analysis.

To produce the Bergen Value contour, the Bergen Values were assigned by the computer when the text analysis program analyzed a data file related to 16:13–23. Table 4 provides a listing of the values associated with each clause of this pericope.

Values assigned to the twenty-nine structures ranged from 4.6 to 23.0. Eight of the twenty-nine were given values that indicated statistically significant deviations from the norm of Hebrew narrative.[12] Six of these eight were present in 23a–g. The other two individual units were 14b.[13]

The first occurrence of particularly unusual constructions is found in 14a–b. Outstanding features of 14a contributing to its score of 13.5 include the information order (WSP), the employment of a relatively rare verbal root (סור 'turn aside'), and the presence of a supernatural subject (Spirit of Yahweh). Clause 14b is actually the construction with the highest Bergen Value in the narrative framework of 1 Samuel (23.0). Besides possessing an unusual information order (WPSf) and containing a rare verbal root (בעת 'be terrified'), a supernatural subject is present (evil spirit) and the verb's stem, piel, is one employed less than seven percent of the time in narrative framework materials.

Table 4. Bergen Value contour of 1 Sam. 16:13-23

Location	Bergen Value	Location	Bergen Value
16:13a	5.9	16:21a	4.6
16:13b	8.1	16:21b	6.5
16:13c	12.7	16:21c	11.1
16:13d	6.0	16:21d	7.0
16:13e	5.1	16:21e	9.1
16:14a	13.5	16:22a	5.8
16:14b	23.0	16:22b	7.2
16:15a	6.1	16:23a	13.8
16:17a	5.0	16:23b	13.9
16:18a	6.3	16:23c	9.2
16:18b	5.7	16:23d	15.7
16:19a	6.3	16:23e	16.5
16:19b	5.1	16:23f	13.8
16:20a	7.8	16:23g	13.5
16:20b	6.8		

The primary section of the text that is highlighted on the Bergen Value contour is 23a–g. Relatively unusual information patterns and verb roots are primarily responsible for the high values here. Worth noting is the fact that the only other non-qal verb present in the twenty-nine constructions studied was located in this section, namely piel, in 23d. As has been previously noted, these verses depict David's ongoing deliverance of Saul from the oppressive spirit.

2.3 Correlating the morphosyntactic contours with the semantics

The contour studies of section 2.2 demonstrate the frequency-based unevennesses that exist among the numerous features of the 1 Sam. 16:13-23 narrative. First, the morphosyntactic contour study showed that, at various points within the text, highly atypical information patterns were employed, often in clusters. As to verbal roots, rarely utilized lexemes were likewise often found packed together in tight configurations. Then the study of the Bergen Values, which reflect the degree of adherence to a broader range of clause-structural norms for Hebrew narrative structures, identified certain parts of 16:13-23 as being much less normal than others.

With these observations now in mind, that quintessentially American question may now be asked, So what? What of value have we gained from all the charts and numbers presented to this point in the paper? The answer to this question lies in the correlation between the morphosyntactic contours and the semantics of the text.

Table 5 suggests a correspondence between the most unusual or thematically significant events of 16:13-23 and the clauses that depart from established norms of Biblical Hebrew narrative framework materials. This observation leads to two tentative conclusions.

First, statements of events without parallel in the Hebrew biblical materials may be couched in highly atypical morphosyntactic structures. Within the passage under consideration, at least two events possess no real analog within the Hebrew Bible: a king being personally tormented by an evil spirit; and an evil spirit being exorcised—through music, no less! Both of these events were expressed using morphosyntactic features rare enough to place them in a class by themselves.

Second, events that are of primary thematic significance may also be couched in grammatical structures that deviate markedly from established norms. Fitting neatly into this category are the narrator's observations that the Spirit of Yahweh penetrated David (13c), that the same Spirit left Saul (14a), and that Saul loved David (21c). Collectively, these three statements summarize three of the most important themes of 1 Samuel:
    (1) David's fitness, as God's anointed, to be Israel's king.
    (2) Saul's unfitness, as God's rejected, to be Israel's king.
    (3) The sterling quality of David's actions toward Saul—his actions evoked even the king's admiration.

Table 5. Value and content correlations for 1 Sam. 16:13-23

Location	Bergen Value	Gramm. Prom. Value	Verb. Prom. Value	Summary of Content
16:13a	5.9	1.9	50.9	Samuel took the horn of anointing oil
16:13b	8.1	1.9	811.4	Samuel anointed David in the midst of his brothers
16:13c	12.7	1.9	1262.1	The Spirit of Yahweh came upon David then and remained on him
16:13d	6.0	1.9	104.2	Samuel arose
16:13e	5.1	1.9	43.7	Samuel went to Ramah
16:14a	13.5	54.1	420.7	The Spirit of Yahweh left Saul
16:14b	23.0	2840.7	11359.0	An evil spirit from Yahweh tormented Saul
16:15a	6.1	1.9	6.4	Saul's servants told him to get someone to relieve him of the evil spirit
16:17a	5.0	1.9	6.4	Saul told his servants to find someone to relieve him of the evil spirit
16:18a	6.3	1.9	147.5	One of Saul's servants answered him
16:18b	5.7	1.9	6.4	Saul's servant told him about Jesse's son, who could help him
16:19a	6.3	1.9	76.8	Saul's servant sent messengers to Jesse
16:19b	5.1	1.9	6.4	Saul told Jesse to send David to the royal household
16:20a	7.8	1.9	50.9	Jesse gathered provisions to send to Saul
16:20b	6.8	1.9	76.8	Jesse sent provisions with David to Saul
16:21a	4.6	1.9	24.4	David came to Saul
16:21b	6.5	1.9	180.3	David attended to Saul
16:21c	11.1	49.0	568.0	Saul liked David very much
16:21d	7.0	29.0	20.4	David became Saul's
16:21e	9.1	43.0	105.2	bearer of equipment
16:22a	5.8	1.9	76.8	Saul sent to Jesse
16:22b	7.2	15.6	6.4	to tell him he wished David to remain in service to him
16:23a	13.8	454.5	20.4	And it was
16:23b	13.9	1623.3	20.4	whenever the evil spirit from God came on Saul

16:23c	9.2	96.3	50.9	David would take the harp
16:23d	15.7	96.3	3786.3	David would play it with his hand
16:23e	16.5	96.3	11359.0	Saul would experience relief
16:23f	13.8	96.3	757.3	Saul would get better
16:23g	13.5	96.3	420.7	The evil spirit would leave Saul

3. Implications for biblical studies

Three implications arise from the previous study. First, biblical exegesis that fails to take into account the morphosyntactic contours of text overlooks significant aspects of the message deposited by the producer(s) of the text. Structural contouring techniques provide information useful for formulating and/or confirming conclusions related to the semantic dimension of text. Author-planted hints present within usually ignored dimensions of language are useful in guiding the reader to author-selected points of significance in a text. Failure to investigate these features increases the probability that flawed conclusions will arise from the exegetical undertaking.

Second, productive sociological research on ancient Israelite culture may be carried out by examining the morphosyntactic contours of Biblical Hebrew narratives. By identifying zones of irregularity within a text and checking the semantic content in these sections, it may be possible with greater objectivity to determine what was considered normal versus exceptional and insignificant versus important for the creator of the text and thus for the society. A new and potentially enlightening chapter in sociolinguistics may now be written.

Finally, artificial-intelligence text-analysis tools that make use of text contouring techniques can be developed to assist in the exegesis and interpretation of the Bible. Hannibal-LaGrange's language-analysis program, which presently interprets Hebrew text-related data files and determines thematically central characters and author-intended thematic centers, is but the first of what may be a long line of artificial intelligence programs for Bible analysis. Using text-contouring techniques in connection with other analysis techniques, reader-response criticism in which the respondent is a computer may be not only a possibility but an inevitability.

Notes

1. Marking may also occur within the semantic domain through the employment of socioculturally significant places, events, times, and persons within certain subunits of a text. Those portions of a text that contain either grammatical or sociocultural highlighting are said to be marked. Often these two forms of "prominencing" will overlap—statistically unusual lexical and structural units will be used to mention events or ideas that are socioculturally significant.

2. Both older and more recent commentaries normally treat v. 13 as the conclusion of one pericope and v. 14 as the beginning of another—most recently Klein (1983:157-67) and, earlier, Kirkpatrick (1891:148-52) and Smith (n.d., 143-50). One exception to this is Gordon (1988:149-53), who treats the chapter as a whole.

I am treating the pericopes 16:1-13 and 16:14-23 as inseparably linked, due to the clause constructions. In Biblical Hebrew narrative the *waw*-subject-perfect-verb construction (here 14a) consistently conveys information that is chronologically consecutive and alternative to materials in an immediately preceding *wayyiqtol* construction (in this case 13c). Assuming this is true, the writer was intending the audience to understand that at the very moment when David was being infused with the Spirit of Yahweh, the Spirit was being withdrawn from Saul and replaced with an evil spirit. For more than a hundred additional examples drawn from the narrative materials of the Pentateuch, see Bergen (1986).

3. Other Israelites portrayed in OT literature as having received a special spirit of enablement include Bezalel (Exod. 31:1-3; 35:30-31); Moses (Num. 11:17); the seventy elders (Num. 11:25); Joshua (Deut. 34:9); Othniel (Judg. 3:10); Gideon (Judg. 6:34); Jephthah (Judg. 11:29); Samson (Judg. 14:6, 19; 15:14); Saul (1 Sam. 10:10; 11:6; 19:23); messengers of Saul (1 Sam. 19:20); Amasa (1 Chron. 12:18); Azariah (2 Chron. 15:1); Zechariah (2 Chron. 24:20); Isaiah (Isa. 61:1); and Ezekiel (Ezek. 3:24; 11:5). Five of these were specifically mentioned as having received the Spirit of Yahweh just prior to the performance of some act of deliverance (Othniel, Gideon, Jephthah, Samson, and Saul). The juxtaposition of David's anointing episode with his exorcistic service to Saul suggests that David was performing this service with divine enablement.

4. Cf. Samson's loss of Yahweh's presence prior to his own downfall (Judg. 16:20). Clearly the narrator intended 16:14 as an allusion to this premonarchical occurrence. For the literate Israelite reader, Samson's disastrous end due to the Philistines following the Lord's departure would cast an ominous shadow over Saul's future. The reader is thus somewhat prepared for Saul's own Philistine-related death.

5. A prominent motif in the Saul cycle (1 Samuel 9-31) is that of the king's spiritual blindness. In the present passage the narrator depicts Saul's servants

as the ones who give definition to his problem and suggest a means of correcting it. Previously (9:6-8) it was another servant who suggested to Saul that he seek a man of God to obtain the needed help. On yet another occasion, Saul's servants were shown to be more insightful than their king when they observed God's hand in Jonathan's deliverance (14:45). Additional examples of Saul's blindness are found in his misjudgment of godly Ahimelech's actions (22:13) and his employment of necromancy (28:7-19). Less spiritual examples of Saul's dullness may be seen in 17:58; 24:4-16; and 26:12-17.

6. Research has indicated that the most prominent zones within a clause are those preceding and including the verb word (see Buth 1985:1).

7. See Table 2. The statistics are based on a study of 11,359 nonquotational clauses taken from the Pentateuch, 1-2 Samuel, and the Book of Jonah. The study was carried out from 1981 until the present by the author working in association with Master's level students at the University of Texas at Arlington and Southwestern Baptist Theological Seminary, Fort Worth, Texas.

8. A comparison of various English translations of the passage reflects this general understanding as well (cf. Douay, RSV, NAS, NEB, TEV, NIV, and NKJV). Major versions not interpreting 16:23 frequentatively are the KJV and ASV.

9. Not only is the grammar associated with this statement unique, so is the event contained in the clause. Nowhere else in the Hebrew Bible is an individual portrayed as being tormented (בעת) by an evil spirit.

10. The verb בעת is employed sixteen times in the Hebrew Bible, making it one of the rarer verbs. Of these occurrences, three of them are in nonquotational stretches of narrative: 1 Sam. 16:14; Dan. 8:17; and Esther 7:6.

11. This program, the "Discourse Sensitive Text Analysis Program," is designed to be operated in a DOS environment and run on an IBM PC-compatible microcomputer. Written in Turbo Pascal, it has been under development since 1985. Besides producing Bergen Values, the program performs a statistical analysis of the data being examined. In its present form it also performs limited artificial-intelligence functions, determining who (or what) is the thematically central character of a text and determining what portion of a text was marked by the author as most significant. A pre-release form of the program and database is available from Hannibal-LaGrange's CSTIM.

Such a chart is of value because it indicates which narrative framework verbs were employed in comparison with a much larger body of Hebrew narrative. Employment of statistically rare verbs gives attestation to atypical events or atypical portrayals of events. Such deviations from norms have the practical effect of highlighting the semantic content.

12. A structure is considered statistically significant if its Bergen Value possesses a standard deviation greater than 1.

13. Two structures are statistically unusual without possessing a standard deviation of 1. The first of these is in 13c. Features of this clause contributing to its relatively high value (12.7) include the occurrence of a rare verb (צלח

'be strong'), an unusual category of subject (supernatural—Yahweh's Spirit), and unit length (eight words). Divine subjects are present in the database just under 10 percent of the time; clauses with eight or more words in them account for about approximately 7.4 percent of those in the database.

The lone spike in the field of otherwise moderate values from 15a–22b is 21c. The value 11.1 was due almost exclusively to an unusual information structure (*wayyiqtol*-plus-pronominal-suffix) and the verb triconsonant (אהב 'love'). Saul's love for David is here expressed.

References

Bergen, Robert D. 1986. Varieties and functions of the Hebrew *waw*-plus-subject-plus-perfect sentence constructions in the narrative framework of the Pentateuch. Ph.D. diss., Southwestern Baptist Theological Seminary, Fort Worth, Texas.

Buth, Randall. 1985. Word order in the Aramaic narratives of Daniel from the perspectives of functional grammar and discourse analysis. Paper presented at the meeting of the Society of Biblical Literature, November 23, 1985, at Anaheim, Calif.

Gordon, Robert. 1988. *1 and 2 Samuel: A commentary*. Grand Rapids: Zondervan.

Kirkpatrick, A. F. 1891. *The First Book of Samuel*. Cambridge: University Press.

Klein, Ralph. 1983. *1 Samuel*. Waco: Word.

McFall, Leslie. 1982. *The enigma of the Hebrew verbal system*. Sheffield: Almond.

Smith, Henry. n.d. *A critical and exegetical commentary on the Books of Samuel*. Edinburgh: T. and T. Clark.

14

A TEXTLINGUISTIC APPROACH TO THE BIBLICAL HEBREW NARRATIVE OF JONAH

Robert E. Longacre and Shin Ja J. Hwang

Using the Book of Jonah for illustration, we present a textlinguistic approach to Biblical Hebrew narrative, dealing with such topics as the discourse type, macrostructure, overall discourse structure (peak and profile), verb and nominal forms, and paragraph structure. We propose that the Jonah story consists of two embedded discourses, each of which has stage, prepeak episode, and peak episode, and claim that chapter 4 is crucial for the unity of the book. Varying verb/clause forms (*wayyiqtol, N + qatal,* and *qatal*) are discussed in terms of their function in discourse, along with flashback mechanisms, motion verbs, and presentative formulas. Especially intriguing is the variation in divine names, which we show to be motivated in the plot structure. Various irrealis constructions encoding "frustration" are correlated with the macrostructure of the story as to how Jonah did not want to be a messenger of mercy but Yahweh caused him to be such. A display of the paragraph structure of chapters 3–4 is given in English at the end.

Narrative discourse is a cultural universal; no culture is without some kind of stories, whether folktales, legends, or just first-person accounts such as "what-happened-to-me-yesterday." In the Bible we find a variety of discourse types, and narrative is certainly a common type, especially in the Old Testament. According to Fee and Stuart (1982:73), "The Bible contains more of the type of literature called 'narrative' than it does of any other literary type ... over 40 percent of the Old Testament is narrative." Understanding narrative structure is an important step toward understanding the Bible.

The purpose of this article is to discuss some methodological concerns in the textlinguistic analysis of Biblical Hebrew narrative, using the Book of Jonah for illustration. Textlinguistic concerns include discourse types; charting; macrostructure; overall discourse structure (peak and profile) with its paragraph and other constituent structures; verb forms (tense, aspect, mood, and voice); and nominal forms (referring to participants and props).[1]

Before we begin, we summarize here some basic assumptions underlying our textlinguistic approach. First, a typology of discourse is considered to be necessary so that rules for each type can be established. Grammatical rules for one type of discourse may be different from the others. For example, different discourse types may have a different word order in the clauses that encode their mainline information, as in Biblical Hebrew, where the order VSO (verb, subject, object) prevails in narrative, but SVO in exposition. A text may show an embedding of discourse types (e.g., a narrative within a sermon) or a skewing (e.g., an expository discourse as to the surface form but with a notional hortatory intent). By establishing such rules, complexity in some texts can be handled systematically, rather than as a chaotic mixture of different types.

Second, we assume that there is no randomness or free variation in the surface structure. Any morphosyntactic form in a text represents the author's choice whether conscious or automatic; we may not know the whys of all such choices, but we may speculate on them as implementations of differing discourse strategies. Thus, as textlinguistic analysts, we try to discern the whats (what forms and constructions occur in text), the hows (how a form like the relative clause is constructed), and the whys (why—for what purpose, in what function—the form is used).

Third, the whole and the parts are mutually elucidating in a constant interplay within a text. "The whole legislates the parts, while, in turn, a study of the parts is necessary to the comprehension of the whole" (Longacre 1989a:42). The parts need to be understood in their context. No language exists in isolation, in a decontextualized vacuum: "language is language only in context" (Longacre 1983:xv). To put it in another way, both top-down and bottom-up strategies are utilized in the processes of production, comprehension, and analysis (van Dijk and Kintsch 1983). In our textlinguistic model, "comprehension of a story results from multiple processing, including top-down (use of schema) and bottom-up (use of content and cues provided by the text)" (Hwang 1984:136); it is interactional in both directions, rather than simply in one direction.

Also, the whole is greater than the sum total of its parts. Thus, in addition to the analysis of the parts, we need to approach a text as a whole. There are three interacting factors in such a holistic approach: *macrostructure* (the overall meaning and thrust), *texture* (peak and profile, mainline and supportive information, participant reference, and other matters related to cohesion and coherence), and *constituent structure* (embedded discourses, as well as paragraphs, sentences, clauses, etc.).

Fourth, in the grammar of language, there are hierarchical levels from morpheme to stem, word, phrase, clause, sentence, paragraph, and discourse. Some of these levels may be collapsed in a given language when they are not contrastive morphosyntactically. Each level has its own unique constituent structure (e.g., subject-verb-object in the clause level; relations such as reason and result in the paragraph; stage, episodes, one of which may be peak, and closure in the narrative discourse).[2] A constituent is like a coin with two sides, one side being the slot-function in the larger structure (e.g., subject), and the other side being the filler-class (e.g., a noun phrase). We believe that textlinguistics should be based on a solid analysis of the morphosyntax of the text, along with semantic and pragmatic considerations.

1. Story as a subtype of narrative discourse

Narrative is agent oriented and action oriented (actions that are contingent–successive). When one or both of these parameters do not have the feature plus, we have procedural (– agent orientation), behavioral (– contingent-temporal succession), or expository (– agent orientation and – contingent-temporal succession, but + topic orientation and + logical succession). A third parameter, projection, distinguishes a story (– projection) from a prophecy (+ projection), and an additional parameter of tension singles out a climactic story from an episodic one (Longacre 1983, chap. 1).

The book of Jonah is a climactic story according to these parameters. It has + agent orientation (mainly oriented toward Jonah and God, along with other participants, namely the sailors and the people of Nineveh), + contingent succession (the events are temporally successive, some of which are caused by, thus contingent upon, earlier events), – projection (dealing with the events that happened, not with what-will-happen), and + tension (permeating the book and in each of the four chapters). Thus, the book is a narrative in general and a story with a climax in particular.[3]

In the book clearly there are also hortatory thematic messages, as in many stories. While there may be texts that are purely narrative, recounting what happened without any teaching implied, biblical stories customarily have some thematic message. This book has other embedded discourse types as well. Jonah's prayer in chapter 2 is poetry, which starts with a form resembling narrative (a kind of recitative) but ends with a promissory type, a subtype of hortatory. The decree of the king of Nineveh in chapter 3 is hortatory.

We add here that a specific discourse typology relevant to a given language and literature needs to be determined emically according to verb forms on the mainlines of each type, as well as other concerns. Thus, in Biblical Hebrew, prophecy (as foretelling) groups with procedural, both having *waw*-consecutive perfect (*weqatal*), rather than with narrative, which has a special tense form, the preterite (*wayyiqtol*), for its mainline material (Longacre 1992a). (Of course, the schematic categories described here in section 1 provide merely an etic starting point for arriving at emic discourse distinctions.)

2. Charting for a systematic display

A text in any language may be charted on large columnar pads into four basic columns: introducer, preposed clause/element, independent clause, postposed clause/element. Within the independent clause, and possibly in pre- and postposed clauses, subcolumns may be set up for constituents like subject (S), verb (V), and object (O), including indirect object (IO) and other elements, according to the basic order of the language. In charting a Biblical Hebrew narrative text, the first two columns (introducer and preposed element) can be combined into one, since neither of these is common. The independent clause column, being most frequent, is allotted the most space. Four subcolumns are set up within it: fronted element (preverbal S or O), V, S, and O (including IO and others). By having a separate subcolumn for fronted elements before the verb, any departure from the normal storyline coding in the verb-initial *wayyiqtol* clauses stands out.

Additional devices like color-coding and notes may be utilized. We may color-code verb forms (e.g., assigning a color for each tense/aspect); participant-reference forms such as the noun phrase, pronoun, verb inflection, and zero; or any discourse particles of interest. A "notes" column at one side is useful to make observations regarding any discourse-relevant morphosyntactic features, such as the introducers that mark section boundaries, preposed elements, and discontinuity in time, location, or participant span.

There are five main characteristics of this charting method (see Longacre and Levinsohn 1978, and Hwang 1993): (1) The sentence (not the clause) is the basic unit.[4] (2) Grammatical constituents are largely kept together. (3) Any irregularity of word order stands out. (4) Independent clauses are clearly separated from pre- and postposed dependent clauses. (5) The text is recoverable from the chart so that we may work directly with the chart in our analysis.

The chart is a tool that helps the analyst see patterns more readily. It may be modified for any particular purpose at hand as long as the charting is done consistently with preservation or indexing of the order of surface constituents.

3. Macrostructure

Any text, including biblical narratives, has a germinal idea, an overall plan at the global level which controls the content structure and the relative elaboration of the various parts of the text. This is called the macrostructure (van Dijk 1977, 1980). (Macrostructures have been posited for several biblical narratives, e.g., Longacre 1985 and 1989a). Exactly how one comes up with a macrostructure is a somewhat open question.

Van Dijk (1980:50) proposes macrorules of deletion, generalization, and construction to derive the macrostructure from an explicit text base, that is, "the text base that is made coherent by the interpolation of propositions from world knowledge." In practice, however, this procedure is problematic due to the enormous amount of material added beyond what is in the text to make all inferential information explicit. Therefore, to formulate a macrostructure for the Flood narrative, Longacre first abstracted all clauses with preterite (*wayyiqtol*) verbs, then eliminated repetitions, preliminary and consequent actions, and paraphrases, and finally reduced direct quotes to indirect summaries. For the Joseph story (Genesis 37, 39–45), however, Longacre assumed that the macrostructure surfaced in the text and surrounding context (in Gen. 45:5–8 and 50:20). Generally, one can intuitively formulate a macrostructure first, and then check this against the information given in the grammatical forms of varying weight and dominance.

We propose the following macrostructure of Jonah: Jonah did not want to become a messenger of mercy to Nineveh but Yahweh caused him to be such by the series of providential occurrences that Yahweh threw across his pathway (see sec. 6).

4. Overall discourse structure

4.1 Peak and profile

The Book of Jonah has two main parts, Jonah's fleeing from God in chapters 1–2 and his obedience in chapters 3–4. The two parts show a symmetry, each with two chapters. Note the close parallelism in setting the stage at the first three verses that begin each part.

(1) 1:1 וַיְהִי דְבַר־יְהוָה אֶל־יוֹנָה בֶן־אֲמִתַּי לֵאמֹר
And-occurred word-of Yahweh to-Jonah son-of Amittai saying

3:1 וַיְהִי דְבַר־יְהוָה אֶל־יוֹנָה שֵׁנִית לֵאמֹר
And-occurred word-of Yahweh to-Jonah (a) second-time saying

(2) 1:2 קוּם לֵךְ אֶל־נִינְוֵה הָעִיר הַגְּדוֹלָה וּקְרָא עָלֶיהָ ...
Arise, go to Nineveh, the-city the-great, and-proclaim against-her (that her wickedness has come up before me)

3:2 קוּם לֵךְ אֶל־נִינְוֵה הָעִיר הַגְּדוֹלָה וּקְרָא אֵלֶיהָ ...
Arise, go to Nineveh, the-city the-great, and-proclaim to-her (the message I give you)

(3) 1:3   וַיָּקָם יוֹנָה לִבְרֹחַ תַּרְשִׁישָׁה מִלִּפְנֵי יְהוָה ...
And-he-arose Jonah to-flee to-Tarshish from-(the)-face-of Yahweh ...

3:3   וַיָּקָם יוֹנָה וַיֵּלֶךְ אֶל־נִינְוֵה כִּדְבַר יְהוָה ...
And-he-arose Jonah and-he-went unto Nineveh according-to-(the)-word-of Yahweh ...

Verse 3 in chapter 3, although very different in content from v. 3 in chapter 1, is nevertheless parallel in structure, starting with "and-he-arose Jonah." This parallel pattern is broken at v. 4 of each passage:

(4) 1:4   וַיהוָה הֵטִיל רוּחַ־גְּדוֹלָה אֶל־הַיָּם ...
And-Yahweh he-sent wind great on the-sea ...

3:4   וַיָּחֶל יוֹנָה לָבוֹא בָעִיר מַהֲלַךְ יוֹם אֶחָד ...
And-he-started Jonah to-go into-the-city journey-of day one ...

In chapter 1, God's action following Jonah's fleeing is reported in a contrastive structure with the fronted noun "Yahweh," marking the onset of the prepeak episode after the stage set in vv. 1–3. In chapter 3, on the other hand, Jonah's action, which is expected in a calling-a-prophet script, is rather routinely reported in the usual storyline form in *wayyiqtol,* continuing on the journey started in v. 3. Thus we may view v. 4 as forming a unit with v. 3 (i.e., Jonah's nonverbal response to God's command), so that both verses function as part of the stage (vv. 1–4) of the second half of the book. The prepeak episode no longer mentions Jonah, but reports on the repenting Ninevites (3:5–9) and God's change of plan (3:10).

One might wonder if there really are stages in the two sections of the book. Admittedly, the first three verses (1:1–3) report happenings: a speech event (God's proposal) occurs followed by Jonah's nonverbal response. However, although the verb is a *wayyiqtol,* וַיְהִי 'and it happened'—the first word in v. 1—is part of a presentative formula, such as we might expect at the beginning of books and sections. Also Jonah is carefully introduced not only by name but also as "son-of Amittai" (1:1), which is typical of the stage of a story. These clues suggest that both 1:1–3 and 3:1–4 function as the stage for each half of the book respectively, while overlapping with the prepeak episode (in a wavelike, nonparticle approach).

As for participants, Jonah and God are major participants who are referred to in all four chapters, while the sailors and Ninevites are minor participants who remain nameless. The sailors and their captain are referred to only in chapter 1, and the people of Nineveh and their king only in chapter 3. The ship and the great fish are important props in the first half, and the city of Nineveh and the place where Jonah sits outside the city are the locales in the second half. In the first part, we see participants and props that may be expected in a sea-voyage script: ship, great wind, storm, sailor, captain, and fish. In the second part, we have a repentance script in the city with a king and his people in sackcloth (chap. 3), followed by a series of props created by God for a lesson on compassion: a vine, a worm, and even a scorching east wind (chap. 4).

Each half of the Book of Jonah has a series of happenings of its own, resulting from Jonah's disobedience and his obedience, with subdivisions in each. Tension is high in each of the four chapters. The reader might wonder midway in each chapter: Will the ship and the people be destroyed? Will Jonah die in the belly of fish? Will Nineveh be overturned? Will Jonah remain angry and wish to be dead? Notice that the dilemma shifts from chapter to chapter, and that the more immediate problems in chapters 1 and 3 have to do with other (pagan) people, while the problems in chapters 2 and 4 have to do with Jonah as an individual.

In the book there is an intricate interplay of an artistic plot structure at several levels. At a higher level of the text, we see Jonah's problem as a runaway from God or as a messenger of God; at a lower level, his interaction with other people and their problems, which are interwoven with his own personal dilemma; and then at an even lower level, for example, his discomfort after the vine withered.

We may postulate that the book consists of two separate embedded discourses, each of which has a stage, a prepeak episode, and a peak episode, as follows.

	Stage	Prepeak episode	Peak episode
Part 1	1:1–3	1:4–16	2:1–11
Part 2	3:1–4	3:5–10	4:1–11

After each stage with its parallel structures, the prepeak episode is highly action oriented and filled with participants. At the peak episode, other participants disappear and only Jonah is left on stage with God, revealing his true being to God. The first peak episode is the psalm-like praise and prayer section in chapter 2, remarkable in such a dramatic situation between life and death in the belly of a fish; then in chapter 4, the second peak episode is a portrayal of Jonah's anger and sullenness even when we, as disinterested observers, might say that all is well.

The peak in part 1 is marked by its being poetry. Normally, poetry outranks prose as a marked surface-structure form in the stream of narrative. Most of chapter 2 consists of poetry (2:3-10), bracketed by two verses at the beginning (2:1-2, in which God causes Jonah to be swallowed by a fish and Jonah prays to God, leading into his prayer in direct speech) and a verse at the end (2:11, in which God causes Jonah to be vomited out of the fish). The poetry itself has its own intricate structure, but is not discussed here; suffice it to note that it is a marked surface structure corresponding to high tension in the plot structure.

The peak in part 2 has its own peculiar features that are contrastive with the peak of the first embedded discourse and the rest of the book. It is here, especially in 4:9, that a real dialogue exchange between Jonah and God occurs for the first time in the book. The chapter is highly interactional in nature, full of dialogues: speech verbs occur seven times. Dialogue is a shift up in the vividness scale (going from narration proper to dialogue to drama) and in many languages is a peak-marking feature. There are a number of quick happenings interspersed among the dialogues: Jonah going out of the city, sitting under a shelter, still waiting to see what would happen to the city (4:5); God preparing a vine for shade, a worm chewing the vine, and a scorching east wind and sun (4:6, 7, 8).

The episode, in fact the whole book, ends with a dialogue paragraph that is unresolved: Jonah's response to God's speech in 4:10-11 is not explicitly given in the book. It may be that the resolution of the story is intended to be left dangling for the reader's own reaction, or it may that the resolution is considered obvious (that Jonah would concede). This type of unresolved dialogue paragraph ending with a question can be poignant, leaving open a range of possible interactions from an active reader. The book of Nahum also ends with a question.

4.2 The role of chapter 4 in the unity of the book

There have been some questions as to the role of chapter 4 in regard to the overall discourse. That is, after the reluctant Jonah played the role of God's messenger and the people of Nineveh repented, isn't the story finished? Why is there another chapter? In our view, the chapter is an integral part of the book, vital for the book's unity, although it might seem extraneous to some readers and scholars.

As we have shown, the book has a symmetrical pattern in two halves, each of which starts with a stage and continues on with inciting incidents involving other minor participants (sailors and Ninevites) and peaks (corresponding to the climax at the notional structure) when Jonah is alone with God. At the peak of the first half, Jonah is inside the fish but prays a song of praise and thanks to God. At the peak of the second half, his mission is accomplished, but he is displeased and angry.

It is of interest to note that chapter 2 is at the height of tension in terms of Jonah's fate (Is he going to die or live?), but its content is calm and even peaceful with a song of praise to God, suggesting the possibility of a thematic peak. Nothing much is going on that can be called events except at beginning and end. At the peak of narrative, however, it is not uncommon for events to stop altogether while the emotional and mental state of a participant is described. Chapter 4, in contrast, is full of actions ("went out," "sat down," "made," "sat," "prepared," "made grow," "chewed," "withered") and speech events ("prayed," "said," "replied," "asked"); it has three emotive verbs in the independent clauses ("was displeasing," "angered," and "was happy"). High tension is shown by the use of direct speech carrying the conflicting mental states and attitudes of Jonah and God; the tension is a present one rather than one induced by future or unknown happenings. The tension in chapter 2 hinges on the physical situation and a bizarre turn of events accompanied by emotional calm; the tension in chapter 4 hinges on an emotional problem, Jonah's failure to understand God's compassion, accompanied by calm (or even finished) physical events. Both peaks, in some sense, are highly thematic.

When we look at the problems in the first three chapters, we see that they are closely related to events and actions and that the resolutions of these local problems are made at the end of each chapter: Both the sailors and the Ninevites are spared, and Jonah is vomited onto dry land after being inside the fish for three days. Both groups of pagan people are brought to God. Yet Jonah, who has been God's instrument for these two groups of people, is not happy. The problem in chapter 4, caused by his unhappiness and anger, is different in kind from the rest of the book. It is mental and emotional rather than action related. Jonah is angry at God's being compassionate, even though he says, "I knew that you are a gracious and compassionate God, slow to anger and abounding in love, a God who relents from sending calamity" (4:2b). In fact, he says, that is why he fled in the first place. But if he *knew* God's characteristics so well, why is he angry? Why does he not rejoice in the fact that his message was heeded so well that the people had genuine repentance? The paradoxical state of his mind points out something basic to human nature: Our feelings are not necessarily based on rational or altruistic thinking. Jonah is angry because God did not destroy Nineveh as he predicted. It is interesting to note in this connection that Jonah's preaching in the book does not include the word "repent" which might be expected of a prophet. The message was simply "Forty more days and Nineveh will be overturned" (3:4b). It seems to be a deliberate choice of wording in anticipation of the content of chapter 4.

To summarize, we believe that chapter 4 is an integral part of the book, both because of the balance and symmetrical pattern of the book and, more crucially, because of the explicit treatment of the mental and emotional problem concerning compassion, an important theme of the book.

5. Verb forms

5.1 Clauses with *wayyiqtol,* N + *qatal,* and *qatal* verb forms

As in any Biblical Hebrew narrative, the single most cohesive textual feature of the story is the sequence of *wayyiqtol* clauses that occur throughout the story from beginning to end. There are, of course, local discontinuities occasioned by the occurrence of other clause types.

The *wayyiqtol* sequence encodes *successive, punctiliar happenings.* In what we might call close context there is a direct and immediate connection from one such *wayyiqtol* clause to another. Each new *wayyiqtol* clause provides *new information* relative to the preceding. Thus,

(5) $wayyiqtol_1$: $happening_1$
       $wayyiqtol_2$: $happening_2$
       $wayyiqtol_3$: $happening_3$, etc.

The "happenings" involve participants and props (in patterns of sameness and replacement) that are either implicitly indicated or are made explicit by use of noun/pronoun. Furthermore, the *wayyiqtol* form, the "prefixal form," is inflected to agree in person, number, and gender with one class of participants/props, namely, the subject. This agreement feature serves to roughly identify at least one entity involved in the happening.

Discontinuities, marked by departure from *wayyiqtol* clauses, introduce further information into the narrative. Unless such further information is parenthetical, the *wayyiqtol* main sequence incorporates it and flows on.

Herein lies the peculiar narrative competence of strongly VSO languages such as Biblical Hebrew: within the chain of such clauses in a narrative, the rhematic element, the verb, occurs first in the clause. The happening is indicated first; then entities involved in the happening can follow encoded as nouns, pronouns, or oblique elements.

One clause type that breaks the continuity of the *wayyiqtol* chain is the N + *qatal* clause. Distinct from the VSO clause, it encodes an entity via the N (the preposed noun), then presents via the verb the happening in which that entity is involved (plus or minus indication of further involved entities in post-verb nouns/pronouns). Thus *wayyiqtol* and N + *qatal* clauses contrast functionally in regard to happening focus (often action) versus entity focus (prop/participant) (see Longacre 1989b, 1992a, 1992b, and Longacre in this volume).

In the Book of Jonah, *N* + *qatal* clauses are rare, but they play a crucial role. We can best illustrate that role by backing up a bit and tying into the storyline. The book begins with a presentative formula of quotation:

(6) וַיְהִי דְבַר־יְהוָה אֶל־יוֹנָה בֶן־אֲמִתַּי לֵאמֹר . . .
And-occurred word-of Yahweh to Jonah son-of Amittai saying . . .

Imperatives follow:

(7) קוּם לֵךְ אֶל־נִינְוֵה הָעִיר הַגְּדוֹלָה וּקְרָא עָלֶיהָ . . .
Arise, go to Nineveh, the-city the-great, and-proclaim against-her (that her wickedness has come up before me)

Verse 3 records the prophet's disobedience in a graphic sequence of *wayyiqtol* clauses:

(8) (a) And-he-arose Jonah to flee to Tarshish from the face of Yahweh.
 (b) And-he-went-down to Joppa.
 (c) And-he-found a ship going to Tarshish.
 (d) And-he-paid its fare.
 (e) And-he-went-down [embarked] on it with them to flee to Tarshish from the face of Yahweh.

The participant reference in this chain of clauses centers around Jonah, the subject of every verb. Jonah is mentioned only in segment a of example 8. Objects occur in segments c and d: "he found a *ship* bound for Tarshish, and he paid *its fare*." An oblique object occurs in segment d: "on it." Place names mark the proposed trajectory: "Joppa" is the point of embarkation, and "Tarshish" is the destination. So far, so good—from Jonah's perspective.

In verse 4, however, strong discontinuities present themselves, encoded in *N* + *qatal*:

(9) (a) וַיהוָה הֵטִיל רוּחַ־גְּדוֹלָה אֶל־הַיָּם
And-Yahweh sent wind great onto the-sea

 (b) וַיְהִי סַעַר־גָּדוֹל בַּיָּם
And-there-was storm great in-the-sea

 (c) וְהָאֳנִיָּה חִשְּׁבָה לְהִשָּׁבֵר
And-the-ship considered breaking-up

The *N* + *qatal* clauses in segments a and c of example 9 underline the shift in the control center (dominance patterns) from "Jonah" to "Yahweh," and the shift of concern to the ship itself, while b, resultant on a, mentions the "great storm" in a וַיְהִי (*wayyiqtol*) clause. Here grammar bends over backwards to register the dramatic shift to a new scenario in which Yahweh *dominates*, and the ship and all in it (including Jonah) are now *dominated* by forces beyond their control.

Are these *N* + *qatal* clauses topic-establishing relative to the ensuing context? On the whole, yes. They do not necessarily establish the subjects of the following clauses, but they point to the main concerns. The ship, established as a concern in segment c, clearly continues to be a concern. The sailors (הַמַּלָּחִים) in v. 5 and the captain (רַב) in v. 6 are clearly implied by the term "ship" and need not be introduced. Their actions—throwing the cargo overboard and eventually throwing Jonah overboard as well—are all reflective of the concern for the ship. But before things come to this desperate expedient, the sailors' discussion with Jonah leads to the recognition that Jonah's God, Yahweh, is responsible for the trouble and to him the sailors sacrifice after the storm. So the concerns eventually circle back to Yahweh, the subject of segment a here. Jonah is, notwithstanding, the subject of clauses in the second half of v. 5 (which is, however, a flashback) and in vv. 9 and 12 as he dialogues with the sailors. Meanwhile, it is of interest to note that further interventions of Yahweh in the balance of the book are not given in *N* + *qatal* clauses but in the more routine grammar of *wayyiqtol* clauses (see the verb וַיְמַן 'prepared' in sec. 5.3.3 with Yahweh/God as subject and with various props as objects).

Qatal verbs occur in clauses in which any particle precedes the verb (i.e., לֹא 'not', אֲשֶׁר 'who, which, that' relative marker, and כִּי 'because, for, that' causal). Whenever such clauses report happenings, they are "demoted" happenings; that is, they are grammatically marginalized in reference to the main clauses or are attributive to a noun head. The particle לֹא 'not' + *qatal* verbs is clearly irrealis in this book (see sec. 6).

5.2 Flashback mechanisms

One more *N* + *qatal* clause occurs: Found in the second half of v. 5, it establishes a flashback that continues via a chain of two *wayyiqtol* clauses. The whole series of three clauses is backset in that they constitute a part of the story that is told out of normal order. At some time between setting sail and the onset of the storm Jonah went below.

(10) (a)   וְיוֹנָה יָרַד אֶל־יַרְכְּתֵי הַסְּפִינָה
And-Jonah had-gone-down to underparts-of the-deck

(b) וַיִּשְׁכַּב
And-he-lay-down

(c) וַיֵּרָדַם
And-he-went-sound-asleep.

Notice also the implicit contrast involved: The *ship* is about to flounder and the sailors are frenziedly working to save it, but *Jonah* is asleep below the deck. Of course, behind it all is *Yahweh,* the sender of the storm. This is the thrust of the three nouns involved in the *N* + *qatal* clauses.

The second half of 1:10 is another flashback, shown here as example 11. It follows upon "This terrified them (the sailors), and they asked him, 'What have you done?'" and is encoded in כִּי 'because, for, that' clauses with *qatal* verbs.

(11) (a) כִּי־יָדְעוּ הָאֲנָשִׁים
for they-knew the-men

(b) כִּי־מִלִּפְנֵי יְהוָה הוּא בֹרֵחַ
that from-face-of Yahweh he was-fleeing

(c) כִּי הִגִּיד לָהֶם
because had-declared-he to-them.

In segments a and b here we see two distinct meanings of כִּי: "*for* they knew *that* he was fleeing from Yahweh." It is possible that a is also flashback in force: "for they had already ascertained . . ." In any case, the third כִּי clause, in segment c, is clearly a flashback: "*for* he had told them."

In summary of the structure of these two flashbacks, we note that a subordinate (here causal) clause is sufficient for encoding a brief flashback of one happening (assuming segment c is the only flashback in example 11). For a more extended flashback that encodes a series of backset happenings, the *N* + *qatal* . . . *wayyiqtol* . . . *wayyiqtol* construction is available. This construction focuses attention on a participant who has been temporarily offstage and reports what he has been doing: Here it focuses on Jonah, who presumably had gone down into the hold before the storm broke. A further flashback possibility is the unmarked one, backtracking within a chain of *wayyiqtol* forms. This could be the case with a shift of participant/subject in the *wayyiqtol* chain.[5] Presumably this is not illustrated in the Book of Jonah. The uncertainty regarding whether segment a is a flashback or not is an uncertainty regarding the interpretation of a *qatal* verb in a כִּי clause.

It is of interest to note that a story once backset by a *N + qatal* clause can continue with *wayyiqtol* clauses as in normal narrative. This is one of these rare cases where *wayyiqtol* functions as a "consecutive" tense.

5.3 Two motion verbs and two presentatives

There are two important verbs and two presentative formulas in the Book of Jonah to which we give special attention here.[6]

5.3.1 קוּם 'arise'

The verb קוּם 'arise' is typically a *script-initiating* verb. Noticeably in 1:3 (example 8), וַיָּקָם is used to initiate a sea-voyage script. Of course, this is no routine sea voyage because in its first and last clauses the script is specifically labeled as a flight/avoidance series of actions. In 3:6, shown as example 12, וַיָּקָם 'and he arose' initiates a repentance script (in this instance royal repentance):

(12)   (a)   וַיָּקָם מִכִּסְאוֹ
              And-he-arose from his-throne

       (b)   וַיַּעֲבֵר אַדַּרְתּוֹ מֵעָלָיו
              And-he-put-aside his-splendor from-off-him

       (c)   וַיְכַס שָׂק
              And-he-put-on sackcloth

       (d)   וַיֵּשֶׁב עַל־הָאֵפֶר
              And-he-sat in the-dust

The sequence thus initiated and carried on ends with a royal proclamation on the part of the king (3:7–9).

5.3.2 יָרַד 'go down'

The verb יָרַד 'go down' is another important motion verb in Jonah —enough to tempt one to homiletic elaboration: The occurrence of this verb marks Jonah's "downward" course:

(13)   1:3a   וַיֵּרֶד יָפוֹ
                And-he-went-down (to) Joppa

       1:3b   וַיֵּרֶד בָּהּ
                And-he-went-down in-it [ship]

       1:5   וְיוֹנָה יָרַד אֶל־יַרְכְּתֵי הַסְּפִינָה
                And-Jonah went-down to underparts-of the-deck

Finally we might add from chapter 2 (the psalm):

(14) 2:7 לְקִצְבֵי הָרִים יָרַדְתִּי
to-roots-of mountains went-down-I

Preacher-like, we might remark that there was no going back up for Jonah until he had gone down as far as possible.

5.3.3 'And Yahweh/God prepared . . .'

The presentative formula . . . וַיְמַן יְהוָה/אֱלֹהִים 'and Yahweh/God prepared . . .' at once emphasizes divine providence and introduces various props. This formula—whatever the divine name used—presents דָּג גָּדוֹל 'great fish' in 1:17, קִיקָיוֹן 'vine' in 4:6, תּוֹלַעַת 'worm' in 4:7, and רוּחַ קָדִים חֲרִישִׁית 'scorching east wind' in 4:8. It is used with frequency in 4:6–8 along with a considerable variation in divine names—shades of early Pentateuchal criticism! (We will consider this variation in sec. 7.)

5.3.4 'And the word of Yahweh occurred to Jonah . . . saying'

A different presentative formula is used in the wording of 1:1 and 3:1: וַיְהִי דְבַר־יְהוָה אֶל־יוֹנָה בֶן־אֲמִתַּי לֵאמֹר 'And the word of Yahweh occurred to Jonah son of Amittai saying'. This occurs rather than וַיֹּאמֶר יְהוָה אֶל־יוֹנָה 'and Yahweh said to Jonah'. Both are formulas that introduce direct speech. But the one in 1:1 and in 3:1 (plus the word שֵׁנִית 'a second time' in the latter) lends a peculiar solemnity and dignity to the context. On other occasions in the book, God's words to Jonah are more simply introduced, with וַיֹּאמֶר יְהוָה אֶל־יוֹנָה 'Yahweh said to Jonah'. Furthermore, the occurrence of וַיְהִי דְבַר־יְהוָה אֶל־יוֹנָה 'And the word of Yahweh occurred to Jonah' serves to mark two main divisions of the book (cf. Parunak re Jeremiah in this volume). The book begins again, as it were, in 3:1 as if God were saying, "Now, to continue with my original plan before interruption . . . "

6. Irrealis constructions and frustration

The first irrealis construction is seen in 1:5b and hinges on a peculiar use of חשׁב 'to think, consider' with an inanimate subject and with an infinitive complement in 1:4b:

(15) וְהָאֳנִיָּה חִשְּׁבָה לְהִשָּׁבֵר
And-the-ship thought-about breaking-up [in the dialect of English spoken in the American South: "the ship was fixin' to break up"]

There is something implicitly modal here: a state of affairs threatens to bring about an event that does not, after all, happen.

Other examples of irrealis can best be handled by what Longacre described some time ago as "the anatomy of frustration" (Longacre 1983:134–43). He represents this symbolically as $(P \supset Q) \wedge (P \wedge \overline{Q}) \wedge R \wedge S$, where there is an implication $(P \supset Q)$, which is broken $(P \wedge \overline{Q})$ since Q is negated; there may also be indicated a blocking circumstance R, and/or a surrogate happening S, as in:

(16) (a) He started out for Paris
    (b) but never arrived;
    (c) a bomb went off in his car
    (d) and they buried him in Calais.

In example 16 segment a states P, which would normally imply Q, namely his arrival in Paris. The latter is negated in segment b, so there is a conjunction of $P \wedge \overline{Q}$; and segment c is the blocking circumstance R, segment d the surrogate happening.

Two such examples in Jonah contain explicit negations ($\overline{Q}$). The first is in 1:13.

(17) (a) וַיַּחְתְּרוּ הָאֲנָשִׁים
       And-rowed the-men

    (b) לְהָשִׁיב אֶל־הַיַּבָּשָׁה
       to-return to the-dry-land

    (c) וְלֹא יָכֹלוּ
       And-not were-able-they

    (d) כִּי הַיָּם הוֹלֵךְ וְסֹעֵר עֲלֵיהֶם
       for the-sea was-continuing and-storming against-them

In example 17, segments a and b establish $P \supset Q$; segment c negates Q, giving $\overline{Q}$; and segment d gives R, the blocking circumstance.

In 3:10, a rather different situation is sketched but summarizable in the same symbolism:

(18) (a) וַיַּרְא הָאֱלֹהִים אֶת־מַעֲשֵׂיהֶם
       And-he-saw the-God ACC their-deeds

    (b) כִּי־שָׁבוּ מִדַּרְכָּם הָרָעָה
       that they-turned-back from-their-way the-evil

    (c) וַיִּנָּחֶם הָאֱלֹהִים עַל־הָרָעָה
       And-he-relented the-God concerning the-judgment

(d) אֲשֶׁר־דִּבֶּר לַעֲשׂוֹת־לָהֶם
which he-had-said to-do to-them

(e) וְלֹא עָשָׂה
And-not did-he [it]

Here God's original intention P is referred to by the noun הָרָעָה 'the evil/judgment' at the end of segment c plus the אֲשֶׁר 'relative marker' clause in segment d. Notice again the pluperfect thrust of the verb דִּבֶּר 'he had said' in segment d. Normally $P \supset Q$, that is, intention to send judgment would be followed by Q, sending judgment. But segment e gives us a negation ($\overline{Q}$): "he didn't do it." So we have $(P \supset Q) \wedge (P \wedge \overline{Q})$. The intention to judge implied judgment, but the intention is stated in conjunction with *not* carrying out the judgment. The blocking circumstance R is encoded in segments a and b: "God saw their deeds, that they turned back from their evil ways." The surrogate happening S is given in segment c, where God extends mercy instead of judgment on Nineveh. We have, then, the full semantic structure $(P \supset Q) \wedge (P \wedge \overline{Q}) \wedge R \wedge S$.

Frustration, as here defined and symbolized, runs through much of the book, even when it is not explicitly presented. We summarize here in prose without resort to symbolization:

(a) God's telling Jonah to go preach to Nineveh should have implied that he would do it, but he didn't; instead he took a ship for Tarshish. The blocking circumstance is indicated in 4:2: Jonah fears that if he preached judgment God wouldn't follow through to bring judgment but would have mercy (1:1-3).

(b) Jonah's embarkation for Tarshish would normally imply his arriving there. But Jonah didn't arrive at Tarshish; there was a blocking circumstance, the storm. Instead, Jonah was thrown overboard into the sea (1:2-16).

(c) Being thrown into the sea should have implied a quick death by drowning; but God sent a great fish to swallow him (1:15-17).

(d) Being in the belly of a great fish should eventually have resulted in death, but instead God caused the great fish to vomit him out onto dry land (1:17; 2:10).

(e) The vine that grew up over the booth where Jonah sat would normally have resulted in Jonah's happiness—and it did for a day. But Jonah wasn't happy for long because God sent a worm to kill the vine and expose him to the sun and hot wind (4:6-8).

Perhaps all this could be summarized in one grand statement, which is, in fact, the macrostructure of the book as presented in section 3: Jonah did not want to be a messenger of mercy to Nineveh, but Yahweh caused him to be such, by the series of providential occurrences that Yahweh threw across his pathway. We might symbolize this as: $(\overline{P} \supset \overline{Q}) \wedge (\overline{P} \wedge Q) \wedge R_1 \ldots R_n$. Positive and negative values are reversed from what we find in example 18 so that the positive values win out in the end. A series of blocking circumstances $(R_1 \ldots R_n)$ leads to the reversal of $\overline{Q}$ to Q. Not only positive intentions can be frustrated but negative ones as well!

7. Variation in divine names

In that יְהוָה 'Yahweh' is the noun employed most frequently in referencing the Israelite deity, departures from this norm are of special interest. Besides יְהוָה, there are in the Book of Jonah occurrences of אֱלֹהִים 'God', אֱלֹהִים with personal pronouns ('your God', 'my God'), אֵל 'God (short form)' once, הָאֱלֹהִים 'the God' four times, and יְהוָה אֱלֹהִים, the compound name, once. The choice of אֱלֹהִים with personal pronouns is, of course, a forced choice; יְהוָה does not occur with possessives. The shorter form אֵל 'God' occurs where Jonah remonstrates with God in prayer concerning what sort of a God he is, namely, a God of compassion. Our interest centers therefore on the other variants, יְהוָה, אֱלֹהִים, and הָאֱלֹהִים.

The God of Israel is typically referred to as אֱלֹהִים in the mouths of non-Israelites or in contexts reflective of their viewpoint. This is noticeable in 3:5, "The Ninevites believed God," and in the king's decrees of 3:8, 9. The narrator, accommodating himself to this context, also referred to "God" in 3:10. Even here, however, there is an interesting complication, namely, the presence of the article with "God" in 3:9 and in 3:10 versus its absence in 3:5 and 3:8 (both of the latter are after prepositions, while the הָאֱלֹהִים forms are subjects of their clauses and refer to God's sovereign act of mercy).

In chapter 1 when the sailors inquire of Jonah concerning his nationality, he answers (1:9) that he is a Hebrew and a worshiper of "Yahweh, the God of heaven, who made the sea and the land." The terrified sailors, having learned the name of Jonah's God, address him as Yahweh twice in 1:14—and when they offer a sacrifice it is to the God of this name (1:16).

The most interesting variation in divine names is in chapter 4:

(19)   4:6   וַיְמַן יְהוָה־אֱלֹהִים קִיקָיוֹן . . .
            And-he-prepared Yahweh God (a) vine (which grew up over Jonah to provide a shade over his head and to ease his discomfort; Jonah's response: great joy)

4:7   וַיְמַן הָאֱלֹהִים תּוֹלַעַת . . .
And-he-prepared God (a) worm (the next day, and it smote the vine so that it dried up)

4:8   (and it came about when the sun rose)
וַיְמַן אֱלֹהִים רוּחַ קָדִים חֲרִישִׁית . . .
And-he-prepared God wind east scorching (and the sun smote on the head of Jonah, and he grew faint and wanted to die; verbal response: "Better for me to die than to live")

4:9   וַיֹּאמֶר אֱלֹהִים אֶל־יוֹנָה . . .
And-he-said God to Jonah ("Is it good for you to be angry about the vine?" And replied Jonah, "It's good for me to be angry unto death.")

4:10 וַיֹּאמֶר יְהוָה . . .
And-he-said Yahweh (in effect: "You've been concerned about this vine which was none of your doing and was perishable. Shouldn't I be concerned about that great city Nineveh, which has 120,000 infants and much cattle?")

(We have reproduced much of the fourth chapter of Jonah in an effort to omit no subtle contextual factors.)

The first thing we notice here is the compound name in 4:6. This striking name reminds us of Jonah's description of Yahweh in 1:9 as "Yahweh, the God of heaven, who made the sea and the land." The compound name in 4:6 has a composite reference to Yahweh, God of Israel and Lord of all nature. As such, this God approaches Jonah with one final ploy to change the sullen prophet's attitude. Holding all the cards, so to speak, he deals Jonah a hand calculated to gain his notice. This, we believe, is the thrust of the occurrence of the compound name here.

The reference to deity in 4:7 is הָאֱלֹהִים 'the God' and the references in 4:8 and 4:9 are אֱלֹהִים 'God' without the article. Keeping in mind that "God" is never pronominalized, we might speculate that we have a two-step simplification: from יְהוָה אֱלֹהִים 'Yahweh God' to the form הָאֱלֹהִים 'the God' (almost deictic in force?), down to אֱלֹהִים as the simplest possible way to refer to God. At any rate, we are brought up short with the name יְהוָה again in 4:10, where a crowning pronouncement of God's mercifulness is made. There may be then a matching of titles to the actions or words indicated: a solemn and sonorous title for God's putting into motion the final string of events in his dealing with Jonah; and יְהוָה again, as God enunciates the great (and at the same time quaint) words of 4:10–11. For intermediate ploys and words, the forms הָאֱלֹהִים and אֱלֹהִים suffice. Furthermore, הָאֱלֹהִים in v. 7 may savor something of "Now the same God who caused the vine to grow sent a worm to destroy it!"

8. Paragraph structure

The following display of the paragraph structure of chapters 3 and 4 in English (according to the NIV) illustrates *the interrelationship of action sequences and dialogue sequences* in the structure of the book.[7] A more detailed analysis—which we have chosen not to give here—would need to be based more squarely on the Hebrew sentence units, a number of which often occur grouped together in the array below. Thus, in the first paragraph, under RU, Sequential Thesis 1 (3:3), an embedded comment paragraph is not indicated; the comment is "Now Nineveh was a very important city—a visit required three days." Notice also the considerable complexity of embedded paragraph structure in 4:2-3 and 4:10.

Part 2: Narrative discourse (3:1-4:11)

Stage: (N) Simple Dialogue P (3:1-4)

Lead-In: 1 Then the word of Yahweh came to Jonah a second time:
IU (Pro): 2 "Go to the great city of Nineveh and proclaim to it the message I give you."
RU (Res, nonverbal): (N) Sequence P
SeqTh1: 3 Jonah obeyed the word of Yahweh and went to Nineveh. Now Nineveh was a very important city—a visit required three days.
SeqTh2: 4 On the first day, Jonah started into the city. He proclaimed: "Forty more days and Nineveh will be overturned."

Prepeak Episode: (N) Result P (3:5-10)

Thesis: (N) Sequence P
SeqTh1: 5 The Ninevites believed God. They declared a fast, and all of them, from the greatest to the least, put on sackcloth.
SeqTh2: (N) Sequence P
SeqTh1: 6 When the news reached the king of Nineveh, he rose from his throne, took off his royal robes, covered himself with sackcloth and sat down in the dust.
SeqTh2: (N) Quote P
Quote Formula: 7a Then he issued a proclamation in Nineveh: "By the decree of the king and his nobles:
Quote: (H) Result P

Thesis: (H) Antithetical P
    Antithesis: 7b Do not let any man or beast, herd or flock, taste anything; do not let them eat or drink.
    Thesis: 8 But let man and beast be covered with sackcloth. Let everyone call urgently on God. Let them give up their evil ways and their violence.
    Result: 9 Who knows? God may yet relent and with compassion turn from his fierce anger so that we will not perish."

Result: 10 When God saw what they did and how they turned from their evil ways, he had compassion and did not bring upon them the destruction he had threatened.

Peak Episode: (N) Sequence P (4:1–11)[8]

Setting: 1 But Jonah was greatly displeased and became angry.
SeqTh 1: (N) Complex Dialogue P
    IU (Rem + Pro): 2 He prayed to Yahweh, "O Yahweh, is this not what I said when I was still at home? That is why I was so quick to flee to Tarshish. I knew that you are a gracious and compassionate God, slow to anger and abounding in love, a God who relents from sending calamity. 3 Now, O Yahweh, take away my life, for it is better for me to die than to live."
    CU (CounterQ): 4 But Yahweh replied, "Have you any right to be angry?"
SeqTh 2: (N) Sequence P
    SeqTh 1: 5 Jonah went out and sat down at a place east of the city. There he made himself a shelter, sat in its shade and waited to see what would happen to the city.
    SeqTh 2: (N) Antithetical P
        Thesis: 6 Then Yahweh God provided a vine and made it grow up over Jonah to give shade for his head to ease his discomfort, and Jonah was very happy about the vine.
        Opposed Thesis: 7 But at dawn the next day God provided a worm, which chewed the vine so that it withered.
    SeqTh 3: (N) Compound Dialogue P
        Ex 1: (N) Complex Dialogue P
            Lead-In: 8a When the sun rose, God provided a scorching east wind, and the sun blazed on Jonah's head so that he grew faint.
            IU (Rem): 8b He wanted to die, and said, "It would be better for me to die than to live."

CU (CounterQ): 9a But God said to Jonah, "Do you have a right to be angry about the vine?"
RU (A): 9b "I do," he said, "I am angry enough to die."
Ex 2: (Unresolved) (N) Simple Dialogue P
IU (Rem + Q): 10 But Yahweh said, "You have been concerned about this vine, though you did not tend it or make it grow. It sprang up overnight and died overnight. 11 But Nineveh has more than a hundred and twenty thousand people who cannot tell their right hand from their left, and many cattle as well. Should I not be concerned about that great city?"

Notes

1. See Longacre's earlier studies on other Biblical Hebrew narrative texts: Longacre 1985 (on the Flood narrative) and 1989a (on the Joseph narrative of Genesis).

2. In contrast, Mann, Matthiessen, and Thompson (1992) posit only one set of text relations—semantic and pragmatic—for the constituents of sentence, paragraph, and discourse. They do not posit any distinct discourse-level schemata.

3. Some authors use the terms *narrative* and *story* interchangeably, preferring the former in order to avoid the fictional connotation that may be associated with the latter. In this article we use *story* as a more specific category within the broader category of narrative.

4. Longacre has argued (1989a:84–85) that Biblical Hebrew has a rather simple sentence structure and that one-clause sentences are frequent.

5. See Randall Buth (in this volume). Ilah Fleming (oral communication) also supports this.

6. See Wilt (1992) for a discussion of repeated lexical items in Jonah (e.g., "go down," "arise," "prepare," "great").

7. See Longacre (1979, 1980, 1989b) and Hwang (1989) for discussions on the analysis of paragraph structures. Part 4 in Longacre (1989a) shows a detailed constituent display—including the paragraph structures—of the entire Joseph text. The following abbreviations are used in the display: A=Answer, CU=Continuing Utterance, Ex=Exchange, H=Hortatory, IU=Initiating Utterance, N=Narrative, P=Paragraph, Pro=Proposal, Q=Question, Rem=Remark, Res=Response, RU=Resolving Utterance, SeqTh=Sequential Thesis.

8. Sasson (1990) sets up a main division in chapter 4 between "Move/countermove" (4:1–6) and "Heat and light" (4:7–11). While his division corresponds with the temporal break between two days, it cuts across the topic of the vine, grown for shade but chewed by a worm. We treat 4:6–7 as forming an antithetical paragraph with two opposed theses.

References

Buth, Randall. 1994. Methodological collision between source criticism and discourse analysis. Elsewhere in this volume.
Fee, Gordon D., and Douglas Stuart. 1982. *How to read the Bible for all its worth: A guide to understanding the Bible.* Grand Rapids, Mich.: Zondervan.
Hwang, Shin Ja J. 1984. A cognitive basis for discourse grammar. *Southwest Journal of Linguistics* 7:133-56.
———. 1989. Recursion in the paragraph as a unit of discourse development. *Discourse Processes* 12:461-78.
———. 1993. Approaching a narrative: Charting and chunking. Ms.
Longacre, Robert E. 1979. The paragraph as a grammatical unit. In *Discourse and syntax* (Syntax and Semantics, 12), ed. T. Givón, 115-34. New York: Academic Press.
———. 1980. An apparatus for the identification of paragraph types. *Notes on Linguistics* 15:5-22.
———. 1983. *The grammar of discourse.* New York: Plenum Press.
———. 1985. Interpreting biblical stories. In *Discourse and literature*, ed. T. A. van Dijk, 169-85. Amsterdam: Benjamins.
———. 1989*a*. *Joseph: A story of divine providence: A text theoretical and textlinguistic analysis of Genesis 37 and 39-48.* Winona Lake, Ind.: Eisenbrauns.
———. 1989*b*. Two hypotheses regarding text generation and analysis. *Discourse Processes* 12:413-60.
———. 1992*a*. Discourse perspective on the Hebrew verb: Affirmation and restatement. In *Linguistics and Biblical Hebrew*, ed. W. R. Bodine, 177-89. Winona Lake, Ind.: Eisenbrauns.
———. 1992*b*. The analysis of preverbal nouns in Biblical Hebrew narrative: Some overriding concerns. *Journal of Translation and Textlinguistics* 5:208-24.
———. 1994. Weqatal forms in Biblical Hebrew prose: A discourse-modular approach. Elsewhere in this volume.
Longacre, Robert E., and Stephen H. Levinsohn. 1978. Field analysis of discourse. In *Current trends in textlinguistics* (Research in Text Theory, 2), ed. W. U. Dressler, 103-22. Berlin: Walter de Gruyter.
Mann, William C., Christian Matthiessen, and Sandra A. Thompson. 1992. Rhetorical structure theory and text analysis. In *Discourse description: Diverse linguistic analyses of a fund-raising text,* ed. W. C. Mann and S. A. Thompson, 39-78. Amsterdam: Benjamins.
Parunak, H. Van Dyke. 1994. Some discourse functions of prophetic quotation formulas in Jeremiah. Elsewhere in this volume.
Sasson, Jack M. 1990. *Jonah: A new translation with introduction, commentary, and interpretation.* New York: Doubleday.
van Dijk, Teun A. 1977. *Text and context.* London: Longman.
———. 1980. *Macrostructures.* Hillsdale, N.J.: Erlbaum.
van Dijk, Teun A., and Walter Kintsch. 1983. *Strategies of discourse comprehension.* New York: Academic Press.
Wilt, Timothy L. 1992. Lexical repetition in Jonah. *Journal of Translation and Textlinguistics* 5:252-64.

PART III

TOPICS RELATING TO NONNARRATIVE GENRES

15

FUNCTIONS AND IMPLICATIONS OF RHETORICAL QUESTIONS IN THE BOOK OF JOB

Lénart J. de Regt

In this article some characteristics of rhetorical questions in Biblical Hebrew are presented, paying attention to their definition, recognition, forms and functions, and bias. The examples are from the book of Job where there are many rhetorical questions of different kinds. They seem to play a part in structuring the poems into sections. Careful interpretation of these aspects of rhetorical questions is important for their translation.

In Job, two disjunctive rhetorical questions (RQs) are often parallel in meaning. This is the case in 38:28-29:

Has (הֲ) the rain a father,
or who (מִי) has begotten (הוֹלִיד) the drops of dew?
From whose (מִי) womb did the ice come forth,
and who (מִי) has given birth (יְלָדוֹ) to the hoarfrost of heaven? (NRSV)

Also, there is "morphological parallelism of word pairs of different conjugation" (Berlin 1979:23-27) because of הוֹלִיד (hiphil) in 28b and יְלָדוֹ (qal) in 29b. The verse relations in this RQ series could be described as follows: *RQ // RQ // RQ // RQ*.

The question in 38:28a primarily presupposes a negative answer but another level of implied meaning is involved. Alter observes "a sort of riddling paradox (no one is the father of the rain, but the rain is the father of life)" (Alter 1985:101). Unlike Alter, however, Mitchell (1992:xxv) sees a different meaning here: "*Does* the rain have a father? The whole meaning is in the lack of an answer ... God's humor is ... subtle beyond words."

These are two different interpretations of the same RQ. While each may be valid, they do call for a more linguistic treatment of RQs. The fact that RQs in Job often occur not only in parallelism but in series (Watson 1984:339-340) raises the issue of their relations and implications.

1. Defining the RQ

Generally, RQ definitions have the following elements in common. "In an ordinary conversation ... a question is assumed to be a request for information. When it becomes evident to the hearer that the 'information' in question is already well known to both of them, he understands that the speaker must be deliberately flouting the expected pattern, and thereby doing something else, namely emphasizing a point" (Koops 1988:418). The (implicit) answer/statement is made all the stronger by the RQ form. Often the answer to an RQ is common knowledge (Beekman and Callow 1976:236).

A "real" question is used to elicit information. A rhetorical question is used to convey or call attention to information, expressing the speaker's attitudes, opinions, etc. (Beekman and Callow 1976:229, 244).

An RQ is really something more than an emphatic statement; it includes the implication that the audience knows the answer, and not only the answer, but also that the audience will be fully cognizant of this implication. Accordingly, a speaker or writer may thus identify with the audience by implying that the audience will obviously agree (Nida et al. 1983:167). In short, RQs "have the form of a question but are not designed to elicit information. The intent, therefore, is not to ask for a response but to make an emphatic declaration" (Nida et al. 1983:39).

With regard to the implied answer, Watson's definition contains a slightly different aspect: "either the speaker or listener (or even both of them) already knows the answer" (Watson 1984:338).

2. Unmarked RQs

In cases where an interrogative particle does not occur, the context may still call for interpreting some clause as an RQ (e.g., Job 2:10; 10:9; 11:11; 17:4b, 16a; 23:17; 30:24; 38:8; 40:24, 25; and probably 12:12 and 21:16). Job 10:11, for instance, simply depends on what precedes, as it is a continuation of the הֲלֹא 'is it not?' question in 10:10 (van Rensburg 1991:242).

An interesting example of how to recognize such an RQ is provided by Job 38:8. Here the RQ is formally unmarked: no interrogative particle occurs in it. But if it were a statement, v. 10 would be unnecessary. Moreover, it would not go with the first person reference in vv. 9–11. The particle מִי 'who?' in 5a is implied or continued here in v. 8. The RQ functions as a challenge and is followed by the speaker's answer in the form of subordinate clauses in 8b–11 (cf. also 21:30): *RQ + subordCl/ answer*.

> Who shut up the sea behind doors
> when it burst forth from the womb,
> when I . . . fixed limits for it
> and set its doors and bars in place . . . ? (NIV)

This illustrates that a speaker may answer his own RQ in a monologue (Longacre 1976:171). Syntactically, the answer in these verses is a subordinate clause to the RQ in the main clause. Although this is not obligatory (as it is in certain languages), RQs in Job are frequently followed by their answer, given by the speaker.

3. RQ forms and functions

RQs take the form of questions. At the same time they are assertions (or the like) by conversational implication. Both the interrogative *form* of RQs and their *function* must be accounted for (O'Connor 1980:12). According to Snell-Hornby (1988:87):

> It is commonly believed that a declarative sentence is automatically a statement, that an interrogative sentence is invariably a question, and that an imperative sentence must essentially be a directive. In fact, the relation between grammatical form and communicative function is far more complex, and for the translator this is a vital insight. A so-called rhetorical question, for example, is in fact an *interrogative sentence* with the force of an emphatic *statement*, while a leading question combines the function of a statement and a question, the focus shifting according to specific factors. Thus form and function exist in *dynamic tension* with each other, and what is important for translation is the fact that this tension varies from one culture, and hence language, to another.

The terms *content* and *intent* may also be used (Nida et al. 1983:39). De Waard and Nida (1986:108) give Eph. 4:26 as an example of "the use of a declarative statement with imperative content": "the imperative . . . is not a command but a type of concessive condition meaning 'even if you do get angry' followed by the result 'still you must not sin.'"

The terms *content, function,* and *intent* may be rather confusing. Koops's distinction between different stages of implied meaning of RQs is more precise (1988:420):

(1) The *rhetorical*, in which the negative-positive polarity is reversed.
(2) The *conventional*, in which a connection is made between a physical state (old or young) or an attitude (you limit wisdom to yourself) and a mental state (wise, foolish or proud).

(3) The *pragmatic*, in which the conclusion is drawn that certain behavior should follow from certain conditions.

Verse 38:8 illustrates the distinction between the levels, or stages, of implied meaning. First, it is made clear that it is God who shut in the sea with doors. Second, this implies that Job or any other human could not possibly have done it. Third, the RQ functions as a challenge.

These levels of implied meaning are also relevant to Alter's remarks on the RQs in 15:7-8. "Eliphaz, in one of the Friends' frequent appeals to the antiquity of received wisdom, upbraids Job" in a "sarcastic hyperbole" (Alter 1985:88). At the rhetorical level, it is implied that Job is not the first man that was born, and that he has not listened in the council of God. At the conventional level, it is implied that wisdom is in the council of God only. At the pragmatic level, Eliphaz makes clear that Job should not be so presumptuous.

4. Bias

The interpretation of Job 12:12 is complex and so it is more difficult to establish whether an RQ is involved in this verse. One could, for instance, maintain that v. 12 is an RQ implying an affirmative answer, still depending on הֲלֹא in v. 11. This is what the NIV has translated and what is suggested by Bobzin (1974:188). For 12:11-13, NIV has:

> Does not (הֲלֹא) the ear test words
>   as the tongue tastes food?
> Is not wisdom found among the aged?
>   Does not long life bring understanding?
> To God belong wisdom and power;
>   counsel and understanding are his.

This rendering of v. 12, however, causes it to contradict v. 13.

If 12:12 is treated not as an unmarked RQ, but as a declarative sentence, it does not contradict v. 13 at all. Rather, it is a contrast: the aged may have wisdom, but only God has the power to go with it. The *Bible de Jérusalem* has translated vv. 12-13 in that way.

> La sagesse est l'affaire des veillards,
>   le discernement le fait du grand âge.
> Mais en Lui résident sagesse et puissance,
>   à lui le conseil et le discernement.

The passage seems most coherent, maintaining the contrast with v. 13, if v. 12 is taken to be an RQ that implies a negative answer. The RQ could have been marked with the particle הֲ. It gives the reason for the preceding RQ in v. 11 and is followed by an answer starting in v. 13. Mitchell has translated accordingly, assuming, as in the *Bible de Jérusalem*, that a new paragraph starts with the RQ in v. 11:

> Doesn't the mind understand
>   as simply as the tongue tastes?
> Do all men grow in knowledge?
>   Are they wise because they are old?
> Only God is wise;
>   knowledge is his alone.

The *Groot Nieuws Bijbel* translates these verses in the same way, except for v. 11, which (in the English backtranslation) is "Should one not test statements, as one carefully tastes food?" The relations of vv. 11-13 can be described as follows: *RQ + RQ/reason + answer*.

In 12:12, the conventional belief that wisdom comes with age is implicitly referred to. On the rhetorical level of implied meaning this belief is repudiated. Koops's rhetorical and conventional levels of implied meaning seem to apply here in reverse order.

At this point something must be said about the bias of RQs. Generally, by asking a yes-no question the questioner often expresses his bias. He does not consider both possible responses to be equally valid but implies or expects that only one of them is right. In English, as Kiefer (1988:259) points out,

> the questioner's bias is signaled by various linguistic means such as tags, particles, negative questions, etc. For example, *Bill is coming tonight, isn't he? Isn't Bill coming tonight? Has she gone to bed already? Did someone call last night?* Normally, in cases when the questioner's expectations are not fulfilled, a more elaborate answer is required.

Hence "real" questions (those asked to elicit information) can be biased, too: a speaker expresses his "belief that a particular answer is likely to be correct" and requests "assurance that this belief is true" (Sadock and Zwicky 1985:180).

In Biblical Hebrew in general, הֲלֹא occurs in questions when an affirmative answer is implied (cf. Latin *nonne*) whereas הֲ is used when a question implies a negative answer (cf. Latin *num*). The latter is also found in real questions where the answer is uncertain (cf. Latin *-ne*) (Lettinga

1976:143 §61b). In addition however, הֲ-questions are found that imply an affirmative answer. This is acknowledged by van Rensburg: RQs with הֲ as well as with הֲלֹא can "elicit a preconceived positive response" (van Rensburg 1991:245). Such instances of הֲ in Job are found in 4:2; 6:26; 11:2 (הֲ...לֹא); 13:25; 15:11; 20:4; 35:2 (disapproval); 41:1; and possibly 22:2-3. Drijvers and Hawinkels (1971) have interpreted vv. 22:2-3 in this way. They therefore render it "Isn't an able man of use to God? Is it no help to Him at all when someone is sensible? Does it not benefit the Almighty when you are righteous?"

The question of bias is important in translation. It would, of course, be wrong to translate a question with a certain bias literally into a language in which its bias would then be different. "Negative yes-no questions are often positively biased questions . . . But in some languages (such as Japanese . . .) they are neutral questions about the negative proposition" (Sadock and Zwicky 1985:182).

Some of the RQs with הֲ imply an affirmative answer. We will now turn our attention to these. For example, in the RQ in 13:25, which starts with הֲ, an affirmative answer is implied: "Will you still frighten a wind-blown leaf and hunt down a piece of straw?" (Drijvers and Hawinkels). This statement is then motivated in the כִּי-sentence of v. 26: "that/For you write bitter things against me and make me inherit the iniquities of my youth." The motivation contains, in fact, what the speaker objects to. The relations of vv. 25-26 can thus be described as follows: *RQ ← objection*. Verse 26, though not an RQ, could be translated as one if that should be the best way to express that its contents are being objected to. This is done in the *Groot Nieuws Bijbel*: "Why do you call me to account for so much, and do I have to pay for the sins of my youth?" (English backtranslation). Van Selms (1971-72:147; 1978:31) refers to v. 25 as a motivated interrogative clause. If the particle הֲ is not taken as implying an affirmative answer, the RQ's relation with the כִּי-sentence would be awkward. Held (1969:79) translates the כִּי-sentence of v. 26 as an RQ and recommends the same for Job 7:12c, 10:6, and other instances.

Job 6:25 shows that "the interrogatory and exclamatory characteristics are often very difficult to keep apart" (van Rensburg 1991:238). The interrogative pronoun מַה occurs in v. 25a as well as in v. 25b. Verse 25a, an exclamation, is antithetically paralleled by the RQ in v. 25b. This RQ expects a strongly negative answer, which follows in v. 26.

> How forceful are honest words!
> But your reproof, what does it reprove?
> Do (הֲ) you think that you can reprove words,

> and treat the words of a despairing man as wind?
> You would even cast lots over the orphan . . .
> (6:25-27, NRSV; v. 26b, NIV)

At the first level of implication, v. 26 is another example of an RQ with the particle הֲ implying an affirmative answer: Job's friends do think that they can reprove his words and treat them just like wind. This is what is implied at the rhetorical level. Koops's terminology is of use here. At the conventional level it is implied that the friends are hard on a desperate man as if his words are just wind, violating the convention that one should not be hard on a despairing man. This implication is continued in v. 27: they would also be hard on an orphan. At the same time, however, v. 26 implies that the friends cannot reprove Job because of his words. At this level, the RQ in v. 25b is answered in the negative by the RQ in v. 26: "But your reproof, what does it reprove? You think you can reprove my words but you can't; and you are so hard as to treat the words of a desperate man as wind." Verse 26 has different implications at different levels and thus functions in more than one way in the context.

This passage illustrates that it is possible to answer an RQ with an RQ that itself constitutes the full answer. This is different from passages like Job 1:9-10 and Matt. 11:7-9 in which after some supplementary RQs the full answer is given but not in the form of an RQ. Nida (1964: 229) points this out:

> In some languages rhetorical questions always require answers. Such a series of questions as that in Matthew 11:7-9 is especially difficult to translate, for three of the questions are expanded by immediately appending supplementary questions, but the full answer is not given until the middle of verse 9.

No answer to the RQ in Job 6:25b is given however, except the RQ in 6:26. Loewen's 1981 translation advice concerning RQs needs to be amplified so as to include instances like Job 6:25b-26. He says that in addition to deciding how to translate a single RQ, you must also decide "whether you can use it unanswered as in the Bible, or whether you can retain it with its answer, or whether you should rewrite it as a statement" (Loewen 1981:149). This should be amplified to include deciding about sequences of RQs, whether all of them, only one, or none of them should be rewritten as a statement or answer.

When receptor-language readers do not recognize that a given question is rhetorical, the translator may need to rewrite it as a statement or it may be possible to make the rhetorical character of the question explicit by using a special construction or particle in translation.

In 6:28-29 Job confronts his friends with a challenge.

> Look me in the face ... (v. 28, TEV)
> my righteousness still stands (29b, NIV footnote)
>   Is (הֲ) there any wrong on my tongue? (30a)
>   Cannot (לֹא ... אִם) my taste discern calamity? (30b)

Job can come up with this challenge for the reason stated in the parallel RQs of 6:30. In 30a the particle הֲ implies a negative answer; in 30b אִם ... לֹא implies a positive answer. Watson (1984:339) quotes v. 30 as an illustration that in Hebrew poetry, which is largely composed of parallel couplets, RQs tend to come in pairs. Yet it is interesting to note that these RQs, though they are parallel, do not have the same bias at the rhetorical level. The verse relations of 6:25-30 could be formulated as follows: *RQ* (25b) + *RQ/answer* (26) + *impl. continued* (27) | challenge (28-29) + *RQ/reason* // *RQ/reason* (30).

After challenging his friends, Job continues his speech in chapter 7 with a complaint about his condition. The RQs in 6:30 thus constitute the closure of this part of Job's first answering speech.

5. Structuring

Chapter 21 illustrates nicely what part RQs can play in the structuring of a text. In 21:2-3, Job announces that he will speak. He starts with disjunctive RQs in v. 4 (Gesenius 1910 §150g). A question, probably an RQ, in v. 7 is the beginning of a lengthy description of the wicked. The virtual quotation put into the mouth of the wicked in vv. 14-15 largely consists of RQs. The description of the wicked ends with the RQ in v. 16 and the one in vv. 17-18.

Job 21:16 consists of an unmarked RQ: it is introduced with הֵן לֹא 'behold, not' and not with הֲלֹא הֵן 'behold, is it not?'. If this verse is not taken as an RQ, the resulting negative statement—"Their prosperity is not in their hand"—would not fit in the context of the chapter. Because of that, an RQ has to be recognized here.

> Behold, (הֵן לֹא) is not their prosperity in their hand?
> The counsel of the wicked is far from me. (21:16 RSV)

As proposed in the *Biblia Hebraica Stuttgartensia*, one could read מֵמֶּנּוּ instead of מֶנִּי at the end of this verse. The whole of v. 16 could then be an RQ. That is how the *Bible de Jérusalem* has translated 21:16:

Ne tiennent-ils pas leur bonheur en main,
et Dieu n'est-il pas écarté du conseil des méchants?

The RQ in 21:17-18—"How often (כַּמָּה) does calamity come upon the wicked ... ?"—is perhaps a transitional element; it also seems to be an introduction to a discussion about punishment. This, in turn, ends with the RQ in v. 21, which gives a reason for what precedes it: "For (כִּי) what (מַה) does he care about the family he leaves behind ... ?" (NIV). The RQ in v. 22 seems to be the beginning of a description of a certain state of affairs in vv. 23-26.

In 21:27 Job speaks to his friends again. This verse is closely connected with the RQs that follow. The RQs in 21:28 with the particle אַיֵּה 'where?' are virtually a quotation explicitly put into the mouth of the friends: כִּי תֹאמְרוּ 'For you say ...'. At the rhetorical level, it implies the negative statement that the house of such a prince and the tent of such prosperous wicked people are nowhere to be found. At the conventional level of implication, it is maintained that the wicked are never prosperous. At the pragmatic level, the view expressed by the quotation is condemned. In the NRSV, 21:27-30 reads:

Oh, I know your thoughts,
and your schemes to wrong me.
For you say, "Where (אַיֵּה) is the house of the prince?
Where (וְאַיֵּה) is the tent in which the wicked lived?"
Have you not (הֲלֹא) asked those who travel the roads,
and do you not (לֹא) accept their testimony,
that (כִּי) the wicked are spared in the day of calamity...

The opposition to 21:28 is introduced in v. 29 by means of RQs, implying that the view of those who travel is opposite to the view put into the mouth of Job's friends. It is the testimony of those who travel that the wicked escape from calamity. Verse 29 is thus followed by the speaker's answer in the form of subordinate clauses in v. 30 as in 38:8-11(discussed in the section of unmarked RQs).

The parallel RQs in 21:31 imply a negative answer: "Who (מִי) declares his way to his face and for what he has done, who (מִי) requites him?" Nobody repays the wicked for what they have done. This answer follows in vv. 32-33, a description of what happens instead: "He is carried to the grave, and watch is kept over his tomb..." (NIV). Finally, the RQ in 34a with the particle אֵיךְ 'how?' constitutes the conclusion of vv. 29-33 and forms the closure of the speech: "How then can you console me with your nonsense when nothing is left of your answers but falsehood?" The verse relations of 21:28-34 are the following: *RQ/virtual quotation* (28) + *RQ/opposition* (29) + *subordCl/answer* (30) + *RQ // RQ* (31) + *answer* (32-33) + *RQ/conclusion* (34).

Other examples in Job of RQs with a structuring function, either starting a section or closing one, are 3:11-12; 4:6-7, 17, 21; 6:11-13; 8:2, 10-11; 9:12; 10:18; 11:2-3, 7; 12:11-12; 13:7-8; 15:7; 18:2-3; 19:2, 22; 22:2-3, 12; 24:25; 28:12, 20; 35:2; 38:2; and 39:5, 9, 19, 26.

In 31:1b, וּמָה 'and what?'—unless one reads מֶהִתְבּוֹנֵן here as is proposed in the BHS—introduces an RQ. The RQ functions as an "exclamation of indignation," as "the indignant refusal of a demand" (Gesenius 1910:§148a):

> I have made a covenant with my eyes;
> how then (וּמָה) could I look upon a virgin? (31:1, NRSV)

The RQ in 31:2, introduced by וּמֶה, is commonly interpreted as the reason for Job's behavior in v. 1. The NIV translates it "For what is man's lot from God above, his heritage from the Almighty on high?" The RQ in v. 3, introduced by הֲלֹא, constitutes the answer: "Is it not ruin for the wicked, disaster for those who do wrong?" (NIV). In vv. 2-3, then, a "virtual quotation" is used by which Job "presents the belief he formerly held in the justice of God, that served as the basis of his code of moral behavior" (Gordis 1978:545). It is a general belief, which is probably why the NIV translated it *"man's* lot . . . *his* heritage" (italics mine). In this view, the verse relations in 31:1-3 would be as follows: *RQ + virtual quotation:* {*RQ/reason + RQ/answer*}.

A different interpretation of 31:2 is followed by the 1982 Willibrord translation (which is Dutch): "*And* what is *my* lot from God, what does the Almighty decree from on high?" (English backtranslation, italics mine). Mitchell translates it "But what good has virtue done me . . . ?" In this view, the conjunction ו introduces what after v. 1 would imply the unexpected. The RQ in v. 2 is then followed by a supposed answer only, a virtual quotation in v. 3. (On the other hand, the view in v. 3 is also the reason for asking the question in v. 2.) The relations in vv. 1-3 are thus as follows: *RQ + RQ/unexpected + RQ/'answer'/virtual quotation*.

At the first level of implied meaning, the bias of the RQ in 31:3 is indeed that it is "expected to be answered in the affirmative," as Brongers (1981:179) maintains. At a further level however, the RQ has a negative bias, implying that it is a virtual quotation the speaker disagrees with. Unlike the virtual quotation in 21:14-15 and 28, the virtual quotation here is implicit. That is, it is not formally introduced as such. In translating, it may be necessary to make this information explicit. This is what the

Willibrord translation does: "Disaster for the wicked—they say—misfortune for all who do evil" (English backtranslation).

The opposition to this is introduced by the RQ in 31:4: "Does he not see my ways, and number all my steps?" (NRSV). Introduced by הֲלֹא, this RQ is expected to be answered in the affirmative at the rhetorical level: He, God, does see Job's ways and number his steps. At what might be called the conventional level, Job implies that he is blameless and this implication is continued in the rest of the chapter. At the pragmatic level it is perhaps implied that God should have rewarded him accordingly.

Verse 31:5 starts with אִם 'if'. If one takes v. 5 to be a conditional protasis, v. 6 can hardly be the apodosis of v. 5. One could then assume that v. 5 is part of a larger conditional structure, formed by a protasis in vv. 5 and 7 and an apodosis in v. 8. The protasis would then be interrupted by v. 6 (NRSV, Bobzin 1974:389-90), in which case the structure of the passage would be awkward.

It would seem more natural to treat 31:5 as Gordis (1978:544) does, as an RQ implying a negative answer: "Ai-je fait route avec le mensonge, pressé le pas vers la fausseté?" (*Bible de Jérusalem*). The answer, then, follows in v. 6: "Let me be weighed in honest scales, and let God know that I am blameless."

Verse 31:5 may illustrate the tension between form and function. The RQ in v. 5 probably functions as an oath. It is thus possible to translate vv. 5–6 as an oath: "I swear I have never acted wickedly and never tried to deceive others . . . he will see how innocent I am" (TEV, *Groot Nieuws Bijbel*).

The verse relations in 31:1-6 can be described as follows: *RQ* (1) + *RQ/unexpected* (2) + *RQ/'answer'/virtual quotation* (3) + *RQ/opposition* (4) // *RQ/oath* (5) + *answer/wish* (6).

6. Conclusion

RQs in Job are frequently followed by their answer, which may itself take the form of an RQ. On the other hand, the answer is often left implicit. A difference in function may or may not be involved.

Some of the functions of RQs in the Book of Job are as follows: RQs can open or close a section and thus play a part in the structuring of the text. They can provide a reason or answer, constitute an opposition or conclusion. RQs may have different implications at different levels and thus function in more than one way in their context. The bias of RQs affects the interpretation of the passages in which they occur.

References

Alter, Robert. 1985. *The art of biblical poetry*. New York: Basic Books.
Beekman, John, and John Callow. 1976. *Translating the Word of God*. Grand Rapids: Zondervan.
Berlin, A. 1979. Grammatical aspects of biblical parallelism. *Hebrew Union College Annual* 50:17-43. (Cincinnati: Hebrew Union College, Jewish Institute of Religion.)
Biblia Hebraica Stuttgartensia. 1967-77. Stuttgart: Deutsche Bibelstiftung.
Bible de Jérusalem: La Sainte Bible traduite en français sous la direction de l'École biblique de Jérusalem. 1986.
Bobzin, H. 1974. Die 'Tempora' im Hiobdialog. Diss., Chicago 16.129. Marburg an der Lahn.
Brongers, H. A. 1981. Some remarks on the biblical particle *hl'*. *Oudtestamentische Studiën* 21:177-89.
de Waard, J. and E. A. Nida. 1986. *From one language to another: Functional equivalence in Bible translation*. New York: Thomas Nelson.
Drijvers, P., and P. Hawinkels. 1971. *Job*. Bilthoven, Netherlands: Ambo.
Gesenius, W., and E. Kautzsch, eds. 1910. *Gesenius' Hebrew grammar*. 2d English ed. Rev. and trans. by A. E. Cowley. Oxford: University Press.
Gordis, R. 1978. *The Book of Job: Commentary, new translation, and special studies*. Moreshet Series, 2. New York: Jewish Theological Seminary of America.
Groot Nieuws Bijbel [The Bible in Today's Dutch]. 1983.
Held, Moshe. 1969. Rhetorical questions in Ugaritic and Biblical Hebrew. *Eretz-Israel: Archaelogical, Historical and Geographical Studies* 9:71-79.
Kiefer, F. 1988. On the pragmatics of answers. In *Questions and questioning*, ed. M. Meyer, 255-79. Berlin and New York: de Gruyter.
Koops, R. 1988. Rhetorical questions and implied meaning in the book of Job. *The Bible Translator* 39:415-23.
Lettinga, J. P. 1976. *Grammatica van het Bijbels Hebreeuws*. Leiden: Brill.
Loewen, J. A. 1981. *The practice of translating: Drills for training translators*. Helps for Translators.
Longacre, R. E. 1976. *An anatomy of speech notions*. Lisse, Netherlands: Peter de Ridder.
Mitchell, Stephen. 1992. *The book of Job: Translated and with an introduction*. New York: Harper Perennial.
Nida, E. A. 1964. *Toward a science of translating*. Leiden: Brill.
Nida, E. A., J. P. Louw, A. H. Snyman, and J. v. W. Cronje. 1983. *Style and discourse: With special reference to the Greek New Testament*. Cape Town: Bible Society.
O'Connor, M. 1980. *Hebrew verse structure*. Winona Lake, Ind.: Eisenbrauns.
Sadock, J. M., and A. M. Zwicky. 1985. Speech act distinctions in syntax. In *Clause structure*, vol. 1 of *Language typology and syntactic description*, ed. T. Shopen, 155-96. Cambridge: University Press.
Selms, A. van. 1971-72. Motivated interrogative sentences in Biblical Hebrew. *Semitics* 2:143-49.
———. 1978. Motivated interrogative sentences in the book of Job. *Semitics* 6:28-35.

Snell-Hornby, M. 1988. *Translation studies: An integrated approach.* Amsterdam: Benjamins.
van Rensburg, J. F. J. 1991. Wise men saying things by asking questions: The function of the interrogative in Job 3 to 14. *Old Testament Essays* 4:227–47.
Watson, W. G. E. 1984. *Classical Hebrew poetry: A guide to its techniques.* Journal for the Study of Old Testament, Supplement Series, 26.
Willibrord Vertaling (Catholic translation in Dutch). 1982.

16

GENRE CRITICISM AND THE PSALMS
What Discourse Typology Can Tell Us about the Text
(with Special Reference to Psalm 31)

Ernst R. Wendland

> How do we "read" (and interpret) biblical texts? This article presents a "structure-functional" methodology within the framework of a generic, typological approach to literary discourse. This is applied to a description and analysis of the lyric-religious poetry of the Psalter, and in particular Psalm 31. After a survey of the notion of "genre-criticism" in relation to biblical poetry, two major psalmic (macro)genres are outlined, the "lament" and the "eulogy." Their structural and functional interaction within Psalm 31 is then examined in terms of the poetic composition as a whole and its central theme, which revolves around the covenantal ḥesed-relationship between Yahweh and his people. Several alternative discourse formats are evaluated, and the hermeneutical importance of adopting such a generic text-stylistic and functionally oriented perspective is pointed out.

In the latter half of this century there has been what Ryken terms a "quiet revolution" taking place in biblical studies as an increasing number of scholars—along with ordinary students of the Word—come to an ever greater awareness that the Bible is literature and that this fact has important implications for interpretation. As Ryken states, "the methods of literary scholarship are a necessary part of any complete study of the Bible" (1984:11).

A problem exists, however, in the application of this insight in biblical studies. The problem, as Wiklander observes, is that although "few scholars—if any—would seriously deny this basic premise ... the extent to which it is allowed to shape exegetical work varies quite considerably" (1984:2). The present study is intended to suggest one important application of a literary-based approach to the text of the Old Testament, whether viewed in its entirety or only with respect to that portion which is the special focus of this particular investigation, the Book of Psalms. A discourse-oriented "generic perspective" forms the crucial first step in the examination of any biblical pericope, large or small; such a comprehensive framework serves to guide the analytical process as the major and minor segments are considered in relation to one another and to the whole of which they are parts.

1. Interpreting the Bible as "literature"

One's understanding of the concept of "literature" will, to some extent, determine the nature and scope of one's investigation. For some, it is restricted to "something written (as the Bible is basically a 'book')" (Maier and Tollers 1979:3); thus "a text is a written work, in contrast to an oral performance" (Sharlemann 1987:7). However, recent studies that draw attention to the "oral overlay" (Achtemeier 1990:3) or "auditory aura" (Silberman 1987:3) of ancient *written* documents suggest that the distinction between the two modes of communication in these texts is not at all easy to maintain since "in practice, interaction between oral and written forms is extremely common" (Finnegan 1977:160) in classical as well as contemporary literature (cf. Finnegan 1970:18). Other scholars would limit the notion of "literature" to "imaginative" or "creative" discourse "in contrast to expository writing," and by this definition "some parts of the Bible are more literary and other parts are less literary" (Ryken 1984:12). I would prefer to operate with a broader definition of literature, combining Neufeldt's with aspects of Webster's: "all of such writings [regardless of the degree of oral influence] considered as having permanent value, excellence of form, great emotional effect... because of their beauty, imagination [adding: content and significance]" (Neufeldt 1988:789).

What then are the implications of such a perspective for biblical interpretation? The case has been well put in general terms by one who ought to know, the great author and literary critic C. S. Lewis: "There is a... sense in which the Bible, since it is after all literature, cannot be properly read except as literature; and the different parts of it as the different sorts of literature that they are" (1958:3).

But what does it mean to read the Scriptures "as literature"? How does literature per se affect reading and interpretation? What it means is, to approach a text with a conscious awareness of the expressive and affective (including the emotive and esthetic) dimensions of semantically significant and stylistically shaped verbal discourse. This is in addition to being aware of the cognitively oriented "information" (i.e., theology) that such writing conveys. When dealing with the Word of God, one would not wish to place too much emphasis on the "imaginative" or "creative" element of the human source or author; but Ryken (1984:14) draws attention to a valid application on the part of all perceptive receptors (listeners/readers): "[Literature] constantly appeals to our imagination (the image-making and image-perceiving capacity within us). Literature *images* forth some aspect of reality."

While this too can be taken too far (as is frequently the case in so-called reader-response criticism), it is important for interpreters to consider those stylistic devices, such as metaphor and sarcasm, which strongly stimulate or appeal to one's perceptions, feelings, moods, and attitudes. These devices are usually bound up with the key aspects of an author's theme or purpose.

Many other, more detailed definitions and descriptions of literature are, of course, available in standard textbooks on the subject, but it suffices to point out what would appear to be the most important characteristic from the standpoint of discourse analysis, namely, the predominant focus upon linguistic form that is typical of a superior literary composition. In other words, there is a special emphasis upon the artistic dimension of discourse—or what Jakobson termed the *poetic function* of the text. According to this principle, "the two basic modes of arrangement used in verbal behavior, selection and combination" (Jakobson 1972:95) are maximized in order to foreground key aspects of the message and to heighten its interest value, emotive impact and persuasive appeal. Verbal artists, including the various biblical authors, frequently exploit the creative, "metaphoric" potential of language in order to present what Paul Ricoeur calls a "re-description" of reality (1975:88) "in which the world is not so much replicated as transfigured in the vision that poet and audience come to share" (Davis 1992:95).

The result of this poetic process, which may be manifested in prose texts as well as in poetry, is normally a discourse that is heavily figured (i.e., with many diverse rhetorical tropes represented), strongly patterned and permeated by recursive syntagmatic and paradigmatic structures of all kinds (i.e., lexical, phonological, syntactic, semantic, pragmatic) on all levels, from the word on up to the composition as a whole. Literature thus maximizes the "how" (or style) of the text in order to highlight the "what" (i.e., content) and the "why" (i.e., intent). This is done by means of such artistic features as "pattern or design, theme or central focus, organic unity (also called unity in variety, or theme and variation), coherence, balance, contrast, symmetry, repetition or recurrence, variation, and unified progression" (Ryken 1984:23–24).

It is this formal but fluid quality of literary writing that we wish to explore more fully in relation to Hebrew lyric discourse, Psalm 31 in particular. We will gradually move from the generic to the specific in the process of analysis in order to demonstrate how diverse rhetorical structures and strategies persistently and progressively shape the reader/listeners' expectations and focus their individual interpretive activities, whether these be implicitly or explicitly realized.

1.1 "Genre criticism" and why it is necessary

Genre criticism is a mode of literary analysis that pays special attention to the distinct compositional forms, or genres, found in a given corpus of literature. The term *genre* refers to "a group of texts similar in their mood, content, structure or phraseology" (Longman 1988:20). Such conventionalized discourse templates, or characteristic feature-sets, tend to "reflect the functions and goals involved in particular social occasions as well as the purposes of the participants in them" (Hatim and Mason 1990:69). Every literary genre observes its own rules or procedures of construction and may therefore be classified on the basis of its distinctive stylistic and pragmatic features. Such attributes pertain largely to linguistic organization; but topical content, such as major themes and motifs, and a progressive illocutionary configuration, or "format" (ibid., 171), are also involved. In addition to these aspects of "outer form," some critics attempt to describe genres in terms of "inner form," that is, "attitude, tone, purpose—more crudely, subject and audience" (Wellek and Warren 1956:219). This is what Hatim and Mason term "discourse" (1990:141). But such an enterprise is more subjective in nature and hence not as helpful in the practice of text exegesis and compositional analysis.

A major problem in genre criticism is one of definition in relation to scope. Simply put, how generic can a "genre" be? A lyric poem, novel, letter, newspaper, recipe, and drama are certainly different kinds of literature, but do these constitute different "genres"? Gerstenberger (1988:243, 258), for example, has a "glossary" of poetic "genres" that range from the abstract "accusation" (*Anklage*) to the specific "Zion hymn" (*Zionshymnus*).

Closely related to this is the question of who sets the standard. In other words, on what basis are the various genre-defining criteria determined? There are two principal perspectives. The first is the alien outsider's *etic* point of view (i.e., a classification which is putatively, perhaps only possibly, universal), a cross-cultural taxonomy defined and described with reference to a behavioral feature, such as literature, that is typical of any human society (see Pike and Pike 1977:484). The second is the insider's *emic* viewpoint in which "an entity is seen from the perspective of the internal "logic" or structure of its containing systems; with contrastive identificational features, variants, and distribution in class, sequence, and system of a universe of discourse" (ibid., 483).

The Pikes' linguistically focused etic/emic dichotomy corresponds in part to what the well-known literary critic E. D. Hirsch terms "intrinsic" and "extrinsic" genres. The former he defines as "that sense of the whole by means of which an interpreter can correctly understand any part in its determinacy" (1967:86). An intrinsic (emic) genre is found within a particular system of literature, for it is grounded in actual usage and related to shared experiences, on the one hand, and meaning expectations, on the other—all of which evoke "a generic conception which controls [one's] utterance" (ibid., 80). By way of contrast then, an "extrinsic genre" is "a generic sense of the whole different from the speaker's...a wrong guess" (ibid., 88). In Hirsch's terms, an "etic" conception would be "a preliminary genre idea that is vague and broad...a preliminary heuristic tool that must be further sharpened before it can discriminate the functions of the partial meanings in their determinacy" (ibid.), that is, with respect to a given language and literature.

One way of differentiating these two perspectives would be to use the expression *discourse type* for the universal, etic classes, such as prose and poetry on the highest level, or more specific classes such as narrative, procedural, hortatory, expository, juridical, and predictive (cf. Longacre's 1989 delineation of types and their application to the Joseph story). The term *genre* would then be reserved for intrinsic, emic, literature-specific categories (Wendland 1985:82–83), such as the ancient system of classification reflected in the superscriptions of the Psalms:

> (1) *mizmor* ("psalm"); (2) *shiggaion* [probably a literary or musical term]; (3) *miktam* [another literary/musical term]; (4) *shir* ("song"); (5) *maskil* [literary/musical term]; (6) *tephillah* ("prayer"); (7) *tehillah* ("praise"); (8) *lehazkir* ("for being remembered"—i.e., before God, a petition); (9) *letodah* ("for praising" or "for giving thanks"); (10) *lelammed* ("for teaching"); and (11) *shir yedidot* ("song of loves"—i.e., a wedding song). (Barker 1985:782)

The problem is that these terms cannot be specified with precision. Indeed, there is much overlapping in the categories as currently defined (e.g., with *shir*). Therefore they are not very useful as analytical designations. A comparative literary approach carried out in the light of other ancient Near Eastern literary traditions is helpful, but not definitive, because their interactive development has not yet been fully established, though additional evidence and associated analyses are slowly accumulating.

For practical purposes, then, in our study of the Psalter, we will have to rely upon a combined etic-emic framework, that is, more or less general category terms, coupled with corpus-specific descriptions of the major formal, semantic, and pragmatic diagnostic features of the several "genres" and "subgenres" posited (see Bergen 1987:335). We will be doing this with particular reference to the text of Psalm 31.

But of what value are such distinctions in the operation of discourse analysis? Hirsch puts the case unequivocally: "All understanding of verbal meaning is necessarily genre-bound" (1967:76). He says more fully (75),

> An interpreter's notion of the type of meaning he confronts will powerfully influence his understanding of details...at every level of sophistication...[Thus] an interpretation is helplessly dependent on the generic conception with which the interpreter happens to start.

This process is simply an instance of the Gestalt principle of figure and ground: One's notion of the meaning potential of the whole (the type or genre) helps to determine one's understanding of the parts (the specific details which constitute any given example of the whole). The converse is also true, thus completing this discourse application of the "hermeneutic circle" (ibid., 76).

"Genre functions as a valuable link between the text and the reader" (Osborn 1991:150), and hence "an understanding of literary forms is crucial to correct biblical interpretation" (Klein et al. 1993:261). All receptors approach a given discourse in their language, whether oral or written, with a certain literary (as distinct from linguistic) "competence," based on learning and past experience, which enables them to recognize and interpret the various stylistic features that are present in the text (Barton 1984:11-19). The more sophisticated the reader/listener, the greater is his or her competence. The typical conventions associated with a particular genre furnish a specific hermeneutical strategy that guides them through the composition—informing, enlightening, motivating, and sometimes even surprising them along the way (i.e., when the expected norms, forms, and structures are deliberately flouted, altered, or ignored). Genre thus acts like a "program" that gives shape to a text and arranges its details into an identifiable, more readily processed pattern—or better, a *system* of linear, concentric, and hierarchically organized patterns which interact and overlap to encompass the literary whole.

The diverse codes and conventions associated with different genres "are capable of different kinds of meaning and offer different kinds of information to a reader" (Tate 1991:64). However, such a significant "meaning potential" exists only in a virtual state until it is actualized by someone who is familiar with the formal system of linguistic and literary signals of the genre and related subgenres or tropes built into the text by the original author.

Robert Alter (1981:47) describes the process thus:

> A coherent reading of any art work, whatever the medium, requires some detailed awareness of the grid of conventions upon which, and

against which, the individual work operates... an elaborate set of tacit agreements about the ordering of the art work is at all times the enabling context in which the complex communication of art occurs. Through our awareness of convention we can recognize significant or simply pleasing patterns of repetition, symmetry, contrast; we can discriminate between the verisimilar and the fabulous, pick up directional clues in a narrative work, see what is innovative and what is deliberately traditional at each nexus of the artistic creation.

Furthermore, an explicit or implicit knowledge of generic organization and operation can lessen the likelihood of one's misinterpreting an artistic piece of literature, for example, one in which the use of irony or hyperbole is a prominent feature.

On the other hand, ignorance of the formal and semantic norms associated with a given genre can lead the reader/interpreter into what James Barr (1973:125) terms a "literary category mistake," which he explains as follows:

> Failures to comprehend the literary genre lead to a use of the biblical assertions with a wrong function... Genre mistakes cause the wrong kind of truth values to be attached to biblical sentences. Literary embellishments then come to be regarded as scientifically true assertions.

One must be careful, of course, not to push this too far in the direction of a denial of the Scripture's capacity to set forth "propositional truth" or inerrant revelation, but the point is well taken. Genre recognition is thus an integral part of the evangelical, "grammatical-historical" method of exegesis. As Vanhoozer (1986:80) says,

> The genre provides the *literary context* for a given sentence [text] and, therefore, partly determines what the sentence [text] means and how it should be taken... Genre thus enables the reader to interpret meaning and to recognize what kinds of truth claims are being made in and by a text.

The present study is intended to show how the special attention devoted to both generic and specific forms in the analysis of Biblical Hebrew poetry can direct one more confidently along the path of a meaningful interpretation of such artistically composed theological literature.

1.2 Genre analysis from a "form-critical" perspective

1.2.1 Background and method

Genre analysis began to be taken seriously as a valid exegetical exercise around the turn of the century. It found its most prominent and influential expression in the critical school known as "Form Criticism" (FC). (In German it is known as *Gattungsforschung* or, in relation to the NT, *Formgeschichte*.)

Though carried on by "outsiders," the FC approach was emic in the sense that it sought to describe and analyze the Bible on its own terms and to develop a system of classification that would reflect the initial, preliterary compositional and performance setting as closely as possible. Accordingly, practitioners of the method attempted to categorize the various types of literature, or "genres" (Ger. *Gattungen*), on the basis of their formal features and the assumed "life-setting" (*Sitz im Leben*) of each one. Although there were several important precursors (e.g., J. G. von Herder 1782), FC was popularized and established largely through the work of the German scholar Hermann Gunkel ([1862–1932] 1967). Gunkel's goal was to describe the religious literary corpus of ancient Israel in a functional manner and on a comparative basis. That is, he particularly emphasized its historical development and oral-aural usage in relation to diverse sociological and cultural settings.

From the very beginning, FC adopted a decidedly discourse-oriented methodology, endeavoring to define and describe each "genre" posited in terms of its original form, meaning, function, and context. "For Gunkel, every genre or literary type has a specific content and mood, a formal language of expression, and a setting in life" (Hayes 1979:128). His process of analysis, which represented a distinct break from prior, author-centered, "source-critical" ("documentary") studies, was founded upon four interrelated presuppositions:

(1) "every written document [of Scripture] was preceded by some oral stage of development; ...
(2) "something can be learned of the oral stage or stages by a study of analogous literary forms [i.e., of other cultures]" (Armerding 1983:44);
(3) "in the earliest usage ... genres were short, oral, and originated in and were employed in general, communal life" (Hayes 1979:129); and
(4) the individual instances of a given genre (e.g., in the Psalms) have similar features of form, content, social setting, and cultic func-

tion, and therefore "by elucidating a whole group, each separate psalm in that group becomes clearer" (Driyvers 1965:36).

John Barton (1984:32) offers a helpful definition of the crucial FC unit or object of analysis:

> A *Gattung* or genre is a *conventional pattern, recognizable by certain formal criteria* (style, shape, tone, particular syntactic or even grammatical structures, recurring formulaic patterns), which is *used in a particular society in social contexts which are governed by certain formal conventions*.

(See also Driyvers 1965:46.)

The major steps that are applied in a typical FC study have been summarized by Tucker (1971:11):

(1) analysis of the structure [i.e., internal form],
(2) description of the genre [i.e., external form],
(3) definition of the setting or settings, and
(4) statement of the intention, purpose, or function of the text.

Following Gunkel, FC analysts such as his renowned student Sigmund Mowinckel (e.g., 1962) soon came to devote most of their attention to an investigation of the implications of their unproven, and currently unprovable, assumptions concerning the genesis of biblical literature. This endeavor has led in turn to much speculation and often a partial vitiation of some of the important insights of their new approach to the composition and operation of the Word of God in its original setting.

1.2.2 Evaluation and conclusion

The Form Critics were among the first to take a "discourse analysis" of the biblical text seriously, viewing pericopes as functioning wholes rather than as a patchwork of diverse "sources" or "documents." The problem was that they practiced this from a distinctive and often disruptive bias whereby a supposedly original oral context often became the determining factor in deciding textual and interpretive issues. In any case, the FC method recognizes that underlying the surface diversity of a number of apparently only loosely related Scripture texts a fundamental similarity may exist with respect to general theological content, emotive mood, compositional structure, and especially communicative function. This principle, augmented by a wide-ranging comparative approach (Knierim 1985:139), enables the analyst to categorize such compositions into a group of related types that can be studied according to a single generic framework and a common set of diagnostic criteria. Such investigations provide many good insights into specific text types and subgenres found in the Hebrew Bible, its lyric poetry in particular, thus giving the reader some idea of "what meanings to look for" (Barton 1984:34), hence also "what type of questions can sensibly be asked of the material" (Tate 1991:64) and, furthermore, what answers can reasonably be expected.

In conjunction with its exploration of the original text, FC studies also help contemporary interpreters to better recognize and understand something of the probable initial oral-aural contextual situations, religious (cultic/ritual) occasions of use, and the likely theological significance to be attached to the various genres identified.

> As Gunkel put it: "To understand a literary type we must in each case have the whole situation clearly before us and ask ourselves, Who is speaking? Who are the listeners? What is the *mise en scène* [French: the setting on stage] at the time? What effect is aimed at?" (Soulen 1976:62)

This enlightening background pertains especially to the different services of worship, both individual and communal, that are prescribed in the Torah and which were practiced in ancient Israel with varying degrees of fidelity, purity, and commitment (Driyvers 1965:43). The FC emphasis upon generic function, though frequently skewed by the positing of certain radical and highly hypothetical settings, did serve to pave the way for more conservative, text-based and communication-oriented, approaches, most notably, the "rhetorical critical" methodology of James Muilenburg (e.g., [1969] 1992).

Although stimulating and informative in a general sort of way, most FC analyses need a rather great deal of correction and supplementation. Their overemphasis on the supposed original *Sitz im Leben*, both historical and sociocultural, often produces very speculative and idiosyncratic reconstructions, with one debatable prop used to support another. "Since in many cases the context can only be conjectured... the crux of the interpretation remains in question" (Greenwood 1970:419). This is a particularly questionable procedure when "there may already be a perfectly clear life-setting for the unit presented in the [Hebrew] text" (Armerding 1983:65), or when such a focus upon the prehistory of the text does little to increase our understanding of the received Masoretic text (Greidanus 1988:54). Furthermore, there tends to be an unsubstantiated concern with the alleged predominant influence of the communal and/or royal cult upon biblical composition (e.g., Mowinckel 1962), a hypothesis that is based to a great extent upon pagan, non-Israelite models. Here too, "in the search for a life-setting, the institutions clearly pictured in Israel's own tradition must provide the basis for objective study" (Armerding 1983:65) and the possibility of individual artistic creation and religious expression must not be lost sight of (cf. Berry 1993:82).

It is somewhat ironic, as Austin Farrar observes, that

> form-criticism [as normally practiced] is rather misleadingly so called, because the name suggests an attempt to appreciate the form of a complete literary unit... Whereas what form-criticism studies is the form of small constituent parts... (cited in Ryken 1984:29)

Thus the results of a typical FC analysis are at times just as "deconstructive" and atomistic, or constituent-oriented, as those of Source Criticism. The main difference is that the fragments or segments posited by FC are supposedly oral and traditional in nature, rather than being inscribed and attributable to specific "authors" (or "redactors"). The adverse, disintegrative effects upon the text of Scripture are largely the same, however. Ryken aptly calls it "textual excavation" (1984:30).

There is also a certain inflexibility of perspective demonstrated, where the possibility of creativity and a deliberate "defamiliarization" in the application of genres is not taken into account, that is, the use of a recognized compositional form in a new or unexpected literary or situational setting. In consequence, form-critical studies suffer as they break the original text down "into fragments so small that any unity of thought is lost" (Armerding 1983:64). On the other hand, there is also the danger that in an effort to determine what is common, typical, and representative of a putative genre, its personal, individual, and unique stylistic features may be overlooked. This tendency towards (over)generalization and an (over)emphasis upon the *Gattung* and its preliterary history may "actually obscure the thought and intention of the writer or speaker" (Muilenburg 1992:54). In other words, "the science of [form] criticism remains uncomfortable with the diversity of the Psalms [and other distinct Hebrew discourse genres]" (Berry 1993:142).

Another general criticism of the FC approach is that an alien ("etic") bias frequently intrudes, especially with regard to certain rationalistic or naturalistic presuppositions that underlie some of the descriptive literary terms used (Greidanus 1988:53). Designations such as "myth," "legend," "fable," and "saga," for example, when employed in reference to some of the older Hebrew narrative texts (e.g., Coats 1985), convey a notion of fictionality and the fantastic that stands in contrast to the strong assumption of historicity and divine action which the Scriptures assert both explicitly and implicitly (in the ten תּוֹלְדֹת 'generations' of Genesis, for example). In addition, FC analysts sometimes take their own theoretical framework too seriously, reading it back into the biblical setting as if under the assumption that "the ancient Israelites made similar psalm [and other] studies and operated consciously with this type of form criticism" (Leupold 1959:11).

In conclusion, early form-critical studies are generally quite deficient due to their lack of a comprehensive, communication-centered, linguistically governed, discourse-oriented method of analyzing and interpreting the biblical text and its sociocultural context. Diachronic and synchronic factors are not clearly differentiated, and historical issues are often emphasized at the expense of the final, received form of the (Masoretic) text. Accordingly, the relationships between form, content, and function are not always explicitly or convincingly drawn, in terms of "speech (text) acts" for example (MacDonald 1992:163). The findings of FC investigation can be profitable, especially those of more recent origin (e.g., Koch, Hardmeier, referred to in Knierim 1985:139ff.). But most must be used with caution—as an initial and tentative guide perhaps—and always with a critical awareness of where they can go wrong. The information supplied tends to be largely of an extrinsic, organizational, or background nature and hence needs to be followed up by an intensive literary-structural and rhetorical-poetic examination of the textual data. The aim of the latter is to reveal precisely how (stylistically) and why (functionally) the original author conveyed a definite ethical and theological message with distinct affective force and esthetic appeal, not only to the initially intended constituency, but also to countless readers and hearers in subsequent ages, right up to the present day.

Such an agenda provides a basis for the study that forms the remainder of this essay, which will proceed from more generic typological observations to a specific textual analysis with the following objectives:

(1) propose a series of criteria for determining the degree of poetry ("poeticality") that is manifested by a given pericope of the Hebrew Scriptures;
(2) describe the two principal genres of lyric poetry to be found in the Psalter, together with several of their major subcategories;
(3) outline a rhetorical, discourse-directed method of text analysis (i.e., a holistic, contextualized, "structure-functional");
(4) apply these procedures in an integrated analysis of Psalm 31 as a way of illustrating this technique;
(5) summarize the possible hermeneutical and practical implications of this sort of methodology for biblical studies. (What can it tell us about the original text with respect to form, content, and function?)

2. The nature of Biblical Hebrew poetry

Before one can adequately investigate the genres of poetry in the Hebrew Scriptures, it is useful to know something of the poetic potential of such discourse. In other words, what are the features that mark a text as being "poetic" as distinct from "prosaic" in nature? The distinction between prose and poetry is important, for it affects how the process of interpreting a given text is carried out, for example, more or less literally, or with a greater or lesser emphasis on formal patterning. However, as in much of art, so also in literary discourse, it is not so much a matter of either-or as it is of more-or-less. That is to say, most verbal art manifests a continuum of characteristics that range between the two putative poles of prose and poetry, a proportion that varies according to the purpose of a given text in relation to both its linguistic cotext as well as its situational context.

As an introduction to the subsequent treatment of a lyric functional typology, ten of the most important features of "psalmodic language" follow. (For a fuller description, see Wendland 1993, chap. 2.) Used in conjunction with one another, these ten enable the analyst to propose an initial "type-setting" of a given pericope as being more or less poetic in quality. If it is quite similar to those of the Psalter in form, a literary text may accordingly be expected to function in a corresponding manner, namely, as a personal or communal expression of petition and/or praise. These ten characteristics will be illustrated in the analysis of Psalm 31 in section 4.

1. *Balanced lineation:* Hebrew poetic lines ("cola") typically occur in symmetrical pairs (i.e., "parallelism") averaging six "words" per couplet/clause and complementing one another through some close correspondence with respect to recursive rhythm (accentual "meter"), phonological quality, morphosyntactic patterning, propositional relations, and/or the meaning in general.
2. *Condensation:* There is a pronounced brevity of expression brought about by apocopation, ellipsis (especially verb "gapping"), semantic laconicity, an absence of the "prose particles" (i.e., the definite article, sign of the direct object, relative pronoun, and inseparable prepositions: *b-*, *l-*, *k-*), as well as a reduction in the incidence of clause-initial *waw* (particularly in the initial, or "A," colon).
3. *Figuration:* Poetry is characterized by a greater concentration of distinctly religious, symbolical language (including allusive "mythological") and imagery such as simile, metaphor, metonymy, synecdoche, merism, apostrophe, personification, and (overlapping with the next category) irony or sarcasm.

4. *Intensification:* Poetic language is frequently heightened emotively by means of emphatic devices such as exclamations, intensifiers, hyperbole, rhetorical questions, cohortatives, and jussives.
5. *Transposition:* One often finds a shift in the expected ("prosaic") order of clausal and even phrasal constituents to form chiastic and other arrangements that serve to foreground selected items of information and also allow the parallel lines to reflect upon each other semantically and pragmatically (while disrupting the normal narrative usage with respect to verbal [*wayyiqtol*] sequence).
6. *Phonesthetic appeal:* The oral-aural qualities of the discourse are maximized through the utilization of reiterated phonological features, resulting in assonance, consonance, rhythm, rhyme, and other sound-based "play," including paronomasia (punning).
7. *Dramatization:* There is a definite inclination towards direct discourse and an "I-you," divine-human interaction, a "personalized" orientation that is emphasized by means of vocatives, separable pronouns, imperatives, embedded quotations, exclamations, and other oral-oriented intensifiers (cf. point 4).
8. *Lexical distinction:* The Psalms are characterized by a conventional, yet internally creative liturgical-cultic ("religious") diction, including certain formulaic expressions, archaic forms, and "universalized" terminology, coupled with many intertextual quotations, allusions, and re-creations or re-applications.
9. *Accentual uniqueness:* Within the Tiberian tradition, the Psalter, along with Job and Proverbs, manifests a system of accentuation or cantillation consisting of seven supra-/subsigns which differs from that of the rest of the Hebrew Bible (Wheeler 1989:15).
10. *Strophic structuration:* The application of Jakobson's poetic principle (1972:93) of correspondence (similarity) superimposed upon sequence (contiguity), results in the formation of additional paradigmatic and syntagmatic structures, on both the macro- as well as the micro-level of textual organization. This greatly increases the semantic "density" of poetic discourse and also serves to segment it into distinct compositional units ("strophes") through the strategic placement of repeated elements, including complete utterances, or "refrains."

3. Two basic psalmic genres: lament and eulogy

The question "Why classify?" has already been addressed: The typological investigation of literature is a proven means of exploring a given poetic text more carefully with regard to its structural organization, from "top-to-bottom" so to speak. This initial procedure in turn provides some important insights into the rhetorical significance of specific stylistic forms and the communicative function(s) of the discourse as a whole in its presumed historical and sociological setting. This is not mere "background information" and hence analytically optional. Rather, it is an essential and integral part of the total "meaning-package" intended to be conveyed by the original author via the specific literary piece that he, under divine inspiration, composed. It is therefore a crucial component of both objective exegetical study and also continued textual transmission today (cf. Bergen 1987:329-30). This text-typing exercise can thus be of aid in the search for a greater measure of "functional equivalence" in the language of translation (de Waard and Nida 1986:119) as well as more "situational correspondence" in relation to the contemporary context in which the biblical message will be received, processed, and responded to.

Before we examine the nature of the two specific genres under consideration, we do well to take note of the ambiguity and uncertainty connected with their own wider literary classification. Are the Psalms lyric "songs" (Berry 1993:107), religious "prayers" (Balentine 1993:13)—whether liturgical or devotional—a mixture of both, or something else? Insofar as they are associated with musical accompaniment and are poems "of limited length expressing the thoughts and especially the feelings of a single speaker" (Beckson and Ganz 1975:135) in a condensed, intensive, and normally picturesque sort of way, the Psalms are lyrics. But they are also prayers since they consist of utterances deliberately directed towards God that deal with the various important moral and theological issues arising out of the faith-life experience of the faithful. Balentine (1993:22) calls them "prose prayers."

This dynamic, functionally fluid equivocality, a distinctive aspect of the Hebrew religion, is admirably reflected in the principal psalmic genres of lament and eulogy: The former, based on petition, are more "prayer-like"; the latter, expressing such motivations as praise and thanksgiving, have a more "lyric," hymnic quality. And yet, as we shall see, such communicative purposes—and the linguistic forms that realize them in poetic discourse—are very closely connected in the Psalter (Westermann 1980:59). Therefore, they are best studied in conjunction with one another, not as rigidly defined structural categories, but as highly flexible and overlapping sets of formal and functional features. These stylistic attributes are rhetorically and artistically varied according to the particular situation as the psalmist freely moves between the two poles of praise and petition in order to give expression to the pair of preeminent religious "tonalities" that encompass the totality of human experience, namely, the "rhythm of joy and sorrow" (ibid., 25). This creative freedom of spiritual expression, a true lyric impulse, is well illustrated in the compositional organization and communicative operation of Psalm 31.

3.1 The lament

A definite form-functional typology is most clearly and extensively manifested in the psalms of lament, in which there is a decided emphasis upon the element of prayer/petition. The latter designates the central "text act," that is, "the predominant illocutionary force [which characterizes] a series of speech acts" (Hatim and Mason 1990:78). Closely associated with a certain text act is its interpretive "frame," a cognitive schema or common "body of knowledge that is evoked in order to provide an inferential base for the understanding of an utterance" (Levinsohn 1983:281) or a related set of them. This would correspond to the characteristic life-setting (*Sitz im Leben*) posited in form-critical studies. The "theory of speech acts" (ibid., chap. 5) thus provides a useful basis for discerning and describing the sequence of stages that a lament psalm in its idealized, prototypical form comprises. According to this pragmatic (text-context oriented) perspective, any utterance, whether literary or not, consists of a tightly knit cluster of four dynamic components:

1. *Locutionary act*, the formal linguistic (phonological, lexical, morpho-syntactic) and semantic features of a given utterance.
2. *Paralocutionary act*, the significant nonverbal elements that accompany an utterance, whether oral (e.g., gestures, facial expressions) or written (e.g., typography, format).
3. *Illocutionary act*, the conventional communicative force that is associated with a particular locution and paralocution, including such general categories as assertives, directives, commissives, directives, and declaratives/performatives (Searle 1979:viii) or specifics such as promise, warning, denial, concession, rebuke, and confession.
4. *Perlocutionary act*, all those effects, intended or unintended, that result from the expression of a given utterance in a specific social situation.

For obvious reasons, especially our lack of access to the original communication event, elements 2 and 4 can play only a minor role in contemporary analyses of the Psalter. They factor in only where explicitly specified or clearly implied by the text itself, an example being the ritual action connected with a certain psalm (e.g., 66:13-15).

The individual (as distinct from the communal) lament may be typologically defined in terms of seven functional, or illocutionary, "stages," some of which are classified as "genres" by FC analysts (e.g.,

Gerstenberger 1988:143ff.). Each stage, which may occur more than once, is in turn realized by either or both of a pair of subconstituents that more precisely describe the type of religious interaction taking place. Only one stage is really obligatory, namely, the central "petition"; but most of the others are usually found, though not necessarily in the order of the seven given below.

I will now describe each stage of the seven compositional stages of the lament with reference to its two possible constituents and illustrate it by means of one or more of the formulaic or typical expressions frequently found associated with it (quotations are from the NIV). Any psalm may therefore be "typified" on the basis of the specific manner in which the sequence of stages is manifested within it, that is, with regard to form, content, function, and occurrence, distribution, or order.

1. Invocation
   a. Divine address or appellation, usually by means of a vocative, with or without a short epithetic description or characterization of God: "Hear us, O Shepherd of Israel, you who lead Joseph like a flock" (80:1); "Surely God is good to Israel" (73:1).
   b. An initial appeal in the form of an imperative, with or without some expression of confident hope or motivation: "Answer me when I call to you, O my righteous God" (4:1); "O LORD my God, I take refuge in you, save and deliver me" (7:1).
2. Complaint
   a. A general description of the distress or plight of the suppliant: "for the godly are no more" (12:1); "how many are my foes, how many rise up against me" (3:1).
   b. A specific expression of grievance concerning the situation of suffering or trial, the enemies or adversaries, or even God himself for his apparent lack or delay in responding to the need: "many are saying of me, 'God will not deliver him'" (3:2); "why have you forsaken me? why are you so far from saving me?" (22:1).
3. Petition
   a. The principal plea or prayer to God for help, expressing the central purpose of the psalm in a further description of the basic problem which the psalmist is facing: "arise, O LORD, in your anger; rise up against the rage of my enemies ...; decree justice" (7:6); "hide me in the shadow of your wings from the wicked who assail me" (17:8-9).
   b. The motivation for divine action, the reason why God should intervene to help the psalmist: "show the wonder of your great

love, you who save by your right hand" (17:7); "or I will sleep in death; my enemy will say, 'I have overcome him!'" (13:3-4).
4. Confession
   a. An admission of personal sin, weakness, or negligence: "I confess my iniquity; I am troubled by my sin" (38:18); "remember not the sins of my youth and my rebellious ways" (25:7).
   b. In contrast to the preceding, an assertion of innocence and righteous behavior before God and man: "I do not sit with deceitful men...I proclaim your praise" (26:4, 7); "though you test me, you will find nothing; I have resolved that my mouth will not sin" (17:3).
5. Profession
   a. Affirmation of trust and confidence in Yahweh and in his power to save: "my eyes are ever on the LORD for only he will release my feet from the snare" (25:15); "in God I trust, I will not be afraid; what can man do to me?" (56:11).
   b. Verbal recognition of God's deliverance in the past and/or hope of a future positive response: "in you our fathers put their trust... and you delivered them" (22:4); "God who is enthroned forever will hear them and afflict them" (55:19).
6. Imprecation
   a. Accusation against the wicked and/or impious enemies: "not a word from their mouth can be trusted; with their tongue they speak deceit" (5:9); "they persecute those you wound and talk about the pain of those you hurt" (69:26).
   b. A call for just recompense or retribution upon all evildoers: "let their intrigues be their downfall; banish them for their many sins" (5:10); "charge them with crime upon crime; do not let them share in your salvation" (69:27).
7. Praise
   a. Promise or vow to personally thank and praise God with or without accompanying sacrificial action: "I will give thanks to the LORD because of his righteousness" (7:17); "I will present my thank offering to you" (56:12).
   b. A call, with or without motivation, for the congregation of the righteous to thank and praise God: "sing praises to the LORD enthroned in Zion...[for] what he has done" (9:11); "you who fear the LORD, praise him...for he has not despised...the suffering of the afflicted one" (22:23-24).

So-called communal laments are much less common than individual laments (Klein 1993:285), at least in the Psalter (examples appear also in the Old Testament prophetic books—see Hos. 6:1-3). It is generally assumed that the individual lament form has been derived or adapted from the communal one (Westermann 1980:30-31). This cannot be determined with certainty, but in any case the same inventory of functional stages may be found in corporate complaints, although, as would be expected, the general orientation is usually national in character, dealing with some widespread drought or plague, enemy invasion, or military defeat. "The anxiety, humiliation, pain, and suffering are those of the community" (Hayes 1976:118). The psalmist typically incorporates the entire congregation of Israel ("we-our-us") in a public expression of repentance, such as a fast, a summons to sacrifice, and/or an exhortation to a revival of hope for the future (as in the Book of Joel). Some representative communal laments are Psalms 44, 58, 60, 74, 80, and 83.

3.2 The eulogy

The eulogy, or song of praise, is distinct from, yet clearly related to, the lament prayer. The most obvious correspondence lies in the final functional unit of the lament sequence, stage 7, "praise," which forms the basis for the eulogy as a whole in its initial stage. But there are other similarities as we see in the generalized set of eulogy elements listed below. For example, some of them are akin to the lament's stage 5, "profession."

It is interesting to speculate about the historical development of these genres. For example, which came first—the lament or the eulogy? Or did they originate together, whether separately or as part of the same larger lyric? But such diachronic issues cannot be decided with reference to the data available, and thus it is more profitable to engage in synchronic studies of the various interrelationships of form, content, and presumably purpose that we are presented with in the extant psalmodic corpus (including of course those that occur outside the Psalter itself such as Exodus 15, Judges 5, Jonah 2, and Habakkuk 3).

The eulogy is also associated with the lament in terms of the basic twofold motivation for which the psalm is sung/prayed, namely, distress/problem and deliverance/solution. In the case of a lament, the individual or group confronted with some major calamity appeals to the Yahweh for relief and rescue. In a eulogy, on the other hand, the psalmist reflects retrospectively in fervent gratitude upon a serious predicament from which Yahweh has already delivered him in his covenantal love. The two genres overlap at the affirmation of faith and/or the (anticipated) act of thanksgiving and praise that marks the major turning point of the typical lament. Thus it is essentially a matter of perspective: with the lament, the

Genre Criticism and the Psalms

petitioner requests and looks *forward* in faith to Yahweh's gracious deliverance; in the eulogy he faithfully looks *back* upon and lauds such divine deliverance received. Another point of correspondence lies in the frequent call to the congregation of the righteous to join the singer in giving a round of heartfelt acclaim to their glorious God.

The discourse of lyric praise is generally not as tightly structured as that of the lament, but the following five bipartite constituents are frequently, though not always, found (roughly in this order):

1. Invitation
   a. A summons to render thanks and praise to Yahweh, directed either to the psalmist himself or his fellow worshipers: "ascribe to the LORD, O mighty ones ... the glory due his name" (29:1-2); "I will exalt you, O LORD" (30:1).
   b. An initial description of Yahweh's praiseworthy attributes: "worship the LORD in the splendor of his holiness" (29:2); "the LORD is my rock, my fortress and my deliverer" (18:2).
2. Motivation
   a. A recounting of the dangerous situation or threatening calamity facing either the individual or the nation as a whole: "the cords of the grave coiled around me" (18:5); "I was overcome by trouble and sorrow" (116:3).
   b. Reference to or even a reiteration of the past plea to Yahweh for help: "in my distress I called to the LORD." (18:6); "to the LORD I cried for mercy" (30:8).
3. Proclamation
   a. Affirmation that Yahweh did respond in an act of deliverance: "you lifted me out of the depths and did not let my enemies gloat over me" (30:1); "you exalted my horn like that of a wild ox; fine oils have been poured upon me" (92:10).
   b. Confident profession of the glorious attributes of Yahweh: "out of the brightness of his presence clouds advanced, with hailstones and bolts of lightning" (18:12); "the LORD is gracious and righteous; our God is full of compassion" (116:5).
4. Promise
   a. A pledge to continually render thankful praise to Yahweh: "I will lift up the cup of salvation and call upon the name of the LORD" (116:13); "you are my God and I will give you thanks" (118:28).
   b. A vow to present some concrete evidence of thankfulness: "I will fulfill my vows to the LORD in the presence of all his people" (116:14); "I will sacrifice fat animals to you and an offering of rams" (66:15).

5. Exhortation
   a. A call to the congregation of believers to offer praise to Yahweh and/or to put their trust in him: "it is better to take refuge in the LORD than to trust in man" (118:8); "rejoice in the LORD and be glad, you righteous" (32:11).
   b. A final moving and motivating testimony to the greatness and goodness of Yahweh: "the LORD is upright; he is my rock, and there is no wickedness in him" (92:15); "the LORD will fulfill his purpose for me; your love, O LORD, endures forever!" (138:8).

The form-functional diversity of the psalmic corpus needs to be reiterated. The several stages, particularly the included segments, may be "mixed and matched" in various ways. Certain compositional elements may be omitted in any given instance, for example, in the sacrificial vow (4b). On the other hand, modifications may be *added* to the basic sequence, such as an initial word of reassurance for the righteous, for example, "Blessed is he whose transgressions are forgiven" (32:1). Some changes may be so similar and occur so frequently as to constitute a distinct subgenre. The "hymn," for example, is a "pure" eulogy (Gerstenberger 1988:15) that omits the closely related stages of "motivation" (2 in the list) and "proclamation" (3 in the list). Thus Yahweh is hailed for his glorious attributes and/or his wonderful works in general, not for some particular act of deliverance, intervention, or blessing either anticipated or already received. (Westermann 1980:25-26 distinguishes between psalms of "narrative praise" and "descriptive praise," or "hymns.").

In any case, variety is the unexpected spice of the Psalter. It is amazing how much artistic diversity is manifested in the composition of so many functionally similar lyric prayer-praises despite the use of a relatively limited set of conventional elements of poetic form and religious content.

3.3 Other subgenres of the lament and eulogy

Form critics have posited anywhere from a half to a full dozen or more additional (sub)genres of Hebrew lyric poetry, especially in relation to the corpus of Psalms. (One example of a list of such subgenres is in Gerstenberger's glossary [1988:243ff.].) Although there is no substantiating historical evidence, a literary-structural comparison would suggest that most if not all of these may have been "generated" or adapted from either one of the two basic forms of lament and eulogy. In other words, each type arose as the result of the creative process of specification or focalization from one or more of the principal stages of the lament or the eulogy according to the particular socioreligious situation and historical setting that pertained.

For example, there may have been the need to musically heighten some special instruction in the Word of Yahweh, specifically the Mosaic Law, or to vocally embellish certain important occasions, whether happy or sad, such as a celebration of the anniversary of the Temple dedication (or some similar festival on the spiritual calendar of ancient Israel); the annual religious journey to the holy city of Jerusalem; the commemoration of some major event in the historical record of God's people; a serious military defeat during a period of widespread moral laxity in the land; the occurrence of a widespread and catastrophic drought, famine, or pestilence; an individual "rite-of-passage" to mark a youth's maturity or marriage; or even a very personal setting of blessing (e.g., the birth of a child) or calamity (e.g., a life-threatening illness). Any of these situations, and many others like them, undoubtedly gave rise to the development of artistic lyric modifications, elaborations, and re-creations of traditional religious expressions and compositional patterns.

Such subgenres are usually named on the basis of some prominent element of form, content, and/or function. Thus we find "royal" (kingship) psalms, hymns "of Zion," songs "of ascent" (pilgrimage), "creation" (nature) psalms, songs of Israel's "salvation history," "penitential" psalms, "didactic" (wisdom/torah) psalms, psalms of "trust," "imprecatory" (vindication) psalms, and "liturgical" songs for public worship. (For a description of these, see any standard commentary on the Psalms or form-critical introduction.) Most instances of such categories are "mixed" in the sense that they do not carry out a particular theme or purpose consistently throughout the text (the didactic psalms, such as Psalms 1 and 119 are, in general, exceptions). But these subgenres are all typical variants, nevertheless, since they can generally be related in one way or another, and more or less, to either the lament or the eulogy.

The point of such FC study of poetic genres is to sharpen the eyes and attune the ears of analysts to the presence of considerable formal, semantic, and intentional diversity in the Psalter as a whole and in any given psalm as a distinctive example of the overall pattern. Such an approach enables us to anticipate, perceive, and interpret lyric meaning in terms of a particular psalm's structure, style, content, and function. With such an understanding of the original text and context we can more effectively convey the essence of its message, including aspects such as affective impact and esthetic appeal, with comparable relevance to a contemporary audience, that is, with "adequate contextual effects at minimal processing cost" (Gutt 1991:30), whether by oral exposition-interpretation or via a written translation into the literary and social setting of another language and culture.

But traditional FC or generic analysis does not take us far enough. The linguistic complexity, rhetorical dynamics, and indeed the esthetic excellence of these Hebrew religious poems requires a more comprehensive methodology that will help us to more fully (yet never completely) discern, describe, evaluate, and apply the original text—in short, plumb its communicative depths.

Any given psalm, for example, must be seen not only as a general type (or some combination of types), but as a unique artistic and purposeful creation. James Muilenburg was one of the first to recognize and explore this hermeneutical exigency in his writings (e.g., [1969] 1992). It remains for us to put his insights into practice today in a more consistent and systematic way than that allowed for by the typical form-critical technique. That will be the main objective of the remainder of this essay, with specific reference then to Psalm 31.

4. A discourse-oriented, "structure-functional" analysis

4.1 Method

Muilenburg built upon the foundation laid by the form critics to investigate "the literary unit in its precise and unique formulation" ([1969] 1992:55). His specific aim was to use a careful textual analysis as the basis for "understanding the nature of Hebrew literary composition, in exhibiting the structural patterns that are employed for the fashioning of a literary unit, whether in poetry or in prose, and in discerning the many and various devices by which the predications are formulated and ordered into a unified whole" (ibid., 57).

Muilenburg termed his modified methodology "rhetorical criticism." He delineated two principal steps: delimitation of the scope or boundaries of the particular unit under analysis, and delineation of the constituent structure of its internal development. As Berry observes, FC had similar concerns but a different motivation: "rhetorical criticism asks the questions [about structure] for the purposes of intrinsic analysis; form criticism asks them in order to assign a *Gattung* [and, we might add, a suitable *Sitz im Leben*]" (1993:83).

To accomplish his objectives, Muilenburg gave special emphasis to the various "rhetorical devices" that indicate "sequence and movement" within the composition, on the one hand, and "shifts or breaks" in thought, on the other (1992:59). Among such stylistic features, he especially noted the inclusio, metrical breaks, clusters of bicola and tricola or strophes, refrains, key-word reiteration, particles, vocatives, rhetorical questions, and general repetition. He also called attention to the need for a functional perspective in order to get "a grasp of the writer's intent and meaning" (ibid., 57).

My analysis of Psalm 31, summarized in section 4.2, is a more text-oriented, functionally motivated version of Muilenburg's "rhetorical-critical" approach. This "structure-functional" method focuses upon the search for spans or stretches of continuity and points of discontinuity within the discourse as a whole (cf. Wendland 1993:138–40 and forthcoming, chap. 2). These two compositional principles govern the generation, organization, and operation of any literary text. However, the various stylistic techniques that realize such objectives tend to be more complexly patterned, artistically crafted, profusely manifested, and strategically positioned in texts that are more poetic than prosaic in nature.

Discourse *continuity* is effected by the diverse modes of repetition that are built into any poetic composition. Such repetition may be either exact (reiteration) or correspondent (recursion) and consist of phonological, lexical, morphosyntactic, semantic, and/or pragmatic (i.e., illocutionary) elements. Furthermore, poetic progression is generally realized on both the micro- and the macrolevels of text structure, in particular, by means of "near" or "far" parallelism of a synonymous, contrastive, or additive (consequential) type.

Discontinuity, on the other hand, is manifested by a special convergence of individual poetic features, such as those outlined in section 2. Normally such a stylistic concentration occurs at some significant point in the structural-thematic-functional development of the discourse, that is, at the beginning ("aperture"), ending ("closure"), or central core ("mesosure") of a given literary unit, wherever this may be in the hierarchical organization of the complete pericope.

The compositional principles of continuity and discontinuity complement each other to define the discourse arrangement and operation of any literary text in terms of three particular structure-functional properties: segmentation, connectivity, and prominence. *Segmentation* deals with the delineation and description of the various discrete units of discourse and their major syntagmatic (progressive/linear) and paradigmatic (recursive/analogical) interrelationships, including the manifold patterns which they form. *Connectivity* concerns the manner in which such individual units are bound together, both externally and internally, through the interlocking techniques of formal "cohesion" and conceptual "coherence" to create unity as well as movement within the whole. *Prominence* then identifies those places within the discourse that are stylistically marked for special thematic focus ("peak") and/or emotive-affective emphasis ("climax").

Such a holistic and heuristic approach attaches great importance to the relative linguistic diversity, density, and distribution of the different poetic devices and rhetorical strategies that are manifested by the pericope under consideration. Their unique deployment and textual interaction are the basis for discovering not only the structural design of the work but also its dynamic communicative effects, as presumably intended by the biblical author in the initial historical setting and socioreligious situation of composition. Any application of the methodology just outlined of course presupposes a prior text-critical study, a thorough microexegesis, literal translation, and a repeated oral reading of the original to properly internalize the discourse.

4.2 Application to Psalm 31

Psalm 31 seems to be a particularly good candidate for a practical exercise of the analytical process described in section 4.1. In the first place, it is a discrete and complete poetic piece; thus there is no controversy over the exact delimitation of the discourse. Second, it is a problematic text, both structurally in terms of its constituent demarcation and also functionally with regard to its generic classification as well as its internal sequence of pragmatic, illocutionary elements. These difficulties and the consequent scholarly divergence which they occasion present a challenge to the interpretive capacity of the methodology being proposed in this investigation. And finally, Psalm 31 is a worthy object in its own right on account of the significant message that it artistically proclaims. This is a highly moving expression of personal commitment to and trust in Yahweh, the ever-present covenant Lord, who upholds his faithful people even in times when there appears to be "terror on every side" (Ps. 31:13).

4.2.1 Functional analysis

A number of recent studies have drawn attention to the difficulties of analyzing the text of Psalm 31. As Gerstenberger concludes, "All commentators agree that Psalm 31 shows neither logical nor literary order" (1988:137). As a result, "there is no firm agreement amongst scholars as to the correct [constituent] analysis" (Craigie 1983:259). Moreover, "the difficulty in determining the literary genre of this psalm has led many scholars to view it as a composite work from anonymous authors" (VanGemeren 1991:262).

Such uncertainty over the form of the text is reflected also in the disparity of situational contexts proposed—settings which supposedly provided the impetus for its original composition. Was it a *Sitz im Leben* characterized by a righteous individual being maligned by "malicious gossip" (Bellinger 1984:36), a state of "deliverance...perhaps from a siege" (Bratcher and Reyburn 1991:289), or "sickness and ostracism" (Gerstenberger 1988:140)? Or indeed was it a more indefinite circumstance of calamity, thus rendering the psalm quite "suitable by any person in distress, whether threatened by enemies (vv. 5, 12), idolaters (v. 7), or sickness and nearness of death (vv. 10–11)" (Craigie 1983:260)? The more inclusive generality of this last suggestion, coupled with the semantic richness and density of the text itself, commends it as being the most appropriate and applicable as a hypothetical contextual description.

Bratcher and Reyburn (1991:289) point out the emotive and motivational diversity of Psalm 31: it "combines elements of sorrow (vv. 9–13), statements of confidence (vv. 3, 4, 14–15), thanksgiving (vv. 7–8, 19–20), and pleas for punishment of enemies (vv. 4, 17–18)." They further analyze the text as an alternating series of affirmations of trust (T) and petitions (P) for deliverance, accompanied by occasional reasons (R) for the two preceding types of discourse. Their analytical perspective is tabulated as follows (ibid.):

Text (verses)	Type (function)
1a	T
1b–2d	P
3a	T
3b–4b	P + R
5a–8b	T + R
9a–13	P + R
14	T
15b–17a	P + R
17b	T + R
17c–18	P
19–22	T + R
23–24	Command to T

Structurally significant in their scheme is of course the concluding double command to "trust" (i.e., "love the LORD" and "be strong"). One could quibble over some of the details of this analysis. For example, it would be equally possible to construe 3a as a "reason" (R) like 4b, which it parallels in content and form. And why is the expression of "hatred" in 6a considered to be an assertion of "trust" (T) such as we have in 6b? Why is a clear panegyric "blessing" categorized as a T statement, rather than as distinctly one of "praise" (Pr)? Or why is 15a excluded from the sequence? Perhaps because it too is ambiguous (i.e., either T or R: "My times are in your hands...")? In any case, the framework is helpful in giving a general overview of the undulating functional progression of this lyric prayer.

Gerstenberger (1988:136-37) offers the following as the structure of Psalm 31 from a typical form-critical perspective:

PSALM 31
COMPLAINT OF THE INDIVIDUAL
Structure

	MT	RSV
I. Superscription	1	—
II. Initial Plea	2-3	1-2
III. Affirmation of confidence	4-7	3-6
A. Confessional statements	4a, 5b	3a, 4b
B. Petitions	4b, 5a	3b, 4a
C. Self-dedication	6a	5a
D. Affirmation of confidence	6b	5b
E. Confession to community	7	6
1. Protestation of innocence	7a	6a
2. Affirmation of confidence	7b	6b
IV. Thanksgiving	8-9	7-8
V. Complaint	10-14	9-13
VI. Petition	15-19	14-18
A. Affirmation of confidence	15-16a	14-15a
B. Petition	16b-18a	15b-17a
C. Imprecation	18b-19	17b-18
VII. Personal hymn	20-22	19-21
A. Communal adoration	20-21	19-20
B. Personal blessing (praise)	22	21
VIII. Thanksgiving	23	22
IX. Exhortation, blessing	24-25	23-24

This analytical schema illustrates both the strengths and the weaknesses of the form-critical approach. On the positive side, it treats the text as "a liturgical unit" (ibid., 137) and takes seriously the interaction of structure and function within the composition as a whole. On the other hand, the overemphasis upon a precise "generic" categorization soon loses the uninitiated in a forest of detail, not all of which is helpful or even correct. For example, the entire psalm is typed as a "complaint of the individual," but this is contradicted by the opening line of v. 23: "Love Yahweh, all you his saints!" The classification "affirmation of confidence" is reiterated on three different levels of the proposed unit covering vv. 3-6 (i.e., III, D, and 2), which is a span that is actually broken structurally at v. 6. The "petition" genre of vv. 14–18 is allegedly composed of three quite diverse constituents, namely, "affirmation of confidence" (again!), "petition" (thus included within itself!), and "imprecation" (another distinct structural unit!). The so-called *"personal* hymn" (VII) leads off with a *"communal* adoration" (A). And finally, vv. 23–24 supposedly contain a "blessing," but if such an element is indeed present, it is quite different from the literal one that initiates v. 21, which is somehow connected with the "communal adoration" of vv. 19–20.

But perhaps the greatest weakness of the preceding FC analysis is that it misses the fundamental structural symmetry which arises out of the psalmist's artistic play upon the typical inventory of elements (or as we have termed them, "stages") of the "lament" genre. Thus a distinct compositional pattern is formed by his unique selection and arrangement of illocutionary functions within the text. Now this may not be "logical" or "literary" from our contemporary perspective (ibid., 137), but the sequence certainly is effective—once recognized for what it is—in terms of its communicative operation, even today. In essence, what we have is an instance of functional "recycling" on the generic level of poetic discourse. Two "cycles" of the lament constituents divide Psalm 31 into two unequal "halves" as indicated on the following table (note that within each cycle there may be an overlapping and/or a polyrealization of a given functional element):

Stage	Cycle I: General (vv. 1–8)	Cycle II: Specific (vv. 9–24)
Invocation	1, 2a	9a
Complaint	4a, 7bc, 8a	9b–13, 22a
Petition	3b, 4a, 2b	15b, 16, 17a
Confession	5a	19–20
Profession	1a, 2b, 3a, 4b, 5b, 6b, 7a, 8b	14, 15a, 17b, (19–20), 23b–24
Imprecation	6a	17c–18
Praise	7a, (7b–8)	21, 22b, (23b–24)

The preceding is not intended to be a precise delineation of the illocutionary structure of this lament. That would require a detailed discussion of each component (and each of its two possible subrealizations) within its textual setting and in relationship to every one of the other stages in both cycles. However, the chart does serve to indicate that the functional "alternation" pointed out by Bratcher and Reyburn (1991:289) may be rather more complex and patterned than first indicated on the surface of the text. Moreover, virtually every one of the stages is closely associated with a particular "reason," whether expressed or implied in the discourse, a motivation that is somehow "related to the notion of trusting" (ibid.). For example, the very covenant name of the LORD, "Yahweh," underlies the initial appeal of the "invocation" in v. 1.

The preceding functional analysis demonstrates both the "logical" order as well as the "literary" quality of Psalm 31 (contra Gerstenberger 1988:137). It suggests that what we have here is a skillfully combined "lament-eulogy": complaint/problem is in vv. 2, 9, 22b (this last is a "flashback" in direct speech) and praise is in vv. 7-8, 21-24. There is a predominant focus upon "profession." This affirmation of complete confidence and personal dedication is clearly the dominant functional constituent within both cycles in terms of both quantity and quality (i.e., not only the amount of text, but also the diversity and intensity of poetic expression that is devoted to it). The focused faith of the pray-er, thus articulated in such a lyric mode, clearly sets the tone for the psalm as a whole and characterizes its entire structural development. The shifting back and forth between "complaint-petition" and "profession," a feature which has caused problems for source- and form-critics alike, is simply, but significantly, a sign of the creative artistry that gives Psalm 31 its distinctive rhetorical force and religious flavor. Its continuation throughout the discourse has a cumulative effect that ultimately breaks forth in the concluding communal call to praise in vv. 23-24, which is in itself an implicit cry of victorious trust, uttered on behalf of "all you who hope in the LORD!"

There is a final point to note in this connection: For one reason or another most scholarly critics and commentators discount the crucial functional significance of the psalm's title or superscription: literally "For the director of music/choirmaster; a psalm [מִזְמוֹר] of/for David." As in the case of similar psalmodic headings, it is either omitted entirely or relegated to a footnote in many major versions (e.g., NEB and GNB, respectively). Whether the title was part of the original text or was added later, perhaps by one of the later compilers of the collection, cannot be determined with certainty. At any rate, such headings formed a part of the Hebrew text from a very early date (cf. Ps. 18:1 and 2 Sam. 22:1; Hab. 3:1, 19b). As a result countless audiences ever since that time have simply assumed certain psalms, such as 31, to be the speech of king David himself. Undoubtedly this formed a vital point of orientation as well as identification for them as they heard or read these words. As Berry observes: "This least important portion of the poem from the contemporary textual critic's viewpoint was likely the most important portion to the worshipping Israelite" (1993:132).

Genre Criticism and the Psalms 403

The point is that David was a man of unshakable faith. His strong confidence in God shone through many dangers and perilous trials as extensively recorded in the Scriptures. His several glaring failures stand out sharply against this general backdrop of fidelity. It is therefore probable that current readers, of whatever age, read this psalm and others like it in the light of David's own experience. In that sense too, his victory becomes theirs as they encounter similar situations of severe testing and serious distress (e.g., v. 13), only to ultimately overcome them through an implicit, heartfelt trust in Yahweh (e.g., v.14).

4.2.2 A structural-thematic summary of Psalm 31

In conjunction with a functional analysis as outlined in section 4.2.1, features of special emotive and/or affective significance (intensity or change) within the text should be noted. As far as Psalm 31 is concerned, several major breaks of this nature occur at vv. 6, 9, 14, 19, 21, and 23. (All verse references to Psalm 31 follow the English versions.) These junctures correspond, in turn, to the psalm's principal stanzaic/strophic divisions as shown in the following overview:

Psalm 31: Commit yourself to the hands of the merciful LORD for refuge from all your enemies!

Cycle One: vv. 1–8
  Stanza One—*Petition* (1–5): Deliver me from my enemies, O LORD!
  Stanza Two—*Praise* (6–8): The LORD has saved me from my enemies!

Cycle Two: vv. 9–24
  Stanza One—*Complaint* (9–13): I am near death (9–10) and surrounded by trouble! (11–13)
  Stanza Two—*Petition* (14–18): Deliver me from my enemies and punish them, O LORD! (2x: 14–16, 17–18)
   Praise (19–20): The LORD keeps his people safe!
  Stanza Three—*Praise, individual* (21–22): The LORD helped me when I was in trouble!
    Praise, communal (23–24): Trust the LORD, you saints, for he will preserve you!

A systematic analysis with respect to the "segmentation" of Psalm 31 as set forth in the preceding outline and the "connectivity" of its various constituent units (stanzas/strophes) (see sec. 4.1) will not be presented here; but such a structural delimitation would depend, in particular, upon major topical and/or illocutionary shifts, usually coupled with a vocative utilizing a confessional reference to the divine name. These indicate initial unit boundaries (i.e., aperture as in vv. 1, 6, 9, 14, 19, 21, 23). Internal cohesion, on the other hand, is built up largely through referential chains, both positive and negative in connotation (e.g., the laudatory depictions of Yahweh as a "rock...refuge...fortress" in the first stanza, vv. 1-5, or the various expressions of physical anguish and personal affliction in the initial stanza of cycle two, vv. 9-13).

At this stage we wish merely to survey several of the devices that promote "prominence" within the text, especially in relation to the principal theme, "Commit yourself to the hands of the merciful LORD for refuge from all your enemies!" A number of instances of synonymous and exact recursion involving key terms operates to tie both cycles of the psalm together conceptually (Craigie 1983:259). These are visually displayed in the diagram below, where a slash mark (/) indicates a stanza break according to the proposed segmentation of the discourse. While the recursive pattern unfolds in a linear fashion in cycle one, it is clustered in the second stanza of cycle two, which approximates the former in length:

	One				Two		
"seek refuge"	1	/		/		19	/
"be ashamed"	1	/		/		17	/
"rescue"	2	/		/	15		/
"deliver"	2	/		/		16	/
"your hand"		5 /	8	/	15		/
"trust"		/ 6		/ 14			/
"mercy"		/ 7		/		16	/ 21

In addition to this considerable repetition, there are other, less exactly reiterated ideas that perform a similar integrative function within the text as a whole, for example, "my rock...a strong fortress" (2) + "O LORD...my God" (14); "free me from the trap" (4) + "deliver me from my enemies" (15). In general, this series, expressing an unbounded trust in Yahweh, acts as a conceptually positive counterbalance to several parallel pessimistic strands, most notably, those articulated in vv. 9-13.

The central theological notion of חֶסֶד, 'unmitigated mercy'/ 'unfailing faithfulness'/ 'continued covenantal commitment'/ 'loving loyalty'/ 'unchanging love', needs special consideration. This conceptual complex, which cannot be adequately rendered by a single term in most languages, represents the motivating force behind Yahweh's deliverance of all those who commit themselves in faith to live according to the basic precepts of his gracious covenant. It acts, in turn, as the foundation for his people's diverse petitions to him in time of need. Driyvers would go so far as to claim that "the supreme fact that formed the basis of every liturgical celebration in Israel was the unchanging faithfulness of Yahweh"

(1965:42). Thus חֶסֶד entails both a socioreligious philosophy, or worldview, and also a closely associated code of conduct for the people of God. The twofold focus of this covenantal relationship (as ideally realized) is tabulated as follows with respect to its primary expression in Psalm 31:

Yahweh provides	the dual motivation	the saints respond in
defense (e.g., 1-4) deliverance (21-22) vindication (17-18)	חֶסֶד	love (23) trust (14) joy (7)

This nucleus of key thematic concepts is articulated progressively as the psalm unfolds. It thus provides yet another testimony to the work's compositional integrity—an overall unity of form, content, and function. This unity needs to be conveyed in any presentation to a contemporary constituency, whether individually or communally apprehended.

The covenantal significance of חֶסֶד plays an important organizational and defining role in relation to all of the psalmodic laments, both personal and public. The term's crucial semantic components of "steadfastness" or "unchangeableness" or "constancy" (with other glosses possible) acts as the foundation for the varied expressions of certainty and anticipated fulfillment which characterize this genre. Moreover, חֶסֶד is closely connected in meaning and import with the concept of 'faithfulness' (אֱמֶת) in its various manifestations.

Bellinger (1984:61) provides the following summary of this mutual interrelationship:

> [Yahweh] is faithful to his promise to deliver, which means that his commitment to his people does not change as circumstances do . . . (Ps. 31:6) . . .). This in turn calls for faithfulness from the people in response to this renewed demonstration of Yahweh's *hesed* to them (31:24 . . .).

This important theological fact may be related in a general way to the thematic structure of many psalms—as well as the Psalter as a whole. Brueggeman (e.g., 1984:21) has provided a useful synoptic formula for showing this. It organizes the lament, in particular, into a series of three relational "movements" involving the psalmist, or God's people, and Yahweh: "orientation-disorientation-new orientation."

Several other points of special lexical prominence within Psalm 31 bear a direct relationship to its central theme of trusting in the LORD of חֶסֶד. These all occur in structurally significant positions. Summaries of them follow.

v. 5 (ending of stanza one, structural midpoint of cycle one):

Here we have the ultimate expression of confidence and a commitment of oneself (i.e., רוּחִי, 'my spirit') into the very hands of Yahweh, the "God of faithfulness and truth" (אֵל אֱמֶת), a double articulation of the divine name. The notion of "depositing" (פקד) one's spirit is unique in the Old Testament. The psalmist's present hope of "redemption" (פדה) is based upon God's covenantal fidelity demonstrated in the past, as at the Exodus deliverance (Deut. 7:8).

v. 13 (ending of stanza one, cycle two):

In graphic contrast to v. 5, this is the ultimate expression of danger and defeat. Indeed, the psalmist was surrounded by terrible terrifying things (cf. Jer. 6:25; 20:3). It was not only a matter of words (דִּבַּת 'slander, whispering'), but his very life (נַפְשִׁי) was at stake. The emotively medial "valley" of the psalm and nucleus of the lament (i.e., vv. 9-13) thus reaches its nadir, the depths of despair. The source of all his physical and social distress, so vividly described in the antecedent verses, is the continual conspiracy of friend and foe alike (cf. v. 11). The treachery of man contrasts markedly with the faithfulness of God in v. 5 (cf. v. 20 at the close of cycle two, stanza two).

v. 14 (beginning of stanza two, cycle two):

The verbal and semantic disjunction with the preceding unit is quite dramatic. With וַאֲנִי 'but I', the psalmist is suddenly transformed from a defeated object to a defiant subject, one whose courage rests upon Yahweh alone. Repetition of the divine name here echoes v. 5 as the central core of the composition is reached. The expression of "trust" (בָטַחְתִּי), highlighted by direct speech, reiterates v. 6 in another significant structural-thematic correspondence. Indeed, the covenantal affirmation "You are my God" (אֱלֹהַי אָתָּה) could stand as the motto of this entire psalm. The psalmist then entrusts everything that happens to him in life into the "hands" of Yahweh (v. 15a), along with his very "spirit" (v. 5a).

v. 21 (beginning of stanza three, cycle two):

The final paean of thanksgiving and praise leads off with a powerful word of blessing. This is characteristic of many psalmic hymns of this nature: בָּרוּךְ יְהוָה 'blessed [be] Yahweh' (e.g., Psalms 103-4, 134, 144; cf. הַלְלוּ־יָהּ in Psalms 146-50). The motivation for this exaltation is encapsulated in the key word חֶסֶד of the next line, which summarizes the fuller description found in the preceding strophe (vv. 19-20) as well as in the remainder of this one (vv. 21c-22).

vv. 23-24 (the psalm's concluding strophe):
These final words provide a most fitting close to this artistically conjoined lament-eulogy. After the initial exhortation to all "his saints" (חֲסִידָיו, related to חֶסֶד, i.e., "those who have been mercied" by Yahweh and who in turn manifest חֶסֶד in their own lives), the theme of Psalm 31 as a whole is set forth in antithetical parallelism: The faithful (אֱמוּנִים) Yahweh is watching over (נֹצֵר), and [= but] he is requiting them (מְשַׁלֵּם) to the utmost, anyone who acts haughtily (גַאֲוָה). Yahweh's חֶסֶד thus turns out to be a double-edged sword—one of sure protection for his people, but one of sharp punishment for all their oppressors. In such confident trust the psalmist has composed this encouragement to personal devotion for the congregation of "all who wait for the LORD (to act on their behalf)" (v. 24b) and "take refuge" in him (v. 1a, i.e., a thematic inclusio).

In conclusion, it is important to emphasize the powerful communicative effect of this coincidence of the two macroconstructs, the structural-thematic and the functional-generic. One complements the other to fully confirm both the organization of the discourse and also its rhetorical dynamics. The elaboration of cycle A in cycle B is a discourse manifestation of the micropoetic principle of "seconding"—"A, and what's more, B" (Kugel 1981:42, 52). The double articulation of a theme which celebrates the blessings of human faith in a faithful God is reinforced by a literary expectation shaped by the genres of lament and eulogy. And yet this expectation is also surprised, so to speak, by the creative variations which the poet-psalmist has introduced into the composition—not as a means of pure artistic expression, but primarily to accent the particular message about the unfailing "covenant love" (חֶסֶד) of Yahweh that he wishes to convey to all who have made themselves part of that covenant through their trust in him. Unity in diversity, strength in adversity—this principle is thus illustrated in Psalm 31 both on a stylistic as well as a theological level. For that reason the prayer endures as a beautiful lyric testimony to the Rock of stability (v. 2, 8, 19), which Yahweh is, and which Yahweh also provides for his people in all the severe trials and worrisome vicissitudes of life (vv. 13, 20-21).

4.2.3 The dilemma of competing discourse designs

One specific application of a structure-functional analysis is its use as a means of evaluating different suggestions for demarcating a particular text into its constituent parts. Intermediate Bible students are often frustrated by the conflicting proposals frequently offered as a compositional outline, chart, or theological summary of a given book, portion, or pericope. (This sort of problem with reference to Psalm 31 has already been presented in secs. 4.2.1 and 4.2.2.) In certain respects, such outlines may, where corresponding, complement one another; if they are detailed outlines, they may supplement one another. But where they differ, how can the student know which scheme is the best? Even though there will always be a certain amount of arbitrariness and pure personal preference involved, in some cases the disparities are of a more serious nature; that is, one of the structural plans may be misleading or even patently erroneous.

When a specific methodology is included along with a detailed exposition to back up a particular analysis and its associated outline, then students can at least go back and test the results for themselves by applying the principles and procedures that have been supplied. They can compare them with another study in support of a different scheme and then choose between them (or some other alternative). With the background material and references provided in the preceding discussion, it is hoped that such an evaluation and critique will be possible.

As an example of how to assess the results of different analyses and understand the structural-functional method behind them, we shall now look at two other proposals for outlining the discourse organization of Psalm 31.

VanGemeren comes to the conclusion, as I did, that "the psalm falls into two parts" (1991:263), but his principal divisions, vv. 1–18 and 19–24, appear to be quite different. What he proposes is two greatly unbalanced sections, the first and larger one manifesting an alternating parallel arrangement as follows:

I. Prayer (vv. 1–18)
  A. Prayer for Yahweh's Righteousness (vv. 1–5)
    B. Expression of Trust (vv. 6–8)
  A'. Prayer for Yahweh's Favor (vv. 9–13)
    B'. Expression of Trust (vv. 14–18)
II. Thanksgiving (vv. 19–24)

It appears that he has overlooked the formal and functional similarities between vv. 1–8 and 9–24 in favor of a more logically ordered format. However, there are several problems with this proposal. First, the title "Prayer for Yahweh's Righteousness" (A) is ambiguous. It is also misleading in that actually Yahweh as a source of "refuge" is in focus here. Similarly, the theme suggested for A' is off the mark since the emphasis of this segment (stanza) is upon the multifaceted affliction being experienced by the psalmist. Furthermore, it is debatable to posit the ultimate expression of "Thanksgiving" (II) as beginning at v. 19 rather than at v. 21. It would seem that vv. 19–20 are more an "Expression of Trust" (i.e., still part of B') than hymnic words of grateful praise. The latter motivation is certainly involved, but of lesser functional priority.

Craigie's analysis (1983:259) also has some serious difficulties. He presents a chiastic framework—logically neat, but hard to substantiate on the basis of the original text (the Hebrew verse numbering is given):

    I. *Prayer*   (1) prayer [2–6]   A
                   (2) trust [7–9]   B
                   (3) lament [10–14]   C
                   (4) trust [15]   B'
                   (5) prayer [16–19]   A'
             (declaration of oracle between v. 19 and v. 20)
    II. *Thanksgiving and Praise* [20–25]

What would appear to be the psalm's principal division between v. 8 and v. 9 is not recognized, and as a result undue emphasis is thrown upon the final thanksgiving portion. This portion is thus detached, as a constituent element, from the lament, which is this psalm's main function. Moreover, as was just pointed out, the structural components of this lament alternate and interact with one another in a much more complex fashion. It is therefore misleading for the commentator to impose an alien schema upon the text, no matter how much simpler or ordered this may seem. As we have seen, expressions of trust permeate the entire poem and cannot be restricted to vv. 6–8 and 14 (the numbering of the English versions will be followed in this discussion). The utterance "my times are in your hands" (15a), to be specific, surely conveys as much trust as the words of v. 14, and yet Craigie classifies it as a prayer—along with such imprecations as "let the wicked...lie silent in the grave" (17). It is also difficult to see how the final verse of the psalm, "Be strong and take heart, all you who hope in the LORD" (NIV), can be regarded as an instance of "thanksgiving and praise." It is obviously a concluding communal exhortation to the congregation of the righteous to celebrate Yahweh's mighty deliverance of his formerly suffering servant and, as such, is a typical element of a lament.

The preceding exercise illustrates both the potential as well as some of the pitfalls of typological analysis: informative if done well, along emic lines; inevitably distortive and deceptive if done otherwise. Do such structures have any objective basis? Or do they, like proverbial beauty, exist merely in the eyes of the beholder (or analyst)? It is hoped that this discourse-based, rhetorically oriented approach, however biased by the perspective of its proponent, will have proved the former, whether one happens to agree with all of its conclusions or not.

5. Concluding evaluation and outlook

The use of a structure-functional set of procedures to coordinate and supplement a traditional form-critical methodology is invaluable. Only within such a wider framework can an adequate typological analysis on both the macro- and microlevels of literary discourse, generic as well as specific, be adequately carried out. This approach has several other advantages. First of all, it is flexible and able to incorporate diverse methods, as long as the dual focus upon larger text form and function is maintained. It is thus also inclusive and comprehensive in scope since only a complete composition or pericope is treated, one that is considered as a whole—as a unified, operational discourse "organism," as it were. Furthermore, the technique is communication centered in terms of both the original as well as the contemporary historicocultural and sociolinguistic settings. This makes it useful in traversing the hermeneutical gap that inevitably hinders a transmission of the original, author-intended message by means of translation and transposition via modern visual and oral-aural media.

A structure-functional perspective can also provide some new and valuable insights into certain familiar texts. With reference to Psalm 31, for example, it highlights the masterful way in which the major elements of the lament and eulogy genres are interwoven into a tightly integrated network of artistic form and emotive expression. It is a dramatic prayer in which the central motivating force of steadfast trust in Yahweh is renewed and reinforced amidst a succession of diverse appeals, complaints, and imprecations. This constitutes the alternate and alternating progression that keeps the discourse moving forward from beginning to end, unpredictable in its details but having a certain eventual outcome, just like life itself—but only for those who "take refuge" in Yahweh (vv. 1, 4, 9)!

The object of such rhetorical-critical analysis then is to convey as much as possible of the major themes, emphases, feelings, and aims of the Scripture message in a manner that will most faithfully represent the original intentions of the Hebrew author, on the one hand, and the relevant needs, desires, and abilities of the present-day receptor community on the other. The total communication of any literary work, let alone the Word of God, is of course an impossibility. But it is a legitimate goal to try and come as close as current linguistic science, biblical knowledge, and cross-cultural studies will allow.

The limitations of the present investigation tend to point in the direction of some important future research. A more detailed and comprehensive (computer/database-aided) text-type analysis of the Psalms and other poetic literature is needed so as to provide a more precise functional typology based upon the speech acts (illocutions), both apparent and implicit, found in the original text. Such a generic analysis would have to be supplemented, whenever possible, by a detailed listing of the formal linguistic markers typically associated with a given functional category (e.g., invocation, appeal, imprecation, vow, and credal profession).

A prerequisite for this sort of analysis would be an explicit definition of the various distinct communicative intentions that are manifested in the biblical corpus. (Any initial inventory would undoubtedly need to be modified as the study proceeds.) Also necessary would be a means of delineating the text's formal span, the span over which a given function, or functional complex, is assumed to operate or apply (e.g., bi/tri-colon, strophe). It would also have to be determined whether an implicit hierarchy or level of prominence exists whereby a certain function (functional set/sequence) may be posited as the dominant one controlling a larger segment of the discourse (e.g., a stanza) or even the composition (psalm) as a whole, thus delineating a particular text type.

Similar form-function-ideational studies then need to be undertaken in receptor languages throughout the world wherever a meaning-centered, popular-language Bible translation is envisaged, planned, or actually under way. But the original form-critical concern for describing indigenous genres (text) in relation to social setting (context) and a given literary tradition, whether oral or written (i.e., the "intertextual cotext"), must be emulated and the necessary research completed *before* such a project gets under way. The results of text analysis should be much more reliable with living people and actual life-settings available to observe, document, and test than the analysis of biblical texts.

Such investigations clearly have to be carried out immediately, especially in the case of oral genres. Otherwise, we will end up with the same problem that FC encountered with biblical literature, namely, a "dead" (extremely hypothetical!) *Sitz im Leben*. A primary goal would be to establish and define emic receptor-language discourse typologies, providing an inventory of literary resources ready for use as potential form-functional equivalents for Scripture translation. The aim would be to match as closely as possible the meaning dynamics of the original text in its assumed context with the nearest sociocultural correspondents available within the receptor life-setting. Although difficult and time-consuming, such a strategy would seem to be the only one that pays due consideration to the message transmission process, which involves bridging two different languages, disparate epochs, environments, ethoi, and ethnic groups. All this in the cause of communicating the covenantal חֶסֶד of the LORD to the multitudes who are desperately searching for something, or someone, upon which to set their hope in a seemingly hope-less world (v. 24).

References

Achtemeier, Paul J. 1990. Omne verbum sonat: The New Testament and the oral environment of late Western antiquity. *Journal of Biblical Literature* 109(1):3–27.
Alter, Robert. 1981. *The art of biblical narrative.* New York: Basic Books.
Armerding, Carl E. 1983. *The Old Testament and criticism.* Grand Rapids: Eerdmans.
Balentine, Samuel E. 1993. *Prayer in the Hebrew Bible: The drama of divine-human dialogue.* Minneapolis: Fortress.
Barker, Kenneth, gen. ed. 1985. *The NIV Study Bible.* Grand Rapids: Zondervan.
Barr, James. 1973. *The Bible in the modern world.* London: SCM.
Barton, John. 1984. *Reading the Old Testament: Method in biblical study.* Philadelphia: Westminster.
Beckson, Karl, and Arthur Ganz. 1975. *Literary terms: A dictionary.* New York: Farrar, Straus and Giroux.
Bellinger, Jr., W. H. 1984. *Psalmody and prophecy. Journal for the Study of the Old Testament,* Supplement Series 27. Sheffield: JSOT Press.
Bergen, Robert D. 1987. Text as a guide to authorial intention: An introduction to discourse criticism. *Journal of the Evangelical Theological Society* 30(3):327–36.
Berry, Donald K. 1993. *The Psalms and their readers: Interpretive strategies for Psalm 18. Journal for the Study of the Old Testament,* Supplement Series, 153. Sheffield: JSOT Press.
Bratcher, Robert G., and Wm. D. Reyburn. 1991. *A translator's handbook on the Book of Psalms.* New York: United Bible Societies.
Brueggemann, Walter. 1984. *The message of the Psalms.* Minneapolis: Augsburg.
———. 1991. Bounded by obedience and praise: The Psalms as canon. *Journal for the Study of the Old Testament* 5:63–92.
Coats, G. W., ed. 1985. *Saga, legend, tale, novella, fable: Narrative forms in the Old Testament. Journal for the Study of the Old Testament,* Supplement Series, 35. Sheffield: JSOT Press.
Craigie, Peter C. 1983. *Psalms 1–50.* Word biblical commentary, vol. 19. Waco, Tex.: Word Books.
Culley, R. C. 1967. *Oral formulaic language in the biblical Psalms.* Toronto: Toronto University Press.
Davis, Ellen. 1992. Exploding the limits: Form and function in Psalm 22. *Journal for the Study of the Old Testament* 53:93–105.
de Waard, Jan, and Eugene A. Nida. 1986. *From one language to another: Functional equivalence in Bible translating.* Nashville: Thomas Nelson.
Driyvers, Pius. 1965. *The Psalms: Their structure and meaning.* New York: Herder and Herder.
Eaton, John. 1984. *The Psalms come alive: Capturing the voice and art of Israel's songs.* Downers Grove, Ill.: InterVarsity Press.
Fee, Gordon D., and Douglas Stuart. 1982. *How to read the Bible for all its worth.* London: Scripture Union.
Finnegan, Ruth. 1970. *Oral literature in Africa.* Oxford: Clarendon Press.
———. 1977. *Oral poetry: Its nature, significance and social context.* Cambridge: University Press.

Gerstenberger, Erhard S. 1988. *Psalms (part 1) with an introduction to cultic poetry.* The Forms of the Old Testament Literature, 19. Grand Rapids: Eerdmans.

Greenwood, David. 1970. Rhetorical criticism and *Formgeschichte*: Some methodological considerations. *Journal of Biblical Literature* 89:418-26.

Greidanus, Sidney. 1988. *The modern preacher and the ancient text: Interpreting and preaching biblical literature.* Grand Rapids: Eerdmans.

Gunkel, Hermann. 1967. *The Psalms: A form-critical introduction.* Trans. Thomas M. Horner. Facet Books, Biblical Series, 19. Philadelphia: Fortress.

Gutt, Ernst-August. 1991. *Translation and relevance: Cognition and context.* Oxford: Basil Blackwell.

Habel, Norman. 1971. *Literary criticism of the Old Testament.* Philadelphia: Fortress.

Hatim, Basil, and Ian Mason. 1990. *Discourse and the translator.* London: Longman.

Hayes, John H. 1974. *Old Testament form criticism.* San Antonio: Trinity University Press.

———. 1976. *Understanding the Psalms.* Valley Forge, Pa.: Judson Press.

———. 1979. *An introduction to Old Testament study.* Nashville: Abingdon.

Hirsch, E. D., Jr. 1967. *Validity in interpretation.* New Haven: Yale University Press.

Jakobson, Roman. (1960) 1972. Style in language. In *The Structuralists from Marx to Levi Strauss,* ed. Richard and Fernande DeGeorge, 85-122. New York: Doubleday.

Klein, Wm. W., Craig L. Blomberg, and Robert L. Hubbard, Jr. 1993. *Introduction to biblical interpretation.* Dallas: Word.

Knierim, Rolf. 1985. Criticism of literary features, form, tradition, and redaction. In *The Hebrew Bible and its modern interpreters,* ed. Douglas A. Knight and Gene M. Tucker, 123-65. Philadelphia: Fortress.

Kugel, James L. 1981. *The idea of biblical poetry: Parallelism and its history.* New Haven: Yale University Press.

Leupold, H. C. [1959] 1969. *Exposition of the Psalms.* Grand Rapids: Baker Book House.

Levinsohn, Stephen C. 1983. *Pragmatics.* Cambridge Textbooks in Linguistics. Cambridge: University Press.

Lewis, C. S. 1958. *Reflections on the Psalms.* New York: Harcourt, Brace.

Longacre, Robert E. 1989. *Joseph: A story of divine providence: A text theoretical and textlinguistic analysis of Genesis 37 and 39-48.* Winona Lake, Ind.: Eisenbrauns.

Longman, Tremper III. 1988. *How to read the Psalms.* Downers Grove, Ill.: InterVarsity Press.

MacDonald Peter J. 1992. Discourse analysis and Biblical interpretation. In *Linguistics and Biblical Hebrew,* ed. Walter R. Bodine, 153-75. Winona Lake, Ind.: Eisenbrauns.

Maier, John, and Vincent Tollers, eds. 1979. *The Bible in its literary milieu: Contemporary essays.* Grand Rapids: Eerdmans.

Miller, Patrick D., Jr. 1986. *Interpreting the Psalms.* Philadelphia: Fortress.

Mowinckel, Sigmund. 1962. *The Psalms in Israel's worship.* Trans. D. R. Ap-Thomas. New York: Abingdon.

Muilenburg, James. [1969] 1992. Form Criticism and beyond. *Journal of Biblical Literature* 88:1-18. Reprinted in *Beyond Form Criticism: Essays in Old Testament literary criticism,* ed. Paul R. House, 49-69. Winona Lake, Ind.: Eisenbrauns.

Neufeldt, Victoria, ed. 1988. *Webster's new world dictionary of American English.* New York: Simon and Schuster.
Osborne, Grant R. 1991. *The hermeneutical spiral: A comprehensive introduction to biblical interpretation.* Downers Grove, Ill.: InterVarsity Press.
Pike, Kenneth L., and Evelyn G. Pike. 1977. *Grammatical analysis.* Dallas: Summer Institute of Linguistics.
Ricoeur, Paul. 1975. Biblical hermeneutics. *Semeia* 4:78-92.
Ryken, Leland. 1984. *How to read the Bible as literature . . . and get more out of it.* Grand Rapids: Zondervan.
Searle, J. R. 1979. *Expression and meaning: Studies in the theory of speech acts.* Cambridge: Cambridge University Press.
Scharlemann, Robert P. 1987. Theological text. *Semeia* 40:5-19.
Silberman, Lou H. 1987. Introduction: Reflections on orality, aurality and perhaps more. *Semeia* 39:1-6.
Soulen, Richard N. 1976. *Handbook of biblical criticism.* Atlanta: John Knox Press.
Tate, W. Randolph. 1991. *Biblical interpretation: An integrated approach.* Peabody, Md.: Hendrickson.
Tucker, Gene M. 1971. *Form criticism and the Old Testament.* Philadelphia: Fortress.
VanGemeren, Willem A. 1991. Psalms. In vol. 5 of *The Expositor's Bible Commentary*, ed. Frank E. Gaebelein, vol. 5, 3-880. Grand Rapids: Zondervan.
Vanhoozer, Kevin J. 1986. The semantics of biblical literature: Truth and Scripture's diverse literary forms. In *Hermeneutics, authority, and canon*, ed. D. A. Carson and John D. Woodbridge, 237-70. Grand Rapids: Zondervan.
Wellek, Rene, and Austin Warren. 1956. *Theory of literature.* 3d ed. New York: Harcourt, Brace.
Wendland, Ernst R. 1985. *Language, society, and Bible translation: With special reference to the style and structure of segments of direct speech in the Scriptures.* Cape Town: Bible Society of South Africa.
———. 1993. *Comparative discourse analysis and the translation of Psalm 22 in Chichewa, a Bantu language of South-Central Africa.* Studies in the Bible and Early Christianity, 32. Lewiston, N.Y.: Edwin Mellen Press.
———. Forthcoming. Continuity and discontinuity in Hebrew poetic design. In *Discourse perspectives on Biblical Hebrew poetry*, ed. Ernst Wendland. New York: United Bible Societies.
Westermann, Claus. 1980. *The Psalms: Structure, content and message.* Trans. Ralph D. Gehrke. Minneapolis: Augsburg.
Wheeler, John. 1989. Music of the temple. *Archaeology and Biblical Research* 2(1):12-20.
Wiklander, Bertil. 1984. *Prophecy as literature: A text-linguistic and rhetorical approach to Isaiah 2-4.* Old Testament Series, 22. CWK Gleerup: Coniectanea Biblica.

17

GENRE AND FORM CRITICISM IN OLD TESTAMENT EXEGESIS

Bo-Krister Ljungberg

Exegetical methods, in general, and form criticism, in particular, are in focus in this article, with the text having priority over methods in interpretations. Another focus is the linking of literary criticism and poetics on the one hand and linguistics on the other. Going beyond the sentence level in discourse analysis and giving close attention to movements such as New Criticism, we find that the respective spheres intermingle. Terminology describing identical phenomena needs to be made compatible. Genre and exegetical methods are examined in hierarchical structure along with linguistics. It is posited that, among exegetical methods, Form Criticism stands the best chance for continued attention since it includes features prevalent in discourse analysis as well. It must, however, be considerably modified. The literary notion of genre is discussed in relation to traditional Old Testament form-critical genres—Law, Wisdom, Prophecy, Psalms, Historical Narrative—and examined from the concept of genre, as a heuristic device. Also discussed is how major linguistic discourse types—Narrative, Expository, Hortatory, and Procedural/Predictive—may be related to exegesis. Poetics and linguistics must not neglect exegesis and its contributions to texts. Neither should texts be held hostage to the methods of biblical exegesis. Exegesis must comply with the new rules of interpretation set up by "linguistic criticism."

One of the earlier thrillers of author John LeCarré, *The Spy Who Came in from the Cold*, dealt with espionage in the early days of the cold war and the Berlin Wall. Coming in from the cold meant climbing over that wall in order to get to the West. In this tale, "the spy" didn't come in to do espionage; he was coming back after having fulfilled a mission, only to find that the West had changed. It wasn't quite like he had known it before. One theme in the story—as I remember it—is his trying to cope with "coming in." Now, theology can be a pretty cold and strictly supervised area, and coming in from it is like getting over a wall (the wall of negligence of the transmitted Text, perhaps). And why not make discourse linguistics the element of change in "the West"?

I hope this metaphor is clear. I—the spy or agent—wish, in a most general manner, to bring up issues which surface for one "coming in from the cold." Actually, I shall not be climbing any wall, but rather "come in" flying 30,000 feet above the ground. My perspective, that of an overview, will become apparent. (Those interested in details are referred to the notes.)

1. Form Criticism as exegesis

Exegetical methods are supposed to support interpretation.[1] They have long held a monopoly over the interpretation of biblical texts.[2]

Exegesis has been practiced under different names. The classical historical-grammatical method ruled as long as churches were in charge of interpretation. Now the historical-critical method rules, crowned and sustained by universities and colleges.

As these names imply, the concern is with what really happened.[3] Both use the word *historical*. In the classical method "historical" is related to "grammatical," and thus to language, and consequently to a linguistic analysis of the text (albeit by means of methods which now seem outmoded). But the "critical" (or "liberal") method had other overruling concerns: the grammar of the texts was replaced by presuppositions such as evolutionism (without which it is difficult to imagine the evolution of Wellhausen's Source Criticism) and later also positivism.

With "the Text" again becoming a center of interest, and with developments in linguistics such as discourse analysis, it has become important to ascertain which method to apply first, as has been demonstrated by several writers (e.g., Berlin 1983 and Longacre 1989). Source Criticism[4] could be said to be "out."[5] The historical-critical method as such has more artillery in store, however. Bypassing Tradition Criticism, which seems mainly to be a Scandinavian or German phenomenon, and putting to the side for the time being Redaction Criticism, that leaves us with Form Criticism. It is also appropriate that this should be so, since Herman Gunkel originally introduced it as a reaction to Wellhausen's Source-Critical approach.

So, if discourse analysis and Form Criticism both share in a negative evaluation of Source Criticism, do they have much in common? Could they mutually benefit? Possibly, but with certain crucial modifications as to Form Criticism.

2. Form Criticism and dimensions of meaning

Form Criticism pays attention in a unique way (compared to other exegetical methods) to several dimensions of meaning that have to be dealt with when doing discourse analysis: meanings of syntax, pragmatics, and semantics.[6] In terms of the communication triangle, focusing on any of these dimensions[7] would mean concentrating on some of its components, as shown in Figure 1.

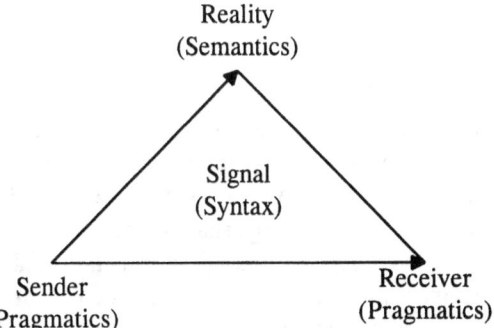

Figure 1. The communication triangle related to dimensions of meaning (direction of arrows indicates flow seen as instruction to speaker)

Different authors apply the very same concept to biblical texts as literary communication, as in Figure 2, is presented by with little variation.[8] This can be seen in Figure 2. Note that *structural* means "syntactic," *situational* means "pragmatic," and *referential* signifies semantic dimensions of meaning.

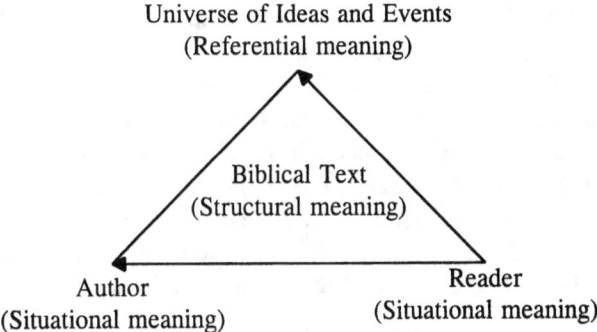

Figure 2. Triangle of literary communication and interpretation of biblical texts (direction of arrows indicates reader's interpretative approach)

2.1 Structural meaning

I shall not dwell long on the obvious, the structural meaning, or on the signal itself, that is, the biblical text. I do, however, strongly affirm the priority of the written text. Suffice it to say that it is through it that we gain knowledge of other dimensions of meaning. It is the text that the reader approaches; it is the text by which he is informed. That is, only the text may inform us of the different dimensions of meaning, including that of the author.[9]

2.2 Referential meaning

Referential meaning[10] involves two communication parameters: that of referent and that of reference. The first equals denotation and signifies "the relationship that holds between (that) lexeme and persons, things, places, properties and activities external to the language-system" (Lyons 1977:207). The second reference "is an utterance-bound relation and does not hold of lexemes as such, but of expressions in context" (Lyons 1977:208, 174).[11] It is the denotational dimension of language that I wish to highlight here (since reference-in-context draws on the input of the other two dimensions of meaning).

2.3 Situational meaning

Situational meaning[12] highlights author and reader. Brown and Yule (1983:1) emphasize discourse-as-process over against text-as-product, viewing a textual record as an attempt by a producer to communicate his message to a recipient: "Text . . . is the verbal record of a communicative event" (p. 190).[13] Some would see discourse analysis as fundamentally concerned with the study of the relationship between language and the contexts of its uses and, as such, study language in use (McCarthy 1991:5, 7, 10). Situational meaning may be subdivided in various ways such as text-external and text-internal (see also Kopesec 1988:15–18).

Text-internal situational meaning is related to terms such as *pragmatics* and *conversational implicature* and *speech act theory*. (Wingate 1991 gives a brief, clear explanation of this.) Text-external situational meaning, on the other hand, may be exemplified by the notions of *Sitz im Leben* and *Gattung* in Form Criticism (see Fig. 3 and secs. 3 and 4).

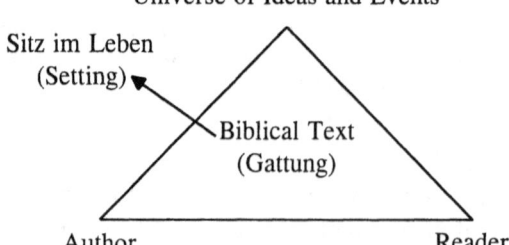

Figure 3. Form Criticism's setting (*Sitz im Leben*) and the triangle of literary communication: text (*Gattung*) bears witness of extratextual situational meaning.

3. Form Criticism and setting (*Sitz im Leben*)

Form Criticism may be characterized as the study of patterns of speech (*Gattungen* 'forms') in relation to their roles in human life (*Sitz im Leben* 'setting') (Buss 1979:1). In Gunkel's (1913) analysis, genres are constituted by their (1) thoughts and moods, that is, content and style; (2) linguistic form, including largely vocabulary and grammar; and (3) connection with life.[14] Gunkel developed the idea that each "form" has a particular "setting"—*Sitz im Leben*—in the life of the community as Longman (1985:63) shows.

A sociological orientation has been central to Form Criticism,[15] and regardless of which specific *Sitz im Leben* may be most appropriate in individual cases, it is always clear that appeal is made to this external reference. Form Criticism as a general phenomenon deals with the environment from which any literary entity might derive its meaning, and within which it might *fulfill* a purpose (Knight 1974:105–7).

Form Criticism was, from the beginning, understood as not only "affording insight into the biblical text by isolating pre-literary stages in its growth, but also a tool in reconstructing the social life and institutions (both sacred and secular) of ancient Israel" (Barton 1984*b*:31). This reasoning, of course, is highly circular.

Gunkel applied his method to literature believed to be oral in origin. Waltke (1988:117) notes that Form Criticism, Tradition Criticism, and Canonical Criticism are all based on the principles that much of the literature in the Pentateuch, especially the stories in Genesis, had a long prehistory before being written down, and that during its oral stage this material was often transposed into new settings with new meanings. According to the standard introductions (e.g., Rast 1972:18), the messages of the Old Testament texts have experienced development over long periods of time: different generations have taken them up, either in oral or written form, and transposed them into fresh settings and understandings. Scholars who examine the texts in this light hold that it is frequently possible to recover meanings buried deeply within them.[16]

Because of the assumed oral origin of texts, the task of interpreting and translating the meaning of a text is, for Form Criticism, very difficult, since the only thing that can be recovered is a dubious kind of situational/pragmatic text-external meaning. Referential meaning in this view can hardly be attributed to the text, and structural meaning can be only of a second-rate order.[17]

Has it been once and for all settled what Form Criticism is? Encyclopedias and introductions give the impression that Form Criticism *is* firmly established. But current specialized literature does not support this. In fact, methodological discussions are prominent (see Wilcoxen 1979:89), and among them a leading concern seems to be to establish the limits of Form Criticism. What is *not* Form Criticism? What other method must be recognized alongside it?

Has Form Criticism aided in interpretation? Knierim (1973:468) is of the opinion that with some modifications Form Criticism might continue to make a contribution to the exegetical disciplines by being subservient to those factors that dominate texts, rather than dominating texts through its own methodological system.

4. Liberating Genre

Knierim (1973:448-49) calls for a critical reevaluation of the Form-Critical dogma of the coherence of genre and setting:

> The problem of the interrelation of genre and setting has not been critically examined enough in Old Testament form criticism to date. It seems as if the coherence of the two can no longer be dogmatically upheld in the sense form criticism has done. Hence, the method must be designed in a way as to allow us to do justice to the nature of all texts. In such a design, the relationship between genre and setting must remain an open one, so that both can be related to, or kept independent of, one another as a text may require.

Genre in literary criticism denotes a type or species of literature. The criteria for classification of genres have been varied during the centuries (Abrams 1988:73). One main difference between the classical and the modern theory of genre is that classical theory was regulative and prescriptive, arguing that genres should be kept apart and not be allowed to mix (Wellek and Warren 1963:233-34). Today the concept of genre is fluid; but in the nineteenth century, genres were considered rigid and pure.[18] When Gunkel, in the early twentieth century, imported a rigid view of genre into biblical studies, this was already a neoclassic position and obsolete (Longman 1987:81). Longman (1985:48-49), therefore, questions Gunkel's contention that genres were "always completely pure."[19] The implication is, that a *Gattung* will not predict a *Sitz im Leben* with any accuracy.

What, then, is genre? Genre theorists have offered many metaphors to describe a communicative understanding of genre. To Wellek and Warren (1963:226), "The literary kind is an institution" as Church, University, and State are institutions. It exists, not as an animal exists or even as a building, chapel, library, or capitol, but as an institution exists. A person can work or express himself through existing institutions, create new ones, or get along, so far as possible, *without* sharing in polities or rituals; a person can also join, but then reshape, institutions. "The totally familiar and repetitive pattern is boring; the totally novel form will be unintelligible—is indeed unthinkable. The genre represents, so to speak, a sum of aesthetic devices at hand, available to the writer and already intelligible to the reader" (ibid., p. 235).

Longman (1985:56-57) argues that "genre exists at all levels of generality . . . and the make-up and nature of a particular genre depends on the viewpoint which the researcher adopts." Decisions arise from research needs.

To Hirsch (1967:76), "All understanding of verbal meaning is necessarily genre-bound." But in what sense? He states (p. 78) that not only understanding but also speaking must be governed and constituted by a sense of the whole utterance. How does a speaker manage to put one word after another unless his choices and usages are governed by a controlling conception? There must be some kind of overarching notion in control of the temporal sequence of speech, and this controlling notion of the speaker, like that of the interpreter, must embrace a system of expectations. Hirsch concludes (pp. 93-121) that the essential component of a context is the intrinsic genre of the utterance.[20]

5. Genre, a heuristic device in canonical context

Can exegesis be operated in isolation from hermeneutics? Traditionally, exegesis establishes the meaning of an ancient text; hermeneutics, the contemporary relevance of this text. But now there seems to be a growing consensus against this, related perhaps to the emphasis on the reader in literary criticism. In order to give the Scripture-as-literature perspective a clear say, we need to let genre enter the discussion. Genre provides the literary context for a given sentence, and thus partly determines what it means. Genre is constitutive of meaning: it conditions reader expectations and thus allows for understanding (Vanhoozer 1986:79).

Osborne (1983:24) sees genre as a hermeneutical device that enables a fusing of the horizons of both text and reader, while maintaining the integrity of both. To him genre helps in determining the *sensus literalis*, or intended meaning; thus genre is more than a means of classifying literary types. "Genre as a whole comes into play at the focal point between the author and the text and then again between the text and the reader. As such it brings together all three elements of the interpretation process: writer, text, reader. The key is for the reader to align himself/herself with the originally intended genre, and as argued . . . this is both a possible and a necessary enterprise" (pp. 26, 27).

Gerhart (1988:41-42, note 1) argues from a reader perspective that genre analysis should be "genric," and not generic, analysis: *genric* emphasizes the functions of the concept of genre in interpretation; *generic*, the conventional form. *Generic* connotes aspects such as nonspecificity and common variety, which are aspects unrelated to the process of interpretation.

And Barton (1984:5-16) suggests that the understanding of a text "depends crucially on decisions about *genre*, about what a text is to be read *as*." Literary competence to him is "the ability to recognize genre."

Now, in interpreting and translating the Old Testament, there are different and probably more difficult issues at stake than in the New Testament. For one thing, the text gives witness to a primary spatio-temporal setting of events which is attributed secondarily to Christ in the New Testament. How does one handle authorial intention and intended audience reception of text?[21] In contrast to NT interpretation and translation, where we, as readers-now, may easily identify with the intended readers, OT interpretation is a bit more complicated. In short, we should be reminded that meaning (according to the NT perspective) is often secondarily attributed to us as readers-now, through Christ. As readers in a canonical context, the meaning we may appropriate is situationally extratextual, as in Figure 4. In my mind, one needs to read the OT from a canonical perspective which includes the NT as well.

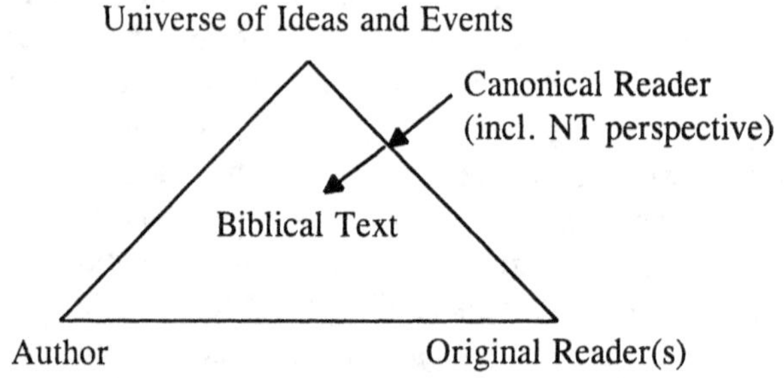

Figure 4. A canonical perspective on the OT in relation to the text-dominated triangle of literary communication.

My assumption is that one has to translate from a reader-response pragmatic/situational perspective of *reading*. The biblical canon (i.e., the Old and New Testaments), which is establishing and being confirmed by the believing community, the church, indicates that this should be so. Newer and pertinent insights of literary criticism, expressed here by Robert Scholes (1989:27), agree: "Reading is not just a matter of standing safely outside texts, where their power cannot reach us. It is a matter of entering, of passing through the looking glass and seeing ourselves on the other side."

6. Register-dominance in traditional OT genres

In trying (hard) to fit traditional exegetical genres (Law, Prophecy, Narrative, Psalms, Wisdom) into this pattern of diverse linguistic meanings, I take help of John Frow (1980:73-79), who reminds us of Halliday's development of the concept of *register* (or *genre*),[22] "a contextual category correlating groupings of linguistic features with recurrent situational features." (This could be paraphrased as: the meaning-potential accessible in a given social context.)

The structure of a situation may be further analyzed in terms of the three variables of *field* (associated with ideational function, i.e., our referential meaning), *tenor* (associated with interpersonal function, i.e., situational meaning), and *mode* (associated with textual function, i.e., our structural meaning). Field governs lexis; tenor governs mood and modality; mode governs forms of cohesion, patterns of voice, and forms of deixis.

Frow also attempts to test the concept for generalization about *kinds* of texts and *kinds* of textual organization. Depending on how field, tenor, and mode receive emphasis, registers may be categorized according to the *dominance* of one of these variables over the others. Frow points out that, whereas each possible genre is characterized by multiple variables, not all sets of variables are significant for each genre. Moreover, there is a constant interimplication of field, tenor, and mode. Tenor relates directly to the processes of field and to the situational determinants of mode (or, couched in my previously employed terminology, situational meaning interacts with referential meaning and with structural meaning). And just as we have seen how genre, as such, is more of a heuristic device than an origin-indicator, the concept of register/genre-dominance "would not necessarily correspond to historical registers. Its purpose is to differentiate, not to produce genre-concepts; and the analysis it makes possible is preliminary to the fuller linguistic analysis which its categories imply" (p. 78).

Now let us return to traditional OT genres and look at *narrative*. Fee and Stuart (1983:74) distinguish between three referential (ideational in Halliday's parlance) levels in biblical narratives:

top level: God's universal plan: creation, fall, sin and redemption, Christ's incarnation and vicarious sacrifice.
middle level: Israel: call of Abraham, exodus from Egypt, life in the promised land, Israel's sin and God's covenant loyalty, exile, return from exile.
bottom level: All the hundreds of individual narratives.

We should know that this characterization of the semantic content is based on theological and canonical presuppositions that are distinctively Christian. The Jews, of course, in describing the top level would not describe the universal plan as Christians do. The fall in Eden, sin, and the role of the Messiah is different in Judaism. [23]

Gunkel's methodological essay on the legends of Genesis (1901) raised the exegetical and hermeneutical question of how the narratives of Genesis should be read, whether as legends or history.[24] Reading the Old Testament from the perspective of the New will not, however, allow us to dehistoricize the biblical narratives; and we must express referential meaning in translation. It is, therefore, important to understand the reasons and the implications when commentators remove referential meaning from narrative. The tendency in certain types of exegesis to ascribe only situational/pragmatic meaning to narrative must be resisted. As for structural meaning in narrative; it is there and it is legitimately explored by discourse analysis.

Prophetic texts present a problem to discourse analysis. Prophetical books are collections of oracles, and it is often difficult to know where one oracle ends and another begins. Often they are presented out of chronological order, and often without indication of historical setting (Fee and Stuart 1982:150-51). However, from an evangelical Christian position, the prophets are seen as "covenant enforcement mediators": they were neither radical social reformers nor innovative religious thinkers, what they said had already been revealed in the covenantal law and their message was therefore not innovative. It was their manner of presenting their message that was innovative. When we read in Hos. 4:2 "There is only cursing, lying and murder, stealing and adultery," this is another way of saying that the Ten Commandments have been broken. The same goes for the Messianic promises: they were also given in the Law, for example in Deut. 18:18 (Fee and Stuart 1982:151-55).

This, of course, goes quite contrary to the inverted scheme inherited by Form Criticism from Wellhausen's Source Criticism, where prophets were prior to priests, and the Law is regarded as a post-exilic reaction. The Form Critical studies by Koch and Westermann contain no discussion of calls to repentance, and Fohrer devotes only one paragraph to the matter. Our working hypothesis *should* be, however, that prophetic oracles are semantically rooted, denotationally as well as connotationally, in the revelation given already to Moses.[25]

Prophecy has many structural features that make any prophecy a coherent entity. Fee and Stuart (1983:158-61) see the isolation of individual oracles as one key to understanding prophecy. Another is establishing forms which is a prerequisite for isolating the individual oracles.

Other authors have gone into greater detail, but I think Fee and Stuart's three most common forms cover the ground: The first is the *lawsuit*. An allegorical literary form called a "covenant lawsuit" is in Isa. 3:13-26. Other examples of lawsuits are in Hos. 3:3-17 and 4:1-19 (summons, charge, evidence, verdict—though elements may be implied rather than explicit). The second of the three terms is the *woe* as in Hab. 2:6-8 (announcement of distress, reason for the distress, prediction of doom). Other examples of the woe are in Hos. 2:16-22; 2:21-23; Isa. 45:1-7; Jer. 31:1-9 (Fee and Stuart's examples).The third form is the *promise,* as in Amos 9:11-15 (reference to the future, mention of radical change, and mention of blessing).

Like the prophecies, the Book of Proverbs is analytically difficult. Proverbs tend not to state things explicitly, but to be rather inexact statements. They point, they carry their message in figurative ways. They do not speak exhaustively about a subject but point toward it (Fee and Stuart 1983:196-98).

The didactic character of the proverb is heightened in admonition, which seeks to impart a desired behavior pattern and right thinking (Crenshaw 1977:235-36). To accomplish this, the admonition uses motive clauses, positive commands, and grounds for conduct. Wisdom texts are most often expressed through poetry with its "careful wordings, cadences, and stylistic qualities that make it easier to commit to memory than prose" (Fee and Stuart 1983:191).[26] Here structural meaning and situational meaning join forces for a greater impact.

In the OT, as it stands, the entire complex of legal literature (the Law, which is embedded in the Pentateuch) is characterized as divine revelation, deriving from the utterances of Yahweh at Sinai. This forms the basis of the subsequent history in which the Israelites often failed to obey that law. This is the traditional view of the OT Law and its significance. But a decisive break came with Wellhausen, who insisted that the prophets belonged to an earlier historical stage than the Law (Høgenhaven 1988:106).[27]

Form Criticism has always been greatly interested in the Psalms (Day 1990:11ff.), since the days of Gunkel, whose five main types (genres) of Psalms were: hymns, communal laments, royal psalms, individual laments, and individual thanksgiving psalms. It was Sigmund Mowinckel, however, who introduced the cultic (*Sitz im Leben*) understanding of Psalms and spurred the Myth and Ritual school, based on the assumption of a common ritual pattern throughout the countries of the ancient east. But Day points out (1990:101–8) that there is "very little if any support in the biblical text itself and . . . the proposed common ancient near eastern ritual pattern is dubious."[28]

7. Traditional OT genres and discourse genres

Discourse linguists have not yet published any literature attempting to correlate discourse text types to traditional OT genres. Edward L. Smith in his article "Text Type and Discourse Framework" (1985:231) examines Longacre's approach to classifying text types: Longacre links the purpose of the discourse with the linguistic features which realize that purpose in the text. Smith argues for "a *discourse framework*, consisting of the functionally dominant, though not necessarily numerically dominant, material surrounding (and developing) a text." This discourse framework should be seen as "the composite of a writer's attitudes and purpose with respect to his or her topic and audience, as well as the particular situation (linguistic and extralinguistic) in which the text is produced" (1985:241–42).

As to how the different discourse analytical methods handle different dimensions of meaning, some have a semantic tilt; others rhetorical; most, I guess, are structural. I am unaware of any that handle extralinguistic (extratextual) features.

8. Conclusion

"Coming in from the cold," I have attempted to pay attention to different dimensions of meaning in the interpretation and translation of OT texts. I have concluded that Form Criticism will not do us much good, save alerting us to extratextual situational meaning, which does have to be taken into account. I have suggested viewing genre as a heuristic device within a canonical context. Also I have sought to point out that traditional OT genres perhaps should be analyzed somewhat less uniformly, and rather in the light of the dominant dimension. I have pleaded for those experienced in discourse analysis and textlinguistics to lend a helping hand to theologians "from the East" as they try to climb over the "Berlin Wall" of textual negligence because even though the wall has already been torn down, to many it is still there in their minds. So don't leave the poor theologians out in the cold. Please invest in the infrastructure of theology. (It may become a bursting market.)

Notes

1. In the restricted and popular sense, exegesis has to do with establishing the meaning of an ancient text as intended by the author and as comprehended by the original audience; hermeneutics, on the other hand, has to do with expounding the contemporary relevance of the text. The two combined will be referred to as interpretation. Sometimes hermeneutics will be an overarching term encompassing exegesis; then the presuppositions of the interpreter will be in focus.

2. The Bible, and foremost the OT, is now being read and interpreted by literary critics from a variety of perspectives. Alter and Kermode's 1989 *Literary Guide to the Bible* is but one example. This has somewhat diminished the monopoly on exegesis as practiced by universities and seminaries.

3. Theology was caught up in the general trend in historiography to find out *wie es eigentlich gewesen (ist)* 'what really happened'.

4. Literary Criticism, rather than Source Criticism, must now be assigned to the study of Poetics in texts.

5. Longacre (1985:170) puts it aptly: "If variations in the text can be explained as simply reflexes of the narrator's art, then those same variations need not be explained as due to differing sources. The latter explanation has become superfluous. The discourse analyst is left, therefore, with an attitude of agnosticism toward the sources: undoubtedly, for whoever wrote the story, sources existed, but just as probably those sources are completely irrecoverable and bear no resemblance to the familiar J, E, P, D of source criticism."

6. It should be pointed out that these three dimensions of meaning are in no way mutually exclusive, but simultaneously and inherently present in a text.

7. This is a well-known fact, one which is sometimes presented in a vastly more complex and elaborate way as in Wiklander (1983:35–36).

8. See Hayes and Holladay (1987:25). A very similar model is found in Longman (1987:18): he makes "historical events and theological ideas" a subtitle under "universe." The arrows go in the same way in both presentations. M. H. Abrams (1953) is reported as the originator of the chart titled "The Orientation of Critical Theories." Abrams uses the terms *Universe, Work, Artist,* and *Audience,* respectively (according to Barton 1984:29).

9. One could, of course, equally well let the arrow go from the text to the reader. My point is that the reader is active in interpretation, but I do by no means wish to say that what meaning there is to the text is inferred by the reader.

10. Kopesec (1988:11–20) gives a chart with alternate designations for referential meaning, such as Semantic, Descriptive, Cognitive, Propositional,

Utterance-type, Ideational/Objective/External. The different terms are related to different authors.

11. Thomson (1988:23) interestingly wants to view translation from the vantage point of reference (here probably in the sense of denotation) rather than universal mental form: "reference-based translation would not involve so much a transfer between languages as a use of two languages to stand for the same external thing." In making mention of it, I merely use it as an illustration of the dimension of language-meaning under discussion. Nida's approach (1975:14) is more common: "the referent of a verbal symbol is not an object in the practical world; rather, it is a concept or a set of concepts which people may have about objects, events, abstracts, and relations." His approach, however, is perhaps carried one step too far; he says, "meaning exists only where systematic sets of contrasts exist."

12. Other designations used by scholars for this concept include "interpersonal" subdivided into "expressive" and "social," "illocutionary act," "occasion meaning," "interpersonal/subjective/internal," and "socio-expressive/socio-stylistic" (Kopesec 1988:11).

13. It is here that the term *reference* comes into its own. It may be "reserved for that function whereby speakers (writers) indicate, via the use of linguistic expression, the entities they are talking (writing) about" (Brown and Yule 1983:204-6). "Despite the fact that, in some analyses, the idea is put forward that some linguistic expressions have unique and independent reference, we shall insist that, whatever the form of the referring expression, its referential function depends on the speaker's intention on the particular occasion of use" (pp. 206-7).

14. Gunkel separated himself from the earlier practice of seeking to discover the historical occasion for a particular text's composition. Instead he focused on its place within the religious-social community. After Gunkel, OT exegetes searched for the place a Psalm occupied in the cultic ritual rather than for the historic event that stimulated its composition (an episode in the life of David for conservative scholars or an event in the Maccabean period for critical ones). Now, however, modern conservatives are less speculative about designating exact events alluded to in a psalm, and modern critics for the most part agree that most Psalms are pre-exilic (so Longman 1985).

15. "Wer die Gattung verstehen will, muss sich jedesmal die ganze Situation deutlich machen und fragen: wer ist es, der redet, wer sind die Zuhörer? welche Stimmung beherrscht die Situation? welche Wirkung wird erstrebt?" (Cited by Knight 1974:195 from Gunkel). My translation: "In order to understand the genre, one will in each case have to get a clear grasp of the entire situation and ask, Who speaks and who listens? What mode is prevalent? What are the effects desired?"

16. Waltke (1988:120) questions the oral base and refers to Whybray (1987), who, in his *The making of the Pentateuch: A methodological study*, takes up and advances the earlier work of Van Seters. Whybray insisted that the alleged earlier forms of the material no longer exist and that there is no

direct evidence of them. All arguments for and against Form Criticism and Tradition Criticism are indirect. Whybray attacked the assumption that it is possible, by studying a written text, to discover whether it is based on oral composition or not.

17. In my estimation, it is highly conjectural, fully comparable to the JEDP of Source Criticism.

18. Up to the eighteenth century genres were thought to be fixed literary types, somewhat like species in the biological order of nature. When new literary types emerged, the neoclassic confidence in the stability of genres weakened, and from the Romantic period until the recent past, genres have been thought of as a convenient but arbitrary way to classify literature. In New Criticism, genre played but a superficial role; and in Structuralism, deep structure is of greater importance (Abrams 1988:73).

19. Buss (1979:53) also views the situation this way: in actual practice Gunkel recognized mixtures, viewing them either as creative borrowings of style or as the decline of a form. Old Testament Form Critics have often not seen, as others have, that genres are abstractions, and that virtually all human experiences involve a combination of categories applied simultaneously.

20. He deems it entirely fit to call an intrinsic genre a system of conventions. This emphasis on the conventional character of all genre expectations and inferences leads back to Wittgenstein's metaphor of a game. (But since there are a great many games *(langue)*, and since it is necessary to know the rules that apply to a particular game *(parôle)*, a problem arises. How does one know which game is being played? To have mastered all rules is not to know which one to apply. Even when people know all the games, they may still disagree about which game they are playing. We can never be sure which game is being played. We must learn, as Wittgenstein insists, by playing. (If we believe that the schemata, or rules of the game, of interpretation are constitutive rather than arbitrary and heuristic, then we have made a serious mistake.)

21. In commenting upon biblical interpretation, Hirsch notes that "The 'sensus plenior', a conception in scriptural interpretation under which the text's meaning goes beyond anything the human author could have consciously intended, is, of course, a totally unnecessary entity. The human author's willed meaning can always go beyond what he consciously intended so long as it remains within his willed type, and if the meaning is conceived of as going beyond even that, then we must have recourse to a divine Author speaking through the human one. In that case it is His willed type we are trying to interpret, and the human author is irrelevant. We must not confuse his text with God's. In either instance the notion of a sense beyond the author's is illegitimate. The same point holds, of course, for inspiration in poetry: either we are interpreting the poet's text or that of the muse who possesses him, one or the other. The fact that two different minds can intend quite different meanings by the same word sequence should not by now be surprising. Nothing is gained by

conflating and confusing different 'texts' as though they were somehow the same because they both use the same word sequence" (1967:126, note 37).

22. Frow prefers Volosinov's term *genre* to Halliday's *register,* since "as a musical term this suggests a scale on a single plane, whereas 'genre', borrowed from poetics, implies the unity of multiple convergent planes" (1980:74).

23. My point here is that the difference is more than one of accepting Jesus as God's Messiah. In terms of sin, the incident in Eden is treated lightly by the rabbis. For Judaism the great sin is the one described in Exodus 32-34, the worship of the golden calf. And the Messiah is not preexistent, incarnated, and vicariously suffering. That the top levels of Christianity and Judaism look different should be admitted as a presupposition. This is what we as readers bring into the surface-level text.

24. Gunkel (1901) used several criteria: oral transmission, common people's interests, depending on tradition and imagination, reporting incredible events, poetic aim to please. He further subdivided the patriarchal narratives and elaborated on the relation of oral legend cycles to sources such as JEDP (Hayes 1980:130-31).

25. It seems to me that the heavy emphasis given to situational meaning and *Sitz im Leben* has been triggered by the evolutionary scheme Form Criticism inherited from Source Criticism, where there would not have been any Law to relate to. Westerman believes that the differences noted between the proclamation of salvation and the oracle of salvation arise from the difference in the original *Sitz im Leben* of each, the oracle being related to the ceremony of individual lament and announced by a priest, while the proclamation was part of the community lament service and was proclaimed by a prophet (Isa. 40-66, 79).There has been agreement that there is a genre properly designated as "trial speech" or "juridical speech," but the quest for the *Sitz im Leben* has led to different conclusions, for example, Würtwein's cultus and Begrich's (followed by Boecker and Westermann) everyday legal custom. Was the *rib* form of address an established genre in the liturgical life of Israel? The most that can be said is that liturgical practice is *reflected* in the OT literature.

26. Traditional Form Criticism, of course, sought to determine the primary forms characteristic of wisdom, and to say from what settings those forms originated (Hayes 1980:151). This approach, however, is contested: "Little precision is possible in specifying settings within which each literary genre functioned, that is, beyond the general category of didactic" (Crenshaw 1977:228). Crenshaw elaborates on the new didactic setting, speaking of possible multi-verse structuring of proverbs, so that the total Book of Proverbs in the product of intentional arrangement (p. 229). The proverb is a result of a collective experience, and as such it is retrospective. Because of this character of observation, it often lacks the imperative. One might say that the didactic intent is skewed or secondary due to its succinct and highly metaphorical style (p. 231). Still, in all wisdom literature, a pragmatic reader-response perspective is built in, since in the process of listening, the word is submitted to

response. The didactic character of the proverb may also be heightened in admonition by the use of motive clauses (pp. 235-36).

27. Alt established a structural distinction. A casuistic law contained an introductory clause that generally began with "if" or "when" and provided an instance of the case. It was then followed by a clause stating the consequence or penalty that was generally introduced by "then" or "he" or "the one" (as in Exod. 22:1-17). Alt argued that Israel shared this type of law with general Near Eastern culture. An apodictic law, on the other hand, could begin with a reference in the second person ("you shall not ...," e.g., Exod. 23:14-19), or with a Hebrew participle ("whoever...," as in Exod. 22:19-20), or with a curse ("cursed be he who...," as in Deut. 27:15-26). Alt took this type of law to be typically Israelite, concerned with the sacral realm and religious matters (Hayes 1979:149-51).

28. The Swedish Bible (1917) has clear traces of this influence in the translation of the phrase יְהוָה מָלָךְ as in 97:1. At the yearly enthronement festival (supposedly as part of a fertility cult inherited from the Canaanites—see Day 1990:75-82 for a full discussion—the king was reinstalled as Yahweh's representative. If one goes along with this thought, the translation would be 'The LORD has become king'; this is mitigated, however, into *Herren är nu konung* 'The LORD is now king'. Elsewhere in the Swedish Bible we read that 'the LORD rules; he is king'. Here this extratextual situational meaning ought to be resisted.

References

Abrams, M. H. [1953] 1973. *The mirror and the lamp: Romantic theory and the critical tradition*. Oxford: Oxford University Press.

———. 1988. *A glossary of literary terms*. 5th ed. Chicago: Holt, Rinehart and Winston.

Alter, Robert, and Frank Kermode. 1989. *The literary guide to the Bible*. London: Fontana Press.

Barton, John. 1984a. Classifying biblical criticism. *Journal for the Study of the Old Testament* 29:19-35.

———. 1984b. *Reading the Old Testament: Method in biblical study*. London: Darton, Longman and Todd.

Berlin, Adele. 1983. *Poetics and interpretation of biblical narrative*. Sheffield: Almond Press.

Brown, Gillian, and George Yule. 1983. *Discourse analysis*. Cambridge: Cambridge University Press.

Buss, Martin J. 1979. The study of forms. In Hayes 1979, 1-56.

Crenshaw, James L. 1977. Wisdom. In Hayes 1977, 225-64.

Day, J. 1990. *Psalms*. Sheffield: JSOT Press.

Fee, Gordon D., and Douglas Stuart. 1983. *How to read the Bible for all its worth*. London: Scripture Union.

Frow, John. 1980. Discourse genres. *The Journal of Literary Semantics* 9:73-77.

Gerhart, Mary. 1988. Generic competence in biblical hermeneutics. *Semeia* 43:29-44.

Gunkel, 1901. The legends of Genesis.

———. 1913. *Reden und Aufsätze*. Göttingen: Vandenhoeck and Ruprecht. (Reprinted in DLZ 27 [1966], cols. 1797ff., 1861ff.)
Hayes, John H., ed. 1977. *Old Testament Form Criticism*. San Antonio: Trinity University Press.
———. 1979. *An introduction to Old Testament study*. Nashville: Abingdon.
Hayes, John H., and Carl R. Holladay. 1987. *Biblical exegesis: A beginner's handbook*. 2d ed. Atlanta: John Knox press; London: SCM.
Hekman, Donald. 1987. Some comparisons between Old and New Testament exegesis. *Notes on Translation* 121:15-31.
Hirsch, E. D., Jr. 1967. *Validity in interpretation*. New Haven and London: Yale University Press.
Høgenhaven, Jesper. 1988. *Problems and prospects of Old Testament theology*. The Biblical Seminar. Sheffield: JSOT Press.
Knierim, Rolf. 1973. Old Testament Form Criticism reconsidered. *Interpretation* 27(4):435-68.
Knight, Douglas A. 1974. The understanding of 'Sitz im Leben' in Form Criticism. *Society of Biblical Literature seminar papers*, vol. 1, ed. George MacRae, 105-25.
Kopesec, Michael F. 1988. A translator's perspective on meaning. *Occasional Papers in Translation and Textlinguistics* 2(1):9-20.
Longacre, Robert. 1985. Interpreting biblical stories. In *Discourse and literature: New approaches to the analysis of literary genres*, ed. Teun A. Van Dijk, 169-85. Philadelphia: John Benjamins.
———. 1989. *Joseph: A story of divine providence: A text theoretical and textlinguistic analysis of Genesis 37 and 39-48*. Winona Lake, Ind.: Eisenbrauns.
Longman, Tremper, III. 1985. Form Criticism, recent developments in genre theory, and the evangelical. *Westminster Theological Journal* 47:46-67.
———. 1987. *Literary approaches in biblical interpretation*. Foundations of Contemporary Interpretations, 3. Grand Rapids, Mich.: Academie Books.
Lyons, John. 1977. *Semantics*, vol. 1. Cambridge: University Press.
March, W. Eugene. 1979. Prophecy. In Hayes 1977, 141-77.
McCarthy, Michael. 1991. *Discourse analysis for language teachers*. Cambridge: Cambridge University Press.
Nida, Eugene A. 1975. *Exploring semantic structures*. International Library of General Linguistics, 11. Munich: Wilhelm Fink Verlag.
Osborne, Grant R. 1983. Genre Criticism—Sensus Literalis. *Trinity Journal* 4(1):1-27.
Rast, Walter E. 1972. *Tradition, history and the Old Testament*. Philadelphia: Fortress.
Scholes, Robert. 1989. *Protocols of reading*. New Haven and London: Yale University Press.
Smith, Edward L., Jr. 1985. Text type and discourse framework. *Text* 5(3):229-47.
Thomson, Greg. 1988. What sort of meaning is preserved in translation? *Notes on Translation* 2(1):1-24.
Vanhoozer, Kevin J. 1986. The semantics of biblical literature: Truth and Scripture's diverse literary forms. In *Hermeneutics, Authority and Canon*. ed. D. A. Carson and John D. Woodbridge, 53-104. Leicester: Inter-Varsity Press.
Waltke, Bruce K. 1988. Oral tradition, inerrancy and hermeneutic. In *A tradition, a challenge, a debate*, ed. Harvie M. Conn, 117-35. Grand Rapids, Mich.: Baker.

Wellek, Rene, and Austin Warren. 1963. *Theory of literature*. 3d ed. London: Peregrine.
Westermann, C. 1969. *Isaiah 40-66*. Philadelphia: Westminster Press.
Wiklander, Bertil. 1983. Prophecy as literature. Ph.D. diss., University of Uppsala (later published in the Coniectanea Biblica Series).
Wilcoxen, Jay A. 1979. Narrative. In Hayes 1977, 57-98.
Wingate, J. Douglas. 1991. How pragmatic is pragmatics? *Notes on Linguistics* 55:4-15.

18

HEBREW PROVERBS AND HOW TO TRANSLATE THEM

Murray Salisbury

This article addresses many of the difficulties involved in analyzing, interpreting, and translating Hebrew proverbs by suggesting step-by-step procedures. Since procedures must be based on a clear understanding of the nature of the proverb, the first section describes the proverb in general, with respect to its distinctive form (concise, striking poetry), and the second section describes the Hebrew proverb in particular. Each proverb is the unique product of complex interactions between several features of its language and poetry. For instance, sound patterns and other poetic devices may function at the discourse level (cohesion and prominence), at the semantic level (linking words which have meaning relations), and at the syntactic level (making up for grammatical ellipsis). So proverb description requires the multivariate perspective of several different linguistic and poetic levels of analysis. Ten steps of a method for analyzing and interpreting Hebrew proverbs are suggested in section three. The procedure is demonstrated in full for three Hebrew proverbs, one of which is difficult to interpret. The overall effects of the interplay between their linguistic and poetic features are explored, as is the way this interplay contributes to the meaning of the cryptic messages. Conclusions about form and its correlation with meaning are tested by slightly changing the form while retaining similar semantic content. Finally, in section four the ten-step methodology is incorporated into a five-step procedure for translating Hebrew proverbs, illustrated with examples and alternative translations into English proverbial form.

Proverbs are alive and well in most of the world's cultures even though we have witnessed their decline and fall in Western culture. Unfortunately, Westerners frequently fail to recognize the proverb's powerfully persuasive potential for many non-Western people groups. The failure to appreciate the proverb's distinctive form has resulted in such poor translations of Hebrew proverbs that the translations often are no longer proverbs at all; and to make matters worse, there are difficulties involved in interpreting biblical proverbs. In fact, the Book of Proverbs has been given scant attention by biblical scholars and translators alike. But before these difficulties can be addressed, the nature of the proverb must be clearly understood.

1. Towards a description of proverbs in general

The proverb has stubbornly defied adequate definition. Many a paroemiologist has floundered in the ocean of proverbial diversity of form, style, and function while the precise definition of what he is investigating eludes him (e.g., Seiler 1922).[1]

Archer Taylor, America's leading proverb scholar, refrains from defining the subject of his famous book entitled *The Proverb*. He begins by saying (1931:3),

> The definition of a proverb is too difficult to repay the undertaking; and should we fortunately combine in a single definition all the essential elements and give each the proper emphasis, we should not even then have a touchstone. An incommunicable quality tells us this sentence is proverbial and that one is not. Hence no definition will enable us to identify positively a sentence as proverbial.

In fact, according to Whiting, "no definition is really necessary, since all of us know what a proverb is" (1952:331). Despite the problems in precise proverb definition, it is important to take steps towards understanding and describing the nature of the proverb.

The first step is to recognize that the proverb is a surface-structure subtype of hortatory discourse.

Longacre (1983:11) describes hortatory discourse as "possibly the least vivid of all the discourse types. We can witness this in a Sunday morning church service." He describes his concept of "skewing" between the notional level and the surface level. One way of making a less vivid discourse more appealing is by skewing it to be a more vivid surface form. Longacre gives the parable and the fable as examples of "well crystallized and recognizable types in the surface structure . . . casting hortatory material into narrative form" (1983:13).

By analogy, a proverb may be described as a well-crystallized and recognizable type in the surface structure designed to cast hortatory material in a special form of concise poetry that is more vivid, appealing, and memorable. The following diagram shows such "skewing," or mismatch, between the deep level and the surface level.[2]

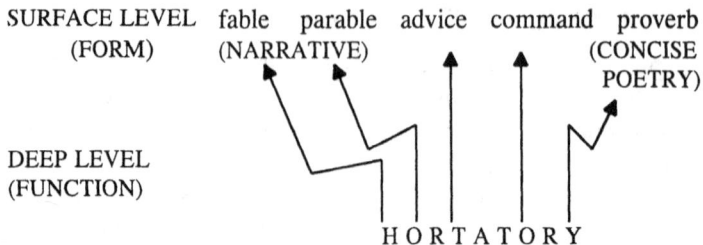

The proverb serves the same pedagogic function as various other hortatory discourse subtypes, such as fable, parable, prophetic exhortation, and wisdom poem. What sets the proverb apart from other subtypes (whether hortatory or not) is its distinctive surface form. For this reason, proverb definitions based on form are preferable to those based on function.

The importance of form may be demonstrated by comparing a well-known proverb with a paraphrase in ordinary prose: compare "Birds of a feather flock together" with "People tend to socialize with those who are similar to themselves." The latter is flat and has none of the features found in proverbs:

1. Conciseness: There is an ellipsis of "similar" before "feather" and an explicit tenor for the metaphor is lacking.
2. Metaphor: "birds" for the implied "people."
3. An extended meaning of "feather" to mean "same kind, sort."
4. Sound patterns: Consonance of the two "f"s and the repetition of "-ether."[3]
5. A correlation between sound and sense: The initial and final sounds in "feather" are repeated in "f[lock tog]ether." This phonic link hints at a semantic link also, namely that because they are of the same kind ("feather") they are flocking together. We could say that the *sounds* "flock together," thus causing the *sense* of the words that carry these sounds to "flock together" as well!
6. Rhythm (aided by the ellipsis).
7. Binary structure: The two parts of the proverb are metrically and phonically balanced and punctuated by the "-ether" rhyme.

The prose paraphrase, lacking an ear-catching form, would be neither remembered nor used by hearers, but be doomed to remain on the page of a textbook. In short, it is not a proverb. Not concise and not poetic. It lacks all the poetic features that give the proverb its striking form.

In order to test this thesis, let us change the form of the proverb by substituting synonyms for three of the words: "Fowls of a plumage band together." This form, though it does show the features of conciseness and imagery, does not affect us in the same way that the well-known proverb does. The sound patterns have been lost, resulting in the loss of rhythm, balance, and the all-important correlation between sound and sense. It lacks a dynamic interplay between its poetic features; its form is neither arresting nor proverbial. The meaningfulness of the first proverb has been lost.[4]

Taylor (1931) speaks of an "incommunicable quality" that characterizes the proverb. We might suggest that that quality is its striking poetic form. In other words, a proverb's high concentration of poetic features collectively produces an arresting form.[5] But a conglomeration of poetic features is not enough. It is the unique fusion of these features and their dynamic interplay and interrelationships that give the proverb its "incommunicable quality" or striking form.

2. Towards a description of Biblical Hebrew proverbs

Like the English proverb just considered, Biblical Hebrew proverbs are also characterized by a striking poetic form. Their features may be summarized by viewing them from various perspectives.

1. *The proverb as a discourse.* A proverb is a self-contained sentence that requires no larger linguistic context to justify its existence.[6] That is to say, adjoining proverbs are not interdependent in the same way that sentences in a paragraph are. Rather, each is a relatively independent discourse that contains no paragraphs and only one sentence. This means that any developmental units of argumentation or exhortation must be very brief. Proverbial discourse is hortatory discourse in a poetic nutshell.

2. *The proverb as a sentence.* The goal in constructing a proverb is to achieve a maximum of meaning with a minimum of words. So the proverb is typically more elliptical than ordinary prose. Syntactic relations within the clause and between clauses are frequently not marked grammatically. That is, grammatical markers (such as prepositions, conjunctions, relatives, and the accusative marker) are often missing or economized. (Since the corpus of biblical proverbs is finite, it is possible to enumerate all of the sentence types, and this has already been done for the admonitions by Nel 1982.)

3. *The proverb as a bicolon.* The typical Biblical Hebrew literary proverb is a bicolon[7] whose two cola are usually metrically balanced and in some

kind of parallelism or chiasmus (inverse parallelism). The parallelism or chiasmus may be at any level: semantic, syntactic, morphological, phonological, or metrical. Often more than one level is involved.

4. *The proverb as a proposition.* Proverbs are normally divided into admonitions and sayings.[8] Admonitions consist of an imperative or a prohibitive plus either a motive clause or a result clause. The saying, however, is a topic-comment composite. At least one topic is introduced and one or more comments are made on that topic. Topics and comments may have either a positive or a negative value according to the ancient Israelite value system. Opposite word pairs (e.g., wise person versus fool) are often used as topics. But it is the comments made about the topics that are the more significant. The semantic relations between the propositions most commonly involve similarity (including comparison and simile), contrast, or consequence.

5. *The proverb as a succession of sounds.* Sound patterns are frequent features of Biblical Hebrew proverbs; they not only help to give them their striking form but also may function at other levels of language. In order to achieve greater brevity, the functions of syntactic markers, discourse markers, and explicit statements of the semantic relationships are often indicated by sound patterns.

6. *The proverb as metaphor.* Imagery, whether simile, metaphor, or personification, etc., is often found in proverbs.

7. *The proverb as poetry.* The proverb has an especially compact poetic form. Except for features of a poem larger than the bicolon (such as the stanza, tricolon, and refrain), it appears that any feature of Biblical Hebrew poetry may be a feature of Biblical Hebrew proverbs.[9] In fact, poetic features are found in an even higher concentration in the proverb than in other types of poetry.

8. *The proverb as wisdom literature.* Many literary proverbs may have originated with a small group of sages, but in any case they have been sanctioned by an entire community.[10] A proverb is a piece of the collective wisdom of a whole community. It is wisdom in a nutshell. Its intended purpose is normally instructive as to codes of conduct, whether in the form of an imperative, a prohibitive, an observation, or an amusing anecdote.

9. *The proverb as a speech act.* Paroemiologists inform us that "The meaning of proverbs is best revealed by actual usage in social situations" (Seitel 1981:122).[11] This dimension is less important for literary proverbs than for popular proverbs, yet even literary proverbs may be used by

parents or teachers in specific social situations. For Biblical Hebrew proverbs we are able only to conjecture what these social situations might have been and how a proverb in a given situation might have affected the hearer(s).[12]

10. *The proverb as rhetoric.* Proverbs utilize a number of rhetorical and poetic devices in order to persuade the hearer(s) to carry out (or refrain from carrying out) a certain course of action. It is necessary that proverbs sound authoritative. It is essential that they feel right and sound absolutely true. This effect is achieved by means of a proverb's form. Its cryptic, elliptical constructions, the structural and metrical balance of its two lines, its neat grammatical and semantic symmetries, its highly patterned sound and word repetitions, the subtle ways it links sound and sense, its witty identifications or contrasts expressed in tightly formulated propositions, the vivid or amusing imagery it conjures up, and the familiarity of its idiom all contribute to the feeling that the insight or idea encapsulated in the proverb must indeed be true and its advice diligently heeded.

Thus far, the proverb has been discussed from a number of different perspectives, providing us with a fairly comprehensive description of what a proverb is. Putting all this together, we may now define the two-line proverb of the Book of Proverbs: The Biblical Hebrew literary proverb is a self-contained, often elliptical sentence in the form of a bicolon, comprising at least one topic and one comment, which normally expresses some kind of similarity, contrast, or consequence. It is pedagogically and rhetorically motivated, having either vivid imagery or a striking and memorable form. This is achieved by the complex interplay between its several poetic features (such as sound patterns, rhythm, parallelism, repetition, and paronomasia).

3. A method for analyzing and interpreting Biblical Hebrew proverbs

The proverb has so far been described (amongst other things) as wisdom in a nutshell. The nutshell is the striking, concise, poetic form of the proverb. The small size of the nutshell imposes constraints on the syntax, semantics, and discourse in such a way that clausal relationships, sense relations, cohesion, and unit breaks are often marked by the sound patterns or some other poetic device.

What is needed now is a nutcracker to crack open the proverb so that the hidden depths of wisdom may be revealed. The proposed nutcracker is of the two-handled kind. Linguistic analysis and poetic (or stylistic) analysis are the two handles.[13] To apply these two kinds of analysis I have devised a ten-step methodology, the final two steps (synthesis and solution) being the hinges of the nutcracker. The ten steps, illustrated with examples, are as follows:

1. *Notice the sound patterns.* Sound repetitions may be of a single sound (a series) or more than one sound (a sequence). Some sequences of sound have intervening sounds. Chiastic sequences involve an exact reversal of the sound sequence (McCreesh 1991, chap. 2). Noticing such sound patterns becomes useful for interpretation only if their function in a particular proverb can be determined. Possible functions[14] of sound patterns include:

   a. *Intracolon cohesion* (McCreesh's "Linking"). One word may be linked to the next by sound repetition. That second word may be linked to a third by a different sound, and so on.
   b. *Key sounds* ("Correlation"). The sound patterns of the key word may be repeated so that the sense of the key word is subtly reiterated.
   c. *Clause markers* ("Tagging Sound Patterns"). Sound patterns may be used to punctuate or to mark off clause boundaries.
   d. *Intercola cohesion* ("Coordinating Proverb"). When syntactic connectors such as conjunctions have been pared away, cohesion between two cola is frequently provided by sound patterns.
   e. *Semantic links.* Sense relations between an agent or a consequence and its event and sense relations between words of similar or opposite meaning may be indicated by means of sound patterns.
   f. *Prominence.* If there is one (or more than one) dominating sound pattern in a proverb, then any word or phrase outside of this pattern is marked as prominent.

2. *Analyze the syntax and morphology.* Syntax and morphology are easily handled together. Grammatical relationships between words and parts of words (subject, object, noun, verb, pronominal suffix, anaphoric reference) are analyzed at the surface level.

3. *Determine the sentence type.* The surface-level grammatical relationship between the two lines or clauses is in focus here. In some cases, the two or more clauses may be juxtaposed without any explicit grammatical marker. In other cases, the relationship may be marked in the surface grammar (-וְ 'and', כְּ... כֵּן 'as ... so', טוֹב מִן 'better than', etc.).

4. *Investigate the syntagmatic and paradigmatic sense relations.* The logical relationships between words are now investigated, including both syntagmatic (agent, patient, consequence, etc.) and paradigmatic (similarity, oppositeness, etc.). Questions of word choice are handled by comparing

each word in the proverb with other words belonging to the same semantic fields (taking into account factors at other levels such as sound patterns).

5. *Determine the proposition type.* This involves the logical relationship between propositions, irrespective of whether or not it is marked in the surface grammar. The semantic structures and the surface-level structures often do not correspond. For instance, both juxtaposition and the *waw* conjunction are used to cover a wide range of notional types (such as exhortation-grounds, means-purpose, condition-consequence, or reason-result). In addition, the sayings are analyzed into topics and comments, which are given positive or negative values.[15]

6. *Analyze the structural relations in the bicolon.* The possible relations between parallel lines seem limitless. Each couplet is a unique composite of two lines that interact with each other in unique ways to form an inseparable unit. Line a anticipates line b; line b intensifies the line a image. The preceding five steps of analysis are prerequisite in determining the unique interrelationships between the two cola of each proverb.

7. *Identify figures of speech.* The distinction between simile and metaphor can be misleading when applied to Biblical Hebrew since the presence or absence of the preposition כְּ 'like, as' often has to do with reasons of conciseness, sound patterns, or rhythm; it is not necessarily a signal of different types of figures. The term *similitude* is, therefore, more useful than *metaphor* or *simile*. Other figures, such as personification, metonymy, and synecdoche, are also used.

8. *Identify all other stylistic devices.* Biblical Hebrew proverbs are replete with poetic devices: sound patterns, parallelism, imagery, paronomasia, hendiadys, repetition, word pairs, inclusio, allusion, ellipsis, paradox, irony, oxymoron, rhetorical question, hyperbole, merismus, delayed identification, enjambment, and the "break-up" of a composite phrase. More important than mere identification of these devices is the determination of their function and effect.

9. *Synthesize and test.* It is not enough to analyze features in isolation; it is also important to determine how they combine and interact with each other to form a compact aphorism with a clear-cut message. In other words, analysis should be combined with regular exegetical methods, looking for cultural clues and cross-references and asking how the original hearer would have perceived all these clues and combined them to solve the proverb's cryptic message. Then, although we cannot know for sure what went on in the subconscious minds of the hearers more than two millennia

ago, we can *test* many of the results of our analysis and synthesis. This is done by changing the form of all or part of the proverb (without changing its semantic content) and seeing the difference that it makes to the overall coherent meaning.

10. *Compose an expanded paraphrase.* On the basis of such analysis and synthesis, it should now be possible to compose an expanded paraphrase of the proverb and arrive at the full, correct interpretation. A proverb is composed according to the principle of a maximum of meaning expressed with a minimum of words. The two handles of linguistic analysis and poetic analysis help us crack open a proverb and expose the hidden depths of meaning, the "maximum of meaning" brought out explicitly, fully, and clearly. To do this, a paragraph of several sentences will usually be necessary.

Now let us apply these ten steps to three examples: Prov. 10:12, 5:12, and 27:19.

Example one: Prov. 10:12.

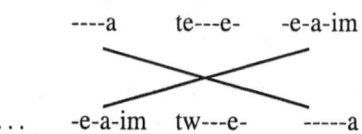

    a. Hatred provokes arguments
    b. but love covers over all offenses.

1. The sound patterns form a chiastic pattern:[16]

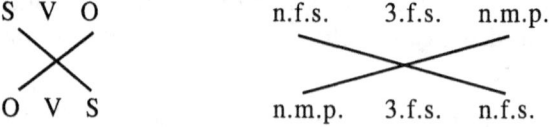

2. Other chiastic patterns are found:[17]

```
S  V  O           n.f.s.   3.f.s.   n.m.p.
 \/                     \  /
 /\                     /  \
O  V  S           n.m.p.   3.f.s.   n.f.s.
```

3. The *waw* conjunction (וְ 'and, but') joins the two syntactically complete transitive predications.

4. As is so often the case with proverbs, this one contains two contrasts: שִׂנְאָה 'hatred' and אַהֲבָה 'love' are opposites, as are תְּעוֹרֵר 'arouse' and תְּכַסֶּה 'cover'. Synonymous terms are another characteristic of

proverbs, and here we find מְדָנִים 'disputes' and פְּשָׁעִים 'offenses'. A chiastic structure links these semantically related terms:

5. At the deeper level of analysis, the relationship between the two propositions is one of contrast, with ambiguous *waw* conjunction (וְ 'and, but') meaning (in this case) 'but, on the contrary'. Both propositions are comprised of a topic and a comment. The topics are שִׂנְאָה 'hatred' and אַהֲבָה 'love', respectively. The comments make up the remainder of each line. The contrast between the two lines involves both the topics and the comments, which have negative values in a, but positive in b. There is yet another chiastic structure, this one involving the topics and comments:

6. As to structural relations in the bicolon, the two lines are related by chiastic structures at several levels: phonological, morphological, syntactic, semantic, and propositional, underscoring the contrast between the two propositions and helping to disambiguate the *waw* conjunction. The chiasm also draws attention to the semantic relationships between שִׂנְאָה 'hatred' and אַהֲבָה 'love', between תְּעוֹרֵר 'arouse' and תְּכַסֶּה 'cover', and between מְדָנִים 'disputes' and פְּשָׁעִים 'offenses'.

7. As for the figures of speech, we can identify metonymy (abstract for concrete): שִׂנְאָה 'hatred' and אַהֲבָה 'love' are abstract nouns representing the persons experiencing these emotions, normally expressed as participles of the verb (שׂוֹנֵא 'hater' and אוֹהֵב 'lover'). This substitution cannot have been made for reasons of sound pattern alone, for the participles would be linked by an even stronger sound pattern (-o-e-). There are several possible reasons for this substitution.[18] It may be simply a device to elevate the style of the proverb[19] and, at the same time, focus the hearer's attention on the two topics and on the contrast between them. A second figure in this proverb is the metaphorical use of the verbs: עוֹרֵר (*pōʿlel*) 'to stir up, rouse, disturb' and כִּסָּה עַל 'to cover over' are used metaphorically to signify "to provoke (strife)" and "to forgive (offenses)," respectively.

8. There are no further stylistic devices in the example unless we include a possible phonic inclusio: -a............-a.

9. The chiastic structure (expressed at all possible linguistic levels) functions at several levels also. At the discourse level, it serves to tie the two lines together (intercola cohesion) while, at the same time, demarcating the boundary between them. At the propositional level, it underscores the contrast between the two propositions. At the semantic level, it draws attention to the sense relations between שִׂנְאָה 'hatred' and אַהֲבָה 'love', between תְּעוֹרֵר 'arouse' and תְּכַסֶּה 'cover', and between מְדָנִים 'disputes' and פְּשָׁעִים 'offenses'. The first of these relationships (between שִׂנְאָה 'hatred' and אַהֲבָה 'love') is particularly prominent. Not only are these two words linked by the chiasmus at five linguistic levels (and by a possible phonic inclusio), but the link is strengthened by virtue of their being the topics of the propositions as well as abstract nouns substituting for concrete participles. All levels of analysis point to the same message. A clear contrast is being made between the first and last words of the proverb—between the attitude of hatred and the attitude of love.

10. This proverb is contrasting two kinds of response to disagreement between people. One response aggravates the disagreement and makes it larger than it should be. The other calms the storm and heals the wounds. This is the true test of love and of hate. In a potentially confrontational situation, are past disputes and hurts revived so that the present grievance is exacerbated? Or is there a willingness to forgive and forget, to overlook past and present offenses?

Example two: Prov. 15:12.

a. A scoffer does not like [anyone] to rebuke him.   לֹא יֶאֱהַב־לֵץ הוֹכֵחַ לוֹ

b. To wise ones he will not go.   אֶל־חֲכָמִים לֹא יֵלֵךְ

1. The sound patterns[20] within each line contribute to intracolon cohesion:

lō' ye'ĕhab	lēṣ hôkēaḥ	lô	'el ḥăkāmîm	lō' yēlēk
lo	l.....o	lo	el	l.....ele
(h	h		k	k)
lo	....	lo	el....	...le

Hebrew Proverbs and How to Translate Them

Sound patterns between the lines form a chiasmus:

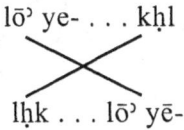

This chiasmus reinforces the intercola cohesion provided by the exchange of the dominant sound sequences in the middle of each colon. That is, the dominant sequence in the first line (*lo*) occurs in the middle of the second line and the dominant sequence in the second (*le*) occurs in the middle of the first.

2. There is no clear morphological chiasmus, parallelism, or repetition. Rather, there is a little of each. Both verbs are *qal* p.c. 3.m.s. Colon a has two n.m.s., while b has one n.m.p. There is, however, a (weak) syntactic chiastic pattern to be seen: VSO versus LocV. The subject is ellipsed in colon b.

3. Ellipsis is unmistakable in this proverb. There are no grammatical markers linking the two clauses. The grammatical subject (לֵץ 'scoffer') is implicit in the second clause. The infinitive absolute (הוֹכֵחַ 'to reprove') replaces the expected finite verb (הוֹכִיחַ 'is reproving' or יוֹכִיחַ 'reproves') which would require a preceding relative pronoun (אֶת אֲשֶׁר 'the one who'). There is a complete lack of definite articles and accusative markers (a common characteristic of Biblical Hebrew poetry). This economy of grammatical markers, along with the use of the infinitive, helps to make the proverb more aphoristic.

4. Contrasts and similarities can be seen in this proverb's lexical items: לֵץ 'scoffer' and חָכָם 'wise person' are opposites, while לֹא יֵלֵךְ 'will not go' and לֹא יֶאֱהַב 'does not love' are similar terms. But here the contrast is not between לֵץ 'scoffer' and חָכָם 'wise person'; neither their deeds nor the consequences of their deeds are being contrasted. Rather, חָכָם 'wise person' is linked to הוֹכֵחַ 'reprover' by virtue of the fact that the לֵץ 'scoffer' is rejecting both. The relationship between חָכָם 'wise person' and הוֹכֵחַ 'reprover' is one of similarity, not of contrast. A chiastic structure links these semantically related terms:

Although חָכָם 'wise person' has a number of synonyms, they are fairly rare. It stands virtually alone in opposition to a wide range of words for "fool."[21] Even though לֵץ 'scoffer' is etymologically related to the verb ליץ 'to mock, ridicule', in terms of its actual usage it does not differ from other words for fool in Proverbs (e.g., כְּסִיל and אֱוִיל).

5. The relation between the two propositions is reason-result: the first gives the reason, the second the result. The proverb has a single topic (לֵץ 'scoffer') and two comments on that topic (the remainder of each line), all of which have negative values.

6. The two lines are related by chiasmus at several of the analytical levels: phonological, syntactic, and semantic levels. Due to the chiasmus, colon b shows an exact reversal of the normal word order in Biblical Hebrew (VSO: לֹא יֵלֵךְ לֵץ אֶל חֲכָמִים).

7. The expression "will not go to wise ones" seems to be idiomatic. That they are going to them for advice is implicit.

8. No further stylistic devices are used.

9. *Intracolon cohesion* is achieved by a thrice-repeated sound sequence. The consonant-vowel sequence *lo* binds colon a together; colon b is tied together by the vowel-consonant sequence *el,* once in the reverse order. The inclusio of the dominant sound sequence of each line reinforces this intracolon cohesion and also acts to mark the boundary between the two cola (on the poetic level), the two clauses (on the syntactic level.) Since this proverb has no explicit syntactic boundary marker, it relies heavily on sound patterns to mark the point of its binary division.[22]

Intercola cohesion is achieved by chiasmus at various levels (sound, syntax, and semantics), as well as by the exchange of the dominant sound sequence in each line.

As to *prominence,* לֵץ 'scoffer' is marked as prominent. It is the only lexical unit outside of the main chiastic sound pattern (lō' ye- ...... kḥl/lḥk ...... lō' ye-), the only n.m.s., the only subject for both clauses, the only experiencer for both propositions, and the only topic for both comments. Word order may be signaling a secondary prominence in line b. While the word order in line a follows the usual VSO pattern, in line b אֶל חֲכָמִים 'to wise ones' is fronted. This may be due to the chiastic structure overriding the normal word order, or it could be that the comment "it is to the wise that he will not walk" is being marked as the more prominent of the two comments.

Hebrew Proverbs and How to Translate Them

There is some *correlation between form and meaning (sound and sense)* in this example. The three or four repetitions of the CV sequence *lo* hints at the negative attitude of the לֵץ 'scoffer' toward the wise. That is, the hearer perceives these repetitions as "no, no, no!" (since that is the meaning of this sound sequence in Hebrew).[23] In addition, there are two levels of chiasmus[24] linking הוֹכֵחַ לוֹ '[anyone] to reprove him' with אֶל חֲכָמִים 'to wise ones', signaling that these concepts should be linked in the hearer's mind. Those who are likely 'to reprove him' are none other than 'the wise ones' (to whom 'he will not go').

In order to test these conclusions and results, let us change the form, but not the content, of colon a, as follows:[25]

*yiśnaʾ lēṣ tôkēḥâ ‎ *יִשְׂנָא לֵץ תּוֹכֵחָה‎*
The scoffer hates reproof

ʾel ḥăkāmîm lōʾ yēlēk ‎ אֶל חֲכָמִים לֹא יֵלֵךְ
To the wise he will not go

This change results in a proverb with no intracolon cohesion in a, no intercola cohesion, the weakened prominence of לֵץ 'scoffer', no phonic allusion to the negative attitude of the לֵץ 'scoffer', and no link between the reproof and the wise. Structurally, the chiasmus all but disappears, resulting in a bicolon that portrays two disjointed, unrelated statements about the לֵץ 'scoffer' rather than a meaningful proverb. It has lost many of its poetic features and the unique dynamic interplay between them that endowed it with its special "incommunicable quality," that striking poetic form.

10. Interpretation of this proverb hangs on the co-referentiality of the wise and the agents of the reproof. It is this relationship (signaled by sound patterns) that provides the relationship between the two clauses (reason-result), not signaled in the grammar. The לֵץ 'scoffer' is afraid to go near the wise and to ask for advice because he knows he will be rebuked, and he does not like rebukes. This seemingly straightforward observation has been placed in a collection of texts which, for the most part, are explicitly hortatory in nature. It is likely, therefore, that this proverb also is hortatory in nature. In other words, it is a more subtle and effective way to say, "Don't be a fool! Go to the wise for advice even if it means reproof!"

A full, expanded paraphrase of Prov. 15:12 is as follows: The לֵץ 'scoffer' is afraid to go near the wise and ask them for advice because he knows he will be rebuked. He does not like rebukes, so he keeps well away, preferring to scoff from a distance. He will remain a fool. By distancing himself from the wise, he has ensured that he will never learn wisdom. Don't be like him; go to the wise for advice even if it means reproof!

Example three: Prov. 27:19.

a. As-the-water the-face to-the-face, כַּמַּיִם הַפָּנִים לַפָּנִים
b. so the-heart-of the-man to-the-man. כֵּן לֵב־הָאָדָם לָאָדָם

The value of a prospective procedure can be tested by applying it to a proverb that is problematic in its interpretation. Proverbs 27:19 is particularly difficult to unravel, a good test for our ten steps.

1. In this verse the sound patterns are broken by כֵּן לֵב 'so the heart of' and especially לֵב 'heart'.

	kammayim	happā-nim	lappā-nim	/ kēn	lēb	hā'ādām	lā'ādām
assonance	-a--a-i-	-a--ā -i-	-a--ā -i-	/ -e-	-e-	-a-a-a-	-a-a-a-
consonance	k-mm---m	h--- ---m	l--- ---m	/ k-n	l-v	h-----m	l-----m
word-initial	k	h	l	/ k	l	h	l
word-final		m	m	/ n	v	m	m
sequence	--------	-appā-nim	-appā-nim	/ ---	---	-ā'ādām	-ā'ādām

Here לֵב 'heart' is marked by means of the sound patterns as the most prominent constituent of the proverb. It is linked to כַּמַּיִם 'as the water' by virtue of the fact that they both break the "sequence pattern" as shown in the foregoing chart. This link is also signaled in the grammar by -כְּ . . . כֵּן 'as . . . so.' Intracolon cohesion is aided by the differing sound patterns of the two cola (-a-a-i- versus -a-a-a- and -appanim versus -a'adam). Intercola cohesion is promoted by the repetition of the a-vowel and the word-initial and word-final sound patterns. These are the same for the two cola except for the protruding כֵּן לֵב 'so the heart of.'

2. In the morphology, a break in the pattern can be seen at the same place. The only noun in construct (and the only one without a definite article) is לֵב 'the heart of'. Intracolon cohesion is reinforced by the fact that line a consists entirely of masculine plural nouns, while line b is exclusively made up of masculine singular nouns. Although there is no ellipsis of

definite articles, prepositions, or conjunctions (unlike most Biblical Hebrew poetry), there is a total elision of verbs in both parts of the bicolon. The use of verbless clauses is not at all uncommon in Biblical Hebrew proverbs, but like those that involve a string of participles, they are often difficult to interpret. At first glance, it appears that the two lines have the same structure (k[en]-nounA ha-nounB la-nounB). But a closer look reveals that לֵב 'the heart of' seems to be in construct with הָאָדָם 'the man', whereas מַיִם 'water' is absolute.

3. As to sentence type, the surface-level grammatical relationship between the two clauses is marked by -כְּ ... כֵּן 'just as ... so' in the surface grammar, normally indicating a comparison, simile, or analogy.

4. The two repeated words פָּנִים 'face' and אָדָם 'man' relate as the things being compared in this simile. Yet, once again, there is a kind of contrast in this context. The word 'heart' in Hebrew is not only the seat of emotions and of will (as in English), but more commonly refers to the seat of thought and reason. It may mean all three here, but if a choice between them has to be made for translation purposes, then the mind should win out. The word מַיִם 'water' has many qualities and associations, but what is in focus here is its ability to reflect and to act as a mirror.

5. Often the semantic- or deep-level structures do not correspond to the surface level of a sentence. The surface structure here indicates a relation of comparison (simile) between the two lines. But at the notional level there is a contrast: the external superficiality of the first line (face, surface of the water) contrasts with the internal profundity of the second (heart, character of man). The deep level signals contrast and is skewed to a surface level that signals similarity.

6. The bicolon has the superficial appearance of being a parallel pair with almost the same structure in each line:

          ka-nounA   ha-nounB   la-nounB
          ken-nounC   ha-nounD   la-nounD.

However, as noted above, the grammatical reality shows a number of differences between them. This interplay between the outward and the inner structure of the bicolon may be intended to reinforce the contrast being made between the outward appearance of man (his face) and the inner workings of his heart. There is similarity, yet there is also differentiation. This paradox is also represented in the clash between the surface-level relationship of similarity (signaled in the grammar by -כְּ ... כֵּן) and the deep-level contrast (apparent at the semantic level).

7. The heart is likened to water: they both act as mirrors. The image of water may also convey something of the contrast between the surface level (with its potentially unstable image) and the depths of unknown mysteries below the visible surface.

8. The most obvious poetic device here is word repetition. Virtually two-thirds of the proverb is made up of repeated words, accentuating the relationship of comparison between the only two unrepeated nouns (namely, מַיִם 'water' and לֵב 'heart'). A word play is recognizable between פָּנִים 'face (of a man)' and פָּנִים 'surface (of water)'.[26] This is reinforced by the use of אָדָם 'man' and מַיִם 'water' in the proverb. This play on words strengthens the idea of superficiality in the first line as against the profundity in the second.

9. The preceding steps of analysis have pointed to the prominence of the same word—לֵב 'heart', and also of the relationship between מַיִם 'water' and לֵב 'heart'. Steps 4–8 point to the contrast being made between the external, surface aspect of man's appearance and the deeper, internal aspect of his character.

10. As to interpretation, the heart is the key. The heart is being likened to water. The heart and the water both act as mirrors. A face sees what it is like by looking at its reflection in the water. In the same way a man comes to know himself by looking into his heart to see what motivates him. What a man thinks about is an accurate reflection of his character. But a contrast is also involved. A man can see what his face is like by looking at the surface of water. But if he wants to know what he is really like, then he must look deeply into his heart and consider what he is thinking about. It is not the outward appearance that is important (1 Sam. 16:7), but rather the inner thoughts, motivations, and feelings that make the man.

4. A proposed procedure for translating Biblical Hebrew proverbs

A comparison of English versions reveals a much greater diversity for the Book of Proverbs than for any other biblical book. Two of the major challenges in Bible translation, namely correctly understanding the original and finding the best way of expressing it in the target language, are greatly magnified in translating proverbs. The ten steps in section 3 help us with the first of these challenges. Now we will consider a five-step procedure that addresses the problem of target-language form:

1. Linguistic analysis (steps 1–5 in sec. 3)
2. Poetic analysis (steps 1 and 6–8 in sec. 3)
3. Synthesis (step 9 in sec. 3)
4. Expanded paraphrase (step 10 in sec. 3)
5. Crystallization in a cryptic form

Form is as essential to rendering a proverb as words are to making a sentence. Appropriate form is especially important for those cultures in which proverbs are revered. In these groups, it is essential that the hearers be given the chance to cue in on familiar proverbial forms that signal wise pieces of advice. A proverb can for many people be an effective heart-opener and life-changer. But unless it is in a form that signals its being a wise saying, then it will not be recalled or reused and the translation will gather dust on the shelf.

Naturally, in addition to the steps mentioned here, the translation of proverbs involves all that is required in translating other kinds of texts, such as an exegetical check and a communication-effectiveness check. But in translating proverbs, or poetry of any sort, the communication-effectiveness check will need to go beyond meaning transfer to include checking that the form is communicating the right signals. For instance, in English-speaking cultures some proverbs may sound priggish (moralizing is out of fashion) or trite. Proverbial form has been trivialized by advertising jingles that mimic its style. Thus its effect may be the exact opposite of the desired effect.

The following examples are intended to demonstrate what can be done in a target language. (Any such suggestions would, of course, need to be tested for communication effectiveness with regard to their form.) The first is Prov. 10:12, which was presented earlier as example 1 with the fairly literal translation "Hatred provokes arguments, but love covers over all offenses." It needs a more striking form than this. To sound like a proverb, this expanded paraphrase could be distilled to read as follows:

Hatred stirs up heated disputes, but love forgives and forgets.

This rendering in English provides intercola cohesion with -ts at the end of each colon, and intracolon cohesion with its sound patterns:

Hatred stirs up heated disputes
h trd   s rs p h td d sp t s   (harsh sounds, repeated sounds)

but love forgives and forgets.
    l v   f g v z nd f g   (softer, comforting sounds;
                                   repetition of *forg*-)

For Prov. 15:12, presented earlier as example 2, a fairly literal translation was offered: "The scoffer does not like anyone to rebuke him; to the wise he will not go." This not only lacks a striking form, but also fails to account for the semantic relationships revealed in the sound patterns and the chiastic structural patterns of the bicolon. A good translation would show the causal relationship, whether explicitly or implicitly, and would strive for rhythm and sound patterns to give it a striking form. Here are several suggestions:

(1) The scoffing fool is no fan of reproof,
```
      f        f          f  f        f
      o       oo          o  o       oo
```
   so to the wise he will not walk!
```
              w    w        w
   o  o                o
```

(2) A scoffer does not favor a reprover,
```
      fer          ver       ver
      o            o          o
```
   so to the wise he will not wander!
```
                              er
   o  o    w       wo    wo
```

(3) Fools are no fans of reproof,
```
   foo-      f         -oof
```
   when the wise advise they say their good-byes!
```
   w      w
          ize   ize                    ize
```

(4) Scoffers disapprove of reproof;
```
   f r      proov ov r proof
```
   avoiding the wise is fair proof!
```
                        f r proof
```

(5) Fools flee from the wise, for they fear their reproof!
```
   foo- f  f         fo-   f              -oof
              th           th    eer theer
   f l  fl  fr       f r   f r            r f
```

(6) Visit the wise for advice; only fools fear reproof!
```
   viz      wize    vise      foo   f       oof
```

The first version makes clear that לֵץ 'scoffer' belongs to the semantic field of fool. There is also an expectancy chain between not being a fan (line a) and not walking, for fans normally want to flock to the people they admire. The fulfillment of this expectancy in line b helps to bind the two cola together. Version 2 has better phonic cohesion, as does 3, which probably sounds too much like a jingle. Version 4 attempts to show the connection between the two statements about the לֵץ 'scoffer'. But all these versions sound contrived and too wordy. Conciseness can be gained by reversing the order of the propositions (as in 5 and 6). In 6 the mitigation has been removed and the underlying exhortation given its full imperative force.[27]

Now let us look at Prov. 27:19, presented earlier as example 3. English translations generally supply a verb here. The implicit idea is "show, reveal," but most recent translations have opted for "reflect." Since modern man does not look into water to see what his face looks like, a "cultural substitute"[28] could be used in this verse for the sake of vividness. I am suggesting four alternative renderings, all of which use repetitions of words and sounds as in the original. The last two emphasize the comparison signaled in the surface grammar. The first two place more stress on the inherent contrast signaled at other levels.[29]

(1) A mirror may mirror the face,
But a man's meditations are the measure of the man.

(2) To see yourself, look in a mirror;
To know yourself, look in your heart.

(3) As a mirror is a mirror for the face,
So a man's meditations are a mirror for the man.

(4) As a mirror mirrors the face,
So a man's reflections reflect the man.

Version 4 employs word repetitions as well as a wordplay on the word *reflect*, causing the hearer to reflect on the meaning of the proverb. The word *reflect* (in line b) hints at *mirror* (in line a) and thereby provides a subtle cohesion between the lines. Version 2, however, employs even more word repetitions, the best rhythmical and semantic balance, and the most impact due to its directness. It is the most effective in pointing the hearer in the right direction.

Proverbs 13:24 is an example that we did not consider before:

The-sparer-of his-rod [is] the-hater-of his-son,	חוֹשֵׂךְ שִׁבְטוֹ שׂוֹנֵא בְנוֹ
But-the-lover-of-him [is] the-goer-out-early-for-him discipline.	וְאֹהֲבוֹ שִׁחֲרוֹ מוּסָר

Let us apply the last three steps of our method for translating a proverb here: (3) synthesis, (4) expanded paraphrase, and (5) crystallization.

3. *Synthesis*. Intercola cohesion results from the chiastic structure at various levels (phonological, morphological, syntactic, semantic, and propositional) as well as from assonance in six out of the seven words and the sibilant consonance (especially the *shi--o* pattern linking 'his rod' to 'goes out early for him'). Intracolon cohesion is realized in line a by the repeated vowel sequence (-o-e- --o), while line b is tied together by the (rounded, back) vowel-sibilant-r sequence (o-o-sh-r o-u-s-r). The word 'discipline' is marked as prominent by its standing outside the dominant sound pattern (the o assonance) and by its bicolon-final position.

Once again a correlation between form and meaning can be seen. In the first colon, there is a relationship between its two halves at both the phonological and the grammatical levels, indicating that a semantic connection should be made in the mind of the hearer. That is, the repetition of the vowel sequence (-o-e- -o) and the grammatical sequence (m.s. participle + object noun m.s. with a 3 m.s. possessive suffix) point to the co-referentiality of the one who holds back his rod of discipline and the one who hates his son. This co-referentiality is implicitly carried into the second line also, where it is only signaled weakly.

The chiastic pattern signals (on the one hand) a contrast between the two lines and (on the other hand) two semantic links which cross over between the four half-lines (AB :: B'A'). The nature of these relationships is one of oppositeness at the phrase level, but there is some similarity too. Holding back from is the opposite of going out eagerly for. Hating is the opposite of loving. On the other hand, using the rod and discipline are the same, and so are "his son" and "him." These various relationships are signaled by sound patterns (A: s sh :: A': sh s; A: shi-o :: A': shi-o. B: o-b-o :: B': o-b-o).

4. *Expanded paraphrase*. Proverbs 13:24, which is a striking example of a literary paradox, counters what may have been the commonly held view of child-rearing by making seemingly incongruous ideas into equivalent ones. Hence the son-hater is equated with one who refrains from beating, and a son-lover with one who disciplines. To be lenient is to hate; to be stern is to love. Indulging a child is in effect to hate him; true love manifests itself in a willingness to discipline early. The link between rod and discipline suggests that verbal counsel or castigation alone are not always effective.[30]

5. *Crystallization in a cryptic form.* Four possible renderings are:

(1) Spare the rod and spoil the child.
   sp-   -d -d sp-   -d

(2) Spare the rod and despise the child:
   sp-   -d -d d-sp   i-d

   you've got to discipline to be kind.
                 d-s   p   i-d

(3) Hate the child by sparing the rod; love him by disciplining early.

(4) Spare the rod and spurn the child;
   sp-   -d -d sp-   -d

   respect him by spanking early.
   sp   sp

Robert Alter (1985:166–67) lauds version 1 here: "the still current proverbial adaptation of the first half of the verse" is a "real translator's find," being closer to the original in compactness. The seven words of version 1 neatly parallel the seven words of the original Hebrew. Nevertheless, literary proverbs are permitted to be longer than popular ones both in Biblical Hebrew and in English, and the "proverbial adaptation" of version 1 is hardly an accurate translation as far as its semantic content goes. Spoiling the child is a result of sparing the rod and this is nowhere suggested in the Hebrew proverb. The original language speaks of hating the child as the cause of sparing the rod.

Version 2 retains some of the tight intracolon cohesion of version 1 and adds a second line based on the proverbial saying "You've got to be cruel to be kind." Version 3 is a fairly flat rendition in terms of sound patterns, but it accurately portrays the abrupt, unexpected identification between leniency and hatred and between corporal punishment and love. It also stresses the contrast between hating the child and loving him. Most of this can be successfully incorporated into a translation that also has sound patterns as in version 4.

Now another example, Prov. 11:22:

A-ring-of gold in-a-snout-of a-pig   נֶזֶם זָהָב בְּאַף חֲזִיר
[Is] a-woman beautiful and-lacking-of-   אִשָּׁה יָפָה וְסָרַת טָעַם
sense.

3. *Synthesis.* Although there are a few sound patterns in this proverb, they are weak, especially in comparison to the striking imagery that is the prov-

erb's main feature. Each colon contains a positive topic and a negative incongruous comment on that topic, designed to jolt the hearer. This effect is all the more forceful for its lack of an explanation for the two contradictory images in each line. The more incongruous of these image pairs comes first, like a riddle that does not make sense until the second line supplies the reason for the puzzling incongruity.

4. *Expanded paraphrase:* It is as inappropriate for a beautiful woman to be found lacking in discretion as it is for a beautiful gold ring to be found in the snout of a pig. Just as pigs do not wear gold, so a pretty lady should not be rash, tactless, or lacking in good taste. A pig's snout is an unseemly place for a gold ring; in the same way, indiscretion is not fitting for a pretty lady. Indeed, the whole idea of a beautiful woman who is indiscreet is preposterous!

5. *Crystallization in a cryptic form.* The target language may require that the metaphor be worded as a simile, as in version 1 below.[31] Or it may be necessary for the point of similarity between the topic and image (incongruity) to be made more obvious, as in version 2. Or the amusing aspect of the discordant imagery could be brought out, as in version 3. If in a given target language rhetorical questions do not communicate effectively, perhaps a more explicit rendering such as version 4 would be the most effective.

(1) A lovely lady lacking in sense
    l li l i l   i   i
                   n s ns

   is like a gold ring in a swine's snout.
   i l   l i i
   s   n s n s sn

(2) Should a ring of gold be worn by a pig?
    Should a beautiful woman be indiscreet?

(3) Do pigs wear wigs? Nor should beautiful women lack sense!

(4) Gold rings should not adorn swine! Nor beautiful women be asinine!

Consider now the two forms of Prov. 13:20:

| One who walks with the wise will become wise, But followers of fools will face their demise. | הוֹלֵךְ אֶת־חֲכָמִים יֶחְכָּם
וְרֹעֶה כְסִילִים יֵרוֹעַ | Qere |

Walk with the wise and you will be wise,	הָלוֹךְ אֶת־חֲכָמִים וַחֲכָם	Kethiv
For followers of fools will face their demise.	וְרֹעֶה כְסִילִים יֵרוֹעַ	

Whether the Qere or the Kethiv form is read, the underlying message is the same. Whichever is more appropriate to target language proverbial forms should be chosen. Both of the English translations that I have given are easy to remember. Only one word (*wise* or *fool*) need be remembered and the rest will come from the opposition of wise and fool, from the rhyme of *wise* and *demise*, and from the *w* alliteration (including "one") in the "wise" line and the *f* alliteration in the "fool" line.

Our final example is Prov. 25:11:

Apples-of gold in-settings-of silver	תַּפּוּחֵי זָהָב בְּמַשְׂכִּיּוֹת כָּסֶף
—a-word spoken in its-proper-form [or -time or -circumstances]	דָּבָר דָּבֻר עַל־אָפְנָיו

(The exact meaning of the proverb's last word remains uncertain.)

A rendering of Prov. 25:11 that would provide a fitting end to this article that encourages experimentation in finding an appropriate proverbial form is the following:

Like gold apricots on a silver tray
    o   pr--o-   o   -er ray

Is a proverb presented in the proper way!
    pro-er pr   -e-   proper ay

The key word in this rendering is *proper*, and thus its sounds occur throughout the proverb. Its link to *proverb* and also to *presented* stresses the need for proverbs to be presented in the proper way.

The use of the word *proverb* here may be restrictive of the general term דָּבָר 'word'. But at least two recent scholars[32] take up an earlier suggestion of Boström (1928), that the obscure final word of this proverb refers to none other than the distinctive proverbial form that has been the topic of our discussion. What is more, the first line's reference to apples hints that the word is no ordinary word, but an especially valuable one. Apples had to be imported from Persia and were food fit for kings. The image speaks of valuable things being enhanced by their placement in expensive settings. In the same way, a proverb that is worth hearing should be presented in a pleasing and appealing way—"like gold apricots on a silver tray."

5. Conclusion

The paroemiologist Wolfgang Mieder pointed out that "the proverb in a collection is dead" (1974:892). Of course, nothing can be done about the fact that biblical proverbs are found in a collection. But instead of gathering dust on the shelf, unread and ignored, translators can give them the chance to live in local languages. If they are given catchy, memorable forms, then there is hope that some of them at least will find themselves on the lips and in the hearts of people.

Translating proverbs takes dedication, hard work, creativity, and a willingness to be innovative and to experiment. Rather than trying to translate them in a block, the translator should ponder them one at a time. May future translations of proverbs indeed be "like gold apricots on a silver tray."

Notes

1. Others also contribute to this pessimistic view of proverb definition, for instance, B. J. Whiting (1952:331), who concludes that "To offer a brief yet workable definition of a proverb, especially with the proverbial phrase included, is well nigh impossible."

2. This figure is necessarily kept simple. Some proverbs (the admonitions) have unmitigated hortatory forms (imperatives or prohibitives with grounds, reason, or result clauses). Others surface as observations or amusing anecdotes.

3. This feature and the following one were noted by McCreesh (1991:16).

4. "Plumage" does not appear to have the extended meaning of "same sort, kind" that "feather" has. Nor does "fowl" have the wide range of meaning of "bird." If it did, the consonance of f (and l) might have been reinforced with "fowls of a feather flock together."

5. There are other necessary ingredients: for instance, the proverb's message must be meaningful, relevant, and applicable to real-life situations. But features relating to form are what is in focus here, because the main concern is the translation of Hebrew proverbs and because proverb description should be based on form, not function.

6. This is not to deny the importance of context for interpretation. Biblical proverbs are better understood when investigated in the context of wisdom traditions in the ancient Near East (including other biblical proverbs and chapters 1-9 of Proverbs). Yet each proverb stands as a separate discourse unit within that tradition. (One proverb may relate to another just as one self-contained narrative discourse may relate to another.) Nor is it to deny that some kind of link can frequently be found between two consecutive proverbs—a repeated catchword, for example.

7. This discussion of biblical proverbs focuses on the literary proverb in the Book of Proverbs and not on the single line popular proverb as found in Gen. 10:9; 1 Sam. 10:12; 19:24; 2 Sam. 5:8; 20:18; Jer. 31:29; Ezek. 18:2; and elsewhere. There are several literary proverbs that are longer than one bicolon in length. They could be described as extended proverbs, while the longer discourses found in the first nine chapters of Proverbs and in chapter 31 could be described as wisdom poems, and not proverbs at all.

8. Admonitions are relatively straightforward to interpret and translate, since they are unmitigated hortatory material. For this reason, the focus in this article is on the saying.

9. Particularly frequent are the features of parallelism (including chiastic or inverse parallelism), sound patterns, rhythm, and such poetic devices as repetition, word pairs, and paronomasia. But others such as irony, allusion, hyperbole, oxymoron, and delayed identification are not uncommon.

10. Little is known about the origin and development of biblical proverbs, though there are many theories. A few of them may have been developed from single-line popular proverbs by the addition of a second line as in "Birds of a feather flock together/ so fools do not fraternize with the wise."

11. Cf. Silverman-Weinreich (1978:6), who writes: "The function of a proverb is *to point out that a given specific situation or occurrence illustrates an accepted general rule with which the hearer must already be acquainted.*" Cf. also Kirshenblatt-Gimblett (1973:825), who states, "It is generally recognized that proverbs ... must be studied in their immediate contexts of use."

12. Proverbial function, though important, is much more difficult to study empirically than proverbial form. This is especially true of proverbs that represent the wisdom of a community that lived two-and-a-half millennia ago! Some understanding of proverbial function can, nevertheless, be gained by studying proverbial form.

13. There is some overlap between the two handles. For example, the linguistic analysis of the phonology overlaps with the poetic analysis of the sound patterns.

14. The first four of these were outlined by McCreesh (1991), who has a chapter devoted to each one (though his terms differ from mine).

15. Admonitions are analyzed into precepts (imperatives or prohibitives) and motive clauses or result clauses. These also are given positive or negative values.

16. Some of these chiastic patterns were also noted by McCreesh (1991: 31). (Sound patterns and abbreviations given in the Latin alphabet are to be read from left to right.)

17. The abbreviations in the first of these two lines are to be interpreted as follows: a noun feminine singular followed by verb in the prefix conjugation (i.e., *yiqtol* or imperfect), third-person feminine singular followed by a noun masculine plural. Other abbreviations are analogous to these and include: s.c. = suffix conjugation (i.e., *qatal* or perfect). SVO = subject–verb–object.

18. Watson (1984:314-16) lists eight reasons for balancing a concrete term with an abstract noun. But here we have two abstract nouns.

19. Watson (1983:316) does not allow for such a purpose: "Generally speaking it can be seen that the use of an abstract noun to balance a concrete term is not simply poetic fancy but demanded by various factors."

20. These sound patterns were also noted by McCreesh (1991:46f.).

21. Semantic fields of לֵיץ 'scoffer' and חָכָם 'wise person' would include:

לֵיץ: בֶּן מֵבִישׁ / עָצֵל / בּוֹגֵד / מְחֻסַּר לֵב / נָבָל / פֶּתִי / אֱוִיל / סְרַח טַעַם / כְּסִיל

חָכָם: מַשְׂכִּיל / בַּר תְּבוּנָה / אִישׁ תְּבוּנָה / נָבוֹן / חֲכַם לֵב / אִישׁ מְזִמּוֹת

22. In contrast, the intercola boundary was clearly marked in Prov. 10:12, both by the chiasmus at all possible levels and by the *waw* conjunction. Its intracolon cohesion could afford to be weaker at the phonological level.

23. It seems that neither word-final א nor word-final ה were pronounced in Biblical Aramaic nor in later stages of Hebrew (Qumranic and Mishnaic). Whether or not the final *aleph* in לֹא 'no, not' was pronounced at the time of these proverbs is perhaps debatable, as is the question of whether or not the hearer would actually perceive the CV sequence that is separated by other sounds. But even if word-final אs were pronounced, the negation could still be conveyed (especially in a sequence involving two occurrences of לֹא 'no, not') in the same way that affirmation is conveyed in English with or without the final *s* in *yes*. (*Yeah* and *yep* still signal affirmation.)

24. One is the larger chiastic pattern at the level of the bicolon and the other is the smaller reversal of order: khl/lhk.

25. This alternative was suggested by McCreesh (1991:47), who also noted most of the following consequences.

26. Cf. Gen. 1:3: עַל פְּנֵי הַמָּיִם 'on the face of the water'.

27. But after testing each of these alternatives, it may be necessary to find a more commonly used substitute for 'reproof', which is nonetheless useful in providing a nice inclusio with 'fool'.

28. The use of 'mirror' here, though possibly more vivid for today, offers a more limited picture than that portrayed by water (at least in the Hebrew). It fails to convey the contrast between the surface and the invisible subsurface.

29. This is not a matter of ignoring the grammar, but of recognizing the different levels of meaning in the proverb.

30. Cf. Prov. 20:30; 22:15; 23:13, 14; 29:15.

31. In version 1 the positive topics are linked by the *l/i* patterns, while the negative comments are linked by the *s/n* sound patterns.

32. See McKane (1970:584) and McCreesh (1991:112-13).

References

Alter, Robert. 1985. *The art of biblical poetry*. New York: Basic Books; Edinburgh: T. and T. Clark.

Barley, Nigel. 1972. A structural approach to the proverb and maxim with special reference to the Anglo-Saxon corpus. *Proverbium* 120:737-50.
Crenshaw, James, ed. 1976. *Studies in ancient Israelite wisdom.* New York: Utar.
Dundes, Alan. 1975. On the structure of the proverb. *Proverbium* 125:961-73.
Fontaine, Carole. 1982. *Traditional sayings in the Old Testament: A contextual study.* Sheffield: Almond Press.
Kirshenblatt-Gimblett, Barbara. 1973. Toward a theory of proverb meaning. *Proverbium* 122:821-27.
Longacre, Robert E. 1983. *The grammar of discourse.* New York: Plenum Press.
McCreesh, Thomas P. 1991. *Biblical sound and sense: Poetic sound patterns in Proverbs 10-29.* Sheffield: JSOT Press.
McKane, William. 1970. *Proverbs: A new approach.* London: SCM Press.
Mieder, Wolfgang. 1974. The essence of literary proverb study. *Proverbium* 123:888-94.
Mieder, Wolfgang, and Alan Dundes, eds. 1981. *The wisdom of many: Essays on the proverb.* New York: Garland.
Murphy, Roland E. 1981. *Wisdom literature: Job, Proverbs, Ruth, Canticles, Ecclesiastes and Esther.* Grand Rapids: Eerdmans.
Nel, Philip Johannes. 1982. *The structure and ethos of the wisdom admonitions in Proverbs.* Berlin: Walter de Gruyter.
Rad, Gerhard von. 1972. *Wisdom in Israel.* London: SCM Press.
Scott, R. B. Y. 1961. Folk proverbs of the ancient Near East. *Transactions of the Royal Society of Canada* 155: 47-56. (Reprinted in Crenshaw, 417-26.)
———. 1965. *Proverbs, Ecclesiastes.* The Anchor Bible. New York: Doubleday.
———. 1971. *The way of wisdom in the Old Testament.* New York: Macmillan.
———. 1972. Wise and foolish, righteous and wicked. *VTS* 123:146-65.
Seiler, Friedrich. 1922. *Deutsche Sprichwörterkunde.* Munich: Beck.
Seitel, Peter. 1981. Proverbs: A social use of metaphor. In *The wisdom of many: Essays on the proverb,* ed. Wolfgang Mieder et al. New York: Garland.
Silverman-Weinreich, Beatrice. 1978. Towards a structural analysis of Yiddish proverbs. *Proverbium* 117:1-20.
Taylor, Archer. 1931. *The proverb.* Cambridge, Mass.: Harvard University Press.
Thompson, John Mark. 1974. *The form and function of proverbs in ancient Israel.* The Hague: Mouton.
Toy, Crawford H. 1899. *A critical and exegetical commentary on the Book of Proverbs.* T. and T. Clark: Edinburgh.
Van Leeuwen, Raymound C. 1988. *Context and meaning in Proverbs 25-27.* Atlanta: Scholars Press.
Watson, Wilfred G. E. 1984. *Classical Hebrew poetry: A guide to its techniques.* Sheffield: JSOT Press.
Whiting, B. J. 1952. Proverbs and proverbial sayings: Introduction. In vol. 1 of *The Frank C. Brown collection of North Carolina folklore,* 331. Durham, N. C.
Williams, James G. 1980. The power of form: A study of biblical proverbs. *Semeia* 171:35-581.
———. 1981 *Those who ponder proverbs: Aphoristic thinking and biblical literature.* Sheffield: Almond Press.

19

UNITS AND FLOW IN THE SONG OF SONGS 1:2–2:6

John Callow

This article applies a semantically based discourse theory to the Song of Songs 1:2–2:6, a span that constitutes a widely recognized major section of the Song. The purpose of the analysis is twofold: (1) to identify the semantic units (of varying sizes) in the section 1:5–2:6 and (2) to describe how the content of the Song progresses from 1:5 to 2:6, using the semantic units identified as the basis for doing so. These units are also used for some structural observations on Biblical Hebrew. In addition, it is proposed that 1:2–4 constitutes the Prologue to the Song of Songs, an analysis that is based on its distinctive metrical form and the relation of its content to the rest of the Song, in particular, 1:5–2:6.

The results of the analysis are then applied to issues affecting the translator, especially the choice of printed divisions of the text and their headings. But attention is also given to some of the implications of the poetic genre for the translator and how the speakers in the Song can be identified in a translation.

A major challenge emerges at the end. Can translation theory handle the issue of the translation of discourse structure? Is source-language discourse structure transferable in the translation process, or is it not?

The purpose of this article is to apply discourse analysis procedures to a section of the Song of Songs and draw some conclusions relating to translation from the results. However, the term *discourse analysis*, or *text analysis*, may be used for a variety of different theoretical positions, all of which operate with different assumptions and procedures. It is therefore necessary, first of all, to identify the approach being used in this article.

The theory exemplified here is based on the semantically or cognitively oriented theory of meaning first propounded by John Beekman[1] and, since his death in 1980, developed by others, particularly Mildred Larson (1984), John Callow, and Kathleen Callow. The theoretical assumptions of this approach are explained in Mann and Thompson (1992:5–15). A more detailed presentation is given in Kathleen Callow's *Man and Message* (forthcoming). Suffice to say here that this theory stresses the communication situation: the author is passing a message on to his or her readers and the meaning that the author desires to communicate determines the form in which the message is cast.

In this article I am not attempting a full-scale discourse analysis of the Song, or even of part of it. My aim is considerably more modest than that.

It is generally agreed among commentators that 2:7, 3:5, and 8:4, by virtue of their identical or near-identical form, constitute the boundary verses of major spans of the Song.[2] With this view I would agree, and my own analysis concentrates on the first such span of the Song, 1:1–2:7, or more strictly 1:2–2:6, since the title in 1:1 is considered to stand outside the body of the Song as does 2:7, a closure unit separate from the material that it concludes.

Semantic theory lays considerable emphasis on the author's purpose in communicating and on the semantic units by which that purpose is expressed. It is these two matters, therefore, that I am addressing in this article. I have used the term *flow*, however, rather than *purpose*, since it would require a detailed analysis of the whole Song to discern the author's purpose in writing it. By *flow* I mean the progression of thought in this first "Cycle" (a conveniently neutral term). What was the author seeking to convey to the reader in this first section of the Song?

1. Criteria for determining the semantic units

So far as semantic units are concerned, my primary interest is in the larger units, those, if I may so put it, next in size to the Cycle itself. In other words, I am trying to establish the major divisions of the text between 1:2 and 2:6. This naturally raises the question of what criteria are being used to establish such major units. The criteria are presented in detail as each major unit is discussed, but a summary is given here in the order in which they are used. (As with all analytical criteria, decisions are, whenever possible, based on several concurrent criteria, not just one.)

1. *Who is speaking and to whom.* A semantic unit is considered to be made up of "same speaker" and "same addressee(s)." Change of addressee, then, signals a change of unit.
2. *Unity of topic.* By "topic" is meant a concept to which reference is found throughout the unit. Switch of topic signals a change of unit.
3. *Stimulus and response.* In this particular body of data, this criterion occurs in two forms: either question and answer (e.g., 1:7–8) or remarks that provoke a (verbal) response of an appropriate sort (e.g., 1:9 onwards). Stimulus and response are considered to be a sort of bonded pair. Without the response, the reader is left dangling, as it were; the message is incomplete at that point.
4. *A common conceptual domain.* For example, 1:7–8 uses a number of concepts appropriate to the semantic field of shepherding. These concepts are not found in either the preceding or following units.
5. *Parallelism.* Experience shows that parallel features, lexical and/or grammatical, are not necessarily a sign of unity; two distinct units may

parallel each other. But together with other criteria, parallelism can be very helpful as a clue to unity. The unit 1:9–17 in the Song of Songs makes considerable use of parallelism.

6. *Ascensiveness.* If the same thing is said twice, it is simply a case of repetition or equivalence. By "ascensiveness" I mean a special form of repetition or equivalence in which the second unit is basically covering the same ground as the first, but with greater emotional intensity as shown by the lexical and grammatical choices. The two units together constitute the ascensive unit.

7. *Tail-head link.* There is just one example in this data of a tail-head link (Unit 4, 2:1–6). It is lexical in nature.

8. *Chiasmus.* This common Hebrew figure of speech is relatively rare in Cycle 1, but is drawn on as evidence for unity in 2:4–6.

2. The "flow" of thought

Having established the major units of the text (and inevitably some minor ones as well), I use these major units as a basis for discussing the "flow" of thought in the Cycle. Inherent in this order of presentation is the assumption that the progression of the author's thought is best seen in the light of his own grouping of his material. As the author moves towards his communicative goal, he does not do so in an undifferentiated string of clauses. The clauses will be grouped and that grouping will be controlled by the author's purpose in writing (not necessarily consciously, though with poetry it could well be so). Hence, the importance of seeking to elucidate the major semantic units first. Not until after that do we study how the units relate to each other.

3. The units of 1:5–2:6

As we turn now to consider the semantic units of the Song of Songs 1:5–2:6, a few words about the presentation of the Hebrew data are necessary. Each verse of the text[3] is divided into lines, identified by the letters of the alphabet following the verse number. Broadly speaking, the lines consist of a verb and its satellite nouns or noun phrases, but this is not narrative, and there are many lines in which no verb is present at all; in fact, of the sixty-two lines of the text, about half are without a verb. It should also be said that each of the six examples of a vocative (1:5b, 7b, 8b, 9b, 15b, 16b) is given a separate line, with the Hebrew text moved to the left, as the analysis indicates that the vocatives stand outside the formal structures described for each semantic unit.

The Hebrew text has been provided with an English interlinear of my own devising. In Cycle 1, at least, discourse analysis of the sort presented here is not affected by the question of what some of the lexical items mean, especially the natural phenomena referred to ("rose," "lily," "apple tree," etc.). The interlinear English is provided simply as a help to anyone who might need it.

Where relevant, each semantic unit is divided into smaller units by broken lines. Capital letters are used to highlight subgroupings within the larger whole, P indicates parallel structures, X a chiastic structure, and arrows indicate dependency. It is hoped that these "visual aids" will make the formal, internal structure of the units more immediately obvious.

Since 1:2-4 presents a number of special problems in the analysis, I am starting the analysis of the major semantic units at 1:5. Verses 2-4 will be considered after 1:5-2:6 has been discussed in detail.

3.1 Unit 1 (1:5-6)

The primary indicator that 1:5-6 is a unit is that there is only one speaker throughout (the Heroine)[4] and that what she says is addressed overtly to one group of addressees, "the daughters of Jerusalem" (v. 5). It is important to stress this *twofold* criterion. As is clear from the Hebrew text forms, the Heroine continues to speak throughout v. 7, and translations that present their text with divisions based on who is speaking make a break after v. 7; that is, they treat vv. 5-7 as a single unit. But v. 7 is overtly addressed to another addressee "(you) on whom I have set my love," and the grammar shows this to be a masculine singular addressee. A switch of addressee is considered an important criterion in establishing units, especially in a discourse that is a dialogue (mostly) between a Hero and a Heroine.

Unity is also provided by the centrality of the concept of the dark-colored skin of the speaker.[5] In v. 5 the fact is stated and supported by comparisons (by a single comparison, if 5d is taken to be a comparison describing her beauty); in line 6b this fact is restated; in lines 6c-e it is explained why she is dark in color. Line 6c gives the immediate (physical) cause, the effect of the sun on her skin; lines 6d-e give the ultimate (non-physical) cause, her brothers making her watch over the family vineyards, which exposed her to the sun.

With vv. 5-6 thus established as a unit by these criteria, it is also possible to discern internal structural patterns. (The vocative of 5b, however, is regarded as standing outside these structural patterns.)[6] Three "subunits" are proposed: 5a-d, 6a-c, 6d-f. In the first two, the second two lines are introduced in the same way: by -כְּ 'like' in the first unit, and by -שֶׁ 'because' in the second; and in both cases, these two lines logically/relationally support the main (initial) line. The third unit does not

Display of Unit 1

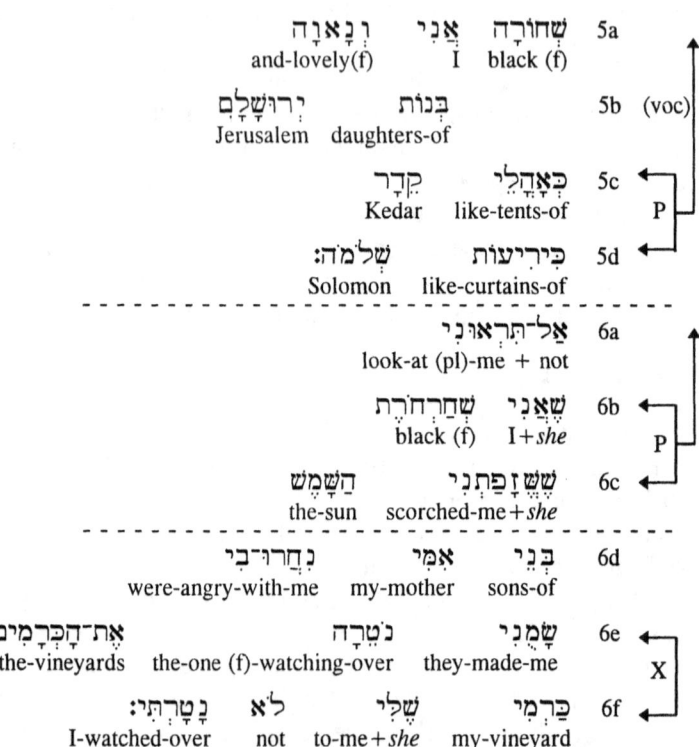

manifest this formal parallelism, but a lexical chiasmus links the lines of 6d–f. It seems likely that the third subunit's departure from the pattern has a prominence purpose. Bliese (1988:56) observes, in connection with a similar lexical chiasmus in Joel, that "such chiastic marking is also characteristic of high points in Hebrew poetry." He also observes that "a series of lines with the same number of feet will normally have its climax as the last line" (p. 52). Lines 6d–f could each be considered to consist of three feet if the negative particle לֹא is linked to the verb in 6f. In this case, line 6f could well constitute the most significant statement in Unit 1. (The fact that the object precedes the verb and that there is emphatic redundancy in "my vineyard which belongs to me" could well provide added support for this view.)

3.2 Unit 2 (1:7–8)

The primary indicator that 1:7–8 is a unit is similar to that proposed for 1:5–6, but with an additional indicator. In v. 7, the Heroine addresses the Hero and, in doing so, asks for information as to the location(s) of his shepherding activities. In v. 8, the Hero addresses the Heroine ("most beautiful of women") and, somewhat indirectly, answers her question. Hence vv. 7 and 8 are not only reciprocal in that the Heroine addresses the Hero and then the Hero addresses the Heroine, but also in that they stand in a question-answer relationship (criterion 3 in sec. 1). This relationship is important. Verse 9 is also addressed to the Heroine by the Hero, so there is continuity in this respect between v. 8 and v. 9; but v. 9 has nothing at all to do with where the Hero shepherds his flock.[7]

The common conceptual domain (criterion 4 in sec. 1) of "shepherding" is found throughout these two verses. It is introduced in line 7c, and again in 7d, 7e, 8c, and 8d.

With the unit thus established, internal structural features can be observed. This unit naturally divides into two subunits: v. 7, in which the Heroine addresses the Hero, and v. 8, where the Hero addresses the

Display of Unit 2

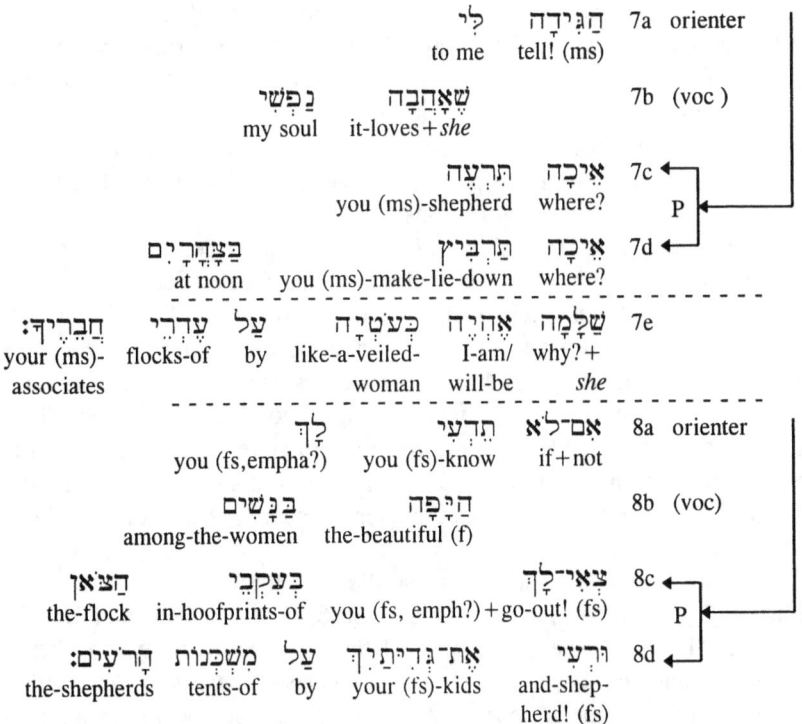

Heroine. In each subunit the opening orienter line is followed by a vocative, and then, as in 1:5-6, two lines that exhibit certain parallels with each other. In 7c and 7d the parallelism is obvious: they are both questions starting with אֵיכָה 'where'. In 8c and 8d, the parallelism consists in their both being commands to the Heroine (in the feminine singular), צְאִי 'go out' and רְעִי 'shepherd'.

These structural patterns isolate 7e, which is also distinguished by being noticeably longer than all the other lines except 8d. In the logical structure of the Heroine's questions to the Hero it appears that 7e provides a rationale for the two questions in 7c and 7d. It gives a sort of grounds for her parallel questions. Its longer form, its logical relationship, and perhaps the opening שַׁלָּמָה 'for why?' raise the exegetical question of whether it has some particular significance in this question-answer exchange. Is the Hero's answer in v. 8 framed in the light of this rhetorical question?

3.3 Unit 3 (1:9-17)

Compared to the two previous units, the criteria that mark 1:9-17 as a unit are more complex. The major issue is whether to treat vv. 9-14 as one unit (a unit not unlike the preceding one) and vv. 15-17 as a second separate unit or whether to combine them into one, vv. 9-17. It is readily conceded that analysis as two units would be quite acceptable within the theoretical framework of this paper; however, I prefer to treat them as one larger unit, for the following reasons.

First, in both 9-14 and 15-17, the Hero describes the beauty of the Heroine, the first time that this is done in this Cycle. Second, in both of them (9b and 15b) the Hero addresses the Heroine as רַעְיָתִי,[8] the first time that this term is used in the Song, and the only times as a vocative in this Cycle. Third, corresponding to the Hero's use of רַעְיָתִי, the Heroine uses דּוֹדִי 'my love/beloved' in each of the two (13 and 14, 16b). This is her regular form of address to the Hero (and her regular form of reference to him), and again it is used for the first time in this Cycle. Thus there is a distinct parallelism in form and content between 9-14 and 15-17 that draws them together.

However, there is more than parallelism: there is also what might be called a degree of ascensiveness (criterion 6) between 9-14 and 15-17. In 9-11 the Hero describes the beauty of the Heroine by comparing her to a richly ornamented royal mare, the comparison having to do with the beauty of the ornamentation. In v. 15, however, he speaks of her beauty directly, using יָפָה 'beautiful': he describes a specific feature, her eyes (15d). For her part, the Heroine moves from the third person term "the king" (12a) and from a third person use of דּוֹדִי 'my beloved' (13, 14) to addressing the Hero directly in the second person and using this term of endearment as a vocative (16a–c). My proposal, therefore, is to analyze vv. 9–17 as an "ascensive couplet," rather than two separate units; the second half thus covers the same ground as the first, but with heightened emotion.

Each half of this couplet consists of a stimulus-response pairing, and in both cases the Hero provides the stimulus, the Heroine the response. The pattern of parallel paired lines seen in the two previous units is not observed in vv. 9–11, but lines 13 and 14 are parallel to each other: both open with a verbless copula clause in the order Complement, Subject/Topic, and in each case the Subject/Topic is דּוֹדִי and the structure of the Complement is Noun-art + Noun.

In the second half of this unit (15–17), however, identical parallelism is used at the beginning of the stimulus-response pairing, not at the end, as previously: הִנָּךְ 'behold' plus pronoun, followed by the appropriate gender form of יָפָה 'beautiful' for the first line, and a vocative for the second line (15a, b and 16a, b).

Display of Unit 3

						Stimulus
דְּמִיתִיךְ	פַּרְעֹה	בְּרִכְבֵי	לְסֻסָתִי			9a
I-have-compared-you (fs)	Pharoah	in-chariots-of	to-my-mare			
		רַעְיָתִי				9b (voc)
		my-delight (f)				
בַּחֲרוּזִים:	צַוָּארֵךְ	בַּתֹּרִים	לְחָיַיִךְ	נָאווּ		10
with-jewels?	your (fs)- neck	with-rows?	your (fs)- cheeks	they-are- lovely		
הַכָּסֶף:	נְקֻדּוֹת	עִם	נַעֲשֶׂה-לָּךְ	זָהָב	תּוֹרֵי	11
the-silver	studs?-of	with	we-will-make +for-you (fs)	gold	rows?-of	
						Response
רֵיחוֹ:	נָתַן	נִרְדִּי	בִּמְסִבּוֹ	עַד-שֶׁהַמֶּלֶךְ		12
its-fragrance	it-gave	my-nard	in-his-circle	while-the-king		
יָלִין:	שָׁדַי	בֵּין	לִי	דּוֹדִי	הַמֹּר	צְרוֹר	13
he-is-lying	my-breasts	between	to-me	my- beloved	the- myrrh	bag (m) -of
עֵין גֶּדִי:	בְּכַרְמֵי	לִי	דּוֹדִי	הַכֹּפֶר	אֶשְׁכֹּל	14
Engedi	in-the-vineyards-of	to-me	my- beloved	the- henna	cluster- of	

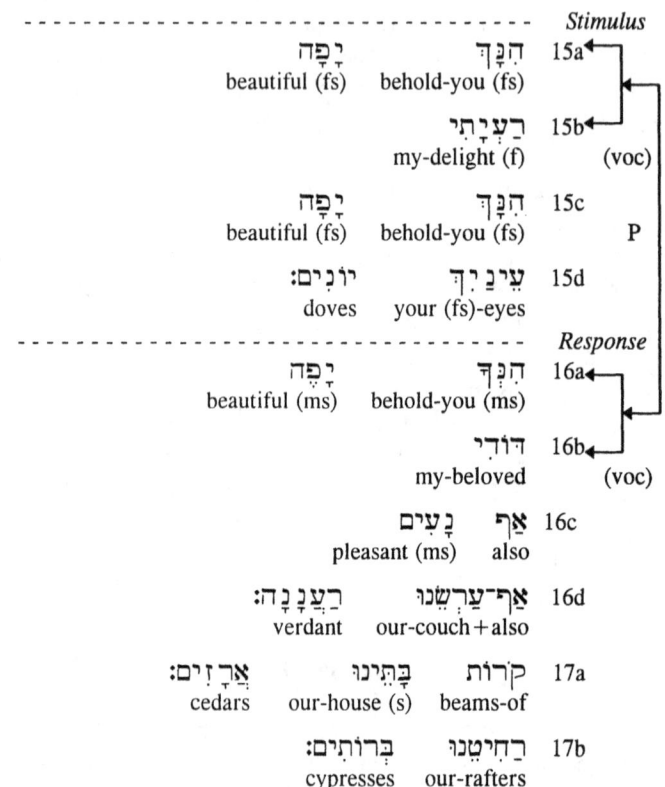

It remains to be pointed out that the subunits within this ascensive couplet (9–11, 12–14, 15, 16–17) are themselves considered to be semantic units for the following reasons: First, in three of the subunits, there is one speaker only (Hero/Heroine) and one addressee (Heroine/Hero), as shown by the vocatives in 9b, 15b, and 16b, supported by the appropriate formal gender markers. Verses 12–14 do not conform to this pattern, however. The Hero is referred to here, but is not addressed directly; note הַמֶּלֶךְ 'the king' in 12, דּוֹדִי 'my beloved' in 13 and 14, and the lack of second person singular masculine forms throughout. (This third person indirectness is part of the evidence for considering this couplet ascensive.)

Second, each subunit draws on vocabulary from one distinctive conceptual domain. In vv. 9–11, it is the domain of decorative jewelry for the head and neck; in 12–14, that of fragrant substances ("nard," "myrrh," "henna blossoms"); in 15 of a dove; in 16–17 there are two interrelated domains: houses and the trees from which they are made. For example, רַעֲנָנָה 'verdant' in 16d collocates with trees.⁹

3.4 Unit 4 (2:1-6)

Since 2:7 is regarded as a separate semantic unit, a closure unit terminating Cycle 1, the last unit to be considered here is vv. 1-6. So far as speakers and addressees are concerned, it is interesting that there are no vocatives in vv. 1-6; the next vocative is in v. 7, "daughters of Jerusalem." Consequently, in these verses, we are concerned with speakers and their referents rather than their addressees:

	Speaker	Referent(s)
verse 1	Heroine	herself (אֲנִי 'I' in 1a)
verse 2	Hero	Heroine (רַעְיָתִי in 2b)
verse 3	Heroine	(a) Hero (דּוֹדִי in 3b)
		(b) 'apple tree' (תַּפּוּחַ in 3a, c, d)
		(c) herself (1 sg. suffixes in 3c, d)
verse 4	Heroine	(a) Hero (masc. sg. affixes in 4a, b)
		(b) herself (1 sg. suffixes in 4a, b)
verse 5	Heroine	(a) unidentified plural persons, addressed with parallel commands in 5a, b
		(b) herself (1 sg. suffixes in 5a, b; use of אֲנִי 'I' in 5c)
verse 6	Heroine	(a) Hero (masc. sg. suffixes in 6a, b)
		(b) herself (1 sg. suffixes in 6a, b)

At first sight, then, we are faced with a string or sequence of verses, all spoken by the Heroine except v. 2 and initially seeming somewhat disjointed. But connections between these verses, though varied in form, can be discerned: (1) Verse 2 is linked to v. 1 lexically by the repetition of שׁוֹשַׁנָּה 'lily' in 2a; the Hero takes up the imagery used by the Heroine of herself, an example of a tail-head link. (2) The first half of v. 3 is strongly parallel to v. 2, with a -כְּ . . . כֵּן 'like . . . so' structure in both, identical word order, and דּוֹדִי in 3b matched with רַעְיָתִי in 2b. (3) The second half of v. 3 is linked to the first half by the continued use of the תַּפּוּחַ 'apple tree' imagery, referring to its shade in 3c and its fruit in 3d. (4) Verses 4-6 exhibit a simple chiastic structure.

    A (v. 4)   references to the Hero as Agent, to the Heroine as Patient
    B (v. 5)   appeal by the Heroine for strengthening
    A' (v. 6)   references to the Hero as Agent (lover), to the Heroine as Patient (being loved).

In addition, אַהֲבָה 'love' links vv. 4 and 5 together (4b, 5c).

Display of Unit 4

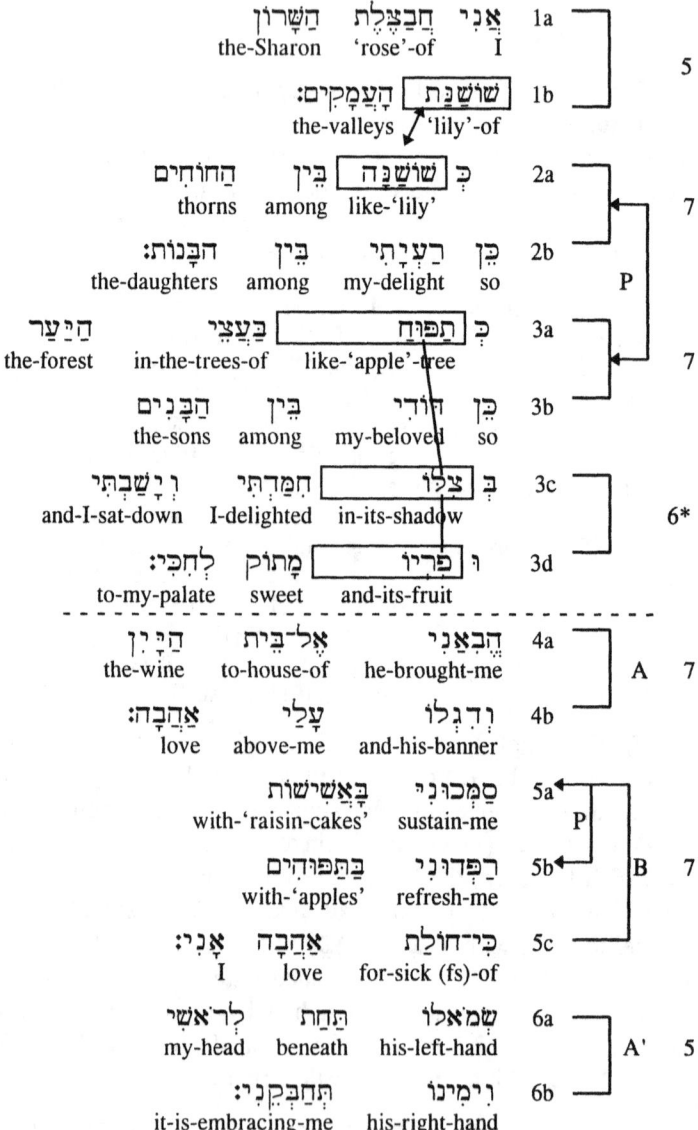

It seems reasonable to posit, therefore, that vv. 1–3 form a larger unit, and that vv. 4–6 do also. These observations lead to the same question as for 1:9–17: Are vv. 1–3 and 4–6 to be analyzed as constituting a larger unit or are they to be treated as two separate smaller units? My own preference is to analyze them in the same way as 1:9–17, as an ascensive couplet. It does not seem necessary to argue strongly for the ascensiveness. As just pointed out, the noun אַהֲבָה 'love' is used twice in vv. 4-6, and the last word of all is the verb חבק in the Pi‛el *yiqtol* form, variously translated as 'embracing', 'caressing', etc., a clear term of physical intimacy. In vv. 1-3, in contrast, the strongest terms used are the verb חמד in the Pi‛el 'to delight in' and the adjective מָתוֹק 'sweet (to the taste)'.

Finally, it is considered significant that vv. 1-6 consist of seven paired lines; only 5c, introduced by כִּי 'for', stands outside the paired system. Although paired lines are characteristic of Biblical Hebrew poetry, this is the first time in the Cycle (and thus in the Song) that they have been used so obviously and frequently. This fact, coupled with the chiastic structure in the final verses of this Cycle,[10] points strongly to vv. 1-6 as the Cycle's "peak" (to use Longacre's well-established term).

In summary then, Cycle 1 (1:5-2:6) is analyzed as comprising four semantic units: 1:5-6, 1:7-8, 1:9-17, and 2:1-6, the final unit being the peak in this opening Cycle. These observations lay the groundwork for tackling the more difficult question of the "flow" in Cycle 1.

4. The "flow" of Cycle 1 (1:5-2:6)

If then, 1:5-2:6 is a major semantic unit, what was the author seeking to achieve by it? What was he communicating to the reader?

In a 1992 article, Eep Talstra discusses the approach of Wolfgang Schneider to Hebrew grammar and states two principles underlying Schneider's approach, the second of which is "Language should not be studied as a means of purely personal expression but as a means of communication" (1992:269). This is a fundamental principle of the text-analysis approach that I am using. Thus the author of the Song wrote *to communicate*; he had a purpose which he sought to achieve by writing the Song. The question is, For Cycle 1 (recognizing that it is only part of the total discourse), can any clear purpose be identified? *What* was the author seeking to communicate by these verses?

It does not need to be argued that the Song is presented almost entirely as either dialogue between the Hero and the Heroine (first person and second person exchanges) or descriptions spoken by one of them about the other (third person material). It thus seems reasonable to assume that the author's purpose is being achieved by these exchanges. It also seems reasonable, since the Hero and the Heroine often address each other in terms of endearment, to work with the further assumption that the writer is presenting a *relationship* between these two people, the Hero and the Heroine. A third assumption is that, in Cycle 1, this purpose is effected primarily via the four constituent units that have just been described. In seeking, then, to discern the author's purpose, we will look at these units again from the perspective of what they reveal about the relationship between the two principal characters.

One is immediately struck by the fact that, in the first unit (1:5-6), the Hero plays no part. It is the Heroine who speaks and she is speaking to the "daughters of Jerusalem." (Who they are does not materially affect the analysis at this point—it is sufficient that they are *not* the Hero.) In this unit she is talking about her dark color, which has evidently caught the attention of the ladies she addresses (6a, b). Their attention is motivated either by surprise or criticism, depending on whether the Heroine's words are considered an explanation or a defense. She points out that her dark appearance does not spoil her beauty (5a, נָאוָה 'lovely') and that it is not her fault. But in any case, it is clear that she is starting off on the wrong foot; these ladies are certainly not extolling her beauty, attractiveness, etc., to the Hero.

In the second unit (1:7-8), the Hero appears and he and the Heroine interact verbally. Two observations are relevant. First, although the vocatives used by the Hero and Heroine to each other ("you whom my soul loves" to the Hero, "most beautiful of women" to the Heroine) are strongly positive in connotation, nevertheless they are not the terms of endearment (דּוֹדִי and רַעְיָתִי) used constantly throughout the rest of the Song. There is a certain "distance" between the Hero and the Heroine here.

Second, the Hero's answer to the Heroine's question as to where he carries out his shepherding activities is by no means intimate. He does not say he will show her. Although he answers her question, he gives the impression that he is keeping her at arm's length.

The third unit (1:9-17) has already been analyzed as ascensive in presentation. The ascensiveness is in terms of an increasingly intimate relationship in which the Heroine is drawn into an ever-increasing intimacy with the Hero. For example, the Hero initiates this particular unit, which is unlike either of the two previous ones; he uses the direct vocative רַעְיָתִי in both halves; he refers to her beauty, but much more obviously and directly in the second half, using the root יפה 'to be beautiful' and introducing it with הִנֵּה, traditionally 'behold!' In this type of context, however, a much more appropriate translation is "How beautiful you are!" (as in GNB, NIV, REV). And this exclamation is promptly repeated in 15a and 15c.

In response to these verbal encouragements, the Heroine moves from *referring* to the Hero as דּוֹדִי (1:13, 14) to addressing him directly (16b) with this explicit term of endearment. And taking her cue from him, she uses יָפֶה of him, and also expresses her delight in his company and their surroundings. In other words, by the end of this third unit, they are addressing each other as lovers and the Heroine is also expressing her pleasure in the Hero's company, which company she was lacking in the two preceding units.

As already pointed out, there is good formal evidence for regarding the final unit as the climactic unit of this Cycle. This is reinforced by the choice of words in 2:4-6, the "peak of the peak," where the Heroine describes herself as collapsing, overwhelmed with the impact of the Hero's love for her (v. 5), and they are described as actually in physical contact (v. 6).

The flow, then, is seen in the author's description of how the Heroine moves from explaining or defending her unusually dark coloring, and from not even being in verbal contact with the Hero, to addressing him as דּוֹדִי 'my beloved' and being in his arms, swooning with the effect of his love on her. In other words, this first Cycle describes how, from the Heroine's hesitant or diffident start, the Hero constantly encourages her to love him openly.

No claim to originality is made for this analysis of the "flow," or purpose, of this first Cycle.[11] What I have done is to seek, through the establishment of semantic units, to give an objective linguistic basis for this analysis.

There are significant implications for the translator in establishing the units and in establishing the "flow." These will be examined in section 9. But before leaving the analysis of 1:1–2:6 of the Song of Songs, vv. 1:1–4 still need to be considered.

5. The title and prologue (1:1-4)

Cycle 1 has 1:5 as its opening verse, in which the Heroine explicitly addresses the "daughters of Jerusalem." What, then, of vv. 1-4?

Verse 1, "the song of songs which is Solomon's," is regarded by all commentators as a formal title. It tells the reader/hearer nothing about the actual content or purpose of the Song. However, it does evaluate it as outstanding (which, of course, arouses interest in it) and it relates it to Solomon in some way, either as the author or as the one to whom the Song is dedicated (less likely, as the one whom the Song is about). Verse 1, then, stands outside the Song itself.

As to vv. 2-4, I view these three verses as the author's prologue to the Song. In general, it is to be expected that an author would use the opening words to orient the reader/hearer to what is to follow, to give them some clues as to what to expect, and hence to enable them to bring to

Display of the title and prologue

פִּיהוּ his-mouth	מִנְּשִׁיקוֹת with-kisses-of	יִשָּׁקֵנִי he-is-kissing-me	2a	A	3
מִיָּיִן: from-wine	דֹּדֶיךָ your (ms)-loves	כִּי־טוֹבִים good (pl)-for	2b	⌉	3
טוֹבִים good (pl)	שְׁמָנֶיךָ your (ms)-oils	לְרֵיחַ concerning-fragrance	3a	B	3
שְׁמֶךָ your (ms)-name	תּוּרַק it (f)-is-poured-out	שֶׁמֶן oil	3b	⌋	3
אֲהֵבוּךָ: they-love-you (ms)	עֲלָמוֹת maidens	עַל־כֵּן that-is-why	3c	C	3
נָרוּצָה let-us-run/we-will-run	אַחֲרֶיךָ after-you (ms)	מָשְׁכֵנִי draw (ms)-me	4a	A'	3
חֲדָרָיו his-inner-rooms	הַמֶּלֶךְ the-king	הֱבִיאַנִי he-brought-me	4b	A''	3
בָּךְ in-you (ms)	וְנִשְׂמְחָה and-we-will-rejoice	נָגִילָה we-will-exult	4c	⌉	3
מִיַּיִן from-wine	דֹּדֶיךָ your (ms)-loves	נַזְכִּירָה we-will-praise	4d	B' ⌋	3
אֲהֵבוּךָ: they-love-you (ms)	מֵישָׁרִים upright (pl)/(up)rightly		4e	C'	2*

the front of their minds relevant frames and concepts within which the author's work is to be understood.

But how can it be established that a given span of discourse is, in fact, a prologue rather than simply the first part of the first unit? Specifically, how are vv. 2-4 distinguished as Prologue rather than part of Cycle 1?

The answer I am proposing to this question is twofold, having to do with *structure* and *content*; that is, vv. 2-4 are seen to be Prologue by how the author puts them together and by what they actually communicate. Although these two factors can readily be distinguished in theory, here they are closely intertwined. Moreover, these verses are not at all easy to interpret; there is a considerable variety of scholarly opinion concerning them.[12] Although there are no serious lexical questions, there are several grammatical ones: the function of the initial לְ in לְרֵיחַ in 3a (approximately, 'with-respect-to fragrance'); the apparent clash of gender in 3b, since שֶׁמֶן 'oil/ointment' is masculine, whereas תּוּרַק 'is poured out' is the feminine form of the third person singular; whether to allocate אַחֲרֶיךָ 'after you' to the preceding or to the following verb in 4a; the interpretation of מֵישָׁרִים in 4f as a (plural) noun 'the upright ones' or as an adverb '(up)rightly'. Where relevant to the discourse analysis, decisions on these questions must be made.

Delitzsch (1885:19) points out that vv. 2-4 consist of "two pentastichal strophes" (i.e., two units of poetic form), each having five lines. What he does not point out is that each of the ten lines consists of three Hebrew words, except the last of all, which has only two. The formal structure, then, distinguishes vv. 2-4 from the unit that follows, which is neither pentastichal nor consisting regularly of three words.

However, there is more to the structure of vv. 2-4 than these numerical observations, important though they are. Verses 2 and 3, the first strophe, pentastich, can be divided formally into three parts as follows:

A (2a) a verbal clause, with the verb in the third person, occurring as the first word in the clause

B (2b-3b) three verbless copula clauses, lexically linked (טוֹבִים 'good' links 2b and 3a and שֶׁמֶן 'oil/ointment' links 3a and 3b)

C (3c) a verbal clause, with the verb in the third person, occurring as the last word in the clause

In addition, lines 2b-3c are each marked, by the occurrence of the second person masculine singular suffix, as being addressed to a singular male addressee. The addressee is not named in these verses, but it would be unreasonable to assume it was someone other than the Hero. Thus, it is generally agreed that 2b-3c express a strong positive evaluation of the Hero, but with the difference that they give the speaker's own evaluation, whereas 3c is the evaluation of others, the עֲלָמוֹת 'young unmarried women, maidens'. The first line, A, is also an evaluation of the Hero, but expressed in terms of longing for his love to be openly expressed to the speaker: the intensive (Piʿel) form of the verb, the cognate verb and noun, and the (apparently) redundant collocation 'kisses of his mouth' are almost certainly devices used by the writer to express the depth of feeling of the speaker, most readily understood as the Heroine herself.[13] Thus, this first strophe can be considered a semantic unit in which the Heroine does two things: she expresses her powerful longings for the Hero to demonstrate his love to her, and she describes, in vivid figurative language, her high view of the love and character of the Hero, a view supported by others.

It would, of course, be very satisfying to any discourse analyst if it could now be said that the second strophe, v. 4, followed the same structural ABC pattern as the first one did. But it does not appear that that is the case. In fact, v. 4 is not at all easy to analyze satisfactorily or convincingly. However, based on the same sort of criteria already applied, the structure appears to be as follows:

A' (4a)   the first verb is second person sg. masc. imperative and has a first person (object) suffix
A'' (4b) the verb is in the third person sg. masc. and has a first person (object) suffix (the expressed subject of the verb is הַמֶּלֶךְ 'the king')
B' (4c, d) first person pl. imperfect verb forms with second person sg. masc. suffixed forms also occurring
C' (4c)   third person pl. perfect verb form with the same second person sg. masc. suffix as in B'

Thus, although an ABC pattern can be discerned, it does not obviously parallel the ABC pattern of vv. 2 and 3 and generally gives a more disjointed impression. Nor is it very obviously a semantic unit, although it shares the same pentastichal form as the first strophe. However, when the *content* of this second unit is considered, the similarities and parallels are much clearer. A' (4a) is similar to A (2a) in that it directly links the Hero and the Heroine: the Heroine (speaking) requests the Hero to 'draw' (מָשַׁךְ) her. This verb can be used both literally and figuratively. (Examples of a figurative use are found in Jer. 31:3 and Hos. 11:4, where God is speaking of how he has drawn Israel to himself with love and compassion.) So A and A' are both requests by the Heroine for the Hero to exhibit his love for her.

The second verb in 4a, נָרוּצָה 'let us run/hurry', is understood by most commentators to express the Heroine's sense of impatient longing for the Hero to respond. With this analysis, the ambiguously placed אַחֲרֶיךָ 'after you (masc. sg.)' would be collocated with the first verb and "we" would be dual inclusive. The other view is to take the verb נָרוּצָה as a simple future, 'we will run', expressing a sort of promise or commitment. However, this view makes it more difficult to interpret "we," since the object of "draw" is clearly "me," not "we." Hence, the first interpretation is preferred.

For the moment, line 4b will be passed over to comment on B' (4c, d). Like B in the first strophe (2b–3b), these two lines are understood to be extolling the praiseworthiness of the Hero, since the suffixed forms are בָּךְ 'in you (masc. sg.)' and דֹּדֶיךָ 'your (masc. sg.) love(making)',[14] and since the three verbs involved are all considered to belong to the conceptual domain of joy and praise. (Although the versions vary as to how they translate the individual verbs, they all agree on the general area of meaning of rejoicing and praise.)

Similarly, C' (4c) corresponds to C (3c) in giving the evaluation of others (in third person form) identified either as 'the upright ones' (taking מֵישָׁרִם as a noun) or unidentified (taking מֵישָׁרִים as an adverb 'rightly'). In either case, what they do is 'love you (masc. sg.)' (אֲהֵבוּךָ).

To return now to A'' (4b) "the king has taken/brought me into his private apartments", this line stands out from all the others with its use of הַמֶּלֶךְ 'the king'. (The only references to a singular male before this have been by suffix or verb form, the referent thus being unidentified.) It also has no obvious corresponding line in the first strophe. My own analysis of these three Hebrew words follows, along with my answer to the obvious question of who "we" refers to in 4c and 4d and who "the upright" or the "they" is in the final line.

The question was raised earlier of how it could be shown that vv. 2-4 constituted the Prologue to the Song, apart from the obvious (though not irrelevant) fact that they are the first three verses. Now we can see that vv. 2-4 are considered to be the Prologue to the Song because *they adumbrate the content of the Song*: they state in brief what the Song states in full.

Two themes have emerged from these strophes in spite of the interpretative problems. One is the Heroine's expressed longing for the love of the Hero; the other is the outstanding quality of the Hero's character. Both of these themes have received clear expression in both strophes. It hardly needs demonstration that the Heroine's love and longing for the Hero's love is found in Cycle 1; in fact, the whole unit climaxes with her finding it and being overwhelmed by it. But there is also expression given to the Hero's "worthwhileness" in 1:13, 14, 16c-17b (his attractiveness), and 2:3 (how outstanding he is compared to other men).[15]

The first of the two themes is more significant that it may seem: "In this song of love the voice of the beloved is dominant. It is her experience of love, both as the one who loves and as the one who is loved, that is most clearly expressed. The Song begins with her wish for the lover's kiss and ends with her urgent invitation to him for love's intimacy" (Stek 1985:1004). The Prologue makes it clear from the start that this Song is written from the perspective of the woman, not that of the man.

Now we are ready to consider A'' (4b) "the king has taken/brought me into his private apartments." If the aforementioned themes were the only ones in the introductory material, it would leave unsaid, and hence unclear, whether the man ever responded. It is clear, however, even from Cycle 1, that he did respond and, in fact, actually encouraged the Heroine in her love for him. Of course, the author could have chosen to reveal the

Hero's response later on in the Song, not in the Prologue. But it seems quite reasonable to interpret 4b as a brief, but effective presentation of a third theme—the Hero's positive response to the requests of the Heroine. So, in this second strophe, his response immediately follows the urgent request for him to show his love for the Heroine. He does so by taking her to a place where they could be private.

One or two final comments. It probably is not necessary to identify the "we" of 4c and 4d; it could simply be the author's way of stating the praiseworthiness of the Hero without its coming from the lips of the Heroine herself. On the other hand, 3c has already stated that the maidens love the Hero. It would therefore be quite appropriate contextually if in v. 4 "we" were taken to be the maidens speaking. In this case, the final line could be understood as referring to the maidens again, especially since the form of the verb אֲהֵבוּךָ 'they love you (masc. sg.)' is identical in 3c and 4e.

The unity of vv. 2-4 lies primarily in their role as the Prologue. However, it is surely not without significance that the final line of each strophe ends with אֲהֵבוּךָ 'they love you (masc. sg.)' and that the second line (2b), "for your (masc. sg.) love(making) is better than wine," is similar to the penultimate line (4d), "we will praise your (masc. sg.) love-(making) more than wine." By echoing the second line of the first strophe in this way, and by using the identical verb form in the final line of the two strophes, the author deliberately links the two strophes and closes off this introduction, preparing the reader for a new start with v. 5.

6. The printed format

Now I would like to address an issue that affects all translators: the final printed form of a translation. Modern translations no longer follow the practice of making each verse a small "paragraph." This practice was abandoned because, it was agreed, it tended to give the reader, experienced or inexperienced, the impression that the biblical text was a series of relatively unconnected small bits of information. So now Bibles are printed in paragraph style, each paragraph spanning a number of verses, and quite commonly some or all of the paragraphs are given headings.

There is a lot of variation in the frequency of headings from one version to another, as can be seen from the chart at the end of this article. And there is also considerable variation in the content of these headings. For example, in the span 1:2-2:7 the NRSV has only two, "Colloquy of Bride and Friends" (1:2-8) and "Colloquy of Bridegroom, Friends and Bride" (1:9-2:7). In contrast, the NKJV has no less than fourteen headings in this same span, the REB thirteen, and the NIV eleven. And the difference in content is just as striking. For example, compare the NRSV headings above with the GNB headings that alternate between "The Woman" and "The Man."

But does it matter all that much? Obviously translators are not bound by what any particular version does in these respects. Nevertheless, it is commonly the practice for translators to follow some modern version, even if not slavishly.[16] Very rarely, I suspect, do translators create their own independent printed units and headings for them.

But how is a team of translators going to make a reasonable and informed choice between competing divisions and headings? As the foregoing analysis has shown, there are certainly questions as to the validity of the divisions and titles used by *all* modern versions in the Song. A fairly brief study of the chart of these versions shows that while there is some agreement among the versions that there is a break between 1:4 and 1:5 and almost total agreement that there is a major break after 2:7, the units that I have argued for between 1:4 and 2:6 command hardly any support at all: *none* at 1:6, and only a little at 1:8, 1:17, and 2:6.

It might be thought that this is a problem peculiar to the Song of Songs. But Louw (1991:102), after presenting a discourse analysis of Rom. 8:1-17, states:

> Verse divisions should not have a prominent place in a translation. Rather, the determining factor should be paragraphing according to the structural features of a text. In Romans 8.1-17 one would think that the paragraphing should be fairly obvious, but if we compare the following chart with the structural analysis discussed above, it is obvious how these translations [he lists seven] differ in this respect.

And what is true of the divisions themselves is equally true of the titles used; and while I have not in this article proposed any titles, I have attempted to describe the "flow" of the Song between 1:4 and 2:6. None of the versions attempt this; they simply identify the speakers with more or less frequency.

You may be thinking, Well, your analysis just adds one more choice to those already facing translators, hardly all that helpful! But I would like to suggest that there is more at stake here than simply selecting something from a set of confusing choices for the final printed version of the Song. It needs to be remembered that readers of the Bible in their own language are definitely influenced by what is presented to their eyes on the printed page. As Louw (ibid., 103) states, "Readers ... are often guided to a considerable extent by the divisions and subdivisions of a text. Accordingly, much more attention should be given to this aspect of translating." Ott (1990:35, 36) puts it very clearly:

Section headings are *part of the message that is presented*... Therefore, translators must use all their skills to create section titles that *support the author's message* in each part of the document... It must be kept in mind that the purpose of writing section titles is to help the readers *understand* the passage... In first editions especially, section titles should attempt to show the author's purpose and the unity that he intended. (Ott's emphasis)

Later (p. 49) he adds, "They [section headings] enable the reader to *distinguish the natural units of the text and read an episode as a whole*" (my emphasis).

The choices made will influence the understanding that the readers of the text will come to. Most, with few exceptions, will accept the divisions and their accompanying headings just as they accept the content of the text. So I am raising the serious issue that in the printed presentation of the Song of Songs, modern versions are at best unhelpful to the reader and at worst actually misleading. A situation, surely, that Bible translators can hardly be happy with.

7. Identifying the speakers

Another interesting issue arises out of this study of part of the Song of Songs. As we have seen, the speakers are not overtly identified in Biblical Hebrew except by the way in which they are addressed in the vocatives, by the gender distinctions of the morphology, and by such occasional references as הַמֶּלֶךְ 'the king'. But many languages do not have gender distinctions as morphological categories. Conclusions concerning the gender of the speaker can only be drawn from some of the contextual statements and comparisons. For such languages, the majority surely, the speaker will need to be identified as is currently done in European versions. This is a rather unusual way for the translation of distinctions in the source language grammar to be expressed, but there does not seem to be any obvious alternative.

8. "Don't put out the fire!"

No one questions that the Song of Songs is poetry, and passionate poetry at that. This raises the issue of how poetry, in general, should be translated (and, possibly, how it should be printed). I would like to raise a related, but different issue, along the lines of a 1991 article entitled "Don't Put Out the Fire!" by Ross McKerras. His opening words are well worth quoting:

The eighteenth-century English poet Alexander Pope said in the preface to his translation of Homer's *Iliad*: "It is not to be doubted that the *fire* of the poem is what a translator should principally regard, as it is most likely to expire in his managing." ... Oh dear, how often is this true of the English translations of the Bible! So often where there is a little bit of fire or feeling in the original, it is doused with mathematical precision.

In the theory on which this article is based, a distinction is drawn between three broad purposes of human communication: to exchange factual information, to share one's own inner values and feelings, and to affect the future. The second of these purposes is termed *expressive* and though from a grammatical perspective the first and second purposes can look very similar, they are really quite different. Compare, for example, "I think she is due to retire soon" and "I think she's a very gifted pianist." The former is factual information, "she is due to retire soon," with the speaker expressing uncertainty about the accuracy of this information; the latter expresses the speaker's evaluation of the pianist. To the first, you could respond, "I'll try and find out for sure," but this would be quite inappropriate for the second.

Since this threefold distinction reflects our human personalities, it is considered to be universal; hence all languages will have appropriate ways of communicating "expressively." This is not to say they all have a recognizable poetic genre (whether written or oral), but they all have ways of sharing their feelings, opinions, and value systems and these will be different from the ways in which facts are exchanged.

Translators need to be aware that the Song of Songs is expressive in purpose. They also need to know how such expressive material would be appropriately translated. An example of this was seen in our discussion of how הִנֵּה and כִּי should be translated into English in the expressive context of the Song. The Song should *not* read like a narrative, or an argument, or a set of commands.

And connected with this, more research needs to be done into Hebrew itself as relates to the effects of expressive material on Hebrew grammatical usage and lexical choices.[17] Such research would enable translators to be more confident in handling the transfer—careful research is always to be preferred to guesswork or intuition.

9. Some final comments

It is my considered opinion, and this study of the Song of Songs has reinforced it, that the (last?) major issue now facing translation theory is the transfer of the discourse structure of the source language to the discourse structure of the receptor language. This was forced on my attention recently when checking Gen. 7:17-24, a part of the Flood account where the Biblical Hebrew style is clearly "overlapping" and one new bit of information is added per clause. This Hebrew discourse feature was faithfully preserved in translation by one team of translators, but was reacted to as "bad style" by the other team. It violated the expected discourse patterns of the receptor language. But what was to be done? Abandon the Biblical Hebrew discourse style for the corresponding natural one? But what *was* the appropriate receptor-language discourse style at that point? Did anyone know? Probably not. And is anyone—consultant or translator—prepared to go that far? Since it was the "overlappingness" that was unacceptable, presumably a natural local equivalent would have produced a much shorter text. Is this acceptable? Is anyone prepared to say?

Bliese's work on "structurally/metrically marked peak" in Hebrew poetry (1990:265-67) makes us think of another example. If the chiastic and homogeneous metrical structure of Hebrew poetry is a means of indicating which information is the most significant, and if that structure cannot be reproduced in a translation (a reasonable assumption), what then? Not signaling the most significant information is surely bad translation. So what is the answer?

Finally, there is a corollary. How many translators, or even consultants, are aware of the many discourse insights that have been developed over the last few years and are still being developed? How are these insights to be effectively conveyed to them? And further, how many translators would be able to make good use of the information even if they had it and understood it? Would they know what the corresponding discourse features would be in the receptor language?

Discourse analysis is fundamental to good translation, both exegetically and from a natural/idiomatic standpoint. But there is a lot yet to be done in the field of discourse analysis of the biblical literature and in the training of translators (local or foreign) in discourse analysis. The need to develop a theoretical framework within which the translator knows how features of the original languages revealed by discourse analysis are to be handled in the translation process is perhaps the biggest challenge of all.

Sections and headings in seven versions of the Song of Songs 1:2–2:7

	JB (1974)	GNB (1976)	NIV (1978)	NKJV (1984)	NJB (1985)	NRSV (1989)	REB (1989)
1:2		the Woman[18]	Beloved	the Shulamite[19]	Prologue	Colloquy of Bride and Friends	Bride
1:3	the Bride						
1:4			Friends[20]	[21]	[no title][22]		companions[23]
1:5	the Bride[24]		Beloved	the Shulamite			Bride
1:6							
1:8	Chorus			the Beloved			
1:9	the Bridegroom	the Man	Lover				Bridegroom
1:10							
1:11				d. of Jerus.	Dialogue of the Lovers	Colloquy of Bridegroom, Friends, and Bride	companions
1:12		the Woman	Beloved	the Shulamite			Bride
1:13							
1:14							
1:15	Dialogue of the Bride and Bridegroom	the Man	Lover	Beloved			Bridegroom
1:16		the Woman	Beloved	the Shulamite			Bride
1:17			Lover				Bridegroom
2:1			Beloved				Bride
2:2		the Man	Lover	Beloved			Bridegroom
2:3		the Woman	Beloved	Shulamite			Bride
2:4				Shulamite to the daughters of Jerusalem			
2:5							
2:6							
2:7							Bridegroom

NB: Divisions/sections without titles are not shown on the chart. My own unit boundaries are shown by extensions to the left of the chart, double lines showing major divisions, a single line minor divisions. The versions are arranged in chronological order from left to right with minor boundaries shown by a thin line, major boundaries by a thick line.

Notes

1. See, in particular, chapters 17–20 of Beekman and Callow's 1974 work.

2. Murphy (1990:77) says, "Each of these occurrences marks what many commentators have judged to be the conclusion of a major poetic unit in the Song."

3. The text used is that of the *Biblia Hebraica Stuttgartensia*, 1983.

4. The terms *Heroine* and *Hero* are used to refer to the two principal participants in the Song, without prejudice to the many interpretations found in the commentaries.

5. Not enough is known about Biblical Hebrew word order in this type of material to make any strong claims, but it certainly seems significant that the first word in this unit is שְׁחוֹרָה 'black', referring to the topic concept.

6. Murphy (1990:88) says, "In 1:5, interestingly, the appellative invocation ... seems to be a supplemental or extrametrical feature."

7. Delitzsch (1885) assigns v. 8 to the "daughters of Jerusalem," as do other commentators and some versions; the NIV assigns it to "Friends," the Jerusalem Bible (1974) to "the Chorus." This is done because in 5:9 and 6:1 the "daughters of Jerusalem" address the Heroine as "the most beautiful of women." However, where the question is addressed to the Hero (7b), it is unnecessary and inappropriate to have someone else answer the question.

8. It is difficult to know how to translate this word into English. However the root may be understood, it occurs in the Song in contexts where it is most naturally interpreted as a term of endearment, and this is how it is translated in English versions. Carr (1984) says, "It occurs nine times in the Song, always on the lips of the lover, and usually in conjunction with an explicit statement about her beauty."

9. Delitzsch (1885:39) says, "רַעֲנָן ... is not a word of color, but signifies to be extensible ... We have no such word as this which combines in itself the ideas of softness and juicy freshness, of bending and elasticity, of looseness and those of overhanging ramification (as in the case of the weeping willow)." Carr (1984) is more succinct: "... the word is not so much used of the color proper, but of a tree that is alive and in leaf. The NEB *shaded with branches* is a good paraphrase."

10. Bliese (1988:77–78) gives chiasmus as one example of "nonmetrical marking of peaks in Joel." The same could well apply here in the Song. Taking Bliese's approach further, however, it would be possible to analyze all of vv. 1–6 as a chiasmus of metrical structure *5776775*, if in 4a אַל is treated as a separate word. In this case, according to Bliese's theory of metrically marked peak, lines 3c–d would be the peak so marked. But this conflicts with the ascensive analysis that I have proposed, which makes vv. 4–6 more significant than 1–3. Assuming Bliese's approach has been correctly applied, this raises interesting questions concerning criteria for identifying the most important information in a given unit/strophe.

11. As far back as 1853, George Burrowes, although he followed the traditional view of the Heroine as representing the believer and the Hero as representing Christ in his summary of the Song, labeled this passage "the way in which the soul...is led along...from one degree to another of pious enjoyment, until attaining the greatest delight possible for the saint in this present world. Chap. i.1; chap. ii.7." More recently, Carr (1984:72) closed his introduction to 1:2–2:7 with this statement: "the general progress towards fulfillment is unquestioned."

12. Murphy (1990:64), for instance, says, "The most questionable passages are the following: 1:2–4 (where an abrupt change of speakers occurs)." However, he does recognize these verses as having some sort of unity when he describes them as "a poem of yearning, spoken by the woman" (p. 60).

13. Delitzsch (1885:19) takes the view that all of vv. 2–4 are sung by the daughters of Jerusalem: "the two pentastichal strophes...are...the table song of the ladies." But, as my chart of versions shows, this view is not widely held (cf. Murphy's observation in the previous note).

14. The noun used here is the same as in the phrase דּוֹדִי 'my beloved', but is in the plural. It is commonly thought that the plural focuses on the various outward expressions of love, and hence is translated by "lovemaking." The same form of the same noun is found in 2b.

15. According to Bliese (1988:52), "a series of lines with the same number of feet will normally have its climax as the last line." In that case, the fact that the last line of the second pentastich is very similar in meaning to the last line of the first pentastich is obviously striking. And both of these lines draw attention to how "loveworthy" the Hero is.

16. See, for example, Barnwell's instructions under the heading "Checking larger units" (1990:27–29).

17. Talstra (1992:283) comments, "the analysis of *nonnarrative* texts is a promising field for further research . . . One has to admit, however, that at several points (*in poetic and prophetic literature*) this approach needs further development. Indeed, this seems to be the case with virtually any existing textgrammatical model" (emphasis mine). In my opinion, research into word-order patterns in nonnarrative texts should be conducted within the context of established semantic units if it is to take all the relevant contextual factors into account.

18. The GNB has a general heading for 1:2–2:7, "The First Song."

19. The NKJV has a general heading for 1:2–2:7, "The Banquet."

20. Lines 4c, d only; line 4e is included under the next division.

21. Verse 4 is divided between the Shulamite in 4a and the daughters of Jerusalem in 4b.

22. The NJB has a general heading for 1:4–2:7, "The First Poem."

23. Lines 4c–e only.

24. The JB has a general heading for 1:5–2:7, "The First Poem."

References

Barnwell, Katharine. 1990. Final checking of a New Testament. *Notes on Translation* 4(2):17-37.
Beekman, John, and John Callow. 1974. *Translating the Word of God*. Grand Rapids: Zondervan.
Bliese, Loren F. 1988. Metrical sequences and climax in the poetry of Joel. *Occasional Papers in Translation and Textlinguistics* 2(4):52-84.
———. 1990. Structurally marked peak in Psalms 1-24. *Occasional Papers in Translation and Textlinguistics* 4(4):265-321.
Callow, Kathleen. Forthcoming. *Man and message: A meaning-based approach to text analysis*. Lanham, Md.: University Press of America.
Carr, G. Lloyd. 1984. *The Song of Solomon*. Tyndale Old Testament Commentaries. Grand Rapids: Eerdmans.
Delitzsch, F. [1885] 1986. *Commentary on Proverbs, Ecclesiates, Song of Solomon*. Reprint. Grand Rapids: Eerdmans.
Larson, Mildred L. 1984. *Meaning-based translation: A guide to cross-language equivalence*. Lanham, Md.: University Press of America.
Louw, Johannes P., ed. 1991. *A receptor's understanding of a reasoned discourse: Romans 8.1-17*. UBS Monograph Series, 5 (Meaningful Translation: Its Implications for the Reader). United Bible Societies.
Mann, William C., and Sandra A. Thompson, eds. 1992. *Discourse description: Diverse linguistic analyses of a fund-raising text*. Amsterdam: John Benjamins.
McKerras, Ross. 1991. Don't put out the fire! *Notes on Translation* 5(2):1-20.
Murphy, Roland E. 1990. *The Song of Songs*. Hermeneia. Philadelphia: Fortress Press.
Ott, Willis. 1990. Section titles in printed Scripture. *Notes on Translation* 4(3):34-49.
Stek, John H. 1985. Notes on the Song of Songs. In *The NIV Study Bible*, ed. Kenneth Barker, 1003-13. Grand Rapids: Zondervan.
Talstra, Eep. 1992. Text grammar and Biblical Hebrew: The viewpoint of Wolfgang Schneider. *Journal of Translation and Textlinguistics* 5(4):269-97.

20

SOME DISCOURSE FUNCTIONS OF PROPHETIC QUOTATION FORMULAS IN JEREMIAH

H. Van Dyke Parunak

Careful readers of the Old Testament are often perplexed about the quotation formulas that the sixth-century B.C. prophets use to identify the messages they receive from Yahweh. For example, the Book of Jeremiah uses "The word of the LORD came to Jeremiah," "The LORD said to me," "The word that came to Jeremiah," "This word came to Jeremiah," "Thus says the LORD," "Hear the word of the LORD," and "Oracle of the LORD" (or "says the LORD"). Why are there so many different formulas? Do they all mean the same thing? Why are they often so deeply nested? Meier (1992:258) laments that "the means for marking D[irect] D[iscourse] in Jeremiah are the most varied, unpredictable, and, quite simply, chaotic of any book in the Hebrew Bible."

This article identifies two kinds of distinctions that these formulas encode: first, the different components within a single oracle (incipit, background, dispatch, and body) that give information on the communication events in which oracles participate; second, what Hollenbach and Longacre have termed a "cline," an ordered paradigm, which in this case indicates the relative semantic ranking and structural clustering of different oracles or repeated components of a single oracle.

Understanding these distinctions is beneficial to the expositor or translator. For one thing, the information that these formulas contain, which may not be evident to the casual reader, aids in understanding the text. For another, the potential confusion arising from the unnaturally deep nesting on the surface of the text (e.g., "The LORD said, 'The LORD said, "The LORD said, '...' " ' ") can be avoided.

Jeremiah 29:30–32 is a good example of the challenge posed by the quotation formulas in the sixth-century prophets.[1]

> 30Then the word of the LORD came to Jeremiah, saying, 31Send to all them of the captivity, saying, Thus says the LORD concerning Shemaiah the Nehelamite; Because Shemaiah has prophesied to you, and I sent him not, and he caused you to trust in a lie: 32Therefore thus says the LORD; Behold, I will punish Shemaiah the Nehelamite, and his seed: he shall not have a man to dwell among this people; neither shall he behold the good that I will do for my people—oracle of the LORD—because he has taught rebellion against the LORD.

Even such a short paragraph poses several knotty questions:

- These three verses contain three different formulas: "the word of the LORD came to Jeremiah," "thus says the LORD (twice)," and the very different phrase "Oracle of the LORD," which is misleadingly rendered "says the LORD" in older translations. Why are these particular formulas used? Why do they appear where they do?
- Another question is, How should the Jer. 29:30-32 paragraph be punctuated? Conventional English punctuation would require four levels of nested quotations, the first beginning with v. 31, the second before "Thus says the LORD," the third before "Because Shemaiah has prophesied," and the fourth before "Behold" in v. 32. Zech. 1:1-4 is even more deeply nested, requiring five levels. From an English perspective, such deep nesting seems unnatural, especially when the speaker does not change.
- What is the connection between Shemaiah's offense in v. 31 and his punishment in v. 32? We expect to read, "Because Shemaiah did wrong, therefore I will punish him." But the most straightforward reading of the text indicates that his offense results in a prophecy of punishment rather than directly in the punishment itself.

The meaning and function of the three formulas that appear in Jer. 29:30-32, along with several others, will be explored in this article based on an exhaustive survey of Jeremiah's usage. In addition to their semantic content (which largely overlaps), the formulas serve very different structural functions, functions that can relieve our frustration over the depth of apparent nesting of quotations and logical connections among paragraphs.

In section 1 I begin with an overview. Then in sections 2 and 3 I describe the overall structure of a prophetic oracle and the kinds of formulas that can appear at each juncture. I discuss each formula in turn, along with more detail concerning its function in the larger structure.

1. Overview of an oracle

A prophetic book, as a result of the process by which it is written, delivers its message on two levels. The structure of the oracles recorded in the Bible reflects this, and the different formulas that occur are assigned with some regularity to the various parts of a typical oracle.

1.1 How the prophetic books were written

The key to understanding the prophetic introductory formulas lies in the nature of the prophetic books as we have them and the process by which they were composed. Like the other major prophets, and most of the minor ones as well, the Book of Jeremiah is a compilation of many "clumps" of oracles and anecdotes. The opening verses of the book tell us that these clumps originated at different times during a forty-year period, from the thirteenth year of Josiah (627/626 B.C.)[2] to the end of Zedekiah's reign at the destruction of Jerusalem (587 B.C.), and many of the individual prophecies are dated to different years or events within this period (e.g., 25:1; 28:12; 33:1). The anecdotes and oracles also come from different places. Some are given by Jeremiah in the royal palace (22:1), others in workshops of the common people (18:1, 2), and still others in the land of Egypt (chap. 44).

Thus the Book of Jeremiah does not have its origin with a decision of Jeremiah to sit down and write a book. In fact, the decision to commit his oracles to writing is not made until 605 B.C., when Yahweh commands him to record the many messages he has already delivered (36:1, 2). For more than twenty years he has carried many different messages from Yahweh to the people and experienced in different ways their response. Now he is to bring them together into an integrated work. Even after writing them down, he is not finished. Jehoiakim burns the original edition (36:23), which is immediately replaced with a longer one (36:32), and that, in turn, must have been subsequently edited and enlarged, for our Book of Jeremiah includes prophecies that were uttered nearly twenty years later.

There are several ways one can combine previously existing oracles into a single collection. At one extreme, successive prophecies retain their individual identity and are presented one after another in simple chronological order. At the other extreme, the writer rearranges the material to produce an integrated book in which the original prophecies lose their individual identity. We know Jeremiah (and his scribe Baruch) did not go to this latter extreme, because they often give the date and place of individual messages. Nor did they follow the strictly chronological approach; some of the oracles are out of chronological order. The prophecies are arranged thematically so that they develop the overall message of the book.

Thus the current literary form of an Old Testament prophetic book is the result of two processes. The first is the delivery of the original prophetic oracle, which involved a set of ideas to convey a specific message to a specific group of people at a specific time and place. The second is the arrangement of these oracles into an integrated collection to bring out the overall message emerging from all the prophecies. This message is larger than that conveyed by any single oracle. We may view it as the synthesis and summary of a prophet's entire ministry, a "life message" that may not have been apparent to him until he paused to look back over his life's ministry.

The New Testament claims inspiration both for the messages of the individual prophecies and for the message conveyed by arranging them into a single integrated collection. Peter focuses on the spoken prophecy, the original individual messages, when he insists that "prophecy came not in old time by the will of man, but holy men of God spoke as they were moved by the Holy Spirit" (2 Pet. 1:21); Paul's insistence that "all scripture is given by inspiration of God" (2 Tim. 3:16) emphasizes "scripture," that is, the written books in their final form. Precisely because both processes are controlled by God to produce his Word, we should give careful attention to discern the meaning of the oracles both in their original settings and in relation to the larger message that emerges from them as they are arranged in the written book.

This study seeks to show that the introductory formulas help us to sort out these two levels of meaning in a prophetic book. In particular, they can give us three kinds of guidance:

1. They enable us to identify the individual oracles and, in some cases, their original settings.
2. They help us analyze the internal structure of individual oracles, thus recovering the message of the original prophecy as it was first given.
3. They show us the logic that connects the different oracles with one another and thus help us recover the prophet's larger message.

The introductory formulas are not the only devices that serve these three purposes. We must also understand the other ones in order to analyze a prophetic book (see Parunak 1981, 1982, 1983, 1993). It should, of course, be remembered that the introductory formulas serve other purposes besides these structural ones; for example, they emphasize the divine origin of the oracles. But though the introductory formulas are not sufficient to determine a book's structure, they are necessary; hence this study seeks to equip Bible students to use them, along with other techniques, to understand the messages of the ancient prophets.

One more caveat. This study is based on an exhaustive survey of the formulas in Jeremiah. The same principles apply throughout the prophetic books wherever these formulas appear, so the conclusions we reach here may be cautiously applied in books other than Jeremiah's. But Meier (1992) quite appropriately emphasizes the diversity of usage in other parts of the Bible, and serious students may wish to do an exhaustive study of these other books to verify whether the formulas have the same meaning there, and if not, how they differ.

1.2 The structure of an oracle

A common phenomenon in human language is the existence of relatively fixed schemas or literary forms for different types of material. For example, a letter usually begins with the sender's address and the date, followed by the recipient's address, a salutation beginning "Dear...," then the body of the letter, and finally a complimentary closing such as "Sincerely yours" and the signature of the sender. Not every letter has all of these parts, and sometimes one part may take different forms in different letters, but enough of the general pattern is repeated often enough that we can reconstruct the "ideal" letter and use it to describe any individual letter. In fact, the ways in which an individual letter varies from the ideal are often important clues to the function and meaning of that specific letter. For example, lack of the recipient's address, and a complimentary close of the form "Love" or "Best Wishes" instead of "Sincerely yours," suggests an informal letter between close friends, while lack of a salutation suggests a brusque, impersonal communication.

In the same way, we can describe the parts of an "ideal" prophetic oracle. As with letters, not every oracle will have every part or always have them in the same form. In fact, deviations from the ideal will be useful indicators of the specific meaning and function of an individual oracle.

At least three communication events (each with a transmitter, content, and receiver) may be involved when we read the record of a prophetic oracle: the *committal*, the *delivery*, and the *report*. Theologically, each of these events reflects a different clause in 2 Pet. 1:20, 21.

1. "Holy men of God... were moved by the Holy Spirit." *God commits* the message to the prophet, often with instructions to pass it on to the people. (Sometimes the Lord and the prophet have a dialogue.)
2. "Holy men of God spoke..." *The prophet delivers* the message to the people, sometimes including a narrative account of the committal. (Again, sometimes the communication is in both directions.) In a few cases,[3] the delivery requires several stages, in which the prophet gives a message to people who are not the final recipients but who are intended to carry it to the final audience.
3. "Every prophecy of scripture is not of private interpretation." *The compiler reports* one or both of these events (i.e., the committal and the delivery) for later readers.

Figure 1 illustrates the relations among these three communication events. Gray rounded squares represent communication events; black circles or ovals represent the communication agents (transmitters or receivers); and black squares with sharp corners represent the content communicated between the transmitter and the receiver. A black square surrounding a communication event is a narrative of the surrounded event.

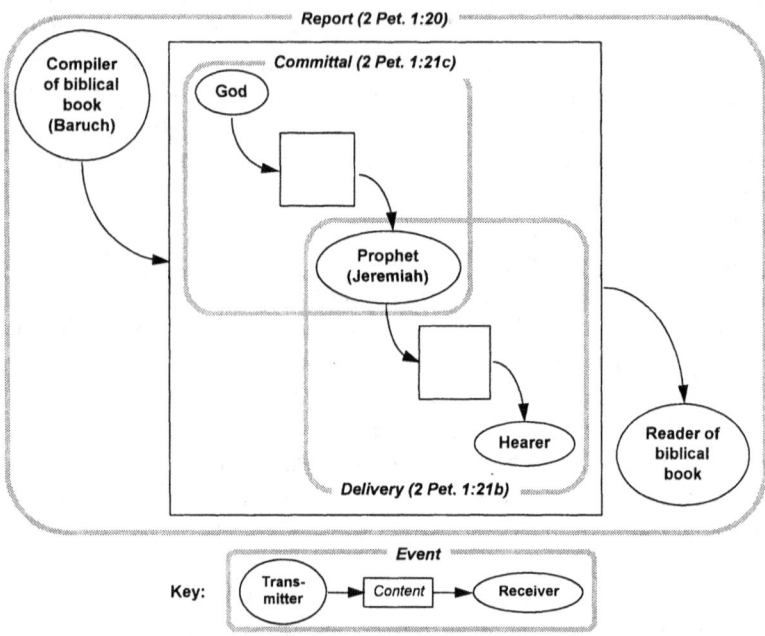

Figure 1. The three communication events in a prophetic oracle.

Usually, the compiler records either the committal of the message to the prophet or its delivery to the final audience, not both. The reader is expected to realize that both have taken place. Thus, there is no statement in 29:30-32 that Jeremiah actually sent the message to the Jews in captivity, but we do not question that he did. Sometimes, as in 2 Sam. 7:4-17, a single verse after the oracle reports that it was indeed delivered. Conversely, as in Jer. 42:7-22, the body of the oracle is sometimes reported to the reader as it is being delivered to the final audience, only a single verse (42:7) having told us that God first gave the message to the prophet. Even the summary of the committal may be omitted, as in Jer. 26:18.

In 19:1-15, we have a rather complete record of the committal of the message to Jeremiah in 1-13, and an abbreviated record of the delivery in 14-15. In 28:12-16, different parts of the message are recorded in the committal and the delivery. In 35:12-19, the oracle has components intended for two different audiences, the men of Judah and the Rechabites; the message to the men of Judah is recorded only when it is committed, and that to the Rechabites only when it is delivered. The sequence found in 21:3-7, 8-10, 11-14, and 22:1-23:40 is similar.

When the compiler simply leaves out one or the other of these two events, we can usually figure out what has happened. Sometimes the compiler of Jeremiah (usually understood to be Baruch) makes matters a little more complicated and blends the first two speech events together.[4]

Prophetic quotation formulas help to elucidate this structure by delimiting and identifying several common components of the three communication events of committal, delivery, and reporting.[5]

1.2.1 Body

The committal and delivery of a prophetic oracle are the body of the oracle, the record of the words originally spoken in the oracle's original setting. As noted in section 1.2, historically these words would have been spoken twice, once by Yahweh to the prophet, and again by the prophet to the audience, but the compiler usually reports them only once. In Jer. 29:30-32, for example, the body begins in the middle of v. 31 with the words "Thus says the LORD."

> [31]...Thus says the LORD concerning Shemaiah the Nehelamite; Because Shemaiah has prophesied to you, and I sent him not, and he caused you to trust in a lie: [32]Therefore thus says the LORD; Behold, I will punish Shemaiah the Nehelamite, and his seed: he shall not have a man to dwell among this people; neither shall he behold the good that I will do for my people—oracle of the LORD—because he has taught rebellion against the LORD.

The oracle's body is our main source of information on what Yahweh wished to tell the people through the prophet. It provides us with the meaning of the original oracle in its original setting.

1.2.2 Dispatch

The biblical prophets are insistent that they deliver their messages not because they compose them and decide who needs to hear them, but because God has given them the message and commanded them to deliver it. Many oracles make this divine dispatch explicit by recording the command by which God sent the prophet to deliver the message. This command usually comes just in front of the oracle body. In Jer. 29:30-32, it consists of the first half of v. 31: "Send to all them of the captivity, saying, ..."

Sometimes a dispatch is repeated just before successive sections of a single oracle. A clear example of this is 2 Sam. 7:4-16, with repeated dispatches in 5a and 8a. In the Book of Jeremiah, this dynamic appears in 21:3-7, 8-10, 11-14; 22:1-23:40. The first part of the oracle is reported only in delivery, as Jeremiah sends Zedekiah's messengers to carry the oracle back to the king, an intermediate prophetic role (cf. 27:4). Each of the next three sections, presented as committal, has its own dispatch, reflecting a different setting and audience to which it is to be delivered.

The dispatch relates to the committal. Sometimes the prophet repeats it in delivery,[6] presumably to add authority to the message. It often gives us detailed information on the setting of the original oracle, information that would not be available if we had only the words that the prophet actually spoke. It was customarily included in written letters, as an instruction to the letter carrier. In both the Mari archives from the eighteenth century B.C. and the Amarna correspondence from the fourteenth century, letters commonly begin with the words "Say to my Lord the King" (Pritchard 1969:482-90). We do not know whether the messenger who carried these letters actually spoke the dispatch to his hearers, or whether he began with the words that the dispatch directs him to speak.

1.2.3 Incipit

As we said before, the *body* records the main message. It is what the prophet heard from Yahweh and the audience heard from the prophet; thus it involves both the committal and the delivery. The *dispatch,* which records what the prophet heard from Yahweh in sending him to the original audience, belongs only to the committal.[7] Both the body and the dispatch represent words that were spoken in the oracle's original context, either to the prophet privately or to the audience.

The third part of an oracle is the *incipit,* the prophet's memorandum that this was, in fact, a message from Yahweh. It often records the date and circumstances of the committal, the event in which Yahweh sent him to carry the message, and sometimes summarizes it. Unlike the body and the dispatch, the incipit need never have been spoken or written down until the final collection was composed. It belongs to the report. Its audience is neither the audience of the original message nor the prophet, but the readers of the overall compilation of prophecies. In our example of Jer. 29:30-32, the incipit is 29:30, "Then the word of the LORD came to Jeremiah, saying, ..."

Like the dispatch, the incipit can help us better understand the setting of the oracle. As this study will show, it can also help us understand the relation of one oracle to another in developing the larger message of the entire compilation.

Just as the incipit gives the setting of the committal, a report of a delivery usually includes information on the setting of the delivery (e.g., 26:18a). Sometimes a delivery is marked in other ways, for example, by a personal exhortation from the prophet to the people given along with the body, as in 13:15-21. In 13:8-25, the committal occupies vv. 8-14; 22-27, marked by "Oracle of the LORD," is clearly a body section. These segments are separated by vv. 15-21, a personal exhortation from the prophet to the people, which shows that the prophet has moved from committal to delivery. So we should understand vv. 22-27 as being delivery as well. Marks of a delivery, such as setting and personal exhortation, are not presented by means of specific quotation formulas.[8]

1.2.4 Background

In some cases, a "background," a brief statement of the state of affairs that leads to the sending of the message, appears between the incipit and the dispatch For example, 3:11-4:18 begins,

> And the LORD said to me [incipit], Backsliding Israel has justified herself more than treacherous Israel [background]. Go and proclaim these words toward the north, and say: [dispatch] ... [body]

Another clear example is 13:8-14:

> Then the word of the LORD came to me, saying [incipit], Thus says the LORD: After this manner will I mar the pride of Judah... [9-11, background]. Therefore thou shalt speak to them this word [12, dispatch]: Thus says the LORD God of Israel, ... [body].

The background communicates a sense of the intimacy between God and the prophet. In the spirit of Gen. 18:17, Yahweh will not hide from Jeremiah what he is doing, but explains the motive for the oracle of judgment. This background (which, unlike the dispatch and body, is not paralleled in ancient secular letters) appears not to have been spoken to the hearers. It never has its own introductory formula[9] and is therefore not discussed further in this article. It may be considered an extension of the subject margin that is often attached to the incipit.

1.2.5 Summary

There are four distinctive components of an oracle: body, dispatch, incipit, background. They reflect three communication events (see sec. 1.2):

1. In the *committal,* God gives the prophet the background, dispatch, and body. A background requires a dispatch, but otherwise any of these

parts can be omitted. That is, sometimes God simply dispatches the prophet on a nonverbal task so that there is no body (e.g., 13:1); other times (at least so far as the text indicates) there is only a body without an explicit dispatch (e.g., 14:1-6).
2. In the *delivery,* the prophet conveys the body (rarely, the dispatch; once, with an incipit) to the audience.
3. In the *report,* the writer may record either the committal, the delivery, or both, and typically introduces the committal with an incipit and the delivery with an appropriate setting or personal exhortation.

Table 1 summarizes the four components. It shows the time they were first verbalized, the communication event with which they are most closely associated, and what they present to the readers of today.

Table 1. The components of a prophetic oracle.

Part of oracle	Time	Communication event	Content
Incipit	at compilation	report (writer to reader)	original message of the book and setting of the original message
Background	with dispatch	committal (God to prophet)	reason for the original message
Dispatch	before original delivery	committal (God to prophet)	setting of the original message
Body	at original delivery	delivery (prophet to original audience)	meaning of the original message

1.3 The formulas

The various formulas do not occur with equal frequency in the different parts of an oracle, as can be seen in Table 2. Table 2 summarizes the distribution of formulas across the three parts of a typical oracle in Jeremiah and introduces the abbreviations by which they will be noted later in this study.[10]

Some Discourse Functions of Prophetic Quotation Formulas in Jeremiah

Table 2. The location of introductory formulas within oracles.

Formula	Incipit	Dispatch	Body
WLC—"The word of the LORD came . . ."	28	0	0
LSM—"The LORD said to me . . ."	15	0	0
WTC—"The word that came to Jeremiah . . ."	14	0	0
TWC—"This word came to Jeremiah . . ."	3	0	0
HWL—"Hear the word of the LORD"	0	0	16
TSL—"Thus says the LORD"	0	10	155
OOL—"Oracle of the LORD"	0	0	175

1.3.1 Formulas for the incipit

The most common formula for an incipit, which appears to be the unmarked one, is "The word of the LORD came to Jeremiah [to me]." Three other formulas are used only in incipits. "The LORD said to me" indicates that this oracle is part of an interchange, either between Yahweh and Jeremiah or between Yahweh and Israel. "The word that came to Jeremiah from the LORD" and "This word came to Jeremiah from the LORD" are more formal than the unmarked formula: They never describe Jeremiah in the first person and never introduce elements in an interchange or dialogue between Jeremiah and Yahweh. They sometimes seem to govern collections of oracles rather than single oracles, thus providing a higher level of grouping in the structure of the book.

1.3.2 Formula for the dispatch

"Thus says the LORD" sometimes introduces the dispatch In some of these cases there is no incipit (e.g., 22:1); in others there is (26:2).

1.3.3 Formulas for the body

Three formulas appear regularly in the body. All may be repeated several times in the course of a single body.

When the addressee of the oracle is to be marked explicitly in the text of the oracle (rather than in the dispatch), the paragraph begins with "Hear the word of the LORD." Following this formula (or beginning the oracle if the addressee is not marked) is the common formula "Thus says the LORD." This is the classical formula to indicate that the prophet is speaking under divine rather than human authority. These formulas always mark the beginning of a paragraph of the oracle and are useful for determining the inner structure of an oracle (though other techniques for marking division are also used).

The third body formula is "Oracle of the LORD." In a few cases this formula appears to replace "Thus says the LORD" in authenticating an entire oracle body (3:6-10; 3:11-4:18; 15:1-9; and in general oracles with an incipit marked by "The LORD said to me"). But more commonly it focuses the reader's attention on individual phrases or clauses within an oracle.

These oracles encode an oracle's basic structure. Furthermore, in terms of the hierarchical decomposition of the text (book, sections, oracles, paragraphs within an oracle, individual phrase or clause within a paragraph) they form a cline.[11]

2. The incipit formulas

2.1 The word of the LORD came to Jeremiah (WLC)

The common incipit formula WLC appears twenty-eight times.[12] It occurs only as an incipit, marking the beginning of a report.[13] Eleven times[14] (all in 25:3 or earlier, with the exception of 32:6, which is embedded in direct discourse by Jeremiah), the prophet refers to himself in the first person rather than by name. References to the proper name "Jeremiah" appear only in 28:12 and later, with the single exception of 14:1. It is tempting to see in this division a reflection of the two editions of the book described in chapter 36, with the first-person incipits dating from the original version composed entirely from the mouth of Jeremiah (36:4), and later additions marked by the third person to indicate the "many words like them," some perhaps recalled by Baruch. The use of third-person identifiers for Jeremiah only with formulas that indicate higher-level structure would confirm their association with a later stage in the book's development. The verb is usually in the suffix conjugation, but the prefix conjugation appears in 14:1; 25:3; 32:6; 39:15; 46:1; 47:1; and 49:34.

The role of the WLC formula in marking distinct oracles is indicated in two ways: (1) its ability to take margins of place and circumstance and (2) the use of "again" (שֵׁנִית) to mark association with a previous oracle. A margin of place appears in only one case, 43:8, but time margins appear eight times, in 25:3; 28:12; 33:1; 36:27; 39:15; 42:7; 47:1; and 49:34. Such margins commonly mark scene changes in narrative literature, and formulas that can carry them serve to punctuate the quasinarrative matrix within which the various oracles are embedded. The formula carries "again" in 1:13, 13:3, and 33:1, indicating that its oracle is closely tied to the previous one.

Sometimes Yahweh speaks to Jeremiah in order to give him a message for the people, but on other occasions the incipit is not followed with a dispatch, and the WLC formula is used simply to introduce Yahweh's utterance in a report of a conversation with Jeremiah (1:4, 11, 13; 13:3; 32:6, 26). Some incipit formulas (WTC, TWC) are never used in interchanges, and one (LSM) appears only in them. Thus the WLC formula appears to be the one that is the most general, the unmarked one. It is Jeremiah's notation that a new utterance of Yahweh is about to be reported, but does not distinguish between full-blown oracles and conversational interchanges.

The WLC formula appears three times in the oracles against the nations in chapters 46–50 (46:1; 47:1; 49:34). Nine oracles are distinguished either by quotation formulas or change in addressee, beginning at 46:2, 13 (Egypt); 47:1 (Philistia); 48:1 (Moab); 49:1 (Ammon); 49:7 (Edom); 49:28 (Kedar); 49:34 (Elam); 50:1 (Babylon).[15] The WLC formula marks two of them, 47:1 and 49:34 (the 47:1 occurrence introduces rather the entire set). Two others, 46:13 and 50:1, are marked by "The word that the LORD spake to Jeremiah." Three of these four indicate the group under discussion,[16] and the fourth (46:13) omits it, perhaps because the subject (Egypt) is unchanged from the previous oracle. TSL introduces 48:1. The other four oracles have no formula, but simply begin with the prepositional phrase identifying the subject of the oracle. Since the formula that introduces the entire series is "The word of the LORD came to Jeremiah," we should probably read the prepositions as elided incipits. In only one other passage (14:1) does this formula carry an indication of the subject, for a total of four out of twenty-nine cases.

2.2 The LORD said to me (LSM)

The incipit formula LSM appears fifteen times.[17] It always describes Jeremiah in the first person except in 9:12 and 15:11, which omit any mention of the addressee (15:11 also is the only case in the suffix conjugation). Its occurrences are all before chapter 25, corresponding with the distribution of the first-person forms in WLC.

The LSM formula marks the oracle that it introduces as an element in an interchange, either between Yahweh and Jeremiah or between Yahweh and Israel. While WLC and less commonly TSL can also introduce an oracle in an interchange, they are unmarked for interchange. Oracles beginning with LSM are always part of an interchange. In 1:7, 9, 12, 14 (alongside WLC in 1:11, 13), 13:6 (alongside WLC in 13:3, 8 and TSL in

13:1), and 24:3, LSM introduces utterances by Yahweh that alternate with Jeremiah's utterances in a conversational interchange. In these cases Yahweh's utterances are relatively short (a verse or two) and contain no oracle body, only words to Jeremiah. Through chapter 20, Jeremiah frequently records his own lamentations on behalf of Israel in the collection of his prophecies. These lamentations are often not marked explicitly for change of speaker, which must be deduced from shifts in person. LSM is sometimes used to call attention to these sections by introducing oracles that adjoin them.

- LSM at 3:6 introduces an oracle that extends through 3:10. The previous oracle extends from 2:1 through 3:4, in which Yahweh addresses Israel, "Wilt thou not from this time cry unto me, 'My father, thou art the guide of my youth'?" From these first and second person references to God, v. 5 shifts to the third person, "Will he reserve his anger for ever? Will he keep it to the end?" The shift in person suggests that at this point Jeremiah breaks in to plead with the people to hear Yahweh's gracious invitation. The following LSM introduces the next oracle as a response to Jeremiah's cry, and in fact that oracle is entirely addressed to Jeremiah, beginning with the question, "Hast thou [singular] seen what backsliding Israel has done?"
- LSM in 9:12 (E.T. 9:13) responds to v. 12, marked as Jeremiah's by the third person description of Yahweh ("Who is he to whom the mouth of the LORD has spoken?"), a shift from consistent first person statements from Yahweh in the previous verses.
- LSM in 11:6 responds to Jeremiah's words (this time marked explicitly with a quotation formula) in 11:5b.
- LSM occurs three times with utterances by Yahweh in an extended interchange between Yahweh and Jeremiah in 14:1–15:21. The successive sections are shown in Table 3. Yahweh's utterances are shown with the appropriate formula and Jeremiah's with QF or NQF depending on whether there is a quotation formula or no quotation formula. While other formulas (WLC and TSL) can introduce utterances in this interchange, LSM is the most common formula so used and appears consistently in the interior of the complex where confusion might be especially likely.

Table 3. Formulas in interchange.

Yahweh		Jeremiah	
14:1–6	WLC	14:7–9	NQF
14:10a	TSL	14:10b	NQF
14:11–12	LSM	14:13	QF
14:14–18	LSM	14:19–22	NQF
15:1–9	LSM	15:10	NQF
15:11–14	LSM	15:15–18	NQF
15:19–21	TSL		

- LSM sometimes introduces an oracle that does not immediately follow Jeremiah's words, but that is interrupted by an otherwise unmarked utterance of Jeremiah and then resumed without a separate incipit. Following immediately on the oracle of 3:6–10, the oracle that begins with LSM in 3:11 extends through 3:22. There it is interrupted by words spoken by Jeremiah on behalf of the nation in 3:22–25, again unmarked except for shift in person. The original oracle resumes without another incipit at 4:1. LSM in 11:9 also immediately follows a previous oracle, but prepares for Jeremiah's words in 11:17–20 which, in turn, are followed by a continuation of Yahweh's words, without another incipit, in 11:21. Thus LSM, in 11:9 as in 3:11, marks an embedded interchange.

The LSM formula does not usually take margins (except for 3:6), but its function in introducing utterances of Yahweh that are discontinuous from their context is clear from its role in interchanges, and we have already seen that in interchanges it can be parallel with WLC. However, its very marking for interchange means that it marks cohesion with adjacent paragraphs in a way that WLC does not, and thus WLC often indicates a stronger break than does LSM. The extended interchange in chapters 14–15 that we have already examined is an example of this. The first oracle in the series begins with WLC, marking a strong disjunction; and subsequent oracles, integrated with one another by interchange, are introduced either by TSL or by LSM. We will see in section 3.1 that TSL, when introducing an entire oracle, also marks for cohesion with context.

2.3 The word that came to Jeremiah (WTC)

The incipit formula WTC occurs fourteen times.[18] In two cases (46:13 and 50:1) the verb is slightly different.[19] In every case but two (25:1 and 44:1) the formula identifies Yahweh as the speaker.[20] The formula carries an explicit notice of the subject of the oracle four times (25:1, 44:1, 46:13, and 50:1), twice as frequently as WLC. Jeremiah is always identified, and always in the third person. A plural form that does not identify Jeremiah as the recipient appears in 30:4, and similar expressions describe Jeremiah's words to other characters in 45:1 (to Baruch) and 51:59 (to Seraiah).

The WTC formula marks a stronger disjunction than any of the formulas thus far considered. In several of its occurrences, it introduces a series of oracles, as shown in the list that follows, including some that begin with WLC, the strongest disjunction thus far encountered.[21] While WLC can also introduce a series of oracles (chaps. 14–15), none of the components there begins with WTC.

1. WTC, in 11:1, supports a summary clause ("Hear ye the words of this covenant") and dispatch that introduce not only the oracle body of 11:3b–5a, but also LSM oracles in 11:6, 9, and perhaps the entire interchange that extends through chapter 12, and perhaps even chapter 13.
2. The occurrence in 32:1 supports the time margin that governs all of chapters 32 and 33, a span that includes WLC oracles beginning in 32:6, 26, and 33:1.
3. WTC, in 34:8, introduces an extended circumstantial margin that supports a WLC oracle in 34:12–22.
4. WTC, in 35:1, introduces the Rechabite episode, which includes, in addition to narrative text, a WLC oracle, 35:12–17.
5. WTC, in 40:1, appears at a major break in the story, the deliverance of Jeremiah from prison as a result of the Babylonian breach of Jerusalem. The formula is not followed by an oracle body (unless vv. 2–3 are to be viewed as the delivery of a message committed by God to Nebuzaradan!), but by extensive narrative; and the next oracular material begins at 42:7.
6. WTC, in 44:1, introduces not only the oracle that extends through v. 14, but also sets the stage for the discussion between the men of Judah and Jeremiah in vv. 15–23, and Jeremiah's subsequent oracle in vv. 24–30.

In several of these cases, the argument turns on WTC's affinity for margins of time or circumstance, which enables it to set the stage for several succeeding oracles. WTC takes such margins much more frequently than any of the formulas considered so far: seven out of fourteen occurrences,[22] or 50 percent, compared with eight out of twenty-eight, or 29 percent, for WLC[23] and one out of fifteen, or 7 percent, for LSM.[24]

2.4 This word came to Jeremiah (TWC)

The incipit formula TWC[25] appears only three times, in 27:1, 36:1, and 26:1 (where Jeremiah is not identified as the addressee). All three instances carry time margins. The instance in 36:1 is very short, introducing only an instruction to Jeremiah rather than a full oracle; but 26:1 and 27:1 do introduce full oracles, and they also set the stage for narrative material. There is no clear evidence to show whether or not the TWC formula can dominate other incipit formulas.

3. The dispatch and body formulas

The formulas discussed in this section do not take margins of time or circumstance, suggesting that they are not diagnostic of an incipit. If an incipit is missing, some of them may be initial to an oracle, but the independent identity of the oracle must be established on grounds other than the presence of one of these formulas. The first can appear either in a dispatch or an oracle body. The other two appear only in bodies.

3.1 Thus says the LORD (TSL)

The TSL formula[26] occurs 155 times in Jeremiah. It can occasionally introduce a dispatch,[27] but is most common in the body of an oracle, where it is one of several devices that can mark off distinct paragraphs within a single oracle.[28] It thus marks less of a disjunction than the previous formulas.

In addition to marking paragraphs within an oracle, TSL validates the message that it introduces as a word from Yahweh. With the occasional exception of HWL, it is the first evidence that the original audience has that the words they are hearing originate with Yahweh rather than with the prophet. A striking example of this function appears in 2 Samuel in Nathan's speeches to David.

- In 2 Samuel 7, Nathan gives David two contradictory instructions concerning the temple: encouragement to build it in v. 3, and instructions not to in vv. 4–16. The latter message comes from Yahweh and is couched in oracular form and introduced with TSL in v. 5. The initial encouragement is not so marked, and we are to understand that this encouragement represents Nathan's own judgment, which Yahweh corrects with an explicit oracle.
- In 2 Samuel 12, when Nathan rebukes David for his sin with Bathsheba, he begins with a parable that betrays no evidence of its divine origin and thus takes David completely off guard. Only when Nathan begins to give the interpretation does he make clear that he

is delivering a word from Yahweh, and he marks his message appropriately with TSL in v. 7.

A peculiar feature of the syntax of TSL can lead to misunderstanding. Frequently, the formula is introduced by an inferential conjunction such as "for" (29 times)[29] or "therefore" (24 times).[30] The naive parsing of such a construction (say, Proposition 1 + "therefore" + TSL + Proposition 2) is that Proposition 1 is the reason for Yahweh's speech, which has Proposition 2 for its contents. Sometimes this parsing is reasonable. For example, when Proposition 1 describes the sin of the people and Proposition 2 describes Yahweh's coming judgment, it is reasonable to see the decree of judgment, and not just the judgment itself, resulting from the sin. However, this parsing seems stilted for many passages. The one with which this study begins, 29:30-32, is a case in point. Schematically, the oracle body there is of the form TSL + "Because Shemaiah has sinned" + "therefore" + TSL + "I will punish him." If the propositions are taken as the direct objects of the preceding TSLs, the conventional reading results in an uncomfortably deep nesting: The LORD says, "Because Shemaiah sinned, therefore the LORD says, 'I will punish him.'"

An even clumsier example is 24:8: "Like the spoiled figs, which are so spoiled that they cannot be eaten," + כִּי + TSL + "So I will deliver Zedekiah . . . to be exiled." The only reasonable sense for כִּי is the asseverative, "surely, indeed," but this in turn makes sense only with respect to the result, "So I will deliver Zedekiah . . ." The comparison is not between the spoiled figs and the fact of Yahweh's speaking, but between the rejection of spoiled figs and the rejection of Zedekiah.

The naive parsing suggests that the major phrase structure break should fall between TSL and its object. Aronoff (1985) has observed from the Hebrew accentual system that this is rarely the case, and argues more generally that quotation formulas in English as well as Hebrew function more as sentence-level adverbs to the quoted material than as governing propositions. This suggests that we should analyze the discourse relations among propositions introduced by TSL as though the formula were not there. The function of the formula is not to participate in the discourse structure marked by conjunctions such as "for" and "therefore" (or in other such relations among the associated propositions), but rather to mark significant breaks in the oracle and to call attention to the divine origin of the expressions that they introduce. Just as Hebrew indicates the adverbial nature through accentuation, so we might in English show this with punctuation: Like the spoiled figs, so—and this is the Lord speaking—so is Zedekiah.

Sometimes, TSL introduces a dispatch rather than appearing in the body. In all of these cases, the dispatch includes a command not just to speak, but to perform some nonverbal action, usually with obvious symbolic overtones.[31] Even when the nonverbal command is simply "go" or "stand,"[32] the intent may be to emphasize the physical presence of Jeremiah, since sometimes he delivered his messages through other intermediaries.[33] These observations suggest that when the message is to be delivered not only by the prophet's words but also by the symbolism of his actions, these actions themselves need to be authenticated as divine revelation.[34]

3.2 Hear the word of the LORD (HWL)

The sixteen occurrences of HWL[35] are always associated with a designation of the addressee in the vocative. This distribution suggests that the primary function of HWL is to name the addressee within the message. The dispatch often names the addressee but is not part of the message, and in the communicative encounter the addressee would ordinarily be designated nonverbally, by the direction in which the prophet faces and by other gestures. When Yahweh wishes to focus attention on the addressee explicitly, the addressee is named within the body with HWL.

Like TSL, HWL is often the first indication in the words actually spoken to the audience that a message is from Yahweh; it thus serves to authenticate the message as divine. A clear example of this function appears in the contradictory recommendations of Micaiah ben Imlah to King Ahab in 1 Kings 22. Faced with a court full of sycophantic prophets who encourage Ahab's desire to go to war, Micaiah initially agrees facetiously with their recommendation in v. 15. Ahab recognizes that he is not speaking sincerely and challenges him to give a genuine oracle. In v. 19, with an introductory HWL, Micaiah then tells Ahab that God is plotting his destruction. There is no such formula in v. 15, which may be how Ahab recognizes Micaiah's facetiousness.[36]

HWL is a stronger disjunction than TSL. Six out of the sixteen occurrences of HWL (38%) appear at the beginning of the body,[37] nearly twice the proportion that TSL exhibits in comparable positions: twenty-two times immediately after a dispatch[38] and twelve times at the beginning of a delivery body,[39] for a total of 34/154 (22%). Also, HWL is almost always followed immediately by TSL,[40] making TSL the introduction to the "word of the LORD" to which HWL calls attention, while TSL is never followed immediately by HWL.

3.3 Oracle of the LORD (OOL)

The formula "Oracle of the LORD"[41] has long been a source of perplexity. The etymology of the word for "oracle" is unclear, and it has no Hebrew cognates other than an apparently derivative verb in Jer. 23:31. Like all of the formulas (and particularly TSL), OOL marks a body of text as coming from Yahweh (and "oracle" is used ten times elsewhere in the OT to identify a prophet or some other human as the speaker), but scholars have felt there must be more to the story. We will survey meanings of the formula proposed by others before presenting a new and rather different view.

3.3.1 Previous suggestions for OOL

Rendtorff (1954) places the occurrences in Jeremiah into six categories: three major uses, two minor ones, and a residue that is assigned to redactorial activity. Baumgaertel (1961) suggests a seventh, and North (1952) hints at an eighth. The eight categories are as follows:

1. *Paragraph conclusion.* Rendtorff counts thirty-five places[42] where OOL concludes "an independent word of the LORD." OOL's role as a concluding formula has often been suggested. Rendtorff himself notes that it is a part of several other functions. It is the only function cited by Waltke and O'Connor (1990:40.2.3a), who feel it is nearly universal (though "the closure may be slight"). The pairing of TSL at the start of an oracle with OOL at the end is a common occurrence (as Baumgaertel 1961 notes), but far from universal. In particular, the uses of "oracle" to describe human speech (e.g., Balaam in Numbers 24) all introduce, rather than conclude, the material that they mark.[43] North (1952) finds a position near the beginning of a paragraph characteristic as well. I will argue in the next section that the frequent position of OOL at the end of an oracle or paragraph is a secondary consequence of another mechanism, not the primary discourse function that is so often associated with it.
2. *Between parallel cola.* Rendtorff assigns forty-two occurrences to parallel structures. OOL often falls between the cola of a parallel pair in poetic passages, and Rendtorff includes here sixteen passages which he scans as prose but considers to be imitative of poetry. He assesses the function here to be a species of closure.
3. *Bound to introductory formulas.* Rendtorff counts thirty-one occurrences of OOL with fixed formulas, usually at the beginning of oracles. These formulas are characteristically either eschatological notices, such as "Behold the days come" or "In those days," or oath forms, such as "As I live" and "By myself have I sworn." It is

difficult to consider these as evidence of a concluding function, since the formulas themselves are seldom utterance final. At most, OOL might be marking the end of the formula, but it is not clear why the language should need such a mark. I shall argue that, instead of being considered exceptions to a general OOL function of marking juncture, these instances are the most characteristic of OOL's underlying function, one that can be traced in other occurrences as well.

4. *Between accusations and consequences.* In 9:5 (E.T. 9:6) and 23:1, 11, OOL stands between an accusation (*Scheltrede*) and the following consequence (*Drohwort*), introduced by "therefore."[44] Rendtorff notes that Jeremiah differs from other prophets in assigning the accusations to Yahweh rather than to the prophet, and thus sees these as an extension of the concluding function of OOL, marking the end of the accusation.

5. *With rhetorical questions.* In 18:6, 22:16, and 23:28 the formula is associated with rhetorical questions (in the first case, separating such a question from a restatement in the indicative).

6. *Redactorial residue.* Apart from a handful of other cases that Rendtorff considers extensions of his three basic rules, he explains the remaining several dozen cases as marks of attachment for glosses or other supplementary material added to the text, identified either by comparison of MT with LXX, or through the consensus of other scholars. North (1952) argues similarly that wherever OOL occurs other than at the end of a sentence or its beginning (usually with a formula), it should be taken to indicate secondary material. The argument in both cases is more than that an editor has misunderstood the phrase and inserted it randomly. North goes so far as to identify four passages that otherwise seem textually sound as secondary, based solely on the occurrence of OOL! The implication seems to be that the redactor was so eager to pass off additions as genuine that he specifically marked them as of divine origin, in a species of "protesting overmuch."

7. *Indicative versus imperative.* Baumgaertel (1961) suggests that TSL without OOL often introduces specific commands, while the material marked by OOL is indicative or, if imperative, only very general. Jeremiah does use OOL ten times to mark imperatives, mostly calls to repent[45] and instructions to fear not,[46] and Baumgaertel's distinction between "specific" and "general" seems difficult to make precise under these circumstances.

8. *Paragraph-initial.* We have already noticed the observation of North (1952) that OOL often appears near the beginning of a paragraph.

3.3.2 A new view of OOL

While some of the characterizations of OOL in section 3.3.1 account for portions of the data, they leave an embarrassingly large residue that must be attributed to the redactorial dustbin. Furthermore, no common thread is proposed to join the various uses together, no shared mechanism or plausible semantic history that explains why the same expression marks them all. Why should a mark of closure also mark fixed expressions that often occur in the middle of a clause? Why should these occurrences with fixed expressions be deemed original while other interruptions of clause structure by OOL be considered redactorial?

Because OOL is so often characterized as a formula of closure, it is interesting to examine in more detail some examples of this closure:

- OOL in 31:14 clearly ends a paragraph, since the next verse begins with TSL. The paragraph that it ends begins in 3:10 with HWL, and describes the future blessings of God on his people. A long list of active clauses itemizing these blessings concludes in 31:14 with a passive clause, "my people shall be satisfied with my goodness," and then ends with OOL. The final clause is distinct from those before it in two ways. First, it is passive rather than active. Second, it does not name specific groups of people or specific blessings but merely asserts a general sense of satisfaction.
- OOL in 9:5 (E.T. 9:6) concludes a paragraph beginning in v. 3 (E.T. v. 4) on the subject of deceit. The final clause, just before OOL, is "through deceit they refuse to know me," where the pronoun refers to Yahweh. This pronoun is the first mention of Yahweh in the paragraph. The previous descriptions of deception all have to do with the social hazards of deception, not with its theological implications.
- In 48:19–25 the coming judgment on Moab is described. After a detailed list of the towns and regions that will be destroyed, the last verse asserts, "The horn of Moab is cut off, and his arm is broken: OOL." The metaphorical imagery and generality of the final bicolon is in contrast with the literal vocabulary of judgment and detailed list of places in the preceding verses.

These three examples are only a few of many that could be cited. Over and over again, when OOL ends a paragraph, it closes a single clause, or at most a verse, that summarizes or draws a conclusion from the previous clauses. The conventional interpretation of OOL as a mark of closure is that its primary function is to close the paragraph, and the proximity of the summary clause is a coincidence of the inner structure of the paragraph itself. That is, the conventional interpretation sees the paragraph syntax as ((Paragraph Detail + Paragraph Summary) + OOL), with the major structural division between the paragraph summary and OOL, and OOL serving the function of paragraph closure. But we have already noted that this function is far from universal, and even conflicts with other functions of OOL.

Some other examples may help to clarify matters:

- In 5:15–17 the coming of Babylon against Israel is described. The paragraph begins with "Behold, I am bringing against you a nation from afar, O house of Israel: OOL." The following clauses describe various details about this foe: its strange language, effective armaments, and rapacious effect on the land. Only in the initial clause is Yahweh mentioned as the agent of the coming disaster.
- In 7:30–31 the idolatrous practices of the people of Judah are itemized: They have set up idols in the temple precincts and also performed infant sacrifices in Tophet. These specific indictments are preceded by a general statement, "For the children of Judah have done evil in my sight: OOL."
- In 50:35–37, Yahweh calls for a sword against the Chaldeans. After a general announcement of the theme, "A sword upon the Chaldeans! OOL," the paragraph details the various groups against whom the sword will come.

Like the paragraphs examined earlier, these all have a summary or theme clause at one extremity, and they all use OOL. In these cases, OOL comes not at the end of the paragraph, but at its beginning, just after the introductory clause. If OOL marks paragraph closure, these cases (and many like them) are anomalous. But if OOL is marking the summary, they are consistent. That is, these two sets of paragraphs offer support for the hypothesis that OOL and a single clause (or at most a bicolon) form a unit, which then relates at the paragraph level to other clauses. OOL frequently ends up at the end of a paragraph because various sorts of concluding or explanatory clauses with which OOL is associated frequently fall at the end of a paragraph, not because OOL itself marks paragraph juncture.

In short, OOL is a marker of what Callow (1974:52) calls "focus": a highly local highlighting of a clause or phrase that merits the recipient's special attention. It sets off the clause or phrase with which it is associated from the context, as though it were printed in italics or boldface type. In the examples we have seen, it marks the summary clause of a paragraph.[47] In its association with fixed formulas, it underscores these formulas, and in particular the two themes that most of them express, Yahweh's faithfulness to his oath and the promise of restoration of his chastened people in a future day. In other cases, it marks a clause containing a noun later explained through relative clauses, comments, or specializing apposition.[48] In more than half its occurrences, OOL follows a clause that explicitly identifies Yahweh, and thus often focuses attention on his agency, whether as a witness to sins,[49] or as the agent behind disasters,[50] or the source of declared blessings,[51] or the judge who will bring consequences for sin,[52] to name only a few of many examples.

This notion of OOL as a mark of focus at the level of the phrase or clause is a common feature that explains other hypotheses about its significance. We have already seen that it subsumes claims that OOL either begins or ends paragraphs, or marks frequent phrases. The hypothesis is consistent with the use of OOL between parallel cola, as highlighting one or the other colon, and between *Scheltrede* and *Drohwort* (in both cases, often emphasizing a reference to Yahweh). The use with rhetorical questions may be a way of reinforcing the claim on the recipient's attention already posted by the skewing of deep and surface function. The explanation of OOL as a redactorial marker of a gloss is methodologically suspect, but putative glosses are often identified on the grounds that the material they introduce is redundant or superfluous; and when such a gloss is claimed following OOL, the material before OOL is frequently the original material with which the commentator finds the gloss redundant. To put it another way, instead of OOL's introducing superfluous material, it may be viewed as highlighting a statement that will be amplified in what follows. In other words, it marks the head of a discourse unit. The only previous characterization of OOL that cannot be explained as focus is Baumgaertel's distinction between specific commands and indicative statements, a distinction not consistently supported by the data.

Space does not permit a detailed review of all 175 instances of the formula in Jeremiah, and the notion of "focus" is sufficiently broad that the cases do not fall into a set of categories that can be easily summarized. Nevertheless, in most cases, the reason for the focus is clear, and in those cases where it is not, nothing in the context precludes understanding the formula as highlighting the clause or phrase to which it is attached.

There is only one occurrence of OOL that cannot be explained as focus. In 9:21 (E.T. 9:22), Jeremiah is instructing the mourning women on how to bewail Zion's coming destruction. In keeping with standard prophetic diction, the formula ought to be TSL, but Jeremiah replaces "says the LORD"[53] with "Oracle of the LORD,"[54] perhaps to create the image of a novice mourner who hasn't quite learned the vocabulary yet, pressed prematurely into her gruesome service.[55]

4. Conclusions

Three broad conclusions emerge from this study: (1) The various quotation formulas in Jeremiah are closely tied to the three communication events that provide the context for an oracle. (2) They form a well-ordered cline of disjunctive markers. (3) They carry other formula-specific meanings.

4.1 Oracle structure and communication events

An oracle in a writing prophet reflects as many as three communication events: the *committal* from God to the prophet; the *delivery* from the prophet to the original audience; and the *report* from the compiler of the prophetic book to the readers. These events are reflected in the different components of an oracle: the incipit (which introduces the report of the committal), the background and dispatch (which belong to the committal), and the body (which is included in both the committal and the delivery). Table 2 shows how the various quotation formulas in Jeremiah are associated with specific components, and thus with specific communication events. These formulas, together with other indications such as delivery settings, enable the interpreter to reconstruct the underlying communication events reflected in the text.

4.2 The disjunctive cline

The quotation formulas not only help identify the communications context of the components of an oracle, but also reflect the hierarchical structuring (e.g., paragraph, section, division, complete work) that regularly characterizes verbal communication. The distinction among the various communication events provides the highest level of this hierarchy: the incipit formulas mark successive reports, within which details about committal and delivery are lower-level sections. Thus the incipit formulas mark stronger disjunctions than do the others.

Within the incipit formulas, WTC is the strongest, since it can introduce extended sections within which WLC occurs. WLC in turn dominates LSM, while none of the reverse orderings appears. The contexts in which the three instances of TWC appear are too restricted to situate this formula in the sequence.

Within the other formulas and within the body of an oracle, HWL dominates TSL, which in turn dominates OOL. The occurrence of TSL but not HWL with dispatches is superficially an exception to this order, since the break between dispatch and body is stronger than that between successive elements of the body. However, the formulas have other functions besides marking disjunction. In particular, the universal use of vocatives with HWL shows that it appears only when there is a need to encode the recipient explicitly, and this need does not arise in the dispatch. OOL is disjunctively the weakest of the formulas, and in fact is not disjunctive at all, but provides focus at the phrase or clause level.

This ordering is consistent with the relative frequencies of the various formulas. In a hierarchical structure with fan-out greater than one, lower-level entities will be more plentiful than higher-level ones. Table 1 shows that if we restrict our attention to just incipit formulas or just formulas besides the rare TWC, the ordering from least common to most common corresponds with that which emerges from our analysis. Furthermore, with the exception of HWL and TWC, the rule holds for the entire set of formulas, and we have already argued that other conditions besides hierarchical structure restrict the appearance of HWL.

The formulas that are disjunctive have consistent relative disjunctive force, but they are not the only markers of hierarchical structure in Jeremiah. For example, three instances of WLC introduce successive sections of chapter 33: vv. 1-18, 19-22, and 23-26, suggesting that these are of parallel hierarchical rank, but semantic and vocabulary correlations suggest that they are really successive extractions and amplifications. The 1-18 section ends in 17-18 with a separate paragraph (introduced by TSL) promising the perpetuity of the Davidic and Levitical ministries. This single theme from the several in 33:1-18 becomes the sole focus of 19-22. Verses 23-26 in turn focus even further, repeating only the promise concerning David. Figure 2 provides a graphic representation:

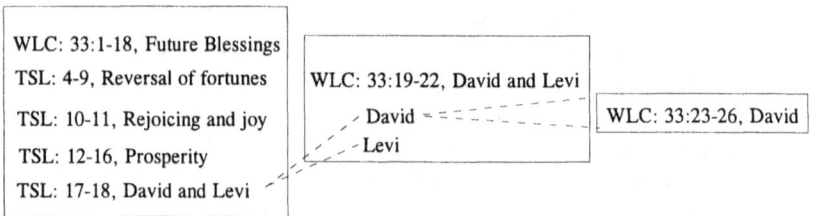

Figure 2: Use of a single formula at different hierarchical levels.

Semantically, each of the three main sections is a component of, and thus subordinate to, the previous one. The effect of introducing each with the same high-ranking quotation formula is the same as that obtained on a stage by successively narrowing the spotlight. The perpetuity of David may be only a part of the promises of chapter 33, but it is the part to which we should pay the closest attention.

4.3 Other formula meanings

In addition to encoding communicative context and reflecting the hierarchical structure of the text, several of the quotation formulas carry specific meanings:

- LSM marks the oracles it introduces as part of a conversational interchange.
- HWL, TSL, and OOL attest the divine authorship of the oracle body (and, in the case of TSL, the symbolic import of the dispatch). The usage of inferential conjunctions ("for," "therefore") with TSL and the occurrences of OOL in the middle of propositions suggest that these formulas stand in an adverbial relation to the material they mark, rather than governing it as direct discourse. This insight relieves the awkwardness that Western readers feel when confronted with the deep nesting that emerges from a traditional parsing.
- HWL explicitly encodes the final recipients within the body of an oracle.
- OOL is a low-level focus formula and often marks a summary that is expanded either earlier or later in the same paragraph.

Notes

1. The renderings are my own, but intentionally follow traditional versions wherever possible to help readers follow the argument in their own texts.

2. Some (e.g., Holladay 1986:1) suggest that this is the date of Jeremiah's birth, rather than of his first prophecy. The difference is immaterial for this study.

3. 21:1-4; 27:1-4; 37:6-10. Compare the paradigmatic description of prophecy in Exod. 7:1-2, in which the message moves from God to Moses to Aaron and then to Pharaoh.

4. Van Selms (1976) describes the phenomenon in chaps. 42, 44, and 45, and suggests that it is unique to the Book of Jeremiah. A mechanism of this sort appears to be involved as well in the confusing discourse structure of chap. 29.

5. Meier (1992:264) recognizes that "there is an intense concern to identify not only who speaks but how this message is transferred from God to his spokesman and subsequently to God's people," but does not leverage this important insight in distinguishing the roles of the various formulas.

6. 21:3; 25:15, 27, 30; 27:2-4; 29:24.

7. Only twice does an incipit formula appear in a delivery, and only once (32:6) is it the incipit for the oracle corresponding to the delivery. In 25:3 there is an embedded report of earlier prophecies, not a description of the committal of the prophecy of which this is a delivery.

8. The solitary exception is 30:4. In this oracle (beginning in 30:1), the Lord dispatches Jeremiah to write out his message, rather than speak it, and the report of Jeremiah's obedience (which corresponds structurally to a delivery, though there is no immediate audience) begins with the formulaic "these are the words that the Lord spoke," וְאֵלֶּה הַדְּבָרִים אֲשֶׁר דִּבֶּר יְהוָה.

9. The syntax of 45:2-3 is complicated by the mingling of different speech events in a single report (Van Selms 1976), and does not constitute a clear exception.

10. In order to make this study more accessible to readers without a detailed knowledge of Hebrew, I have used simple English translations in the body of the text. The Hebrew forms of the formulas, together with their variants, are discussed in notes to the detailed discussion of each formula in sec. 2.

11. Compare the relation of indicatives with other moods in paragraph structure, the analysis of binding of clause modifiers in Greek by Hollenbach (1985), and the exposition of the structure of the Hebrew paragraph by Longacre (1989).

12. וַיְהִי/הָיָה דְבַר־יְהוָה (אֵלַי/אֶל־יִרְמְיָהוּ]) 'the word of Yahweh came (to me/to Jeremiah)': 1:4, 11, 13; 2:1; 13:3, 8; 14:1; 16:1; 18:5; 24:4; 25:3; 28:12; 29:30; 32:6, 26; 33:1, 19, 23; 34:12; 35:12; 36:27; 37:6; 39:15; 42:7; 43:8; 46:1; 47:1; 49:34. While 1:2 (with prefixed אֲשֶׁר 'which, that') is superficially similar to 14:1; 46:1; 47:1; and 49:34, its position as an embedded relative clause is unique, and it is not included here.

13. In 25:3 Jeremiah is including a report of an earlier oracle in a later one, and in 32:6 an unusually full delivery includes a complete report of the committal. These may appear to be exceptions, but they are not.

14. 1:4, 11, 13; 2:1; 13:3, 8; 16:1; 18:5; 24:4; 25:3; 32:6.

15. This last section may consist of as many as six oracles, but the distinction among them must be made on more subtle grounds, and is not marked by formulas (Aitken 1984).

16. With עַל 'on' or אֶל 'to'.

17. וַיֹּאמֶר יְהוָה (אֵלַי) 'Yahweh said to me)': 1:7, 9, 12, 14; 3:6, 11; 9:12; 11:6, 9; 13:6; 14:11, 14; 15:1, 11; 24:3.

18. הַדָּבָר אֲשֶׁר (הָיָה [מֵאֵת יְהוָה/דִּבֶּר יְהוָה]) אֶל/עַל/בְּיַד יִרְמְיָהוּ 'the word which (was from Yahweh/Yahweh spoke) to/on Jeremiah': 7:1; 11:1; 18:1; 21:1; 25:1; 30:1; 32:1; 34:1, 8; 35:1; 40:1; 44:1; 46:13; 50:1.

19. דִּבֶּר 'spoke' instead of הָיָה 'was': הַדָּבָר אֲשֶׁר דִּבֶּר יְהוָה אֶל־יִרְמְיָהוּ 'the word which Yahweh spoke to Jeremiah'.

20. Either as the subject (in the דִּבֶּר 'spoke' cases) or with מֵאֵת יְהוָה 'from Yahweh' (when the verb is הָיָה 'was').

21. 25:1 (WTC), 3 (WLC), is only superficially an example of this phenomenon, since the WLC oracle is not a component of the WTC section, but simply a report of an earlier oracle that has been embedded in the delivery of a later one. However, the pattern is amply attested in other passages, as outlined below.

22. 21:1; 25:1; 32:1; 34:1, 8; 35:1; 40:1.

23. 25:3; 28:12; 33:1; 36:27; 39:15; 42:7; 47:1; 49:34.

24. 3:6.

25. הָיָה הַדָּבָר הַזֶּה (אֶל־יִרְמְיָה[וּ]) מֵאֵת יְהוָה 'there was this word (to Jeremiah) from Yahweh'.

26. כֹּה אָמַר יְהוָה 'thus said Yahweh': The count includes 46:25, which omits כֹּה, but otherwise functions in the same way as other instances. The divine name is often augmented with other titles.

27. 13:1; 17:19; 19:1; 22:1; 26:2; 27:2, 4; 30:2; 34:2; 35:13 (27:4 is interesting because it is a dispatch given by Jeremiah to the ambassadors of the confederate kings, embedded in the body of a commission!).

28. Drawing on the analysis of Haggai and Zechariah in Clark (1985), Meier (1992:297) is uncomfortable relying on TSL (and OOL) as "a guide to the macrostructure of the text." This caution is certainly appropriate in the case of OOL, but in Jeremiah TSL is regularly paragraph initial.

29. כִּי 'that': 4:3, 27; 6:6; 10:18; 16:3, 5, 9; 20:4; 22:6, 11; 24:8; 25:15; 27:19, 21; 28:14; 29:8, 10, 16; 30:5, 12; 31:7; 32:15, 42; 33:4, 17; 42:18; 48:40; 49:12; 51:33.

30. לָכֵן 'therefore': 5:14; 6:21; 7:20; 9:7, 15; 11:11, 21, 22; 14:15; 15:19; 18:13; 22:18; 23:2, 15, 38; 28:16; 29:32; 32:28; 34:17; 35:17, 19; 44:11; 50:18; 51:36.

31. 13:1 (wear a linen girdle); 19:1 (get a clay bottle); 25:15 (take a wine cup); 27:2 (make bonds and yokes); 30:2 (write the words in a book); 32:14 (seal real estate documents in a jar).

32. 17:19; 22:1; 26:2; 34:2; 35:13.

33. 21:1–4; 27:1–4; 37:6–10.

34. The converse is not true. In all the following examples the prophet is dispatched to perform some nonverbal action, but without attaching TSL: 1:17; 2:2; 3:12; 7:2 (cf. 17:19; 26:2!); 13:3, 6; 18:2; 19:10–11; 28:13; 36:2,28; 39:16; 43:9. More study is needed into the conditions for attaching TSL to a dispatch.

35. שִׁמְעוּ דְבַר־יְהוָה 'hear the word of Yahweh': 2:4; 7:2; 9:19; 17:20; 19:3; 21:11; 22:2, 29; 29:20; 31:10; 34:4; 42:15; 44:24, 26. The count also includes רְאוּ דְבַר־יְהוָה 'heed the word of Yahweh' (2:31), and also אֶת־הַדָּבָר אֲשֶׁר דִּבֶּר יְהוָה שִׁמְעוּ 'hear the word which Yahweh speaks' (10:1), which also carry vocatives; 50:45 is different both in form and function. The inflection of the verb varies according to the addressee.

36. This example differs from the instances in Jeremiah in that it contains no explicit reference to the addressee, reminding us of the need to be cautious in extrapolating results from one writer to another.

37. 7:2; 17:20; 19:3; 21:11; 22:2; 44:24.

38. 2:2; 8:4; 11:3; 13:12, 13; 15:2; 18:11; 19:11; 21:4, 8; 25:27, 28; 26:4; 27:4; 28:13; 29:25, 31; 34:2b; 36:29; 39:16; 43:10; 45:4.

39. 19:15; 26:18; 27:16; 28:2, 11; 29:2; 32:3, 14; 35:18; 38:2, 17; 42:9.

40. Exceptions are 2:31; 9:19; 31:10; 44:26. The first three of these are elaborated or varied beyond the basic formula.

41. (יְהוָה) נְאֻם, rendered "saith [Yahweh]" in older translations. Jeremiah uses the expression 175 times, including four cases where יְהוָה 'Yahweh' is preceded by אֲדֹנָי 'my Lord' and three cases where it is replaced with הַמֶּלֶךְ 'the king'.

42. All counts from Rendtorff are in Jeremiah.

43. These other instances are critical to the suggestion of Baumgaertel (1961) that the differences between TSL and OOL can be traced to the two major sources of revelation in Israel, the priestly organization (which gave rise to the TSL formula), and the ecstatic *Nabiʾ* (from which OOL originated). His argument is weakened somewhat by the regular occurrence of OOL with specific commands in Ezekiel 43–48, a decidedly priestly section. It may be refined to a more acceptable form if we notice that throughout the prophets OOL tends to be utterance final, while outside of the prophets (for example, in the histories of David and Balaam), it is utterance initial. If we restrict our attention to comparing utterance-initial formulas, OOL is indeed associated strongly with the ecstatic prophets and TSL might well be assigned to the priests. By the time of the writing prophets, any such distinction has disappeared. In the eighth century, Isaiah arguably uses OOL both to begin (1:24; 56:8?) and to end utterances, but by the sixth century OOL has become specialized as a post-utterance formula, and in this position has gained a new function, which will emerge from our analysis in the next section. Meier (1992:305-6) cites Jer. 9:21 and Zech. 12:1 as examples of later utterance-initial OOL, but the explanation developed in this paper can apply to Zech. 12:1 as utterance final, and Jer. 9:21 (כֹּה נְאֻם יְהוָה 'thus saith Yahweh') is discussed as a special case below.

44. לָכֵן.

45. 3:1, 12, 13, 14.

46. 30:10; 42:11; 46:28. The other instances are 2:12 (call for cosmic witnesses in a רִיב 'law case'); 49:30 (warning to Hazor to flee from Nebuchadnezzar); and 50:21 (command to an unspecified army to attack Babylon in the last times).

47. Compare also 8:13; 17:24; 34:22; 39:17.

48. 7:13; 15:3; 16:5; 21:13; 23:30, 31; 29:11, 19a; 34:17; 44:29; 51:25.

49. 7:11; 23:11; 29:23; 48:30.

50. 5:15; 8:13; 23:12; 48:38, 44.

51. 32:44; 34:5.

52. 5:9, 29; 23:2; 27:8.

53. אָמַר יְהוָה 'says Yahweh'.

54. נְאֻם יְהוָה 'oracle of Yahweh'.

55. The converse interchange, with the phrase אָמַר יְהוָה 'says Yahweh' appearing where נְאֻם יְהוָה 'Oracle of the LORD' would be expected, occurs in 30:3 and 49:2.

References

Aitken, K. T. 1984 The oracles against Babylon in Jeremiah 50-51: Structure and perspectives. *Tyndale Bulletin* 35:25-63.

Aronoff, M. 1985. Orthography and linguistic theory: The syntactic basis of Massoretic Hebrew punctuation. *Language* 61:28-72.

Baumgaertel, F. 1961. Die Formel *ne'um jahwe*. *Zeitschrift für die alttestamentliche Wissenschaft* 73(3):277-90.

Callow, K. 1974. *Discourse considerations in translating the Word of God.* Grand Rapids: Zondervan.

Clark, D. 1985. Discourse structure in Zechariah 7:1-8:23. *Bible Translator* 36:328-35.

Holladay, W. L. 1986. *Jeremiah 1: A commentary on the book of the prophet Jeremiah chapters 1-25.* Philadelphia: Fortress.

Hollenbach, B. E. 1985. Two constraints on subordination in New Testament Greek. *Selected Technical Articles Related to Translation* 14:1-16.

Longacre, Robert E. 1989. *Joseph: A story of divine providence: A text theoretical and textlinguistic analysis of Genesis 37 and 39-48.* Winona Lake, Ind.: Eisenbrauns.

Meier, S. A. 1992. *Speaking of speaking: Marking direct discourse in the Hebrew Bible. Vetus Testamentum Supplements* 46. Leiden: Brill.

North, F. S. 1952. The expression the oracle of Yahweh as an aid to critical analysis. *Journal of Biblical Literature* 71.

Parunak, H. V. D. 1981. Oral typesetting: Some uses of biblical structure. *Biblica* 62(2):153-68.

———. 1982. Transitional techniques in the Bible. *Journal of Biblical Literature* 102(4):525-48.

———. 1983. Some axioms for literary architecture. *Semitics* 8:1-16.

———. 1993. The dimensions of discourse structure: A multidimensional analysis of the components and transitions of Paul's Epistle to the Galatians. In *Linguistics and New Testament interpretation,* ed. D. Black. Nashville: Broadman.

Pritchard, J. B. 1969. *Ancient Near Eastern texts relating to the Old Testament.* Princeton, N.J.: Princeton University Press.

Rendtorff, R. 1954. Zum Gebrauch der Formel *ne'um jahwe* im Jeremiabuch. *Zeitschrift für die alttestamentliche Wissenschaft* 66:27-37.

Van Selms, A. 1976. Telescoped discussion as a literary device in Jeremiah. *Vetus Testamentum* 26:99-112.

Waltke, B. K., and M. O'Connor. 1990. *An introduction to Biblical Hebrew syntax.* Winona Lake, Ind.: Eisenbrauns.

21

THE POETIC PROPERTIES OF PROPHETIC DISCOURSE IN THE BOOK OF MICAH

Francis I. Andersen

This is an analysis of the prosody of the prophetic compositions in the Book of Micah, using criteria of grammar, rhythm, and thematic patterns. It shows that Micah's poetic units are of variable shapes and sizes. The preferential use of shorter lines in some poems is associated with greater emotional intensity.

In this article four tables are presented to show from different perspectives that Micah used many kinds of units to build his poetry. His *words* range in length from one to six syllables. *Cola* range in length from one to eight words and from three to fifteen syllables. Any number of cola, from one upwards, make the next highest units. *Monocola* range in length from four to fourteen syllables; *bicola* from 8 to 27; *tricola* from 14 to 30. (In the tabulation a quatrain of four cola is treated as two bicola and larger units similarly as various combinations of colon, bicolon, tricolon.)

These estimates of the number of syllables in the cola of Micah are, of course, no better than the division of the text into the cola for which counts have been made. (I have followed the Masoretic cantillations in nearly every case.) The compositional units of a poem in the Hebrew Bible can be identified and described with reference to at least four features of verbal art—quantity (syllable counts), prosodies or speech rhythms (Masoretic accent signs), rhythm (words, beats, pauses), and theme (parallelism, matching terms). Sometimes these considerations work together to yield an identification of poetic units that no one will dispute. But sometimes the structures indicated by these several rhetorical dimensions do not coincide; they might even pull against one another. Then the researcher must decide which feature dominates the others.

The individual oracles or poems can be isolated with reasonable assurance; these units are likewise varied. (We do not find it appropriate to talk of strophes.) In Table 1 twenty-seven such "poems" are recognized, ranging in length from four to thirty-three cola (36 to 262 syllables). The entire book is characterized by variety throughout; there is no section that shows a marked preference for any particular pattern. The average colon length for the whole book comes out at 7.6 syllables. This is a little below the classical norm of 8 syllables (better, 16 syllables per bicolon). Each of the "Books" has a different average: Book I has 7.3, Book II 8.1, Book III 7.7 (Table 1). There is a range within each book for the average length of cola in each of its "poems." For Book I it is 5.5–8.0, for Book II 6.8–9.8, for Book III 6.9–8.5.

Table 1. Colon length in terms of syllables in the Book of Micah

Unit	Syllables	MT	Cola	Syl./Colon	Monocola	Bicola	Tricola
1:2-9	262	263	33	7.9	-	15	1
1:10-16	182	179	33	5.5	-	15	1
2:1-5	165	166	22	7.5	1	9	1
2:6-11	159	161	22	7.2	-	5	4
2:12-13	80	78	10	8.0	-	2	2
3:1-4	136	134	17	8.0	-	4	3
3:5-8	151	150	19	7.9	-	8	1
3:9-12	132	134	17	7.8	-	7	1
Total 1	*1267*	*1265*	*173*	*7.3*	*1*	*65*	*14*
4:1-5	220	218	28	7.9	2	10	2
4:6-8	104	104	13	8.0	1	3	2
4:9-10	75	75	11	6.8	1	2	2
4:11-13	106	106	12	8.8	1	4	1
4:14	29	29	4	7.3	-	2	-
5:1-3	105	101	14	7.5	-	7	-
5:4-5	85	84	10	8.5	-	2	2
5:6	45	43	6	7.5	-	3	-
5:7-8	64	64	8	8.0	-	4	-
5:9-14	127	140	13	9.8	1	6	-
Total 2	*960*	*964*	*119*	*8.1*	*6*	*43*	*9*
6:1-5	145	150	17	8.5	2	6	1
6:6-7	68	65	8	8.5	-	4	-
6:8	33	36	4	8.3	-	2	-
6:9-12	86	88	11	7.8	1	2	2
6:13-16	123	127	17	7.2	1	8	-
7:1-6	178	180	25	7.1	-	11	1
7:7-12	173	175	25	6.9	-	11	1
7:13-17	135	141	17	7.9	-	7	1
7:18-20	85	86	10	8.5	2	4	-
Total 3	*1026*	*1048*	*134*	*7.7*	*6*	*55*	*6*
Total	**3253**	**3277**	**426**	**7.6**	**13**	**163**	**29**

As shown in Table 2, one-word cola range in length from 3 to 5 syllables, two-word cola from 3 to 10 syllables, three-word cola from 7 to 11, and so on. The longest colon by syllables (15) has only four words (5:12a—we would be forcing it to read a bicolon); and the longest by words (eight words) has only 13 syllables (6:5a)—hardly enough for a bicolon unless there are strong indications from parallelism, which accounts for the fairly large number of bicola of 13 syllables or fewer that we have recognized in Table 3.

Table 2. Colon length measured by number of words

Syllables per colon	Words per colon								Cola	Sylla-bles
	1	2	3	4	5	6	7	8		
3	3	2	-	-	-	-	-	-	5	15
4	1	15	7	-	-	-	-	-	23	92
5	1	20	16	2	-	-	-	-	39	195
6	-	30	32	10	-	-	-	-	72	432
7	-	14	28	16	1	-	-	-	59	413
8	-	6	51	28	4	1	-	-	90	720
9	-	7	29	25	4	2	-	-	67	603
10	-	1	10	15	3	2	-	-	31	310
11	-	-	2	9	9	1	-	-	21	231
12	-	-	-	3	8	-	-	-	11	132
13	-	-	-	-	2	-	-	1	3	39
14	-	-	-	-	2	2	-	-	4	56
15	-	-	-	1	-	-	-	-	1	
Total cola	5	95	175	109	33	8	-	1	426	
Total words	5	190	525	436	165	48	-	8	1377	
Total syls.	18	565	1287	931	354	85	-	13		3253
Syl./word	3.6	2.8	2.5	2.1	2.1	1.8	-	1.6	Mean 2.4	

Most bicola fall in the range 12–18 syllables (Table 3). There is no distinct peak in the histograph. The colon lengths that occur most often are 17 syllables (22×) and 14 syllables (21×). There are just as many 12-syllable cola as 15-syllable cola (16×), just as many 18-syllable cola as 13-syllable cola (15×). The length of all the units we have recognized as bicola ranges from 8 to 27 syllables.

Of the three spectra shown in Table 3, the shortest and longest cola are problematical. A colon of one word, or of 3 or 4 syllables, would not pass muster with most students of Hebrew prosody. The overlap of the three spectra in Table 3 suggests that a long monocolon (say, 12 syllables or more) might be construed as a bicolon. Since 8 syllables is the standard length of a colon, an 8-syllable bicolon calls for justification. Why not read it as a colon? Our reason for retaining most short bicola is usually the occurrence of classical parallelism between two short cola. The alternative is to have a monocolon with *internal* parallelism as a *single* unit.

Table 3. Length of poetic units measured by syllables

Length	Colon	Bicolon	Tricolon
4	1		
7	1		
8	2	2	
9	2	3	
10	1	4	
11	1	8	1
12	2	16	
13	1	15	
14	2	21	1
15		16	1
16		19	1
17		22	1
18		15	4
19		6	3
20		5	3
21		4	2
22		3	1
23		1	2
24		1	1
26		1	2
27		1	1
28			1
29			3
30			1
Total	13	163	29
Syl./colon	10	7.7	7.1

Length, however measured, is not the only thing to be taken into account for the identification of poetic units, certainly not in prophetic poetry, unless we declare that prophets had to keep to the rhythmic severity of Hebrew epic, lyrical, wisdom, and cultic poetry, in which the majority of bicola have sixteen syllables. All the features and devices that contribute to the total artistic effect of oracular poetry have to be considered when we try to map the patterns and structures of prophetic compositions.

Throughout the analysis that yielded the data in these tables we have recognized continually that there is a margin of indeterminacy involved in identifying any kind of unit—except the orthographic word (we have no warrant for revising this most ancient part of the textual tradition). Although the delimitation of poetic cola is often unequivocal, it is often enough for an assurance that we have poetry in the Book of Micah. Some scholars have considered other options, including the dismal conclusion that it is bad poetry, or not poetry, or a corrupted text. The margins of uncertainty are ineluctable; but no matter how we negotiate the options, a wide variety of formal features would remain in the outcome. Micah's poetic art is not the result of "regularity." He does not prefer any particular kind of colon, nor any particular kind of bicolon.

A typical dilemma is presented by a unit that is a clause with no parallelism and that is long enough to be one bicolon—the notorious "synthetic" parallelism of Lowth (1971). Some such periods in Micah are almost long enough for three cola (e.g., 4:5b with its nineteen syllables). There may be no natural break in such a unit to assist location of the caesura so that it can be laid out as a bicolon. Here the cantillations are of prime value. They map the prosodies or speech melodies heard in reading; that is, they reflect the rhythms and cadences that make a text poetic, even when the assistance usually afforded by parallelism is lacking. To all intents such a clause is indistinguishable from prose. The retention of such a portion of text as an integral part of the poem has to be argued on the basis of thematic cohesion rather than prosody. Considerations of length or rhythm (in terms of beats) might have some weight if we knew that these must be regular. But this guideline does not help much because there are so many indications that Micah uses cola of a wide range of length, even when poetry is recognized by everyone.

There is another dilemma related to this question of the bounds of colon length. We see it in a concentrated form in 1:10–16, which can be read as thirty-three short cola or as sixteen long cola. Perhaps two very short clauses were recited as just one colon, even when there was parallelism *within* that colon. In the limit case, one word, usually a verb, is enough for a whole clause. But in many instances two verbs in succession are coordinated in one colon: other factors override a purely grammatical analysis. Here grammar and quantity and parallelism work against one another.

It follows from all this that the analysis can sometimes be done plausibly in more than one way, depending on which consideration is believed to be paramount. It is a false escape from this predicament arbitrarily to declare one property of poetry to be definitive and dominant, yielding the "correct" result. All factors are present, now in harmony, now in discord. More than one display might be needed to exhibit concomitant, but incongruent, structures. The aggregation of the syllable counts in Table 1 is only one of several possible ways of reading the data. Alternatives have been considered in the preparation of the data. If we had joined up more contiguous pairs of short cola to make long cola, the mean colon length would have been greater. With a bit of ingenuity, they could have been adjusted nearer to the classical norm. But it would have been begging the question to have gone in that direction. We cannot and should not force the issue. All we can say is that the mean length of cola for the whole book could be as short as 7 syllables (but hardly shorter) or as long as 8 (but hardly longer). In any case, the lengths are distributed around the classical norm. This is partly because a lot of unequivocal cola are just like what we meet in Psalms and wisdom poems (two-thirds are in the range of 6 to 9 syllables); partly because a very short and very long colon often make a standard bicolon (three-quarters of bicola are in the range of 12 to 18 syllables). The position of the caesura is quite variable.

As we see in Table 1, each of the three "Books" in Micah has a different mean length for cola. The "poems" within each Book similarly disclose a range of mean colon lengths (Table 4). In Book I, five of the poems are near enough to the norm of 8 syllables per colon; two (2:1–5, 2:6–11) have shorter cola on the average; one (1:10–16) is the outlier, with 5.5 syllables per colon. The outlier at the other extreme is 5:9–14, with 9.8 syllables per colon. Both of these outliers have been studied closely to see if some other reading of the prosody might be feasible. We could have joined up the short cola in 1:10–16 in pairs to make as few as sixteen long cola; but then the mean (11.4 syllables per colon) would have been just as far away from the norm on the other side. It would have been patently bending the evidence if we had chosen the second reading just to make the average for the whole book come out nearer the standard of 8 syllables per colon. We see no way of avoiding the conclusion that in 1:10–16 Micah has deliberately and consistently used very short cola. It is different with the thirteen cola in 5:9–14. Each colon (except 5:14b) is a complete clause; none lends itself to identification as a bicolon. Here we must accept the conclusion that Micah has deliberately and consistently used long cola. We must therefore soften the stipulation of Geller (1982:66), who says, "The only surviving indisputable phonetic limitation of biblical verse is the relative brevity of the poetic line in relation to prose."

The range in Book III is not as wide as in the rest of Micah. Book III begins and ends with long cola. In the middle are three sections (6:13–7:12) in which the length of the cola is much shorter than average. Examination of the seven "poems" that have a mean length of 7.3 syllables or less per colon (Table 4) shows that colon length and mood are in complementary distribution. The seven poems with the shortest cola are the most emotional in the book, and the poetic lines are short and jumpy—to the point of incoherence in the case of 1:10–16. They register profoundly disturbed states of mind: grief (1:10–16; 7:1–6), anguish (4:9–10; 4:14), indignation (2:6–11; 6:13–16, which is also rather incoherent), and in one case jubilation (7:7–12). In contrast, oracles of salvation and hope achieve

Table 4. Mean colon length of the sections of Micah

Mean colon length	Sections (Book I, *Book II*, **Book III**)
5.5 syllables	1:10–16
6.8 syllables	*4:9–10*
6.9 syllables	**7:7–12**
7.1 syllables	**7:1–6**
7.2 syllables	2:6–11; **6:13–16**
7.3 syllables	*4:14*
7.5 syllables	2:1–5; *5:1–3; 5:6*
7.8 syllables	3:9–12; **6:9–12**
7.9 syllables	1:2–9; 3:5–8; *4:1–5*; **7:13–17**
8.0 syllables	2:12–13; 3:1–4; *4:6–8; 5:7–8*
8.3 syllables	**6:8**
8.5 syllables	*5:4–5;* **6:1–5; 6:6–7; 7:18–20**
8.8 syllables	*4:11–13*
9.8 syllables	*5:9–14*

stately and serene effects through the use of longer cola. The calm deliberation of the judgment speech in 5:9–14 is awesome.

Renaud (1977:65) finds this kind of contrast even between successive lines of the same oracle. "The slowness of [chap. 2] v 1a (with four stresses) contributes very well to the solemnity of an oracle's beginning, just as in v 2 the *qînâ* rhythm (3+2) translates admirably the lamentable situation created by the exactions of the rich."

These observations bring into view an interesting structural relationship within Book II. The unit 4:11–13 has very long cola (the mean being 8.8 syllables per colon). It is flanked by pieces characterized by very short cola. In colon length, 4:14 has affinity with 4:9–10, and the two pieces can be identified as one poem wrapped around 4:11–13. The latter is thus the centerpiece of the Book of Visions, with a positive note matching that of the opening and closing visions.

Of the 426 cola isolated, 384 have been paired to yield 192 bicola. (Some of these bicola are discontinuous, making an envelope construction around one or two cola; 29 are in tricola as shown in Table 3.) The remaining 42 cola are either real one-colon units in the structure (we count 13) or else might link with a nearby unit (not necessarily contiguous) to make a tricolon. We recognize that these smallest discrete units often join together to make tetracola, pentacola, and larger; but here we are interested mainly in the size of the bicola, which are most frequent. The only thing that we have omitted from the reckoning is the title (1:1).

When there is good parallelism, the identity of a bicolon and the place of the caesura that breaks it into its constituent cola are rarely in doubt; and there are enough of these to warrant the hypothesis that the prophecy is poetic—a poem or a collection of oracular poems. When there is little or no parallelism, the identity of the unit might still be clear (sometimes because it is a well-formed grammatical unit, often because its boundaries are marked by default at the clear bounds of its more poetic neighbors). When there is little or no parallelism, which is often the case, the position of the caesura is indeterminate; and in some cases we do not make strong claims for the display of such a unit as two cola. When the grammar is unclear, the boundaries of a unit and of its constituent cola may be hard to map.

The thirteen units identified as each just one colon range from 4 to 14 syllables in length (Table 1). (The range would extend even to 19 if we had included 4:5b.) A colon length of 14 syllables might seem overly long by classical standards, but this upper limit for a stand-alone colon is inside the range of length found for cola within bicola and tricola; it is not just a peculiarity of single cola. A longer individual colon might have been called a bicolon, but it is not appropriate to use that term if the unit consists of just one clause with no break. The long clause in 6:4b, "And I sent before you Moses, Aaron, and Miriam," is certainly part of the poem, but it would be artificial to scan it as two cola in parallel.

The range in the length of units we have identified as bicola is similarly wide (8 through 27 syllables). The very short ones have been classified as bicola because of their undeniable inner parallelism; the two short bicola in 7:8b and 7:9a, for example, have clearly marked clause boundaries. At the other end of the range the very long bicola have not been patient of division into three or four well-marked cola, not even the 27-syllable bicolon in 2:3.

We have identified twenty-nine units as tricola because each is one integral grammatical period divisible into three parallel pieces. The tricola range in length from 11 (1:11a) to 30 syllables. The next shortest (4:8a) is admittedly problematic; but for the next shortest (4:10b) we have followed the Masoretic punctuation as well as the parallelism and evident meter, all of which show that it is a tricolon. The longest tricolon (3:3a) can hardly be read any other way. Yet, compared with the large number of bicola with more than 20 syllables, a tricolon with a average colon length of 10 syllables is not out of the field. In fact 5:12, with 26 syllables, can only be read as two cola, one of which has 15 syllables.

Another interesting feature of Micah's poetry is revealed in Tables 2 and 3. The number of syllables in any poetic unit depends on both the number of words and the length of those words. *The more words used in a colon, the shorter those words tend to be.* When there is only one word in a colon, the mean length is 3.6 syllables per word (Table 2); when there are eight words, the mean length is 1.6 syllables per word. The average monocolon has 10 syllables; the average tricolon has 7.1 syllables per colon (Table 3). Thus the range of length in terms of the number of syllables does not go up in proportion to the range of length as measured by the number of words. Amazingly, the longest colon by word count (6:5a), which is eight words long, has only 13 syllables.

The extraordinary range of the lengths of Micah's poetic units, by any method of counting, is matched by a similar range of patterns used, covering everything from bicola of classical size and shape with all kinds of parallelism, including little or none, up to long proselike units with no parallelism at all. The conventions for prophecy, whether spoken messages or written texts, resemble only partly the conventions of classical Hebrew poetry. There is more freedom, more room for originality, more variety. Instead of expecting the prophet to speak or write like a psalmist, we should let him do it his own way and accept the result for what it is.

I wish to repeat that these units were isolated in the first place by considerations of both grammar and prosody. They are portions of text that are grammatically complete and marked off by disjunctive cantillations, and they often exhibit parallelism of a familiar kind. The prophet was clearly not driven by any obligation to frame his poetry in cola of regular length. The wide range of lengths as shown in the four tables is spread throughout the whole book. Leaving the text as we find it, we conclude that this is how the prophet did his work. The fact that the whole text can be broken up into cola of a manifest poetic character should not be belittled by pointing out how diverse these cola are in design and length. Nor does the fact that in some places the text reads like classical prose diminish its poetic quality. Poetry is not always completely different from prose. One can find clauses in almost any poem that would not be poetic if they were embedded in prose, just as any literary prose will occasionally have a poetic phrase.

References

Geller, S. A. 1982. Theory and method in the study of biblical poetry. *Jewish Quarterly Review* 73:65–77.

Lowth, Robert. [1753] 1971. *Lectures on the sacred poetry of the Hebrews.* Translated by G. Gregory. New York: Garland.

Renaud, B. 1977. *La formation du livre de Michée.* Traditions et actualisation. Études Bibliques. Paris: Gabalda.

22

VISION AND ORACLE IN ZECHARIAH 1-6

David J. Clark

> This article, building on the author's previous work on Zechariah 7-14, Haggai, and Obadiah, applies the same principles to the study of Zechariah 1-6. Although the main discourse units in this text are clearly marked and have long been recognized, the linguistic position is more complicated than in the other texts studied in that there appear to be two distinct genres involved. These are termed *vision* and *oracle*. The entire text is examined in detail from a discourse standpoint (with diagrammatic displays). Then the structural differences between the two genres are discussed as well as the location of the oracles in relation to the visions and the possible implications of this for the redactional history of the text.

In previous articles, I have attempted analyses of the discourse structure of the following passages: Zechariah 7-8 (1985), Zechariah 9-14 (1988), Obadiah (1991), and Haggai (1992). The present article is another in the same series, applying the same principles to Zechariah 1-6. A major presupposition is that the Masoretic Text has to be taken seriously, and its present form has to be examined carefully, with no quick resort to emendation or transposition. Somebody, be it author or redactor, had some purpose in putting the text into the form in which it has been transmitted, and the assumption is that discourse cohesion was part of that purpose.

The problems in Zechariah 1-6 are somewhat different from those in the rest of the book; the main units, as in Haggai, are clearly marked in the text itself and are not in dispute. The application of the principles derived from the earlier studies may sharpen some boundaries, but do not call them into question. The main interest in Zechariah 1-6 lies in the intermingling of self-designated visions and apparently nonvisionary strands, for which the label *oracle* is often used. As we examine the order and interrelationships of the eight visions, the focus will be on the distinction between these two types of material and on the location of the oracles.

The passages that need to be quoted do not require a detailed knowledge of Hebrew. They will be cited generally in a relatively literal English rendering rather than in Hebrew. (The Hebrew equivalents for each word or phrase are given at the first occurrence.)

1. Overall structure

As in Zechariah 7-8 and Haggai, the highest rank of marker is a date. The date in Zech. 1:1 is different from the other dates in Haggai and Zechariah in that it specifies the year and the month but not the day. There is no reason to suppose that this affects its status as a discourse marker, especially as it comes at the beginning of the book. This first date covers only the material in the first six verses, which can be said to form an introduction to the whole discourse. This introductory unit is termed a section and, as it contains no visions, it can appropriately be labeled oracular. A more detailed discussion of the 1:1-6 unit is given in sec. 2.1.

The next date is in 1:7; it covers the large section from 1:7-6:15, within which there are eight visions. The beginning of each vision is clearly marked: at 1:8, 2:1 (English numbering 1:18), 2:5 (Eng. 2:1), 3:1, 4:1, 5:1, 5:5, and 6:1. Some form of the Hebrew verb "to see" occurs at or near the beginning of each vision. A more detailed discussion of the 1:7-6:15 unit is given in sec. 2.2.[1]

1.1 Layering in the visions

As has been noted by other scholars (e.g., Baldwin 1972:85; Butterworth 1992:251-52, 299-300; Stuhlmueller 1988:60-61), a broadly chiastic arrangement of the visions can be discerned. The first and eighth visions both contain horses and both deal with the Lord's concern for the world at large; they constitute the outer layer. The second and third visions are both short and relatively simple and both deal with the welfare of Yahweh's people. The sixth and seventh visions are also both short and relatively simple and again deal with the welfare of the Lord's people. This group of four visions constitutes the middle layer (according to Baldwin). The fourth and fifth visions are longer and more complex; they deal with the leadership of Yahweh's people. They constitute the inner layer.

In general, despite various problems, this outline forms a useful framework. Though it may not be "proved" by discourse analysis, it certainly receives support from it, and nothing is suggested by a discourse analysis that would discredit the outline.

1.2 Embedded oracular material

Within the general framework of the visions, there are some pieces of text that do not appear to be part of a vision, but which are juxtaposed with, or even embedded within, a vision. There is general agreement that 2:10-17 (Eng. 2:6-13) and 6:9-15 fall into the first category, and 4:6b-

10a, and perhaps some or all of 1:14-17 and 3:6-10 into the second (Amsler 1981, Chary 1969, Delcor 1964, Petersen 1984, R. L. Smith 1984, Stuhlmueller 1988). The structural characteristics and placement of the oracular material will be examined in section 2.[2]

2. The discourse units

2.1 The first section (1:1-6)

The short first section manifests no features that would require it to be subdivided into any smaller units. It could be described in the terms used in my previous studies as a *section* consisting of a single *division* consisting of a single *paragraph*. However, in respect to the number of degrees of quotation it contains, it is more complex than any of the visions. It begins with a date (1:1), which is the highest level of discourse marker in Zechariah 1-8.[3] The date is immediately followed (as also in 1:7; 7:1)[4] by the formula which in my earlier studies has been recognized as the highest-level quotative formula, ... וַיְהִי דְבַר־יְהוָה אֶל־ לֵאמֹר 'the word of Yahweh came to ... saying'. The content of the oracle follows at once (1:2), and leads into second- and third-degree quotations (1:3) with וְאָמַרְתָּ אֲלֵהֶם 'you shall say to them' immediately followed by the already familiar second-ranking quotative formula כֹּה אָמַר יְהוָה צְבָאוֹת 'thus says Yahweh of hosts'. (According to the syntax, the antecedent of "them" in "you shall say to them" should be "ancestors"; the sense, in contrast, demands that the antecedent must be the "you" underlying "your." This is but the first of many stylistic infelicities in the book of Zechariah.)

If the second-ranking quotative formula "thus says Yahweh of hosts" is to be attributed a function similar to that recognized elsewhere, then the material it introduces is best analyzed as something not encountered in earlier studies, namely a downward rank-shifted embedded paragraph, which extends to the end of 1:4. The first sentence of the embedded paragraph in the third-degree quotation embraces two other quotative formulas נְאֻם יְהוָה צְבָאוֹת 'oracle of Yahweh of hosts' and אָמַר יְהוָה צְבָאוֹת 'says Yahweh of hosts'. The first of these two formulas has three functions, all three of which are exemplified in Hag. 2:23 (Clark 1992:21). The occurrence here in Zech. 1:3 fits with the first of the three functions already identified, namely reinforcing an opening marker. As for the second formula, it can be attributed the same function it has in Zech. 4:6; 7:13; and 8:14,[5] namely marking a climax.

The first sentence of the oracle in 1:3 "return to me ... and I will return to you" (NRSV) is an imperative, and is paralleled by a negative imperative, "Do not be like your ancestors" in the next sentence (1:4).

This leads into a fourth-degree quotation: "to whom the former prophets proclaimed" (NRSV), which cites a stereotypical oracle from earlier prophets, and begins with the same quotative formula as the second-degree quotation in 1:3, that is, "thus says Yahweh of hosts." The cited oracle (a fifth-degree quotation) is a doubly embedded paragraph, that is, an embedded paragraph within the existing embedded paragraph. It begins with the same imperative ("return...") as the (third-degree) oracle into which it is embedded, and appears to extend over only one clause (NRSV, "Return from your evil ways and from your evil deeds"). The next clause (NRSV, "But they did not hear or heed me") balances "to whom the former prophets proclaimed," and is thus best interpreted as continuing the original embedded paragraph in the third-degree quotation. In view of the interruption of the doubly embedded paragraph, it may be better to identify this clause as a second subparagraph within the first embedded paragraph.

There follows at the end of 1:4 the quotative formula "oracle of Yahweh," the function of which is somewhat unclear at this point. The next three sentences are syntactically distinct from anything earlier in that they are interrogative rather than imperative. Semantically they may anaphorically resume either the topics of the third-degree quotation, the ancestors and the prophets (1:4), or the topic of the first-degree quotation, the ancestors (1:2). The formula may therefore be analyzed in either of two ways. It may have its second function, namely marking some climax within the third-degree quotation, which would then continue to the end of 1:6. Or else it may have its third function, and mark the closure of some unit. This would be the third-degree quotation (the original embedded paragraph), introduced by "Thus says Yahweh of hosts" in 1:3. It would thus mark the end not only of the third- but probably also of the second-degree quotation. In that case, the ensuing questions would be a continuation of the first-degree quotation in 1:2. If "oracle of Yahweh" does have such a closure function at this point, then one could argue that 1:5-6, with its change of syntactic mode to interrogative, should be regarded as a new subparagraph. This would be structurally tidier, in that it would provide a more explicit "unwinding" of the multiple degrees of quotation. There appears to be no indication in the text that would tilt the analysis decisively one way or the other, but my intuition inclines towards the closure function on the subjective basis that closure seems more aesthetically satisfying at this point. This is the analysis that will be represented in the display of Zech. 1:1-6 that follows.

Whichever analysis is preferred, there is a further quotation (treated as second degree, but it is possibly fourth degree) within the remaining part of the oracle. This is structured as a comparison with כַּאֲשֶׁר...כֵּן... 'as...' and 'so...', and seems to indicate a climax, like the similarly

Vision and Oracle in Zechariah 1-6

expressed comparisons in 7:13 and especially 8:14. There is no final formal closure marker, though the occurrence of the date at the beginning of the next verse leaves no room for doubt that this is the end of a section. In the display of the first section, the various degrees of quotation are indicated by indentation:

1:1 **Section 1** Date
    Division 1, Paragraph 1 *The word of Yahweh came to . . . saying*
1:2–3a   **1st degree, Subparagraph 1**
    Yahweh was very angry . . .
    you shall say to them
1:3b   **2nd degree**
        Thus says Yahweh of hosts
            3rd degree, embedded paragraph 1:1, subpara. 1
            Imperative: *Return to me, oracle of Yahweh of hosts,*
            and I will return to you, says Yahweh of hosts
1:4   Imperative: *Do not be . . . the prophets called saying*
                4th degree
                Thus says Yahweh of hosts
                      5th degree, doubly embedded paragraph 2:1
                      Imperative: *Return . . . from your evil deeds*
            3rd degree, embedded paragraph 1:1, subpara. 2
            But they did not hear . . . oracle of Yahweh
1:5–6a   **1st degree, Subparagraph 2**
    Interrogative x 3
    they . . . said
1:6b   **2nd degree**
        As . . . so . . .

2.2 The second section (1:7–6:15)

The second section is much longer than the first; it is clearly marked off into at least eight units which, as before, will be termed *divisions*. The date in 1:7 separates this section from the previous section (1:1–6), and unites it as a unit at some level. The unit continues until the next date in 7:1. Internally, the section is divided into smaller parts by occurrences of some form of the verb "to see." In seven of the eight divisions there occurs the formula רָאִיתִי (הַלַּיְלָה) וְהִנֵּה 'I saw (by night) and behold' (1:8; 2:1, 5; 4:2; 5:1, 9; 6:1), which in five of the seven cases is extended to וָאֶשָּׂא (אֶת־)עֵינַי וָאֵרֶא וְהִנֵּה 'I lifted up my eyes and I saw and behold' (2:1, 5; 5:1, 9; 6:1). There are minor variants in the longer formula: in 2:1 only (the first occurrence), "my eyes" is preceded by the object marker אֶת; in 5:1 and 6:1 only the formula is extended further to ... וָאָשׁוּב/וָאָשֻׁב 'I returned and lifted up my eyes and I saw and behold'. The word "I returned" is spelled with a long *û* in the first instance and a short *u* in the second; and in both occurences, the word "I saw" that follows is spelled with a short *e* rather than a long *ê* in the first root syllable, and with a final ה. It is hard to see any significance for discourse analysis in these orthographic variants. The division where the above formula does not occur, the fourth, nevertheless does begin with a form of the verb "to see," namely וַיַּרְאֵנִי 'he made me see'. The identical form of the verb has already occurred in the middle of the second division at 2:3, where it may mark the beginning of a lower-level unit (cf. Amos 7:1, 4, 7; 8:1).

2.2.1 The first division (1:7-17)

As in the first section (1:1-6), the date in the first division is followed immediately by the formula "the word of Yahweh came to ... saying," which is the highest level quotative formula, and may be taken as a paragraph opener. It recurs in 4:8 and 6:9, though it is not immediately clear whether in either of those places it is functioning at the same rank as here. Next occurs the formula that introduces the first vision, expanded only in this occurrence to "I saw by night and behold." The content of the vision is narrative interspersed with dialogue. It is not as clear as it could be how many participants there are. But in my view, as argued elsewhere (Clark 1982), there are two angels in addition to the prophet himself. For present purposes, it suffices to note that down to the end of 1:13, the structure is straightforward with no more than one degree of quotation in each turn of the dialogue. Each turn can be regarded as a separate subparagraph, there being six such subparagraphs. The last turn in 1:13 supplies no direct speech, but gives a narrative evaluation of what was said. It seems quite probable that the change from direct speech marks some kind of closure. This is the interpretation of the *Français Courant,* which, unlike the Good News Bible or *Die Gute Nachricht,* not merely treats 1:14 as the beginning of a new paragraph, but even inserts a new section heading.

The 1:14-17 unit is more complex, and may indeed be best treated as a new paragraph. After an introduction presented as a continuation of the vision narrative (וַיֹּאמֶר אֵלַי הַמַּלְאָךְ הַדֹּבֵר בִּי 'The angel who spoke with me said to me'), it consists of two parts which may be regarded as subparagraphs. They are second-degree quotations, both introduced by an imperative clause not previously encountered as a quotative formula: קְרָא לֵאמֹר 'call saying' (cf. 1:4), leading to third-degree quotations. In both parts, this clause is followed by another quotative formula which elsewhere has functioned as a second-ranking formula, namely "thus says

Yahweh of hosts" (cf. 1:3, 4; 3:7; 7:9; 8:2, 3, 4, 6, 7, 9, 19, 20, 23), leading into a fourth-degree quotation (cf. 1:4). In both cases, the fourth-degree quotation can be interpreted as a rank-shifted paragraph embedded within the subparagraph.

The position in the first part is further complicated by the occurrence in 1:16 of "Therefore thus says Yahweh." This may be hierarchically coordinate with "thus says Yahweh of hosts" (without "therefore") in 1:15. In Hag. 1:10 a similar expression for "therefore" (עַל־כֵּן rather than לָכֵן as here) appeared to function as a low-level opening marker, so a similar situation here cannot be excluded. However, semantically it seems more probable that "therefore" links the quotative formula closely with the immediately preceding content of the fourth-degree quotation, and if so, "therefore thus says Yahweh" would introduce a fifth-degree quotation, and another doubly embedded paragraph, as in 1:4. This is the analysis represented in the display of 1:7–17 that follows. It has been found that כִּי in Hag. 2:6 and Zech. 8:14 functions in a similar way, rank-shifting the quotative formula downwards; conceivably different discourse functions motivate the choice between לָכֵן and עַל־כֵּן, the one conjunctive, so to speak, and the other disjunctive. Proof would await extensive investigation of their distribution, but the possibility seems attractive in the present context. In the last part of 1:16 "oracle of Yahweh of hosts" has its third function, that of closure. In all probability it closes not just the fifth-degree quotation (the doubly embedded paragraph), but also the fourth- (the singly embedded paragraph) and third-degree quotations. The structure of the first division of the second section, with indentation showing the various degrees of quotation, is shown in the following display:

1:7   **Section 2** Date
        Division 1, Paragraph 1 *The word of Yahweh came to ... saying*
1:8   **1st degree, Subparagraph 1**
        I saw by night and behold a man ...
1:9   *I said*
            2nd degree
            Interrogative + Vocative: *What are these, sir?*
        1st degree, Subparagraph 2
        The angel who spoke with me said
            2nd degree
            Answer: *I will make you see ...*
1:10   **1st degree, Subparagraph 3**
        The man ... replied and said
            2nd degree
            These are ...

1:11	**1st degree, Subparagraph 4**
	They replied ... and said
	2nd degree
	We have patrolled ... and behold ...
1:12	**1st degree, Subparagraph 5**
	The angel of Yahweh replied and said
	2nd degree
	Vocative + Interrogative: *LORD of hosts, how long ... ?*
1:13	**1st degree, Subparagraph 6**
	Yahweh replied ... with good and comforting words
1:14a	**1st degree, Paragraph 2**
	The angel who spoke with me said to me
	2nd degree, Subparagraph 1
	Imperative: *Call saying*
	3rd degree
	Thus says Yahweh of hosts
1:14b–15	**4th degree, embedded paragraph 1:1**
	Statement: *I am jealous ...*
1:16	**4th degree**
	Therefore thus says Yahweh
	5th degree, doubly embedded paragraph 2:1
	I will return ... oracle of Yahweh of hosts
1:17	**2nd degree, Subparagraph 2**
	Imperative: *Call again saying*
	3rd degree
	Thus says Yahweh of hosts
	4th degree, embedded paragraph 1:2
	My cities ...

It is notable that 1:14–17, which many scholars have classified as oracular rather than visionary, is now seen to be structurally more akin to the oracular material of 1:1–6 than to the visionary material of 1:7–13. To this extent its treatment as a separate paragraph may have significant formal support.

2.2.2 The second division (2:1–4, Eng. 1:18–21)

The second division opens with the first occurrence of the longer vision-introducing formula "I lifted up my eyes and I saw and behold." We may note that this formula and the corresponding ones in all the subsequent visions are technically parallel with "I saw by night and behold" in 1:8. This means that each vision is strictly speaking already a first-degree quotation when it begins. However, in order to prevent the displays from becoming more complicated than necessary, this is henceforth indicated only once, at the beginning of each division. The content of the present vision is described very briefly as "four horns." There follows a dialogue of only two turns, with only one further degree of quotation in each turn. The prophet asks a question and the interpreting angel answers it. Each turn is treated as a separate subparagraph. Then a second element of the vision is introduced with the narrative clause "Yahweh made me see" (2:3), which may be regarded as beginning a new paragraph. Its content is described, also very briefly, as "four smiths," and followed, as was "four horns," by a dialogue of only two turns with but one further degree of quotation in each. Again the prophet poses a question and the angel answers it, and again each turn is treated as a separate subparagraph. Thus this short division may be considered as two paragraphs of parallel structure, each with two subparagraphs. It will be displayed (in sec. 2.2.3) together with the third division to show the similarity of structure.

2.2.3 The third division (2:5–17, Eng. 2:1–13)

The third division opens with the same formula as the previous one. It is again followed by a simple question-and-answer dialogue of two turns (and therefore two subparagraphs), with one further degree of quotation in each turn. As in the previous division, a further visionary element is introduced (2:7) in a narrative sentence, this time beginning with הִנֵּה 'behold'. This word in initial position has been noted to function as a unit opening marker (in Zech. 9:4, 9; 11:6, 16; 12:2; 14:1; Obad. 2), and it is reasonable to see it as opening a new paragraph here. Two angels are mentioned in 2:7, and a monologue from one of them is addressed to the other beginning in 2:8. In another of Zechariah's obscurities, it is not entirely clear who speaks to whom. (See the comments on 4:1 in sec. 2.2.5, which however, do not affect the discourse analysis here.)

The monologue has two further degrees of quotation. The problem is to decide where it ends. It certainly extends at least to the end of 2:9 and may perhaps extend to the end of 2:17. Many modern translations, of which NRSV is typical, print closing quotation marks at the end of 2:9, thus indicating that they consider the angel's words to end there. Some, like NIV, punctuate in such a way as to show that they consider the monologue to go on to the end of the chapter. What can discourse analysis say on this matter?

The quotative formula "oracle of Yahweh" occurs in the last sentence of 2:9; and although this is not always a closure marker, there is no reason in this context why it could not be. We note also that 2:10 begins with the repeated interjection הוֹי הוֹי (NRSV, "up, up") and an imperative. This interjection has a unit opening function in Zech. 11:17, and an imperative verb also has a unit opening function in Zech. 9:9, 12; 10:1; 11:1; 13:7; Hag. 1:7; 2:15, 18; and Obad. 12. There is therefore adequate reason to posit a new unit at the beginning of 2:10, though its rank has yet to be determined. We may note also that there seems to be a change of addressee in 2:10, 2:9 being addressed to one individual and 2:10 to more than one as shown by the second person plural. A further pointer is the double occurrence in 2:10 of "oracle of Yahweh." The second occurrence may well mark closure since it is immediately followed by הוֹי, opening another unit. (The earlier occurrence can be interpreted as having its first function, reinforcing an opening marker.) So far, then, there are several indications that a new unit does indeed begin at 2:10, and nothing that would indicate a close link with the explicitly visionary material in 2:5–9.

In 2:11, the interjection הוֹי (NRSV, "up") recurs and may be taken as opening the next unit. It is followed by the name "Zion" and an imperative verb. NRSV follows LXX in interpreting "Zion" as directional, "to Zion." This would be a syntactically odd place for a directional term to occur, especially with no directional suffix, and the interpretation of "Zion" as a vocative (with Vg, NIV, NJV, NJB, REB, TOB, FC, DGN) is syntactically much to be preferred. Vocatives and imperatives (in either order) collocate quite readily at the opening of a unit (Zech. 9:9 twice; 11:1–2 three times; also in Hag. 1:7, 2:18; and Obad. 12). The next verse, 2:12, begins with the quotative formula preceded by "for": "for thus says Yahweh of hosts." Elsewhere, namely in Zech. 8:14 and Hag. 2:6 (cf. Obad. 18), "for" before this quotative formula has been found to rank-shift its function downwards. This analysis fits the present context well. The oracle introduced by the quotative formula gives the reason for the command in 2:11. The next "for" (also in 2:12) simply links its clause closely with what has preceded.[6]

The word "for" recurs a third time before הִנְנִי 'behold me' at the beginning of the next sentence in 2:13. In other contexts (e.g., 2:7; 9:4; 12:2; 14:1) "behold" opens a new unit, but after "for," this function can be rank-shifted downwards to mark the opening of a subunit (as in 11:16). That appears to be the case here also. Such a subunit is a continuation of the oracle introduced at the beginning of 2:12, as shown by the fact that Yahweh continues to speak of himself in the first person. At the end of 2:13 is the first occurrence of a clause which will be labeled a self-assertion formula: וִידַעְתֶּם כִּי־יְהוָה צְבָאוֹת שְׁלָחָנִי 'you shall know that Yahweh of hosts has sent me (to you)'. With minor variations, it occurs four times in Zechariah 1–6 (2:13, 14; 4:9; 6:15). The change of person suggests that this sentence may not be part of the oracle that began in 2:12, and certainly not part of the words of the angel beginning in 2:4–5. The prophet is here speaking in the first person; however, "you" is second person masculine plural and must have the same referents as the two occurrences of "you" in 2:12. It seems necessary then, despite the awkwardness, to treat this clause as part of the oracle beginning in 2:12.

The opening words of 2:14 are two imperatives plus a vocative, forms which have regularly marked the beginning of a new unit. It is not certain whether the imperatives open a unit coordinate with that which began in 2:11, or a subunit within a larger unit covering the whole of 2:11-16. The absence of an interjection here, in contrast with 2:10, 2:11, and 2:17, suggests the latter. The expression "for behold me" in 2:14b seems clearly linked in a result-reason relationship with the preceding imperative, so we have to assume that, as in 2:13, the word כִּי 'for' in this case overrides any opening function which "behold me" may have in other contexts. The quotative formula "oracle of Yahweh" in 2:14c does not seem to be near enough to the beginning of a unit to be interpreted as having its first function, nor does it appear to close any unit, so we have to conclude that it has its second function, that of marking a climax.

The unit beginning at 2:14 extends to the end of 2:16. In 2:15 occurs the phrase בַּיּוֹם הַהוּא 'n that day', which in Zechariah 12-14 often has an opening function. Its opening function, however, can be attributed only when it occurs in clause-initial position, as in Zech. 12:4, 6, 8, 11, and 14:20 (cf. Hag. 2:23 and Obad. 8). Elsewhere (Zech. 14:4, 9, 21) it has what I call a face-value function, and that is also the case here. The second occurrence of the self-assertion formula "you will know that Yahweh of hosts has sent me to you" in 2:15 may seem to interrupt the unit 2:14-16. But this time "you" is feminine singular, referring back to the feminine vocative "daughter of Zion" in 2:14; the statement therefore can hardly be taken as anything other than an integral part of the 2:14-16 unit. However, this is another example of Zechariah's stylistic clumsiness, as the first person "I" referring to the prophet himself jars with "I" referring unambiguously to "Yahweh" in the previous clause. It is conceivable that 2:16, in which "Yahweh" continues to be the subject of a clause, is a continuation of the statement of what "you will know"; but if this were the case, one would expect a repetition of כִּי rather than of יְהוָה 'Yahweh' in 2:16. Therefore it is more probable that 2:16 continues the unit begun in 2:14 and that the prophet's personal remark is an aside.

The interjection הַס (NRSV, "be silent") at the beginning of 2:17, followed as it is by a vocative, can be taken as a new unit. It is parallel in structure with the unit consisting of 2:10, namely a command followed by a reason. If 2:11-16 is regarded as one unit, as suggested, then 2:10-17 has a simple chiastic structure; in the middle is a long unit (2:11-16), probably best labeled a paragraph with two subparagraphs (2:11-13, 14-

16), and enclosing it are two short units (2:10, 17) similar to each other, which would be interpreted as coordinate paragraphs.

As is seen more clearly in the display that follows, which includes both the second and third divisions, 2:10–17 has no close connection in meaning or structure with 2:5–9. Indeed it shows more formal similarities with chapters 9–11 than with any of the first three visions. Thus there is no reason to regard it as part of the monologue in 2:8–9, and there are good reasons for interpreting it as a unit in its own right, outside of the visions, though for the moment the matter will be left open.

2:1	**1st degree, Division 2, Paragraph 1, Subparagraph 1**
	I lifted up my eyes and I saw and behold . . .
2:2	*I said to the angel who spoke with me*
	2nd degree
	Interrogative: *What are these?*
	Subparagraph 2
	He said to me
	2nd degree
	Answer: *These are . . .*
2:3	**Paragraph 2, Subparagraph 1**
	Yahweh made me see . . .
2:4	*and I said*
	2nd degree
	Interrogative: *What . . . ?*
	Subparagraph 2
	He said saying
	2nd degree
	Answer: *These are . . .*
2:5	**1st degree, Division 3, Paragraph 1, Subparagraph 1**
	I lifted up my eyes and I saw and behold . . .
2:6	*I said*
	2nd degree
	Interrogative: *Where . . . ?*
	Subparagraph 2
	He said to me
	2nd degree
	Answer: *To measur . . .*
2:7	**Paragraph 2**
	Behold . . .
2:8–9	*He said to him*
	2nd degree
	Imperative: *Run, speak . . . saying*

	3rd degree
	Jerusalem . . . oracle of Yahweh
2:10	**Paragraph 3**
	הוֹי הוֹי + Imperative: *Flee . . . oracle of Yahweh*
	for . . . oracle of Yahweh
2:11	**Paragraph 4, Subparagraph 1**
	הוֹי + Vocative: *Zion* + Imperative: *Escape . . .*
2:12	*for thus says Yahweh of hosts*
	2nd degree
	Statement (content not clear)
2:13	*for behold me . . .*
	you shall know that Yahweh of hosts has sent me
2:14	**Subparagraph 2**
	Imperatives: *Sing and rejoice* + Vocative: *daughter of Zion*
	for behold me . . . oracle of Yahweh
2:15–16	Statement: x 3
	you shall know that Yahweh of hosts has sent me to you
	Statement: x 2
2:17	**Paragraph 5**
	הַס + Vocative: *all flesh*

2.2.4 The fourth division (3:1–10)

The fourth division is the least typical in terms of structural features in common with other divisions. But its structure is not as complex as some of the others and there is no reason to see more than one paragraph. The opening expression "he made me see" has already occurred in 2:3. There is no noun subject in the present context, and there is some grammatical uncertainty about who the subject referent is. The last mentioned noun is "Yahweh" in 2:17, but it is not in subject position, and does not seem a very likely antecedent. It is possible that "the angel who spoke with me" in 2:7 is the antecedent, though this is not very convincing (it is adopted by LB). The most probable antecedent is "Yahweh" in 2:3, where the very same verb occurred. Translations which commit themselves on this point (TEV, NJB, TOB, FC, DGN) almost all regard "Yahweh" as the subject, whether or not they take the occurrence of the name in 2:3 as the direct antecedent.

The division alternates narrative with speech, but the speech turns are a succession of monologues rather than a dialogue. An opening narrative description (3:1) leads into a second-degree quotation (3:2). There follows a further narrative description (3:3) and two second-degree quotations addressed by an angel to different participants (3:4), and a third second-degree quotation spoken by the prophet himself, then another narrative description (3:5). It is not clear whether the angel in 3:3 is the same as "the angel of Yahweh" in 3:5, 6. From 3:6 onwards, the angel of Yahweh delivers a monologue with second- and third-degree quotations. Since all the monologues are separated from each other by at least a brief narrative, it may be best to regard each piece of narrative plus monologue as a separate subparagraph.

Within the long third-degree quotation in the final subparagraph, we may recognize an embedded paragraph divided into four subparagraphs. The beginning of each subparagraph is identified by items that usually function elsewhere as lower-level-unit opening markers, namely an imperative (3:8), "behold me" (3:9b) and "in that day" (3:10).

It remains to comment briefly on the two occurrences of "oracle of Yahweh of hosts" in 3:9, 10. The first one may be interpreted as having its second function of marking a climax, or it may be interpreted as having its first function of reinforcing "behold me" as an opening marker. The second occurrence is clearly reinforcing "in that day" as an opening marker, so it may be preferable to interpret the first occurrence in the same way.

The structure of the fourth division is as follows:

3:1   **1st degree, Division 4, Paragraph 1, Subparagraph 1**
He made me see . . .

3:2   *Yahweh said to Satan*
        2nd degree
        Jussive: *Yahweh rebuke you . . .* + Vocative: *Satan*
        + Interrogative: *Is not . . .*

3:3   **Subparagraph 2**
Joshua was dressed . . .

3:4   [The angel] *replied and said to . . . saying*
        2nd degree
        Imperative: *Take off . . .*
    Subparagraph 3
    [The angel] *said to him*
        2nd degree
        Imperative: *See* + Statement: *I have taken away . . .*

3:5   **Subparagraph 4**
I said
        2nd degree
        Jussive: *Let them put . . .*
They put . . .

3:6	**Subparagraph 5**
	The angel of Yahweh assured Joshua saying
	2nd degree
3:7	*Thus says* **Yahweh** *of hosts*
	3rd degree, embedded paragraph 1:1, subparagraph 1
	If . . . and if . . . then . . . and then . . .
3:8	**3rd degree, embedded paragraph 1:1, subparagraph 2**
	Imperative: *Listen* + Vocative: *Joshua . . .*
	for behold me . . .
3:9	*for behold . . .*
	3rd degree, embedded paragraph 1:1, subparagraph 3
	behold me . . . oracle of Yahweh of hosts
3:10	**3rd degree, embedded paragraph 1:1, subparagraph 4**
	In that day, oracle of Yahweh of hosts . . .

2.2.5 The fifth division (4:1-14)

The visionary part of the fifth division is straightforward, consisting mainly of dialogue with only one degree of quotation. The main problem lies in deciding the status of 4:6b-10a. Is it or is it not an integral part of the vision? And if it is not, is there any plausible explanation for its present location?

The division opens with an initiative from "the angel who spoke with me," waking the prophet up as from sleep. It is not clear whether the opening Hebrew verb (וַיָּשָׁב) is to be understood as a genuine verb of motion that is rightly translated "came back" (NJV, NJB, REB; cf. DGN) or "returned" (NAB, NIV; cf. TOB), or whether it is to be understood as a paraphrastic way of saying "again." Neither view is free of problems: "came back" or "returned" implies that the angel had been somewhere. If he had, this is not recorded, unless the distant command to run and speak to the young man with the measuring line in 2:8 (Eng. 2:4) is taken as addressed to the interpreting angel. On the other hand, if וַיָּשָׁב is taken to mean "again," the objection can be raised that it is not possible to wake the prophet again since there is no mention of his having been wakened once. However, in the light of the clear use of the verb שׁוּב in the sense of "again" at the beginning of a vision (5:1; 6:1), it seems more probable that that is its sense here (certainty is impossible). GNB and NRSV sit neatly on the fence with "came again." This is yet another of Zechariah's stylistic oddities.

The first stage of the dialogue reverses the pattern found in 2:2, 4, 6; 5:6, 10; 6:4. This time the angel asks a question and Zechariah answers (cf. 5:2). The question is simply מָה אַתָּה רֹאֶה 'What do you see?' In introducing his answer, the prophet uses the shorter formula "I saw and behold" as in 1:8 (cf. the longer formula in 2:1, 5; 5:1, 5, 9; 6:1), with a description of what he saw, a lampstand. The description is not very clear as is typical of Zechariah, but the problems do not appear to affect the discourse structure, so we will not linger over them. As before, each turn of the dialogue is regarded as a separate subparagraph.

The next stage of the dialogue consists of two turns by each speaker, with Zechariah asking a question, the angel answering it with another question, Zechariah responding, and finally the angel answering the original question. There is thus a simple chiasmus in the dialogue: question 1 + question 2 + answer 2 + answer 1. This is repeated in 4:12-14. In the first turn, the opening formula is וָאַעַן וָאֹמַר ... לֵאמֹר 'I replied and said ... saying'. The Hebrew verb ענה is not exactly equivalent to *reply* in English, as the latter implies a previous utterance by someone else. The Hebrew can imply this, as in 1:10-13 or 4:5, 6a, and 11, but does not necessarily do so. For instance, in 3:4 and 6:4, this verb introduces direct speech which is not a response to any previous recorded utterance. Only here and in 4:12 (at least within chapters 1-6) is the verb ענה used to introduce a second utterance by the same speaker. In this context it should strictly speaking be translated "spoke again," but we retain "replied" in order to keep the formula consistent in English.

The main problem in this division is that the question asked by Zechariah in 4:4 is not answered until 4:10b. In the text as it has come to us, however, the angel's apparent response to the question begins in 4:6b, but vv. 6b-10a have nothing to do with the vision or the question. Has the text been dislocated in transmission as many scholars believe, or is this some literary technique? The view that it may be a literary technique can be supported by the occurrence of a similar structure in chapters 7-8, where the question in 7:3 is not answered until 8:19. The parallel is only an approximate one, as the intervening material in chapters 7-8 is not as alien to the question-answer sequence as it is in 4:6b-10a. Discourse analysis can perhaps best approach the problem by examining the structure of 4:6b-10a and seeing what affinities it may have with other parts of chapters 1-6.

The angel's reply opens with an expression that has a formulaic ring, זֶה דְּבַר־יְהוָה אֶל ... לֵאמֹר 'This is the word of Yahweh to Zerubbabel saying', but in fact it is unparalleled in any of the material studied so far. The quotation introduced by this phrase opens with an elliptical and epigrammatic sentence followed by the formula "says Yahweh of hosts." As elsewhere (Zech. 1:3; 7:13; 8:14; Hag. 1:8; 2:7, 9), this formula can be said to mark a climax. The utterance continues in 4:7 with a rhetorical question and a vocative, followed by a statement generally taken to be an answer to the rhetorical question.

The next sentence (4:8) is a normally high-ranking quotative formula, "the word of Yahweh came to me saying." It therefore suggests a unit of rank not less than coordinate with the unit that began in 4:6b, and furthermore suggests that that unit is also high ranking. Moreover, if, as seems almost certain, it is an utterance of Zechariah, then it cannot be part of the angel's words. This formula is followed by a two-clause statement and the self-assertion formula which occurs elsewhere only in nonvisionary material (2:13, 15; 6:15), "you (masculine singular) shall know that Yahweh of hosts has sent me to you (masculine plural)." The masculine singular subject is presumably Zerubbabel, and thus forms a cohesive link between 4:8-10a and 4:6b-7. The dissonance with the masculine plural "to you" is awkward, but not unintelligible: Zerubbabel would recognize that Yahweh had sent Zechariah not just to him personally but to the people at large. A few Hebrew manuscripts and several ancient versions read masculine plural in both places; the effect of this would be to separate 4:8-10a not only from the vision but also from 4:6b-7. Either way, this sentence is irrelevant in the context of the vision and can hardly be given a sensible interpretation unless it is regarded as something outside the structure of the vision. The unit 4:8-10a ends with a clause beginning with "for" (4:10), which links it with what has gone before.

It is clear that 4:10b is the answer to the question in 4:5, or at least part of the answer. In 4:11, the prophet asks a supplementary question and, before the angel answers, he adds a third question. There are striking parallels with the dialogue sequence in 4:2-5. As in 4:4, so in 4:12 the prophet speaks twice in succession without the angel taking a turn. The second utterance is again introduced by the verb ענה: "I replied a second time and said . . ." As in 4:5, so in 4:13 the angel asks the prophet whether he knows the meaning of the vision. The sense is the same in both places though the wording is not identical, not in the quotative formulas and not in the questions. In both cases the prophet denies that he knows. Finally in 4:14 the angel answers the original question. Thus in 4:12-14 there is the same chiastic sequence as in 4:4-6: question 1 + question 2 + answer 2 + answer 1.

In the display of the proposed structure of 4:1-14 that follows, double lines are inserted to indicate the extent of the nonvisionary material, which is tentatively considered to be two paragraphs. If these two paragraphs are extracted from their context and treated as a separate unit, then the quotations within them would be second degree rather than third degree, but they are shown as third degree in deference to the textual tradition.

Internally, these two paragraphs have more in common with chapters 7–8 than with the visions of 1–6.

4:1–2a	**1st degree, Division 5, Paragraph 1, Subparagraph 1**	
	The angel wakened me . . . and said to me	
		2nd degree
		Interrogative: *What do you see?*
4:2b–3	**Subparagraph 2**	
	I said	
		2nd degree
		Answer: *I saw and behold . . .*
4:4	**Subparagraph 3**	
	I replied and said to the angel who spoke with me saying	
		2nd degree
		Interrogative + Vocative: *What are these, sir?*
4:5	**Subparagraph 4**	
	The angel who spoke with me replied and said to me	
		2nd degree
		Interrogative: *Don't you know what these are?*
	Subparagraph 5	
	I said	
		2nd degree
		Answer: *No, sir.*
4:6a	**Subparagraph 6**	
	He answered and said to me saying	
		2nd degree

===================================

4:6b	**Paragraph 2?**	
	This is the word of Yahweh to Zerubbabel saying	
		3rd degree/2nd degree
		Not . . . not . . . but . . . says Yahweh of hosts
4:7		Interrogative + Vocative: *Who are you, great mountain?*
		Statement: *Before Zerubbabel . . .*
4:8	**Paragraph 3?**	
	The word of Yahweh came to me saying	
4:9		**3rd degree/2nd degree**
		Statement: *The hands of Zerubbabel . . .*
		and you shall know that Yahweh of hosts has sent me to you
4:10a		*for . . .*

===================================

4:10b	Answer: *These are . . .*
4:11	**Subparagraph 7**
	I answered and said to him
	2nd degree
	Interrogative: *What . . . ?*
4:12	**Subparagraph 8**
	I answered a second time and said to him
	2nd degree
	Interrogative: *What . . . ?*
4:13	**Subparagraph 9**
	He said to me saying
	2nd degree
	Interrogative: *Don't you know what these are?*
	Subparagraph 10
	I said
	2nd degree
	Answer: *No, sir.*
4:14	**Subparagraph 11**
	He said
	2nd degree
	Answer: *These two are . . .*

2.2.6 The sixth division (5:1–4)

The sixth division opens with the longest form of the vision-introducing formula: "I returned and I lifted up my eyes and I saw and behold." In 5:1 the content of the vision is very briefly described as "a flying scroll" (NRSV). There follows a simple dialogue with only one degree of quotation in each turn. As in the fifth division, the angel (identified only by a third-person verb ending, not by a noun) takes the initiative and asks the prophet, "What do you see?" (5:2; cf. 4:2). The prophet answers, supplying more detail than in 5:1. Then the angel provides, without being asked, an explanation that the scroll represents a curse on evildoers. This takes the form of two statements, with "oracle of Yahweh of hosts" in the second one. This formula is not reinforcing an opening formula, nor is it near enough to the end of the utterance to be attributed a closure function. Therefore it must be seen as marking a climax. This fits the context well, as the formula is emphasizing Yahweh as the source of the curse. There is no reason to break this division into more than one paragraph, but as before each turn of the dialogue is analyzed as a separate subparagraph. This division will be displayed with the seventh division (in sec. 2.2.7).

2.2.7 The seventh division (5:5–11)

The seventh division opens in a manner not paralleled in any of the other visions. Instead of the prophet describing his experience, the angel takes the initiative and commands him to look, using an imperative form of the familiar formula: ... שָׂא נָא עֵינֶיךָ וּרְאֵה 'Lift up your eyes and see ...' This first degree quotation is set in the context of the angel "going out" (or perhaps "coming out"), though if this is a genuine verb of motion, it is not clear where the motion is to or from. Possibly, from the point of view of semantics, the verb is no more than an almost vacant device for resuming the sequence of the visions. (However, if that is so, there is no obvious reason for departing from the established formula for introducing a vision.) There follows a dialogue in which the prophet asks for an explanation, and the angel answers in two consecutive turns of the dialogue (cf. 4:2–4, 11–12). Each turn is treated as a separate subparagraph.

In 5:7, there is another occurrence of "behold." This opens a sentence that is not part of the angel's speech; it can be considered a further subparagraph. There follows another turn from the angel, which is rounded off by a short narrative description. Then in 5:9, there occurs the formula "I lifted up my eyes and I saw and behold," which elsewhere (2:1, 5; 5:1; 6:1) introduces a new vision and, in discourse terms, a new division. But here, this analysis will not hold, as the content of what is seen is integrated into the vision already in progress. However, the relatively high rank of this formula elsewhere suggests strongly that here it initiates a new paragraph that consists of a two-turn dialogue with a second-degree quotation in each turn. Thus the seventh division is analyzed as comprising two subparagraphs.

The following display includes both the sixth and seventh divisions:

5:1	**1st degree, Division 6, Paragraph 1, Subparagraph 1**
	I returned and I lifted up my eyes and I saw and behold . . .
5:2	*He said to me*
	2nd degree
	Interrogative: *What do you see?*
	Subparagraph 2
	I said
	2nd degree
	Answer: *I see* . . .
5:3a	**Subparagraph 3**
	He said to me
	2nd degree
5:3b–4	Statement: *This is* . . . *for* . . .

Vision and Oracle in Zechariah 1–6

> *I have sent it out, oracle of Yahweh of hosts . . .*

5:5 **1st degree, Division 7, Paragraph 1, Subparagraph 1**
The angel who spoke with me went out and said to me
    2nd degree
    Imperative: *Lift up your eyes and see . . .*

5:6 **Subparagraph 2**
I said
    2nd degree
    Interrogative: *What is it?*
Subparagraph 3
He said
    2nd degree
    Answer: *This is . . .*
Subparagraph 4
He said
    2nd degree
    Answer: *This is . . .*

5:7 **Subparagraph 5**
Behold . . . + Narrative
5:8 *He said*
    2nd degree
    This is . . .
Narrative

5:9 **Paragraph 2, Subparagraph 1**
I lifted up my eyes and I saw and behold . . .
5:10 *I said to the angel who spoke with me*
    2nd degree
    Interrogative: *Where . . . ?*
5:11 **Subparagraph 2**
He said to me
    2nd degree
    Answer: *To build . . . in the land of Shinar . . .*

2.2.8 The eighth division (6:1–15)

The eighth division begins, like the sixth division (5:1), with the longest introductory formula: "I returned and I lifted up my eyes and I saw and behold." The description of the vision that follows is long and detailed, with four chariots each pulled by different-colored horses. We need not enter the discussion about the exact color of the horses pulling the last chariot. The prophet opens the dialogue by asking the angel for an interpretation (cf. 1:9; 2:2; 4:4; 5:6). The question is introduced with the use of the verb ענה even though it is the first utterance of the vision: "I replied and said . . ." The rest of the vision is dominated by three utterances, all by the interpreting angel. The first is addressed to the prophet (6:5-7a), the second to the horses (6:7b), and the third to the prophet again (6:8). If we apply the analytical criteria used in the previous visions, and there are no contraindications to this procedure, 6:1-8 would consist of one paragraph with four subparagraphs.

In 6:9 we meet with the formula which elsewhere is the highest-level quotative formula, "the word of Yahweh came to me saying." This suggests at the least the beginning of a new paragraph; and since the content of what follows has no perceptible connection with the preceding vision, this may well be the beginning of a higher-level unit. In the absence of any evidence to compel the recognition of a unit of a rank between paragraph and division, we label this unit a paragraph. The second-degree quotation that follows contains what may be called procedural discourse, with a series of instructions conveyed by "imperative substitute" forms, namely an infinitive absolute and five second-person singular future verb forms ("you shall . . ."). In the first of these five clauses occurs the phrase "in that day," but it is not in initial position and is therefore taken as having only a face-value function, and no discourse relevance. (This paragraph will be a first-degree quotation if it is regarded as not part of the vision in v. 6 and v. 8.)

The last of these five second-person future clauses, "you shall say to him saying" (6:12; cf. 1:3), introduces a third-degree (or second-degree) quotation. This consists solely of the next-lower-ranking quotative formula "thus says Yahweh of hosts saying," introducing a lengthy oracle in a fourth-degree (or third-degree) quotation. We treat it as an embedded paragraph. It opens with הִנֵּה, 'behold,' and continues with a series of thirteen clauses with third person verbs. The seventh and thirteenth of these (6:13b, 15) are both וְהָיָה (glossed rather unsatisfactorily as 'it shall be'), which functioned as a lower-ranking unit opening marker in Zech. 13:8; 14:7, 9, 16, 17, and 21. It would seem reasonable to interpret it here as marking the beginning of new subunits within the oracle, that is to say, subparagraphs within the embedded paragraph, as in 3:7-10.

The twelfth clause is the self-assertion formula "you (masculine plural) shall know that Yahweh of hosts has sent me to you (masculine plural)," which here as elsewhere is a strong hint that this paragraph is not part of a vision. The masculine plural forms do not fit the context very well, since the oracle as a whole is identified in 6:12 as addressed to one individual, the high priest Joshua. Perhaps the mention by name of four other men in 6:14 may be taken as implicitly broadening the range of those addressed. The subparagraph consisting only of the final clause in the series specifies obedience as the general condition for the fulfillment of the oracle. This division is displayed as follows:

6:1–3	**1st degree, Division 8, Paragraph 1, Subparagraph 1**
	I returned and I lifted up my eyes and I saw and behold...
6:4	*I replied and said to the angel who spoke with me*
	2nd degree
	Interrogative + Vocative: *What are these, sir?*
6:5–7a	**Subparagraph 2**
	The angel replied and said to me
	2nd degree
	Answer: *These are...*
6:7b	**Subparagraph 3**
	He said
	2nd degree
	Imperative: *Go, patrol the earth*
	Narrative
6:8	**Subparagraph 4**
	He cried out to me and said to me saying
	2nd degree
	Imperative: *See....*
6:9	**Paragraph 2, Subparagraph 1**
	The word of Yahweh came to me saying
6:10–12a	**2nd degree/1st degree**
	Imperative substitute x 6: *...you shall say to him saying*
6:12b–13a	**3rd degree/2nd degree**
	Thus says Yahweh of hosts saying
	4th/3rd degree, embedded paragraph 1:1, subparagraph 1
	Behold... + Statement x 6
	4th/3rd degree, embedded paragraph 1:1, subparagraph 2
6:13b–14	*It shall be...*
6:15	*you shall know that Yahweh of hosts has sent me to you*
	4th/3rd degree, embedded paragraph 1:1, subparagraph 3
	It shall be...

3. Vision and oracle

The next task is to attempt to establish the presence of structural features that might distinguish the parts of the text that are indisputably visionary in content from the parts that are not (or possibly are not). It is worth noting that chapters 1-6 of Zechariah form the longest series of visions in the OT, and there is little else to compare with it. The closest parallels are in Amos 7:1-9 and 8:1-3 where there are four visions, and Jer. 1:11-19, where there are two. There are visions recorded in the books of Ezekiel and Daniel also, but they are much longer and quite different in content. In the following discussion, comparison with the material in Amos and Jeremiah will be made where appropriate, but comparison with the texts of Ezekiel and Daniel is beyond the scope of this article.

3.1 Structural features of the visions

The clearest and most frequent feature of the visions, both in Zechariah and in Amos and Jeremiah, is the occurrence of the verb ראה 'see' in the introduction. Several formulas are attested (two co-occurring in a few visions) with no distinction of purpose observable between them. They include the following (presented in composite form where possible):

1. I saw (by night) and behold רָאִיתִי (הַלַּיְלָה) וְהִנֵּה (1:8; 4:2)
2. I lifted up my eyes and I saw and behold
   וָאֶשָּׂא (אֶת־)עֵינַי וָאֵרֶא וְהִנֵּה (2:1, 5; 5:1, 9; 6:1)
3. he/Yahweh made me see (יְהוָה) וַיַּרְאֵנִי (2:3; 3:1; cf. Amos 7:1, 4, 7; 8:1)
4. What do you see? מָה אַתָּה רֹאֶה (4:2; 5:2; cf. Amos 7:8; 8:2; Jer. 1:11, 13)
5. Lift up your eyes and see . . . שָׂא נָא עֵינֶיךָ וּרְאֵה . . . (5:5)

A second feature of the Zechariah visions is the occurrence of dialogue, often but not always in the form of question and answer. This is true of the visions of Amos and Jeremiah as well.

A third feature of the visions, which is found only in Zechariah, is the presence of an interpreting angel. It is not certain whether the angel in the fourth vision of 3:1-10 (see sec. 2.2.4) is the interpreting angel or not, but even if not, at least there is an angel present.

3.2 Structural features of the oracles

When we come to examine the passages that seem to have the least formal connection with their adjacent visions, 2:10-17 (Eng. 2:6-13) and 6:9-15, it is interesting to note that none of the features just mentioned (in

Vision and Oracle in Zechariah 1–6

sec.3:1) occur in them. They do contain three of the four occurrences of the self-assertion formula (2:13, 14; 6:15), which never occurs in any indisputably visionary text. As already noted in section 2.2.3, 2:10–17 has more structural features in common with chapters 9–11 than with any of the visions. There does thus seem to be a *prima facie* reason for treating this stretch of text as a unit in its own right (perhaps best labeled a division) apart from the preceding vision. It has been further noted (in sec. 2.2.8) that 6:9–15 begins with וַיְהִי דְבַר־יְהוָה אֵלַי לֵאמֹר 'the word of Yahweh came to me saying', the formula which elsewhere (e.g., Zech. 1:1; 7:1, 4; 8:1, 18; Hag. 1:1; 2:1, 10, 20) functions only at the highest discourse level and is not attested within any vision (except at 4:8 in a unit whose visionary status is debatable). This passage also contains more degrees of quotation than any of the visions, and in this respect has more in common with 1:1–6 than with any of them. This strongly suggests that it too would be better regarded as a separate unit (again perhaps a division) than as part of the preceding vision.

As for the other three passages of debatable status, 4:6b–10a is not only very awkward in its present setting, but also displays none of the features that characterize the visions. At 4:8 it contains the same formula as 6:9, indicating a high-level unit, and at 4:6b it contains a similar expression: זֶה דְּבַר־יְהוָה אֶל־זְרֻבָּבֶל לֵאמֹר 'This is the word of Yahweh to Zerubbabel saying'. This expression, while not attested as an opening formula in any other passage studied, is certainly similar enough to other such formulas to be credible in such a function; it is clearly parallel in function with the formula in 4:8. The fourth occurrence of the self-assertion formula is in 4:9; this formula never occurs in any unquestionably visionary passage. There are therefore good reasons for maintaining that 4:6b–10a should be treated as a unit (once more perhaps a division) separate from the vision in which it is embedded. These reasons are strengthened by the fact that the cohesion of the context is not merely undisturbed by the hypothetical removal of 4:6b–10a, but is actually enhanced. The angel in whose mouth this oracle appears to be placed still has a complete and fully intelligible utterance without it.

This last feature is not true of the two remaining debatable passages, 1:14–17 and 3:6–10. They both constitute a complete angelic utterance, and their removal would leave an opening quotative formula with nothing to follow. We may say that these two passages are more fully integrated into their present context than 2:10–17, 4:6b–10a, or 6:9–15. Moreover, neither contains the self-assertion formula, which seems to be a distinctive feature of the separable oracular sections. However, 1:14–17 does have several degrees of quotation, and manifests כֹּה אָמַר יְהוָה צְבָאוֹת 'thus says Yahweh of hosts', the formula which is common in oracular material such as Zechariah 7-8 and is here analyzed as introducing an embedded paragraph. We can thus recognize 1:14-17 as having some oracular features, but can find no ground for treating it as a unit separate from the vision of which it is a part in the traditional text. Indeed, it is thoroughly integrated into its context and in this respect has more in common with such "mini-oracles" as 2:8b-9 and 5:3-4 than with 2:10-17, 4:6b-10a, and 6:9-15. Much the same is true of 3:6-10. It does not have a high degree of quotation, though it does have the formula "thus says Yahweh of hosts," introducing another embedded paragraph. In this case too there is no real ground for separating the material from its traditional context in the vision. Parallels to such passages may perhaps be seen in Amos 8:3 and Jer. 1:14-19.

4. Structural patterns

Baldwin is one of several scholars who have discerned a chiastic arrangement in the visions. (Baldwin 1972:85 shows this diagrammatically.) She links the first and last visions (1:7-17 and 6:1-15) as an outer layer of the chiasmus. The middle layer is composite, consisting of the second and third visions (2:1-4 and 2:5-17, Eng. 1:18-21 and 2:1-13) together with the sixth and seventh visions (5:1-4 and 5:5-11). The inner layer consists of the third and fourth visions (3:1-10 and 4:1-14).

We will now examine the validity of Baldwin's schema. In the light of my foregoing analysis, her view seems oversimplified. It takes no structural account of the contrast between vision proper and oracle, though the distinction is recognized. The oracles are simply swallowed whole into the visions.

4.1 Prologue and epilogue

The first point to notice is that the 6:9-15 paragraph shows no features suggestive of its being regarded as part of the last vision. In fact, it is not linked with the vision series by anything other than the date in 1:7, which is not changed till 7:1. In terms of both its size and its internal structure, 6:9-15 is more comparable with 1:1-6 than with anything else in 1:7-6:8. Therefore, if 1:1-6 is seen as a prologue to the visions, 6:9-15 can be seen, structurally and perhaps semantically, as an epilogue. The prologue deals with the punishment that was the consequence of past disobedience (1:4), and the epilogue deals with the blessing that can be the consequence of future obedience. This layer falls outside the chiastic structure proper, yet can be seen as enclosing it within a larger pattern covering the whole of 1:1-6:15, as in the outline that follows.

If this analysis is accepted, it may be more appropriate to regard 6:9-15 as a separate division rather than as a paragraph within the eighth division of the second section. To mark this change from the analysis presented in section 2.2.8 while retaining a link with it, 6:9-15 will now be re-labeled as "Division 8X":

Prologue: Section 1 (1:1-6)
8 Visions: Section 2, Divisions 1-8 (1:7-6:8)
Epilogue: Section 2, Division 8X (6:9-15)

4.2 The middle and outer layers

Next we turn our attention to the middle layer of Baldwin's chiasmus. Is it justified to link pairs of visions in the way she suggests? In structural terms, there is no objection. All four are short and relatively simple in structure, and none has any embedded oracular material. The second (2:1-4) and seventh (5:5-11) visions both fall clearly into two parts (the horns and the smiths in the one case, and the barrel and the flying women in the other), which are identified as two paragraphs. They thus have some structural resemblance to each other, and both deal with the suppression of forces inimical to the welfare of the people of God. The third (2:5-9) and sixth (5:1-4) visions are unitary in theme, though the third is analyzed as two paragraphs and the sixth as one. They are somewhat complementary in topic, one dealing with Yahweh's protection of his people, and the other with his judgment of them. It would be possible to regard the second and seventh visions as one layer, and the third and sixth as another (cf. Stuhlmueller 1988:61 and Butterworth 1992:299), but there is no strong reason for doing this, nor any obvious advantage. Baldwin's analysis may as well be accepted as it stands.

As to 2:10-17 (Eng. 2:6-13), if the inner layer of Baldwin's chiasmus (3:1-4:14) is imagined as removed, then the oracle of 2:10-17 stands in the center of the middle layer. This perspective offers some structural rationale for its location, which otherwise appears random. We may now turn back to the outer layer of the chiasmus (1:7-17 and 6:1-8). If we imagine both the inner and middle layers of the chiasmus removed, then the "mini-oracle" of 1:14-17 stands in the center of the outer layer, though incorporated into the first vision (it is not a separate unit). In other words, the visions and the embedded oracular material in the outer layer occupy similar positions in terms of the chiastic structure to the parallel material in the middle layer.

In the following diagram of these portions of the second section, the oracle in 2:10-17 is re-labeled as: "Division 3X, Paragraphs 1-3," instead of "Division 3, Paragraphs 3–5" (as it was in sec. 2.2.3). Note that the embedded oracle is shown in square brackets.

> **Outer Layer:** Division 1, Paragraph 1 (1:7–13)
> [Embedded oracle: Division 1, Paragraph 2 (1:14–17)]
>
> > **Middle Layer:** Division 2, Paragraphs 1–2 (2:1–4)
> > Division 3, Paragraphs 1–2 (2:5–9)
> > > Oracle: Division 3X, Paragraphs 1–3 (2:10–17)
> >
> > Division 6, Paragraph 1 (5:1–4)
> > Division 7, Paragraphs 1–2 (5:5–11)
>
> **Outer Layer:** Division 8, Paragraph 1 (6:1–8)

4.3 The inner layer

When we move to the inner layer of the chiasmus, the previously noted pattern appears no longer to hold. The oracle that may be regarded as a separate unit (4:6b–10a) is inserted in the middle of the fifth vision, and the embedded oracular material (3:6–10) is at the end of the fourth vision. At first sight, this seems merely untidy and purposeless. But if we make a closer examination of this structure in the light of the relative placement of the visions and oracles in the middle and outer layers, something of the redactional history of the text may be inferred.

Some scholars (e.g., Amsler, Chary, Delcor, Elliger) have proposed that the fourth vision (3:1–10) is a later addition to an original inventory of seven visions. Their arguments are based mainly on the differences of content between the fourth vision and the others. Structural analysis would seem to offer some support for this position. If we imagine the series of visions as originally seven in number with what is now the fourth one removed, then the oracle in 4:6b–10a, curiously inserted as it is into the fifth vision, is seen to be at the center of the inner layer just as the oracle in 2:10–17 is at the center of the middle layer and the embedded oracle in 1:14–17 is at the center of the outer layer. Though the insertion is rather clumsily executed, it does thus have some rationale in terms of its location.

If we then suppose a later redaction with the fourth vision included in its present position to make a total of eight visions, the inner layer would then consist of the fourth and fifth visions. The oracle of 4:6b–10a would no longer be at the center of the inner layer, but interestingly the embedded oracle of 3:7–10 would now be in this position. Thus the overall structural pattern would be in a measure maintained, though distorted by the now structurally inappropriate location of 4:6b–10a. There is nothing very novel in such a view of the redactional history of the text. The interesting feature is that a discourse analysis of the text can suggest (but of course not prove) why the text should have come to be in the order in which it has been transmitted. Probably nothing more than tradition would be required to keep 4:6b-10a where it was in the first redaction, even when the reason for its being there was no longer valid.

This structural perspective can also offer a comment on why some modern translations (e.g., TEV, TOB, FC, DGN, NJB, and PS) transpose 4:6b-10a to follow 4:14. Though a transposition may in itself be justified for clarifying the identity of 4:6b-10a as a separate discourse unit, possibly the structural intention of the author/redactor would be better respected if this unit were transposed to precede 4:1 rather than follow 4:14. It would then be back at the center of the chiasmus where we suggest it may have started.

Other modern versions (e.g., NAB, REB) have transposed 4:4-10 to precede 4:1. (REB is much more restrained in its transposition than its predecessor, NEB. NEB's transpositions in chapters 3 and 4 are so complex and wild that they will not be discussed. The fact that they have been abandoned by REB is sufficient indication that they were no more than a transitory quirk of scholarship.) The addition of 4:4-6a to the transposed unit has the effect of relating the question of 4:5 not to the seven lamps or seven lips of the lamps in 4:3, but to the seven facets of the stone in 3:9. This seems to be overriding the structural indicators in 4:6b and 8 in an arbitrary manner. It gains no support from a discourse analysis.

This view of the redactional process says nothing about authorship. Amsler (1981:46) is of the view that such a redaction could well have been carried out by the prophet himself. Nowhere does Zechariah state how many visions he had, nor does he ever claim that he has recorded them all. It is perfectly credible that he first recorded a set of seven, keeping one or more others to himself. Later in the light of changed circumstances (such as the disappearance of Zerubbabel), he could have produced a "second edition," recording a further vision which gave more prominence to the role of the High Priest. It is not essential to presuppose that Joshua was still alive when 3:1-10 was incorporated into the series of visions. He may well have been, but even if he were not, he could have been understood as symbolizing the High Priesthood, which, unlike the line of Davidic rulers in which Zerubbabel stood, continued unbroken.

Some scholars (e.g., Elliger, Petersen) go further than this in their identification of stages in the redactional process, and indeed in their identification of units of text smaller than those recognized in the present analysis as elements in that process. Such confidence appears to go beyond what the evidence adduced from a structural analysis will support, and will not be discussed here.

The display that follows is of the inner layer of the chiasmus according to our analysis. The oracle in 4:6b–10a is here re-labeled as: "Division 5X, paragraphs 1 and 2," instead of "Division 5, Paragraphs 2 and 3" (as it was in sec. 2.2.5).

Inner Layer: First Redaction
    Division 5, Paragraph 1, Subparagraphs 1–6 (4:1–6a)
    Oracle: Division 5X, Paragraphs 1–2 (4:6b–10a)
    Division 5, Paragraph 1, Subparagraphs 6–11 (4:10b–14)

Inner Layer: Second Redaction
    Division 4, Paragraph 1, Subparagraphs 1–4 (3:1–5)
    [Embedded Oracle: Division 4, Paragraph 1, Subpara. 5 (3:6–10)]
    Division 5, Paragraph 1, Subparagraphs 1–6 (4:1–6a)
    Oracle: Division 5X, Paragraphs 1–2 (4:6b–10a)
    Division 5, Paragraph 1, Subparagraphs 6–11 (4:10b–14)

5. Summary and conclusion

The detailed discourse analysis presented in this article leads to the conclusion that there is a recognizable structural distinction between visionary and oracular genres. Of the oracular passages in Zech. 1:7–6:15, three and only three (2:10–17; 4:6b–10a; 6:9–15) can justifiably be considered as separate units of the structure. These units are treated as coordinate with the visions and labeled as divisions. The chiastic framework of the visions finds some support from a structural analysis, and thus the separate oracular divisions are seen as located among the visions in a pattern that respects that chiastic framework. These divisions may even offer some rationale for the supposed redactional development of the text. The overall structural analysis is summed up in the following display:

Prologue Oracle: Section 1 (1:1–6)

  Outer Vision Layer: Section 2, Division 1, Paragraph 1 (1:7–13)
  [Embedded oracle: Section 2, Division 1, Paragraph 2 (1:14–17)]

    Middle Vision Layer:
    Section 2, Division 2, Paragraphs 1–2 (2:1–4)
    Section 2, Division 3, Paragraphs 1–2 (2:5–9)

    Oracle: Section 2, Division 3X, Paragraphs 1–3 (2:10–17)

      Inner Vision Layer: (Second Redaction)
      Section 2, Division 4, Paragraph 1, Subparagraphs 1–4 (3:1–5)
      [Embedded Oracle: Section 2, Division 4, Paragraph 1, Subparagraphs 5 (3:6–10)]

Section 2, Division 5, Paragraph 1, Subparas. 1-6 (4:1-6a)
Section 2, Oracle: Division 5X, Paragraphs 1-2 (4:6b-10a)
Section 2, Division 5, Paragraph 1, Subparas. 6-11 (4:10b-14)

Middle Vision Layer:
Section 2, Division 6, Paragraph 1 (5:1-4)
Section 2, Division 7, Paragraphs 1-2 (5:5-11)

Outer Vision Layer: Section 2, Division 8, Paragraph 1 (6:1-8)

Epilogue Oracle: Section 2, Division 8X (6:9-15)

Notes

1. Where the Hebrew verse numbers differ from the English, the Hebrew numbering will normally be used, with occasional cross-references to English.

2. This article was completed without knowledge of Parunak's work on Jeremiah also published in this volume. It is interesting and gratifying to see that his conclusions reached independently and based on a much larger textual corpus are generally compatible with my own.

3. A date occurs again only in 1:7 and 7:1, and also in Hag. 1:1; 2:1, 10, 20.

4. And in Hag. 1:1; 2:1, 10.

5. Also in Hag. 1:8; 2:7, 9.

6. For the purposes of discourse analysis, we do not need to discuss the exegetical problems surrounding the words rendered "after his glory sent me" in the NRSV.

References

Amsler, Samuel. 1981. *Aggée, Zacharie 1-8.* Commentaire de l'Ancien Testament XIc. Neuchâtel-Paris: Delachaux and Niestlé.
Baldwin, Joyce G. 1972. *Haggai, Zechariah, Malachi.* Tyndale Old Testament Commentaries. London: Tyndale Press.
Butterworth, Mike 1992. *Structure and the Book of Zechariah. Journal for the Study of the Old Testament,* Supplement Series, 130. Sheffield: JSOT Press.
Chary, Théophane 1969. *Aggée-Zacharie-Malachie.* Sources Bibliques. Paris: Gabalda.
Clark, David J. 1982. The case of the vanishing angel. *The Bible Translator* 33(2):213-18.
———. 1985. Discourse structure in Zechariah 7:1-8:23. *The Bible Translator* 36(3): 328-35.
———. 1988. Discourse structure in Zechariah 9-14: Skeleton or phantom? In *Issues in Bible translation,* ed. Philip C. Stine, 64-80. UBS Monograph Series, 3.
———. 1991. Obadiah reconsidered. *The Bible Translator* 42(3):326-36.
———. 1992. Discourse structure in Haggai. *Journal of Translation and Textlinguistics* 5(1):13-24.

Delcor, M. 1964. *Zacharie. La Sainte Bible,* vol. 4. Paris: Letouzey and Ané.
Driver, S. R. 1906. *The minor prophets.* The Century Bible. Edinburgh: T. C. and E. C. Jack.
Elliger, Karl. 1982. *Das Buch der zwölf kleinen Propheten II.* Das Alte Testament Deutsch. Göttingen: Vandenhoeck and Ruprecht.
Mason, Rex. 1977. *The Books of Haggai, Zechariah and Malachi.* The Cambridge Bible Commentary. Cambridge: Cambridge University Press.
Mitchell, Hinckley G. 1912. *A critical and exegetical commentary on Haggai and Zechariah.* International Critical Commentary. Edinburgh: T. and T. Clark.
Petersen, David L. 1984. *Haggai and Zechariah 1-8.* The Old Testament Library. Philadelphia: Westminster Press.
Smith, George Adam. 1928. *The book of the twelve prophets,* vol. 2. London: Hodder and Stoughton.
Smith, Ralph L. 1984. *Micah-Malachi.* Word Biblical Commentary. Waco, Texas: Word.
Stuhlmueller, Carroll, C. P. 1988. *Rebuilding with hope: A commentary on the books of Haggai and Zechariah.* International Theological Commentary. Grand Rapids: Eerdmans; Edinburgh: Handsel Press.

www.ingramcontent.com/pod-product-compliance
Lightning Source LLC
Chambersburg PA
CBHW071218290426
44108CB00013B/1212